THE WORLD'S GREATES

K

25TH ANNIVERSARY EDITION

KNIVES
2005

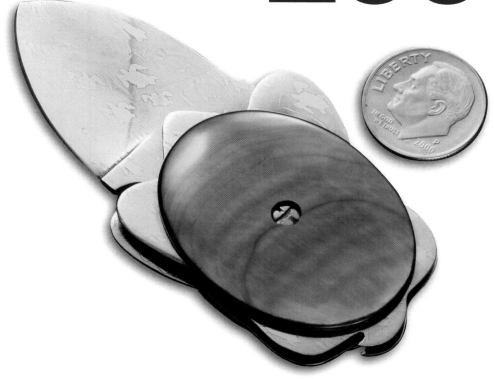

Edited by
Joe Kertzman

The Cover Knives

What a lineup of fine knives assembled for this cover! At far left is a Kenneth King dagger with more gold, emeralds and diamonds than the red carpet on Oscar night. In addition to inlaying precious stones, Kenneth worked mokumé magic on the bolster, carved a fantastic mother-of-pearl handle and inlaid 18-carat gold into the raindrop-damascus blade by Devin Thomas. To its immediate right is the "Venetian Carnival," a deeply carved Arpad Bojtos knife, with bolsters and blade revealing exotic characters boating and showboating in Venice. It also features a lapis-lazuli handle and a Devin Thomas damascus blade. Larry Lunn carved coral daisies and screwed them (using gold screws) into the mother-of-pearl handle of his window-frost-damascus folding knife, complete with lace-mosaic-damascus bolsters. Can you believe John Perry's six-sided black-lip-pearl handle anchoring a 13 1/4-inch O-1 blade? Finishing the handle of the geometric wonder took him two weeks alone. If you're looking for a big, strong frame-lock folder, then you'll find the R.J. Martin Avenger (far right) to be a fantastic knife of the groovy kind. It sports a cut-like-crazy CPM S30V blade, a bead-blasted titanium handle with grooved G-10 overlays and a shapely deep-carry pocket clip.

© 2004 by Krause Publications

Published by

kp books

An imprint of F+W Publications, Inc.

700 East State Street • Iola, WI 54990-0001
715-445-2214 • 888-457-2873

Our toll-free number to place an order or obtain
a free catalog is (800) 258-0929.

Library of Congress Catalog Number: 2004093865

ISBN: 0-87349-867-4

Designed by Patsy Howell, Kara Grundman, Paul Birling
Edited by Joe Kertzman & Ken Ramage

Printed in the United States of America

Introduction

They've done it! Everyone is walking around in shock, like zombies half unwrapped and staggering about blindly, squinting at the sun and wondering where they've been the last 100 years. Truth be told, it's mass confusion out there, but one thing is for certain. Among the pages of this book lies the answer to an age-old question, one that has baffled scientists and metallurgists for centuries. It's uncovered. It's known—it's the meaning of knife. That's right—knife. We now know the meaning of knife, and like the answer to that other riddle occupying great minds since the dawn of civilization—the meaning of life—the solution is simultaneously simple, astounding and elusive.

Knifemakers are the ones who uncovered the truth, and to do so, they looked within. Thinkers from across the universe tackled the task of solving the riddle, with several camps coming to similar conclusions at the same time. Like countries racing against time to send astronauts to the moon, build nuclear weapons or launch satellites into space, their success occurred during a momentary revelation of reason—a genesis of genius, so to speak. And here it is, revealed at last. The meaning of knife, like life, is found by baring one's soul. That's it. We'll give you a moment to grasp the concept, to let it sink in, to absorb the enormity, beauty, meaning and clarity of it all.

Knifemakers bear their souls, revealing all that is true in the universe, allowing the great unknown to escape from within themselves. To allow emanation of such insight, all they had to do was peer inside, and there it was all along, the meaning of knife waiting to be discovered. It's buried within their very being, among their cells, their makeup, their consciousness and ego. To be true to their art, they have to be true to themselves.

When a knifemaker forges a blade from steel, he must become the steel and allow it to dictate form and function. While shaping it with hammer and heat, he or she must also listen to the steel, allow it to breathe and speak. When a scrimshaw artist stipples ivory, pricking colorful pinholes into its pores, painting pictures, that creative person must also understand the ivory and all that it has to offer.

Engravers who take hand files to knife bolsters must first acknowledge the presence of the bolsters, discover their purpose, allow them their space and respect their individualism. Only then can an artist complement them with cuts and carvings. When applying a handle to edged steel, the knifemaker must learn the nature of the steel, inquire as to its intentions, uncover its goals and understand what it means to do. Then the handle becomes apparent. The soul of the knife must be revealed to understand the meaning of knife. That's when the knife unravels like the scrolls of scripture in the hands of a prophet.

Only skilled artists, the best forgers, the most aware blade builders in the world can dig so deep into the steel as to understand its very being. Those are the ones whose work is featured within the pages of this book, hidden between covers, waiting like shiny pennies to be plucked from the pavement and admired under inspecting eyes. They're yours for the taking, the works of art and manifestations of soul baring. They are useful tools, so much more than mere cutting apparatuses, but taking on lives of their own, sprouting guards, points and edges, growing toward the sun like seedlings in spring drizzles. Their forms are mysterious works of wonder, but only if their masters remained true to their souls. No hybrids have ever equaled the natural knife. Master smiths realize this universal truth. It's the meaning of knife, captured here, in Knives 2005. It's alive, not pictures printed on paper, but images left after the knives graced us with their presence. Benefit from their beings, and rejoice in their inner meaning, the meaning of knife!

Joe Kertzman

Contents

FACTORY TRENDS

KNIVES MARKETPLACE 187

DIRECTORY

2005 WOODEN SWORD AWARD

When knifemaker Tim Britton finished forging an L-6, O-1 and mild-steel raindrop-pattern damascus blade, he wasn't crystal clear about what he wanted to do for a handle. Soon, it became "crystal" clear—glass, that is, transparent gold, bubblin' goo. Britton employed the services of his good friend and master glass blower John Nygren to shape what has to be one of the most stunningly beautiful knife handles in the world, and perhaps the first blown-glass blade grip from an artist of Nygren's renown. Britton's knife ferrule is sterling silver inlaid with 24k-rose-gold vines and leaves to match the flowering plant life on the blows-your-mind, blown-glass handle. The Master's Series #1 knife is the first of 10 knives Britton plans to build with handles fashioned by well-known art-

ists who don't traditionally work with cutlery. For such aspirations, as well as for a blow-the-hinges-off –the door, blown-glass knife handle, the editor of Knives 2005 awards Britton the 2005 Wooden Sword Award. For a larger picture of the Master's Series #1 knife, see the "Bling Bling Blades" section of "Trends." (PointSeven photo)

A Forge Where Magic Knives Are Made

A Spaniard and a hand-forged navaja take the author to real and imagined places

By James Ayres

BARCELONA IS AN ancient city of light and shadow, a hidden city, one that does not easily give up its secrets. It sits at the edge of the Mediterranean and has seen centuries of conquerors and kings, tourists and lovers. Many of life's dramas are played out in its narrow, shaded alleys and twisted, winding streets.

Sometimes, when the hot afternoon sun cuts through the shadowed corners and hidden courtyards of the Gothic Quarter, the light seems to half reveal things that should have remained concealed. The stones of the buildings breathe secrets—trysts, duels, war, love affairs and betrayal. When I think of Barcelona, I think of nightfall and the anticipation of the evening ahead, of watered steel and mysteries. I went there once in search of a knife, a magic knife.

I first heard of Barcelona when I was 12 years old. I lived in a small Midwestern town where nothing ever happened, and where no one ever came. I had never met a person from another country, until one day I became acquainted with a man who spoke English with a slight accent that I later learned was Spanish. Like many travelers, he had stories to tell.

One day around lunchtime, I saw him sitting in the shade of one of the leafy sycamore trees that surrounded the county museum. I used to go to the museum and spend hours looking at dinosaur bones, muskets, Minie balls, a thousand butterflies in glass boxes and, best of all, swords, knives and daggers from all over the world.

The Spaniard I saw there was a thin, quiet man who occupied his space with weight and authority. He was dressed in a black suit, a brilliant white shirt

On a recent visit to Barcelona, the author scoured the streets for a hand-forged clasp knife—a navaja—like the one a personable Spaniard showed him when he was a child. The only navajas he found were in a knife store—Gran Cuchilleria—leading into the Gothic Quarter, right off Las Ramblas.

and a tightly knotted tie. His face was pale, dominated by dark, almost black eyes. I stumbled on the stairs when he caught me staring at him. He smiled, and with a curious hand motion, fingers down, brushing the air, motioned for me to come to him.

Sr. Aguilar introduced himself, offering me half of his sandwich. In answer to my questions, he told me that he taught Spanish at the nearby university, that he came from Spain and that, yes, Spain was very different from Indiana. He liked America, and Indiana, very much. After we finished his sandwich, he took a long, slender folding knife from his pocket and peeled an apple all in one long spiral, something I had only seen my grandfather do.

He was, to a small town boy, a fascinating find, a look outside at the wide world beyond the borders I knew. But it was the knife that captured me. I begged him to tell me about it. Over the next couple of weeks I managed to find time to meet him each day at lunch, and little by little, he told me his story and the background behind his knife.

The knife had a blade about 5 inches long, with a bowie-like, up-swept tip. The blade folded into a thin handle with honey-colored horn scales pinned in place. There was a silver tip on the handle, and a lock with a lever on the back where the blade and handle joined. All in all, it was like no other knife I had seen. I was more accustomed to Barlows and scout knives. Daggers and other exotic knives were only to be seen in museums. But here in this dignified man's hand was a knife that spoke of romance, far away places and events I could only imagine.

"This is a gypsy knife, a navaja (clasp knife)," he said. "In the old days, especially during the war, Spain was a very dangerous place, and most people went armed, either with blade or gun. But this knife is more than a weapon. It is a symbol of independence and a willingness to defend your person. It speaks of pride in your life. We

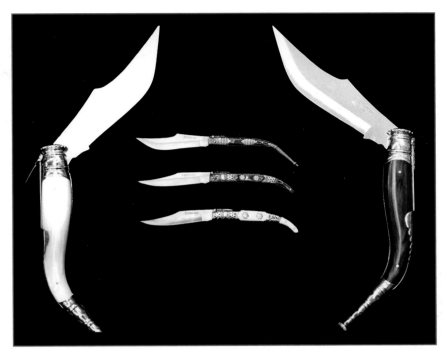

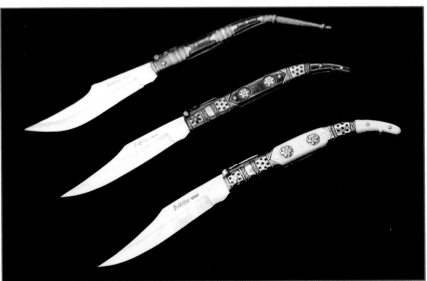

At the Gran Cuchilleria knife shop in Barcelona, one can find large and small navajas, expensive navajas, cheap navajas, decorated navajas and plain navajas. But none are hand forged and as mysterious or magical as the first navaja the author laid eyes on, yearning to have and hold.

are a very proud people, we Spanish. We have a long history, and steel is part of that history."

He meant the Spanish civil war, but I did not yet know that. He taught me history as effortlessly as he taught me language and geography. Navaja was the first word of Spanish I learned. His teaching and my learning were to become the center of our relationship.

Carry Navaja With You

"In those days," he said, "gypsies, poor people, and others who needed a weapon but did not wish to have, or were not permitted to have, a firearm, would obtain a knife like this to protect themselves. There were many criminals. Sometimes soldiers became criminals. One had to take care

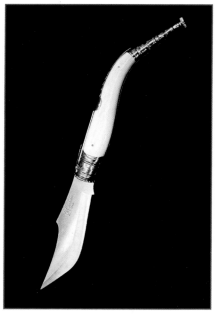

A typical Spanish navaja features a blade about 5 inches long with a bowie-like, upswept tip. The blade folds into a thin handle, often with honey-colored horn scales pinned in place, though myriad handle materials are used. There is a silver tip on the handle, and a lock with a lever on the back where the blade and handle join.

of one's self and his [or her] loved ones. Classes were taught in the use of this kind of knife. Swords could no longer be carried, but the navaja could always be with you, companion and protector. In time, the navaja, once a poor man's weapon and tool, came to be carried by rich and poor alike." He smiled, "Of course, you can also peel an apple with it."

He continued his story over the next few days. "Seville was famous as the town where the best steel in Spain was made, but there were fine blades made elsewhere in the country. This knife and others like it were fashioned in Barcelona, which was once my home," he said. "This particular knife has a life of its own. The blade was forged in fire and hammered until there was no weakness in it. The man who forged this knife did so in the old way, with ancient knowledge and magic. It will cut like no other steel. It will bend without breaking, and spring back to true after it's bent. The blade is what we call *'acero de Damasco.'*"

It was to be many years before I learned anymore about damascus steel.

The knife did look alive. He held it lightly, but carefully, in his hand. Its blade was thin, the handle looking almost fragile. Like a raptor, the long-bladed folder looked as if it might leap from his hand and strike whatever it wanted.

I was convinced that this was, indeed, a magic knife. In my mind it was related to Excalibur, Durandel, Jim Bowie's knife, and all the great swords and knives of myth. I never saw him do anything more than peel an apple or cut a sandwich with it, but I believed every word he told me.

He went on with his story: "I once used this knife to take a man's life, and to save a woman's life. It was the life of my mother that I saved, and the life of a soldier I took. It was during the war, when all of Spain went crazy. The communists were fighting the republicans, the republicans were fighting the anarchists, and the communists, along with everyone

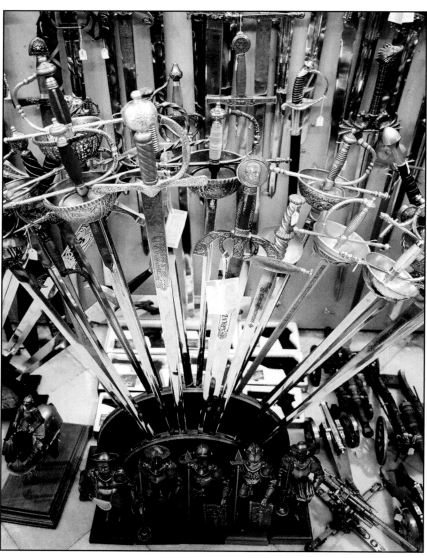

A typical Spanish navaja features a blade about 5 inches long with a bowie-like, upswept tip. The blade folds into a thin handle, often with honey-colored horn scales pinned in place, though myriad handle materials are used. There is a silver tip on the handle, and a lock with a lever on the back where the blade and handle join.

Right and Below: Early Spanish navajas, though significantly smaller than swords when closed, were nearly equal to small swords when opened.

who got in the way, were killed. My mother was not political, but my older brother was, and that was enough for the communists to issue death warrants for the whole family. They had already killed my father.

"The communists came and took my mother one night while I was away," Sr. Aguilar continued. "When I returned home, my neighbor told me what had happened. They were holding her in a building not far away. They planned to shoot her at dawn, as they had already shot so many.

"I went to the building where they held her late that night," he said. "I climbed across the rooftop. When the moon was behind clouds, I slipped down into the courtyard of the building. I was only 15 then. I was small and thin, and could move very quietly. I knew that there would be no mercy from the communists, and that there was no use to ask for any, not for my mother or myself.

"The whole neighborhood knew where they kept the women," he claimed. "I had no trouble finding her. I hoped to open the door quietly and sneak out with her. But I was only a boy and I had not thought it all through. Of course, there were other women condemned to death the next morning. My mother could not leave without them, nor could I.

"We made too much noise," said Aguilar. "A soldier who was standing in shadow heard us. You might think that a small boy of 15 would have no chance against a man with a rifle. But you would be wrong to think that. I had determination and fear, and anger for my father's death on my side. I also had a magic knife. Perhaps more importantly, I believed that God was with me because what they planned to do was wrong. It would have been a mortal sin for them to kill my mother and the other women who had done no wrong."

Knife-And-Folk Lore

He would never tell me the whole story, how he overcame the soldier and escaped with his mother. But the parts of the story he did tell me, and the vision of his knife, are still with me, even today, over 40 years later.

A dozen years after I met Sr. Aguilar, I rode into Barcelona on my chuffing-and-rumbling Triumph motorcycle. It was a blue and white 650cc that I had bought in England and which, along with a small green tent, had been my magic carpet and my home for many months.

My first night in Barcelona was filled with sangria, laughter and dancing on the sand till dawn, when my dark-eyed girl led me back to our room in the Gothic Quarter, just off Las Ramblas near Placa Espania. In those days, they served dinner on the beach in small thatched-roof buildings. From the fresh catch that came in on wooden boats, they cooked paella in black iron skillets, over open fires, on the sand. Wine was drunk from clear glass *pourons* (blown-glass goblets) held at arm's length so that the clear, cold white wine fell in a smooth stream, and ran down your face and into your mouth. El Cordobes, the matador, was the talk of Barcelona, and everyone danced until dawn.

My reasons then for coming to Barcelona were many. I wanted to meet Sr. Bulto, the founder of Bultaco motorcycles, for whose mark I had raced for two years. I wanted to see a bullfight and a Spain that was lost in time under its dictator, Gen. Franco. I wanted to carry a leather *bota* (a wine bottle made of leather) full of rich red wine, ride my bike to tiny white villages in the Sierra and through lion-colored hills, and see the blue of the sea from a high mountain pass.

I wanted to find the man who forged the knife I had seen so many years ago in Sr. Aguilar's hand.

Although 12 years might not seem so many or so long to those of us who are on the far side of the matter, they seemed both many

The first Spanish navaja the author saw looked alive. The Spaniard who showed it to him held the navaja lightly but carefully in his hand. Its blade was thin, the handle appearing almost fragile. Like a raptor, the long-bladed folder looked as if it might leap from the Spaniard's hand and strike whatever it wanted.

and long to me then. Since I had left Indiana as a small boy, I had traveled Latin America and Asia, heard shots fired in anger, and seen our nation's capitol torn apart by riots. I had buried friends and was more than a little burned out. I felt old. Childhood quests seemed just the right thing at the time.

I started my search the day after I arrived. I stopped a group of gypsies and asked them if they knew about such knives as navajas. They looked at me as if I was crazy and tried to pick my pocket. From a friendly waiter with a potbelly who served me *café con leche* (coffee with milk) each morning, I heard a rumor of knives forged in the old ways.

In a knife store, I was told that there might be such a man making knives somewhere, but no one knew where. A gray-haired woman in the bakery said that she thought there was a man who still fashioned knives in the old way, and who worked somewhere deep in the Gothic Quarter, but no one knew exactly where he was to be found. I followed directions that led nowhere. I wandered the crooked streets listening for the sound of a forge.

Once, while walking in the old town, I heard the sound of

steel on steel. I followed the clashing sounds from street to alley to courtyard. But I never found the two men who, from the sound, must have been sword to sword. Whether practice or duel, I will never know.

I talked to the proprietors of knife shops across the city. I learned that everything Sr. Aguilar told me about navajas was true. Those knives were just what he said they were to the people of Spain. There were stories told about special navajas, as there were about certain swords. But there were no such knives to be found.

I never did find the man who forged that knife. I didn't meet Sr. Bulto, either. But life and travel will always bring you what you did not expect. I did find some healing magic in that city, and young love under a star-filled night sky at the edge of an ancient sea.

A few months ago, I again went to Barcelona, this time to make a short film. When the work was done, I took a day to myself to resume my search for a man who forged damascus steel, and who made navajas in the old way.

I would like to tell you that I did, finally, more than 40 years after I first heard the story, find such a man. But I did not.

Never in Barcelona did I find a forge, or a man who could make knives with magic in them. When I first went to Barcelona, many men still carried navajas, and they were sold in several stores. In today's Barcelona, the only navajas I found were in a knife store leading into the Gothic Quarter, right off Las Ramblas.

Barcelona has changed in many ways. But the old part of town is still there. Mian Muhammed Shahrawaz and Sunil Khatri operate the Gran Cuchilleria at Calle Ferran, number 16. Gran Cuchilleria might have been one of the stores I visited over 20 years ago, but I cannot say for sure; there were many knife stores then.

Sunil, Mian and Walls of Knives

Sunil and Mian have more knives in one small room than you would think possible. They have swords, kukris, bayonets, Solingen folders, Spydercos and Benchmades. Their walls are covered with knives, and their cases full of steel.

They also have navajas. They have large and small navajas, expensive navajas, cheap navajas, decorated navajas and plain navajas. If you go to Barcelona, you should visit their store. They are amiable fellows, and they have some unusual knives that any aficionado of steel would enjoy seeing. But they do not have any hand-forged navajas like the one I saw in a small town in Indiana so long ago.

Sometimes I wonder what happened to Sr. Aguilar, the professor with the hidden past, the man with the magic knife, the man who couldn't go home again. He told me his brother was killed before they could get out of the city. I imagine Sr. Aguilar, still in his black suit, with his mother alive and well, somewhere under my Midwestern sky, and still carrying his Spanish steel. And I imagine that somewhere deep in the Gothic Quarter of Barcelona, in some hidden secret place, there is a forge where magic knives are made.

When the author first visited Barcelona more than 25 years ago, it was a different city from what it is now, having changed in many ways. But the old part of town is still there, and though the number of knife shops has dwindled, the walls of Gran Cuchilleria are covered with knives, and display cases are full of steel.

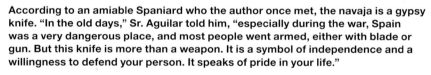

According to an amiable Spaniard who the author once met, the navaja is a gypsy knife. "In the old days," Sr. Aguilar told him, "especially during the war, Spain was a very dangerous place, and most people went armed, either with blade or gun. But this knife is more than a weapon. It is a symbol of independence and a willingness to defend your person. It speaks of pride in your life."

At Gran Cuchilleria, swords are lined up against the walls like Spanish soldiers fighting for their independence.

Always Heat Your Leftovers

Knifemaker Loyd Thomsen forges beautiful damascus blades from leftover scraps of steel

By Durwood Hollis

MOST KNIFEMAKERS HARBOR a certain reluctance to throw anything away. Knifemaking leftovers, like last week's casserole, seem to hold the promise of fulfillment somewhere down the line. Still, that moment in time when the scraps will serve a purpose never comes to pass, and based on my firsthand observations, those who forge damascus knife blades are the biggest junk collectors of the lot.

Somewhere in most knifemakers' shops, maybe up on a top shelf or in a dusty corner, you're sure to encounter old coffee cans. Within their confines are leftover bits and pieces of steel billets that were brought to life under the hammer. Some are damascus, or pattern-welded steel, fragments showing contrasting lines, swirls, shapes and layers. The tiny fragments are too small to be of use as knife blades, but the beauty of their individual hand-forged patterns is enough to discourage damascus forgers from simply pitching them out with the trash.

During a recent visit to the shop of Loyd Thomsen, proprietor of Horsehead Creek Knives and a damascus maker of some renown, I spent an entire afternoon watching him take his own personal collection of worthless odd-shaped steel bits and pieces, and forge them into a priceless edged treasure.

Looking over the scraps of steel that were scattered across the top of Loyd's workbench, it was evident that the individual pieces varied in thickness. Likewise, they were configured in every shape imaginable. The damascus patterns were equally as varied—ranging from as few as 80 layers to as many as 320 layers of forged steel. Furthermore, each piece contained varying amounts of 15N20, 1084HC, 1095HC, L-6 and D-2 steels. Collectively, the whole lot didn't look like something that could be forged together. If there was ever such a thing as a diverse jumble of steel, the accumulation that Loyd poured out onto his workbench was all that and then some!

"I knew if I thought on it a while, something would come to mind," Thomsen stated. Apparently, a solution to the problem of what to do with the leftover steely scraps, aside from discarding them like most reasonable in-

Knifemaker Loyd Thomsen stands at the forge, demonstrating his own method of forging leftover scraps of damascus into quite strikingly beautiful mosaic-Damascus knife blades.

dividuals would have done, had come to Loyd's mind. And he insisted that I observe his resolution to a perplexing problem of "knife-making proportions."

Rummaging around in his shop, he came up with a section of four-sided tubular 1018 carbon steel. I recognized the material from the time my sagging garage door had been replaced. It was nothing more than a section of mild strap steel, designed for minimal stress and used often as bracing material.

"This will do," Loyd said.

Knowing when to keep one's mouth shut is an art unto itself and that talent is something that generally escapes my mastery. Just as my lips began to form a question about the squared tube of steel, Loyd said, "Don't ask. You'll find out find out in good time."

The Creative Process

Loyd wasn't trying to be impolite. On the contrary, he was in the midst of a creative idea. The process by which that particular concept was brought to life was best observed rather than explained. Therefore, I kept quiet and watched as he worked.

First of all, Loyd cut a 5-inch length of 1018 tubular steel, a section that measured 2 inches wide and 1 inch high. He then cut off one of its four sides and set the whole works aside for later use. Taking two pieces of 2-inch-by-1-inch flat steel, he welded plates onto both ends of the now three-sided hollow tube. A rectangular steel box, complete with a separate flat lid, was created.

"You'll notice that this looks just like the inside of a box of farmer's matches," Loyd said, drawing my attention to his creation. I had a difficult time with the term "farmer's matches" (how is one match box any different from another?), so I kept my mouth shut and nodded in agreement.

Setting the new creation aside, Loyd spread the tag end contents of his coffee can out on the workbench. Sorting through the various

After forging bits and pieces of leftover damascus into a new billet of steel, Thomsen pounds the resulting red-hot bar into the shape of a blade.

During a recent visit to the shop of Loyd Thomsen, the author spent an entire afternoon watching Loyd take his own personal collection of worthless odd-shaped steel bits and pieces, and forge them into a priceless edged treasure. Looking over the scraps of steel that were scattered across the top of Loyd's workbench, it was evident that the individual pieces varied in thickness. Likewise, they were configured in every shape imaginable. The damascus patterns were equally as varied—ranging from as few as 80 layers to as many as 320 layers of forged steel. Furthermore, each piece contained varying amounts of 15N20, 1084HC, 1095HC, L-6 and D-2 steels. Collectively, the whole lot didn't look like something that could be forged together.

sizes, he selected those that fit easily into the little steel box. He then carefully arranged the different-size pieces into a single, flat layer in the bottom of the box. The empty spaces between each piece were filled with powdered steel (15N20 or 1084HC). He then tapped the box a time or two, which allowed the contents to settle into place (it's important to make sure there are no open voids between the individual pieces of steel).

After he completed the first layer, the next tier was laid in place. Once again, the voids between the pieces of steel were filled with powdered steel. Layer by layer, this procedure was repeated until the box was filled to the top.

It was time now to enclose the box with the flat lid. Since the sides of the metal container had a tendency to spring open, flaring slightly, when the top was cut off, Loyd used his vise to pinch it back to its original shape. The top was then welded into place, which made the steel container airtight. Then he drilled a 1/16-inch hole in one end of the closed box to allow the gases to escape when the entire steel package was placed into the forge. Finally, a short length of Re-bar® was welded onto one end of the box. This would serve as a handle during the forging process.

From past experience, I knew that forging the steel container and its content was going to take time. Loyd fired up his forge and waited a half-hour until it reached the right temperature (2300 degrees Fahrenheit). Putting on his heat-resistant gloves, he grabbed the Re-bar handle of the boxed bits and pieces and placed it into the forge.

"It will take about 30 more minutes for the heat to thoroughly penetrate the box and its contents. After that, I can start on it with the hammer," Loyd commented.

He went on to explain that the individual pieces of steel, the powdered steel and the containment box would "melt together" in the forge. After that, he would be able to manipulate the molten steel with hammer pressure. However, when the steel was removed from the forge, he only had about 10 seconds to work. After which, the steel had to be returned to forge once again.

Blow By Blow

When Loyd began to work, I noted that he initially used light hammer pressure on the edges of the box. This apparently was done to keep the top from bursting open at its previously welded seams. Once the hammer work began in earnest, however, greater force was implemented. Over a period of about an hour, he repeated the constant cycle of forging and hammering. Slowly, the combined pieces of steel were condensed and flattened into a single billet about 8 inches long and 3/4-inch thick.

The next step was to remove the outer layer of boxed steel that originally held all of the tiny bits of damascus. This was 1/8-inch thick, so Loyd set his milling machine to that dimension. In short time, he removed the outer shell on all sides of the billet.

He then tested the integrity of his work by running an 80-grit belt across all surfaces of the billet. After soaking it in ferric chloride (etching solution) for about five minutes, and carefully scrutinizing the billet for any evidence of de-lamination, cold shuts and trapped flux, Loyd was happy with his work. If surface imperfections had been observed, the billet would have to be returned to the forge. Then the entire process of heat, hammer and flux would have to be repeated over again to hopefully fix the problem.

When Loyd had accomplished this assignment, he returned the bar to the forge and brought it up to welding temperature (again,

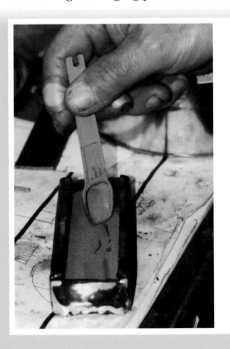

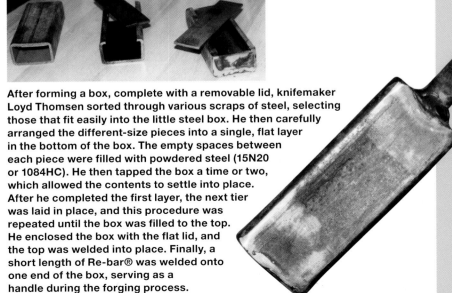

After forming a box, complete with a removable lid, knifemaker Loyd Thomsen sorted through various scraps of steel, selecting those that fit easily into the little steel box. He then carefully arranged the different-size pieces into a single, flat layer in the bottom of the box. The empty spaces between each piece were filled with powdered steel (15N20 or 1084HC). He then tapped the box a time or two, which allowed the contents to settle into place. After he completed the first layer, the next tier was laid in place, and this procedure was repeated until the box was filled to the top. He enclosed the box with the flat lid, and the top was welded into place. Finally, a short length of Re-bar® was welded onto one end of the box, serving as a handle during the forging process.

2,300 F). The bar was then removed, taken quickly to his vise, clamped securely and then twisted one full turn. This was done to enhance the complexity of the pattern within the steel. During and after the twisting process, Loyd sprinkled "20 Mule Team Borax" as a cleansing agent (flux) on the steel. He then used a steel brush to remove any crust of impurities that was formed.

"When the fluxing agent begins to bubble up and looks like melted honey, you'll know that it's done its job," he commented.

Once again, a combination of heat and hammer work, and fluxing, took the corkscrew-looking billet down in size until it was about 12 inches long, 2-1/2 inches wide and 3/4-inch thick. The newly forged damascus steel billet was about three times the size of what Loyd actually needed for a final finished blade.

To continue the work, however, it would be necessary to anneal the billet. He returned the length of steel to the forge, turned off the heat, plugged the ends to prevent premature heat escape and let the forge cool down over the next four-to-five hours.

Looking over the newly formed steel billet, Loyd exclaimed, "Hot damn, it's a winner."

I took it from his carefree moment of exuberance that he was satisfied with his efforts. For my part, I was amazed to see a jumble of worthless scrap steel become transformed into a workable billet of exquisite damascus.

Steel Surprise

The one unfortunate part, or perhaps the fun aspect, of forging a billet of damascus in this manner is that you have no idea what it will look like in the end. You'll never be able to replicate a particular pattern. The end product is a billet of blade steel that is truly one-of-a-kind and representative of every type of damascus pattern you've ever seen or made.

Once again, Loyd placed the length of steel in the mill and ma-

The final product of forging scraps of damascus steel together is a knife blade of unique and exquisite beauty.

chined it perfectly flat on both sides. While he was at it, the thickness of the steel was reduced to what he wanted in his finished knife blade. Moving over to the grinder, he worked steadily until all of the hammer marks, imperfections and slag were removed from the surfaces of the steel.

The creation of the knife blade, itself, involved tracing the required shape on the surface of the steel billet. Loyd then used a metal band saw to rough profile the blade blank. Of course, a grinder could be used for the same purpose.

While we were waiting for the blade to anneal, Loyd had cut out and shaped a guard for the knife from a piece of nickel silver. After profiling the blade, he fit the guard into place. Watching him work, it was obvious that he wanted the hand guard to fit perfectly square in relation to the blade. When he was satisfied that the guard was fitted properly, he set it aside.

The Horsehead Creek logo and knife serial number were both stamped into the blade, on opposites sides, just forward of where the guard would be soldered (or pinned) in place. The rest of the blade shaping, decorative file work, edge formation (hollow or flat grind) and drilling of the tang for handle attachment were all done on the annealed blade. Finally, Loyd took the blade to the buffing wheel and used a 600-grit belt to polish out all of the sanding, grinding and tool marks.

The final process in blade formation was heat-treating. Loyd used foil tool wrap to enclose the blade in an airtight envelope. Before the foil seal was closed, however, a small piece of tissue paper was placed inside. During

the heat-treating process, the tissue would burn and consume any trapped oxygen within the foil envelope. After the blade was fully enclosed in foil, it was placed into an Even-Heat kiln that was preheated to 1400-1500 degrees for five minutes.

The blade was then removed from the forge and quenched in light hydraulic oil, at room temperature, for five more minutes. The blade was air cooled on a fire-brick for approximately 30 minutes, after which the foil wrap was cut off with a pair of scissors. If any "hot spots" (areas where the blade may have had contact with the surface of the firebrick during the heat treat process) arose, then those areas would have to be rebuffed prior to etching. Finally, ferric chloride was used to etch the blade, thereby bringing out the layered pattern within the damascus steel.

The final steps in the knife-making process included attaching the guard and handle. Once in place, the guard and handle were shaped, buffed and polished. All of the diverse elements—layered steel blade, nickel-silver guard and handle scales (wood, horn, antler, etc.)—had been formed into a single, bonded unit. Lastly, the blade edge was sharpened.

"Personally, I've found the entire process gratifying. So much so, that as soon as enough tag-ends of steel accumulate, I am back at again," Loyd concluded.

If you're a damascus steel maker, then give some thought to your own collection of bits and pieces. It's possible to turn all of that worthless junk into priceless treasure. Loyd Thomsen found a way. All you have to do is work outside of the box!

Land the Finest in Fish Knives

Casting for the big ones nets the author a trophy catch of "steel heads"

By Richard D. White

FISHING . . . TALK ABOUT a specialized occupation or hobby. You have your floaters and your boaters, your waders and your walkers, those who cast and those who cast-off, some who fish using flies, and others who fly to fish. You have fishermen who swear by bait, and those who swear at bait. You have "catch and release" fisher people and other folks who keep all they catch.

Some walk and stalk, and others splash and thrash.

Some prefer to sit on the bank watching their bobbers, while fellow fishermen tramp through the woods trying to avoid branches that slap painfully at their faces. You have warm water hook dippers and people plying their trade in the chilling waters of glacial runoff. Some fishermen spend thousands of dollars on specialized

boots, boats, rods and reels, while others are perfectly comfortable with bib overalls and long-sleeve wool shirts.

Even among general fishing categories, there is specialization. Some prefer wet flies, others dry flies. You have fishermen who opt for "poppers," while others gravitate toward spinners. On the one hand, there is the vacation fisherman, and on the other is the guy

A group of Texas-toothpick-style fishing knives include those made by, from left, Camillus Cutlery; Ulster Cutlery (red handle); Ulster (yellow), complete with a sharpening stone; Camillus (with cap-lifter main blade); Hoffritz; and Kutmaster. The two Camillus Cutlery models are engraved with "Fisherman's Luck" on yellow-celluloid handles.

or gal who fishes on a daily basis. Some fish for sport, and others fish for food, whether bringing fillets to their own tables or to the plates of those willing to pay for the tasty treats. Some mount their trophies while others consume theirs. You have fishermen who use minute flies, barely big enough to be seen with a naked eye, and those who throw pounds of gear into the water behind trolling boats.

Despite this tremendous variety of fishing types, styles and individual preferences, there is one common denominator among all fishermen—they need knives to cut bait, remove hooks from toothy mouths, prepare fish for consumption or trim the hackles (tufts of feathers from rooster necks used in making fishing flies).

In fact, given the tremendous variety of fishing styles, locations, fish species and fish sizes, you would think it natural that knives made to skin, fillet and prepare fish for consumption would have the same degree of variety and specialization. You'd be right, and therein lies the joy of collecting pocket and sheath knives made specifically with the fisherman in mind.

Even as early as the late 1920s, several well-known cutlery manufacturers recognized that the production of specialized and unique knives for fishermen might provide a viable market niche. And, because of the tremendous variety of fish and fishermen, perhaps several fishing knives could be developed to meet the specialized needs.

A "Zane-y" Fish Knife

As a recognized leader in the cutlery industry, Union Cutlery Co., located in Olean, N.Y. (and famous for the KA-BAR tang stamp), was the first to openly court someone in the fishing industry to consult on the design of a fish knife. Union Cutlery's choice of an expert in the field proved

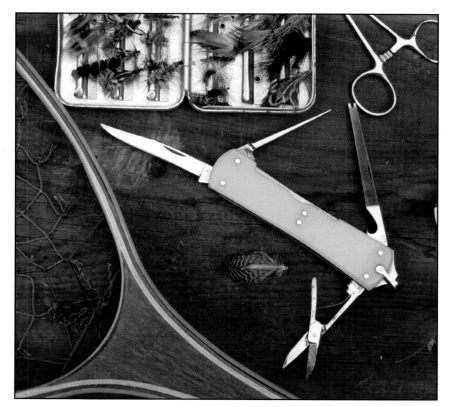

a stroke of genius. The chosen world-famous trophy fisherman had an even greater reputation as a western novel writer. Union Cutlery's new employee was none other than Zane Grey.

Grey authored 66 novels, including "Riders of the Purple Sage," "The Last of the Plainsmen," "The Spirit of the Border" and "The Call of the Canyon." With a reputation to match an exciting writing style, his novels were practically guaranteed to sell over a million copies each. In his time, Grey held 10 world records for trophy fishing. His name, both for his novel writing and fishing, was a household word.

Not only was he a brilliant choice for name recognition and fishing prowess; at the time, Union Cutlery was in desperate need of a "second wind."

The partnership between Union and Grey was formed during the darkest years of The Great Depression, soon after the stock market crash of 1929, at a time when approximately 25 million workers were unemployed and money was almost non-existent. The result of this partnership was the production of a fishing knife that carried an endorsement by Grey, himself, in the form of a signature etched on the master blade.

The resulting edged tool was a two-blade, Texas-toothpick-style fishing knife, handled in bright yellow celluloid. The knife commonly referred to as a "Texas toothpick" is a large, slender, serpentine jackknife with two blades unfolding from one end of the handle. It features a rather pointed handle butt opposite the blades, and is generally 5 inches in length.

Union's Zane Grey knife sported a master blade for cleaning fish, and a secondary blade outfitted with a hook disgorger and scaler. The total package was a great success. An additional feature manifested itself in the form of a hook-sharpening stone inset into one side of the yellow-celluloid grip.

Although Grey died approximately seven years after the "endorsed by Zane Grey" knife was first manufactured, the edged tool brought Union Cutlery a welcome association with a larger-than-life fishing folk hero.

The Texas toothpick style of fishing knife has become one of the most popular models, and has been duplicated by a number of cutlery companies. In fact, a serious enthusiast could put together a significant and impressive collection of Texas toothpick fishing knives without a great deal of effort. In addition to Union Cutlery fishing knives, collectors can find edged examples stamped by Imperial; Kutmaster; Utica; Colonial; Hoffritz; W. R. Case; Remington; Ulster; Primble; Clauss; Camillus; and a host of other companies.

Generally, traditional Texas toothpick-style fishing knives were handled in yellow celluloid, and since the knife-grip material was and is rather rare, the question arises as to why it was chosen. The answer is surprisingly simple: yellow is a bright color that can be seen in the water if a fishing knife is dropped while gutting. Some older Texas toothpicks showcase red-celluloid grips for the same reason.

Bonkers Over Fish Bonkers

In addition to the Texas toothpick style of fishing knives, the cutlery industry developed several other unique patterns designed for various types of fishing. The strangest of these is known as the "fish bonker," and made by Puma, a well-regarded German cutlery manufacturer. The imposing and impressive all-metal knife sports a large, solid-metal ball attached to the end of the handle opposite a folding blade. The metal knob is often referred to as the "priest," because it administers the "last rites" by bonking the fish on the head.

In addition to this unique feature, the Puma fish-bonker has another, even-more-unusual characteristic. With the blade in the open position, one can see a series of small, regularly spaced square notches cut into the top of the blade. At the base of these notches are etched numbers representing pounds. By hanging a fish on a stringer from one of these notches, and holding the knife by an integral leather strap, a fisherman can move the stringer along the notches and accurately weigh a

Shown are two examples of three-bladed fish gaff knives. The model at left is a Western States Cutlery Co. pattern, and the other, handled in brilliant red celluloid, was made by Hoffritz Co., Germany.

rather large fish. In use as a scale, the heavy metal bonker acts as a counterweight to the poundage of the fish, making this Puma knife scale a rather useful gadget.

Using the Puma fish bonker as a prototype, the Italians came up with a "knockoff" (pun intended), designing their own fish-bonking knife with the tang stamp "LUNA." This folding knife is almost the same size as the Puma, and contains not only a master blade, but also a secondary fish-disgorger/scaler blade and, as an added attraction, a spring-loaded tape measure located inside of the bonker. This knife doesn't provide a scale for weighing fish, but does allow the owner of the edged tool to claim bragging rights by providing a tape measure to arrive at an accurate length of catch—those clever Italians.

There has been a recent discovery of yet another bonker knife model. The newly unearthed bonker is a miniature Puma fish knife with an overall length of less than half that of the full-size Puma. The miniature model parades Micarta® handle scales, a full-size bonker and a most unusual blade etching. In addition to the Puma tang stamp, the mini-bonker knife

is clearly etched "Abercrombie and Fitch, Made in Germany." Now that's a real catch!

For those who tempt fish with small, artificial flies, several specialized fly fishing knives have been

developed. For most fishing knife collectors, these edged tools are in an elite category by themselves. Made by CASE, Union Cutlery (KA-BAR), HARDY (an English company) and several other Ger-

In mint condition is KA-BAR's answer to the fish gaff knife. The three-blade pocketknife is stamped "T33" on yellow celluloid, and the unusual shape results from a need to house the large gaff hook when the blade is closed.

Below: Notice the large "priests," or balls, attached to the backs of the handles on two "fish bonker" knives. The balls were used to "bonk" fish on the head after they were caught. Both are Puma knives, and the smaller example is stamped "Abercrombie and Fitch" on the blade. Abercrombie and Fitch was a major sporting goods distributor, not a teenage clothing manufacturer.

man manufacturers, the knives contain several different tools designed for the fly fisherman.

First is the prerequisite master blade for gutting fish, and second is a small, metal toothpick for undoing knots in fly line. Thirdly, the necessary folding scissors are at the ready for trimming hackles and hairs on dry flies, and for snipping loose ends off fly-line leaders. A long file blade/hook disgorger is perfect for removing hooks from the mouths of fish prior to releasing them back into the water. Finally, a small, stubby screwdriver is built into one end of the knife liner.

Generally, these knives parade an attached bail, which allows a fly fisherman to hook a knife to a fishing vest. The KA-BAR originally came in a choice of a bright-yellow-celluloid handle or a jigged, black-celluloid grip. The CASE came with metal side plates, as did the British "Hardy" model.

As a fishing knife innovator, Union Cutlery manufactured a unique edged fixed blade outfitted with a sheath. It showcases a yellow-celluloid handle, and the small knife, measuring only 6 inches from point to aluminum pommel, is stamped "KA-BAR" in chrome. It initially came with a genuine leather sheath embossed with "KA-BAR TROUT KNIFE." The back of the sheath had two slits so that the knife could be attached to a fisherman's belt for easy access.

This unique German knife, called the "Overland Fisherman's Friend," features not only a master blade, but also a sinker- or weight-crimping tool, a file blade, cap-lifter and pliers.

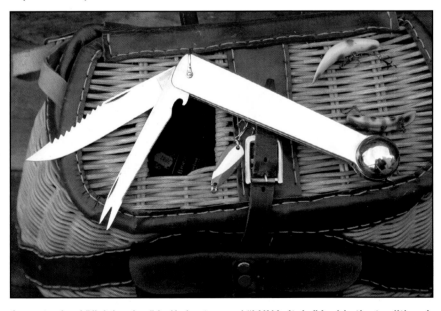

A most prized "fish bonker" knife is stamped "LUNA, Italy." Inside the traditional "priest," or metal ball, is a tape measure, making this particular piece highly collectible. It also sports two blades, including a master blade with fish scaler. The secondary blade employs a cap-lifter and hook disgorger.

No Guffawing Over the Gaff

The Puma fish bonker knife might be a strange looking contraption, but so is another edged specialty tool, the "Fish Gaff Knife." Although there is seldom any need for a fish gaff when landing trout, fishermen who aim for pike and northern in and around the Great Lakes apparently have plenty of use for a fish gaff.

Early fish gaff knives were made by KA-BAR, Western States Cutlery Co. of Boulder, Col., and several different German outfits. Later, the Japanese copied the gaff knife under the name "BEST-MADE, Japan."

Unlike most fish knives, which incorporate two blades, the gaff knife has three, including a master blade for cleaning fish, a secondary blade with hook disgorger and scaler, and a most unique third blade. Protruding from the handle, the third blade is an imposing fish gaff with a sharpened hook. By hooking or "gaffing" the fish, it becomes easier to land it in the boat.

To accommodate the gaff blade, the shape of the fishing knife handle was modified to a pistol-grip configuration, which seemed

Each of the four outstanding examples of fish bonker knives is quite rare, especially in good condition. They form the basis for a serious fishing-knife collection.

like a good compromise and was employed as the final shape of all such fishing knives. Not only was the pistol grip good for enclosing the gaff-hook blade, but the shape also helped the user hold onto the knife while hooking a large fish. Gaff knives are rather rare and quite expensive.

Western Cutlery's description of a gaff knife (from its 1931 catalog) is, *"Fisherman's knife, 5 inches long overall. Amber cream-colored non-breakable handle. Includes a large fish gaff, scaler, hook disgorger and bottle capper. Also large, slim clip-shaped blade. An absolutely new item that fills a long felt need. Hole for ring in end of handle."*

The list of other unique fishing knives is quite extensive, with the Marbles Safety Axe Co. developing several unique varieties, including the Marbles Handy Fish Knife, the Marbles Safety Fish Knife

and a small, simple blade called the Marbles Trout Knife. The Trout Knife has a small, round hold in the end of the handle that fits over a pinky finger to secure it and avoid dropping it into the water while gutting slimy fish. All of these fish knives are in high demand by collectors who seek the famous "Marbles" name. Western Cutlery and Manufacturing Co. produced a similar wedge-shaped fish scaling knife, several models of sheath knives with fish scaler blades, and several Texas tooth-pick-style fishing knives in both red and yellow celluloid. One of Western's Texas-toothpick-style fishing knives has a bottle opener built into the master blade, as does a similar piece built by W. R. Case and Co. of Bradford, Pa.

The collecting of fish knives has been generally limited to fishermen who appreciate the refinements

found in several knife varieties, or to collectors of gadget knives who have taken a liking to the uniqueness of built-in gaff hooks, tape measures and "bonkers." Because of tremendous variety, both in brand names and styles, available on the marketplace, the future of fish knife collecting is wide open both to experienced collectors and those just entering the arena. Particularly with the "Texas toothpick" varieties, mint examples can still be found on a regular basis, some with original etchings on the master blades. Resulting from increased interest in fish knives over the last several years, those pieces in outstanding condition will surely increase in value over time.

The key to fish knife collecting is not waiting until the spring thaw, but jumping in now and getting your feet wet.

Bear Hunting with a Virtual Ed Fowler

A bear hunt in the Algonquin wilderness tested the author's mettle, and he was glad to have Ed along, in spirit

By Evan F. Nappen, Esq.

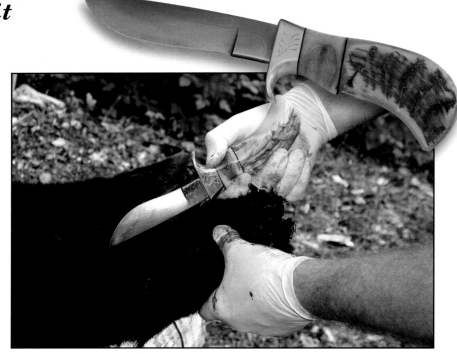

I RECENTLY HAD THE opportunity to go bear hunting in the Canadian Algonquin wilderness with knifemaker Ed Fowler. Ed wasn't physically present with me, but I had one of his famous Pronghorn knives in its heavy-duty, waxed-harness-leather sheath riding on my hip. Frankly, that's a lot like having Ed with you. This is because Ed builds his knives with indomitable spirit and purpose. He uses the finest 52100 ball bearing steel, which is hand-forged, multi-thermal treated and pushed to its penultimate limit in performance. Ed is always trying to go one better.

One of Ed's test blades was clamped in a vise and bent 11 times 180 degrees right and left. After returning to true, there were no cracks or stressors in the

Top Right: Carrying an Ed Fowler Pronghorn knife while bear hunting is much like having the maker alongside you in the woods. Everything about a Fowler knife has a purpose and a reason for being there. A Pronghorn fits the hand like an old friend. There is no surface on the knife that is uncomfortable to the touch, and the guard protects the user in the most effective, yet unobtrusive way.

Bottom Right: Hunting for bear in the Algonquin wilderness, the author could not have foreseen downing a 300-pound black bear, a trophy even in that neck of the woods, especially one that was charging right at him from 35 yards away!

steel. That's tough! The functional full guard of the Pronghorn is hand-sculpted brass marked with Ed's brand on one side, and on its obverse, the distinguished "Willow Bow" etch (the name of his ranch is the Willow Bow, and the etch is of a willow bow branch). The handle is from the most rugged and beautiful horn of Ed's Rambouillet buck sheep.

The high performance knife is created for grueling cutting tasks. Ed makes his knives to USE, and use hard. Everything about a Fowler knife has a purpose and a reason for being there. A Pronghorn fits the hand like an old friend. There is no surface on the knife that is uncomfortable to the touch, and the guard protects the user in the most effective, yet unobtrusive way.

Most importantly, the knife cuts and cuts and cuts. The steel is second to none.

Ed's voice speaks to you through his knives, "Hunt the way of the high performance knife." If you have ever had the good fortune to attend one of his BLADE Show seminars on high performance knives, you know what this means. It means not failing.

Notice the Rambouillet-buck-sheep-horn handle of the Ed Fowler Pronghorn knife sticking up above the leather sheath on the author's hip.

It means meeting the challenge. It means being tough and ready for whatever comes your way.

A bear hunting experience in the Algonquin wilderness tested my mettle, and I was glad to have Ed along with me.

On opening day of fall bear season in Canada, I sat alone wearing a full camouflage "bug suit" in a ground blind on a small rise in the verdant forest of the Algonquin wilderness. The area was a low cedar wetland and the aroma of white pines luxuriously flavored the air. The weather was crisp and clear.

A Crossbow and the Pronghorn

I was overlooking a baited log pile about 35 yards away down an old logging cut that veered to my right. I was armed with a crossbow and the Pronghorn. I sat from 2 p.m. until dark and saw no bears, but nonetheless I enjoyed my front row seat on nature.

By that first night, approximately half of the hunters at the Kanukawa Lodge (affectionately known as the "K.O.") took bears. My friend and associate Richard Gilbert took his first bear that night from a tree stand. The K.O. has been bringing premier hunts to outdoorsmen for over 30 years. The lodge is the proud recipient of a top recommendation (five stars) from the Ontario tourism board.

K.O. owner and manager, Ed Fick, assured me my bait was "active" for six weeks prior to my ar-

The author let his hunting guide use the Pronghorn to skin out the trophy black bear. Having personally skinned over 800 bears, the guide knew a good "using" knife when he saw it. He started at the bear's paw and opened him up like he was taking off the bear's clothes.

The bear-hunting guide meticulously removed the hide and took extreme care around the bear's head. Ed Fowler's Pronghorn knife performed flawlessly. Before giving the Pronghorn back to the author, the guide carefully examined it, and he stated that it was the finest knife he had ever used.

rival. Bears had been visiting the site regularly. He explained that bears often run their routes in three-day cycles. Given the K.O.'s outstanding reputation and success rate, I was confident I would see some action. Little did I know that my wishes for action would shortly be fulfilled "to the hilt."

The next day I was back in the ground blind at 2 p.m. It was sunny, about 70 degrees Fahrenheit, and most importantly, there was virtually no wind. If anything is detrimental to bear hunting, it is wind. I made a switch from the crossbow (the scope sight was malfunctioning) to my back-up weapon, a Marlin Model 1895 lever-action Guide Gun in 45-70. It's a darn good thing I switched from the crossbow to a gun because of what happened next.

At about 3:15, I heard a lot of crunching around in the woods and I knew it was a bear. I wondered if it was a cub being careless or a big bear that just did not care. I quietly eased the safety off and peered low over the blind waiting for the bear to lumber out of the thick woods to the log pile bait. Suddenly the woods to my left exploded and a black tornado charged me from 12-15 yards to the left of the ground blind. He must have thought I was another bear. I had only enough time to jump up and fire from the hip, a la Chuck Connors.

The bear was directly in front of the ground blind when I fired. It almost came down to having to use the Pronghorn to fight off the bear. He was so close that some

blood spattered back onto my gun and scope. The Garrett Cartridges Super-Hard-Cast Gas-Checked Hammerhead 420-grain slug at 1850 feet-per-second knocked him back hard on a roll down the hill and he lit into the woods. I then heard two unforgettable death moans.

I hiked out to the old logging road and marked it with an orange plastic ribbon and some dead logs so when the guide took a run he would see that I had shot a bear. My adrenaline was so pumped that when a chipmunk darted out in front of me, I almost blasted him with my 45-70. When the guide arrived, he commented that he never before had to begin a track right from the blind.

We tracked the bear 30-40 yards into the forest. We came upon him lying down dead on the forest floor of pine needles and leaves. He was a large 300-pound male black bear! He had an enormous head and a beautiful coat. This is a fine trophy size for Canada. It took four guys to drag the bear out of the woods and onto the 4x4 pickup truck.

The High-Performance Mindset

If my experience can make a difference for folks who are planning to do the same kind of hunt, then the key to surviving an aggressive bear encounter is to be well prepared, having the right equipment and being mentally ready to use it to one's best advantage. This is what very probably saved me from

a serious collection of impressions from bear teeth, claws and the like. Always be prepared for the worst-case scenario by pre-planning and keeping your eyes open.

Any hunt can result in the kind of jackpot I found myself in. The right gun, ammunition and knife can make all the difference. High performance is a mind-set that begins with reliable tools and ends with a purposeful attitude.

The next morning, I let my guide use the Pronghorn to skin out my bear. He has personally skinned over 800 bears and he knows a good "using" knife when he sees it. He is a highly-skilled bear skinner. He started at the bear's paw and opened him up like he was taking off the bear's clothes. He meticulously removed the hide and took extreme care around the bear's head. He butchered out the hams and back straps. He even packaged the hide and meat to be frozen for the long ride home.

Fowler's Pronghorn performed flawlessly. Before giving the Pronghorn back to me, my guide carefully examined it, and he stated that it was the finest knife he had ever used. He intends to acquire one for himself. (I was not about to tell him there is a seven-year wait.)

I was honored to have Ed Fowler with me on this exhilarating bear hunt. His high-performance philosophy is expressed through his workmanship on his outstanding knives. Ed's way of thinking can accompany you on any outdoor adventure, even if you cannot get your hands on a Pronghorn.

Family Forges

Find out how and why knifemaking runs in the blood

By Linda Moll Smith

THERE IS ONE verse in the Bible that has become a bit of a family joke around our house. It is from a time during the reign of Israel's King Saul, when the neighboring tribe of Philistines held sway in the land, and proclaims, "Now there was no smith found through all the land . . ." In response to which we always say, "We are making up for it now—why do you think there are so many Smiths around?"

Of course, the above scripture doesn't refer to Smith as a surname, but to a period of history during which the Philistinian oppressors forbade the Israelite men to forge copper, "lest they make themselves swords and spears." Those silly Phili oafs apparently didn't welcome the edged competition that finely drawn blades would have afforded Saul's underlings, either in the kitchen or on the battlefield, which may be why, even today, we refer to the uncultured and non-erudite (not to mention un-knifed) as Philistines!

The curious fact is, "smithing," as not merely a name but an occupation, does seem to run in family circles. Knifemakers themselves are always the first to grasp the point of bladesmithing as an art and a science. Their passion, distilled into a collectable and usable cutting edge, begs to be passed on to loved ones as a working inheritance. Sometimes the crafty connections are relatively evident, the most obvious being the tie between a father knifemaker and his son (or occasionally, vice-versa). Another trend is husband-wife teams.

Dellana and Van Barnett distinguish themselves from other knifemakers, not only because they're a married couple, but also by building blades with fine art designs that feature breathtaking gold and fine jewelry accoutrements, those certain knives that make collectors' eyes gleam.

Yet another common bond occurs when the overwhelming urge to meld fire and hammer to mould metal pauses and then leaps over a generation, passing from grandparent to grandchild. An invisible law of sorts, you might call it "the training clause for grandfathering in new knifemakers."

A Sharp Grandson

Such is the case with Wally Watts and his grandson, Johnathan, from Flat, Texas, near Gatesville, deep in Central Texas. Wally was working in computer operations as a night shift supervisor, with what he describes as "absolutely no background in metallurgy or machine shop design," when he was abducted one night by an alien desire to make knives. No, not really, but even he seems to remain a bit puzzled by his rapid transition from computer operator to knifemaker. "Well, I was always interested in the beauty of a good working folder," he allows with a soft Texas drawl.

That was 1986, and by 1988, he was a full-time maker of what he calls "family knives," folding knives ranging in design from traditional to custom, crafted from ATS-34 stainless steel. Wally ap-

Knifemaker Dale Cannon (left) is full of pride for his grandson, Chad Heddin, who has also been bitten by the blade-building bug.

plies his own heat treatment and temper, and he tests every blade for Rockwell hardness. When asked what makes his knives special, he says with modest pride, "They sharpen easy and hold an edge real well."

While Wally was steadily honing his craft, to the point that he received the "Best Handmade Functional Knife" award at the 1992 BLADE Show, holding onto his leather apron strings (so to speak) was Johnathan. First trying his hand at making knives when he was just 10 years old, the now 17-year-old senior at Gatesville is the only one in his class of 200 who can get by carrying a knife to school. (Ssshhh, we won't tell, either!) His very first year of knifemaking, the youngster sold enough edged tools to pay for a flight to Richmond, Va., for the national riflery matches, another interest of his.

At the 2004 BLADE Show in Atlanta, in June, Johnathan sold his entire lot of eight knives, also working folders like his grandfather's, and was busy taking orders for late summer delivery. One of his knives found a home with Susan Kreiser, herself a BLADE Show exhibitor.

How does his grandfather/tutor feel about the pupil's work?

His congratulatory grin says it all without words. But Wally allows, "When he's working, he turns up the radio in the shop real loud. That's when Grandpa has to leave to make a run into town." He glances knowingly at the object of his consternation, and for a moment, includes his audience in what is obviously a family joke.

Johnathan says that the profit from his knife sales helps pay for his truck and school expenses. Wally agrees: "Knifemaking is a good way for me to pay for my bad habits like golf and fishing. Everybody needs two jobs. I'm a bit of a professional bass fisherman after winning a big tournament."

When Wally is asked if Johnathan's father was ever taken with bladesmithing, he says, with a slight twinkle, "Naw, my son was always more interested in fishing. I think I passed that onto him, though."

Ancestral Art

By far the most common family connection in the knife business is that between father and son (or occasionally, son and father). Walk the aisles of any major knife show, or check out publications such as this one, and a person frequently notices the "& Son(s)" appellation tacked on the end of business names.

Lonesome Pine Knives, owned by Larry Harley of Bristol, Tenn., is a similar example. Harley's son, Richard, owns an offshoot business, Richard's Lonesome Pine Knives.

Larry offers immediate insight into knifemaking as an ancient and ancestral art. "Did you know that knifemaking is the second oldest profession?" He chuckles. "It's next to building fires, of course."

He declares that both his and his son's urge to forge must be genetic knowledge. "I think there's something to having it in the blood," he says. "I think my ancestors way back when were sitting around chipping flint and making knives. It seems natural to me."

Larry waxes most enthusiastic about his son's budding design eye. "I made him practice long and hard on railroad spikes, and when he satisfied me on those, I encouraged him to try knifemaking, more as a lucrative hobby, not full-time, like me, and he's been interested in it since he was nine years old."

Richard, who was displaying his first batch of knives at the 2004 BLADE Show, says he completed his first knife this year. "I've been hanging around the shop at home for so long and it looked easy, so I thought I would try it," he remarks.

He first tried forging at the most recent slate of classes held at the American Bladesmith Society's (ABS) School of Bladesmithing in Texarkana, Ark., and has turned out artistic results, with special

High school sweethearts, Dan and Carol Harrison have been married for 49 years and have worked together as knife and sheath makers, respectively, for 40 of those years.

touches like hand-made mesquite handles and textured copper.

His dad points out the Japanese temper line on one of his son's knives, and says, "I'm proud of him, not because he does good work, but because he works so hard. It takes a lot of work and concentration to finish out a knife, and he takes three or four days." He winks. "It also helps keep him plumbed up and away from the cars and those girls his age."

Larry himself has followed the creative urge away from stainless steel and towards damascus and what he calls "organic appeal." One of his knives, echoing Celtic lines, was forged using three cups of river sand from a friend of his. Another uses an Eskimo halibut weight as a functional design element on the handle. He also designed the prototype for the Browning Liberty Tree Bowie, including a handle fashioned from the original Liberty Tree in Maryland, with permission from the rare wood society that oversees it.

"I have a philosophy about dressing knives. They should be like clothing," says Larry. "You don't wear a tux shirt with jeans or jeans with a tux jacket. No, if you are putting on the Ritz, then you should look like Gary Cooper wearing a tux—everything goes together. Knives should be like that—everything belongs, not like sticking a striped tie on a hillbilly. It should 'stay purty,' like I always tell my friends."

Interestingly, another son of a father-son knifemaking combo echoes those exact sentiments. "When it comes to knife work, I'm big on the flow," says ABS journeyman smith Jody Muller. "Everything should look smooth."

Jody, and his father, Pat, along with the assistance of other family members, form the Muller Forge of Pittsburg, Mo. In this instance, it was son Jody who first began making knives in 1984, at the ripe old age of 12. He says, "I always liked knives, and my dad was a crafty-type guy. He bought me cheap knives and pocketknives, and finally I made a knife

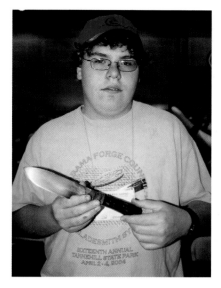

myself, an ugly thing with a wood handle screwed to it."

Jody soon enlisted the assistance of Pat, and started Jody Muller Knifeworks. As it turns out, 1994 was a banner year— the son-father team built a forge, began making damascus and changed the family business name to Muller Forge. Jody and Pat collaborate to make cleavers, swords and custom knives limited only by the imagination.

Muller Forge knives stand out, down to the tips of their hand-forged (1095 and L6) damascus blades, because most exhibit the

While Wally Watts was steadily honing his knifemaking craft, holding onto his leather apron strings (so to speak) was grandson, Johnathan. First trying his hand at making knives when he was just 10 years old, the now-17-year-old Johnathan sold his entire lot of eight knives at the 2004 BLADE Show. One of his knives found a home with Susan Kreiser, herself a BLADE Show exhibitor.

Larry Harley says he's proud of his son, Richard, shown with a fixed blade he fashioned, not because the youngster does good work, but because he works so hard. "It takes a lot of work and concentration to finish out a knife, and he takes three or four days," Larry says.

quality of hand carving, engraving and/or inlay work most often seen in fine jewelry. Such comes naturally, because Jody is a custom jewelry designer and watchmaker by trade, as well as a national-award-winning jewelry designer.

This is a family process. Pat grinds blades and fabricates handles and sheaths, while "Mom," Sue, updates the brochure and web site and waxes enthusiastic over Muller Forge products to anyone within earshot. Jody's wife, Ginger, serves as accountant and treasurer for the forge. Everyone at Muller Forge also welcomes visitors, which they say are happily frequent."

In the Family Way?

Speaking of familial processes, one former seamstress-turned-knifemaker is known in the indus-

try for engaging her entire brood in bladesmithing. Audra Draper, husband Mike, and their children, of Riverton, Wyo., all design, fabricate or dream about knives.

It all started 12 years ago when Audra hired onto the ranch of Ed Fowler and found herself drawn to the mechanic's shop, tinkering soon with custom leatherwork and some knife grinding. She received her ABS journeyman's stamp in 1996 and her master smith mark in 2000, and in between, moved and began her own knife shop.

Mike, a heavy equipment mechanic, had already been "playing" with knives on weekends, when in 2000 he injured his back in an accident and underwent surgery. Rather than be classified as disabled, he sought retraining as a knife designer. Audra says, "We had to beg the state of Wyoming to classify knifemaking as a bona-fide occupation." Adds Mike, "We had to educate them on all aspects of our knife operation—it was interesting that at first they didn't consider it a real job."

By 2001, Mike had become a journeyman smith. But that's only the beginning. In August 2003, son Gregory, 15, won the "Best New Knifemaker" at the Professional Knifemakers Association Show in Denver for a knife he styled with African water buffalo horn, turquoise, brass and damascus. Nephew, Jeremy, now 16, won "Best Miniature Knife" at the same show. Christopher, 14, designs fantasy knives, and 13-year-old daughter Melis-

sa's damascus jewelry took the "Grand Champion" award in the 4-H competition at the Wyoming State Fair this year. In addition to a son in the military, Mike has two daughters, Elizabeth and Rebecca, both of whom have also forged knives.

When not heating up the forge, the entire clan kicks back and cools down with typical Wyoming outdoorsy pursuits, including bow hunting, fishing, camping, and shooting rifles and pistols.

Knifemaking seems as natural as taking breath to this family that Audra laughingly describes as "real country hicks." Hicks? Not judging by their sophisticated knife designs, such as Mike's Sabra folders in anodized titanium, ladder-pattern

damascus and exotic black ash or box elder burl handles, or Audra's cowgirl design and classic jigged bone or mineralized deer horn handles.

Conjugal Creativity

Marriage is a blessed union, and no more so than when husband and wife combine to produce truly divine knife designs. Within the cutting edge industry, a partnership between spouses is a decided trend.

One way in which connubial connections make a statement in the smithy is when both spouses design and make knives. Just such a couple is Dellana, a bladesmith, and her partner in both love and knife 'crime,' Van Barnett, of St. Albans, W.Va.

An ABS journeyman smith and master smith, respectively, Mike and Audra Draper are a skilled husband-and-wife knifemaking team, so skilled, they've passed their knowledge down to their children who all make or dream about making knives. The three damascus folders pictured together are Audra's creations, and Mike made the mix of damascus and non-damascus folders in the other photo.

Jody, and his father, Pat, along with the assistance of other family members, form the Muller Forge of Pittsburg, Mo. In this instance, it was son Jody who first began making knives in 1984, at the ripe old age of 12. He says, "I always liked knives, and my dad was a crafty-type guy. He bought me cheap knives and pocketknives, and finally I made a knife myself, an ugly thing with a wood handle screwed to it." Jody soon enlisted the assistance of Pat, and started Jody Muller Knifeworks, now known as Muller Forge.

In July 1997, Dellana, who hails from Upstate New York, met Van at a Knifemaker's Guild Show in Las Vegas. She says, "We were both exhibiting, and I was set up across the aisle from him. We kept meeting eyes. In true West Virginia fashion, he hollered across the aisle, 'Are ya married?'"

"That may not sound romantic, but it worked. I went to visit him in West Virginia that Christmas," she pauses, "and didn't make it back home until March. By August, I had completely moved from New York to West Virginia."

Dellana, an award-winning original goldsmith who wears her own jewelry, and Van distinguish themselves from other knifemakers by building blades with fine art designs that feature breathtaking gold and fine jewelry accoutrements, those certain knives that make collectors' eyes gleam. These include hunting knives with elegant twists, damascus folders on the order of the deceased Jim Schmidt and limited-edition classics. A tribute to the popularity of her work, Dellana sold out of knives at the 2004 BLADE Show and added commissions to her five-year waiting list.

Speaking of years, perhaps one of the longest-lived partnerships in all of "knifedom" is the husband-wife team of Dan and Carol Harrison of Edom, Texas. High school sweethearts, the two have been married 49 years and have worked together for over 40 of those years.

Dan's knife work and Carol's custom sheath making are difficult to categorize, but that may be because the couple brings so much background and influence to the product. Dan, in addition to a military background, has served as riflery coach for a team of female marksmen, as a policeman, salesman, justice of the peace and bullmastiff owner.

He and Carol set up shop years ago in rural East Texas, in Van Zandt County, near the artsy community of Edom, and both have been heavily involved in local drama productions. All of this experience is distilled into Dan's final edged products, housed in Carol's leather sheaths. Son, Adam, and daughter, Dana Harrison Simmons, assist in the family business.

Dan first earned a niche as a stock-removal knifemaker after starting out forging his own D-2 steel. Along with revered fellow knifemaker Bob Dozier of Arkansas, Dan is using a triple-draw heat-treating process on D-2 that he believes makes for the newest great steel.

Because It's Fun

Time was, blacksmithing was a family-run institution. Fathers reared sons before the forge, and grandsons were born within earshot of the ringing anvil.

At this point in history, knives are just as necessary as they always were, but the methods of making them have been refined and industrialized so that hand forging has diminished in importance. The only exception is the enlightened craftsman, and spouses and family members, who cling happily to the old ways enriched with modern methods and materials.

Ancient tribal urges, genetic wisdom, artistic outlets or economic necessity aside, why would anyone, especially entire families, tackle the time, expense and fiery discipline required to join the sacred brotherhood of knifemakers?

One answer comes from a junior exhibitor at the Spirit of Steel knife show in Mesquite, Texas, last September. At his second show, displaying his two first knives—a mesquite-handled drop point hunter and 'just a hunter' with a jigged-bone handle—young Chad Heddin, only 14 at the time, said, "This is fun!"

A Bloke Who Builds More Than Blades

Meet an Australian knifemaker who is bound by no restrictions, no notions and certainly no limitations

By Keith Spencer

DAVID BRODZIAK STARTED out handcrafting collectible but serviceable knives in 1989. I like to call them "practical collectibles" (PC's)—knives that are equally suited for use or keeping in a display cabinet. Right from the outset, David had the mark of a maker who was going somewhere.

For years, he diligently labored, turning out PC's, experimenting with all sorts of innovative ideas, before inevitably drifting into the realm of creating art knives, which is now David's forte. His unique items of edged art are in demand all over the world, with about 80 percent of the sales generated via the Brodziak Knives Internet website www.omninet.net.au/-brodziak.

Ask David what's new in the workshop, and you'll be fascinated by what he tells you. Those of us familiar with his knives get used to seeing the endless array of stylish blade shapes, many of them ground from beautiful Swedish Damasteel, but it is the embellishment of David's furnishings that really grabs your imagination.

Many of his early knives featured scrimshawed images stippled into handles by renowned scrimshaw artist Gary Tonkin, whose fabulous marine artistry adorns ivory in galleries around the world. Both Gary and David live on the southwest corner of Australia, at Albany, a historic whaling and sealing port since before it was settled in 1827. The art of scrimshaw, practiced on whale teeth and bone, was spawned by

Two exquisite David Brodziak medieval daggers showcase artwork by Carol Ann O'Connor, marine scrimshaw by Gary Tonkin, engraving by Rashid El Hadi and highly patterned Damasteel blades.
(Brodziak photos)

crewmembers during downtime onboard whaling ships working the waters of the Atlantic Ocean and beyond.

So, at this place on the edge of the southern ocean, best known for its whaling and sealing history, David the custom knifemaker and Gary the marine artist combined their skills to "make some magic," adorning ivory knife handles with pictures portraying life at sea in a bygone era.

Ever on the lookout for new ways to market his wares, David went into full-time custom knifemaking in 1993, introducing unusual, upscale working knives with clear-resin handle scales. Each intricately developed knife featured fascinating objects from the South Sea encapsulated forever in clear-resin handle inserts.

In addition to his newfound vocation as a knifemaker, David was also a part-time diver. He inset and integrated colorful seashells into the clear-resin knife handles, along with a few other things the ocean gave up. Each one-of-a-kind knife could be as surely identified as a fingerprint, which is great for insurance purposes. For a time David took to forever encapsulating Australia's dangerous red-back spider in knife handles. It looked fantastic—a jet-black arachnid with a bright-red stripe on its back. Once seen, a knife collector just "'ad to 'ave one!"

No Greenbacks for Red-Backs

But David "got the chat" from the authorities for doing it. It seems you aren't allowed to encapsulate the ecology, even though we Australians swat and spray redbacks on sight to avoid being bitten by the buggers. Deterred, but not fazed, David ceased creeping around in dark places under the house with a jar in one hand and a lid in the other, and looked for new things to do.

By the time David became a full-time maker at age 45, he had been there and done that a bit. Mostly though, David was involved in the

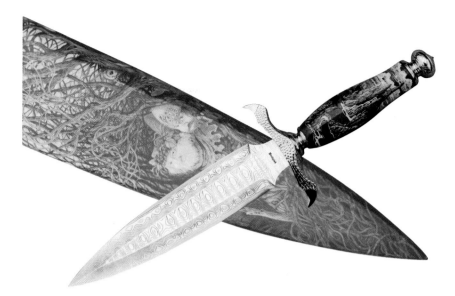

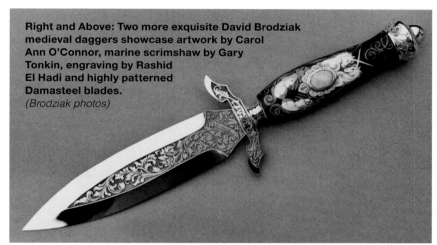

Right and Above: Two more exquisite David Brodziak medieval daggers showcase artwork by Carol Ann O'Connor, marine scrimshaw by Gary Tonkin, engraving by Rashid El Hadi and highly patterned Damasteel blades.
(Brodziak photos)

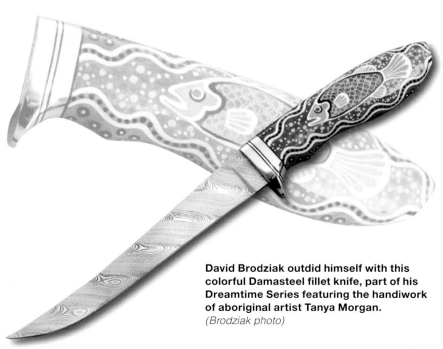

David Brodziak outdid himself with this colorful Damasteel fillet knife, part of his Dreamtime Series featuring the handiwork of aboriginal artist Tanya Morgan.
(Brodziak photo)

sheep industry, which included working with shearing teams in the harsh Northwest, traveling on a sheep ship to the Middle East, and employment as a dyer and colorist at the Albany Woolen Mills. He says he's always been interested in art, woodwork and metalwork, and David's aptitude to work with these mediums manifests itself in exceptional knives.

A deeply thinking, quiet-natured fellow with a real sense of humor, David never gets ruffled. Like everyone else, he occasionally gets bothered over things, but you need to ask him if he is angry because he doesn't show it. David is perhaps the most even-tempered person I know. I am the opposite. You will know if I'm ratty about something, which is why David and I probably get along so well—unlike poles attract and all that stuff.

This is not to say David is passive. Quietly determined, he is passionate about his lifestyle and livelihood. I can tell you he's a great bloke to be with on a boat fishing at sea, and he enjoys a beer—what more can I say?

I once quizzed David about where he gets his knifemaking inspiration and he told me he wakes up early in the morning and the ideas begin to flow. Armed with intuitive guidance for the day, he heads off to the workshop to bring them to fruition. However, don't try to telephone David in the middle of the day, because lunch is followed by a siesta, and you won't get past his wife, Gail, who also works in the business.

As a full-time knifemaker, David batch-makes his knife orders and speculative show knives, but he directs his attention to the handles later. For example, he might grind 20 blades, and then, to ensure complete compatibility, he sets about designing and fashioning each handle to specifically suit individual blades. Naturally, David takes into account the special requirements of a buyer and, if possible, factors those features into the finished product.

For a period, David engaged the services of Albany aboriginal artist Tanya Morgan to adorn knife handles with traditional images of our indigenous culture. It is an excellent concept. I remember writing David a check while waiting at a Perth City traffic light to obtain the first (unfinished) Dreamtime Series knife that he showed me while driving in the car.

"How much do I make it out for Broddy?"

"I dunno, mate...it isn't finished yet."

"C'mon, how much...the lights will change in a second and you'll lose the sale."

That did it. David dreamt up a price and I tossed him the check just before the joker in the car behind us impatiently tooted his horn.

David has always liked to participate in art, craft and custom-knife shows and travels extensively to meet collectors face to face.

A valuable David Brodziak showpiece parades marine scrimshaw by Gary Tonkin, and engraving and gold inlays by Rashid El Hadi. (Spencer photo)

A close look at the grip of Brodziak's stylized Middle Eastern dagger reveals a resin-encapsulated, fossilized fish in handle. The knife also sports a Gary Wood damascus blade. (Spencer photo)

BOY, DOES THIS BITCH...

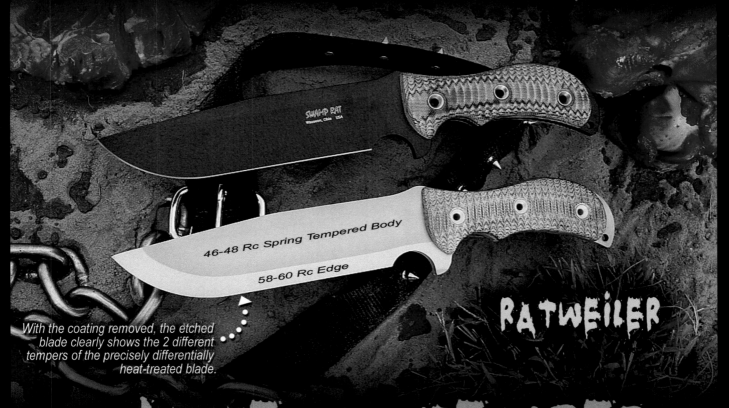

46-48 Rc Spring Tempered Body

58-60 Rc Edge

RATWEILER

With the coating removed, the etched blade clearly shows the 2 different tempers of the precisely differentially heat-treated blade.

...HAVE A TEMPER.

IN FACT, SHE HAS 2 COMPLETELY DIFFERENT TEMPERS!!!

NAME:	BLADE LENGTH:	OVERALL LENGTH:	HANDLE:	PRICE:
RATWEILER	7.5 INCHES	13 INCHES	CANVAS MICARTA	$178.95

The Ratweiler easily chopped through a concrete block with no major damage to the edge.

Locked in a steel jaw vise, the Ratweiler was bent past 70 degrees without breaking.

The Ratweiler chopped through 8 2 x 4's and maintained a shaving, sharp edge.

Shows have been good to him, not only for direct sales and to promote his work, but also for the knife awards he accumulated. Such awards further enhance David's widening reputation in the custom cutlery marketplace.

At the Australian Knifemakers Guild Millennium 2000 Show in Melbourne, David blitzed the field by winning Best Art Knife, Best Kitchen Knife, Best Hunter and Best Small Game Knife awards. Later in the year, he took home Best Art Knife at the Adelaide Custom Knife Show. In all, David's knives have won over 16 show awards since 1995.

David journeyed to the United States, in 1997, to attend shows.

One of them was the 5th Annual Custom Knife Show run by the Professional Knifemakers Assoc. in Denver, where he received an award for Best Fillet Knife. Enlightened and enthused by the overseas experience, David returned to his workshop and set about taking his art knives to a new level of quality and presentation.

Staggering Price for a Dagger

David altered his knife designs and became more selective in the materials he used in order to better accommodate the brilliant skills of those with whom he elected to work. The exquisite adornments of Tonkin and world-class engraver Rashid El Hadi came together on a fabulous Brodziak dagger that carried a price tag of $6,500. A discerning collector quickly snapped up this unique showpiece.

David learned that such showpieces, which were essentially conceived to draw buyers to his show tables, were always among the first to sell. Over time, his heavily adorned patterns have become the knives for which he is best known.

Inspired by his own success selling up-market art knives beautified by only the best embellishers, David harnessed the fantastic talent of a fine artist, Carol Ann

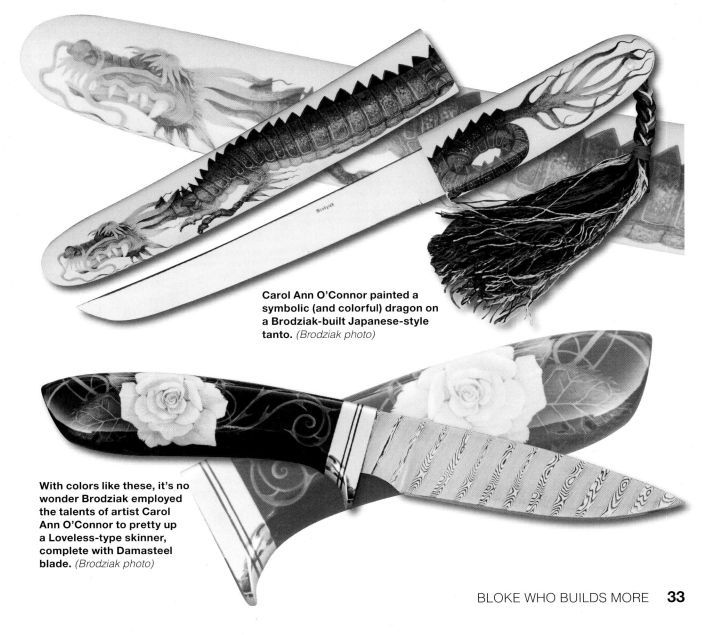

Carol Ann O'Connor painted a symbolic (and colorful) dragon on a Brodziak-built Japanese-style tanto. (Brodziak photo)

With colors like these, it's no wonder Brodziak employed the talents of artist Carol Ann O'Connor to pretty up a Loveless-type skinner, complete with Damasteel blade. (Brodziak photo)

O'Connor, to intricately paint images on the handles and scabbards of his medieval dagger series. It turned out to be a masterstroke by David.

Carol Ann, originally a wildlife artist, turned her hand to producing medieval mystical/fantasy art. Her phenomenal imagination and incredible creativity manifests in fascinating images embracing old-world mythology and symbolism. Surreal, intriguing impressions sometimes drift into the dark side, yet always there exists the element of mystique.

For Carol Ann, decorating David's large daggers has proven to be a unique, challenging and rewarding extension of her work; the more knives she paints, the more David sells, and the more new ideas they can dream up. And the collectors are lining up for Brodziak creations, which means collectively David and the artists he commissions have got the formula right!

I guess it can be seen as a measure of success when opportunist manufacturers copy your work and inject cheap replicas of your masterpieces into the global market. A Chinese company brazenly flogs "knock-offs" of at least two scaled-down Brodziak-O'Connor one-of-a-kind art knives at silly prices. Presented in colorful and attractive packaging, the clever devils have made the knives just

Take a walk on the dark side with this Brodziak dagger of unorthodox design. The handle and sheath embellishment is by Carol Ann O'Connor. *(Brodziak photo)*

An Arabian Jambiya-inspired knife by Brodziak not only demonstrates what can be done with a Damasteel blade, but also how subtle-yet-detailed artwork, in this case by Carol Ann O'Connor, can take a knife to new levels. *(Brodziak photo)*

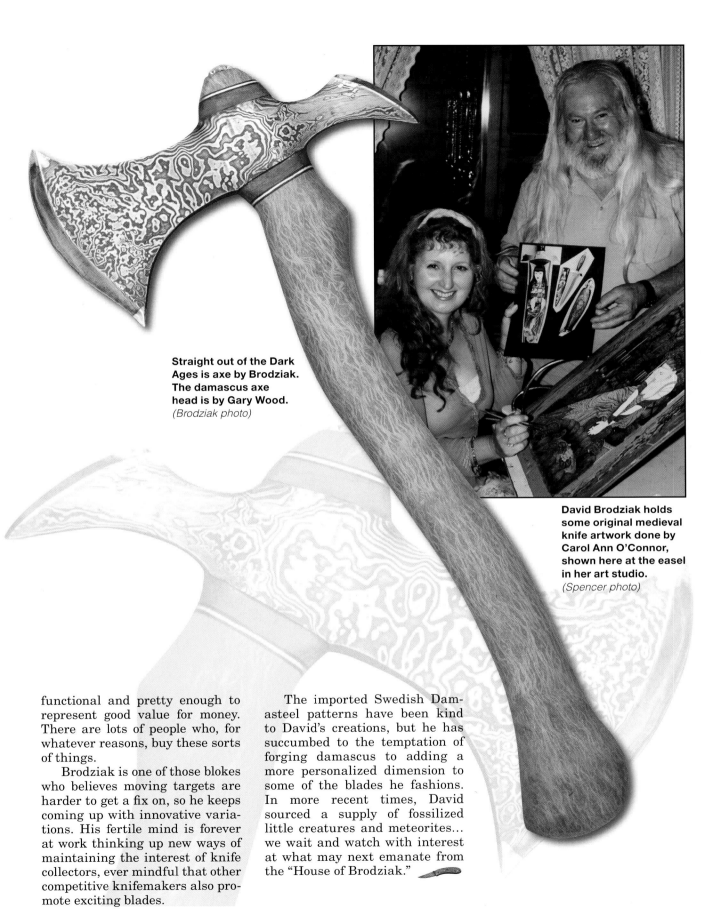

Straight out of the Dark Ages is axe by Brodziak. The damascus axe head is by Gary Wood.
(Brodziak photo)

David Brodziak holds some original medieval knife artwork done by Carol Ann O'Connor, shown here at the easel in her art studio.
(Spencer photo)

functional and pretty enough to represent good value for money. There are lots of people who, for whatever reasons, buy these sorts of things.

Brodziak is one of those blokes who believes moving targets are harder to get a fix on, so he keeps coming up with innovative variations. His fertile mind is forever at work thinking up new ways of maintaining the interest of knife collectors, ever mindful that other competitive knifemakers also promote exciting blades.

The imported Swedish Damasteel patterns have been kind to David's creations, but he has succumbed to the temptation of forging damascus to adding a more personalized dimension to some of the blades he fashions. In more recent times, David sourced a supply of fossilized little creatures and meteorites... we wait and watch with interest at what may next emanate from the "House of Brodziak."

A Meeting of the Mosaic Damascus Minds

Experimentation and sharing of information between smiths led to significant changes in the damascus world

By Joe Szilaski

MY FIRST EXPERIENCE with damascus was in trade school, back in 1963. My teacher, who was a third-generation blacksmith, taught me how to forge. After so many months, he showed me how to make damascus out of horseshoe nails the way his grandfather had taught him. On my first try, I made a big mess. He encouraged me to keep working on it, because out of that black, charcoal-looking thing I'd made, some magic would come.

In my mind, the only magic would be if anything at all came out of that ugliness. But he was right. When we ground and etched the billet, something was magical—my first damascus forged from horseshoe nails. At 14 years old, I thought that it was the most beautiful thing, and I felt like king of the hill. Some 40 years later, I still feel that magic.

However, a lot has changed in the last 40 years, due to advances in technology, better steels, and a lot of dedicated bladesmiths who push their skills and the steel to the limits. While the fundamental techniques of blacksmithing have not changed in thousands of years, bladesmiths are now developing new techniques in the making of mosaic damascus that are well suited to this art form.

It is known that mosaic damascus has been made for centuries.

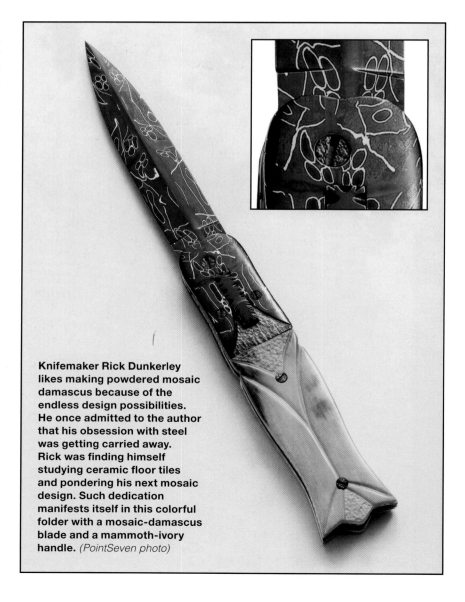

Knifemaker Rick Dunkerley likes making powdered mosaic damascus because of the endless design possibilities. He once admitted to the author that his obsession with steel was getting carried away. Rick was finding himself studying ceramic floor tiles and pondering his next mosaic design. Such dedication manifests itself in this colorful folder with a mosaic-damascus blade and a mammoth-ivory handle. *(PointSeven photo)*

Steve Schwarzer started experimenting with powdered steel in the 1980s, and he's gotten quite good at forging the stuff, as evidenced by the "Killer Whale" mosaic-damascus blade of his folder. The fossil-walrus-ivory handle is carved, and the knife liners showcase heavy file work by the maker. (*PointSeven photo*)

Old swords and daggers have been found with lettering and initials forged into the blades. How this was done was a well-kept secret.

Nevertheless, such mystery has not stopped modern blade-smiths from learning the ancient technique. Just to name some of today's pioneers in mosaic da-mascus, such would include Daryl Meier, Steve Schwarzer, George Werth, Hank Knickmeyer and others who contributed to this beautiful art.

When you first look at a blade with lettering forged into the steel, it's a common reaction to scratch your head wondering how this was done, similar to the feeling you had as a kid the first time you saw a ship-in-a-bottle. But upon studying the steel pattern more closely, you can usually figure out the way things were done.

The old technique of making mosaic damascus involved the use of rectangular- or square-bar stock. Back then, the oddly shaped bars necessary to form the design had to be forged or filed into their required shapes. Today, bar stock is readily available in various sizes, though there may still be some need to forge different sizes and shapes to suite your needs.

In the mosaic-Damascus world, guessing is not really an option, and planning is. Using graph paper to plan mosaic de-signs or lettering is a good start. This old-style of mosaic-damascus making is an extremely time-con-suming process. The smith has to give careful consideration to what type of steel is used. Just like a marriage between two people, the steels, either high or low carbon, have to be compatible with each other in order to fashion a strong forge weld. A lot of time, planning and dedication goes into this type of art form.

The letters can be lined up to form words, or combined with oth-er designs. A bladesmith should remember that each letter or design is one separate steel billet, at least until he or she starts slic-ing and dicing in the final forging stage to form the whole billet.

I remember back in the early 1990s, when Werth and Joe Knuth collaborated on a knife that ap-peared on the cover of *BLADE Magazine*. George forged a damas-cus billet with Jim Weyer's name in the steel, the letters stretching from the hilt to the point. Joe de-signed and executed the knife, and many years ago, he and I sat at my dining room table discussing the great number of hours and pieces of bar stock George spent to create just one element of that design.

Damascus Worth Fighting For

Then our conversation drifted to Meier and the unforgettable mosaic-Damascus bowie he fash-ioned with the U.S. flag, including

In the author's opinion, the earliest form of mosaic damascus was multi-bar damascus, where more than one bar of pattern-welded steel is put together to create the whole. One of the best modern examples of a bladesmith using such a technique is Jerry Rados, who forges multi-bar twist patterns, known as Turkish damascus. For his "Metamorphosis" locking-liner folder, knifemaker Steve Hill employed Rados's Turkish damascus. (*SharpByCoop.com photo*)

the stars and stripes, forged into the steel. When I saw that bowie in *BLADE*, I could feel the power and freedom we enjoy. Forget the Alamo, that bowie would have been reason enough for Samuel Bell and his buddies to fight!

All this was made possible due to the amount of experimentation done by all blacksmiths who came before our time. In my opinion, the earliest form of mosaic damascus was multi-bar damascus, where more than one bar of pattern-welded steel was put together to create the whole. One of the best modern examples of a bladesmith using such a technique is Jerry Rados, who forges multi-bar twist patterns, known as Turkish damascus. His steel, sought by makers and collectors alike, emulates the charm of this almost lost art, while maintaining the beauty and function of the alloys he blends.

As time has progressed, some smiths have started experimenting with new steel technologies, pushing the mosaic-damascus envelope even further. Today, we have computerized laser and wire EDM (Electrical Discharge Machining) units available to cut out complicated designs that were previously not feasible.

Another new avenue in the making of mosaic damascus is the use of powdered steels. Technology is definitely giving the modern smith a huge advantage compared to what was. Computer-guided lasers and advanced, powdered-steel technology serve as huge steppingstones for the mosaic-Damascus world.

This is where some questions must be raised. I initially viewed the use of laser-cut designs as a form of cheating. What happened to the good old-fashioned way of forging and hand-filing bar stock to achieve design? Some of the more skeptical may ask, "How can this be handmade when the designs are cut by computer-controlled machines?" Well, this is a fair question.

After pondering the issue for some time, with a cup of coffee in my hand, I decided my first

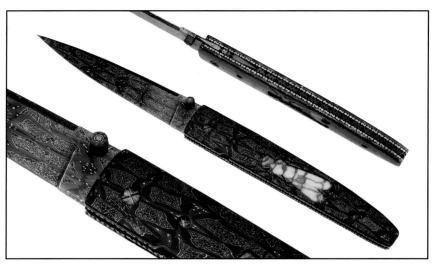

As if the "Bug Splats"-pattern mosaic damascus blade and handle of a Barry Gallagher folder weren't enough to look at, the knifemaker continued the theme with a fly-shaped window frame on the handle. *(BladeGallery.com photo)*

For the blade of his "Riptide" folding fantasy fighter, John Lewis Jensen combined checkerboard-flower-pattern mosaic damascus with George Werth worm-hole damascus. The Riptide also showcases two different damascus patterns for the bolster—paisley and crossroads—both forged by Robert Eggerling. Other knife features include sapphires set into 18-carat-gold bezels and an exhibition-grade fossil-mastodon-ivory handle.

impression was incorrect. Yes, the use of computer technology makes creating more complicated designs faster and simpler, but this does not mean it is easy, not at all. I agree we cannot call this process "handmade," and it is true

that a bladesmith practicing such techniques is not actually cutting, drilling, filing or completing other handiwork needed in creating the design.

It is also true that no matter what method is used, the mosaic design is only a raw material until the smith puts his or her skill into forging the billet, which is only the first step in making a knife. This is how a non-handmade material transforms to handmade.

In the making of any type of mosaic damascus, numerous things can go wrong and careful preparation is required. For powdered damascus, a smith needs to make a forge box to contain the handcrafted or laser-cut designs in whatever order he or she prefers. Then, it is necessary to tightly fill the box with powdered steel. Before sealing the box, most smiths will place cigarette paper or a few drops of oil to burn out the small amount of oxygen trapped inside the box.

Now the steel-filled box, complete with mosaic patterning in the form of shapes, letters or other designs in neat rows, is ready for forging. Forge welding temperature and timing is extremely important to have a strong weld. The other key factor is for a smith to make certain he or she forges as evenly as possible in all six directions, keeping the billet perfectly square, or the design will be distorted. This all takes time and experience.

Though I have over 40 years experience with metal work, I do not consider myself the most advanced person in the field of powdered damascus. So I asked a few questions of the mosaic pioneers.

Scene Steelers

Schwarzer and I attended a few hammer-ins together and had some time to shoot the breeze. Steve mentioned he was the first smith to start experimenting with powdered steel in the 1980s. By 1990, he was making powdered damascus. In 1991, BLADE Magazine featured Steve's beautifully done "Gent's" powdered damascus folder with a hunting scene in the blade.

Steve shared this technique with a few smiths, who, for a while, managed to keep the secret under their hats. But like everything else, sooner or later the

rabbit jumped out of the hat and the process became more popular. Steve went to Germany in 1993 to demonstrate the making of powdered mosaic damascus to European bladesmiths.

In 1998, Steve and Matt Diskin got together and took a different approach to making powdered mosaic. Instead of using 2- or 3-inch-thick steel stock to cut the male and female designs, they started using thinner flat stock and pierced the design through. The advantage of this technique is that you can create more detail for your design and it is a lot more efficient.

My next interviewee was Knickmeyer. Hank makes complicated and intricate mosaic damascus. I save only the highest of compliments for his work. Hank likes the new powdered mosaic process because it gives him the freedom to develop extremely complex designs, not to mention the efficiency of such a technique. Hank reinforces the strength of

his blades by using a solid-steel or damascus cutting edge.

I already mentioned Werth's work. I had the opportunity to visit George at his shop many years ago. The careful drawing and planning of his work impressed me. George used powdered steel only a few times. He feels you can create smoother curves and some more complicated designs with powdered steel, but he still prefers to make his mosaic out of old-fashioned bar stock. After asking him why, he explained that he has better luck forging from bar stock and feels it is structurally better.

Rick Dunkerley also likes making powdered mosaic damascus because of the endless design possibilities. Rick is dedicated to the art of creating new mosaic patterns, and about 10 years ago, he and I got into a conversation about his mosaic damascus. Rick mentioned his obsession with steel was getting carried away. He was finding himself studying ceramic floor tiles and pondering his next mosaic design. It is

Right: The bolsters of a Jason Howell locking-liner folder are deer-skulls-patterned mosaic damascus. The knife also sports a blue-mammoth-ivory grip, a damascus thumb stud and vine file work inside the liners. *(PointSeven photo)*

Left: The author will never forget a mosaic-Damascus bowie Daryl Meier fashioned with an image of the U.S. flag, including the stars and stripes, forged into the steel. Paul Jarvis incorporated a strikingly handsome Daryl Meier damascus blade on an exotic dagger, complete with a carved African-blackwood handle. *(PointSeven photo)*

true—inspiration can come from many sources. Anyone who sees or owns one of Rick's knives realizes the time and effort that goes into one of his pieces.

As for myself, I am an old-fashioned dinosaur. I only use high-carbon tool steels in my damascus, with just enough carbon difference in the steels to obtain a nice contrast. Sometimes I employ some nickel damascus designs for decoration along the spine or center of the blade, but the cutting edge is always high-carbon steel or damascus.

Most mosaic damascus is fragile compared to other types of damascus due to the nature of this type of construction. I do not mean fragile like glass that, if you drop it, will fall apart, but being made of a lot of small pieces that must be properly forged together in order to make a whole. Mosaic steel can only be as strong as its weakest weld.

Another reason mosaic is not as strong as it could be, is that nickel is often used in the designs. Nickel gives a beautiful contrast in a pattern-welded billet and in the design itself, but it does not create as strong of a forge weld. Like I mentioned earlier, the materials have to be compatible to have a strong weld, and nickel is not one of the stronger components.

Knifemaker Jerry Grice fashions a pair of folders, one with a crisscross-pattern mosaic-damascus blade, and the other revealing images of stars, stripes and guns within the blade steel. *(PointSeven photo)*

Steel Reinforcements

Most bladesmiths agree that mosaic is not made for heavy use unless it is reinforced. Reinforcing the steel can be done by one of several methods, and only then does a bladesmith achieve a strong, functional knife.

Just because some of us strive for higher standards in the making of art knives does not mean we sacrifice the true form and function of a knife, or in my case, a tomahawk. Anybody can achieve elegance, grace and function in their product as long as they are willing.

Experimentation and sharing of information between smiths led to a significant change in the damascus world. Though some may take different approaches, there is a time and place for all in the world. Computers save us time and effort while making new things possible, but hopefully the heart of the forge will live on for generations.

Bladesmithing is not just brute force or strength. One has to have imagination, visualization and some brains. To achieve mosaic damascus takes great skill and dedication. It does not matter what technique or modern technology is used. So I would like to congratulate all pioneers and bladesmiths for their contribution to this beautiful art form.

Thanks to our ancestors whose needs sparked ingenuity in solving everyday intangible problems, perhaps a small, prehistoric seed has been planted in all of us to carry on in the modern world.

The **Bill Fiorini slicing machine** sports a 7-inch pinwheel-pattern mosaic damascus blade forged from 1095 and L-6 high-carbon steels. The bolster is sterling silver with 14-carat-gold pinwheel-shaped inlays, and the handle is blue/green mastodon ivory.
(BladeGallery.com photo)

Pop Open A Serious Auto Knife

As edged steel slams home by the push of a button, a smile spreads across the knife nut's face

By Dexter Ewing

THEY WON'T MIND if you call them knife nuts—no more than a switchblade minds being called an "automatic knife" or an "auto." It's all the same to them. To anyone who likes gadgets, and in particular, those who can appreciate the shine of new steel and an edge so sharp it's dangerous to the touch, autos are by far the coolest things cutting.

Now, quite probably more than ever before in history, autos are popular with knife aficionados. It's not difficult to figure out why. It's the thrill of pressing a button and seeing a flash of steel as the blade is unleashed and rotates out of the handle with force, and being able to fully deploy a folder blade just by pressing a button. The blade is out in the blink of an eye, locked and ready for use. Through the advancements of modern metalworking machinery (CNC-controlled laser cutters, milling machines and grinders), autos have become slick, sleek and serious.

Automatic knives are subject to strict federal regulations. The sale, ownership and even the shipping of automatic knives is strongly controlled by the government. Technically, the only

people legally allowed to possess, carry and use automatic knives are law enforcement, firefighters, emergency medical personnel and those in the military. Even within these agencies, there are also laws governing the use of automatic knives by their members, and not all participants are allowed to carry autos. Interstate commerce of automatic knives is also strictly regulated. Direct sale of such knives from authorized dealers to any of the exempted agencies is the exception. With this being said, let's sit back and take a look at the latest offerings in tactical-style automatic knives that can be found on the market today.

The Scarab is MicroTech's latest out-the-front (OTF)-opening automatic. The OTF design permits for a slender, flat-profile handle, which makes the knife easy to carry. This is one of the finest OTF knives on the market. *(Hoffman photo)*

The Pro-Tech Knives Godson
The Godson is Pro-Tech's scaled-down version of its popular Godfather automatic. The Godfather design was inspired by the classic Italian-style stiletto and came to fruition through the use of modern-day materials like titanium, aluminum, carbon fiber and 154CM steel.

Dave Wattenberg, president of Pro-Tech Knives, says that there is a "vintage appeal to the Godson," with its unique blend of historic design interpretation mated with modern manufacturing techniques. Another aspect of the Godson that appeals to knife nuts is "the size [of the overall knife], especially the width of the handle," Wattenberg points out. "We planned that out and kept the handle very slender."

The Godson sports a 3-inch blade with a nice tumble finish, and comes in several models featuring different looks and materials. There is an all-black tactical-style Godson, and full-blown, dressed-out versions featuring pearl, gold-lip-pearl and carbon fiber handle inserts coupled with titanium frames.

Blade options include hand-rubbed, satin-finished 154CM steel, and Devin Thomas stainless

Each knife in the 685 Series from Masters Of Defense is a compact, tactical automatic folder featuring a 2.9-inch blade. *(Hoffman photo)*

damascus in reptilian and fireball patterns. One Godson model features an anodized-aluminum frame and bolsters, and a smooth, black G-10 handle. A steel pocket clip is affixed to the butt end of the handle for carrying the knife deep in a pants pocket.

Those familiar with Pro-Tech's knives know that they have strong springs, and when the blades are activated via buttons, they have a bit of recoil to them. The Godson is no exception. Its smooth action and strong spring equate to the blade popping out real fast, with the type of sound and action that would make any hard-core automatic knife fanatic grin from ear to ear.

Benchmade 5000 Auto Presidio

Benchmade has long been an authority in the realm of factory automatics. The company doesn't mess around, taking seriously the production of real-world autos for law enforcement and military personnel. In 2003, Benchmade took the wraps off its latest automatic folder, the Model 5000 Auto Presidio. Designed by custom knifemaker Mel Pardue, the heavy-duty, robust Auto Presidio incorporates Benchmade's exclusive Axis Lock mechanism that props the blade open.

At the 2003 S.H.O.T. (Shooting Hunting Outdoor Trade) Show, I had an opportunity to visit at length with Bill McHenry and Jason Williams, two accomplished makers who designed the Axis Lock. The mechanism is significant, as Benchmade also incorporates the Axis Lock into numerous of its manual, non-automatic-opening folders. I asked the design pair for their insight into the use of the Axis Lock for an automatic knife. The Model 5000 and new 4200 were Benchmade's first automatics to employ the Axis Lock, and hopefully, they will not be the last! "The 5000 is a tactical, weapons-grade automatic knife," declared Bill McHenry.

"The Axis Lock," began Jason Williams, "transfers force from the lock bar to the [steel] liners, thus creating a folding knife that possesses the strength of a fixed blade." "It became a stronger, more reliable platform for an automatic knife," McHenry summed up.

What is particularly interesting is the underlying concept of the 5000's lock design, along with its integrated safety that prevents accidental lock movement in the blade-open or blade-closed positions.

McHenry explained that the 5000 has "fail safe redundancy," meaning, no matter which springs (those in the Axis mechanism, main blade coil spring or the safe-

ty) may break in the field, the user still has a fully functional, folding lock-blade knife. What's the mere price to pay for all this innovation? The manufacturer's suggested retail price (MSRP) is $220 for a satin-finished-blade version, and $230 for a blade with a black BT2 coat.

Another exciting automatic to come from the Benchmade stable is the new 4200 Auto Resistor. Custom knifemaker Mike Snody designed the Resistor to be a substantial folding work knife with a comfortable grip and handy blade shape. Benchmade infused the design with its exclusive Axis Lock mechanism that also acts as the blade release, just like the Model 5000 Auto Presidio.

The 4200 Auto Resistor features a 3 3/4-inch 154CM blade in a shape that Benchmade calls a "Gotham-swedged clip point." Machined, black G-10 handle overlays give a unique appearance to the knife, while adding to the hand-filling grip quality. A pocket clip mounted at the extreme end of the handle allows for toting the 4200 tip-up in a pants pocket, and as deep as possible for maximum concealment.

It's a bit deceiving, but the Auto Resistor has a big, thick handle. The backbone of the knife comes in the form of 6061-T6 hard-anodized aluminum scales with 420J2 liners. Pick up a 4200 Auto Resistor and feel how the handle fills your grip nicely. It's definitely powerful cutlery for those qualified to carry it. The MSRP for the 4200 is $180 for the satin-finished-blade version, and $190 for one with a black BT2-coated blade. Each model comes with a plain or partially serrated edge.

Gerber-Emerson Alliance

Ernest Emerson is the president of Emerson Knives, Inc., a company with a reputation solidly grounded in the building of top-notch factory tactical folders. Emerson is also an accomplished custom knifemaker whose designs are in demand among the "high-speed, low-drag" circles. Thus, it made sense that Gerber Legendary Blades would hook up with Emerson to collaborate on Gerber's first automatic knife.

Says Mark Schindel, marketing services manager for Gerber, "The Gerber-Emerson Alliance was the logical next step in our progression of knives. We work very closely with the Spec Ops teams and law enforcement, and they were requesting an automatic knife."

Appropriately named the Alliance, this fistful of knife features a 6061-T6 aluminum handle with an integral hand guard, and it's given a tough, Type III hard-anodized finish. The 4-inch, clip-point blade is of premium 154CM steel treated with a black-oxide coating to ward off corrosion and reduce glare.

"The knife was designed as ruggedly and heavy-duty as possible," Schindel points out. "We wanted a knife that could be depended on when the going gets tough."

Some of the automatic knives on the market have a built-in safety that prevents accidental firing of the blade. The Alliance's safety is unique in the sense that it is of a cross-bolt type activated by a push button, and the mechanism is located in close proximity to the firing button. When the safety is engaged, and the blade is in the closed position, the user simply puts his/her thumb over the two buttons and gives them both a firm press simultaneously. In one fell swoop, the safety is disengaged and the blade is fired. A black pocket clip allows for tip-up carry and, thus, easy access and blade deployment. The Alliance is yours for an MSRP of $228.

Microtech QD Scarab OTF

Microtech's QD Scarab is classified as an OTF (out the front) automatic. The Scarab is an offshoot of the Ultratech, another OTF that is still a part of the MicroTech line.

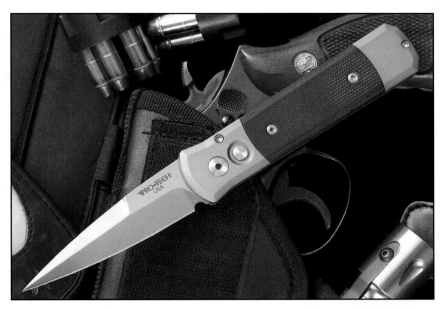

Pro-Tech built the Godson to be a scaled-down version of its popular Godfather model. The 3 1/4-inch, stiletto-style blade of the Godson tapers to a precise point, and heavy-duty handle construction involves G-10 scales with double aluminum bolsters. *(Hoffman photo)*

"There was great demand for a wider blade, and a knife for utility use," explains Microtech president Tony Marfione on why the company brought out the Scarab. "We upgraded the blade steel [from the Ultratech], and utilized the hardest coating for the handle."

As "OTF" designates, the blade of the Scarab shoots straight out from the front end of the handle, as opposed to swinging out from the handle on a pivot like the other automatics reviewed for this article. The OTF design permits for a slender, flat-profile handle, which makes the knife easy to carry. One downside to this design is the handle shape itself, which is limited outside of a rectangle. The second disadvantage, though more of a personal preference more than anything else, is that when the blade is extended, there is slight side-to-side play in the locked-open position. The play is necessary to assure quick, fluid-like action of the blade sliding out of the handle.

Most OTFs are single actions, meaning each has a blade that automatically pops out of the handle by sliding or pressing a release button. Then, to retract the blade, one must pull a cocking lever that brings the edged steel back into the handle. The Scarab is a double-action OTF. Not only does the blade automatically extend out of the handle, it also retracts automatically. Marfione explains that there are dual kick springs in the handle to automatically control both the extend and retract actions of the blade, and there are two locks—one to lock edged steel open and one to lock the edge closed.

As for strength of the locks, Marfione says, "There is no way to collapse the blade when open." The blade is controlled via an oversized thumb slide switch. A quick push on it will make the blade instantly appear. A firm tug back on it retracts the blade at equal speed. It seems to magically extend and retract, complete with a metallic noise that will delight any auto knife enthusiast! The Scarab's blade is 3-1/2 inches long and is flat ground from CPM S30V steel. One particular sample exhibits an attractive, two-tone, black-and-silver blade finish. MicroTech does its own black coating in-house, using a molybdenum disulfide. "Corrosion resistance is phenomenal," Marfione proudly declares.

The Scarab's handle is milled out of 6061-T6 aluminum and subjected to a Type II, Class III hardcoat anodizing, called "Hard Tuff X-20," which includes a Teflon impregnation. Inlays of grip tape on both sides of the handle, along with the milled-in traction notches on the perimeter, provide secure, non-slip hand purchase.

There are two carry modes for the Scarab. A black, steel pocket clip is affixed to the end of the handle and can be switched to the other side of the grip for left-hand carry. With each Scarab, Microtech also includes a high quality nylon belt sheath sporting a Velcro® flap closure. Each sheath also contains a diamond-coated sharpening file and a takedown key for reversing the pocket clip. These two accessories ride securely in their own pockets on the sheath. The file is a nice bonus that allows easy edge maintenance while in the field, and for added versatility, a steel glass breaker is screwed into the end of the handle for rescue applications. The latest and greatest from the company that helped popularize production OTF automatics will cost you $595.

In 2004, the company also released the MTX2 double-action folder, a stout, working folder done up in typical Microtech fashion. The modified-clip-point blade stretches 3 1/2 inches, with premium CPM S30V stainless steel being the material of choice. With an overall length of just under 8 inches, the MTX2 offers powerful cutting performance in a compact, easy-to-carry package.

The blade can be opened in one of two modes. Regular, manual opening is achieved by coaxing the blade out of the handle and forward via one of the dual, ambidextrous thumb studs. Edged steel can be fired automatically by pressing the left-hand bolster forward. If firm pressure is placed on the rear of the bolster, it will pivot slightly, therefore releasing the leaf spring inside the handle and kicking the blade up and out to the locked position.

The MTX2 is available in a green-linen-Micarta® or carbon-fiber handle with titanium bolsters, or an all-carbon-fiber handle version. Blade finishes include a satin finish, stone wash, two-tone black polymer coating, or an OD green coating. As an added touch of aesthetic quality is an inlay on each

blade, just underneath the thumb stud, that matches the handle material of choice. That's neat!

The MTX2 represents Microtech's ongoing commitment to designing and executing the finest double-action folding knives on the production market. One would be hard pressed to find another knife in this class, with such excellent fit, finish and action, as the MTX2. The MSRP is $600.

Masters Of Defense 875 Series

Masters of Defense (MOD) is another top name in the tactical auto folder arena. Each of its edged products is manufactured with precision and quality, two characteristics that have helped the MOD name climb to the top. New is the 875 Series of auto folders.

With a blade length of 3-3/4 inches, making it a formidable folder, the 875 LTF has a 154CM flat-ground, fighter-style blade set into a stylish Zytel® handle with heat-treated stainless steel liners.

"The 875 series was designed to provide the customer with an extremely well made knife without the expense involved in milled-aluminum handles," said Jim Ray, CEO of MOD.

MOD wanted a knife that was not only cost conscious, but also stylish. Ray indicated that he aimed for a balance between performance and aesthetics. With the 875 series, MOD has accomplished the balance with not one, but three handsome-looking variations. In addition to a fighter-style blade, MOD also offers striking clip-point and aggressively styled tanto blades. There is certainly something for everyone!

In the handle department, an inlay of grip tape enhances hand purchase. "The ergonomics of the 875 series is exceptional and allows the user to employ several different grips with equal comfort and effectiveness," Ray noted. One aspect of the handle design that helps with the user's grip is the handle width. The knife has the widest handle of the knives re-

Gerber's initial foray into tactical automatic folders comes in the form of the Alliance. Knifemaker Ernest Emerson was called upon to guide the company through this project, and this resulted in a nice, substantial folder that incorporates Emerson's signature handle design with a highly utilitarian clip-point blade. *(Hoffman photo)*

In its 875 Series, Masters of Defense offers a large auto-opening folder exhibiting a perfect blend of performance and value. A sliding safety switch prevents accidental opening.
(Hoffman photo)

viewed for this article. The 875 series will fill a knife user's grip while instilling confidence.

MOD went as far as to include a safety for the lock on the 875, located on the handle spine close to the thumb rest area. It is refreshingly easy to engage and disengage because it's in the area where the user's grip lies, and, of course, the safety insures against accidental opening and closing of the blade.

The LTF 875 is a great all-around working knife with plenty of blade belly to facilitate slicing chores, and there is still enough tip remaining for precise, detailed cuts. A pocket clip on the pivot end of the handle is purpose designed for tip-down carry, and an extra set of screw holes in the butt end of the grip caters to knife users who prefer tip-up carry.

For those who might find the 875 series to be too big, MOD offers a blade length of 2.9 inches in the 685 series. The compact frame size of the 685 series makes each knife in the line a breeze to car-

ry in the pocket. The 875 series comes in both plain-edge and serrated configurations, with only one blade finish—black. The tanto, clip point, or fighter blade styles each carries an MSRP of $199.98. The 685 series autos go for $149.98 apiece.

The Triton is an all-business out-the-front-opening automatic knife from MOD. Knifemaker Jeff Harkins is known for his stealth, well-crafted automatic and double-action folders. Harkins designed the symmetrical OTF automatic, employing a 3.6-inch, double-edged, dagger-shaped 154CM blade. A tungsten DLC finish provides superior corrosion resistance and enhanced cutting performance.

Fueling the Automatic Fire

The auto-opening mechanism is similar to that of the Microtech Scarab. The blade juts out and retracts back into the handle automatically via an oversized thumb

slide switch on the grip. The 6061-T6-aluminum handle is hard-coat anodized to thwart scratches and scuffs. Grip tape inlay portions of the handle provide excellent hand purchase with either wet or dry hands, gloves or not. With a MSRP of $450, this technologically advanced automatic knife isn't cheap, so if you want to play, you have to pay! Any way you look at it, automatics are heavy-duty work knives that serve their roles well for those qualified individuals who can legally possess and carry them. They serve as primary tools and back-up weapons, and are carried by police officers, firefighters, emergency medical technicians and the military. Pro-Tech, Benchmade, Gerber, MOD and MicroTech are some of the major players in this genre. The selection of automatic knives are not limited to those discussed, as there are many good brands and models on the market. The automatic-knife fire is fueled annually by new and innovative designs such as the knives represented here.

The Knifemaker Who Never Works

Building traditional Scottish dirks and daggers isn't at all tedious for this talented 'smith

By Greg Bean

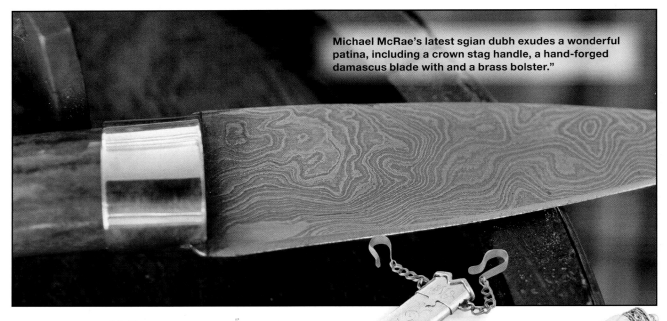

Michael McRae's latest sgian dubh exudes a wonderful patina, including a crown stag handle, a hand-forged damascus blade with and a brass bolster."

McRae says this is one of the best two or three pieces he's made, noting that the twist-damascus blade, the fluted-ivory handle, sterling silver, 18-carat gold and cultured pearl are displayed to perfection.

MICHAEL MCRAE WAS ruined the day he was introduced to the forge, and he hasn't worked a day since. Such ruination hasn't kept him from playing hard for 40 or 50 hours a week, though.

Michael, whose business operates under the name of Scotia Metalworks, is equal parts proud Scotsman and professional knifemaker. Since both pursuits are full time, he is a busy Scot. He combines the two pursuits by making "fine blades in the traditional Scots style"—dirks, daggers and sgian dubhs (literally "black knives," with black referring less to a color and more to the practice of Scotsmen secreting, or hiding, knives in the tops of their hose).

Most of his output is traditional in look, but includes damascus from his own forge, differentially tempered edges, precious metals and woods from around the world. The modern touches don't dilute his work, but create a product with a broader appeal, rather like offering blended Scotch whiskey instead of single malt. Purists be forewarned.

Michael jokes about the career moves that led him to knifemaking as if they represent an addict's

The "Stubby Skinner" is one of the few pieces McRae has named. With the bulbous handle cupped in the palm of a knife user's hand, and with the person's forefinger laid on the blade spine, the knife is ideally suited for separating a deer from its hide.

The hardwood dirk, with a handle of South American bocote wood, has a fuller on the back edge and a blued finish that's burnished with steel wool to simulate sheath wear. These traits are found on a lot of 18th-century dirks made from cut-down backsword blades. The ivory-handled dirk is typical of the Victorian-era civilian knives.

descent from respectability to a halfway house. Knifemaking is definitely an addiction, but look close; you'll see a buildup rather than a breakdown.

Michael's career-building started with a solid job as a telephone linesman. Working with his hands and developing a healthy respect for his work environment was a great training ground for laboring in a metal shop and forge. From climbing poles, he progressed to selling wine as a shop manager. It would be a stretch to correlate this to making knives, but it did provide the experience for running a business.

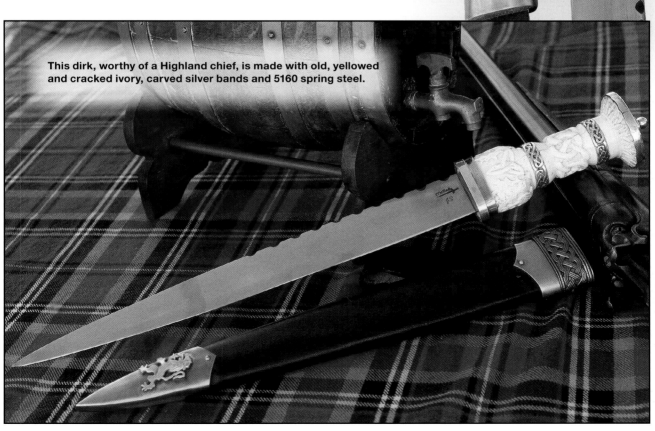

This dirk, worthy of a Highland chief, is made with old, yellowed and cracked ivory, carved silver bands and 5160 spring steel.

Examples of McRae's work include a rifle knife, three sgian dubhs and a hunter.

As McRae forges a blade, he remembers to put on his ball cap to keep sparks from setting his hair on fire (there's no substitute for experience). Notice how, in the last two slides, the color of the heated metal changes according to temperature.

His next stint, which he has yet to recover from, was making custom jewelry. Michael reports, "I went into the jewelry business with more ambition than skill."

As a jewelry maker, Michael was in business for himself, usually working for commission directly from sales to the end user. He also owned several stores in his port of origin, Charlotte, NC. With much

of his work being carriage-trade output, such as high-carat gold, platinum and diamonds, the jewelry business was more lucrative than knives, but was also a high-stress line of work.

Displayed at a Highland's games is Mike's personal knife.

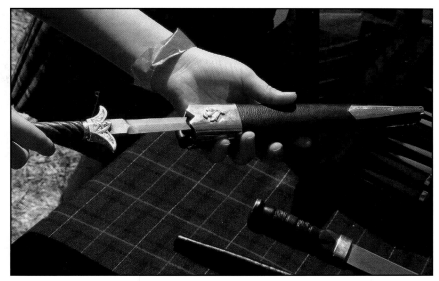

This commissioned piece features 9 inches of twist-patterned damascus, sterling silver furniture, progressive twist fluting of California buckeye burl and a piece of fire agate in the pommel.

This is a close-up of the chief's old dirk (Michael's personal knife).

A dozen years or so ago, Michael became involved in Scots heritage (proper Scots aren't "Scotch," they are "Scots"). As an introductory gift when he joined a group of folks who study Scottish heritage and practice its traditions, Michael was honored with a "bad sgian dubh," as he puts it. He realized he could make a better one. So he bought a piece of bar-stock damascus, ground it to shape and put an ebony handle on it. People who saw it asked him to make them similar sgian dubhs.

One of Michael's jewelry customers, who also happened to be a knife collector, asked him to make a butterfly knife. Michael said it was awful; it looked okay but the handle was too light for the blade. It apparently impressed the collector who came back and asked for more. Michael has made 12 to 15 butterfly knives, all as giveaways.

Sharp And To The Point

Like the proper Scot he is, Michael started going to various Highland games where, as a vendor, he showed a small line of Celtic-oriented jewelry developed for the games. Since most people there were wearing two or three pieces of edged weaponry, he began laying out a few knives and discovered the first things sold off the table were sharp and pointy. "I didn't have to be hit over the head," he jokes.

At that point, half his inventory turned into knives. "One thing led to another, and I started to make traditional Scottish dirks to go along with the sgian dubhs. Today, as a full-time bladesmith, the bulk of my income is generated from men in kilts," McRae says.

Michael made the leap to full-time knifemaking five or six years ago when he started fashioning dirks in earnest. "My first love is the dirk. The shape talks to me," he relates. Early dirks were not especially traditional in the finished look, but, instead, were Michael's own take on the genre. As he evolved, Michael realized dirks were not really what he wanted to build, and he began making historically accurate pieces. His goal was to forge the "kind of knife that a warrior from 350 years ago would pick up and be comfortable with."

Michael studied knives from historical collections, recreating many of the weapons illustrated in John Wallace's monograph, "Scottish Swords and Dirks," one of the definitive resources on the genre. "The dirks I make today,

"You've gotta love a woman who's armed to the teeth," McRae says. "All four carry a blade of mine."

One of Mike's customers, who already totes a McRae fighting dirk, still can't resist the eye candy.

unless direct museum pieces, have the flavor of a given period without being slavish to a particular style," he notes. Michael doesn't incorporate a spear point into a knife reproduction from the late 17th century, for example. He says, "I want it to look like it's supposed to look. Early dirks were heavy. After 1715, they were made from cut-down sword blades and much lighter."

Aside from the fighting dirks, Michael makes sgian dubhs, the little knives that first made their appearance as concealed weapons. These fixed-blades were also used as camp knives, where their blackened, stained appearance helped give rise to their name. As time went on, such pieces became fashionable adornments that were worn in the stocking bands of kilted men.

Michael's sgian dubhs have a traditional look but display craftwork beyond the needs of defense or kitchen duty. Along with the Scottish offerings, he makes daggers that look as if they'd be part of a pre-Celtic religious ceremony, perhaps a ceremony held at night with unwilling participants. While Druids are in short supply, women who admire their elegant profile and jewelry-like finishing are not. Even their admitted im-

practicality enhances their appeal as items of personal decoration.

One of the ways Michael diverges from tradition is his use of modern steels. "Three hundred years ago, their steel was garbage," he reports. "Old swords and knives have holes in the blades and are shot through with rust, a bunch of rusty holes holding hands." The ancient blades haven't lasted, so he uses modern steels and modern methods.

Michael employs 1095, 1084 and 5160 for single-steel blades, such as his fighting dirks, with his prime steel being 5160. "It's really forgiving. But don't quench it in water," he warns. "It comes out with cracks, but quenched in oil, it will scratch glass."

Historical accuracy takes another hit with damascus, which he forges himself. "I don't believe there was a Highland Scot that ever had a damascus blade, even coming back from the Crusades. But every now and then I make one, just because I like the way it looks," Michael relates.

When making damascus, Michael forges 1084 and 15N20 steels, which are not so coincidentally the materials he will incorporate into blades to test for his master smith stamp from the

American Bladesmith Society. The 15N20 gives a great contrast with the 1084 and hardens nicely, which is a failing of pure nickel.

Edgy with a Temper

Expect to see edge tempering on all the Scotia Metalworks blades. Michael uses a torch to heat the blade, the full width on a narrow blade, but just the cutting edge on a wide blade. He then uses a combination of non-detergent, 30-weight motor oil, automatic transmission fluid and diesel fuel for quenching. While not as exotic as bull's blood or urine produced during a full moon, he says the same process of experimentation and testing led him to this equally unpleasant combination.

Differential tempering done in a Japanese style involves clay and a bit of artistic bent. While Michael does not lack on the artistic side, his method is straightforward and produces just a few missed hits, though they can be spectacular. In his quench pan—a valve cover from a Ford Fairlane—he sets a stop block adjusted to the depth he needs for each specific blade.

Michael draws the blade by heating it to 400 degrees for an

The elegant lady didn't find what she wanted on this day, but commissioned a custom design, asking for a feminine dagger. If only all women considered the knifemaker's art as a necessary accessory.

Father passes on tradition, or as McRae puts it, "ruination," to the next generation of knife collector—his son.

hour, and then he lets it cool to the point where he can handle it. He runs both steps three times in a row. He finds the triple heat-treating, "gives you an unbelievably tough blade that cuts and cuts very well for a long time."

The Scots used the local woods for their grips. Most were bog oak or boxwood root, which is incredibly dense, according to Mike. "Mine have the look of the old stuff, but I use rosewood or African blackwood to get that dark look," he notes. Michael especially likes blackwood, as do the makers of clarinets and oboes, as it carves well and doesn't splinter or crack.

Occasionally but rarely were grips made of ivory or bone. Michael offers ivory as an option. He likes working with the stuff, asserting, "Ivory carves like no other material."

Another wood he works with, especially for his daggers, is stabilized California buckeye burl root. Just out of the ground, it is unusable, with no weight to it, even though it is beautiful. It is stabilized by placing it in a high vacuum, with the vacuum drawn through the wood. The wood soaks up the synthetic stabilizing compound rendering it impervious to temperature and humidity.

Thuyu, another wood from off the beaten path, adds the aromatic touch of cinnamon to its visual appeal. Michael makes a point of using a respirator when sanding thuya. As he says, "Anything that smells that good when sanding can't be good for you."

Michael willingly gives credit and blame for his education and influences. His first class on sword forging was taught by knife and sword maker Don Fogg and precipitated a life-changing revelation for Michael. Before this class, Michael had been making knives by stock removal, but he was so intrigued by what he saw that he skipped lunch to try his hand at forging.

Since picking up the hammer that first time, he hasn't ground but two knives. "Don got me into it. I can lay it at his feet that he ruined me," he complains. "He's also taken classes from Jim Batson, "an authority, maybe the authority on bowie knives. He used to be a rocket scientist, so it really is rocket science."

Once you add master smith Bill Moran into the mix of Michael's tutors, you've got a world-class education. "I've been fortunate," he observes, "that these teachers have been first-rate bladesmiths, but also have a knack for imparting their knowledge and don't mind sharing it."

Self-Reliant and Improvisational

Improvisation and self-reliance are part of the calling to the forge and Michael wouldn't have it any other way. A tinkerer and experimenter by nature, when he started out, he used a piece of railroad track for an anvil, vise grips for tongs, and made his own propane forge. You add that to the salvaged quench pan and his homemade tongs and clamps and you've got a good start for a village blacksmith.

Like all knifemakers, Michael is proud of what he does and where he comes from. "The blacksmith's ability to make his own tools is the same ability that put men on the moon," he says, "and I am proud to be part of that brotherhood."

The Search for the Perfect Pocket Knife

Seek and you shall find the best edges to add to your collection, but are they the perfect blades?

By Mac Overton

THERE IS SOMETHING within us that makes us seek the different, the view that "the grass is always greener on the other side of the fence," or that something better than what we have is waiting just around the bend.

The search for the perfect woman is one of those areas. Unfortunately, as I have learned since my divorce a decade ago, all the desirable ones seem to be taken!

Another area of my life, full of possibilities that are safer to pursue, however, is the search for the perfect pocketknife! The search involves finding the perfect handles, perfect blades, perfect combinations of the two and ideal materials for both. It involves an odyssey into high tech, then a journey back to the traditional!

It began when I was maybe 6 years old and found a tiny, three-blade Camillus stockman knife, about 2 3/4-inches wide, on the playground of the country school I attended. I still have that little knife, although it hasn't been carried for nearly 45 years. Instead of a spay blade and sheepsfoot blade common to the style, my pocketknife sports a coping blade and a pen blade, in addition to the main clip-point blade, and a stockman-style handle. The plastic, bone-textured handle is closer to maroon than brown in color.

I had some great adventures with that knife, including crawling under several tables in the old farmhouse where I grew up and doing battle with the huge spiders that had set up camp there. My grandparents raised me, and

The author has found that, among the folding knives that find their way into his pocket or onto his belt consistently, are Bob Dozier's Small Trapper (top) and Folding Hunter. Both have triple-drawn D-2 blades, and titanium frames and locks.

while I waged war with arachnids, they visited with friends who came over for frequent fish dinners in the evenings.

I think my grandfather legitimized the tiny stockman as a "real knife" for me by borrowing it a time or two to skin squirrels or clean bream.

It was also the knife that suffered as I began to "hone" my sharpening skills. I mimicked my

grandfather's method, using a 3-inch Carborundum pocket stone. My technique took some time to develop, and I finally learned that it was not wise to let the ends of my fingertips stick up over the ends of the sharpener. Close examination of my left fingers will still reveal some tiny scars there. I tried to always make sure that I concealed the damage from my grandparents, out of fear that

One folder currently vying to make the list of the author's favorites is the Cold Steel Ozark Hunter, at left, a reproduction of a Remington Bullet Knife but in Carbon V steel. In center, from top, are a Bear MGC large trapper, a Moore Maker three-blade whittler and a Queen single-blade trapper. At right is the Columbia River Knife & Tool Lake's P.A.L. folder.

they might not let me try to sharpen a knife again.

I had my own stash of Band Aids, and I stayed out of sight until the bleeding stopped.

That little Camillus was retired on a snowy Friday afternoon when school was dismissed early. My grandfather surprised me with what I still consider my first "true pocketknife"—an Imperial Barlow! My grandfather had been to town before the snow hit and made travel difficult, and bought it off one of those then-ubiquitous cards behind the counter at almost every country grocery or dry goods store. I think he paid a dollar for it in 1960, probably the equivalent of $10, or so, today.

The little shell-handled Imperial with its high-carbon steel blades gave good service. Like the stockman, I still have the Imperial, handles loosened and cracked, and its blades darkened and worn down from countless sharpening sessions. I used it to clean hundreds of fish, squirrels, birds and other small game.

Cutting Class

In those less-politically correct days, knives were not frowned upon at rural schools, and either the Camillus or Imperial was my constant companion. Teachers often borrowed my pocketknives for various cutting needs.

The Imperial was relegated to a backup piece in 1963, when I bought a Schrade Walden No. 293 from the now-

defunct mail order house, Maher and Grosh. That two-blade trapper served for years, until I thoughtlessly caused one of the backsprings to snap by opening and closing the folder repeatedly.

By the late 1960s, Schrade-Walden had introduced its first Uncle Henry model, the 897UH. Schrade's legendary chairman, "Uncle Henry" Baer once called the stockman "the finest three-blade knife his company or any other has ever produced." The 897UH remains in the Schrade product line. It was one of the first popular folders to incorporate "Razor Blade Stainless" blades.

Several of those were in my future, but to replace the 293, I bought a Schrade 285UH, an Uncle Henry trapper made using the same frame as the 897UH stockman. It showcased a "Staglon" (stag-patterned Delrin®) handle, which was the synthetic most closely resembling real stag. The backs of the liners paraded mechanically applied decoration that resembled hand file work, I guess.

In those days, blades of the 285UH were of 1095 steel. I kept mine until 1995, when I gave it to one of my daughters who, in turn,

lost it somewhere along the way. Oh, well!

By the late 1970s, Schrade had discontinued the 293 in favor of an Old Timer Trapper with carbon-steel blades. I was then working in the personnel department of a Westinghouse transformer factory in Jefferson City, Mo.

A department supervisor showed me his Old Timer Trapper, which had recently been used to cut ends out of chemical drums to suffice as makeshift stoves for the unheated sections of the factory. I promptly traded him a Western locking-liner folder—a good knife, but one that didn't fit my needs—for the Old Timer. I still own and occasionally carry that fine Old Timer. Unfortunately, as Schrade has joined other cutlery makers in vying to debut the latest in space-age-looking knives, the fine traditional design is no more!

During the same time frame, I bought and began carrying Schrade's single-blade Old Timer trapper, with a split-liner lock. I still carry it a lot, the blade thinned by nearly 30 years of sharpening, and darkened by use. Now, it's just about perfect.

The job with Westinghouse "went south" during one of the frequent reorganizations that eventually led the company to corporate extinction, and I moved to Texas to become a community newspaper editor.

This was shortly after I had published my first couple of knife articles in "Knife World" magazine, and I began to get more and more into testing and reviewing pocket cutlery. This opened new doors to me, as I was able to try out dozens of knives over the years, in the search for the perfect blade.

It was also in the early 1980s that I got my first Victorinox Swiss Army folder, the original Tinker model, with large and small spear-point blades, large and small screwdrivers, a Phillips screwdriver, an awl, tweezers and a toothpick—all encompassed in an incredibly durable, red-plastic handle. That knife became a favorite companion, not so much as a cutting instrument, but because of the assortment of screwdrivers immediately at hand. The way I usually use a knife, a spear point is not that versatile. I like a needle-sharp point, in addition to a length of cutting edge.

Engineering Marvels

Engineers I worked with at Westinghouse in the late 1970s and early '80s found the assemblage of tools to be truly wonderful. Today, they would probably carry the Leatherman models, or one of the many imitators.

The first Tinker model was 3-1/4 inches closed, and unfortunately for the U.S. market, Swiss Army Brands soon discontinued it in favor of a 3 1/2-inch model, which was not nearly as comfortable in the pocket or on the belt! That proved one of my knife truisms that bigger is not always better!

Since then, I have owned many other Swiss Army knives, from both Victorinox (The Original) and Wenger (The Genuine). In general, I find that smaller is better, in width more than length. The multi-tools I keep going back to are similar to the Tinker. I carried that Tinker for maybe 15 years or so, simply to have such an assemblage of screwdrivers at hand, until Leatherman brought

The author carried the Victorinox Tinker (top) almost daily until more-modern Leatherman Squirt (left) and Micra models displaced it.

out the Micra, followed closely by the Squirt.

During that time, the early 1980s, a major trend was extremely lightweight knives, with the Gerber Bolt-Action and LST (the latter said to stand for "Light, Smooth, Tough") Zytel®-handle models leading what was to become a crowded niche market.

Gerber ran ads featuring company founder and then-president Pete Gerber, stating that, of all the knives his company made, the LST was the

The A.G. Russell FeatherLite, at top, sports a fine general-purpose, Wharncliffe-style blade. Below it are the A.G. Russell Acorn-Shield small lock-back folder, the Spyderco Kiwi and a Robert Blasingame trapper.

only one he carried—an excellent endorsement!

I owned many LSTs over the years, and found them to be quite serviceable and convenient to carry. They weighed about an ounce-and-a-half each, and rode flat in the pocket. The blade, at 2 1/2-inches, was big enough to do a lot of serious work. The major problem was that whenever someone saw me using an LST, they tried and often succeeded in talking me out of it.

Buck also introduced its own ultra-light variations on major models, the chief of which was a version of their trend-setting 110 Folding Hunter. I liked the knife, although I never could figure out why it was introduced in a dull-maroon color. Later, a black version was offered. That was a favorite folder for big jobs.

Schrade brought out one of the best post-LST lightweights. The SP3 model was slightly larger closed, with more comfortable contours and a bigger blade.

When Spyderco introduced the FRNR-handled Endura and Delica as the first of its lightweights in the late 1980s, the company upped the ante, and SOG, Benchmade and Cold Steel soon had their own excellent entries in the ultralight competition. "FRNR" is short for "fiber-reinforced nylon resin," a more generic term for glass-fiber reinforced plastic. Spyderco explained to me

Among the many high-tech knives the author has encountered and favored over the past two decades is, at top, the Cold Steel Land and Sea Rescue knife. From left are a Schrade SP3; a Fallkniven U2; a Benchmade Axis Lock; a Camillus EDC (Every Day Carry); two Spyderco models with G-10 handles; and a Dan Harrison model featuring a D-2 blade attached to a Columbia River Knife & Tool handle.

that ultralight handles might not always be made of Zytel (DuPont) or Valox (General Electric) glass-fiber-reinforced resin, so this covered all the bases.

Still, today, anyone who wants a plastic-handled ultralight knife for most any chore still can't go wrong with either the Gerber LST, the Schrade SP3 or any of the myriad lightweight knives from Spyderco, Cold Steel, SOG or any of the others.

Ferrari Blade

The latest in the genre is an impressive little drop point from Fallkniven, which the company calls its "Ferrari blade in a Ford body." The laminated stainless blade has a core of something called Super Gold Powder Steel, the specifications of which are similar to the current U.S. fad steel, CPM S30V. The handle is Zytel. Rockwell on the blade is 64 Rc, so, once it dulls, it's best to plan on spending some time re-sharpening it, and it's much more costly than the others.

Buck had introduced its incredible 500 series of folders in the late 1970s, incorporating extremely heavy frames and representing what Buck said was a step up in quality from the 300-series folders made on contract for them.

The Buck 500 line included two sizes of stockman pocketknives, a little single-blade "gent's" knife and other variations. The models, most with laminated-wood handles, seemed designed to compete directly with Kershaw's original heavy-framed line.

Alas, in short order, I found that the weight-to-blade ratio was too heavy for my tastes, and the knives got shelved. In other words, they were too heavy for the amount of cutting edge they provided.

Western Cutlery, once a fine old-line knife manufacturer, hit on hard times and was bought out by Coleman. Coleman-Western,

as the new enterprise was trade-marked, brought out some interesting things, including ultra-light trappers. For some reason, Coleman-Western decided to make the handles thick and the blades relatively short for the handle size. While a good idea, it wasn't executed well. Western ended up being sold again, this time to Camillus, and Western products now are mainly just variations on the Camillus line. Of course, with Camillus' quality, nobody can go wrong with one of today's Westerns.

Speaking of Camillus, the Yello-Jakt trapper and other models came along, and, for a time, blew away everything else I carried in the way of work knives. The 4-inch trapper has been discontinued, although larger Camillus trappers and variations thereof continue to be produced with 440A stainless blades. While I love carbon steel, the rust resistance is a real advantage in the summer in places with searing, humid climates like East Texas. That 4-inch Yello-Jakt trapper still finds use when I need a tough work knife.

As the 1990s dawned, the rage was G-10 handles on "tactical knives," most of them featuring Tanto blades copied from the successful Cold Steel fixed-blade designs. For all-around use, I never really liked the Tanto blade, but did appreciate some of these folders when they were offered with clip- or drop-point blades.

Among the many full-size trapper knives that have found favor with the author over the years are those from Queen, Schrade and Robert Blasingame.

Still, the search for perfection continued. The ones from the tactical-knife arena that remain in contention for a place in my pocket as I wrote this (spring 2004) were Kershaw's Ken Onion series, including the Leek and the Chive, and various assisted-opening models from SOG and Camillus, which entered the fray with various Darrel Ralph designs.

Custom collaborations became common in the 1990s, and continued on into the new century.

New World Designs

This opened up a whole new world for knife fanciers like me, as production knives, designed by some of the great makers of this age, became available at reasonable prices. Michael Walker, Ron Lake, Pat Crawford, Ken Onion, Dan Harrison and Bob Loveless were only a few of the many whose designs suddenly were affordable!

I've tried designs from all them, and others, as brought to market by Columbia River Knife & Tool (CRKT), Schrade, Lone Wolf, Benchmade and more. All had their pluses and minuses. The minuses generally had to do with weight (steel frames, required to house the locking mechanisms on some, don't come light).

Today, I often carry a Kershaw Leek or a CRKT Ron Lake Signature, in addition to more tradition-

al knives on my person. I usually have at least four, and sometimes up to seven folders on me at any one time. Even before the current level of airport security, I had to be careful when traveling by air.

Just a few days ago, as I wrote this, CRKT's new Lake's P.A.L. (Piston Activated Lock) arrived, and it blew me away. The folding knife is the best blend of traditional and high-tech I've seen yet, and, with its semi-skinner blade (which CRKT erroneously calls a modified clip point in its catalog), should be very versatile.

After all these five decades of testing, reviewing and evaluating literally hundreds of folders, what am I carrying currently?

I realize I've returned to my cutlery roots.

In one pocket, I have a Schrade 5OT with a drop-point, carbon-steel blade. It was purchased at a gun show for $15. I had several similar Schrades, but all of them were in stainless. The only way Schrade could make this 3 3/4-inch-closed, brass-framed masterpiece any better would be to offer the blade with an oak handle similar to the design the company makes for Ducks Unlimited.

In a slipcase in another pocket, I tote a Moore Maker small trapper with a yellow jigged-bone handle. In the same pocket is a slim Queen single-blade trapper with a bone-stag handle.

Riding in a sheath on my belt is a Bear MGC large trapper in damascus blade steel and the company's trademark Sambar stag handle. Also on my belt is a Cold Steel Ozark Hunter, the spittin' image of the famous Remington Bullet lock-back done up in proprietary Carbon V steel. It is the latest version of this style I've carried. Two others of the genre, equally serviceable, if not as authentic, are a Rigid in 440A stainless steel, and an A.G. Russell work knife with a yellow Delrin handle and a 154CM blade.

In a pocket today is the Leatherman Squirt, which is nearly identical to the company's Micra model. I rarely carry my Victorinox Tinker anymore, since I learned that the Micra and Squirt provide the screwdrivers and other tiny tools I need in a smaller, handier package.

Sometimes, for old time's sake, I carry a Schrade Uncle Henry 897UH, and I find it serves everyday cutting needs just as well as ever.

I'm sure there will be other knives in the near and far future to titillate my interest and get a spot in the review pocket, but the ones I keep coming back to, the ones that I find are the greatest when I need to cut something, are those tried and true designs from knifemaking's past.

And, the perfect pocketknife remains easier and safer to pursue than the perfect woman!

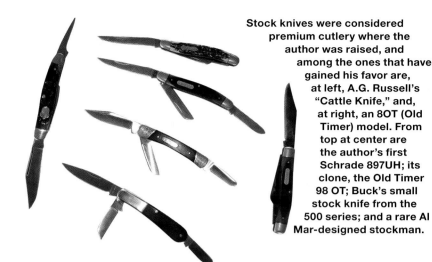

Stock knives were considered premium cutlery where the author was raised, and among the ones that have gained his favor are, at left, A.G. Russell's "Cattle Knife," and, at right, an 8OT (Old Timer) model. From top at center are the author's first Schrade 897UH; its clone, the Old Timer 98 OT; Buck's small stock knife from the 500 series; and a rare Al Mar-designed stockman.

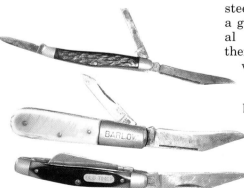

Three of the author's first knives, going back to the late 1950s and early '60s, include, from bottom, a tiny Camillus three-blade folder, an Imperial Barlow with stamped shell handles, and one of the early Schrade Walden 34 OT small stockman knives.

TRENDS

Y ou can try to predict them, laying your money down, letting it ride on whims and conjecture. You might even have an educated guess as to which knife styles, materials, gadgets, accessories, blade shapes or edged historic recreations will be hotter than a forge fire. It's a bit like playing the stock market. "If I take stock of these knives now, they're sure to go up in value over the next few months and I can turn them around for a quick profit." Are you ready? Who's got their fingers on the pulse of the knife industry? Are you willing to ante up some hard-earned cash on that intuition?

For most non-clairvoyant folks, predicting trends in the knife industry is much like a weatherman's seven-day forecast—not all that reliable. That's what makes the job of the KNIVES 2005 editor a bit easier than that of a weatherman, or woman, if that's possible. The editor of the KNIVES annual book series recognizes, or "spots," trends after they've already emerged. It's a bit like being a weather watcher, only not as dangerous.

Some piping-hot trends have emerged this year, and one is the direct result of heat itself—blue blades. Hot-blued blades are screaming for your attention until they're, well, blue. Speaking of trendy, "Bling Bling Blades" are as "chingy" as a "gansta" rapper's gold chains. And how about those nifty pearl knife handles that entrepreneurs are intricately "checkering," placing a pin in the center of each check? Then again, mosaic-damascus might just be the long-shot pick of the week. It has staying power, and those little checker-shaped pictures in the steel are hard to brush off as passing fads. Maybe checks, in general, are in, or is it swirls? Are you ready to invest that wad of sweaty bills?

Joe Kertzman

Blue Blades

THE CAMPFIRE IS so mesmerizing. Fingers of yellow-orange flame flicker against the dark, starry sky. Demons reside inside the orange-red flames, and the blue ones, oh the blue ones—they're the hottest. I heard that once from a fellow camper. It makes me cringe to think of such scarring, destructive heat so close at hand, my lawn chair being only feet from the fire. The warmth, though, the inner glow, manifests itself in a false sense of security—safeness—and solitude, the fire lulling all who gaze upon it into semi-consciousness on a damp, dark night. Yes, mesmerizing, it's mesmerizing.

The blue flame is the hottest.

Blue blades, much like blue bloods who demand respect, whether earned or not, are the penultimate in the hierarchy of fiery-hot edges. And heat has everything to do with their existence. They don't call them hot-blued blades for nothing, and nothing but heat has the ability to create such hues of blue. Whether they most closely resemble the innermost blue flames of a well-fed fire, or the blue-green saltwater of the Caribbean Sea, blue blades are by far the most colorful, stunning and energetic of all cutting edges in the knife industry. And they're hot! They're popular. They're everywhere a knife collector looks.

Say it isn't so, Joe. Tell us that blue blades haven't invaded the land, trampling all other inbred stainless or serf-class high-carbon steels! Is the hue so royal that all folding blades must bow before the blue class, allowing them to point the direction the masses must follow?

From deep within the fire, energy is born, and the fuel that feeds it allows it to grow. From the forge of the knifemaking magician, such energy is harnessed and directed into heat-bluing blade steel to its most favorable hue—blue! It's the blue of the ocean, the blue of the sky, a South Sea blue, a boy blue and a big blue. It's a blue born from the hottest flames, a mesmerizing blue, one with an inner glow, manifesting itself into a false sense of security, a safeness, like a blue blanket enveloping us all with its warmth.

Joe Kertzman

▶ **JASON TIENSVOLD:** The mosaic damascus is as blue as the ocean and just a wavy. *(PointSeven photo)*

▶ **RICK EATON:** The Celtic-style sticker deserves a gold medal, a purple heart and a **blue ribbon.** *(PointSeven photo)*

◀ **JOSH SMITH:** One of the more spectacular of the blue blades, the damascus pattern continues up the handle and out the end of the knife, too busy, as it was, to say goodbye. *(PointSeven photo)*

THEUNS PRINSLOO: The blue, red, purple and gold hues create a rainbow effect over the South African hunters stalking game on a sun-bleached strip of land. *(PointSeven photo)*

GARY HOUSE: He probably swore a blue streak forging this integral twist-damascus dagger. *(PointSeven photo)*

VAN STECK: The Blue Grotto is a heat-anodized titanium fillet knife named after a swimming hole on Saipan. It is distal tapered and shaving sharp.

RICK DUNKERLEY: The pearl finally came out of its shell to partner up with an ocean-blue bolster and blade. *(Custom Knife Gallery of Colorado photo)*

LOYD THOMSEN: Here's hoping you're not blue-green color blind.

◄ TOM FERRY: The born-to-be-blue Persian Flames folder is blued damascus on one end, and carved and textured Timascus on the other. *(BladeGallery.com photo)*

▼ SHANE TAYLOR: The Forces of Darkness folder is a thematic masterpiece, including a gold-inlaid dagger sticking through a skull like a crooked blue-veined finger pointing you out as its next victim. *(Custom Knife Gallery of Colorado photo)*

▲ JOHN W. SMITH: The carbon-damascus blade is as blue as the Caribbean Sea, and complemented by an ancient blue-walrus-ivory handle. *(Glassman & Son photo, Custom Knife Gallery of Colorado)*

▲ GERALD CORBIT: Mirror, mirror on the wall, who's the bluest of them all? *(Custom Knife Gallery of Colorado photo)*

◄ RICK DUNKERLEY: Rubies, gold and a sapphire made the blade blue with envy. *(PointSeven photo)*

WADE COLTER: The honey-hued wooly-mammoth-bark handle contrasts starkly with the hot-blued mosaic-damascus blade and bolster. *(Custom Knife Gallery of Colorado photo)*

MICHAEL WALKER: Flames really are blue when they're at their hottest. *(PointSeven photo)*

DES HORN: The Ittore Gianferrari damascus blade and handle were hand carved by Des until he was blue in the face. *(PointSeven photo)*

BOB BIZZELL: The colors vary from blade to handle, but it's all heat-blued W's-pattern Damascus and if it doesn't woo you, it will wow you. *(BladeGallery.com photo)*

BARRY GALLAGHER: Stars are diamonds and the Big and Small Dippers are gold in Barry Gallagher's galaxy of blue steel and meteorite. The smart money says collectors get a Big Bang out of this one. *(BladeGallery.com photo)*

TED MOORE: The pearl is at home in the sea.

Cowboy and Indian Knives

LET'S PLAY COWBOYS and Indians. The cowboy is an American icon, with hands and face like leather, the brute strength of a bucking bronco, a will to survive, the backbone of a battering ram and a heart as big as Texas. The dust on his hands is permanent, the squint in his eyes omnipresent. He represents pain for gain, work for reward, the claim to a stake and a dream fulfilled.

The Indian chief stands totem pole stiff, a most brave warrior, he who padded across the Plains, the original tribesman, the honorable, wise and all-knowing. He holds the secrets of the world, answers only to his gods, respects the land,

obeys natural boundaries and stalks game like a leopard.

Is the view of history slanted, contorted? Can we ever gain back what we have lost?

The new cowboys, the braves, the red and white, the blue, the fierce, the spirited and the determined are putting out some of the most piercing weapons of peace and destruction. They hone their skills on stone and steel, awaiting the Great Spirit in the sky to send them a sign. Their actions are deliberate, their burdens heavy, their outlook positive, and their purpose defined.

Knives, tomahawks, hunters, skinners and bowies are born from their hands, products of rhythmic

hammer blows and heat so hot it singes the land and evaporates all moisture around it. Dust and dirt are drunk like wine, and the lips of modern warriors are moistened by ash and soot. Their edged tools and weapons are awe-inspiring gifts to the greater beings who reside in the wind and dance across the clouds.

Not a shot has been fired in this game of cowboys and Indians, not an arrow released. Edges are stockpiled, collected, admired and forfeited for a greater cause.

Joe Kertzman

▼ **MUDD SHARRIGAN:** The selectively heat-treated 5160 blade of the Mountain Man Knife is left rough for a primitive look and feel. *(Mitchell photo)*

▼ **JAMES BARRY III:** The "Mystic Warrior" is a "gunstock" war club, so named because it resembles the stock of a rifle. Barry says such war clubs were widely spread among the semi-nomadic Native American Plains tribes, and many such pieces were outfitted with knife blades.

◄ **GLEN SMIT:** The "Blackfoot Dag," complete with raindrop-Damascus blade and black-bear-jaw handle, will lead you to the happy hunting grounds.

◄ **NORMAN BARDSLEY:** The sculpted-metal head of the tomahawk features a bleeding heart cutout, while the 26-inch kingwood haft showcases bead strands and horsehair dangles. *(Caldwell photo)*

► **CARLTON EVANS:** The "Cowboy" is a modern warrior donned in Spirograph damascus and some of the greenest giraffe bone this side of Tombstone.

► **HEATHER HARVEY:** The blade of the Mountain Man Folder went down in a blaze of glory. *(BladeGallery.com photo)*

▼ **E. JAY HENDRICKSON:** The fine silver handle inlay, as well as the copper and nickel-silver eye in the blade, are feathers in Jay's headdress. *(PointSeven photo)*

▼ **RIK PALM:** Rotating spurs take the guard for a twirl, while a 6-inch clay-hardened blade, with Spanish notch and a full-length distal taper, is as light and lively as a young buck. With a "Ranch Hand" like this, roundups, roping and branding won't seem like chores.

▲ **RICK SMITH:** Wearing the Cowboy Boot Knife and the Stocky Cowboy Bowie would be like packing twin six-shooters.

◄ DANIEL WINKLER: The "primitive" damascus steel is anything but, and crown stag gives this one as much charm as the fringed-leather sheath. Yee Haa! *(PointSeven photo)*

▲ MIKE MANN: There's a new sheriff in town and he's protected by 350 layers of steel. *(BladeGallery.com photo)*

▲ LEON TREIBER: The Lone Star State is represented here, as an ivory inlay set into a Texas ebony handle and flanked by mokumé bolsters. *(Ward photo)*

▲ WADE COLTER: It's called "Not a Bell," but over 10 inches of 1084 carbon steel anchored by ebony and pure silver will ring anyone's bell. *(BladeGallery.com photo)*

▼ TOM FERRY: Stars flit across the mosaic damascus blade of the Deputy Marshal Bowie, and the heat-blued oval guard matches the hand-forged spur set. *(BladeGallery.com photo)*

► BERNARD BERTHOLUS: The hammer marks, or file cuts, or whatever was left on the forged blade give the knife as much character as the boxwood grip. All in all, any rough rider would take pride in ownership.

Mammoth Handles

THEY ARE MAMMOTH not only in size, but also in looks and feel. They come in droves, the earth rumbling under their massive frames, leaving clouds of swirling dust behind them. The beasts flatten the earth where they trod and swallow up vegetation as a drought dries up the land. They are knives with mammoth handles, and what they lack in size, they make up for in figure, pattern, style, color and character.

Step aside stag. Move over Micarta®. Out of the way wood. Mammoth ivory is reserving a shelf of its own at the local knife store. For one, it's ancient, which makes it a relic with certain benefits the youngsters can't claim for themselves. It has seniority over such mundane handle materials as bone and even stone. In fact, it's the stone that helps push the mammoth tusks to the earth's surface, allowing them to break through the crust in far northern Alaska

where few other things penetrate the permafrost. Only local Alaskans with roots dating back to ancient tribes can harvest the stuff, so it leads a storybook existence.

Only the earth can form such colorful characters. They're blue, brown, beige, green, black, gold and red. They've survived quakes and mudslides, and they've been lifted from the center of the earth for purposes known only to Mother Nature. Taking full advantage of their reappearance are opportunistic knifemakers with an eye for inherent beauty.

Mammoth ivory is flooding the knife

market like great walls of water known to wash away islands and move shorelines at will. Don't try to stop it. Just follow in its wake and enjoy the ride.

Joe Kertzman

◄ **DOC HAGEN:** Few inter-frame folders feature mammoth-bark-ivory inlays, but judging by the green, blue, gold and beige colors of this pretty piece of tusk, more should. *(Glassman of customknifegallery.com photo)*

▼ **JENS ANSO:** Only one side of the locking-liner folder has a mammoth-ivory overlay. The other is the titanium frame equipped, instead, with a pocket clip.

► **LUDWIG FRUHMANN:** He used the mammoth ivory sparingly on an all-damascus integral fixed blade, saving the bulk of tusk for knives to come.

BILL RUPLE: Think about how far knifemaking has come when collectors and enthusiasts come to expect such things as double Devin Thomas raindrop-damascus blades, reptilian-damascus bolsters, blue-mammoth-ivory handles and file-worked liners. *(Garrett Edged Productions photo)*

SHANE TAYLOR: In "Bat Wing Blue River," Shane accomplished total-knife patterning that appeals to even the more conservative knife buyer. *(BladeGallery.com photo)*

AAD VAN RIJSWIJK: Gold engraving was deserving of a golden handle.

LEON TREIBER: He inset a mammoth-ivory handle with a mammoth-ivory inlay, and it actually worked! *(Weyer photo)*

JASON HOWELL: The mammoth ivory is actually the most subdued part of this locking-liner folder. *(Ward photo)*

▼**J.W. RANDALL:** Just when you thought you saw every color of mammoth ivory there was, along comes a rusty one to win you over with its charm and good looks.

▲ **J.D. BARTH:** With so much busyness—a Spirograph damascus blade, sunburst-mosaic-damascus bolster and mammoth ivory grip with a lot of character—it's amazing how subtly all of the effects blend together.

▼**CARLTON EVANS:** The "Gentleman Cowboy" dismounted, shook off the dust and sauntered into the saloon on bowed mammoth-ivory legs.

▲ **RUSS SUTTON:** The black damascus called for an equally peppery section of mammoth ivory.

▲ **ROBERT BIZZELL:** The jellyroll-damascus blade met its eye-appealing equivalent in the presentation-grade, mammoth-ivory-bark handle.
(BladeGallery.com photo)

Whiz-Bang Folding Blades

MUCH ATTENTION IS paid, and rightly so, to the artistry of knives. From their simplistic forms with smooth angles and gentle curves, to embellishments ranging from scrimshaw and engraving, to precious stone and gold-wire inlay, knives are often works of art. Time is also spent debating, and for good reason, the performance of knives. After all, if a knife looks good but won't perform, it's worthless for cutting tasks and emergency situations where good blades save the day.

Often overlooked is the wizardry of knives, especially folders. Add a folding blade to a knife, and the dimension of moving parts becomes part of the equation. Suddenly there are inner workings, mechanics and resulting "operations," whether smooth or disastrously awkward and clunky. Those who master the wizardry of folding knives tend to be mechanically inclined. They don't buff the skin off their thumbs at the grinding wheel as often as the rest of us. They think in terms of pivots, tolerances, clearances, and material viability and compatibility.

Recently, Michael Walker was inducted into the BLADE Magazine cutlery Hall Of Fame® by fellow knifemaker Frank Centofante. Frank credited Walker, as was expected, with the invention of the LinerLock® for propping open the blades of folding knives. What wasn't expected was the amount of time and kudos Frank dedicated to other Walker offerings, like ball detents and bushings. While such small knife parts seem insignificant, the crowd gathered at the BLADE Show banquet couldn't help but feel Frank's enthusiasm for the subject matter, and most folks walked away with a greater appreciation for the mechanics of the knife and for the type of people who, like Walker, think outside the blade, so to speak.

Merlin has his hat on, and he's waving the magic wand so fast, a smoke trail swirls behind and rises up into the air in a cloud of intrigue and imagination. Don't let the funny outfit fool you, he's a wise old fellow with a devious mind and a smile to match. The steel magicians don't practice his trickery, but their hands are faster than the eye, so pay close attention, or you'll miss what makes the folding blades flick!

Joe Kertzman

► **PHIL BOGUSZEWSKI:** The stylish titanium-handle stiletto is ready to capture your heart and loosen your purse strings. *(BladeGallery.com photo)*

▼ **BOB DOZIER:** All Bob Dozier folders are about performance, even his fancy damascus pieces with wood-inlaid ivory handles. *(Weyer photo)*

▲ **JOHN KUBASEK:** Just the shapes of the folding Karambit-style knives give enough bang for the buck. These babies are titanium frame locks with CPM S30V blades, and carbon fiber and G-10 inlays. *(PointSeven photo)*

▼ **KIT CARSON:** Materials like heat-colored Timascus qualify some folders as whiz-bang blades. The matching ring is fashioned by Kristi Obenauf. *(Weyer photo)*

▲ **JOHN FRAPS:** John achieved a whiz-bang blade using hot-blued raindrop-pattern damascus, Timascus and pre-ban elephant ivory. *(BladeGallery.com photo)*

▲ **PAUL FOX:** The rear-lock folder features a bi-metal blade of Darrel Ralph damascus and purple-anodized titanium, which makes perfect sense if you're a knife wizard. *(PointSeven photo)*

◄ **MICHAEL WALKER:** Michael's Zipper blades are the results of fusing steels together, and the visual effect is as awesome as it is thought provoking. This model's called "Shark Tooth." *(Weyer photo)*

▲ **BRIAN TIGHE:** The folding single-edge dagger is as easy to open as one ... two ... three. *(PointSeven photo)*

▼ **KEN ONION:** The inventor of the Speed-Safe assisted-opening mechanism for folding knife blades builds a titanium-handle folder that incorporates so many smooth inner workings, it all had to be tied together like a Victorian-era corset. *(Weyer photo)*

▲ **RALPH TURNBULL:** Four colorful folders are a feast for the eyes and perplexing enough to qualify for the category. *(PointSeven photo)*

▼**GEORGE MULLER:** It wasn't that much work. Meteorite and damascus collided in the atmosphere and formed a locking-liner folder through natural combustion. *(Custom Knife Gallery of Colorado photo)*

▼**BILL KING:** Mechanical wizardry wasn't enough for Bill, who tore the circuit boards out of the computer as knife handles.

▼**PAT CRAWFORD:** The Merlin-like knifemaker combined a locking liner with his own lift lock. The bigger self-defense blade is kept sharp because the knife user will theoretically use the small utility blade for everyday cutting jobs. *(PointSeven photo)*

◀**HOWARD HITCHMOUGH:** The name for Howard's "Spirit Of Freedom" folding dagger results from the fact that, while he was building the whiz-bang blade, he had his final interview with the INS to become a naturalized U.S. citizen. The double-ground blade of Odin's Eye stainless damascus is complemented by a hot-gun-blued steel handle that acts as a dark background to set off the white pearl and gold wire inlays. *(PointSeven photo)*

▼**DOC HAGEN:** You need a good grip—in this case molded stingray skin—to work a scale-release automatic. Which part of the handle scale do you think moves to release the spring-activated blade? *(Custom Knife Gallery of Colorado photo)*

▶**JACK LEVIN:** Jack has won acclaim as of late for his French poinard-style folders with shields that open automatically when the blades are opened. The engraving and sculpting isn't too shabby, either. *(PointSeven photo)*

▼ **DES HORN:** Whether the knifemaker's Damasteel folders exhibit snowflake-Alphen-damascus or 4.6-billion-year-old Gibeon meteorite bolsters, they're impressive. *(PointSeven photo)*

▼ **GORDON CHARD:** Sure it's a high-tech, double-action, scale-release, hollow-ground folder with a false edge and anodized-titanium bolsters, Gordon. It sounds like double speak to me. *(Hopkins photo)*

◄ **RAY ROGERS:** Break out the shaving cream, it's a party, and the ladies should be impressed by the titanium-frame, burgundy-linen-Micarta®-handled, locking-liner razor with a BG-42 blade. *(Hoffman photo)*

▼ **LEE FERGUSON:** The bolsters are anodized gold, the liners anodized blue and the handle naturally white.

▲ **TOM FERRY:** The "Persian Flame" incorporates a laddered-chains-pattern damascus blade and a carved, sculpted and heat-blued Timascus handle. Ferry's the sole author and blade builder. *(BladeGallery.com photo)*

► **RICHARD S. WRIGHT:** From a Persian blade of Jerry Rados Turkish twist damascus, to Robert Eggerling mosaic-Damascus bolsters, to carved cross-guard and circular-sterling-silver rear bolsters, the ambidextrous bolster-release switchblade is a mechanical wonder.

▲ **DARRIEL CASTON:** A little engraving and some green jade, and you have it made in the shade with a whiz-bang blade. *(BladeGallery.com photo)*

Hunt and Peck

▶ **ART TYCER:** Water buffalo horn provides a natural grip for a damascus hunter. *(Ward photo)*

▲ **DICK FAUST:** Upswept hunters are a favorite among those who like to sweep up in the woods.

▲ **BURT FOSTER:** The lightning-like temper line was achieved through clay hardening, and the wood-grain pattern from finding the right tree.

▼ **CHAD CARROLL:** Chad loved the blade so much he hand rubbed and satin finished it.

▲ **BOB DOZIER:** Bob rarely fancies them up much, but he sure makes 'em clean and shiny. *(Weyer photo)*

▼ **ROBERT BEATY:** Robert gave a bighorn handle to a Rocky Mountain Hunter. *(BladeGallery.com photo)*

▼ BRUCE ALLRED: The reconstituted stone handle on the Cheetah model is the cat's pajamas.

▶ GEORGE TICHBOURNE: A fillet knife, deer knife and moose knife stand ready to prepare fish, venison and Bullwinkle burgers.

▲ WALLY WATTS: The horn handle and leather thong give it away as a hunting knife.

▶ RUSS SUTTON: It's amazing what a little stag and some mosaic pins can do for a full-tang ATS-34 hunter.

▼ THAD BUCHANAN: Whether a semi-skinner or drop-point hunter, the knife is nothing short of sharp. *(BladeGallery.com photo)*

▼ FRED ROWE: Picture yourself holding onto the maple handles of this pair of small, kukri-style skinners.

▼**AL LAWRENCE:** The fierce 4-inch damascus hunter has a wolf-tooth-patterned edge. *(Hoffman photo)*

▲ **SCOTT GOSSMAN:** To handle a knife like this, you need to get a good grip.

▶ **ED BAUMGARDNER:** The blade grinds are as gorgeous as the slabs of stag. *(PointSeven photo)*

▼**JOHN HUTCHESON IV:** The stag-handle hunter is a colorful character. *(Hoffman photo)*

▼ **HEATHER HARVEY:** Here's a hand-forged honey-of-a-knife covered in copper, burl and brown cowhide. *(BladeGallery. com photo)*

▲ **JOHN HUTCHESON IV:** The stag-handle hunter is a colorful character. *(Hoffman photo)*

▼ **BILL LEVENGOOD:** The trout-and-bird knife sports an oosik and crown-stag handle.

▼ DAVID BANKS: Here's a wolf in sheep's clothing. The gold-anodized-titanium guard emulates brass and blends the damascus blade into the horn handle. *(BladeGallery. com photo)*

▼ DAN HOCKENSMITH: It took 1,200 layers of damascus to achieve such a pretty pattern, and Dan didn't spoil it with a busy handle, but bowed instead to black ebony. *(BladeGallery.com photo)*

▼ JOHN YOUNG: It's all eyes, ears, tongue and groove. *(Weyer photo)*

▼ RIK PALM: Shaping the blade wasn't enough for the energetic maker. He clay-hardened the 1084 carbon steel, differentially heat-treated it, resulting in a terrific temper line, and scalloped its bolsters, dovetailing them into a fossil-mammoth-bark handle. *(BladeGallery.com photo)*

▼ RONNIE FOSTER: Several knife-show attendees strained their necks trying to get a good look at the giraffe-bone handle.

◄ ROB HUDSON: "The Bird" is named not for how it looks, but for the fine-feathered friends its 7-inch blade is built to prepare for dinner.

▲ LEE FERGUSON: Allow the olive wood to penetrate the pores of your palm before sliding the 4-inch blade into the downed beast.

◀ **BILLY WATSON:** A slice of stag complements a slicer of damascus.

▲ **JACK FULLER:** Judging by the modified-spear-point blade, the maker of the crown-stag slicing machine might have hunted a time or two in his life.

▶ **ROBERT NELSON PARKER:** The drop-point hunter is stainless now, but wait until it gets into its first game.

▼ **GERT VAN DEN ELSEN:** It might be a Mouse Skinner, but this blade will scare the cat and the dog.

▲ **LAWRENCE LITTLE:** The antler-and-wood grip is as natural as the hunt itself.

▼ **REGGIE BARKER:** The W-pattern damascus blade will make you whistle. *(Hoffman photo)*

▼ **PAUL LEBATARD:** The skinner is slimmer than most, but that doesn't mean it can't cut through the fat.

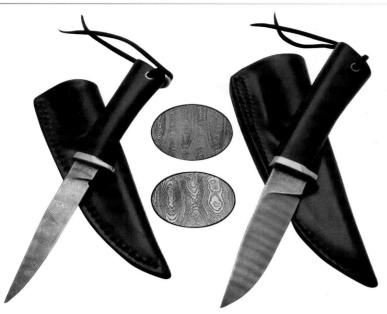

▼ CORBIN NEWCOMB: The stag grips are as polished as the multi-bar damascus blades.

▲ A.C. RICHARDS: The African blackwood handles of a skinner and caper set match the dyed-cowhide sheaths, but who'd want to hide the damascus blades? *(Custom Knife Gallery of Colorado photo)*

◄ LARRY MENSCH: Green means go to town.

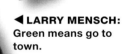

▲ CHARLES "DICKIE" ROBINSON: The steel skinner went stag to the hunting party.

▼ RUSTY POLK: Rusty didn't try to offset the clean ATS-34 drop-point blade with a showy handle, but rather accessorized it tastefully using a mastodon-ivory grip with just enough character. *(Ward photo)*

▲ LYNN MAXFIELD: The sheep was domestic, but its horn was wild.

▼ **MARVIN SOLOMON:** Ironwood and damascus were decent enough to grace an O-1 hunter with their presence. *(Ward photo)*

▲ **FRANK SELZAM:** Frank says he lives near Schweinfurt, Germany, the ball-bearing center of the world, so he has access to steel that he selectively hardens to show the temper lines. Thanks for uncovering its beauty, Frank!

▶ **NORMAN BARDSLEY:** With turquoise, coral, lapis, Charoite, pearl and abalone, Norman put together a 14-piece American flag for the handle of his hunter.

▲ **S.R. JOHNSON:** Stag and mammoth ivory team up to contain a narrow-tang hunting blade. *(BladeGallery.com photo)*

▲ **DON MAXWELL:** One has to wonder if, when Devin Thomas forges damascus, he has any idea how primo it will look on the knives these makers are constructing?!

◀ **ED FOWLER:** Ed spent so much time perfecting the 52100 blade, he achieved a damascus effect with one steel. *(BladeGallery.com photo)*

Lords of the Swords

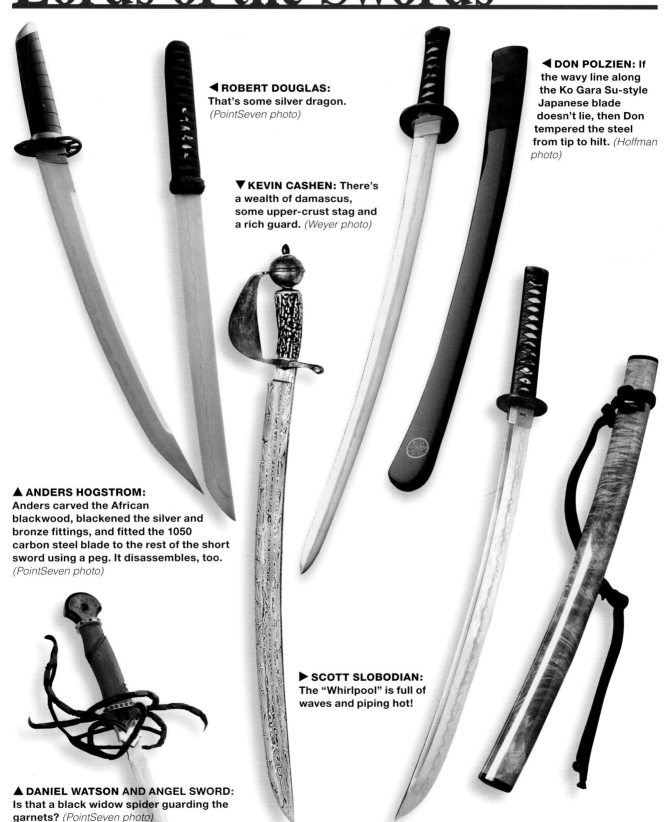

◀ ROBERT DOUGLAS: That's some silver dragon. *(PointSeven photo)*

▼ KEVIN CASHEN: There's a wealth of damascus, some upper-crust stag and a rich guard. *(Weyer photo)*

◀ DON POLZIEN: If the wavy line along the Ko Gara Su-style Japanese blade doesn't lie, then Don tempered the steel from tip to hilt. *(Hoffman photo)*

▲ ANDERS HOGSTROM: Anders carved the African blackwood, blackened the silver and bronze fittings, and fitted the 1050 carbon steel blade to the rest of the short sword using a peg. It disassembles, too. *(PointSeven photo)*

▶ SCOTT SLOBODIAN: The "Whirlpool" is full of waves and piping hot!

▲ DANIEL WATSON AND ANGEL SWORD: Is that a black widow spider guarding the garnets? *(PointSeven photo)*

Take Hold'a Some
TIMBER

▲ **CORBET SIGMAN:** Take hold'a some desert ironwood and let 'er rip.

▶ **ROB AND DENISE SPROKHOLT:** The Ultimate Thuya backpack knife is a burly boy, complete with powdered-damascus blade in a random pattern.

▲ **MIKE MCCLURE:** A length of 5160 blade (7 full inches) is anchored by a curly maple handle. *(PointSeven photo)*

▶ **JAMES (SEAMUS) HARRISON:** You can always tell snakewood by the scaly grain structure and the way it strikes out at you. The blade is Talonite, and the bolsters dovetailed.

▶ **ROGER HARRINGTON:** The blade's flat Scandinavian grind is offset by the highly figured Thuya-burl grip.

▲ **MAIHKEL EKLUND:** This one's a burl-esque show.

▶ **BILL BEHNKE:** Curly maple burl advances the curlicue theme of the ladder-pattern damascus blade and bolster. *(Weyer photo)*

▼ **LYNN MAXFIELD:** Does combining Babinga wood and curly maple on a knife handle count as cross-pollination?

▶ **BRIAN TOMBERLIN:** Bacote wood is like a fancy robe on a prizefighter. *(Hoffman photo)*

▲ **EDMUND DAVIDSON:** The BG-42 integral is as sweet as sugar maple, Honey, and you should see the way it glides through a pot roast. *(PointSeven photo)*

◀ **KEVIN HARVEY:** Even the "Moth Antennae"-pattern damascus blade can't lessen the impact of the redwood burl handle. *(BladeGallery.com photo)*

▼ **DONALD H. OSBORNE:** "Atta-boy" for building it with amboyna burl. *(Richmond photo)*

▲ **COLTEN TIPPETTS:** The cleanliness of blade and bolster called for a bit of burl—ironwood. *(PointSeven photo)*

▲ **FRED ROWE:** The damascus hunter sports some curl and some burl.

▲ **LOYD THOMSEN:** A matched pair of foot-long damascus fixed blades don desert-ironwood grips.

▼ **GLEN SMIT:** A red spalted-maple handle is the focal point of a clip-point hunting/utility knife.

◄ **LAWRENCE LITTLE:** A finger-grooved cocobolo handle is book-ended by antler spacers and nickel-silver guards.

▼ **RALPH TURNBULL:** The fluted desert ironwood is like the earth below a starburst and its aftereffects.

▼ **ANDERS HOGSTROM:** The snakewood benefits from antiqued copper fittings, and the damascus sleeve knife benefits from snakewood.

▼ **RONNIE FOSTER:** The trailing-point hunter only trails off at one end. *(Ward photo)*

◄ **EDDIE STALCUP:** File-working the blade, dimpling the guard and polishing the mesquite burl handle are the extras it took to create a **winner.** *(Hoffman photo)*

▼ **RAYMOND L. SMITH:** Raymond obviously went with the grain when sanding the tulipwood.

▼ **ROBERT ROSSDEUTSCHER:** The handle is engineered wood from Italy attached to a 1084 blade with brass pins.

▼ **JOHAN VAN DER MERWE:** The classy olive color of the green-dyed and stabilized burl wood pays the gold mokumé bolster its compliments. *(BladeGallery.com photo)*

► **RIK PALM:** The Gentleman's Bowie is one of Rik's journeyman test knives, and the coffin-style maple-burl handle is a good way to start the **blade.** *(BladeGallery.com photo)*

▲ **JERRY LAIRSON SR.:** Jerry's war hawk chose tiger-striped camouflage in which to do battle.

▶ **TODD BEGG:** The rounded, sculpted curly-maple grip forms to the hand and feels grand. *(Lum photo)*

▼ **S.R. JOHNSON:** The Big Country Hunter stole some desert ironwood from the neighboring countryside.

▲ **J. NEILSON:** Presentation-grade ironwood couldn't even slow down that chainsaw-damascus blade.

▲ **SCOT MATSUOKA:** A leaf sprouts from a curly Koa stem. Does that make the knife a leafcutter? *(Weyer photo)*

◀ **ALAIN MIVILLE-DESCHENES:** Lace wood and brass secure an O-1 blade, allowing it to point the way.

► **GEORGE BAARTMAN:** The sandblasted titanium bolster is a perfect match for the olivewood handle.

◄ **THOMAS HASLINGER:** This one belongs in the woods, so the stabilized Caragana will feel right at home.

▼ **LOWELL LOCKETT:** Mosaic pins and a brass guard accent a Koa-wood handle.

► **MIKE TAMBOLI:** It's the first combination of a Cholla-cactus handle, an Indian penny bolster and a raindrop-pattern-damascus blade the author can remember seeing. And it's nice to see. *(Garrett photo)*

▲ **PEDRO GIBERT:** Ironwood and buffalo horn make for a good grip.

▲ **MIKE ZIMA:** The mirror-polished stainless blade and bolster needed a little spicing up from stabilized black ash.

▲ **DAVID BOYE:** This one isn't a lemon. *(Weyer photo)*

Take Hold'a Some Timber

▶ **PAOLO SCORDIA:** The lignum-vitae grip is as essential to the knife as the temper line of the forged XC100 steel blade.

▶ **A.C. RICHARDS:** The choice of Chakte Vega wood, which is rare (it's not just you), is no longer a mystery. *(Custom Knife Gallery of Colorado photo)*

◀ **CHUCK WARD:** Mansions can be built with hammer and nails, and paramount knives with walnut and A-2. *(Ward photo)*

▼ **MIKE O'BRIEN:** With one of these wooden whackers in the waistband, bandits beware. *(PointSeven photo)*

◀ **GEORGE S. COPELAND:** He sectioned the snakewood and framed it in aluminum.

▲ **DOC HAGEN:** Who knew the old box elder tree had such inner beauty? *(Custom Knife Gallery of Colorado photo)*

Dagger Management

DAGGERS ARE BLOODY old beasts, are they not? Think about it. No self-respecting member of high society uses one to remove a splinter, cut some yarn or notch a belt. They're disgustingly sharp and pointy, with no forgiving blade spines on which to rest well-manicured fingertips. The evil things have two edges, as if one wasn't bad enough, and they're usually so sharp, they'll bite before you even brush against them. They have no manners whatsoever and stick their pointed tips into whatever business they please.

No well-regarded gentleman or proper young lady would carry such brutal weapons of mass destruction. They're neither refined nor blood-lined. Do away with them is what I say. Society will be better off without the wretched, sordid things. They are what ills the social order. They have no respect and are really quite savage when you think about it. They're better off with their own kind. They can wallow in their own stench and squalor.

There, now that I've said it, I feel much better. Call me a self-absorbed snob if you will, but I see no reason to acknowledge such lower life forms. I've heard that some beggars, paupers and thieves wear daggers in their boots, while others tuck the blasted things into the waistbands of their filthy rags.

Imagine such primitive practices. If I ever need such a knife, though I can't fathom what on earth for, I'll borrow one from a blacksmith, knifemaker or collector who's into that sort of thing.

Round them up and *ooh* and *ahh* over them if you want. I'll turn my back and you can have all the fun your little hearts desire. I'm certainly not going to partake in such sinful pursuits. Well, go ahead, whoop it up if you wish. Don't let me spoil your fun. It's your life, not mine. I'm above all that.

Joe Kertzman

◄ **BOB PATRICK:** The solid-damascus push dagger wasn't forged to shape. It got that way from sawing, filing and sanding, as well as a little sweating. *(Twig photo)*

◄ **MIKE MCCLURE:** The double-hollow-ground damascus blade wasn't whipped up overnight, and the mammoth-ivory grip was a few years in the making, too. *(PointSeven photo)*

► **J.W. MCFARLIN:** The handle is actually ebony with a white mother-of-pearl overlay, like a cloth draped over the coffin of the faithfully departed. How 'bout that damascus blade, anyway? *(Weyer photo)*

▼ ROBERT ROSSDEUTSCHER: Since there were only 176 layers of damascus steel, he added a few rings of curly ash.

▼ HEATHER HARVEY: The bronze guard and pommel thought they were going to be the golden children, but then they saw the fluted box elder-wood handle and took their places in line.
(BladeGallery. com photo)

◀ PAUL LEBATARD: Here's one of those alternative-ivory handle daggers folks wear in their boots. It must be an alternative lifestyle thing.

◀ TAI GOO: It's a galactic dagger, including a meteoric-damascus blade and a silver ferrule with moonstone settings.

▼ J. NEILSON: This chessboard push dagger just called checkmate.

◀ BRUCE BUMP: Bruce's ABS mastersmith dagger dons a fluted-ivory handle with nickel-wire overlay, a lathe-turned guard, quillions and pommel, and a 12-inch, 300-layer damascus blade. He calls it a "take-down" model, and I don't doubt it.
(PointSeven photo)

◄ MIKE MCRAE: It took sterling silver, 18-carat gold, garnets from Mozambique and damascus steel to make a dagger this beautiful.

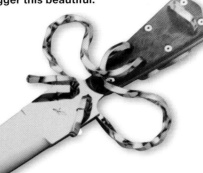

▲ LARRY MENSCH: Twisting the guard was no big deal. He was already crazed after shaping and finishing the ATS-34 blade and the lace she-oak handle.

▼ HANK KUBAIKO: Three damascus push daggers come in multi-hued handle choices of ivory, pink ivory and African black wood.

▼ ED LARY: Ed could have stopped at the five-bar-composite Nick Smollen Turkish-twist damascus blade and we'd all be impressed. Those are garnets and rubies inlaid into the damascus pommel, by the way. *(Custom Knife Gallery of Colorado photo)*

▼ THOMAS HASLINGER: The fancy EK Dagger sports ironwood scales with black-lip pearl inlays. It's a pretty cool C. Chisan damascus guard, as well.

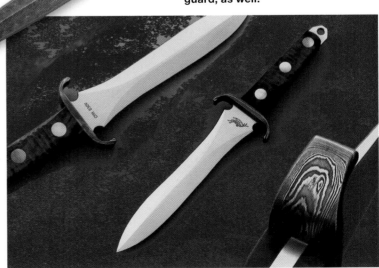

◄ LEE FERGUSON: The handle and sheath were made from one piece of book-face mastodon ivory, then the grip was inlaid with silver wire and given an Awabi shell spacer.

▲ PAUL TRUDEL: Paul put his thumb print in the base of the 210-layer damascus blade, added an alternative-ivory handle and a gold-plated brass guard and pommel, and he called it a **dagger.** *(Baril photo)*

▼ BRENT BESHARA: It's O-1 carbon tool steel, some Japanese cord wrap and a whole lot of attention to detail. The blade is actually diamond-shaped when viewed from the tip, and it's **stunning!** *(PointSeven photo)*

▲ DON HANSON III: Mastodon, mosaic and a good 'magination.

◀ JOHN WALKER: The "Nordic Song" belts out a sad ballad of steel and stabilized myrtle.

▲ JOHN POYTHRESS: The fluted-ebony dagger didn't need any dressing up, but the purple- and blue-anodized titanium spacers are the cummerbunds of this tuxedo. *(Hoffman photo)*

◀ KEVIN HARVEY: The scroll dagger reads from top to bottom and includes a twist-pattern damascus blade, a wrought-iron scroll guard, a twisted-iron, copper and silver-wire handle, and a bronze pommel with copper accents. *(BladeGallery. com photo)*

▲ ED BRANDSEY: Make mine a mule-deer push dagger with a side of turquoise, some nickel-silver caps and a mink-skin sheath. Joe Hauck did the damascus honors. *(PointSeven photo)*

▲ LARRY MENSCH: He trimmed this Western wonder out in red, white and blue recon stones, impala horn and nickel. Go get 'em, cowboy.

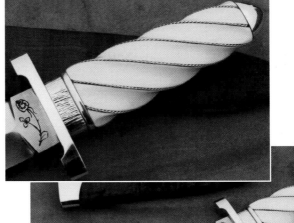

▲ PEDRO GIBERT: The fluted elephant-ivory handle is so tasty, it's like getting the twist cone at the ice cream parlor.

▼ DARREL RALPH: The Mike Norris stainless damascus gets gold accents and gold-lip pearl inlays. The dagger is reminiscent of the Italian stiletto that James Dean made so popular in the 1950s.

◄ RICHARD SUNDERLAND: Fossil oosic found a home on a soldier-stiff dagger that'll make you stagger.

◄ MUDD SHARRIGAN: The "Black Widow Dagger" wags its scorpion-like tail and claws at a 12-inch, hot-blued blade. *(Mitchell photo)*

Culture Clashers

DO GERMAN, JAPANESE and American car manufacturers share ideas? It's not likely. Does the president of General Electric call Sanyo to find out how the company's televisions are manufactured so inexpensively? That's doubtful. It's not that Americans couldn't learn a few tricks of the trade from the Japanese, or vice-versa. It's just that neither party is willing to share trade secrets. They're greedy, or "profit-driven," or they have good "business sense." They're team players, savvy and want their slice of the global economic pie. Such bottom-line theories and philosophies are the subjects of entire business summit meetings.

In other words, Toyota and Chevy aren't planning any car collaborations in the near future!

So, why does U.S. knifemaker George Tichbourne build a Persian hunting knife, and what would possess South African knifemakers Kevin and Heather Harvey to sweat over an Arabian fixed blade? Are they traitors, turning their backs on their own countries? Are they defectors, agents or spies?

Maybe knifemakers are more culturally minded than most. Perhaps they recognize quality traits in knives built elsewhere that aren't often incorporated into blades at home. Knifemakers might have an appreciation for ethnic art, exotic styles and foreign traditions. Maybe the world, especially the knife world, is becoming smaller, more accepting, friendlier, open-minded and willing to share experiences and ideologies.

World powers, religious leaders and extremist factions on all sides should take note. Knifemakers are bringing people together, forming common bonds and breaking down barriers. Their industry is richer, not poorer, for it, and not everyone is starving from lost jobs because an American shared an idea with someone from China.

The earth's axis is still at the same tilt it was before Brent Beshara made a Japanese tanto.

Joe Kertzman

► **CAREL SMITH:** Imagine heading for the Highlands with a Scottish sgian dubh tucked inside the boot. The black-ivory grip is meticulously carved in a checkered pattern, and the pommel parades a faceted, smoky topaz. What a gem! *(BladeGallery.com photo)*

► **BRENT BESHARA:** The Japanese cord-wrapped tanto is an efficient design, indeed. *(PointSeven photo)*

▲ **KEVIN AND HEATHER HARVEY:** Though the Arabian Janbiyya was traditionally used for everything from slaughtering livestock to repairing camel harnesses, the sheik might have laid claim to this ornate piece. *(Custom Knife Gallery of Colorado photo)*

▼ **YASUTAKA WADA:** This is a 1/3-size scale reproduction of a W.W. Cronk "Arabian Night." The file work, stainless guard, twisted silver wire and fluted-ivory handle are all impressive.

▼ **GEORGE TICHBOURNE:** This pearl-handle Persian hunter might be more apt for carpet riding than lamb sacrificing.

▼ **MARDI MESHEJIAN:** Mardi pays tribute to Nepalese Gurkhas, building a Kukri Fighter from 5160 blade steel, and strategically insetting a green tourmaline into the center of a fossil-walrus-ivory handle, as if it's a warrior's eye scanning enemy territory. *(Weyer photo)*

▼ **GERT VAN DEN ELSEN:** The Nordic Puukko is at home in a bog-oak and beech wood handle.

▼ **TEX SKOW:** It's hard to decide which is more amazing on this culture clasher, the upswept blade with false edge, the gnarly grip or the horn scabbard.

▲ **VINCENT EVANS:** With 5160 blade steel, stingray skin and silver wire, Vincent styled a Scottish Basket Hilt after an original 18th-century piece built by Walter Allan of Stirling, Scotland. *(Weyer photo)*

▼ANDERS HOGSTROM: Wavy temper lines along blade edges and spines, antiqued guards and natural handles speak of a proud people, those who would carry puukkos and upswept fighters to defend their lands and feed their fellow countrymen. *(PointSeven photo)*

▲VINCE EVANS: Only the most sophisticated 10th-century Vikings—those with neatly trimmed beards and good sea etiquette—could have appreciated such a sword. *(Weyer photo)*

▼JODY AND PAT MULLER: The 18-inch tanto showcases a strikingly handsome 800-layer damascus blade, a buffalo-horn spacer and a traditional stingray-skin handle with a silk-cord wrap.

▼ WALLY HAYES: Like a Samurai in the shadows, a silver menuki (charm or decoration) peeks out from behind the nylon wrap of a blue-stingray-skin handle. *(Hiro Soga photo)*

▶ DANIEL WATSON: The jasper handle of the Celtic sword is a head-turner, and the Celtic-knot-pattern Wootz blade is a headhunter. *(Weyer photo)*

▲ SCOTT SLOBODIAN: Whether the Devin Thomas damascus blade of the Koto Tanto bedazzles you, or the swirl-some handle, titanium bolsters and flowerlike thumb stud, the folder is flavorful, for sure.

▼ SCOTT SLOBODIAN: The tempered blade and curly-koa handle make the most un-Japanese want to bow down in pure respect.

▲ VAN STECK: Even an unskilled warrior would have the edge in battle carrying the tanto and spear.

▶ MIKE MCRAE: Mike was inspired to build the steel, brass and rosewood dirk after seeing such a piece in John Wallace's book "Scottish Swords & Dirks." *(Hoffman photo)*

▲
MICHAEL BELL: The 23-inch, cable-damascus blade is accompanied by a wood and stingray-skin handle, and a shibuichi collar. Shibuichi is an alloy of silver and copper, traditionally used in Japanese sword furniture, and is stronger than silver or copper alone.

◀ ANDERS HOGSTROM: Here's a Wharncliffe Kwaiken of premium ironwood, bronze and clay-tempered 1050 blade steel.

▲ DAVID MIRABILE: Two views of a Tlinget Indian dagger show that the forged blade is concave on one side and has a fuller on the other, the way such pieces were originally built. *(PointSeven photo)*

◄ **ALAIN MIVILLE-DESCHENES:** "Le Centaure" is an African-blackwood-handle beauty with a hollow-ground 440C blade, brass mosaic pins and a black- and salmon-leather sheath.

▼ **HARALD SELLEVOLD:** The "Rattle Knife" rattles when shaken, having steel balls in the top of the ferrule, an old Norwegian tradition used to warn that the knife was ready to be used.

▼ **DON POZIEN:** The matched pair of Chinese swords, made for Horace Greeley IV, showcases ivory grips carved in the forms of dragonheads.

▲ **GERT VAN DEN ELSEN:** From the Netherlands comes the Loki, complete with a Ziricote wood handle, a stabilized-maple spacer and sterling-silver trimmings.

▼ **HEATHER HARVEY:** The "Gaucho" wears a box-elder handle and a powerful damascus blade, slips into a cowhide sheath and accessorizes with cubic zirconium. *(Custom Knife Gallery of Colorado photo)*

▲ **MARDI MESHEJIAN:** Seldom a slave to conventionalism, Mardi builds a chainsaw-damascus dirk, adding anodized-titanium fittings and a Shakuido hibachi (blade collar). *(Weyer photo)*

Mighty Mites

▼ LEE FERGUSON: He measured the ivory-handled mini-knife and still couldn't believe it.

▶ MIKE TAMBOLI: Decked out in duds of mastodon ivory, synthetic emeralds and Robert Eggerling mosaic damascus (bolsters), this short but fancy folder is ready to trim a fingernail or two in the board room.

▲ VERNON RED: It might not help you improve your golf swing, but the stag-handle folder with a mini-but-mighty 1-inch damascus blade and file-worked liners is a hole-in-one from the get-go (and it cuts through the rough). *(Ward photo)*

▲ CLIFF POLK: Cliff had no intentions of letting the little piece of abalone go to waste, and engraving by Everett Smith sets it off nicely.

▶ BERNARD BERTHOLUS: A pair of capers is game for any capers that might come along.

▼ TILL AND RUTH CALVIN: The bowie is a bit undersized for reenacting the fighting at the Alamo.

▶ MIKE TAMBOLI: Engraved by Bruce Shaw, the Mini-Hunter with fireball-damascus blade and ram-horn handle fills a room with its presence. *(PointSeven photo)*

Cut from the Same Cloth

"LIKE MIKE, I wanna be like Mike." Some of you might remember that catchy jingle from Michael Jordan's heyday with the Chicago Bulls. It's true. People want to emulate those they admire, whether by slight or large degrees. One person might want to be a good speaker like his or her favorite orator, and another might want to be strong and sleek like an Olympian. You could strive to be brave and bold like a soldier, or meek and mild-mannered like a librarian.

Most knifemakers have someone they admire, usually another knifemaker who's been in the business longer than they have, or one who taught them the ropes. Some go as far as building replicas of their mentors' or heroes'

knives. Just like that little boy on the playground you saw giving his young opponents a head fake one way, pivoting another, dribbling twice, leaping and shooting a fade-away jump shot Jordan-esque style, complete with his tongue hanging out of his mouth, a few blade builders emulate their icons' every move.

It's fun to envision Dr. James Lucie in his shop, which is equipped with original William Scagel handle materials he inherited from the legendary Michigan knifemaker, swinging the hammer to the same beat as Scagel swung his. Knowing Dr. Lucie, it might even be the same hammer. He might go as far as grinding and polishing blades using the same methods as Scagel,

or perhaps the habits he picked up from his knifemaking mentor are more subtle or subconscious, like the way he wipes the dust from his hands with a rag, or the manner in which he inspects a finished blade.

One thing is for sure, looking at modern handmade replicas of classic knife patterns, a good number of knifemakers have perfected the art of flattery. Some modern versions of classic knives are as high quality as the originals. Maybe the next television commercial will be a group of leather-apron-wearing youngsters singing, "Like William. I wanna be like William." It's sort of catchy, isn't it?

Joe Kertzman

▼ **JIM BATSON:** It's not William Scagel's personal pocketknife, but it sure does look like it.

▲ **RON WELLING:** Ron makes a living off building Scagel-style knives, and he's living in an ivory, brass and red-spacer world. *(Weyer photo)*

► **CLESTON SINYARD:** Scagel would have appreciated the flow of the damascus. *(Long photo)*

▼ **EDMUND DAVIDSON:** Edmund might not be cut from the same cloth as Bob Loveless, but he drinks from a similar cup and builds 'em like he sees 'em. This one's got a black-ash-burl handle and a BG-42 blade. *(PointSeven photo)*

▼ **LARRY MENSCH:** Larry replicated a knife style of someone who is probably the most copied knifemaker in the world—William Scagel—and to do that, you must do it well.

◄ **KOUJI HARA:** Bob Loveless will recognize his Big Bears, those with 7- and 20-inch claws. *(Weyer photo)*

▶ **JOE CORDOVA:** The recognition of a classic design, like a Marble's Woodcraft Style Hunter, is only half the fun. Forging an eagle-feather blade from 1095 and L-6 carbon steels, and stacking a stag and maroon-Micarta® handle is the other half of the fun. *(BladeGallery.com photo)*

▼ **RICK SMITH:** It's almost as if Michael Price, himself, had a hand in building the San Francisco Bowie, his spirit forging a mirror-polished O-1 blade and adding an alternate-ivory handle. The mosaic pins are definitely his.

▼ **RENDON GRIFFIN:** Rendon's San Francisco Folding Knife has all the right elements, an 18-carat-gold handle frame and studs, engraving, red stone inlays and a 5-inch blade built to just the right shape. *(Weyer photo)*

▲ **RON WELLING:** What else would a "Cowboy Camp Knife" wear but stag, leather and brass? *(Weyer photo)*

Cut From The Same Cloth

▼ **S.R. JOHNSON:** The shapes are just as stunning as Robert Loveless originals. Even Bob's probably shaking his head in disbelief. *(PointSeven photo)*

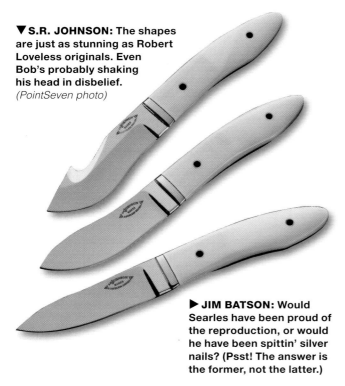

▶ **JIM BATSON:** Would Searles have been proud of the reproduction, or would he have been spittin' silver nails? (Psst! The answer is the former, not the latter.)

▼ **ROGER MUDBONE JONES:** The replica of a Scagel Persian hunter/fighter is a fistful of stag and fine 5160 blade steel.

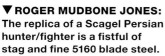

▲ **MICHAEL VAGNINO:** The "California Sheffield" bowie borrows from both blade-making meccas—California and Sheffield, England—then ventures off into a damascus and stag land of its own.

▶ **KEVIN HARVEY:** The Samuel Bell Bowie might be in the Stafford Style, but Kevin is the one who worked, forged and heat-beat the mosaic damascus, and planted the mother-of-pearl where it counts. *(BladeGallery. com photo)*

▲ **STEVEN R. JOHNSON:** If you could only take one knife into the woods, wouldn't it be a Bob Loveless-style Wilderness? This one's dressed in ironwood for just such an occasion. *(PointSeven photo)*

▼ **DR. JIM LUCIE:** The utmost authority on William Scagel knives, Dr. Jim builds "exact replicas," like this Trout & Bird, and he begs you to differ.

▼ **DR. JIM LUCIE:** The doctor has a supply of original William Scagel handle parts, but he forges his own blades and blazes his own trails.

▼ **TEX SKOW:** California was all about pomp and circumstance, and still is, come to think of it. The inlays and engraving would even turn heads on Hollywood Boulevard.

▼ **LAWRENCE LITTLE:** Before building knives, Lawrence was a William Scagel mind reader.

▼ **RAYMOND L. SMITH:** This wow-me Woodcraft-style fixed blade has that polished look—brass, leather, stag and steel.

▶ **ART TYCER:** Though it's a Loveless style, this one's fashioned with Thunderforged damascus and a buffalo-horn handle, definite departures from the knives made in Oceanside, Ca.

Pearls in the Rough

G IVE A GIRL a pearl necklace, and many of your faults may be forgiven. There's something so pure, pretty, pristine and pleasant about the natural substance that even man can't destroy it. Yes, nacre outshines lacquer. Women know these things. They know nature's beauty firsthand. Don't try to trick them with fake diamonds, fool's gold or manmade pearl. Love will be lost, and at a cost. Such is the way of Mother Nature. She forgives no fool.

In the hands of knifemakers, pearl is put to the test. Can it really retain its natural glow when butted up against bolsters, blades, guards and pommels? Can sharp steel be a bedfellow to black-lip pearl? Why on earth would gold-lip pearl be chosen to decorate a dirk or dagger? Should mother-of-pearl grace the grips of a big-bladed bowie? Mightn't a mollusk head for higher ground? How dare the bladesmith subject the pearly whites to perilous whittlers? For the sake of the sea, make them stop!

Ah, but knifemakers are artisans. They bring out more beauty from the pearl than is immediately apparent upon laying eyes upon the clammy growth. They cut it, polish it and protect it. They take off the rough exterior and uncover its inner beauty. They give it gold and silver, shower it with diamonds, rubies and emeralds, and surround it with carving, etching and engraving. Blade builders place pearl on a pedestal. They pay homage to it, honor it and enrich it with the fruits of their labor.

Give a girl a pearl-handle pocketknife, and many of your faults will be forgiven. There's something so sweet, safe, sensuous and splendid about it. Not even knifemakers can destroy it.

Joe Kertzman

▶ **GEORGE MULLER:** As if a damascus blade and meteorite bolster weren't exotic enough, they're anchored by a green, red, gold, pink, blue, purple and yellow grip called "black-lip pearl." *(Custom Knife Gallery of Colorado photo)*

▼ **GEORGE COPELAND:** It was a golden opportunity to frame gold-lip pearl.

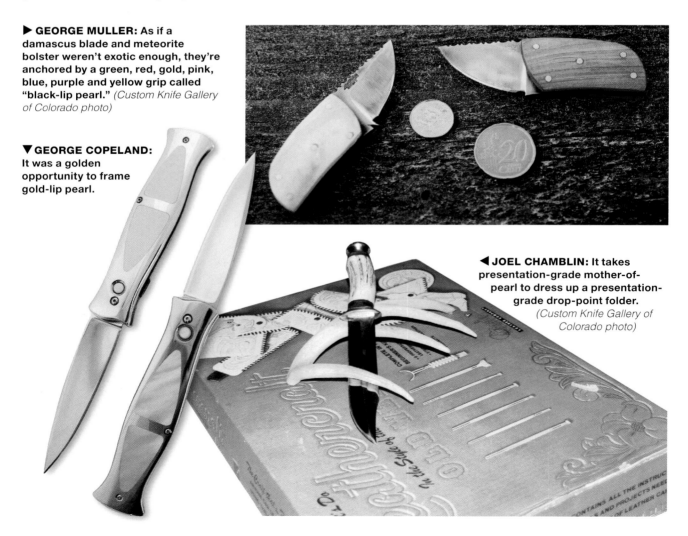

◀ **JOEL CHAMBLIN:** It takes presentation-grade mother-of-pearl to dress up a presentation-grade drop-point folder. *(Custom Knife Gallery of Colorado photo)*

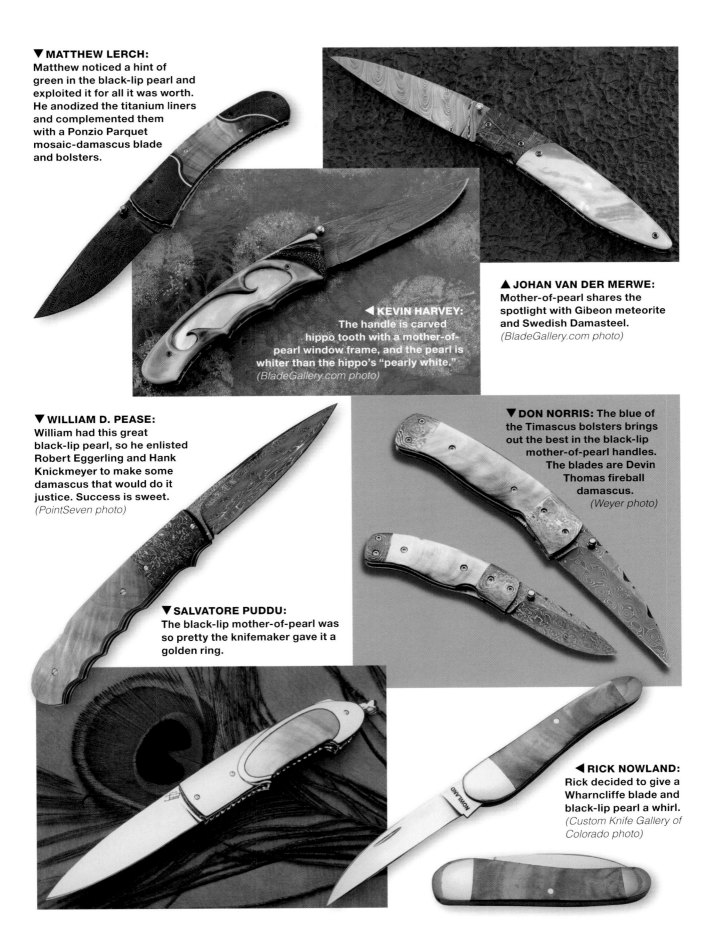

▼ MATTHEW LERCH: Matthew noticed a hint of green in the black-lip pearl and exploited it for all it was worth. He anodized the titanium liners and complemented them with a Ponzio Parquet mosaic-damascus blade and bolsters.

◄ KEVIN HARVEY: The handle is carved hippo tooth with a mother-of-pearl window frame, and the pearl is whiter than the hippo's "pearly white." *(BladeGallery.com photo)*

▲ JOHAN VAN DER MERWE: Mother-of-pearl shares the spotlight with Gibeon meteorite and Swedish Damasteel. *(BladeGallery.com photo)*

▼ WILLIAM D. PEASE: William had this great black-lip pearl, so he enlisted Robert Eggerling and Hank Knickmeyer to make some damascus that would do it justice. Success is sweet. *(PointSeven photo)*

▼ DON NORRIS: The blue of the Timascus bolsters brings out the best in the black-lip mother-of-pearl handles. The blades are Devin Thomas fireball damascus. *(Weyer photo)*

▼ SALVATORE PUDDU: The black-lip mother-of-pearl was so pretty the knifemaker gave it a golden ring.

◄ RICK NOWLAND: Rick decided to give a Wharncliffe blade and black-lip pearl a whirl. *(Custom Knife Gallery of Colorado photo)*

▼ **RUSS SUTTON:** A rather complex black-lip-pearl handle enlivens an otherwise clean slip-joint folder.

▶ **BILL LEVENGOOD:** It's an abalone handle, but the back bar is inlaid with pearl, and the whole thing has me feeling kind of clammy.

▲ **LARRY NEWTON:** Raindrops splatter the damascus blade of the dagger and pool up at the carved-pearl grip.

▶ **JOSH SMITH:** Josh might be subtle about his steel making, but when it comes to the handles, he holds nothing back. *(PointSeven photo)*

▶ **ROGER DOLE:** As purple as the bolster is, the pearl is equally as white. *(BladeGallery.com photo)*

▲ **BARRY DAVIS:** Who says checks and stripes don't go together? *(PointSeven photo)*

◀ **T.R. OVEREYNDER:**
Swirly steel = subtle handle.
Swirly handle = subtle steel.
(PointSeven photo)

◀ **JOHN POYHRESS:** Pink pearl is the
centerpiece, literally, of a stain-free
statement in steel.

◀ **MATSUSAKI TAKESHI:**
It was a plain planer until
he planted the pearl.

▶ **AL DIPPOLD:** From green
to pink to black, the
damascus locking-liner
folder is a lesson in
graduating colors.
(PointSeven photo)

◀ **DON HANSON III:** Take
me to where the grass is
green and the swirls are
pretty. *(PointSeven photo)*

▼ **BOYD ASHWORTH:** What a shell
on that turtle! *(PointSeven photo)*

▲ **MICHAEL VAGNINO:** He traveled
to Damascus dressed in pink, yet he
feared no man.

Them's Fightin' Knives

IN THE WORLD of knives, there is nothing quite so raw, unpolished or untamed as the fighter. It's not that all other knives are more refined, although some are, it's just that the fighter pattern is as straightforward as they come. To fight with a knife, one needs a good grip, a guard to protect the hand and fingers, and a long, thin blade for pointing, stabbing, slashing and otherwise wielding.

Don't be fooled. Only fools fight with knives, and it's not recommended. The Knives 2005 editor and publisher go on record as saying that fighting of any kind, especially with knives, is not condoned in any way, shape or form, and the said parties take no responsibility for any injuries, including pokes in eyes, stabbed palms, sliced wrists,

bleeding fingers or other severed extremities from folks who try to simulate knife fighting, or who actually fight with knives. Knife-fight simulations should always be conducted with dull rubber or plastic knives. It's also a good idea to take training courses first.

No trained knife fighter uses a traditional fighting-style knife, anyway. Today tactical folders, Karambit-style knives, tantos, daggers and other claw and concealable knives do the trick. A fighter is old school. It's for those folks who remember what their great-grandfathers tucked in their belts or boots for a night at the saloon, or what heroic soldiers did battle with in the world wars.

The fighter-style knife is legendary, but it's also sensuous

in a "sticker shock" kind of way, and we're not talking price. These stickers are actually shocking. Their very forms remind us of what they're meant to do. Their curved C- and S-guards are for reflecting enemies' slashing blades. The grip is for pulling back as well as pointing, stabbing or slashing forward. Thrusting and parrying even come into play with skilled knife fighters, those who saw plenty of Errol Flynn films. These puppies excel at exacting punishment. When you see a few of the edged demons that make you cringe a little, you'll know right away that them's fightin' knives.

Joe Kertzman

▼ **DICK FAUST:** You can bust his chops, but not his steel and stabilized box elder bastion of a knife.

◀ **PETER DEL RASO:** Decked out in engraved armor and ancient ivory, the warrior fought with the grace and style of a well-trained professional. His personal engraver is P. Vinnecombe. *(KnifeArt.com photo)*

▲ **ED CAFFREY:** Think of icebergs breaking up, or of ice crystals forming on a storm window, and look into the blade, realizing why the maker calls it a "Winter Thaw" Mosaic Damascus Fighter/Bowie.

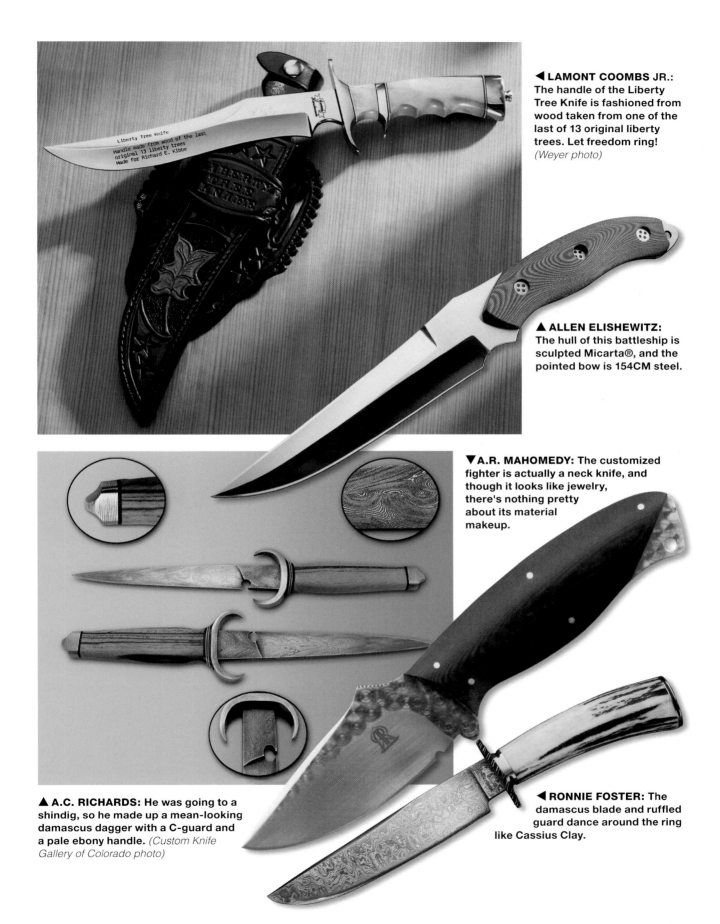

◀ **LAMONT COOMBS JR.:** The handle of the Liberty Tree Knife is fashioned from wood taken from one of the last of 13 original liberty trees. Let freedom ring! *(Weyer photo)*

▲ **ALLEN ELISHEWITZ:** The hull of this battleship is sculpted Micarta®, and the pointed bow is 154CM steel.

▼ **A.R. MAHOMEDY:** The customized fighter is actually a neck knife, and though it looks like jewelry, there's nothing pretty about its material makeup.

▲ **A.C. RICHARDS:** He was going to a shindig, so he made up a mean-looking damascus dagger with a C-guard and a pale ebony handle. *(Custom Knife Gallery of Colorado photo)*

◀ **RONNIE FOSTER:** The damascus blade and ruffled guard dance around the ring like Cassius Clay.

▶ **TOM LEWIS:** The guard brings to mind a musical note and the blade the reverberations.

▼ **BILLY D. MADISON II:** Don't worry. The 440C blade is cryogenically quenched. It won't break. You can venture out into the cold, cruel world with nary a thought to your own wellbeing.

▲ **FRANS VAN ELDIK:** Full-integral fighters are like armored tanks, only better looking and the embellishments go past pinup girls. *(Tienhoven photo)*

◀ **J.P. HOLMES:** As smooth and sculpted as the front and rear bolsters appear to be, as sharp and sleek as the fighting blade is, to such an extent also is the Afzelia-lay handle polished and highly patterned. *(BladeGallery.com photo)*

▶ **WALLY HAYES:** Wally's going in well armed, complete with battle axe and fighting bowie, the pair being of the forged-timing-chain and curly maple variety. *(Soga photo)*

Proven Pocketknife Patterns

"WITH HIS GUNSTOCK in one hand and saddle-horn in the other, the cowboy ventured into orange blossom land, whittled a stick with a Wharncliffe and took a pull from the old Coke bottle."

One could easily mistake such a statement as an excerpt from a weird sci-fi Western flick, unless he or she had knowledge of proven pocketknife patterns. With names like "trapper" and "stockman," the old folding knives rested in the pockets of blue jeans and overalls until called upon to cut a leather harness or castrate a bull. There wasn't any room for sissy knives in those days.

The pocketknife patterns were time-honored, tested and true. Each blade had a purpose. Edges were honed on oilstones. Springs were stiff, and when the folding blades were pulled from the handles via nail nicks, they snapped into place like soldiers ready for battle. Breaking cute little manicured fingernails was not a concern. Men considered pocketknives tools, not showpieces. Cowboys reserved pearl-handle six-shooters and penknives for getting all gussied up and going to town. Knives were about cut, not cute.

Proven pocketknife patterns were specialized, not all-purpose or utilitarian. Sounds like a baseball lineup, doesn't it—the utility player—the one that will do everything? There were no tactical folders. Fists, not knives, were for fighting.

In the barn, a farmer used a stockman or saddlehorn-pattern pocketknife. In the field, a cowboy toted a trapper, sowbelly or bullet knife. At home, he used a whittler, orange blossom or penknife. Neck knives would have gotten a chuckle or two, and gent's pocketknives were too fancy to use.

In some ways, things made more sense in those days, back when a spade was a spade, and it was used to dig dirt.

Joe Kertzman

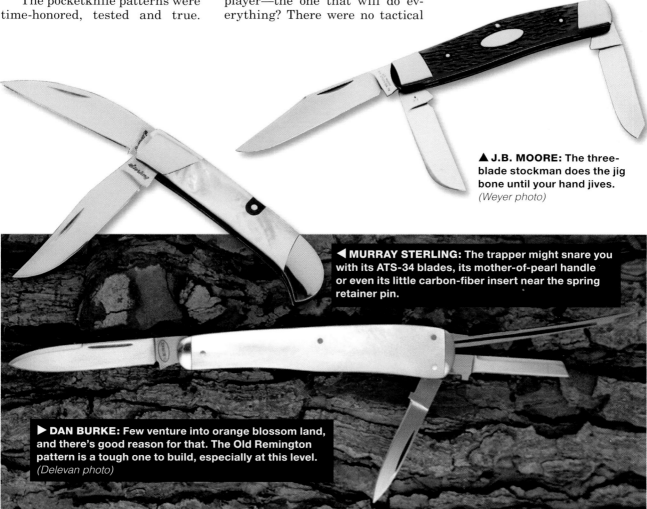

▲ **J.B. MOORE:** The three-blade stockman does the jig bone until your hand jives.
(Weyer photo)

◄ **MURRAY STERLING:** The trapper might snare you with its ATS-34 blades, its mother-of-pearl handle or even its little carbon-fiber insert near the spring retainer pin.

▶ **DAN BURKE:** Few venture into orange blossom land, and there's good reason for that. The Old Remington pattern is a tough one to build, especially at this level.
(Delevan photo)

▶ **JEFF CLAIBORNE:** Long pulls and half stops help work this 3-inch congress-pattern pocketknife.

◀ **MATSUSAKI TAKESHI:** Some guys just know what a traditional multi-blade is supposed to look like. Take this pearly pocketknife, for example.

◀ **BILL LEVENGOOD:** The slip-joint folder, with amber-bone-stag grip, and stainless blade, bolsters and liners is worth pocketing, don't you think?

▶ **RICHARD ROGERS:** The two-blade Gunstock gets it done with an ATS-34 blade, a green jigged-bone handle, domed pins and an inlaid shield.

▼ **DAN BURKE:** A bird takes flight from the pearl and bronze inlays of a buffalo-horn-handle penknife. *(Delevan photo)*

▶ **RICHARD ROGERS:** A man needs Coke-bottle glasses to see all the fine detail in this ATS-34 Coke Bottle-style cutter.

▲ **JOHNATHAN WATTS:** In order to fashion such a fancy raindrop-pattern-damascus two-blade trapper, and fancily file-worked to boot, you'd think he had a good teacher.

▼ MATSUSAKI TAKESHI: Bring on the bubbly, the bartender's knife is open.

◄ JOHN HOWSER: One way to build a Wharncliffe Barlow would be with a cocobolo handle and integral bolsters.

▲ BARRY DAVIS: Barry dealt a pair of ace blades, flush bolsters and a spade-colored jackknife, complete with handle shield. *(PointSeven photo)*

▲ BILL RUPLE: A miniature Saddlehorn Trapper stretches a mere 1-1/4 inches open but stands tall in the stirrups. *(BladeGallery.com photo)*

▼ T.R. OVEREYNDER: The premium Wharncliffe whittler awaits a few sticks and some time on your hands. *(PointSeven photo)*

► HARUMI HIRAYAMA: Leave it to Harumi to create a Bouquet manicure knife, and allow her to build it in silver and gold, engrave it and touch it up with pearl handle scales. *(Hasegawa photo)*

► BARRY DAVIS: With damascus scissors and tweezers, and a gold toothpick and button, Barry set out to build a pocketknife. *(PointSeven photo)*

Dangerous Curves Ahead

SOME ADULTS MIGHT feel silly admitting that the S-curve is their favorite, that the figure-8 holds a fascination for them, or that curlicues get them giddy. After all, aren't the days of sliding down the curly slide, weaving in and out of the yellow lines in the road and making ssss-ounds like a ssss-nake over by the time we reach our 20s? Most people graduate to finding hourglass figures and the curves of a Corvette a bit more appealing. I guess folks never quite outgrow their admiration for dangerous curves, or at least for smooth, gentle, sloping or sexy ones.

Enter the knife blade. The Persians sure knew a shapely blade when they saw one. And the Malaysians didn't miss a beat with curvy kris blades. Upswept blade tips sure did tickle the fancies of patch-eyed pirates. The forward-weighted kukri blades of the Gurkhas had a bend or two in them, as well, didn't they? Some blades are just plain ssss-erpentine. They ssss-lither like a ssss-nake. There I go again.

Combine a tendency toward bends and breaks with an infatuation for edged tools and weapons, and you have some of the shapeliest blades in the universe. Some knife and sword makers go as far as making the handles curve right along with the blades. Others dip the grips in opposite directions to the blades, counterbalancing the edged tools of their liking. When whirling, winding and wickedly wavy guards get into the action, then a knife can curve around like a dragon too far from its lair and caught in a snare.

So, what's your favorite blade shape? Is it the Ssss, the 8, or an even more curvaceous variety of cut?

Joe Kertzman

▲ **TODD BEGG:** Hand rubbing the curvy CPM S30V blade was likely more difficult than designing the dashing handle. *(Lum photo)*

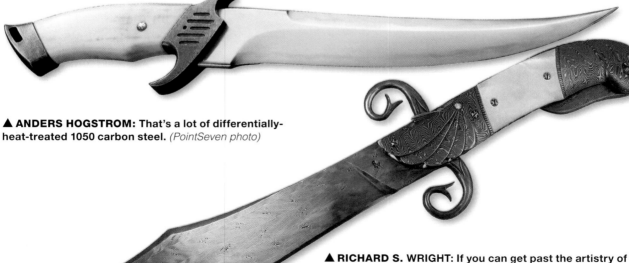

▲ **ANDERS HOGSTROM:** That's a lot of differentially-heat-treated 1050 carbon steel. *(PointSeven photo)*

▲ **RICHARD S. WRIGHT:** If you can get past the artistry of the bolster carved like feathers, the branched-out guard and the beak of an extra blade, then you're sure to notice the long, flowing damascus tail on this bird. Jerry Rados supplied the damascus.

▶ **JOHN POYTHRESS:** The clip-point-style blade has always had all the right curves. *(Hoffman photo)*

▶ **MATT CUCCHIARA:** The titanium handle is sculpted in a way that gives the wildly curved Devin Thomas stainless damascus blade credence and clearance. *(Hoffman photo)*

◀ **ANDRE DE VILLIERS:** With the smooth abalone handle insert and curvaceous blade, things are shaping up nicely.

▶ **SCOT MATSUOKA:** You can cut so much more area when the blades curve around like that, but each handle fills the palm so well, the work is easy. *(Weyer photo)*

▶ **DONALD H. OSBORNE:** The blade reaches far beyond arm's length to sever things one doesn't want too close to his person. *(Richmond photo)*

▲ **AARON FREDERICK:** This one's got more dangerous curves than the Indianapolis 500 Speedway. *(PointSeven photo)*

Shatterproof Synthetics

UNLIKE A BOOK, you can judge a blade by its cover. Canvas Micarta® is my favorite example of a knife-handle material that is tough looking and tough acting. Canvas Micarta is a synthetic formed by layering canvas and, through heat and pressure, much like forging damascus from layers of steel, compressing the layers of canvas until they are one, impenetrable mass of incredible strength and wear resistance. Carbon fiber is a handle material used in the knife industry comparable to fiberglass, so tough, it's shatterproof. G-10 is one of those ultra-strong synthetics that will hold up to hammer blows.

These are all modern materials that have evolved to the demise of another synthetic knife-handle material thought to have ultra-strength—celluloid. Celluloid could be bent, molded, twisted and pressed into form. Celluloid's ability to conform to a specific shape after being subjected to heat and pressure turned out to be one of the material's greatest assets.

It was the perfect pocketknife handle material, right? No, that's wrong. Through trial and error, it was discovered that celluloid billiard balls would literally explode once they hit each other because of the unstable nature of the substance. Though modern, more stable forms of celluloid are still used on a small number of knife handles today, it wasn't uncommon for old celluloid-handle blades to eventually rust near the grips due to gases emitted from the handles as they aged.

As with steels, improvements have been made to synthetics used on knives. Why do knives need to be bulletproof? Should a knife be able to survive a nuclear holocaust? That depends. Do you want to be able to cut something afterwards if you survive such a disaster? Or, more realistically, if you are caught in a house fire, trapped inside a vehicle, pinned below a fallen tree or stuck on a cliff, would you rather have a shatterproof or delicate knife handle?

Unlike a book, you can judge a blade by its cover, and to follow are some of the edgiest tales ever told.

Joe Kertzman

▲ **DAVID DEMPSEY:** It's not that the burgundy linen Micarta® needed bead blasting, but the machine was already fired up to put a grainy finish on a dual-hollow-ground, spear-point blade, so why not?

▼**R.J. MARTIN:** They say CPM S30V steel makes for some of the toughest knife blades, so butting it up against a titanium frame and grooved carbon fiber was a wise choice. *(PointSeven photo)*

▲ **DANIEL GRAY:** As with the 154CM blade, it's the way he shaped and finished the black-Micarta handle that softened its rough exterior. *(Weyer photo)*

◀ **WALLY HAYES:** Not only is the Tactical Knife unbreakable, with an O-1 blade and G-10 handle, but it incorporates a red LED light that shines toward the tip of the edged steel, a compass and a fire starter. Natural disasters have nothing over this puppy. *(Soga photo)*

▶ **KEVIN HOFFMAN:** It's all about patterns with Kevin, whether blade, handle or knife, all are pretty and practically impenetrable.

▼ **DONALD H. OSBORNE:** The knife may be impenetrable, but its character isn't. See how the mosaic pins and multi-colored chord play off the colors of the green-canvas-Micarta handle. *(Richmond photo)*

▲ **ALLEN ELISHEWITZ:** Allen's Striker II is a soft, little, fancy folder built bulletproof-like, complete with an appealing but shatterproof carbon-fiber handle, titanium bolsters and a 154CM blade. She's a looker and a lopper.

▼ **ALLEN ELISHEWITZ:** No one said synthetics had to be ugly, just sturdy and strong.

▲ **BURT FOSTER:** A backpacker can rest assured that the knife won't be his demise if lost in the woods.

▶ **ERIC FEHRMAN:** The "Peace Maker" doesn't intend to deliberate between negotiations.

▲ **SEAN O'HARE:** The green-and-black G-10 handle invites you to "set a spell" and cut, if you like.

▼ **MACE VITALE:** Blue G-10 gives more bite to an already toothy neck knife.

▲ **FARID MEHR:** No matter the blade steels, Farid can't get enough of the carbon-fiber stuff.

◀ **LOWELL BRAY:** Seeing a red-linen-Micarta handle is as rare as spotting a pair of scarlet macaws in the wild.

DWAINE CARRILLO: The 154CM blade, anchored by a black G-10 handle, will chomp through anything, especially considering the offset, dual-action reciprocating saw teeth with built-in cleaning channels. Who needs TV for entertainment? *(PointSeven photo)*

ERIC FEHRMAN: Fehrman outfitted his "Final Judgment" fixed blade with a textured linen-Micarta handle in case it's judged unfairly. *(Hoffman photo)*

JENS ANSO: He calls the knife the "Rebel," and if it gets into trouble, it should fare well with a blue-denim Fibermascus handle and titanium liners.

GEORGE TICHBOURNE: The dive knife isn't for hanging on the wall. It's for diving.

WILLIAM HEATH: The grip is "butterscotch Micarta," and it's sweet.

JENS ANSO: No titanium frame-lock folder before or since has caught as many knife enthusiasts in its pincers as "The Rock Lobster," complete with a green-camouflage-Fibermascus body.

▼ RICK FRIGAULT: In case one bulletproof handle material wasn't enough, Rick overlaid a black G-10 grip with blue G-10, and anyone who cares to differ with his methods might end up the same colors.

▼ ANDRE DE VILLIERS: A green G-10 handle allows the damascus "Warhog" to root around in the mud with nary a nick.

▼ PAUL LEBATARD: LeBatard doesn't wear any leotards, and neither do his knives.

▼ BILL SNOW: The hot-rolled surface texture from the steel mill was left as is on the ATS-34 blade for a rough exterior, and a canvas-Micarta handle was added to back up its image.

▼ PAT CRAWFORD: It took Pat quite some time to draw out the plans for this "Quick Draw" steel, titanium and carbon fiber locking-liner folder, complete with double guard and "Flipper" blade-opening mechanism. *(PointSeven photo)*

▲ JOHN HUTCHESON IV: You can envision this one skinning a moose, and you might even be able to feel the blade glide along as you steady it with the Micarta handle. *(Hoffman photo)*

Fierce and Fantastic

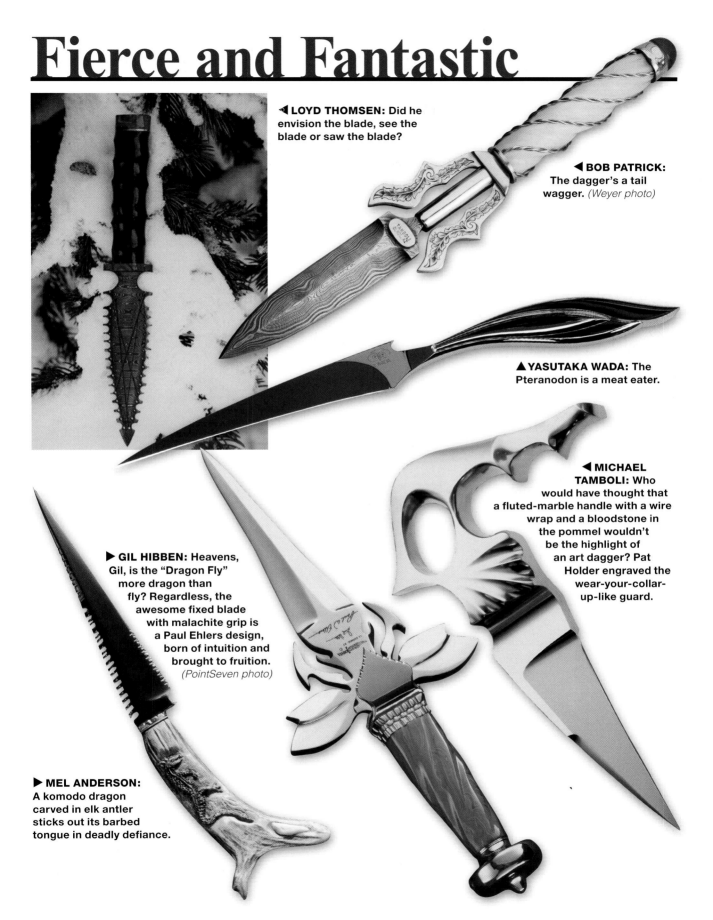

LOYD THOMSEN: Did he envision the blade, see the blade or saw the blade?

BOB PATRICK: The dagger's a tail wagger. *(Weyer photo)*

YASUTAKA WADA: The Pteranodon is a meat eater.

MICHAEL TAMBOLI: Who would have thought that a fluted-marble handle with a wire wrap and a bloodstone in the pommel wouldn't be the highlight of an art dagger? Pat Holder engraved the wear-your-collar-up-like guard.

GIL HIBBEN: Heavens, Gil, is the "Dragon Fly" more dragon than fly? Regardless, the awesome fixed blade with malachite grip is a Paul Ehlers design, born of intuition and brought to fruition. *(PointSeven photo)*

MEL ANDERSON: A komodo dragon carved in elk antler sticks out its barbed tongue in deadly defiance.

Big Bad Bowies

IT'S NO WONDER bowies are the most recognizable, ever-popular, collectible, desired, studied and reproduced blades in the country and probably on the planet. With handles the size of baseball bats, guards that do their jobs instead of just looking pretty and blades, oh the blades, well, they speak for themselves. They're so deep and thick at the guards, and they don't taper much at all, until reaching the clip–that clip, the way it swoops down and then lifts, like a bird looking for prey–and, eventually, the point. Then there's the underside of the blade, the edge, with a belly bulged out like a bowl full of jelly. It has just as hard a time lifting up as Santa has scaling the chimney after too many cookies.

And what you can do with a bowie–that's the other amazing aspect of the kicking-its-heels-up knife of Western repute and cowboy lore. Gut a deer–sure you can. Cut tent stakes–a bowie will do it. Clear a path-yup, it's built for that. Defend your honor-that's its main purpose. Slice a thread, open a box, cut carpet, sever a rope, cut leather, chop a board, notch a belt–a bowie excels at such practices. In short, a bowie is a big, bad blade. It pierces when held point out, slices when rolled downward, chops when brought down hard, slashes when whipped, details when choked up on and even minces when tapped.

Then there's the best part–wearing a bowie. Put that puppy on your hip and strut around like a rooster in the hen yard. Let the sheath hang down and bump up against the outside of your thigh as you walk purposefully from workshop to the field, to the barn and back to the living room. If you should happen upon a neighbor, or even a stranger, on the way, just smile and pass by, your demeanor ever more confident with 10 inches of sharp steel at your side.

Bowies are as American as John Deere, red barns and hayfields. They're as big as short swords and as bad as schoolyard bullies. They're big, bad bowie blades, and they're cutting the life fantastic.

Joe Kertzman

▼ **BURT FOSTER:** The rust-colored, 100-year-old wrought iron guard matches perfectly the colors of the stabilized English walnut grip.

◄ **MICK WARDELL:** If you can't get enough of the high-carbon-damascus blade, grip it by the crown-stag handle and look down at it from the nickel-silver guard.

▶ **RON HEMBROOK:** For the well-dressed cowboy in all of us is a stag-handle 440C bowie with an engraved guard and tail piece.

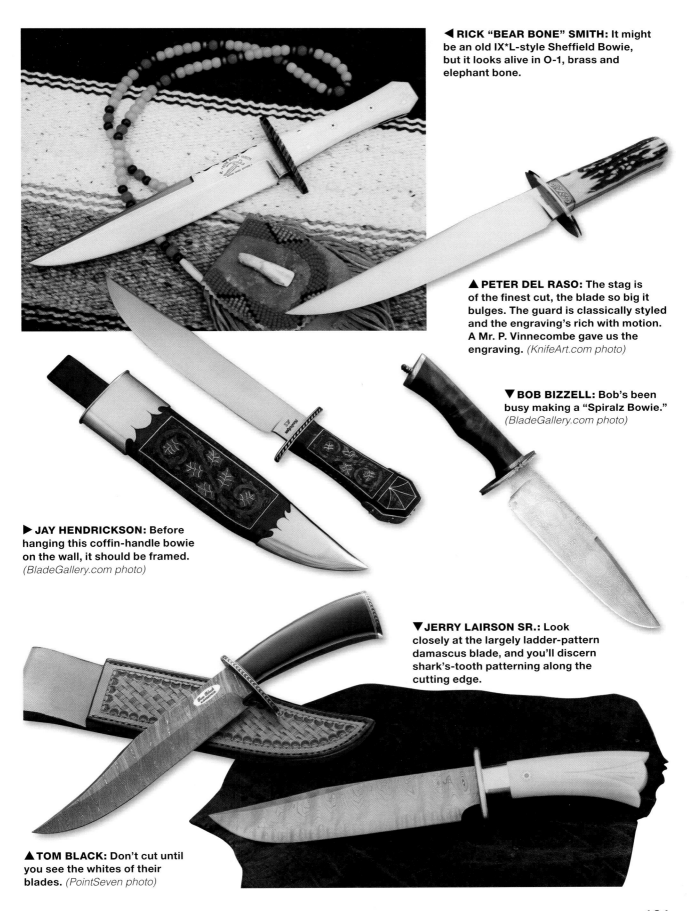

◄ RICK "BEAR BONE" SMITH: It might be an old IX*L-style Sheffield Bowie, but it looks alive in O-1, brass and elephant bone.

▲ PETER DEL RASO: The stag is of the finest cut, the blade so big it bulges. The guard is classically styled and the engraving's rich with motion. A Mr. P. Vinnecombe gave us the engraving. *(KnifeArt.com photo)*

▼ BOB BIZZELL: Bob's been busy making a "Spiralz Bowie." *(BladeGallery.com photo)*

► JAY HENDRICKSON: Before hanging this coffin-handle bowie on the wall, it should be framed. *(BladeGallery.com photo)*

▼ JERRY LAIRSON SR.: Look closely at the largely ladder-pattern damascus blade, and you'll discern shark's-tooth patterning along the cutting edge.

▲ TOM BLACK: Don't cut until you see the whites of their blades. *(PointSeven photo)*

▶ **MUDD SHARRIGAN:** Cold, blue steel stares you in the eye, a D-guard flares its nostrils, and the elk stag handle trumpets loudly enough to cut through the silence. *(Mitchell photo)*

▼ **MILTON CHOATE:** The 5150 steel blade is deep and thick at the guard and puffs out even more before tapering slowly to the point. The clip is subtle but there.

▼ **STEVE DUNN:** It's not the engraving, the ivory or the damascus that gives it class, but the combination of all three, and the way the guard and ferrule flow into the handle, that brings it up a notch. *(PointSeven photo)*

▲ **GERT VAN DEN ELSEN:** Bravo to the Brazos Bowie, caped in random damascus, nickel-silver trimmings and a Cape buffalo-horn handle.

▼ **MARK NEVLING:** The blade had a two-bar heat explosion and the result was fantastic. A fossil-walrus-ivory grip tries to hold it down. *(Ward photo)*

▼ **BOB PATRICK:** These pieces of eight share the same, basic bowie blade style with slight and not-so-subtle handle differences. *(Weyer photo)*

▶ **MIKE TAMBOLI:** The popcorn-stag handle is easy to grip, and the O-1 blade easy to take. *(PointSeven photo)*

▼**PEDRO GIBERT:** Goodness gracious, it's curvaceous. The coffin-style handle is elephant ivory book-ended by black-ebony spacers and flavored by flowery file work.

▼**JAMES CONNOLLY:** He calls it a "Hunter's Bowie," and with a buffalo-horn handle, it may have very well done its job.

▼**JEROME ANDERS:** The bone on the end of this lengthy damascus blade has been around long enough to gain some character. *(Hoffman photo)*

▼**JAMES SCROGGS:** The 10-inch Southwest Bowie is all brawn, including a Daryl Meier clad-steel blade, a copper guard and a walnut handle.

▶**HANK KUBAIKO:** Remember the Alamo bowie? Here's a repro in damascus and African black wood.

▼**CRAIG CAMERER:** The "Lucky 13 Bowie" has a baker's dozen inches of 1080 sharpened steel, and it lived up to its name by winning "Best Bowie" at the 2003 Professional Knifemakers Assoc. Show. *(Hoffman photo)*

▲**KEVIN HARVEY:** Kevin got the Searles style down, and even the black-wood handle with copper pins and silver escutcheon plates, but he blew it when it came to the blade. Searles could have never gun-blued it like that, and heartbeat-pattern Damascus was more than a heartbeat away. When Kevin blows it, he blows it good. *(BladeGallery.com photo)*

▼ **RICHARD LUDWIG:** Ron Nott engraved the gorgeous bowie blade, complete with ironwood grip and ivory butt. The mokumé guard is by Mike Sakmar. *(Weyer photo)*

▲ **JIM WALKER:** Sometimes ironwood, steel and nickel silver are all you need to best your last bowie. *(Engaged Productions photo)*

◀ **BILL WATSON:** Dog-bone-handle bowies are becoming a fast favorite, and 10 inches of damascus doesn't hurt the cause.

▼ **CHRISTOPHER CAWTHORNE:** The tiger-striped maple handle got some sun, and the W-2 blade was exposed to fire before the edge was quenched.

◀ **EDWARD BRANDSEY:** It's the perfect bowie blade, protected by a crescent guard, balanced by whitetail antler and topped off by turquoise inlays. Nothing but elk hide could sheath such a delight. *(PointSeven photo)*

▲ **WILLIAM DEAN MITCHELL:** The forged 5160 blade was subjected to a little file work and attached to a stag handle with iron fittings.

◄ DANIEL GRAY: The antiqued finish on an O-1 blade is just too much, and German silver and stag make it a classic before it even cuts. *(Weyer photo)*

▲ DEAN HARVEY: Harvey was well on his way to riches when he hit the mother lode by adding the gold escutcheon plate to the mammoth-ivory handle. *(PointSeven photo)*

▼ TIM FOSTER: The blue, flame-pattern-damascus blade is blistering hot. *(Ward photo)*

▲ MARVIN SOLOMON: Did Devin Thomas know his damascus would look this good in bowie blade form? *(Ward photo)*

▼ JASON HOWELL: The giraffe bone and damascus are the same colors, so Jason built a little heat-blued wrought-iron guard to show where one ends and the other begins. *(Ward photo)*

▲ MICHAEL M. SANDERS: This bowie is bad to the bone. *(Ambany photo)*

STATE OF THE ART

I**T ISN'T AS** if the majority of knifemakers have studio apartments, drink cappuccino, frequent music hot spots each night, divide time between art museums, bead stores, smoke shops, parks, galleries, lecture halls and cafés during the day, and sleep in hammocks at night. Few of them paint canvases or decorate parchment paper until the wee hours of the morning. Most don't wear sandals and hemp necklaces, recite poetry, practice body piercing, read palms or attend Green Peace and Green Party rallies. Not all of them live or practice alternative lifestyles (other than knifemaking). They're not preppie, yuppie or hippie. Yet, their artwork transcends generations. Their message—through carving, engraving, scrimshaw, etching and forging—is expressive and thought provoking. Their handwork is colossal.

A minority of knifemakers holds art degrees. Handfuls sprinkled here and there throughout the world have any formal training whatsoever. Common phrases in the knife industry include "self-taught knifemaker," "shared knowledge," "shop visits," "trial and error," "reject pile," "homemade forge" and "scrap metal." Some learned to make knives by watching others in the field. A good number began plying their trades after reading books on knifemaking. Quite a few attended "hammer-ins," forging seminars and knifemaking classes. Several have jewelry making, gunsmith and blacksmithing backgrounds. It's an eclectic group of people.

Incredibly, if any given collector of edged tools and weapons, with unlimited resources and a good eye for art, were to walk through the average knife show, cherry-picking the most artistic, highly embellished, fantastic, beautiful and inspiring pieces, he or she could probably exhibit the lot at any art gallery in the country to the awe and admiration of the local community.

Knifemakers know no bounds. While limited by blades, bolsters, guards and handles, they allow their imaginations to run wild, their fingers to sculpt, form and create, their arms to pound, twist, wrestle and maneuver, and their chisels and needles to poke, carve, scrape and groove. Beauty is brought to the surface by cutting away what is already there. Insetting, inlaying, overlaying and encrusting are common practices. It's the way of the knife and the state of the art. The state of the art is good, real good. And you don't have to be eccentric to appreciate it, either, just open-minded.

Joe Kertzman

Bling-Bling Blades

Bling-Bling adj. *[American slang, regional, popular]* **1**. Thick, gaudy gold necklaces, precious metals, gems and other jewels and jewelry, esp. worn by pop culture icons like the Notorious B.I.G. and Puff Daddy; **2**. Knives heavily laden with precious metals and stones, esp. carried by pop-cutlery icons like Dirk, Kris and *Blade*.

◀**WEBSTER WOOD:** The Red Mistress Dagger discreetly discloses a Ron Bishop twist-damascus blade, a red-maple-burl handle wrapped with twisted silver wire, and a blued-steel guard and pommel inlaid with red garnets and silver wire.

▲ **GLENN WATERS:** "Madame Butterfly" took time out from the opera to grace us with her gold-inlaid Barry Gallagher damascus blade, 18-carat-gold thumb opener, and an engraved and gold-inlaid Timascus handle, across which flit green-gold butterflies.

▶ **PAUL JARVIS:** This piece reflects five months of craftsmanship and features a 13-inch Daryl Meier twist-damascus blade, a mammoth-ivory handle, carved-sterling silver and bronze fittings in high relief with gold inlays, six peridots and 13 garnets.

► **MICHAEL WATTELET:** The Dress Knife is dressed to the hilt, including a Damasteel blade, and a sterling silver and gold handle inlaid with amethyst cabochons.

▲ **GARTH DUNCAN:** The handle is fossil ivory carved like knot work and inlaid with gold. The blade is a sharp dresser, too. *(PointSeven photo)*

► **RICK EATON:** His horse-and-rider gold inlay work is strides ahead of artistry by mere mortals. Black lip pearl is surrounded by mosaic-damascus and more golden touches. *(PointSeven photo)*

▲ **PAUL JARVIS:** Carved sterling silver, damascus and mammoth ivory is augmented by 22 garnets and 18 tourmalines.

◄ **J. NEILSON:** The tusk knife is outfitted with a nickel-silver guard and an azurite/malachite stone throat.

◀ **HARUMI HIRAYAMA:** Dragonflies and butterflies are singing in the wind with flowers, according to Harumi, who simply says that the ironwood and mastodon ivory grips are inlaid with many natural materials. *(Hasegawa photo)*

▲ **JURGEN STEINAU:** Within the angular gold are geometric windows revealing precious stone and other natural inlays. The blade isn't bad, either.

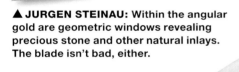

▲ **DELLANA:** Not wanting to skimp, Dellana built a damascus fixed blade using gold for the bolster, pearl for the handle, and diamond, ruby and gold inlays. *(SharpByCoop.com photo)*

▲ **PAUL JARVIS:** Paul is the king of "bling-bling," as evidenced by the Daryl Meier twist-damascus dagger showcasing a mammoth-tooth handle, including gold bezels inset with garnets, and carved sterling silver and gold fittings. *(PointSeven photo)*

Checkers Anyone?

IT'S A PRACTICE held over from long-deceased builders of antique bowies, pocketknives, daggers, dirks and other edged instruments with checkered-pearl, ebony and hardwood grips. It seems checks never go out of style. A pretty piece of pearl, checked up and down, then secured to a knife frame with gold pins, is as classy as cutlery gets. Such detailed file work is a sign of a dedicated knifemaker, one who takes his or her craft seriously.

People still engrave rifles. They insist on insetting precious stones, gold and silver into knife handles and bolsters. They continue to scrimshaw ivory and forge damascus. True craftsmen sand off all rough edges. They polish parts until they reflect images like mirrors. Skilled artisans embellish their work until every part of it outshines the other. Knives sparkle. Their forms are timeless, their blades pointed and sharp.

It is work to make steel sparkle, glimmer and gleam. Knifemakers use no paints, stains or polyurethanes. Why do they torture themselves by sweating the small stuff? Some insignificant steps can be skipped with nary a knife enthusiast being the wiser. Why not cut corners?

Some makers consider knives to be works of art, reflections of their own inner beings, showcases of their skills and manifestations of their active imaginations. For some, a knife is a tool used by men who work hard and deserve the finer things in life. Knife craftsmen strive for greatness. They check pearl that is almost as pretty plain and smooth as it is carved. They use only gold pins to fasten the nacre to knife handles. They make all the checks the exact same size, and the lines between the checkered patterns are straight and even. It's not a silly game, but a learned skill. It's like mastering chess, or checkers.

Joe Kertzman

▼ **JOEL CHAMBLIN:** Checks that were all one size weren't challenging enough. Joel even file worked outside the checks. *(PointSeven photo)*

◄ **BILL KELLER:** He started with steel from Devin Thomas and Delbert Ealy, found common ground between them, carved the bolsters just right, inset the perfect pearl, checkering it first, and used red, white, blue and gold presets and pins to hold it all together. *(Edged Productions photo)*

► **BARRY DAVIS:** Putting gold pins in every check of a checkered-pearl handle is called "pique" work, and it's piquing interest. *(PointSeven photo)*

◄ **KEN STEIGERWALT:** Forget mother-of-pearl with carved checks, how about black-lip-pearl with raised checks? The clamshell bolsters and long-pull nail nick are nice touches. *(PointSeven photo)*

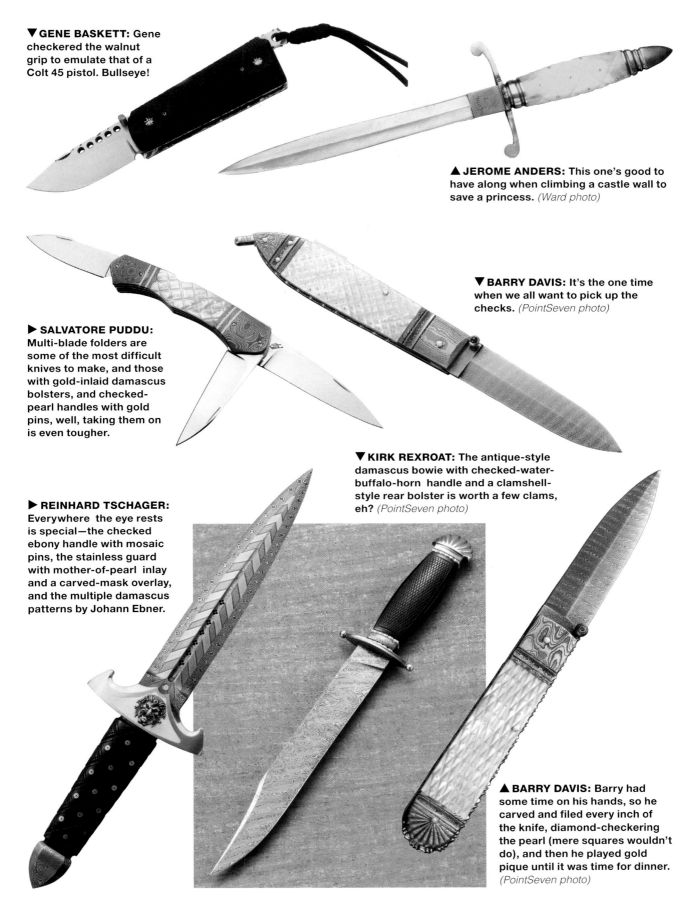

▼ **GENE BASKETT:** Gene checkered the walnut grip to emulate that of a Colt 45 pistol. Bullseye!

▲ **JEROME ANDERS:** This one's good to have along when climbing a castle wall to save a princess. *(Ward photo)*

▶ **SALVATORE PUDDU:** Multi-blade folders are some of the most difficult knives to make, and those with gold-inlaid damascus bolsters, and checked-pearl handles with gold pins, well, taking them on is even tougher.

▼ **BARRY DAVIS:** It's the one time when we all want to pick up the checks. *(PointSeven photo)*

▼ **KIRK REXROAT:** The antique-style damascus bowie with checked-water-buffalo-horn handle and a clamshell-style rear bolster is worth a few clams, eh? *(PointSeven photo)*

▶ **REINHARD TSCHAGER:** Everywhere the eye rests is special—the checked ebony handle with mosaic pins, the stainless guard with mother-of-pearl inlay and a carved-mask overlay, and the multiple damascus patterns by Johann Ebner.

▲ **BARRY DAVIS:** Barry had some time on his hands, so he carved and filed every inch of the knife, diamond-checkering the pearl (mere squares wouldn't do), and then he played gold pique until it was time for dinner. *(PointSeven photo)*

Steels of Swirl

IT WAS ONLY a matter of time before someone—Devin Thomas—came up with Spirograph damascus. After all, pattern-welded steel has so much in common with the children's game of Spirograph. In Spirograph, patterns are made on paper with pen using interconnected wheels, like gears, so the patterns are both planned and random, just like damascus.

So many damascus patterns have proven their worth, and the "old standbys" are still impressive in their very makeup and aesthetic beauty. Raindrop-pattern damascus gives the illusion of a blade having little pools, or drops, of liquid up and down its face. Ladder-pattern damascus tends to loop up and down, from spine to edge on a knife blade, like the rungs of a ladder viewed through a circus mirror. Twist damascus does a Chubby Checker dance within the pattern-welded mix of forged and etched steels.

The newest damascus patterns are even more complex and attractive. Thomas's "reptilian" damascus snakes around a blade, leaving its scaly-skin-like marks all over the steel. "Snake skin" damascus and "baby dragon" damascus are two others that remind one of reptile epidermis in need of lotion. Robert Eggerling's "paisley" damascus is like a '70s suit coat, and "vines-and-roses" damascus clings to a knife blade like ivy on a trellis.

Other variations of damascus, including random patterns, do twists and turns that just aren't possible to plan and execute using "steel recipes."

There is no recipe for adding swirls to steel, at least none that can be followed step-by-step with the same results every time. Like grandmas in their kitchens, bladesmiths add a dash of steel here, a pinch of nickel there and some more steel here, mix it all together and "voila," steels of swirl. Bon appetite!

Joe Kertzman

▲ **ED BAUMGARDNER:** Billy Merritt's damascus pattern looks like cells under a microscope, and the knife, itself, would stand up well under close inspection. *(PointSeven photo)*

▶ **AAD VAN RIJSWIJK:** Eating is easier with stainless damascus utensils, and a lot more fun with golden Jugendstill-style engraving on the rear bolsters of the knife and fork.

▲ **JASON HOWELL:** It's difficult to decide what's more impressive—the 1084 and 15N20 damascus or the Australian Gidgee wood grip. *(Custom Knife Gallery of Colorado photo)*

▲ **REINHARD TSCHAGER:** Four snakes crawled along the Devin Thomas damascus blade, leaving trails of skin behind them. The smooth oosic handle, gold inlay and clean bolster of this Reinhard piece deserve mention.

▶ **RON CAMERON:** Devin Thomas's reptilian damascus crawls all over the locking-liner folder. *(Custom Knife Gallery of Colorado photo)*

▶ **JOSH SMITH:** Follow the looping line from tip to guard and across the carved mammoth-ivory grip. *(PointSeven photo)*

▶ **CHRIS BOOYSEN:** Some of the pink from the gold-lip-pearl handle rubbed off onto the baby dragon damascus blade. *(Custom Knife Gallery of Colorado photo)*

▲ **LUDWIG FRUHMANN:** Ludwig left the handle clean as to not distract from the Schneider damascus.

▲ **JOHN FRAPS:** With a white-as-white mother-of-pearl handle and a small sapphire in the thumb stud, the heat-colored Timascus doesn't distract nearly as much as you'd think it would from the Devin Thomas raindrop-damascus blade. *(BladeGallery.com photo)*

▲ **BRUCE BUMP:** Independence Day damascus is a celebration of steel. *(BladeGallery.com photo)*

▼**JODY AND PAT MULLER:** Here's some aptly named Canyon Bend damascus married with a black-wood handle, engraved guard, a sterling silver throat and copper trim.

▶**JAMES COOK:** The S-guard has gold S's in it, and the blade employs W's, O's, S's, U's and a few Q's. *(Ward photo)*

▼**R.F. DODD:** Above the blade's grind line is jelly-roll-pattern damascus, and within the grind area is ladder-pattern damascus. *(Custom Knife Gallery of Colorado photo)*

▲**GENE LORO:** An elk-stag handle and turquoise spacer give this damascus bowie a frontier feel. *(Hoffman photo)*

▲**THOMAS HASLINGER:** You'd think that ironwood, mokumé and C. Chisan damascus would clash, but instead it's all about class.

▲**KEVIN CASHEN:** The damascus dagger stands regally waiting for its royal highness to beckon for a blade. *(Weyer photo)*

▶**J. NEILSON:** The knife is an actual railroad spike with other steels forged in, and the blade has a core of 1084 high carbon steel sandwiched between layers of damascus.

▶ **GEORGE MULLER:** Snakeskin damascus is cold to the touch and smoother than you'd think. *(Custom Knife Gallery of Colorado photo)*

▲ **DOC HAGEN:** The knife is all about contrast, between the layers of steel, as well as within the buckhorn burl handle. *(Custom Knife Gallery of Colorado photo)*

◀ **HARLAN SUEDMEIER:** The Don Hanson damascus blade is made up of steel from the old Missouri River bridge, files from the historic Morton House kitchens, meteorite from South America and W-2 tool steel. Cliff parker created the powdered-steel element in the form of a Little Giant power hammer. *(PointSeven photo)*

▶ **ALAN TIENSVOLD:** Alan etched the random-pattern-damascus blade with ferric chloride to bring out its true character. *(Custom Knife Gallery of Colorado photo)*

◀ **RICK FRIGAULT:** It's not so much the random pattern of the Damasteel, but rather the overall shape of the knife that makes the eyes smile.

▲ **CLIFF PARKER:** Eye-popping patterns like this take some forging, steel etching and knife know-how. *(BladeGallery.com photo)*

▼TODD BEGG: When dealt such a select piece of Gerome Weinand damascus, you use as much of it as you can, even on a small integral fixed blade. There's just enough giraffe bone to grip. *(Lum photo)*

▼CHARLES SAUER: Two damascus drop-point hunters draw the eyes into the steel. *(PointSeven photo)*

▶JEROME ANDERS: Galaxy-pattern damascus is out of this world. *(Ward photo)*

◀DON MAXWELL: Could the damascus pattern actually help decide the blade shape? Robert Eggerling supplied the pattern-welded steel.

▶GEORGE BAARTMAN: Slipped inside the pocket of pleated pants, the pearl-handled folder with Robert Eggerling damascus blade would be a party hit when pulled out for just the right cutting occasion.

◀GERALD CORBIT: Robert Eggerling's paisley-pattern damascus, checkered pearl, gold pins and ruby inlays dress up a rocker-bar automatic folder. *(Custom Knife Gallery of Colorado photo)*

MATTHEW LERCH: This raindrop-pattern Damasteel knife has more backbone than a Gila monster.

GARY HOUSE: Gary has gotten so good at forging damascus, he combines multiple patterns on a single knife blade. *(PointSeven photo)*

ART TYCER: Devin Thomas vines-and-roses damascus climbs the Big Creek Fighter like it's the facade of a stone mansion.

KEN ONION: Mike Norris damascus makes a trio of Speed Safe folders stand out a bit more than the others on the Wal-Mart rack. *(Lum photo)*

WADE COLTER: If you count them all, you'll come up with 180 layers of damascus, or at least that's how many were forged together. *(BladeGallery.com photo)*

DAN HOCKENSMITH: It's funny how the bird-and-butterfly damascus just seems to flutter around on the blade. *(BladeGallery.com photo)*

▲ **RUSS KOMMER:** With the pearl handle and raindrop-pattern damascus blade, it's a whitewash. *(BladeGallery.com photo)*

◄**TODD KOPP:** The mammoth-tooth handle is streaked with many colors, including the silver of the Jim Ferguson damascus blade. *(Weyer photo)*

▶ **KIRK REXROAT:** This knife is so hot, there's a firestorm across its 13-inch dagger blade. The mastodon is as highly figured as the guard and fancy file work. *(PointSeven photo)*

◄**STEVE DUNN:** The engraved bobcat on the bolster licks its lips in anticipation of what the damascus might cut up for dinner. *(PointSeven photo)*

▶ **DON HANSON III:** The edge and spine slope in blade-like directions, but the steel in the middle is all over the place.

▲ **JIM MEROLA:** Wildwood burl meets wild-pattern damascus and they cut a rug together. Ingemar Nordell contributed the damascus. *(PointSeven photo)*

Carving Out A Niche

I**T'S EASY TO** say you're going to carve a knife handle, a blade, bolsters or an entire edged instrument. It's not too difficult to make a decision on what types of materials to use. Coming up with a pretty, pointed pattern is a bit more tricky, but manageable. Trying to decide how to carve the knife once it's built, however, is nearly impossible, and actually sculpting it into a familiar form is out of the question.

For those of us non-visceral visionaries, the ones who can't see the trees for the leaves, the monumental task of carving a plain knife handle into a glitzy grip would be like creating a picture with anything other than finger paint. We might be able to carve out a niche for ourselves, claw our way to the top or scrape together two nickels, but that's as far as the carving gene was passed down.

If we did carve something, it would NOT be a pretty sight, which sort of defeats the purpose. It would have rough edges, and on a knife, there needs only be one rough edge, maybe two or three, but definitely not where you don't intend the blasted thing to cut.

In short, carving takes a steady hand, some creative genius, an eye for flow, form and function, a little style and a lot of artistic ability. A knife handle has to feel good in the hand. A blade must cut. A bolster or guard must protect the fingers from the edge, and a folder should function smoothly and easily. To make a knife that works well takes years of practice, or a lot of luck, and to carve it into an appealing edged instrument takes talent that escapes the average Joe.

It's a simple exercise to say you're going to carve a knife. It's another matter altogether to shape into an arousing steely sculpture that awakens the senses and sends spine-tingling messages to the brain.

Joe Kertzman

◄ **JOHN POYTHRESS:** He carved the stag until it looked nothing like its former self, adding a turned guard and head-turning blade. *(Hoffman photo)*

▲ **DONALD BELL:** The blade and body of "Thunderbird" are carved in the Haida Indian style. When Robert Eggerling and Ed Schempp see their damascus steels, they'll swell with pride. *(PointSeven photo)*

▲ **AL DIPPOLD:** It's risky to carve pearl and damascus that are so beautiful to start with, but when you've got it, you've got it. *(PointSeven photo)*

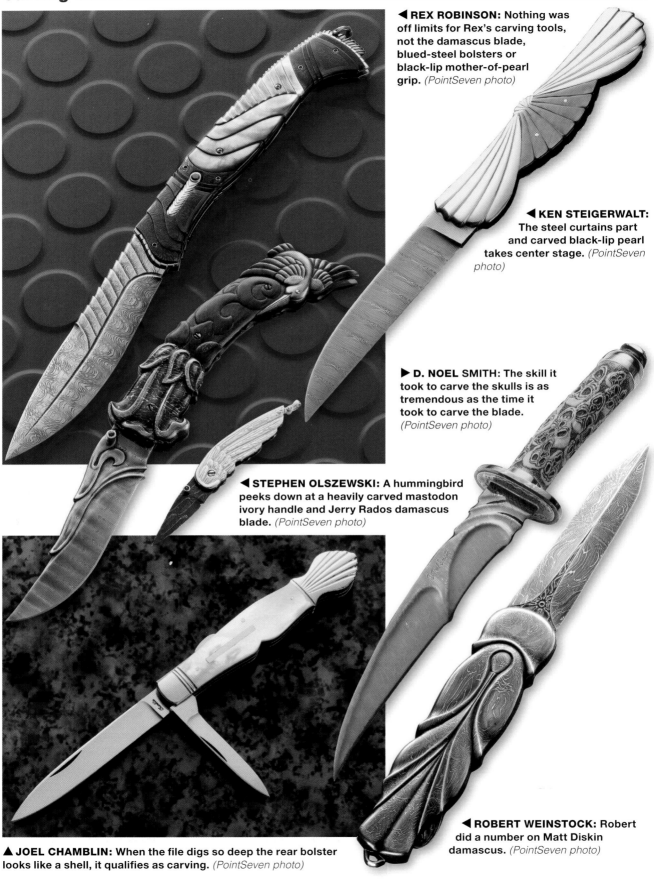

◄ **REX ROBINSON:** Nothing was off limits for Rex's carving tools, not the damascus blade, blued-steel bolsters or black-lip mother-of-pearl grip. *(PointSeven photo)*

◄ **KEN STEIGERWALT:** The steel curtains part and carved black-lip pearl takes center stage. *(PointSeven photo)*

► **D. NOEL SMITH:** The skill it took to carve the skulls is as tremendous as the time it took to carve the blade. *(PointSeven photo)*

◄ **STEPHEN OLSZEWSKI:** A hummingbird peeks down at a heavily carved mastodon ivory handle and Jerry Rados damascus blade. *(PointSeven photo)*

▲ **JOEL CHAMBLIN:** When the file digs so deep the rear bolster looks like a shell, it qualifies as carving. *(PointSeven photo)*

◄ **ROBERT WEINSTOCK:** Robert did a number on Matt Diskin damascus. *(PointSeven photo)*

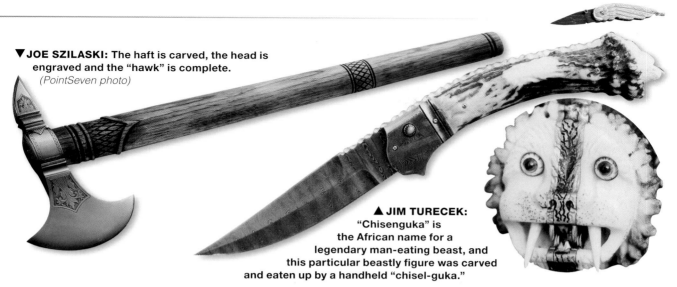

▼ JOE SZILASKI: The haft is carved, the head is engraved and the "hawk" is complete. *(PointSeven photo)*

▲ JIM TURECEK: "Chisenguka" is the African name for a legendary man-eating beast, and this particular beastly figure was carved and eaten up by a handheld "chisel-guka."

▲ HARUMI HIRAYAMA: The cat woman carved another knife grip, and this time it's purrr-fect. The little ball of fur rests on an **ivory bed.** *(Hasegawa photo)*

▲ HANK ISHIHARA: Carved titanium bolsters make nice eye rests between a damascus-inlaid blade and a pearl-inlaid handle.

▲ DON NORRIS: Scorpions scale the bone handles of a bowie and folder, thanks to the carving skills of Shandar, but the real stingers are the Jim Ferguson damascus blades. *(Weyer photo)*

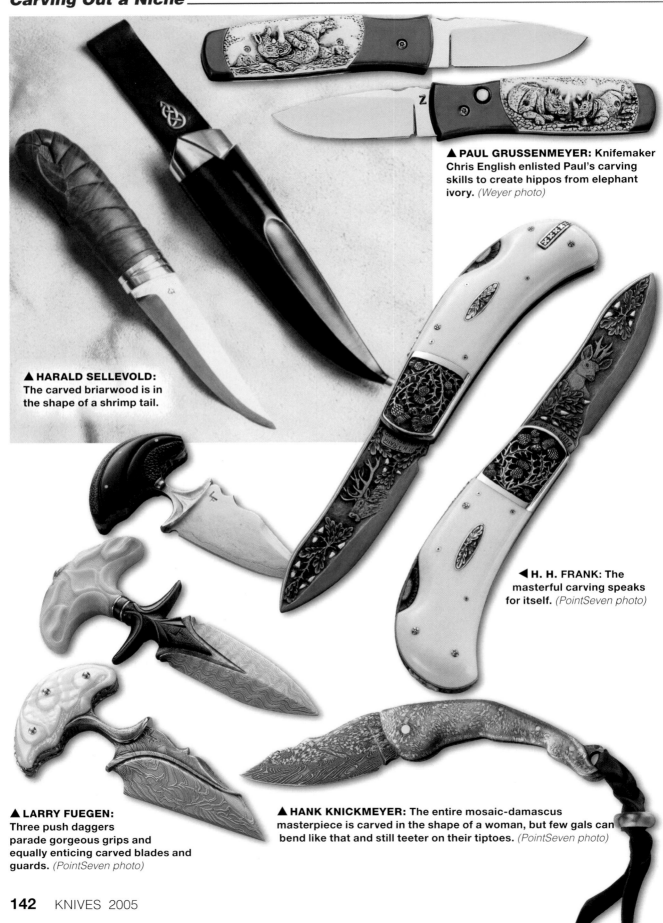

▲ **PAUL GRUSSENMEYER:** Knifemaker Chris English enlisted Paul's carving skills to create hippos from elephant ivory. *(Weyer photo)*

▲ **HARALD SELLEVOLD:** The carved briarwood is in the shape of a shrimp tail.

◄ **H. H. FRANK:** The masterful carving speaks for itself. *(PointSeven photo)*

▲ **LARRY FUEGEN:** Three push daggers parade gorgeous grips and equally enticing carved blades and guards. *(PointSeven photo)*

▲ **HANK KNICKMEYER:** The entire mosaic-damascus masterpiece is carved in the shape of a woman, but few gals can bend like that and still teeter on their tiptoes. *(PointSeven photo)*

DONALD BELL: This hot rod of a knife, called "California Dreamin'," fires up fully carved flames of sterling silver, 14-carat gold and Barry Davis twist damascus. *(PointSeven photo)*

YASUTAKA WADA: Either the whale ate too much squid, shell and seaweed, or Yasutaka carved its tooth in a spiral fashion.

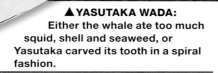

KEVIN HOFFMAN: The fine-feathered blade is accompanied by a fine-feathered bracelet.

RIK PALM: The "Dragonfly" knife was carved with needle files, chisels and ball burrs. The handle is carved blackwood, in a bamboo theme, with an oil finish.

JACK FULLER: The handle is relief carved from ebony, while the blade was forged, with grief and eventual relief, from a half-inch round bar of steel.

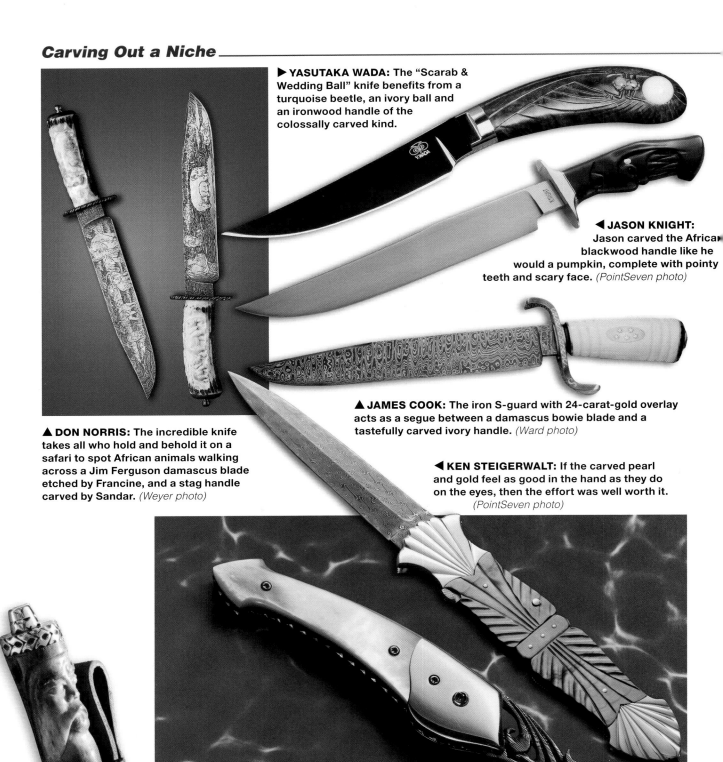

► YASUTAKA WADA: The "Scarab & Wedding Ball" knife benefits from a turquoise beetle, an ivory ball and an ironwood handle of the colossally carved kind.

◄ JASON KNIGHT: Jason carved the African blackwood handle like he would a pumpkin, complete with pointy teeth and scary face. *(PointSeven photo)*

▲ DON NORRIS: The incredible knife takes all who hold and behold it on a safari to spot African animals walking across a Jim Ferguson damascus blade etched by Francine, and a stag handle carved by Sandar. *(Weyer photo)*

▲ JAMES COOK: The iron S-guard with 24-carat-gold overlay acts as a segue between a damascus bowie blade and a tastefully carved ivory handle. *(Ward photo)*

◄ KEN STEIGERWALT: If the carved pearl and gold feel as good in the hand as they do on the eyes, then the effort was well worth it. *(PointSeven photo)*

◄ RICHARD SUNDERLAND: The king is crowned.

▲ DONALD BELL: What knife did he use to carve through the Ed Schempp damascus blade? *(PointSeven photo)*

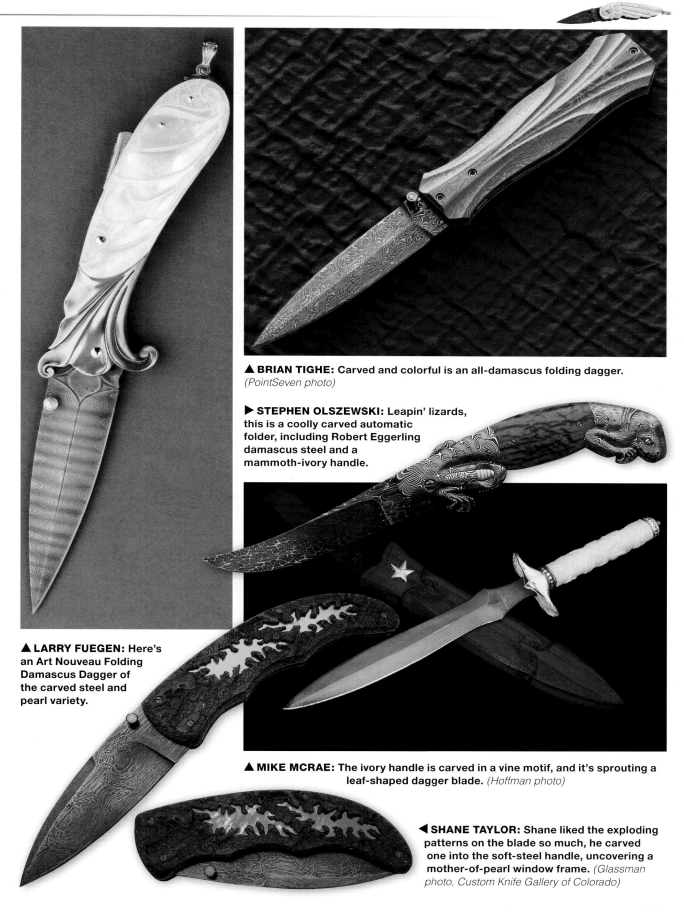

▲ **BRIAN TIGHE:** Carved and colorful is an all-damascus folding dagger. *(PointSeven photo)*

▶ **STEPHEN OLSZEWSKI:** Leapin' lizards, this is a coolly carved automatic folder, including Robert Eggerling damascus steel and a mammoth-ivory handle.

▲ **LARRY FUEGEN:** Here's an Art Nouveau Folding Damascus Dagger of the carved steel and pearl variety.

▲ **MIKE MCRAE:** The ivory handle is carved in a vine motif, and it's sprouting a leaf-shaped dagger blade. *(Hoffman photo)*

◀ **SHANE TAYLOR:** Shane liked the exploding patterns on the blade so much, he carved one into the soft-steel handle, uncovering a mother-of-pearl window frame. *(Glassman photo, Custom Knife Gallery of Colorado)*

Filed And Styled

"**L**EAVE WELL ENOUGH alone." That's an admonition many a spouse, friend and doting mother have bestowed upon their loved ones. "If it's not broke, don't fix it." That's another saying people often use in situations where extra work might be involved. "Leave a sleeping dog lie." "Don't stir up the pot." "Watch what you wish for." "Do what you have to do and no more." "Choose whatever involves the least amount of effort." "I'd rather be fishing." Those last six overused sayings all have to do with "taking the easy way out." Knifemakers seldom take the easy way out.

The average, hard-working, honest American would be happy to be given, to own, to buy or to use a sharp, shiny pocketknife, maybe with a wood, bone or stag handle, possibly with nickel silver bolsters and some etching on the blade. They'd take care of it, treasure it, bring it out when the occasion arose, cut with it, clean it off and put it back in their pocket or purse, or in a sheath on their belt. They'd be glad to have it. No fancy file work, carving or engraving would be necessary—nice but not necessary.

The following knives are not average. They are made by knifemakers who can't leave a sleeping dog lie or pass a pot without stirring it. The knifemakers took extra steps. They skipped the fishing trips. They took little hand files to steel and didn't stop until the dust settled hours, days, weeks and months later. Then, they started polishing, buffing and sanding. And when they were done, when their muscles ached and their eyes bled, they stepped back and admired their work. Let's do the same.

Joe Kertzman

▲ **CARLTON EVANS:** Since Devin Thomas forged the damascus, Carlton concentrated on filing the blade, spacer and titanium liners.

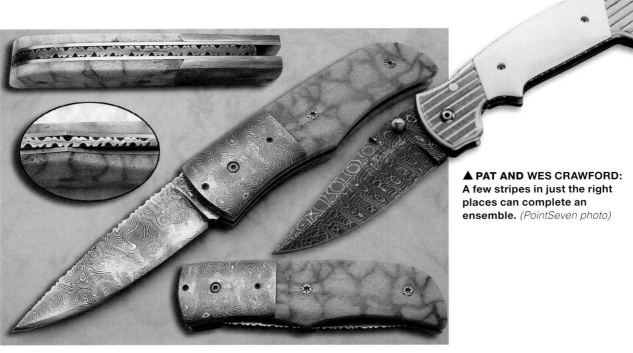

▲ **PAT AND WES CRAWFORD:** A few stripes in just the right places can complete an ensemble. *(PointSeven photo)*

▲ **DOC HAGEN:** While veins run through the tiger coral, vines climb the blade spine. *(Custom Knife Gallery of Colorado photo)*

◄ FRANCINE LARSTEIN: Francine uses fine-point, needle-tipped drawing tools and burnishing files to carve her design into beeswax and an asphaltum ground that covers the surface of a knife blade. When the work is completed, the blade is submerged into an acid bath that etches away the exposed steel, but not the areas covered by the resist. This eight-piece David Boye kitchen set is etched with images of Georgia wildlife. *(Weyer photo)*

► GENE BASKETT: This one has a spinal cord effect.

▲ RICHARD WRIGHT: The front and rear bolsters are carved to match, and the blade spine, spacer and liners are filed to catch the eye. All visible screws are also filed for good measure.

◄ MATT DISKIN: The window into the knifemaker's world often reveals the artist forging and filing for hours on end. The results are often worth the wait. *(Custom Knife Gallery of Colorado photo)*

▶ **SHANE TAYLOR:** Shane's "Leviathan" has reptile-like scales that didn't get there accidentally. Do you see sea monsters in the blade? *(PointSeven photo)*

▲ **MICHAEL SANDERS:** Selective file work is as effective as the extensive stuff. *(Ambany photo)*

▲ **JIM DOWNS:** Jim got so involved in filing the heat-colored-titanium liners he was a third of the way up the blade before he remembered to stop. How cool are the Thunderforged damascus blade and giraffe-bone handle? *(Custom Knife Gallery of Colorado photo)*

▶ **JEFF CLAIBORNE:** Like treads on a tank, the filed liners and spacers keep the two-blade folder moving in the right direction. *(Hoffman photo)*

Enslaving Engraving

◀ BERTIL AASLAND: Bertil got to doodling on an R.F. Dodd hunting knife, and before it was over with, the scrollwork commanded as much attention as the wooly-mammoth-bark-ivory handle. *(Custom Knife Gallery of Colorado photo)*

◀ JERE DAVIDSON: The bolsters of a Frank Centofante lock-back folder are black, silver, gold and oh-so scrolled. *(Custom Knife Gallery of Colorado photo)*

▲ N.C. FOSTER: Jim Barnes built a nice knife, and Foster beautified it.

▲ AAD VAN RIJSWIJK: A good engraver can make an eagle seem so lifelike, even the feathers look real.

▲ DELLANA: When you're the sole author of a knife, using gold is a good start to success, and engraving and texturing it bodes well for the cause. *(SharpByCoop.com photo)*

▲ **RON NOTT:** By adding a little file work along the guard, knifemaker Richard Ludwig fancied up the knife, but the scroll engraving solidifies it as a bona fide beautified bowie. *(Weyer photo)*

▲ **WARREN SMITH:** The big Bob Lay bowie with the box-elder handle is graced with a little engraving. *(Edged Productions photo)*

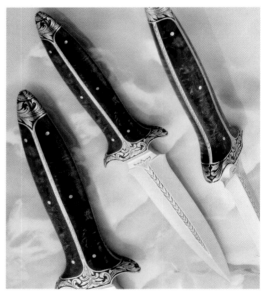

▲ **JIM WHITEHEAD:** Upon first glance, the engraving seems to blend right in with the Robert Eggerling damascus blade of the Don Maxwell knife, and on second glance, it still does.

▲ **JERE DAVIDSON:** It's amazing enough that Edmund Davidson built an all-integral Van Karl Death Star Dagger, and it's as sculpted as they get, but when Jere did the engraving honors, it lifted it to even higher heights. *(PointSeven photo)*

◄ **SHAUN AND SHARLA HANSEN:** Complementing engraving with color anodizing, file work and inlays gets the job done on a pearl-handle folding dagger with blued-damascus blade. *(PointSeven photo)*

◄ **JOYCE MINNICK:** Joyce likes to scribble a little on her husband Jim's knives, in this case in an aquatic theme on the bolsters. But the real surprise hides within the sea-blue handle insert. Look closely. *(PointSeven photo)*

▲ **H.H. FRANK:** They might make up a matched set of folding daggers, but the engraving is exclusive to each and elusive to all but the most skilled.

▶ **TIM HERMAN:** Tim wrote the book on color engraving knives, and it has a happy ending. *(PointSeven photo)*

◀ **RUSS KOMMER:** The fighter is prettied up between pearl and power. *(BladeGallery.com photo)*

◀ **GEORGE GIBO:** Engraving the titanium grip gave him a good start toward that totally cool stainless damascus blade. *(Weyer photo)*

▲ **T.R. OVEREYNDER:** A couple horned beasts, some skulls and a mask come to life on the bolsters of two highly embellished folding daggers. *(PointSeven photo)*

▲ **BILLY BATES:** The bighorn sheep that gave up its horn for the good of the knife grip is immortalized on the guard of the E.G. Peterson fixed blade.

▲ **PAT HOLDER:** The animals on the bolsters of D' Holder knives look caged in by engraving, but they can escape. *(PointSeven photo)*

▲ **JOE KEESLAR:** It's an interesting combination to employ the embellishing techniques of wire inlay and engraving, and then leave the file marks on the blade. But it works real well. *(PointSeven photo)*

▶ **WALTER BREND:** A far out sub-hilt fighter is built to bite and look good doing it. *(PointSeven photo)*

▼ **JACK LEVIN:** The two-layer carved shield opens automatically as the blade is unfolded. One layer of the shield is carved like a scallop shell, and the second layer is carved and engraved as a mythological sea creature with a double tail. A grotesque medieval personage—Breughel's frog—is singing a song and playing the lute on the handle.

▲ **JODY AND** PAT MULLER: Relief engraving gives no relief from the ink-blot-damascus blade, but it does blend the impressively wild steel in with the giraffe-bone handle.

▲ **DUSTY MOULTON:** The "Phantom" is ready for the opera, and the blue giraffe bone getup will fit right in with the rest of the pageantry.

▲ **C.J. CAI:** When engraving can do this much for an already impressive Ken Onion folder, then it's more than just a fashion statement. *(Weyer photo)*

▲ **HARRY LIMINGS:** Gene Baskett's ivory-handle locking-liner folder is forever flavored with enslaving engraving.

▲ **MEL FASSIO:** A flower blooms where the engraving seed was planted.

▼ **DONALD BELL:** The handles scales are pierced and engraved 14-carat gold over pink pearl.

▲ **SIMON LYTTON:** Eugene Shadley's fancy senator folder features a solid-gold handle inset with 19 diamonds—about a half-a-carat's worth—and is copiously engraved by Lytton. *(PointSeven photo)*

▶ **JERE DAVIDSON:** Joe Kious doesn't hold back when building folding inter-frame daggers. He uses presentation-grade black-lip pearl, Mike Norris stainless damascus and arguably one of the best engravers in the business. *(Custom Knife Gallery of Colorado photo)*

▲ VLADIMIR PULIS: Engravings of African animals fit in well with an ostrich-bone handle and they bump up nicely against a hot damascus blade. *(Cillik photo)*

▲ GIL RUDOLPH:
Engraving of this magnitude is often seen on firearms, and this W.E. Ankrom folder just so happens to be a replica of a Beretta Sidelock Shotgun. The bolsters are nitre-blued, another gun carryover.

▲ JONNY WALKER NILSSON: Few knifemakers try or even have the ability to engrave reindeer horn, nor do they have access to such incredible mosaic damascus, like the blade forged by Conny Persson. *(PointSeven photo)*

▲ TIM GEORGE: Obviously, George was inspired by the pearl and Paua inlays of a Scott Sawby folder, and for good reason, and he did his darnedest to make them feel like they're back at home in the sea. *(PointSeven photo)*

▲ JOHN W. SMITH: Tortoise shell shares the blade stage with gold inlay, engraving and damascus. *(PointSeven photo)*

◄ LOVENBERG LIEGE: The Frans van Eldik full-integral hunter had a lot going for it before the engraving, and now it's winning popularity contests all over Amsterdam. *(Tienhoven photo)*

▲ AAD VAN RIJSWIJK: To recreate the colors of nature, you either have to use a natural lapis lazuli handle inlay, be a master engraver, or both.

▲ JULIE WARENSKI: Knifemaker Warren Osborne wanted the bolsters engraved and, with the engraving, got a color and curvature theme that runs like a secret pattern throughout the knife. The blade is Mike Norris' ladder-pattern damascus. *(PointSeven photo)*

◄ GLENN WATERS: The Liquidmetal blade is engraved with Fu Jin, the wind god, and Rai Jin, the thunder god. Here and there, it's also inlaid with 24-carat gold—the gods like that.

▲ BILLY BATES: One of the seeds from the gorgeous guard of an Art Tycer chute knife blew off and landed in the middle of the handle, where it bloomed.

▲ AMAYAK STEDANYAN: Owen Wood works up some naturally flowing folding knives, and, in this case, has some help in engraving them to further the format. *(PointSeven photo)*

▲ DWIGHT TOWELL: The great gods of engraving saw the carved pearl inlay and bestowed the knife with their offerings. *(PointSeven photo)*

Scene-Stealing Scrimshaw

THEY SAY, IN order to wile away the hours aboard ship for months at a time, sailors of all sorts used to scrimshaw images on whale teeth. No one ever adds that, if the images even looked close to what the sailors wanted to portray, then those men of the sea must have had a whole lot more talent than the average salty dog. Not just anyone infatuated with salt water can pick up a needle, a little bit of ink and, dot-by-dot paint pictures on whale teeth (especially not if the pearly whites are still attached to the sizeable sea mammal). It makes for a great story, though, doesn't it? Lonely sailors create scenes with the only materials they have available.

In fact, scene stealing is what scrimshaw is all about. It's not scene stealing in the literal sense of the words, in which an actor gives such an incredible performance that he or she becomes the center of attention, but in a loosely translated sense, in that an artist captures what's around him and recreates its image. Such images invite us into the world where the artist lives. We can become enraptured with a scrimshawed scene and lose ourselves in its imagery, experiencing second-hand what the scrimshaw artist knew and recaptured.

Scrimshaw scenes also bring back to life people who are long gone, like Native American warriors, Victorian-era ladies and even the "Fab Four" (Beatles) walking across the street. Some scrimshawed knife handles portray mythological or fantastic creatures doing equally exotic things.

Scene-stealing scrimshaw is much like painting, only with extremely small brushes, limited pallets and equal parts passion and patience. Having the ability to scrim a scene on a knife handle is a gift few possess. It would be comparable to pricking holes in whale teeth, filling them with ink, to create pictures on the deck of a rocking, pitching, diving and rolling ship.

Joe Kertzman

◀ **CARINA CONOVER:** The J.D. Barth knife and the scrimshawed deer both wave white tails. Devin Thomas is responsible for the Spirograph damascus.

▲ **BOB HERGERT:** "Micro-scrimshaw" is what Bob calls the tiny dots he stippled just below the surface of an ivory grip on a Don Maxwell folder.

▲ **DALE WHITE:** It took three knives to make room for everything Dale wanted to show us.

▶ **GAETAN BEAUCHAMP:** Leopard eyes peer out from a water-buffalo-horn knife handle.

◀ **MAIHKEL EKLUND:** He knew her well enough to immortalize her in moose horn.

◀ **BARBARA ROBERTS:** The Indian girl would pretty up any knife, and Jack Roberts is lucky to have such a talented scrimshaw artist close at hand.

▲ **BARBARA ROBERTS:** Barbara had a howling-good time scrimshawing the ivory-Micarta® handle of a Jack Roberts drop-point hunter.

▲ **GAETAN BEAUCHAMP:** The personality of Cheyenne chief "Two Moon" is as complex as a double-edged damascus fixed blade.

GARY WILLIAMS: It's hard to believe Gary could scrimshaw polar bears with more personality than the ivory grip and engraved bolsters of a Gene Baskett Alaskan Hunter. The engraving is by Harry Limings.

▲ **BOB HERGERT:** Barbaric babes in blade-land complete the theme of a pair of Willie Rigney knives.

▲ **MAIHKEL EKLUND:** A toothy grin, outlined by the furry hood of a parka, graces the whale-tooth grip of a steely sticker.

▲ **GAETAN BEAUCHAMP:** He scrimshawed what he wants to hunt on a pair of knives built for the occasion.

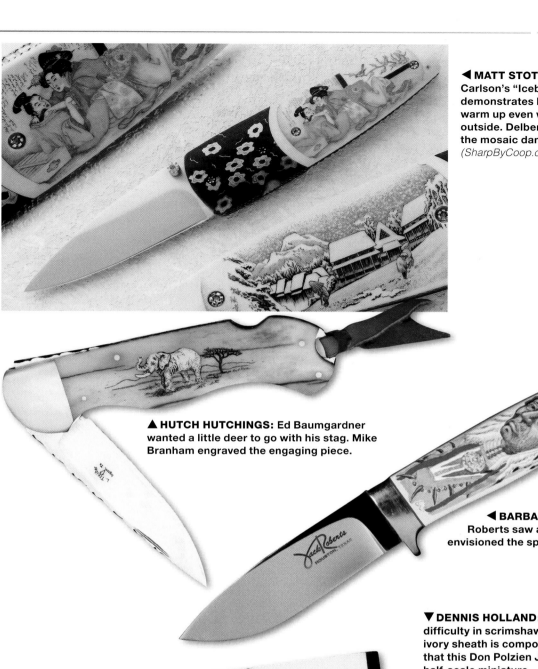

◀ **MATT STOTHART:** Kelly Carlson's "Iceberg" folder demonstrates how things can warm up even when it's cold outside. Delbert Ealy forged the mosaic damascus bolsters. *(SharpByCoop.com photo)*

▲ **HUTCH HUTCHINGS:** Ed Baumgardner wanted a little deer to go with his stag. Mike Branham engraved the engaging piece.

◀ **BARBARA ROBERTS:** Jack Roberts saw a knife, and Barbara envisioned the spirit behind the steel.

▼ **DENNIS HOLLAND:** The degree of difficulty in scrimshawing an alternate-ivory sheath is compounded by the fact that this Don Polzien Japanese tanto is a half-scale miniature.

▲ **LINDA KARST STONE:** Knifemaker Ed Love needed a gift for his daughter's wedding.

◄ BOB HERGERT: The "Fab Four" stroll across the grip of a Mike Dilluvio damascus folder. Even the license plate is legible when looking at the actual knife.

◄ BOB LAY: It's a beautiful bunch of big horns. *(BladeGallery.com photo)*

◄ LORI RISTINEN: A medieval king sits at his throne, with dagger in his belt, and overlooks the kingdom of Damascus, pondering the possibilities of a knife that would fold, or better yet, a scale-release auto like this Doc Hagen piece. *(Custom Knife Gallery of Colorado photo)*

► DENNIS HOLLAND: Upon scrimshawing Don Polzien's "Arabian Nights" knife, he imagined what he'd like his evenings in exotica to be like. *(Hoffman photo)*

▲ LINDA KARST STONE: Not even the damascus blade or mokumé bolster are as wild as the proud Native American gracing the ivory grip of a Leon Treiber folder.

Mokumé And Mosaic Magic

THEY AREN'T PATCHWORK quilts that keep you warm at night. They're not mosaic floor tiles that are tread upon and admired simultaneously. These are knives. In some ways, though, the knives, quilts and floor tiles share likenesses. Common ground is found in the way squares of steel are bonded together to form blades and bolsters, much like patches are lined up side by side and top to bottom to make quilts. Steel squares are welded together through forging, much like floor tiles are held together with mortar or grout.

There's another similarity. Mosiac damascus knives, or those with mokumé bolsters, or both, are artistic expressions of the blade smiths who forged them, just like the quilts and floors are the crafters' and tile layers' creative expressions. Part of putting together the floor or sewing the quilt is creating something that is beautiful. Though some knife-makers and enthusiasts think all knives are beautiful, not all people share that opinion, so steel forgers have decided to change the minds of holdouts who see nothing pretty in bladed tools and weapons.

To reach their goals, blade smiths add artistic touches. They forge mokumé. They perform mosaic magic, forge welding together squares of steel to create pictures. Often they cut steel bars lengthwise into star shapes, or in the forms of birds, turtles, bats, boots, spurs, ghosts, goblins, Jerry Garcia bears, flames, elephants and even letters or words. They line the bars up, forge them together, cut from the ends, and eventually fashion blades with repeated square images, like the impressive tiled floors of art galleries, government office buildings, museums and mansions. They are the patchwork quilts of the knife industry.

Why does mokumé fit in with mosaic damascus? Maybe it fits in better with other damascus, but it is a beautiful bolster material that furthers the aesthetic appeal of knives. It is often married with mosaic damascus, and there's nothing better than buying a knife made through mokumé and mosaic magic.

Joe Kertzman

▲ **BOYD ASHWORTH:** Seldom is the pattern in the blade steel extended to the overall form of the knife, but Boyd stuck his neck out. *(PointSeven photo)*

▲ **MIKE ZSCHERNY:** The blued-mosaic-damascus bolster is electrifying. *(Custom Knife Gallery of Colorado photo)*

▲ **CLIFF PARKER:** Cliff is a star when it comes to forging mosaic damascus. *(PointSeven photo)*

▶ **ED CAFFREY:** The "Pearl Swish" mosaic damascus folder is a steel swashbuckler with a swabbed deck and a slippery gangplank.

▶ **TERRY DAVIS:** Robert Eggerling dreamt up this mosaic damascus pattern in the wee hours of the morning when everything seems to run together. The planets were aligned right for this one, though. *(Engaged Productions photo)*

▲ **RICK DUNKERLEY:** Blued "cowboy-pattern" mosaic damascus reveals spurs, hats, boots and bits. *(Custom Knife Gallery of Colorado photo)*

▲ **DON BELL:** The mosaic carbon-damascus blade is a moving steel scene. *(Custom Knife Gallery of Colorado photo)*

▲ **MATT DISKIN:** Jerry Garcia would have loved this Grateful Dead folder—enough said. *(BladeGallery.com photo)*

▶ **C. LYLE BRUNCKHORST:** The "Goddess of Fire" spews flames from her guard onto her pointed tongue of a blade. *(BladeGallery.com photo)*

▲ **GEORGE BAARTMAN:** Many knifemakers incorporate Robert Eggerling mosaic damascus into their bladed tools and weapons, and looking at the bolster of this piece, it's easy to understand why.

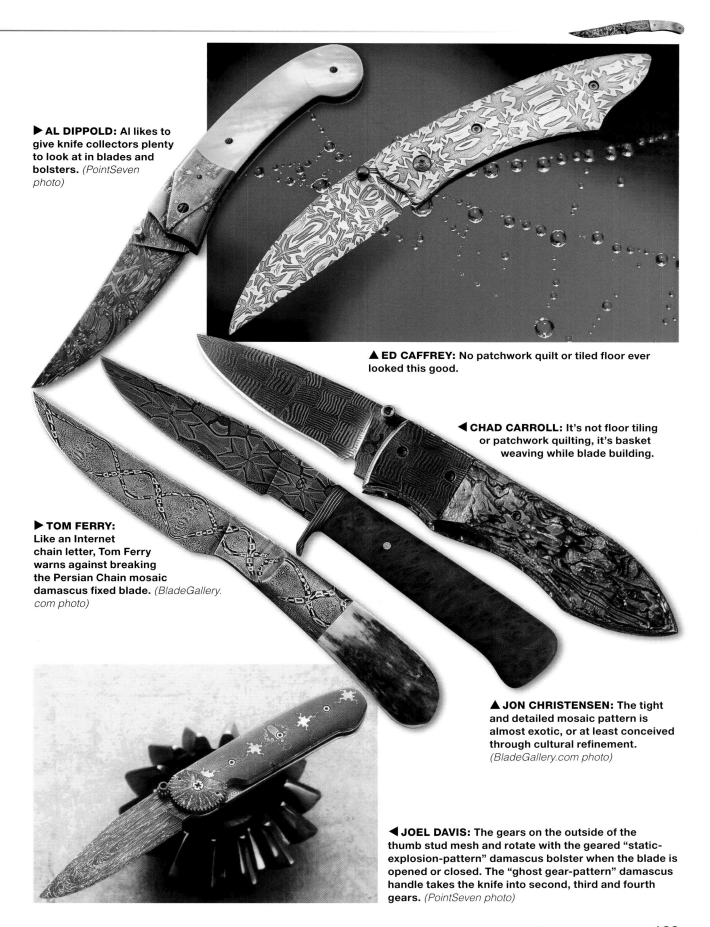

▶ **AL DIPPOLD:** Al likes to give knife collectors plenty to look at in blades and bolsters. *(PointSeven photo)*

▲ **ED CAFFREY:** No patchwork quilt or tiled floor ever looked this good.

◀ **CHAD CARROLL:** It's not floor tiling or patchwork quilting, it's basket weaving while blade building.

▶ **TOM FERRY:** Like an Internet chain letter, Tom Ferry warns against breaking the Persian Chain mosaic damascus fixed blade. *(BladeGallery. com photo)*

▲ **JON CHRISTENSEN:** The tight and detailed mosaic pattern is almost exotic, or at least conceived through cultural refinement. *(BladeGallery.com photo)*

◀ **JOEL DAVIS:** The gears on the outside of the thumb stud mesh and rotate with the geared "static-explosion-pattern" damascus bolster when the blade is opened or closed. The "ghost gear-pattern" damascus handle takes the knife into second, third and fourth gears. *(PointSeven photo)*

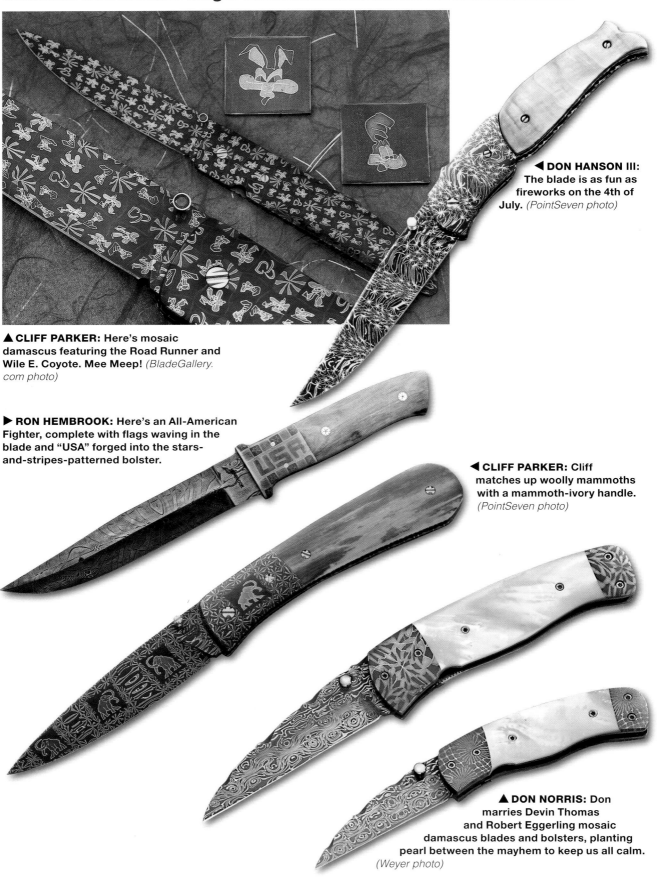

▲ **CLIFF PARKER:** Here's mosaic damascus featuring the Road Runner and Wile E. Coyote. Mee Meep! *(BladeGallery. com photo)*

► **RON HEMBROOK:** Here's an All-American Fighter, complete with flags waving in the blade and "USA" forged into the stars-and-stripes-patterned bolster.

◄ **DON HANSON III:** The blade is as fun as fireworks on the 4th of July. *(PointSeven photo)*

◄ **CLIFF PARKER:** Cliff matches up woolly mammoths with a mammoth-ivory handle. *(PointSeven photo)*

▲ **DON NORRIS:** Don marries Devin Thomas and Robert Eggerling mosaic damascus blades and bolsters, planting pearl between the mayhem to keep us all calm. *(Weyer photo)*

▲ **DON HANSON III:** Don had a lot of demons he needed to work out, and he feels much better now. *(Custom Knife Gallery of Colorado photo)*

▲ **BILL LEVENGOOD:** The locking-liner folder is lovely in yellow-lip pearl, but it's the Al Pendray mokumé that makes the men whistle.

▶ **DAN HOCKENSMITH:** Heat colored damascus helps make the transition from the blue-mammoth-ivory-bark handle to the twist-mosaic-damascus blade. *(BladeGallery.com photo)*

▲ **JOHAN VAN DER MERWE:** He forged his own dragon-skin mosaic damascus, made his own mokumé from brass, copper and pure nickel, built a knife around it and basked in the glory of it all. *(BladeGallery.com photo)*

◄ **RAY RYBAR:** Do you think Ray was trying to tell us something about the American Bladesmith Society's 2nd annual forged blade exposition? *(Custom Knife Gallery of Colorado photo)*

◄ **JASON TIENSVOLD:** If a blade that will blur your vision is what you seek, look no further. *(Custom Knife Gallery of Colorado photo)*

▲ **CLIFF POLK:** Cliff mapped and maxed this one out in mosaic and mokumé. *(Rusty photo)*

▲ **MIKE ZSCHERNY:** Mike Norris provided sun-storm-mosaic damascus for the blade, and Chris Mark lent a hand with mosaic damascus for the bolster. Check out the browns in the blade that match the mammoth-ivory grip. *(Custom Knife Gallery of Colorado photo)*

▲ **J.W. RANDALL:** The D-guard saves the fingers, but not the wandering eyes, from the blade.

▶ **CORRIE SCHOEMAN:** The mokumé stands out on the bolsters of two folders like gold nuggets on a creek bed. Ettore Gianferarri did the damascus honors.

▲ **MURRAY STERLING:** Mosaic bolsters and an oosic handle are enough to get the knife-enthusiast juices flowing.

▼ **RUSS SUTTON:** The Robert Eggerling mosaic bolster helps transition from the tiger coral handle to the Devin Thomas damascus blade.

▶ **RALPH TURNBULL:** Mokumé, walrus ivory and damascus are fine bedfellows.

▲ **SHANE TAYLOR:** He's got bats in the blade steel. *(Custom Knife Gallery of Colorado photo)*

Potentates of Totin' Blades

▼ **ROBERT NIX:** And he wore black leather.

▼ **BOB SCHRAP:** The cowhide pouch sheath was just the place for a Lake Superior agate.

▼ **RICK BRUNER:** From a beaded rosette in the center of a buckskin sheath hang brass cones and antler tips. Madonna, eat your heart out.

▶ **JUDY CHOATE:** It's as "tanned" as a leather knife sheath gets.

▼ **RUSTY POLK:** It's liberty leather, and just stitched for all!

▲ **THOMAS HASLINGER:** When you love a blade, you house it in hand-stitched, premium cowhide lined with ultra-suede and overlaid with Atlantic salmon skin.

▼ ROBERT NIX: The leather sheath and braided-leather tie down secure a knife and make it feel at home.

▲ CHAD CARROLL: His head wasn't in the sand when he outfitted the damascus chopper with an ostrich-leg-overlaid sheath.

▼ JUDY CHOATE: The sheath, itself, is a badge of honor.

◄ KAREN SHOOK: Daniel Winkler's neck dagger is a lesson in forging, dimpling and patterning. But Karen is the one who brought out the colors of a mammoth ivory handle, using a deerskin fringe, a band of quills, a small bone dangle, snake vertebrae and antique glass beads. That's one potent potion. *(PointSeven photo)*

▼ TESS NEILSON: Is it easier to skin a frog or an ostrich leg?

► TODD BEGG: They packed the stag in leather and hauled it off the mountain. *(Lum photo)*

► CHUCK BURROWS AND **GIB GUIGNARD:** The frontiersman's knife and war club slide silently into a rawhide sheath and buckskin drop, respectively. Each sheath is beaded using 19th century reproduction pony beads in the Northern Plains style, and then decorated with tin cones, hawk bells and copper beads—that's all! *(BladeGallery.com photo)*

▼**JAY MAINES:** The handcrafted water-buffalo-hide sheath was built, mountain-man style, for an old Civil War bowie, complete with three rows of domed stainless steel tacks.

▶**ROGER AND TERESA JONES:** The leatherwork includes a cross-draw holster for a Colt SAA, a pouch sheath for a stag hunter and a complex holder for an art knife.

▼**TILL AND RUTH CALVIN:** If you concentrate, you can smell the leather and hear the snap of the strap closing around the knife handle.

▼**DAVE COLE:** A water moccasin shed its skin for the good of the cause.

▲**DAVE COLE:** Dave worked up a wraparound sheath for a stag-handle skinner.

▶**JOANN KELLY:** A cowboy or Indian would like this.

▲**JOANN KELLY:** The turquoise cross matches the handle of the lucky knife with a new home.

▼ **KENNY ROWE:** One has to wonder if Kenny wrestled the anaconda or just happened across its skin.

◄ **BOB SCHRAP:** After fashioning a cross-draw pouch sheath, Bob tooled around the perimeter for awhile.

▼ **CHRIS KRAVITT:** A turquoise-handle knife calls for drastic sheathing matters—in this case classic western floral carving.

◄ **KENNY ROWE:** Netherlands knifemaker Andrew Jordan never imagined Kenny would inlay the sheath with Caiman crocodile skin, or did he?

▲ **LOYD THOMSEN:** Call it the sheath of the cross.

◄ **CHRIS KRAVITT:** The Mexican loop-style sheath fans out its scalloped skirt. The inlay is all rattlesnake.

▲ **TESS NEILSON:** They're black and tanned.

FACTORY TRENDS

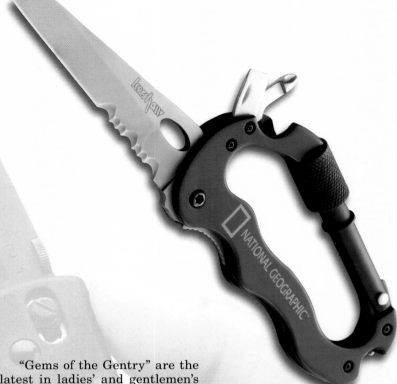

Knife factories have done themselves proud, and it's not the old cliché coming back to haunt again, either. This time, real pride comes to the surface, a soldier type of pride. There might be those cynics who say the reason knife factories are building increasingly more edged weapons and stealth field knives for active soldiers in Iraq and Afghanistan is because they are capitalizing on the conflicts for their own monetary gains. They couldn't be more wrong. Anyone in the knife industry, familiar with the people behind the company headquarters, storefronts and factory machinery, knows that production cutlery companies are making quality, high-tech, inexpensive and safe knives for our boys abroad. There are many such edged tools out there, and the troops are glad for it. Several knife companies are giving knives to the troops!

"Beacon Blades" make up another factory knife trend worth noting. Knives that integrate lights for cutting at night or in dark places are the hottest things under the setting sun. Tactical folders are old hat, but not the "Unusual Tactics" seen today, each unique for a different reason, and all with that mean, black-or-gray, one-hand-opening, pocket-clip-and-thumb-stud look we've grown accustomed to and have learned to love.

"Gems of the Gentry" are the latest in ladies' and gentlemen's knives, a few of which have won major favor with the more refined members of knife society. "Game Getters" are ready for the hunt and eventually the hunter's cabin or tent after a day in the woods. Speaking of the woods, "Exchange-A-Blades" and "Field & Food Knives" are perfect companions for the outdoors person in you.

Some folks familiar with knives say that custom, or handmade, knifemakers saved many production knife companies from ill fates by lending (or selling) them their designs, bringing innovation back into a stale marketplace. Others, also in the know, say that custom knifemakers borrow just as many ideas from what they see in the production knife industry. Either way, the factory knife buyer comes out a winner, and judging by this year's lineup, it's quite a haul.

Joe Kertzman

America Grows Gorgeous Hunting Knives

Good-old American ingenuity reveals itself in the best bladed hunters butchering game

By William Hovey Smith

IN TODAY'S HIGH-TECH world, it is easy to forget that the development of a thin, chipped-stone blade hafted to a wooden handle was a revolutionary technical advance over stone choppers and hand axes. Primitive knives knapped from stone allowed hunters to conveniently carry butchering tools with them, more efficiently process their animals and be exposed for less time to predators that considered man another source of fresh meat.

To the delight of collectors, each area of the world evolved its own version of such eternally useful cutting tools, and North America was no different. Below are some examples of modern hunting knives that changed the way hunters thought about edged tools for the woods. In some cases, the knives are upgrades to traditional designs, while others represent new departures in the engineering of fixed-blade hunters. It is a tribute to the lasting utility of the historically rooted styles that they are still made today.

Buck's Special Bowie, illustrated herein as a Master Series variation with a checkered, impregnated-wood handle and a 6-inch blade, harkens back to the famous Bowie (Col. James Bowie) fighting knives of the 1800s. Evident in Buck's redesign is a

Here's a selection of American hunting-knife blade styles for all occasions. Clockwise from top-center are a clip-point blade, a drop point, an upswept edge, a gut hook and a combination of an upswept and drop-point blade.

thicker-than-customary blade with a strong, needle-sharp, clip-style point.

The Special Bowie is smaller than the average bowie knife, retaining the utility of a camp knife, while still being light enough to carry on the hunt. This knife is sufficiently robust to process even the largest of game, and the blade has enough curvature to be useful for skinning.

This variation on a bowie includes hollow-grinding to lighten the blade and yield a sharper edge. The hollow-ground design also means that the blade offers less support to the cutting edge, making it more likely to chip if called upon to perform hard chopping duties. This is a blade made for slicing and cutting, not for chopping.

Buck knives set a new standard for sharpness. For the Master Series, Buck employs a hardened BG-42 blade that, while slightly more difficult to sharpen,

America's homegrown hunting knives are exemplified by, left, a Buck Master Series Bowie, a Marble's Woodcraft fixed blade, Schrade Sharpfinger, Remington Gut-hook Skinner and Spyderco Bill Moran Skinner.

retains its edge better than the knives of its competitors. Manufactured to meet aerospace standards for purity and strength, Buck's BG-42 is double vacuum melted and heat treated to ensure steel that will take a sharp but strong cutting edge. Dulled Buck blades can be returned to the factory for sharpening, or diamond-impregnated honing steels will restore the edges to true.

The Special Bowie is as large a knife as any hunter needs to burden himself with unless one of three conditions applies: 1. He or she is hunting with hounds and the knife is going to be used to kill deer or hogs; 2. The hunt takes place on the ground with a single-shot muzzleloader, and a knife might be useful for protection and self-preservation; 3. It will likely be necessary to clear an area big enough to pitch camp and gather firewood.

Short swords (*hurstfangers*, literally stag stabbers) are better blades for hunting, and camp axes are the preferred choice for clearing campsites.

Frontier Blades of the 21st Century

Marble's Woodcraft is a distinctive knife brand and pattern that I will always relate to the Alaskan gold rush. Marbles began as a company in 1898, and the "last frontier" was a ready market for its increasingly diverse line of knives and other edged products. The heavy, relatively short, 4 3/4-inch, sharply curved Woodcraft blade allowed the hunter to quickly skin out large animals like moose and walrus. Native Alaskans knew a good blade when they saw one and particularly prized the knives.

Webster Marble's blades were the first hunting knives that looked like models many outdoors enthusiasts use today, and most came with palpable, lasting leather-washer handles. Prior to the Marble's Woodcraft introductions, game was processed with pocketknives, butcher knives or belt knives, the latter or which tended to be large, utilitarian blades often toted in homemade sheaths.

Marble's designs were instantly copied, and post-World War II knifemakers, like Bo Randall, adopted the leather-washer grip for their own knives.

The Marbles knife pictured herein sports a traditional stacked-leather-washer handle, but the company's newer models are also available in bone, wood or no-slip safety grips. Marbles temporarily discontinued knife production shortly after World War II. However, the basic designs have been revived with longer grips and improved high-carbon steel that reaches a Rockwell hardness of between 58-60 Rc, resulting in long-lasting cutting edges.

The new Fieldcraft model employs the same blade shape as the Woodcraft, but is an inch shorter for those who desire a lightweight knife for dressing deer.

The largest of Marbles knives, the Trailmaker, incorporates blade

For its Master Series Bowie, Buck employs a hardened BG-42 blade that, while slightly more difficult to sharpen, retains its edge better than the knives of its competitors.

In addition to having a cool name, the Schrade Sharpfinger is designed to be a small, rugged knife that's ideal for cleaning deer.

The heavy, relatively short, 4-3/4-inch, sharply curved Marble's Woodcraft blade allows the hunter to quickly skin out large animals like moose and walrus.

Spyderco's first entry into the fixed-blade hunting knife market comes in the form of the Bill Moran Featherweight Drop Point Skinner. It combines a no-slip grip that nicely fills the hand, and a thin, deep-bellied 4-inch blade.

steel with a hardness between 57-58 Rc to better handle chopping chores. When introduced, this was the first American-designed "bush knife," and it can still be used for the task today.

With its thick, upswept, 3 1/2-inch high-carbon-steel blade, and nearly indestructible synthetic handle, the Schrade-Walden Old Timer Sharpfinger, when it debuted, was a new departure in American knife design. The Sharpfinger was made to be a small, rugged knife that would be ideal for cleaning deer. Although markedly different in appearance from other post-World War II sporting knives, the Sharpfinger was an instant success. Hunters appreciated that they didn't need a bigger knife to handle 90 percent of their cutting chores. Any cutting chore that could not be accomplished with this knife was better done with a hatchet or saw.

In cross-section, the Sharpfinger's blade is like a thin chisel, offering maximum support to the cutting edge. Using a block of wood as a mallet, the flat spine of the blade allows the edge to be driven through the breastbone of a deer. Such rough use will dull the blade, but not break it. Likewise, the point is well supported, and can be used to disjoint backbone segments if needed.

Prices on the Old Timer products, like the Sharpfinger, were kept competitive through the use of high-carbon steel. The steel is quickly sharpened, but by present standards, easily dulled. If the plan is to process a hog or large animal, such a blade will need to be touched up often before the task is complete. Nonetheless, the knife feels good in most hunters' hands, and it provides such a fine degree of control during skinning and butchering, the Sharpfinger is still sold today, and many such models make it into the woods every year.

Sharpfinger in Sheep Country

My most memorable experience with a Sharpfinger was on a sheep hunt in Alaska, where my partner and I joined a fly-in to a gravel bar. We fought our way up through the alders to sheep country and camped out until we got our rams. Anyone who has ever carried heavy packs through alders can appreciate the need for things small and light. The sheep head and rifle I hauled off the mountain wanted to catch on every alder branch.

Both rams were carefully caped, and the meat completely boned out before being packed down the mountain. This was a lot of precision work for one blade to perform, but it did its job. I carried a lightweight sharpening steel and touched up the blade whenever it seemed to lose its edge. I wiped the blade often, but did not put it in water as contact with water seemed to dull the edge.

As is the case with most blades, it was fairly easy to keep the edge razor sharp by using a sharpening steel and then stropping the blade on a piece of cardboard. Once sharp, I put a light coat of cooking oil on the blade to prevent rusting and stored the knife outside of its leather sheath.

Remington's fixed-blade Gut Hook knife is representative of a design that is now sold by almost every maker of sporting knives. The utility of the design was first recognized by custom knifemakers and popularized by writers who particularly liked the knives for skinning elk.

Remington's version of a gut hook features a hollow-ground, high-carbon-steel blade with a dropped point, an aluminum guard and pommel, and a resin-impregnated wood handle. The result is an excellent elk-processing blade without a custom-knife price.

Remington's gut-hook design makes it more difficult to use this blade as a stabbing knife, but although I have finished off and even hunted game with a blade, this is something that most hunters will never attempt. If you are close enough to stab an animal, you are surely close enough to shoot it— a much safer prospect for killing anything with horn, claws, teeth or hooves.

Give an experienced hunter a Remington Gut-hook Skinner, and he or she will recognize it as an excellent elk-processing blade without a custom-knife price. It features a hollow-ground, high-carbon-steel blade with a dropped point, an aluminum guard and pommel, and a resin-impregnated wood handle.

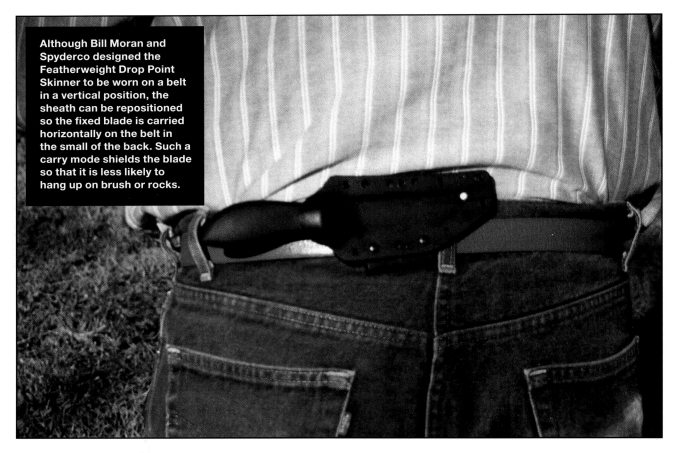

Although Bill Moran and Spyderco designed the Featherweight Drop Point Skinner to be worn on a belt in a vertical position, the sheath can be repositioned so the fixed blade is carried horizontally on the belt in the small of the back. Such a carry mode shields the blade so that it is less likely to hang up on brush or rocks.

Once, when hunting with a single-shot muzzle-loading pistol, I shot a deer and it went down. The deer was still struggling, but after I reloaded, the gun hammer refused to stand at full cock. I later found that a fragment of the percussion cap had blocked the sear. I approached the deer from the back, grabbed the head to keep from being hooked by the horn and thrust my knife blade behind the shoulder to quickly end its struggle. In this instance, there was no need to stab the animal a second time, and the presence or absence of a gut hook would have made no difference.

Spyderco's first entry into the fixed-blade hunting knife market comes in the form of the Bill Moran Featherweight Drop Point Skinner. It combines a no-slip grip that nicely fills the hand, and a thin, deep-bellied 4-inch blade. Despite being a company known for folding tactical knives with pocket clips, Spyderco achieved an ideal sportsman's blade in the Moran Featherweight.

Moran and Spyderco designed the knife to be worn on a belt in a vertical position, but the sheath can be repositioned so the fixed blade is carried horizontally on the belt in the small of the back. Such a carry mode shields the blade so that it is less likely to hang up on brush or rocks.

The VG-10 stainless steel blade reaches a Rockwell hardness of about 60 Rc, and its flat-ground profile results in good edge support. The overall thinness of the blade, combined with its sharpness, allows for easy cutting. When used for its intended purposes of skinning and slicing, a better blade in a lighter package would be hard to find. However, this is not the blade for hacking and prying.

Bear Cutlery offers damascus blades for many of its hunting knife designs, and the company even briefly made stainless-damascus hunters. Such knives proved poor sellers and Bear discontinued production. Bear's 250-layer damascus blades cut well, just as the original damascus knives did a thousand years ago. The company's nicely shaped blades sell briskly to modern users at a fraction of custom-knife prices.

A Nation of Knife Collaborations

Although not unique to Spyderco, the Featherweight Drop Point Skinner is representative of a trend toward production knife companies teaming with custom knifemakers on blade designs. Another such trend is in the outsourcing of knife production overseas. Some of Spyderco's knives are made in Japan, and while the United States still has a viable knifemaking industry, more production is coming from offshore makers. Companies like Browning, Beretta and Frost depend on foreign cutlers to supply product needs. European and Japanese imports are generally of high quality, but edged products from China and Southeast Asia are sometimes lacking (in the author's opinion).

Modern American hunting knife designs have diverged. One path leads toward reproducing historic knife patterns with more-or-less modernized manufacturing methods. Another path points toward high-tech blades designed to handle the toughest of cutting chores under the most challenging conditions.

Present trends include the combination of a cutting edge with a gut hook and saw on the spine of a blade. While such blades might eliminate the need to also carry a saw, the overall utility of the edged steel is reduced because it is no longer possible to use a thumb or forefinger for leverage and added pressure on the blade spine. Partially serrated fixed-blade knives look sexy and do help when cutting through breastbones, but they make it difficult to use the

knife for whittling a fine point on a stick.

Game dressing tools that combine the double-swept-back blade of the Eskimo Ulu look more like hatchets or axe heads than knives, but are useful for field dressing large animals like moose. These are specialized tools, as are the thick, cleaver-style blades combined with large gut hooks and initially popularized by Knives of Alaska. Some game-processing tools without handles have more than a passing resemblance to the stone hand axes of 10,000 years ago. The technology has changed, but the basic needs remain.

Never in history has the hunter had a wider choice of quality knives, whether interpretations of traditional blades, or innovative modern designs.

Soldier Steel

▲ **GERBER LEGENDARY** BLADES: More than one reliable source has confirmed that multi-tools like the all-black Pro Scout 600 DET are popular among U.S. troops for carry in and around the battlefield.

▲ **KERSHAW:** There are few knives stronger than the one-piece, hot-drop-forged Military Boot Knife, complete with a molded thermoplastic handle riveted onto the full tang.

▶ **SIMONICH KNIVES LLC:** Rob Simonich's "Gunner Grip" handle texturing became popular among blade aficionados before the knifemaker passed away, and Simonich Knives LLC still offers such rugged pieces. The Urban Raven is an integral, full-tang CPM S30V cutting machine. (PointSeven photo)

▶ **EMERSON KNIVES,** INC.: From its bull-nose tip and re-curved blade to the G-10 handle with integral hand guard, the CQC-11 UTCOM is an efficient tactical folder for use in the field, whether that happens to be a desert or not.

▲ **BENCHMADE KNIFE** CO.: Benchmade is proud of its "fish-scale" handle texture, just one of the features incorporated into the Mel Pardue-designed 5000 Auto Presidio. The automatic folder sports a 3.42-inch 154CM drop-point blade and a slide-switch safety to prevent inadvertent opening.

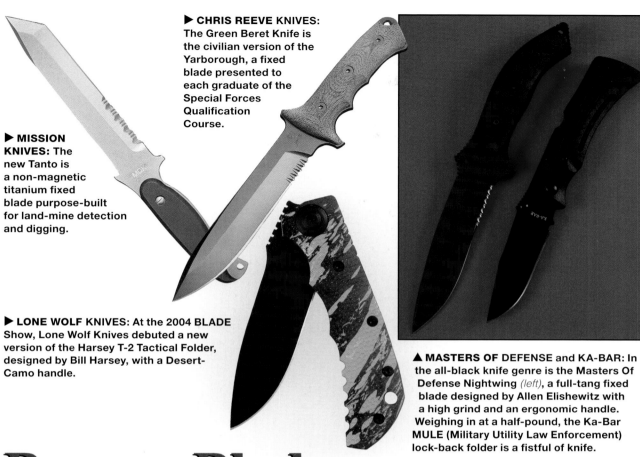

► CHRIS REEVE KNIVES: The Green Beret Knife is the civilian version of the Yarborough, a fixed blade presented to each graduate of the Special Forces Qualification Course.

► MISSION KNIVES: The new Tanto is a non-magnetic titanium fixed blade purpose-built for land-mine detection and digging.

► LONE WOLF KNIVES: At the 2004 BLADE Show, Lone Wolf Knives debuted a new version of the Harsey T-2 Tactical Folder, designed by Bill Harsey, with a Desert-Camo handle.

▲ MASTERS OF DEFENSE and KA-BAR: In the all-black knife genre is the Masters Of Defense Nightwing *(left)*, a full-tang fixed blade designed by Allen Elishewitz with a high grind and an ergonomic handle. Weighing in at a half-pound, the Ka-Bar MULE (Military Utility Law Enforcement) lock-back folder is a fistful of knife.

Beacon Blades

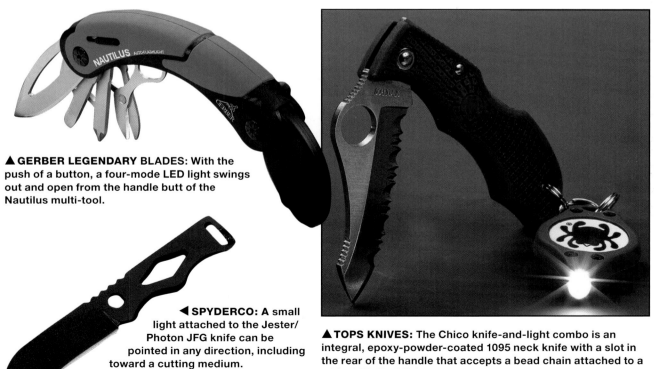

▲ GERBER LEGENDARY BLADES: With the push of a button, a four-mode LED light swings out and open from the handle butt of the Nautilus multi-tool.

◄ SPYDERCO: A small light attached to the Jester/Photon JFG knife can be pointed in any direction, including toward a cutting medium.

▲ TOPS KNIVES: The Chico knife-and-light combo is an integral, epoxy-powder-coated 1095 neck knife with a slot in the rear of the handle that accepts a bead chain attached to a white LED flashlight.

► **VICTORINOX:**
The Huntsman Lite is a Swiss Army Knife that employs, among other tools, two knife blades, a saw and a white LED light.

▲ **TOOLLOGIC:**
A brilliant white LED flashlight is built into the handle of the SL1 Mini Light and designed to shine toward the tip of the razor-sharp, 2-inch 420J2 blade.

Unusual Tactics

▼ **COLUMBIA RIVER** KNIFE & TOOL: Designed by Steve Ryan, the Ryan Model Seven Black features an AUS-6M blade and a textured Zytel® handle.

◄ **MICROTECH: THE** WSF2 Whale Shark Folder is aptly named for its whale-like shape and shark-like bite.

▲ **VATLANTA CUTLERY:** The Balisong showcases a 4-inch stainless steel blade and metal handles with plastic overlays.

▲ **BUCK KNIVES:** Buck teamed up with Strider Knives and police training authority Steve Terani to develop the 882 SBT, a knife designed to suit the needs of law enforcement and emergency response professionals.

▶ **BOKER:** A push-button folder, the Magnum Top Lock model B0017 sports a 3 1/4-inch blade of 420 stainless with a black Teflon™ coat.

◀ **RANDALL KING KNIVES:** Designed in the shape of a lion's claw, the Tsavo-Wraith employs a triple-ground, mirror-polished ATS-34 blade.

▶ **GERBER LEGENDARY BLADES:** Both the clip-point blade and "skeletonized" handle of the Paraframe I are stainless steel in a bead-blast finish.

▶ **BOKER:** Boker's new line of Heckler & Koch lock-back folders features design elements common to the P2000 pistol.

▶ **COLD STEEL:** The Recon 1 is both a working knife and a tactical folder with a mean-spirited, 4-inch, Teflon-coated 440A stainless steel blade.

▶ **IMPERIAL SCHRADE:** Schrade was so proud of the blade-locking system of its new Cable Lock, the company left the mechanism showing on the outside of the handle for all to view.

Game Getters

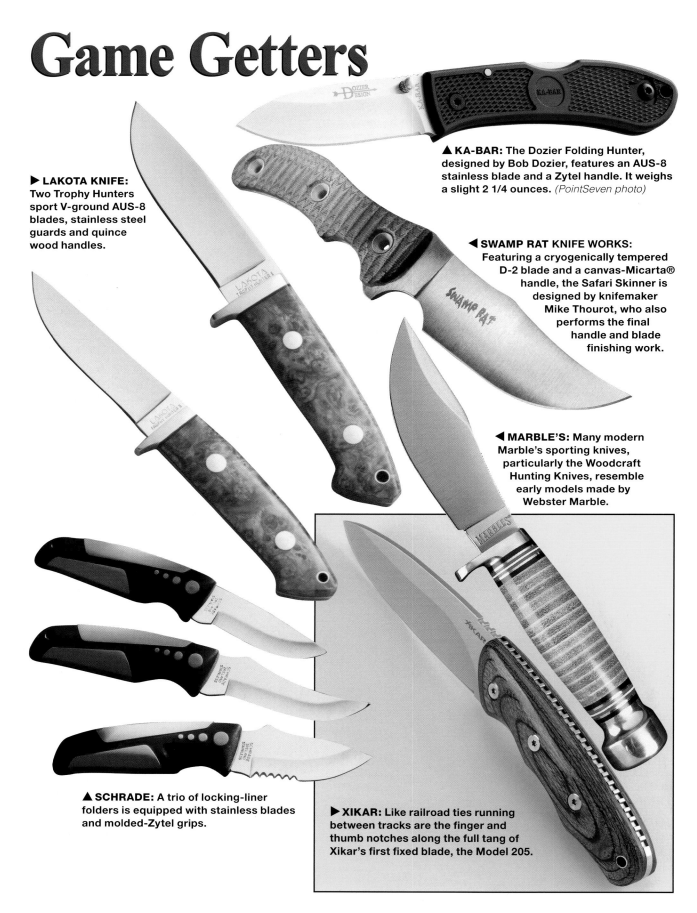

▲ KA-BAR: The Dozier Folding Hunter, designed by Bob Dozier, features an AUS-8 stainless blade and a Zytel handle. It weighs a slight 2 1/4 ounces. *(PointSeven photo)*

► LAKOTA KNIFE: Two Trophy Hunters sport V-ground AUS-8 blades, stainless steel guards and quince wood handles.

◄ SWAMP RAT KNIFE WORKS: Featuring a cryogenically tempered D-2 blade and a canvas-Micarta® handle, the Safari Skinner is designed by knifemaker Mike Thourot, who also performs the final handle and blade finishing work.

◄ MARBLE'S: Many modern Marble's sporting knives, particularly the Woodcraft Hunting Knives, resemble early models made by Webster Marble.

▲ SCHRADE: A trio of locking-liner folders is equipped with stainless blades and molded-Zytel grips.

► XIKAR: Like railroad ties running between tracks are the finger and thumb notches along the full tang of Xikar's first fixed blade, the Model 205.

Gems of the Gentry

▲ **KERSHAW:** With a choice of a quince wood or red-and-black aluminum handle, the Splinter is a sleek, handsome folder, complete with a 3-inch AUS-8A blade and stainless liners.

▲ **CHRIS REEVE KNIVES:** Whether it sports a damascus or CPM S30V blade, and no matter the handle configuration and decoration, the Sebenza is a classic frame-lock folder. *(PointSeven photo)*

▶ **WILLIAM HENRY KNIVES:** The high-tech look of the Westcliff is backed by a button-lock mechanism, a cut-out titanium handle to reduce weight and a tungsten DLC-coated blade. It weighs 1.2 ounces. *(PointSeven photo)*

▶ **KUTMASTER:** Through a licensing agreement with Caterpillar, Kutmaster offers one-hand-opening folding knives carrying the "CAT" brand.

◀ **WILLIAM HENRY KNIVES:** For the investor and collector is the B5 Monarch button-lock folder, including a Mike Norris stainless damascus blade, a mother-of-pearl handle and a Mike Sakmar mokumé bolster. *(PointSeven photo)*

◀ **SOG SPECIALTY KNIVES:** This SOG collector's piece—the Damascus SCUBA/Demo—sports a double-edged, laminated blade hand forged by Saji Takeshi. The price tag is $600.

◄ **SPYDERCO AND KELLAM KNIVES:** The Spyderco Stretch *(top)* was unveiled at the 2004 BLADE Show and features a flat-ground VG-10 blade, a finger choil and Spyderco's patented one-hand-opening hole in the blade. Oozing with traditional styling, the Kellam Otter sports a stainless otter-shaped blade, a brass bolster and a dyed-birch handle.

▲ **W.R. CASE & SONS:** The new Tony Bose saddlehorn reproductions come in handles of red bone, stag and green bone, giving the well-dressed lady or gentleman choices with which to accessorize.

◄ **QUEEN CUTLERY:** Queen's Schatt & Morgan Yankee Muskrat is the third in a line of "President's Choice" knives featuring blades laser engraved with Queen president Robert Breton's signature.

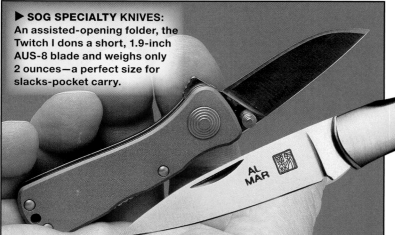

► **SOG SPECIALTY KNIVES:** An assisted-opening folder, the Twitch I dons a short, 1.9-inch AUS-8 blade and weighs only 2 ounces—a perfect size for slacks-pocket carry.

▲ **AL MAR KNIVES:** Blending utility with aesthetics is the mother-of-pearl-handled 1002P Hawk front-lock folder.

Exchange-A-Blades

▲ KERSHAW: The Alaskan Blade Trader sports three stainless steel blades—a large gut hook/skinner, clip point and saw—all of which can be exchanged for the other in a molded copolymer handle.

▲ BOKER: Anywhere from two-to-six blades are available with the Optima, including a saw, and clip-point, drop-point, gut-hook, ceramic and stainless-damascus patterns.

▲ COLUMBIA RIVER KNIFE & TOOL: The Serengeti is several knives in one. A Mike Franklin design, the frame-lock folding hunter sports a main skinning blade, and a single-ground hawk-bill and a detail-skinning blade that attach to the sides of the handle.

▲ KATZ KNIVES: In the Safari Kit, Katz offers a drop-point blade and an axe head that exchange out of the handle. An optional Safari Accessory Kit provides a wood and bone/meat saw, and boning and fillet blades.

Field And Food Knives

▼ BUCK KNIVES: The lightweight, locking aluminum handle of the Revolution XT rotates to double as a sheath, and includes a hanging, or carabiner, clip for attachment to just about any clothing or gear. *(PointSeven photo)*

▲ BUCK KNIVES: A collaborative piece with mountaineer Peter Whittaker, the Summit is a multi-tool with a 2 1/2-inch, partially serrated 420HC blade, a screwdriver, bottle opener and other tools.

▲ TEXAS RANGERS: Taylor Cutlery unveils a wood-handle bowie parading a 440C blade color etched in the law enforcement organization's logo.

▲ KERSHAW: Designed as a mountaineering knife, the National Geographic Carabiner Tool sports a knife blade, screwdrivers and a locking screw latch that secures a spring-loaded "gate" into position for use as the knife's grip. *(PointSeven photo)*

▲ ONTARIO: ONTARIO'S Old Hickory line of kitchen knives dates back to 1889. The name "Old Hickory" is stamped onto hardwood handles, which are secured to blade tangs with rivets.

KNIVES MARKETPLACE

INTERESTING PRODUCT NEWS FOR BOTH THE CUTLER AND THE KNIFE ENTHUSIAST

The companies and individuals represented on the following pages will be happy to provide additional information — feel free to contact them.

SHIVA

When only the best will do, show your customer the fit and finish. After that, the unique designs AMK is known for, and finally the value they get in an AMK knife. To close the sale, tell them how well AMK stands behind their product, including their lifetime warranty.

Cut out articles on AMK from *Blade* magazine or show your customer the *Wall Street Journal* where "Al Mar" was judged to be the "best brand" recently for Father's Day gifts.

Then your customer can see that they're getting more for their money when they buy:

AL MAR KNIVES
P.O. Box 2295, Tualatin, OR 97062
Phone: 503-670-9080 • Fax: 503-639-4789 • www.almarknives.com

---

Sheath making made easy at Jantz Supply

Jantz Supply offers a wide range of sheath making supplies. Whether you wish to make a custom sheath from raw materials or want the simplicity of a kit, Jantz has everything you need to complete your project.

Materials offered by Jantz Supply include leather, Kydex, dyes and finishes, laces and threads, stamps, needles, adhesives, fasteners and setters, oils, space markers, sliders, leather knives, anvils and the Tippmann Boss Hand Stitcher. Jantz also has a good selection of leather crafting books to choose from.

Sheath and pouch kits include pre-shaped leather with needle holes, needle and thread, and fasteners. There are two different sizes each style of kit to choose from. To customize your kit, Jantz offers a variety of dyes and stamps you can purchase separately.

Send $5.00 for their complete catalog, visit them in person, or on the web. Their goal is your success! Same day shipping, their huge warehouse allows them to stock what they sell.

Jantz Supply
PO Box 584
Davis, OK 73030-0584
Phone: 800-351-8900 • Fax: 1-580-369-3082
Web: www.knifemaking.com

A. G. RUSSELL™ KNIVES

2004 *BLADE* THE WORLD'S #1 KNIFE PUBLICATION — Most Innovative Imported Design

The Oldest mail order knife company, celebrating over 40 years in the knife industry, has a tradition of offering the finest quality knives and accessories worldwide. Lines include Randall, Dozier, William Henry, Leatherman, Case, Gerber, SOG, Ka-Bar, Kershaw, CRKT, Al Mar, Klotzli, Boker, Marbles, Schatt, & Morgan, A.G. Russell and more. Call for a free catalog or shop online to see the entire inventory of products at agrussell.com

A. G. RUSSELL KNIVES, INC.
1920 North 26th Street, Dept. KA05
Lowell, AR 72745-8489
Phone: 479-631-0055 • Fax: 479-631-8493
E-mail: ag@agrussell.com
Call For A Free Catalog
(479) 571-6161
agrussell.com

KNIVES MARKETPLACE

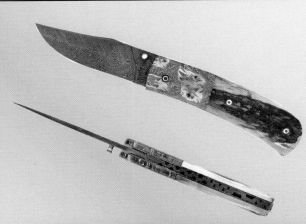

HAWES FORGE

Chuck Hawes
P.O. Box 176, Weldon, IL 61882
Your Style or Mine

Custom Knives
217-736-2479
High Carbon, Damascus
Evenings After 6

Carlton R. Evans Handmade Knives

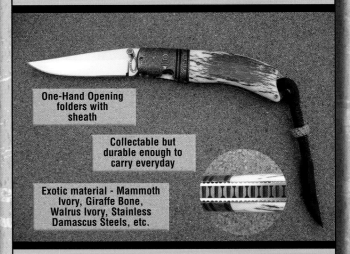

One-Hand Opening folders with sheath

Collectable but durable enough to carry everyday

Exotic material - Mammoth Ivory, Giraffe Bone, Walrus Ivory, Stainless Damascus Steels, etc.

P.O. Box 815, Aledo, Texas 76008
crevanscustomknives.com

(817) 441-1363
(817) 223-8556 cell
carlton@crevanscustomknives.com

KNIVES MARKETPLACE

KNIVES MARKETPLACE

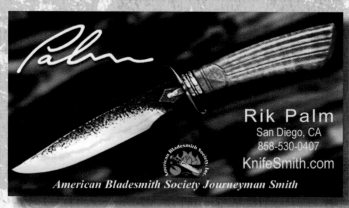
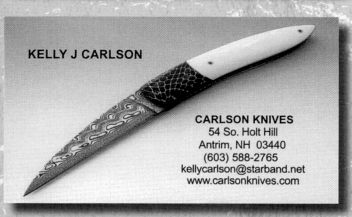

KNIVES MARKETPLACE

DIRECTORY

custom knifemakers

a

ABBOTT, WILLIAM M., Box 102A, RR #2, Chandlerville, IL 62627, Phone: 217-458-2325
Specialties: High-grade edged weapons. **Patterns:** Locking folders, Bowies, working straight knives, kitchen cutlery, minis. **Technical:** Grinds D2, ATS-34, 440C and commercial Damascus. Heat-treats; Rockwell tests. Prefers natural handle materials. **Prices:** $100 to $1000. **Remarks:** Part-time maker; first knife sold in 1984. **Mark:** Name.

ABEGG, ARNIE, 5992 Kenwick Cr., Huntington Beach, CA 92648, Phone: 714-848-5697

ABERNATHY, PAUL J., 3033 Park St., Eureka, CA 95501, Phone: 707-442-3593
Specialties: Period pieces and traditional straight knives of his design and in standard patterns. **Patterns:** Miniature daggers, fighters and swords. **Technical:** Forges and files SS, brass and sterling silver. **Prices:** $100 to $250; some to $500. **Remarks:** Part-time maker. Doing business as Abernathy's Miniatures. **Mark:** Stylized initials.

ACKERSON, ROBIN E., 119 W Smith St., Buchanan, MI 49107, Phone: 616-695-2911

ADAMS, LES, 6413 NW 200 St., Hialeah, FL 33015, Phone: 305-625-1699
Specialties: Working straight knives of his design. **Patterns:** Fighters, tactical folders, waw enforcing autos. **Technical:** Grinds ATS-34, 440C and D2. **Prices:** $100-$500. **Remarks:** Part-time maker; first knife sold in 1989. **Mark:** First initial, last name, Custom Knives.

ADAMS, WILLIAM D., PO Box 439, Burton, TX 77835, Phone: 713-855-5643, Fax: 713-855-5638
Specialties: Hunter scalpels and utility knives of his design. **Patterns:** Hunters and utility/camp knives. **Technical:** Grinds 1095, 440C and 440V. Uses stabilized wood and other stabilized materials. **Prices:** $100 to $200. **Remarks:** Part-time maker; first knife sold in 1994. **Mark:** Last name in script.

ADDISON, KYLE A., 809 N. 20th St, Murray, KY 42071, Phone: 270-759-1564
Specialties: Hand forged blades including Bowies, fighters and hunters. **Patterns:** Custom leather sheaths. **Technical:** Forges 5160, 1084, and his own Damascus. **Prices:** $175 - $1500. **Remarks:** Part-time maker, first knife sold in 1996. **Mark:** First and middle initial, last name under "Trident" with knife and hammer. **Other:** ABS member.

ADKINS, RICHARD L., 138 California Ct., Mission Viejo, CA 92692-4079

AIDA, YOSHIHITO, 26-7 Narimasu 2-chome, Itabashi-ku, Tokyo 175-0094, JAPAN, Phone: 81-3-3939-0052, Fax: 81-3-3939-0058
Specialties: High-tech working straight knives and folders of his design. **Patterns:** Bowies, lockbacks, hunters, fighters, fishing knives, boots. **Technical:** Grinds CV-134, ATS-34; buys Damascus; works in traditional Japanese fashion for some handles and sheaths. **Prices:** $400 to $900; some higher. **Remarks:** Full-time maker; first knife sold in 1978. **Mark:** Initial logo and Riverside West.

ALBERICCI, EMILIO, 19 Via Masone, 24100, Bergamo, ITALY, Phone: 01139-35-215120
Specialties: Folders and Bowies. **Patterns:** Collector knives. **Technical:** Uses stock removal with extreme lavoration accuracy; offers exotic and high-tech materials. **Prices:** Not currently selling. **Remarks:** Part-time maker. **Mark:** None.

ALDERMAN, ROBERT, 2655 Jewel Lake Rd., Sagle, ID 83860, Phone: 208-263-5996
Specialties: Classic and traditional working straight knives in standard patterns or to customer specs and his design; period pieces. **Patterns:** Bowies, fighters, hunters and utility/camp knives. **Technical:** Casts, forges and grinds 1084; forges and grinds L6 and O1. Prefers an old appearance. **Prices:** $100 to $350; some to $700. **Remarks:** Full-time maker; first knife sold in 1975. Doing business as Trackers Forge. **Mark:** Deer track. **Other:** Knife-making school. Two-week course for beginners; will cover forging, stock removal, hardening, tempering, case making. All materials supplies - $1250.

ALDRETE, BOB, PO Box 1471, Lomita, CA 90717, Phone: 310-326-3041

ALEXANDER, DARREL, Box 381, Ten Sleep, WY 82442, Phone: 307-366-2699
Specialties: Traditional working straight knives. **Patterns:** Hunters, boots and fishing knives. **Technical:** Grinds D2, 440C, ATS-34 and 154CM. **Prices:** $75 to $120; some to $250. **Remarks:** Full-time maker; first knife sold in 1983. **Mark:** Name, city, state.

ALEXANDER, EUGENE, Box 540, Ganado, TX 77962-0540, Phone: 512-771-3727

ALEXANDER, JERED, 213 Hogg Hill Rd., Dierks, AR 71833, Phone: 870-286-2981

ALLEN, MIKE "WHISKERS", 12745 Fontenot Acres Rd., Malakoff, TX 75148, Phone: 903-489-1026
Specialties: Working and collector-quality lockbacks, liner locks and automatic folders to customer specs. **Patterns:** Hunters, tantos, Bowies, swords and miniatures. **Technical:** Grinds Damascus, 440C and ATS-34, engraves. **Prices:** $200 and up. **Remarks:** Full-time maker; first knife sold in 1984. **Mark:** Whiskers and date.

ALLRED, BRUCE F., 1764 N. Alder, Layton, UT 84041, Phone: 801-825-4612
Specialties: Custom hunting and utility knives. **Patterns:** Custom designs that include a unique grind line, thumb and mosaic pins. **Technical:** ATS34, 154CM and 440C. **Remarks:** The handle material include but not limited to Micarta (in various colors), natural woods and reconstituted stone.

ALVERSON, TIM (R.V.), 4874 Bobbits Bench Rd., Peck, ID 83545, Phone: 208-476-3999
Specialties: Fancy working knives to customer specs; other types on request. **Patterns:** Bowies, daggers, folders and miniatures. **Technical:** Grinds 440C, ATS-34; buys some Damascus. **Prices:** Start at $175. **Remarks:** Full-time maker; first knife sold in 1981. **Mark:** R.V.A. around rosebud.

AMERI, MAURO, Via Riaello No. 20, Trensasco St. Olcese, 16010 Genova, ITALY, Phone: 010-8357077
Specialties: Working and using knives of his design. **Patterns:** Hunters, Bowies and utility/camp knives. **Technical:** Grinds 440C, ATS-34 and 154CM. Handles in wood or Micarta; offers sheaths. **Prices:** $200 to $1200. **Remarks:** Spare-time maker; first knife sold in 1982. **Mark:** Last name, city.

AMES, MICKEY L., 1521 N. Central Ave., Monett, MO 65708-1104, Phone: 417-235-5941
Specialties: Traditional working and using straight knives of his design and to customer specs. **Patterns:** Bowies, hunters and utility/camp knives. **Technical:** Forges 5160, 1084, 1095 and makes own Damascus. Filework; silver wire inlay. **Prices:** Start at $100. **Remarks:** Part-time maker; first knife sold in 1990. Doing business as Ames Forge. **Mark:** Last name.

AMMONS, DAVID C., 6225 N. Tucson Mtn. Dr., Tucson, AZ 85743, Phone: 520-307-3585
Specialties: Will build to suit. **Patterns:** Yours or mine. **Prices:** $250-$2000. **Mark:** AMMONS.

AMOR JR., MIGUEL, 485-H Judie Lane, Lancaster, PA 17603, Phone: 717-468-5738
Specialties: Working and fancy straight knives in standard patterns; some to customer specs. **Patterns:** Bowies, hunters and tantos. **Technical:** Grinds 440C, ATS-34, carbon steel and commercial Damascus; forges some in high-carbon steels. **Prices:** $125 to $500; some to $1500 and higher. **Remarks:** Part-time maker; first knife sold in 1983. **Mark:** Last name. On collectors' pieces: last name, city, state.

AMOS, CHRIS, 550 S Longfellow, Tucson, AZ 85711, Phone: 520-271-9752
Specialties: Traditional and custom, user-friendly working knives. **Patterns:** Hunters, utility, camp, and primitive. Your design or mine. **Technical:** Forged high-carbon steel, multiple quench differential hardening. **Prices:** $150 and up. **Remarks:** Part-time maker, member ABS, first knife sold in 1999. **Mark:** CAK (Chris Amos Knives).

AMOUREUX, A.W., PO Box 776, Northport, WA 99157, Phone: 509-732-6292
Specialties: Heavy-duty working straight knives. **Patterns:** Bowies, fighters, camp knives and hunters for world-wide use. **Technical:** Grinds 440C, ATS-34 and 154CM. **Prices:** $80 to $2000. **Remarks:** Full-time maker; first knife sold in 1974. **Mark:** ALSTAR.

ANDERS, DAVID, 157 Barnes Dr., Center Ridge, AR 72027, Phone: 501-893-2294
Specialties: Working straight knives of his design. **Patterns:** Bowies, fighters and hunters. **Technical:** Forges 5160, 1080 and Damascus. **Prices:** $225 to $3200. **Remarks:** Part-time maker; first knife sold in 1988. Doing business as Anders Knives. **Mark:** Last name/MS.

ANDERS, JEROME, 155 Barnes Dr., Center Ridge, AR 72027, Phone: 501-893-9981
Specialties: Case handles and pin work. **Patterns:** Layered and mosaic steel. **Prices:** $275 and up. **Remarks:** All his knives are truly one-of-a-kind. **Mark:** J. Anders in half moon.

ANDERSEN, HENRIK LEFOLII, Jagtvej 8, Groenholt, 3480, Fredensborg, DENMARK, Phone: 0011-45-48483026
Specialties: Hunters and matched pairs for the serious hunter. **Technical:** Grinds A2; uses materials native to Scandinavia. **Prices:** Start at $250. **Remarks:** Part-time maker; first knife sold in 1985. **Mark:** Initials with arrow.

ANDERSON, MEL, 17158 Lee Lane, Cedaredge, CO 81413-8247, Phone: 970-856-6465, Fax: 970-856-6463
Specialties: Full-size, miniature and one-of-a-kind straight knives and folders of his design. **Patterns:** Bowies, daggers, fighters, hunters and pressure folders. **Technical:** Grinds 440C, 5160, D2, 1095 and Damascus; offers antler, ivory and wood carved handles. **Prices:** Start at $145. **Remarks:** Knife maker and sculptor, full-time maker; first knife sold in 1987. **Mark:** Scratchy Hand.

ANDERSON, GARY D., 2816 Reservoir Rd., Spring Grove, PA 17362-9802, Phone: 717-229-2665
Specialties: From working knives to collectors quality blades, some folders. **Patterns:** Traditional and classic designs; customer patterns welcome. **Technical:** Forges Damascus carbon and stainless steels. Offers silver inlay, mokume, filework, checkering. **Prices:** $250 and up. **Remarks:** Part-time maker; first knife sold in 1985. **Mark:** GAND, MS. **Other:** Some engraving, scrimshaw and stone work.

ANDERSON, TOM, 955 Canal Rd. Extd., Manchester, PA 17345, Phone: 717-266-6475
Specialties: High-tech one-hand folders. **Patterns:** Fighters, utility, and dress knives. **Technical:** Grinds BG-42, S30V and Damascus. Uses titanium, carbon fiber and select natural handle materials. **Prices:** Start at $400. **Remarks:** First knife sold in 1996. **Mark:** Stylized A over T logo with maker's name.

ANDRESS, RONNIE, 415 Audubon Dr. N, Satsuma, AL 36572, Phone: 251-675-7604
Specialties: Working straight knives in standard patterns. **Patterns:** Boots, Bowies, hunters, friction folders and camp knives. **Technical:** Forges 1095, 5160, O1 and his own Damascus. Offers filework and inlays. **Prices:** $125 to $500. **Remarks:** Part-time maker; first knife sold in 1983. Doing business as Andress Knives. **Mark:** Last name, J.S. **Other:** Jeweler, goldsmith, gold work, stone setter. Not currently making knives.

ANDREWS, DON, N. 5155 Ezy St., Coeur D'Alene, ID 83814, Phone: 208-765-8844
Specialties: Plain and fancy folders and straight knives. **Technical:** Grinds D2, 440C, ATS-34; does lost wax casting for guards and pommels. **Prices:** Moderate to upscale. **Remarks:** Full-time maker; first knife sold in 1983. Not currently making knives. **Mark:** Name.

ANDREWS, ERIC, 132 Halbert Street, Grand Ledge, MI 48837, Phone: 517-627-7304
Specialties: Traditional working and using straight knives of his design. **Patterns:** Full-tang hunters, skinners and utility knives. **Technical:** Forges carbon steel; heat-treats. All knives come with sheath; most handles are of wood. **Prices:** $80 to $160. **Remarks:** Part-time maker; first knife sold in 1990. Doing business as The Tinkers Bench.

ANDREWS II, E.R. (RUSS), 131 S. Sterling Av., Sugar Creek, MO 64054, Phone: 816-252-3344

ANGELL, JON, 22516 East C .R .1474, Hawthorne, FL 32640, Phone: 352-475-5380

ANKROM, W.E., 14 Marquette Dr., Cody, WY 82414, Phone: 307-587-3017, Fax: 307-587-3017
Specialties: Best quality folding knives of his design. **Patterns:** Lock backs, liner locks, single high art. **Technical:** ATS-34 commercial Damascus. **Prices:** $500 and up. **Remarks:** Full-time maker; first knife sold in 1975. **Mark:** Name or name, city, state.

ANSO, JENS, GL. Skanderborgvej, 116, 8472 Sporup, DENMARK, Phone: 45 86968826
Specialties: Working knives of his own design. **Patterns:** Hunters and tacticals. Folders and straight blades. Tantos, drop point, Sheepfoot and hawkbills. **Technical:** Grinds RWL-34 Damasteel ATS-34, B6-42, 530V. Hand rubbed finish on all blades. **Prices:** $100 to $600, some up to $1000. **Remarks:** Full-time maker since January 2002. First knife sold 1997. Doing business as ANSOKNIVES. **Mark:** ANSO. **Other:** Full-time maker since January 2002.

ANTONIO JR., WILLIAM J., 6 Michigan State Dr., Newark, DE 19713-1161, Phone: 302-368-8211
Specialties: Fancy working straight knives of his design. **Patterns:** Hunting, survival and fishing knives. **Technical:** Grinds D2, 440C and 154CM; offers stainless Damascus. **Prices:** $125 to $395; some to $900. **Remarks:** Part-time maker; first knife sold in 1978. **Mark:** Last name.

AOUN, CHARLES, 69 Nahant St., Wakefield, MA 01880, Phone: 781-224-3353
Specialties: Classic and fancy straight knives of his design. **Patterns:** Fighters, hunters and personal knives. **Technical:** Grinds W2, 1095, ATS-34 and Damascus. Uses natural handle materials; embellishes with silver and semi-precious stones. **Prices:** Start at $290. **Remarks:** Part-time maker; first knife sold in 1995. Doing business as Galeb Knives. **Mark:** G stamped on ricasso or choil.

APELT, STACY E., 8076 Moose Ave., Norfolk, VA 23518, Phone: 757-583-5872
Specialties: Bowie, Damascus blade. Mammoth tusk handle with sterling silver and gold overlay. D-guard.

APPLEBY, ROBERT, 43 N. Canal St., Shickshinny, PA 18655, Phone: 570-542-4335
Specialties: Working using straight knives and folders of his own and popular and historical designs. **Patterns:** Variety of straight knives and folders. **Technical:** Hand forged or grinds O-1, 1084, 5160, 440C, ATS-34, commercial Damascus, makes own sheaths. **Prices:** Starting at $75. **Remarks:** Part-time maker, first knife sold in 1995. **Mark:** APPLEBY over SHICKSHINNY, PA.

APPLETON, RAY, 244 S. Fetzer St., Byers, CO 80103-9748
Specialties: One-of-a-kind folding knives. **Patterns:** Unique folding multi-locks and high-tech patterns. **Technical:** All parts machined; D2, S7, 440C, and 6a14v. **Prices:** Start at $8500. **Remarks:** Spare-time maker; first knife sold in 1986. **Mark:** Initials within arrowhead, signed and dated.

ARBUCKLE, JAMES M., 114 Jonathan Jct., Yorktown, VA 23693, Phone: 757-867-9578
Specialties: One-of-a-kind of his design; working knives. **Patterns:** Mostly chefs knives and hunters. **Technical:** Forged and stock removal blades using exotic hardwoods, natural materials, Micarta and stabilized woods. Forge 5160, 1084 and 01; stock remove D2, ATS-34, 440C. Make own pattern welded steel. Prices; $150 to $700. **Remarks:** Forge, grind, heat-treat, finish and embellish all knives myself. Do own leatherwork and wood work. Part-time maker. **Mark:** J. Arbuckle or Arbuckle with maker below it. **Other:** ABS member; ASM member.

ARCHER, RAY AND TERRI, PO Box 129, Medicine Bow, WY 82301, Phone: 307-379-2567
Specialties: High finish working straight knives and small one-of-a-kind. **Patterns:** Hunters/skinners, camping. **Technical:** Flat grinds ATS-34, 440C, D2; buys Damascus. **Price:** $100 to $500. **Remarks:** Make own sheaths; first knife sold 1994. **Mark:** Last name over city and state. **Other:** Member of PKA.

ARDWIN, COREY, 4700 North Cedar, North Little Rock, AR 72116, Phone: 501-791-0301, Fax: 501-791-2974

ARNOLD, JOE, 47 Patience Cres., London, Ont., CANADA N6E 2K7, Phone: 519-686-2623
Specialties: Traditional working and using straight knives of his design and to customer specs. **Patterns:** Fighters, hunters and Bowies. **Technical:** Grinds 440C, ATS-34 and 5160. **Prices:** $75 to $500; some to $2500. **Remarks:** Part-time maker; first knife sold in 1988. **Mark:** Last name, country.

ARROWOOD, DALE, 556 Lassetter Rd., Sharpsburg, GA 30277, Phone: 404-253-9672
Specialties: Fancy and traditional straight knives of his design and to customer specs. **Patterns:** Bowies, daggers and hunters. **Technical:** Grinds ATS-34 and 440C; forges high-carbon steel. Engraves and scrimshaws. **Prices:** $125 to $200; some to $245. **Remarks:** Part-time maker; first knife sold in 1989. **Mark:** Anvil with an arrow through it; Old English "Arrowood Knives".

ASHBY, DOUGLAS, 10123 Deermont, Dallas, TX 75243, Phone: 214-238-7531
Specialties: Traditional and fancy straight knives of his design or to customer specs. **Patterns:** Bowies, fighters and utility/camp knives. **Technical:** Grinds 440C, ATS-34 and commercial Damascus. **Prices:** $75 to $200; some to $500. **Remarks:** Part-time maker; first knife sold in 1990. **Mark:** Name, city.

ASHWORTH, BOYD, 1510 Bullard Place, Powder Springs, GA 30127, Phone: 770-422-9826
Specialties: Turtle folders. Fancy Damascus locking folders. **Patterns:** Fighters, hunters and gents. **Technical:** Forges own Damascus; offers filework; uses exotic handle materials. **Prices:** $500 to $2500. **Remarks:** Part-time maker; first knife sold in 1993. **Mark:** Last name.

ATKINSON, DICK, General Delivery, Wausau, FL 32463, Phone: 850-638-8524
Specialties: Working straight knives and folders of his design; some fancy. **Patterns:** Hunters, fighters, boots; locking folders in interframes. **Technical:** Grinds A2, 440C and 154CM. Likes filework. **Prices:** $85 to

custom knifemakers

$300; some exceptional knives. **Remarks:** Full-time maker; first knife sold in 1977. **Mark:** Name, city, state.

AYARRAGARAY, CRISTIAN L., Buenos Aires 250, (3100) Parana-Entre Rios, ARGENTINA, Phone: 043-231753
Specialties: Traditional working straight knives of his design. **Patterns:** Fishing and hunting knives. **Technical:** Grinds and forges carbon steel. Uses native Argentine woods and deer antler. **Prices:** $150 to $250; some to $400. **Remarks:** Full-time maker; first knife sold in 1980. **Mark:** Last name, signature.

b

BAARTMAN, GEORGE, PO Box 1116, Bela-Bela 0480, Limpopo, SOUTH AFRICA, Phone: 27 14 736 4036, Fax: 27 14 736 4036
Specialties: Fancy and working liner lock folders of own design and to customers specs. Specialize in pattern filework on liners. Specialize in pattern filework on liners. **Patterns:** Liner lock folders. **Technical:** Grinds 12C27, ATS-34, and Damascus, prefer working with stainless damasteel. Hollow grinds to hand-rubbed and polished satin finish. Enjoys working with mammoth, warthog tusk and pearls. **Prices:** Folders from $260-$800. **Remarks:** Part-time maker. Member of the Knifemakers Guild of South Africa since 1993. **Mark:** BAARTMAN.

BABCOCK, RAYMOND G., 179 Lane Rd., Vincent, OH 45784, Phone: 614-678-2688
Specialties: Plain and fancy working straight knives.Will make knives to his design and to custom specifications. **Patterns:** Hunting knives and Bowies. **Technical:** Hollow grinds L6. **Prices:** $100 to $500. **Remarks:** Part-time maker; first knife sold in 1973. **Mark:** First initial and last name; R. Babcock.

BACHE-WIIG, TOM, N-5966, Eivindvik, NORWAY, Phone: 4757784290, Fax: 4757784122
Specialties: High-art and working knives of his design. **Patterns:** Hunters, utility knives, hatchets, axes and art knives. **Technical:** Grinds Uddeholm Elmax, powder metallurgy tool stainless steel. Handles made of rear burls of Nordic woods stabilized with vacuum/high-pressure technique. **Prices:** $430 to $900; some to $2300. **Remarks:** Part-time maker; first knife sold 1988. **Mark:** Etched name and eagle head.

BACON, DAVID R., 906 136th St. E., Bradenton, FL 34202-9694, Phone: 813-996-4289

BAGLEY, R. KEITH, Old Pine Forge, 4415 Hope Acres Dr., White Plains, MD 20695, Phone: 301-932-0990
Specialties: High-carbon Damascus with semi-precious stones set in exotic wood handle; tactical and skinner knives. **Technical:** Use ATS-34, 5160, 01, 1085, 1095. **Patterns:** Various patterns; prefer all Tool-Steel and Nickel Damascus. **Price:** Damascus from $250 to $500; stainless from $100 to $225. **Remarks:** Farrier for 25 years, blacksmith for 25 years, knife maker for 10 years.

BAILEY, RYAN, 4185 S. St. Rt. 605, Galena, OH 43021, Phone: 740-965-9970
Specialties: Fancy, high-art, high-tech, collectible straight knives and folders of his design and to customer specs; unique mechanisms, some disassemble. **Patterns:** Daggers, fighters and swords. **Technical:** Does own Damascus and forging from high-carbon. Embellishes with file work and gold work. **Prices:** $200 to $2500. **Remarks:** Full-time maker; first knife sold in 1999. Doing business as Briar Knives. **Mark:** RLB.

BAILEY, JOSEPH D., 3213 Jonesboro Dr., Nashville, TN 37214, Phone: 615-889-3172
Specialties: Working and using straight knives; collector pieces. **Patterns:** Bowies, hunters, tactical, folders. **Technical:** 440C, ATS-34, Damascus and wire Damascus. Offers scrimshaw. **Prices:** $85 to $1200. **Remarks:** Part-time maker; first knife sold in 1988. **Mark:** Joseph D Bailey Nashville Tennessee.

BAILEY, KIRBY C., 2055 F.M. 2790 W., Lytle, TX 78052, Phone: 830-772-3376
Specialties: All kinds of knives folders, fixed blade, fighters. **Patterns:** Hunters, folders, fighters, Bowies, miniatures. **Technical:** Does all his own work; heat treating, file work etc. **Prices:** $200 to $1000. **Remarks:** Builds any kind of hand cutlery. Have made knives for 45 years; sold knives for 28 years. **Mark:** K.C.B. and serial #. **Other:** Have sold knives in Asia and all states in U.S.

BAKER, VANCE, 574 Co. Rd. 675, Riceville, TN 37370, Phone: 423-745-9157
Specialties: Traditional working straight knives of his design and to customer specs. Prefers drop-point hunters and small Bowies. **Patterns:** Hunters, utility and kitchen knives. **Technical:** Forges Damascus, cable, L6 and 5160. **Prices:** $100 to $250; some to $500. **Remarks:** Part-time maker; first knife sold in 1985. **Mark:** Initials connected.

BAKER, RAY, PO Box 303, Sapulpa, OK 74067, Phone: 918-224-8013
Specialties: High-tech working straight knives. **Patterns:** Hunters, fighters, Bowies, skinners and boots of his design and to customer specs. **Technical:** Grinds 440C, 1095 spring steel or customer request; heat-treats. Custom-made scabbards for any knife. **Prices:** $125 to $500; some to $1000. **Remarks:** Full-time maker; first knife sold in 1981. **Mark:** First initial, last name.

BAKER, WILD BILL, Box 361, Boiceville, NY 12412, Phone: 914-657-8646
Specialties: Primitive knives, buckskinners. **Patterns:** Skinners, camp knives and Bowies. **Technical:** Works with L6, files and rasps. **Prices:** $100 to $350. **Remarks:** Part-time maker; first knife sold in 1989. **Mark:** Wild Bill Baker, Oak Leaf Forge, or both.

BAKER, HERB, 14104 NC 87 N., Eden, NC 27288, Phone: 336-627-0338

BALBACH, MARKUS, Heinrich - Worner - Str. 3, 35789 Weilmunster-Laubuseschbach/Ts., GERMANY 06475-8911, Fax: 912986
Specialties: High-art knives and working/using straight knives and folders of his design and to customer specs. **Patterns:** Hunters and daggers. **Technical:** Stainless steel, one of Germany's greatest Smithies. Supplier for the forges of Solingen. **Remarks:** Full-time maker; first knife sold in 1984. Doing business as Schmiedewerkstatte M. Balbach. **Mark:** Initials stamped inside the handle.

BALDWIN, PHILLIP, PO Box 563, Snohomish, WA 98290, Phone: 425-334-5569
Specialties: One-of-a-kind elegant table cutlery; exotics. **Patterns:** Elegant or exotic knives. Likes the challenge of axes, spears and specialty tools. **Technical:** Forges W2, W1 and his own pattern welded steel and mokume-gane. **Prices:** Start at $1000. **Remarks:** Full-time maker; first knife sold in 1973. **Mark:** Last initial marked with chisel.

BALL, KEN, 127 Sundown Manor, Mooresville, IN 46158, Phone: 317-834-4803
Specialties: Classic working/using straight knives of his design and to customer specs. **Patterns:** Hunters and utility/camp knives. **Technical:** Flat-grinds ATS-34. Offers filework. **Prices:** $150 to $400. **Remarks:** Part-time maker; first knife sold in 1994. Doing business as Ball Custom Knives. **Mark:** Last name.

BALLESTRA, SANTINO, via D. Tempesta 11/17, 18039 Ventimiglia (IM), ITALY 0184-215228
Specialties: Using and collecting straight knives. **Patterns:** Hunting, fighting, skinners, Bowies, medieval daggers and knives. **Technical:** Forges ATS-34, D2, O2, 1060 and his own Damascus. Uses ivory and silver. **Prices:** $500 to $2000; some higher. **Remarks:** Full-time maker; first knife sold in 1979. **Mark:** First initial, last name.

BALLEW, DALE, PO Box 1277, Bowling Green, VA 22427, Phone: 804-633-5701
Specialties: Miniatures only to customer specs. **Patterns:** Bowies, daggers and fighters. **Technical:** Files 440C stainless; uses ivory, abalone, exotic woods and some precious stones. **Prices:** $100 to $800. **Remarks:** Part-time maker; first knife sold in 1988. **Mark:** Initials and last name.

BANKS, DAVID L., 99 Blackfoot Ave., Riverton, WY 82501, Phone: 307-856-3154/Cell:307-851-5599
Specialties: Heavy-duty working straight knives. **Patterns:** Hunters, Bowies and camp knives. **Technical:** Forges Damascus 1084-15N20, L-6-W1 pure nickel, 5160, 52100 and his own Damascus; differential heat treat and tempers. Handles made of horn, antlers and exotic wood. Hand-stitched harness leather sheaths. **Prices:** $300 to $2000. **Remarks:** Part-time maker. **Mark:** Banks Blackfoot forged Dave Banks and initials connected.

BARDSLEY, NORMAN P., 197 Cottage St., Pawtucket, RI 02860, Phone: 401-725-9132
Specialties: Working and fantasy knives. **Patterns:** Fighters, boots, fantasy, renaissance and native American in upscale and presentation fashion. **Technical:** Grinds all steels and Damascus. Uses exotic hides for sheaths. **Prices:** $100 to $15,000. **Remarks:** Full-time maker. **Mark:** Last name in script with logo.

BAREFOOT, JOE W., 117 Oakbrook Dr., Liberty, SC 29657
Specialties: Working straight knives of his design. **Patterns:** Hunters, fighters and boots; tantos and survival knives. **Technical:** Grinds D2, 440C and ATS-34. Mirror finishes. Uses ivory and stag on customer request only. **Prices:** $50 to $160; some to $500. **Remarks:** Part-time maker; first knife sold in 1980. **Mark:** Bare footprint.

BARKER, REGGIE, 603 S. Park Dr., Springhill, LA 71075, Phone: 318-539-2958
Specialties: Camp knives and hatchets. **Patterns:** Bowie, skinning, hunting, camping, fighters, kitchen or customer design. **Technical:** Forges car-

bon steel and own pattern welded steels. Prices $225 to $2000. **Remarks:** Full-time maker. Winner of 1999 and 2000 Spring Hammering Cutting contest. Winner of Best Value of Show 2001; Arkansas Knife Show and Journeyman Smith. **Mark:** Barker JS. **Other:** Border Guard Forge.

BARKER, ROBERT G., 2311 Branch Rd., Bishop, GA 30621, Phone: 706-769-7827
Specialties: Traditional working/using straight knives of his design. **Patterns:** Bowies, hunters and utility knives, ABS Journeyman Smith. **Technical:** Hand forged carbon and Damascus. Forges to shape high-carbon 5160, cable and chain. Differentially heat-treats. **Prices:** $200 to $500; some to $1000. **Remarks:** Spare-time maker; first knife sold in 1987. **Mark:** BARKER/J.S.

BARLOW, JANA POIRIER, 3820 Borland Cir., Anchorage, AK 99517, Phone: 907-243-4581

BARNES, MARLEN R., 904 Crestview Dr.S., Atlanta, TX 75551-1854, Phone: 903-796-3668
Specialties: Hammer forges random and mosaic Damascus. **Patterns:** Hatchets, straight and folding knives. **Technical:** Hammer forges carbon steel using 5160, 1084 and 52100 with 15N20 and 203E nickel. **Prices:** $150 and up. **Remarks:** Part-time maker; first knife sold 1999. **Mark:** Script M.R.B., other side J.S.

BARNES, AUBREY G., 11341 Rock Hill Rd., Hagerstown, MD 21740, Phone: 301-223-4587
Specialties: Classic working and using knives of his design, to customer specs and in standard patterns. **Patterns:** Bowies, hunters, fighters, daggers and utility/camping knives. **Technical:** Forges 5160, 1085, L6 and Damascus, Silver wire inlays. **Prices:** $300 to $2500. **Remarks:** Full-time maker; first knife sold in 1992. Doing business as Falling Waters Forge. **Mark:** First and middle initials, last name, M.S.

BARNES, JACK, PO Box 1315, Whitefish, MT 59937-1315, Phone: 406-862-6078

BARNES, ERIC, H C 74 Box 41, Mountain View, AR 72560, Phone: 501-269-3358

BARNES, WILLIAM, 591 Barnes Rd., Wallingford, CT 06492-1805, Phone: 860-349-0443

BARNES, GREGORY, 266 W. Calaveras St., Altadena, CA 91001, Phone: 626-398-0053

BARNES, GARY L., Box 138, New Windsor, MD 21776-0138, Phone: 410-635-6243, Fax: 410-635-6243
Specialties: Ornate button lock Damascus folders. **Patterns:** Barnes original. **Technical:** Forges own Damascus. **Prices:** Average $2500. **Remarks:** ABS Master Smith since 1983. **Mark:** Hand engraved logo of letter B pierced by dagger.

BARNES, WENDELL, 2160 Oriole Dr., Missoula, MT 59808, Phone: 406-721-0908
Specialties: Working straight knives. **Patterns:** Hunters, folders, neck knives. **Technical:** Grinds 440C, ATS-34, D2 and Damascus. **Prices:** Start at $75. **Remarks:** Spare-time maker; first knife sold in 1996. **Mark:** First initial and last name around broken heart.

BARNES JR., CECIL C., 141 Barnes Dr., Center Ridge, AR 72027, Phone: 501-893-2267

BARNETT, VAN, Barnett Int'l Inc., 1135 Terminal Way Ste. #209, Reno, NV 89502, Phone: 866 ARTKNIFE or 304-727-5512, Fax: 775-201-0038
Specialties: Collector grade one-of-a-kind / embellished high art daggers and art folders. **Patterns:** Art daggers and folders. **Technical:** Forges and grinds own Damascus. **Prices:** Upscale. **Remarks:** Designs and makes one-of-a-kind highly embellished art knives using high karat gold, diamonds and other gemstones, pearls, stone and fossil ivories, carved steel guards and blades, all knives are carved and or engraved, does own engraving, carving and other embellishments, sole authorship; full-time maker since 1981. **Mark:** V. H. Barnett or Van Barnett in script. **Other:** Does one high art collaboration a year with Dellana. Voting Member of Knifemakers Guild. Member of ABS.

BARNGROVER, JERRY, RR. #4, Box 1230, Afton, OK 74331, Phone: 918-257-5076

BARR, A.T., 153 Madonna Dr., Nicholasville, KY 40356, Phone: 859-887-5400
Specialties: Working and collector grade liner lock folders. **Patterns:** Liner lock folders. **Technical:** Flat grinds S30V, ATS-34, D-2 and commercial Damascus; hand rubbed satin finish. **Prices:** Start at $300. **Remarks:** Full-time maker, first knives sold in 1979. **Mark:** Full name.

BARR, JUDSON C., 1905 Pickwick Circle, Irving, TX 75060, Phone: 972-790-7195
Specialties: Bowies. **Patterns:** Sheffield and Early American. **Technical:** Forged carbon steel and Damascus. Also stock removal. **Remarks:** Associate member of ABS. **Mark:** Barr.

BARRETT, CECIL TERRY, 2514 Linda Lane, Colorado Springs, CO 80909, Phone: 719-473-8325
Specialties: Working and using straight knives and folders of his design, to customer specs and in standard patterns. **Patterns:** Bowies, hunters, kitchen knives, locking folders and slip-joint folders. **Technical:** Grinds 440C, D2 and ATS-34. Wood and leather sheaths. **Prices:** $65 to $500; some to $750. **Remarks:** Full-time maker. **Mark:** Stamped middle name.

BARRETT, RICK L. (TOSHI HISA), 18943 CR .18, Goshen, IN 46528, Phone: 574-533-4297
Specialties: Japanese-style blades from sushi knives to katana and fantasy pieces. **Patterns:** Swords, axes, spears/lances, hunter and utility knives. **Technical:** Forges and grinds Damascus and carbon steels, occasionally uses stainless. **Prices:** $250-$4000+. **Remarks:** Full-time bladesmith, jeweler. **Mark:** Japanese mei on Japanese pieces and stylized initials.

BARRON, BRIAN, 123 12th Ave., San Mateo, CA 94402, Phone: 650-341-2683
Specialties: Traditional straight knives. **Patterns:** Daggers, hunters and swords. **Technical:** Grinds 440C, ATS-34 and 1095. Sculpts bolsters using an S-curve. **Prices:** $130 to $270; some to $1500. **Remarks:** Part-time maker; first knife sold in 1993. **Mark:** Diamond Drag "Barron".

BARRY III, JAMES J., 115 Flagler Promenade No., West Palm Beach, FL 33405, Phone: 561-832-4197
Specialties: High-art working straight knives of his design also high art tomahawks. **Patterns:** Hunters, daggers and fishing knives. **Technical:** Grinds 440C only. Prefers exotic materials for handles. Most knives embellished with filework, carving and scrimshaw. Many pieces designed to stand unassisted. **Prices:** $500 to $10,000. **Remarks:** Part-time maker; first knife sold in 1975. Guild member (knifemakers) since 1991. **Mark:** Branded initials as a J and B together.

BARTH, J.D., 101 4th St., PO Box 186, Alberton, MT 59820, Phone: 406-722-4557
Specialties: Working and fancy straight knives of his design. Liner lock folders, stainless and Damascus, fully file worked, nitre blueing. **Technical:** Grinds ATS-34, 440-C, stainless and carbon Damascus. Uses variety of natural handle materials and Micarta. Likes dovetailed bolsters. Filework on most knives, full and tapered tangs. Makes custom fit sheaths for each knife. **Mark:** Name over maker, city and state.

BARTLOW, JOHN, 5078 Coffeen Ave., Sheridan, WY 82801, Phone: 307 673-4941
Specialties: New liner locks, working hunters, skinners, bird and trouts. **Patterns:** Working hunters, skinners, capers, bird and trout knives. **Technical:** Working on 6 new liner lock designs. **Prices:** $200 to $2000. **Remarks:** Full-time maker; first knife sold in 1979. Field-tests knives. **Mark:** Bartlow Sheridan, Wyo.

BARTRUG, HUGH E., 2701 34th St. N., #142, St. Petersburg, FL 33713, Phone: 813-323-1136
Specialties: Inlaid straight knives and exotic folders; high-art knives and period pieces. **Patterns:** Hunters, Bowies and daggers; traditional patterns. **Technical:** Diffuses mokume. Forges 100 percent nickel, wrought iron, mosaic Damascus, shokeedo and O1 tool steel; grinds. **Prices:** $210 to $2500; some to $5000. **Remarks:** Retired maker; first knife sold in 1980. **Mark:** Ashley Forge or name.

BASKETT, LEE GENE, 427 Sutzer Ck. Rd., Eastview, KY 42732, Phone: 270-862-5019
Specialties: Fancy working knives and fantasy pieces, often set up in desk stands. **Patterns:** Fighters, Bowies and survival knives; locking folders and traditional styles. **Technical:** Liner locks. Grinds O1, 440C, S-30-V; buys Damascus. Filework provided on most knives. **Prices:** Start at $195 and up. **Remarks:** Part-time maker; first knife sold in 1980. **Mark:** Last name.

BATLEY, MARK S., PO Box 217, Wake, VA 23176, Phone: 804 776-7794

BATSON, RICHARD G., 6591 Waterford Rd., Rixeyville, VA 22737, Phone: 540-937-2318
Specialties: Military, utility and fighting knives in working and presentation grade. **Patterns:** Daggers, combat and utility knives. **Technical:** Grinds O1, 1095 and 440C. Etches and scrimshaws; offers polished, Parkerized finishes. **Prices:** $300 to $1200. **Remarks:** Semi-retired, limit production. First knife sold in 1958. **Mark:** Bat in circle, hand-signed and serial numbered.

BATSON, JAMES, 176 Brentwood Lane, Madison, AL 35758, Phone: 540-937-2318
Specialties: Forged Damascus blades and fittings in collectible period pieces. **Patterns:** Integral art knives, Bowies, folders, American-styled blades and miniatures. **Technical:** Forges carbon steel and his Damascus. **Prices:** $150 to $1800; some to $4500. **Remarks:** Semi retired full-time maker; first knife sold in 1978. **Mark:** Name, bladesmith with horse's head.

custom knifemakers

BATTS, KEITH, 450 Manning Rd., Hooks, TX 75561, Phone: 903-832-1140
   Specialties: Working straight knives of his design or to customer specs. **Patterns:** Bowies, hunters, skinners, camp knives and others. **Technical:** Forges 5160 and his Damascus; offers filework. **Prices:** $245 to $895. **Remarks:** Part-time maker; first knife sold in 1988. **Mark:** Last name.

BAUCHOP, PETER, c/o Beck's Cutlery Specialties, 107 Edinburgh S #109, Cary, NC 27511, Phone: 919-460-0203, Fax: 919-460-7772
   Specialties: Working straight knives and period pieces. **Patterns:** Fighters, swords and survival knives. **Technical:** Grinds O1, D2, G3, 440C and AST-34. Scrimshaws. **Prices:** $100 to $350; some to $1500. **Remarks:** Full-time maker; first knife sold in 1980. **Mark:** Bow and axe (BOW-CHOP).

BAUCHOP, ROBERT, PO Box 330, Munster, Kwazulu-Natal 4278, SOUTH AFRICA, Phone: +27 39 3192449
   Specialties: Fantasy knives; working and using knives of his design and to customer specs. **Patterns:** Hunters, swords, utility/camp knives, diver's knives and large swords. **Technical:** Grinds Sandvick 12C27, D2, 440C. Uses South African hardwoods red ivory, wild olive, African blackwood, etc. on handles. **Prices:** $200 to $800; some to $2000. **Remarks:** Full-time maker; first knife sold in 1986. Doing business as Bauchop Custom Knives and swords. **Mark:** Viking helmet with Bauchop (bow and chopper) crest.

BAUM, RICK, 435 North Center St., Lehi, UT 84043, Phone: 801-431-7290

BAUMGARDNER, ED, 128 E. Main St., Glendale, KY 42740, Phone: 502-435-2675
   Specialties: Working fixed blades, some folders. **Patterns:** Drop point and clip point hunters, fighters, small Bowies, traditional slip joint folders and lockbacks. **Technical:** Grinds O-1, 154CM, ATS-34, and Damascus likes using natural handle materials. **Prices:** $100-$700. **Remarks:** Part-time maker, first knife sold in 2001. **Mark:** Last name.

BAXTER, DALE, 291 County Rd. 547, Trinity, AL 35673, Phone: 256-355-3626
   Specialties: Bowies, fighters, and hunters. **Patterns:** No patterns: all unique true customs. **Technical:** Hand forge and hand finish. Steels: 1095 and L-6 for carbon blades, 1095/L-6 for Damascus. **Remarks:** Full-time bladesmith and sold first knife in 1998. **Mark:** Dale Baxter (script) and J.S. on reverse.

BEAM, JOHN R., 1310 Foothills Rd., Kalispell, MT 59901, Phone: 406-755-2593
   Specialties: Classic, high-art and working straight knives of his design. **Patterns:** Bowies and hunters. **Technical:** Grinds 440C, Damascus and scrap. **Prices:** $175 to $600; some to $3000. **Remarks:** Part-time maker; first knife sold in 1950. Doing business as Beam's Knives. **Mark:** Beam's Knives.

BEASLEY, GENEO, PO Box 339, Wadsworth, NV 89442, Phone: 775-575-2584

BEATTY, GORDON H., 121 Petty Rd., Seneca, SC 29672, Phone: 864-882-6278
   Specialties: Working straight knives, some fancy. **Patterns:** Traditional patterns, mini-skinners and letter openers. **Technical:** Grinds 440C, D2 and ATS-34; makes knives one-at-a-time. **Prices:** $75 to $450; some to $450. **Remarks:** Part-time maker; first knife sold in 1982. **Mark:** Name.

BEATY, ROBERT B., CUTLER, 1995 Big Flat Rd., Missoula, MT 59804, Phone: 406-549-1818
   Specialties: Plain and fancy working knives and collector pieces; will accept custom orders. **Patterns:** Hunters, Bowies, utility, kitchen and camp knives; locking folders. **Technical:** Grinds D-2, ATS-34, Dendritie D-2, makes all tool steel Damascus, forges 1095, 5160, 52100. **Prices:** $100 to $450; some to $1100. **Remarks:** Full-time maker; first knife sold 1995. **Mark:** Stainless: First name, middle initial, last name, city and state. Carbon: Last name stamped on Ricasso.

BEAUCHAMP, GAETAN, 125, de la Rivire, Stoneham, PQ, CANADA G0A 4P0, Phone: 418-848-1914, Fax: 418-848-6859
   Specialties: Working knives and folders of his design and to customer specs. **Patterns:** Hunters, fighters, fantasy knives. **Technical:** Grinds ATS-34, 440C, Damascus. Scrimshaws on ivory; specializes in buffalo horn and black backgrounds. Offers a variety of handle materials. **Prices:** Start at $125. **Remarks:** Full-time maker; first knife sold in 1992. **Mark:** Signature etched on blade.

BECKER, STEVE, 201 1st Ave. N.W., Conrad, MT 59425, Phone: 406-278-7753

BECKER, FRANZ, AM Kreuzberg 2, 84533, Marktl/Inn, GERMANY 08678-8020
   Specialties: Stainless steel knives in working sizes. **Patterns:** Semi- and full-integral knives; interframe folders. **Technical:** Grinds stainless steels; likes natural handle materials. **Prices:** $200 to $2000. **Mark:** Name, country.

BECKETT, NORMAN L., 102 Tobago Ave., Satsuma, FL 32189, Phone: 386-325-3539
   Specialties: Fancy, traditional and working folders and straight knives of his design. **Patterns:** Bowies, fighters, folders and hunters. **Technical:** Grinds CPM-S30V and Damascus. Fileworks blades; hollow and flat grinds. Prefers mirror finish; satin finish on working knives. Uses exotic handle material, stabilized woods and Micarta. Hand-tooled or inlaid sheaths. **Prices:** $125 to $900; some to $2500 and up. **Remarks:** Full-time maker; first knife sold in 1993. Doing business as Norm Beckett Knives. **Mark:** First and last name, maker, city and state.

BEERS, RAY, 8 Manorbrook Rd., Monkton, MD 21111, Phone: Summer 410-472-2229, Fax: 410-472-9136

BEERS, RAY, 2501 Lakefront Dr., Lake Wales, FL 33898, Phone: Winter 863-696-3036, Fax: 863-696-9421

BEETS, MARTY, 390 N. 5th Ave., Williams Lake, BC, CANADA V2G 2G4, Phone: 250-392-7199
   Specialties: Working and collectable straight knives of his own design. **Patterns:** Hunter, skinners, Bowies and utility knives. **Technical:** Grinds 440C-does all his own work including heat treating Uses a variety of handle material specializing in exotic hardwoods, antler and horn. **Price:** $125-$400. **Remarks:** Wife, Sandy does handmade/hand stitched sheaths. First knife sold in 1988. Business name Beets Handmade Knives.

BEGG, TODD M., 420 169 St. S, Spanaway, WA 98387, Phone: 253-531-2113
   Specialties: Hand rubbed satin finished 440c stainless steel. Mirror polished 426 stainless steel. Stabilized mardrone wood.

BEHNKE, WILLIAM, 8478 Dell Rd., Kingsley, MI 49649, Phone: 231-263-7447
   Specialties: Hunters, belt knives and folders. **Patterns:** Traditional styling in moderate-sized straight and folding knives. **Technical:** Forges his own Damascus, cable, saw chain and 5160; likes brass and natural materials. **Prices:** $150 to $2000. **Remarks:** Part-time maker. **Mark:** Bill Behnke Knives.

BELL, MICHAEL, 88321 N. Bank Lane, Coquille, OR 97423, Phone: 541-396-3605
   Specialties: Full line of traditional Japanese swords. **Patterns:** Complete Japanese line; Tanto, Katana etc. **Technical:** All forged, cable and hand-made steel. **Prices:** Swords from $4000 to $20,000. **Remarks:** Full-time maker; first knife sold in 1972. Served apprenticeship with Japanese sword maker. Doing business as Dragonfly Forge. **Mark:** Dragonfly in shield or tombo Kuni Mitsu.

BELL, DONALD, 2 Division St., Bedford, Nova Scotia, CANADA B4A 1Y8, Phone: 902-835-2623
   Specialties: Fancy knives: carved and pierced folders of his own design. **Patterns:** Locking folders, pendant knives, jewelry knives. **Technical:** Grinds Damascus, pierces and carves blades. **Prices:** $500 to $2000, some to $3000. **Remarks:** Spare-time maker; first knife sold in 1993. **Mark:** Bell symbol with first initial inside.

BENDIK, JOHN, 7076 Fitch Rd., Olmsted Falls, OH 44138

BENJAMIN JR., GEORGE, 3001 Foxy Ln., Kissimmee, FL 34746, Phone: 407-846-7259
   Specialties: Fighters in various styles to include Persian, Moro and military. **Patterns:** Daggers, skinners and one-of-a-kind knives. **Technical:** Forges O1, D2, A2, 5160 and Damascus. Favors Pakkawood, Micarta, and mirror or Parkerized finishes. Makes unique para-military leather sheaths. **Prices:** $150 to $600; some to $1200. **Remarks:** Doing business as The Leather Box. **Mark:** Southern Pride Knives.

BENNETT, PETER, PO Box 143, Engadine N.S.W. 2233, AUSTRALIA, Phone: 02-520-4975 (home), Fax: O2-528-8219 (work)
   Specialties: Fancy and embellished working and using straight knives to customer specs and in standard patterns. **Patterns:** Fighters, hunters, bird/trout and fillet knives. **Technical:** Grinds 440C, ATS-34 and Damascus. Uses rare Australian desert timbers for handles. **Prices:** $90 to $500; some to $1500. **Remarks:** Full-time maker; first knife sold in 1985. **Mark:** First and middle initials, last name; country.

BENNETT, BRETT C., 1922 Morrie Ave., Cheyenne, WY 82001, Phone: 307-220-3919
   Specialties: Hand-rubbed finish on all blades. **Patterns:** Most fixed blade patterns. **Technical:** ATS-34, D-2, 1080/15N20 Damascus, 1080 forged.

Prices: $100 and up. **Mark:** "B.C. Bennett" in script or "Bennett" stamped in script.

BENNETT, GLEN C., 5821 S. Stewart Blvd., Tucson, AZ 85706

BENNICA, CHARLES, Chemin du Salet, 34190 Moules et Baucels, FRANCE, Phone: +33 4 67 73 42 40
Specialties: Fixed blades and folding knives; the latter with slick closing mechanisms with push buttons to unlock blades. Unique handle shapes, signature to the maker. **Technical:** 416 stainless steel frames for folders and ATS-34 blades. Also specializes in Damascus.

BENSON, DON, 2505 Jackson St., #112, Escalon, CA 95320, Phone: 209-838-7921
Specialties: Working straight knives of his design. **Patterns:** Axes, Bowies, tantos and hunters. **Technical:** Grinds 440C. **Prices:** $100 to $150; some to $400. **Remarks:** Spare-time maker; first knife sold in 1980. **Mark:** Name.

BENTLEY, C.L., 2405 Hilltop Dr., Albany, GA 31707, Phone: 912-432-6656

BER, DAVE, 656 Miller Rd., San Juan Island, WA 98250, Phone: 206-378-7230
Specialties: Working straight and folding knives for the sportsman; welcomes customer designs. **Patterns:** Hunters, skinners, Bowies, kitchen and fishing knives. **Technical:** Forges and grinds saw blade steel, wire Damascus, O1, L6, 5160 and 440C. **Prices:** $100 to $300; some to $500. **Remarks:** Full-time maker; first knife sold in 1985. **Mark:** Last name.

BERG, LOTHAR, 37 Hillcrest Ln., Kitchener ON, CANADA NZK 1S9, Phone: 519-745-3260 519-745-3260

BERGER, MAX A., 5716 John Richard Ct., Carmichael, CA 95608, Phone: 916-972-9229
Specialties: Fantasy and working/using straight knives of his design. **Patterns:** Fighters, hunters and utility/camp knives. **Technical:** Grinds ATS-34 and 440C. Offers fileworks and combinations of mirror polish and satin finish blades. **Prices:** $200 to $600; some to $2500. **Remarks:** Part-time maker; first knife sold in 1992. **Mark:** Last name.

BERGH, ROGER, Eklangsvagen 40, 12051 Arsta, SWEDEN, Phone: 070 5941570
Specialties: Collectible all-purpose straight-blade knives. Damascus steel blades, carving and artistic design knives are heavily influenced by nature and have an organic hand crafted feel.

BERGLIN, BRUCE D., 17441 Lake Terrace Place, Mount Vernon, WA 98274, Phone: 360-422-8603
Specialties: Working and using straight knives of his own design. **Patterns:** Hunters, boots, Bowies, utility/camp knives and period pieces, some made to look old. **Technical:** Forges carbon steel, grinds carbon and stainless steel. Prefers natural handle material and micarta. **Prices:** Start at $200. **Remarks:** Part-time maker since 1998. **Mark:** First initial, middle initial and last name, sometimes surrounded with an oval.

BERTHOLUS, BERNARD, Atelier Du Brute, De Forge 21, Rue Fersen 06600, Antibes, FRANCE, Phone: 04 93 34 95 90
Specialties: Traditional working and using straight knives of his design. **Patterns:** Bowies, daggers and hunters. **Technical:** Forges ATS-34, 440, D2 and carbon steels. **Prices:** $750 to $7500. **Remarks:** Full-time maker; first knife sold in 1990. **Mark:** City and last name.

BERTOLAMI, JUAN CARLOS, Av San Juan 575, Neuquen, ARGENTINA 8300
Specialties: Hunting and country labor knives. All of them unique high quality pieces and supplies collectors too. **Technical:** Austrian stainless steel and elephant, hippopotamus and orca ivory, as well as ebony and other fine woods for the handles.

BERTUZZI, ETTORE, Via Partigiani 3, 24068 Seriate (Bergamo), ITALY, Phone: 035-294262, Fax: 035-294262
Specialties: Classic straight knives and folders of his design, to customer specs and in standard patterns. **Patterns:** Bowies, hunters and locking folders. **Technical:** Grinds ATS-34, D3, D2 and various Damascus. **Prices:** $300 to $500. **Remarks:** Part-time maker; first knife sold in 1993. **Mark:** Name etched on ricasso.

BESEDICK, FRANK E., R.R. 2, Box 802, Ruffsdale, PA 15679, Phone: 724-696-3312
Specialties: Traditional working and using straight knives of his design. **Patterns:** Hunters, utility/camp knives and miniatures; buckskinner blades and tomahawks. **Technical:** Forges and grinds 5160, O1 and Damascus. Offers filework and scrimshaw. **Prices:** $75 to $300; some to $750. **Remarks:** Part-time maker; first knife sold in 1990. **Mark:** Name or initials.

BESHARA, BRENT, 207 Cedar St., PO Box 1046, Stayner, ON, CANADA L0M 1S0
Specialties: Tactical fighting fixed knives. **Patterns:** Tantos, fighters, neck and custom designs. **Technical:** Grinds 0-1, L-6 and stainless upon request. Offers Kydex sheaths, does own Paragon heat treating. **Prices:**

Start at $150. **Remarks:** Part-time maker. Active serving military bomb tech driver. **Mark:** "BESH" stamped.

BETHKE, LORA SUE, 13420 Lincoln St., Grand Haven, MI 49417, Phone: 616-842-8268, Fax: 616-844-2696
Specialties: Classic and traditional straight knives of her design. **Patterns:** Boots, Bowies and hunters. **Technical:** Forges 1084 and Damascus. **Prices:** Start at $400. **Remarks:** Part-time maker; first knife sold in 1997. **Mark:** Full name - JS on reverse side. **Other:** Journeyman Smith, American Bladesmith Society.

BEUKES, TINUS, 83 Henry St., Risiville, Vereeniging 1939, SOUTH AFRICA, Phone: 27 16 423 2053
Specialties: Working straight knives. **Patterns:** Hunters, skinners and kitchen knives. **Technical:** Grinds D2, 440C and chain, cable and stainless Damascus. **Prices:** $80 to $180. **Remarks:** Part-time maker; first knife sold in 1993. **Mark:** Full name, city, logo.

BEVERLY II, LARRY H., PO Box 741, Spotsylvania, VA 22553, Phone: 540-898-3951
Specialties: Working straight knives, slip-joints and liner locks. Welcomes customer designs. **Patterns:** Bowies, hunters, guard less fighters and miniatures. **Technical:** Grinds 440C, A2 and O1. **Prices:** $125 to $1000. **Remarks:** Part-time maker; first knife sold in 1986. **Mark:** Initials or last name in script.

BEZUIDENHOUT, BUZZ, 30 Surlingham Ave., Malvern, Queensburgh, Natal 4093, SOUTH AFRICA, Phone: 031-4632827, Fax: 031-3631259
Specialties: Traditional working and using straight knives of his design and to customer specs. **Patterns:** Boots, hunters, kitchen knives and utility/camp knives. **Technical:** Grinds 12C27, 440C and ATS-34. Uses local hardwoods, horn - kudu, impala, buffalo - giraffe bone and ivory for handles. **Prices:** $150 to $200; some to $1500. **Remarks:** Spare-time maker; first knife sold in 1988. **Mark:** First name with a bee emblem.

BIGGERS, GARY, Ventura Knives, 1278 Colina Vista, Ventura, CA 93003, Phone: 805-658-6610, Fax: 805-658-6610
Specialties: Fixed blade knives of his design. **Patterns:** Hunters, boots/fighters, Bowies and utility knives. **Technical:** Grinds ATS-34, 01 and commercial Damascus. **Prices:** $150 to $550. **Remarks:** Part-time maker; first knife sold in 1996. Doing business as Ventura Knives. **Mark:** First and last name, city and state.

BILLGREN, PER, STALLGATAN 9, S815 76 Soderfors, SWEDEN, Phone: +46 293 17480, Fax: +46 293 30124
Specialties: Damasteel, stainless Damascus steels. **Patterns:** Bluetounge, Heimskringla, Muhammed's ladder, Rose twist, Odin's eye, Vinland, Hakkapelliitta. **Technical:** Modern Damascus steel made by patented powder metallurgy method. **Prices:** $80 to $180. **Remarks:** Damasteel is available through distributors around the globe.

BIRDWELL, IRA LEE, PO Box 1135, Bagdad, AZ 86321, Phone: 520-633-2516
Specialties: Special orders. **Mark:** Engraved signature.

BIRNBAUM, EDWIN, 9715 Hamocks Blvd. I 206, Miami, FL 33196

BISH, HAL, 9347 Sweetbriar Trace, Jonesboro, GA 30236, Phone: 770-477-2422

BIZZELL, ROBERT, 145 Missoula Ave., Butte, MT 59701, Phone: 406-782-4403
Specialties: Damascus. **Patterns:** Composite, mosaic and traditional. **Technical:** Only fixed blades at this time. **Prices:** Start at $150. **Mark:** Hand signed.

BLACK, EARL, 3466 South, 700 East, Salt Lake City, UT 84106, Phone: 801-466-8395
Specialties: High-art straight knives and folders; period pieces. **Patterns:** Boots, Bowies and daggers; lockers and gents. **Technical:** Grinds 440C and 154CM. Buys some Damascus. Scrimshaws and engraves. **Prices:** $200 to $1800; some to $2500 and higher. **Remarks:** Full-time maker; first knife sold in 1980. **Mark:** Name, city, state.

BLACK, TOM, 921 Grecian N.W., Albuquerque, NM 87107, Phone: 505-344-2549
Specialties: Working knives to fancy straight knives of his design. **Patterns:** Drop-point skinners, folders, using knives, Bowies and daggers. **Technical:** Grinds 440C, 154CM, ATS-34, A2 and Damascus. Offers engraving and scrimshaw. **Prices:** $185 to $1250; some over $8500. **Remarks:** Full-time maker; first knife sold in 1970. **Mark:** Name, city.

BLACK, SCOTT, 570 Malcom Rd., Covington, GA 30209
Specialties: Working/using folders of his design. **Patterns:** Daggers, hunters, utility/camp knives and friction folders. **Technical:** Patterns pattern welded, cable, 1095, O1 and 5160. **Prices:** $100 to $500. **Remarks:** Part-time maker; first knife sold in 1992. Doing business as Copperhead Forge. **Mark:** Hot mark on blade, copperhead snake.

custom knifemakers

BLACK, SCOTT, 27100 Leetown Rd., Picayune, MS 39466, Phone: 601-799-5939
Specialties: Friction folders; fighters. **Patterns:** Bowies, fighters, hunters, smoke hawks, friction folders, daggers. **Technical:** All forged, all work done by me, own hand-stitched leather work; own heat-treating. **Prices:** $100 to $2200. **Remarks:** ABS Journeyman Smith. **Mark:** Hot Mark - Copperhead Snake. **Other:** Cabel / Damascus/ High Carbone.

BLACKTON, ANDREW E., 12521 Fifth Isle, Bayonet Point, FL 34667, Phone: 727-869-1406
Specialties: Straight and folding knives, some fancy. **Patterns:** Hunters, Bowies and daggers. **Technical:** Grinds D2, 440C and 154CM. Offers some embellishment. **Prices:** $125 to $450; some to $2000. **Remarks:** Full-time maker. **Mark:** Last name in script.

BLACKWOOD, NEIL, 7032 Willow Run, Lakeland, FL 33813, Phone: 863-701-0126
Specialties: Fixed blades and folders. **Technical:** Blade steels d-2 Talonite, Stellite, CPM S30V and RWL 34. Handle Materials G-10 carbon fiber and Micarta in the synthetics: giraffe bone and exotic woods on the natural side. **Remarks:** Makes everything from the frames to the stop pins, pivot pins-everything but the stainless screws; one factory/custom collaboration (the Hybrid Hunter) with Outdoor Edge is in place and negotiations were under way at press time for one with Benchmade.

BLANCHARD, G.R. (GARY), 8900 Condotti Ct., Las Vegas, NV 89117, Phone: 702-645-9774
Specialties: Fancy folders with patented button blade release and high-art straight knives of his design. **Patterns:** Boots, daggers and locking folders. **Technical:** Grinds 440C and ATS-34 and Damascus. Engraves his knives. **Prices:** $1500 to $18,000 or more. **Remarks:** Full-time maker; first knife sold in 1989. **Mark:** First and middle initials, last name or last name only.

BLASINGAME, ROBERT, 281 Swanson, Kilgore, TX 75662, Phone: 903-984-8144
Specialties: Classic working and using straight knives and folders of his design and to customer specs. **Patterns:** Bowies, daggers, fighters and hunters; one-of-a-kind historic reproductions. **Technical:** Hand-forges P.W. Damascus, cable Damascus and chain Damascus. **Prices:** $150 to $1000; some to $2000. **Remarks:** Full-time maker; first knife sold in 1968. **Mark:** 'B' inside anvil.

BLAUM, ROY, 319 N. Columbia St., Covington, LA 70433, Phone: 985-893-1060
Specialties: Working straight knives and folders of his design; lightweight easy-open folders. **Patterns:** Hunters, boots, fishing and woodcarving/whittling knives. **Technical:** Grinds A2, D2, O1, 154CM and ATS-34. Offers leatherwork. **Prices:** $40 to $800; some higher. **Remarks:** Full-time maker; first knife sold in 1976. **Mark:** Engraved signature or etched logo.

BLOOMER, ALAN T., 116 E. 6th St., Maquon, IL 61458, Phone: 309-875-3583
Specialties: All Damascus folders, making own Damascus. **Patterns:** Bowies, Folders, chef etc. **Technical:** Does own heat treating. **Prices:** $400 to $1000. **Remarks:** Part-time maker; Guild member. **Mark:** Stamp Bloomer. **Other:** No orders.

BLOOMQUIST, R. GORDON, 6206 Tiger Trail Dr., Olympia, WA 98512, Phone: 360-352-7162

BLUM, KENNETH, 1729 Burleson, Brenham, TX 77833, Phone: 979-836-9577
Specialties: Traditional working straight knives of his design. **Patterns:** Camp knives, Hunters and Bowies. **Technical:** Forges 5160; grinds 440C and D2. Uses exotic woods and Micarta for handles. **Prices:** $150 to $300. **Remarks:** Part-time maker; first knife sold in 1978. **Mark:** Last name on ricasso.

BLUM, CHUCK, 743 S. Brea Blvd., #10, Brea, CA 92621, Phone: 714-529-0484
Specialties: Art and investment daggers and Bowies. **Technical:** Flat-grinds; hollow-grinds 440C, ATS-34 on working knives. **Prices:** $125 to $8500. **Remarks:** Part-time maker; first knife sold in 1985. **Mark:** First and middle initials and last name with sailboat logo.

BOARDMAN, GUY, 39 Mountain Ridge R., New Germany 3619, SOUTH AFRICA, Phone: 031-726-921
Specialties: American and South African-styles. **Patterns:** Bowies, American and South African hunters, plus more. **Technical:** Grinds Bohler steels, some ATS-34. **Prices:** $100 to $600. **Remarks:** Part-time maker; first knife sold in 1986. **Mark:** Name, city, country.

BOATRIGHT, BASEL, 11 Timber Point, New Braunfels, TX 78132, Phone: 210-609-0807
Specialties: Working and using knives of his design. **Patterns:** Hunters, skinners and utility/camp knives. **Technical:** Grinds and hand-tempers 5160. **Prices:** $75 to $300. **Remarks:** Part-time maker. **Mark:** Stamped BBB.

BOCHMAN, BRUCE, 183 Howard Place, Grants Pass, OR 97526, Phone: 503-471-1985
Specialties: Working straight knives in standard patterns. **Patterns:** Bowies, hunters, fishing and bird knives. **Technical:** 440C; mirror or satin finish. **Prices:** $140 to $250; some to $750. **Remarks:** Part-time maker; first knife sold in 1977. **Mark:** Custom blades by B. Bochman.

BODEN, HARRY, Via Gellia Mill, Bonsall Matlock, Derbyshire DE4 2AJ, ENGLAND, Phone: 0629-825176
Specialties: Traditional working straight knives and folders of his design. **Patterns:** Hunters, locking folders and utility/camp knives. **Technical:** Grinds Sandvik 12C27, D2 and O1. **Prices:** £70 to £150; some to £300. **Remarks:** Full-time maker; first knife sold in 1986. **Mark:** Full name.

BODNER, GERALD "JERRY", 4102 Spyglass Ct., Louisville, KY 40229, Phone: 502-968-5946
Specialties: Fantasy straight knives in standard patterns. **Patterns:** Bowies, fighters, hunters and micro-miniature knives. **Technical:** Grinds Damascus, 440C and D2. Offers filework. **Prices:** $35 to $180. **Remarks:** Part-time maker; first knife sold in 1993. **Mark:** Last name in script and JAB in oval above knives.

BODOLAY, ANTAL, Rua Wilson Soares Fernandes #31, Planalto, Belo Horizonte MG-31730-700, BRAZIL, Phone: 031-494-1885
Specialties: Working folders and fixed blades of his design or to customer specs; some art daggers and period pieces. **Patterns:** Daggers, hunters, locking folders, utility knives and Khukris. **Technical:** Grinds D6, high-carbon steels and 420 stainless. Forges files on request. **Prices:** $30 to $350. **Remarks:** Full-time maker; first knife sold in 1965. **Mark:** Last name in script.

BOEHLKE, GUENTER, Parkstrasse 2, 56412 Grossholbach, GERMANY 2602-5440
Specialties: Classic working/using straight knives of his design. **Patterns:** Hunters, utility/camp knives and ancient remakes. **Technical:** Grinds Damascus, CPM-T-440V and 440C. Inlays gemstones and ivory. **Prices:** $220 to $700; some to $2000. **Remarks:** Spare-time maker; first knife sold in 1985. **Mark:** Name, address and bow and arrow.

BOGUSZEWSKI, PHIL, PO Box 99329, Lakewood, WA 98499, Phone: 253-581-7096
Specialties: Working folders—some fancy—mostly of his design. **Patterns:** Folders, slip-joints and lockers; also makes anodized titanium frame folders. **Technical:** Grinds BG42 and Damascus; offers filework. **Prices:** $550 to $3000. **Remarks:** Full-time maker; first knife sold in 1979. **Mark:** Name, city and state.

BOJTOS, ARPA D., Dobsinskeho 10, 98403 Lucenec, Slovakia, Phone: 00421-47 4333512
Specialties: Fantasy and high-art knives. **Patterns:** Daggers, fighters and hunters. **Technical:** Grinds ATS-34. Carves on steel, handle materials and sheaths. **Prices:** $2000 to $5000; some to $8000. **Remarks:** Full-time maker; first knife sold in 1990. **Mark:** Stylized initials.

BOLD, STU, 63 D'Andrea Tr., Sarnia, Ont., CANADA N7S 6H3, Phone: 519-383-7610
Specialties: Traditional working/using straight knives in standard patterns and to customer specs. **Patterns:** Boots, Bowies and hunters. **Technical:** Grinds ATS-34, 440C and Damascus; mosaic pins. Offers scrimshaw and hand-tooled leather sheaths. **Prices:** $140 to $500; some to $2000. **Remarks:** Part-time maker; first knife sold in 1983. **Mark:** Name, city, province.

BOLEWARE, DAVID, PO Box 96, Carson, MS 39427, Phone: 601-943-5372
Specialties: Traditional and working/using straight knives of his design, to customer specs and in standard patterns. **Patterns:** Bowies, hunters and utility/camp knives. **Technical:** Grinds ATS-34, 440C and Damascus. **Prices:** $85 to $350; some to $600. **Remarks:** Part-time maker; first knife sold in 1989. **Mark:** First and last name, city, state.

BOLTON, CHARLES B., PO Box 6, Jonesburg, MO 63351, Phone: 636-488-5785
Specialties: Working straight knives in standard patterns. **Patterns:** Hunters, skinners, boots and fighters. **Technical:** Grinds 440C and ATS-34. **Prices:** $100 to $300; some to $600. **Remarks:** Full-time maker; first knife sold in 1973. **Mark:** Last name.

BONASSI, FRANCO, Via Nicoletta 4, Pordenone 33170, ITALY, Phone: 0434-550821
Specialties: Fancy and working one-of-a-kind straight knives of his design. **Patterns:** Hunters, skinners, utility and liner locks. **Technical:** Grinds CPM, ATS-34, 154CM and commercial Damascus. Uses only titanium foreguards and pommels. **Prices:** Start at $250. **Remarks:** Spare-time maker; first knife sold in 1988. Has made cutlery for several celebrities; Gen. Schwarzkopf, Fuzzy Zoeller, etc. **Mark:** FRANK.

BOOCO, GORDON, 175 Ash St., PO Box 174, Hayden, CO 81639, Phone: 970-276-3195
Specialties: Fancy working straight knives of his design and to customer specs. **Patterns:** Hunters and Bowies. **Technical:** Grinds 440C, D2 and A2. Heat-treats. **Prices:** $150 to $350; some $600 and higher. **Remarks:** Part-time maker; first knife sold in 1984. **Mark:** Last name with push dagger artwork.

BOOS, RALPH, 5107 40 Ave., Edmonton, Alberta, CANADA T6L 1B3, Phone: 780-463-7094
Specialties: Classic, fancy and fantasy miniature knives and swords of his design or to customer specs. **Patterns:** Bowies, daggers and swords. **Technical:** Hand files O1, stainless and Damascus. Engraves and carves. Does heat bluing and acid etching. **Prices:** $125 to $350; some to $1000. **Remarks:** Part-time maker; first knife sold in 1982. **Mark:** First initials back to back.

BOOTH, PHILIP W., 301 S. Jeffery Ave., Ithaca, MI 48847, Phone: 989-875-2844
Specialties: Folding knives, various mechanisms, maker of the "minnow" series small folding knife. **Patterns:** Auto lock backs, liner locks, classic pattern multi-blades. **Technical:** Grinds ATS-34, 440C, 1095 and commercial Damascus. Prefers natural materials, offers file work and scrimshaw. **Prices:** $200 and up. **Remarks:** Full-time maker; first knife sold in 1991. **Mark:** Last name or name with city and map logo.

BORGER, WOLF, Benzstrasse 8, 76676 Graben-Neudorf, GERMANY, Phone: 07255-72303, Fax: 07255-72304
Specialties: High-tech working and using straight knives and folders, many with corkscrews or other tools, of his design. **Patterns:** Hunters, Bowies and folders with various locking systems. **Technical:** Grinds 440C, ATS-34 and CPM. Uses stainless Damascus. **Prices:** $250 to $900; some to $1500. **Remarks:** Full-time maker; first knife sold in 1975. **Mark:** Howling wolf and name; first name on Damascus blades.

BOSE, TONY, 7252 N. County Rd., 300 E., Shelburn, IN 47879-9778, Phone: 812-397-5114
Specialties: Traditional working and using knives in standard patterns; multi-blade folders. **Patterns:** Multi-blade slip-joints. **Technical:** Grinds commercial Damascus, ATS-34 and D2. **Prices:** $400 to $1200. **Remarks:** Full-time maker; first knife sold in 1972. **Mark:** First initial, last name, city, state.

BOSE, REESE, PO Box 61, Shelburn, IN 47879, Phone: 812-397-5114
Specialties: Traditional working and using knives in standard patterns and multi-blade folders. **Patterns:** Multi-blade slip-joints. **Technical:** ATS-34, D2 and CPM 440V. **Prices:** $275 to $1500. **Remarks:** Full-time maker; first knife sold in 1992. Photos by Jack Busfield. **Mark:** R. Bose.

BOSSAERTS, CARL, Rua Albert Einstein 906, 14051-110, Ribeirao Preto, S.P. BRAZIL, Phone: 016 633 7063
Specialties: Working and using straight knives of his design, to customer specs and in standard patterns. **Patterns:** Hunters, fighters and utility/camp knives. **Technical:** Grinds ATS-34, 440V and 440C; does filework. **Prices:** 60 to $400. **Remarks:** Part-time maker; first knife sold in 1992. **Mark:** Initials joined together.

BOST, ROGER E., 30511 Cartier Dr, Palos Verdes, CA 90275-5629, Phone: 310- 541-6833
Specialties: Hunters, fighters, boot, utility. **Patterns:** Loveless-style. **Technical:** ATS-34, 60-61RC, stock removal and forge. **Prices:** $200 and up. **Remarks:** First knife sold in 1990. **Mark:** Diamond with initials inside and Palos Verdes California around outside. **Other:** Cal. Knifemakers Assn, ABS.

BOSTWICK, CHRIS T., 341 Robins Run, Burlington, WI 53105
Specialties: Slipjoints ATS-34. **Patterns:** English jack, gunstock jack, doctors, stockman. **Prices:** $300 and up. **Remarks:** Enjoy traditional patterns/history multiblade slipjoints. **Mark:** CTB.

BOSWORTH, DEAN, 329 Mahogany Dr., Key Largo, FL 33037, Phone: 305-451-1564
Specialties: Free hand hollow ground working knives with hand rubbed satin finish, filework and inlays. **Patterns:** Bird and Trout, hunters, skinners, filet, Bowies, miniatures. **Technical:** Using 440C, ATS-34, D2, Meier Damascus, custom wet formed sheaths. **Prices:** $250 and up. **Remarks:** Part-time maker; first knife made in 1985. **Mark:** BOZ stamped in block letters. **Other:** Member: Florida Knifemakers Assoc.

BOURBEAU, JEAN YVES, 15 Rue Remillard, Notre Dame, Ile Perrot, Quebec, CANADA J7V 8M9, Phone: 514-453-1069
Specialties: Fancy/embellished and fantasy folders of his design. **Patterns:** Bowies, fighters and locking folders. **Technical:** Grinds 440C, ATS-34 and Damascus. Carves precious wood for handles. **Prices:** $150 to $1000. **Remarks:** Part-time maker; first knife sold in 1994. **Mark:** Interlaced initials.

BOUSE, D. MICHAEL, 1010 Victoria Pl., Waldorf, MD 20602, Phone: 301-843-0449
Specialties: Traditional and working/using straight knives of his design. **Patterns:** Daggers, fighters and hunters. **Technical:** Forges 5160 and Damascus; grinds D2; differential hardened blades; decorative handle pins. **Prices:** $125 to $350. **Remarks:** Spare-time maker; first knife sold in 1992. Doing business as Michael's Handmade Knives. **Mark:** Etched last name.

BOWEN, TILTON, 189 Mt Olive Rd., Baker, WV 26801, Phone: 304-897-6159
Specialties: Straight, stout working knives. **Patterns:** Hunters, fighters and boots; also offers buckskinner and throwing knives. All his D2-blades since 1st of year, 1997 are Deep Cryogenic processed. **Technical:** Grinds D2 and 4140. **Prices:** $60 to $275. **Remarks:** Full-time maker; first knife sold in 1982-1983. Sells wholesale to dealers. **Mark:** Initials and BOWEN BLADES, WV.

BOWLES, CHRIS, PO Box 985, Reform, AL 35481, Phone: 205-375-6162
Specialties: Working/using straight knives, and period pieces. **Patterns:** Utility, tactical, hunting, neck knives, machetes, and swords. **Grinds:** 0-1, 154 cm, BG-42, 440V. **Prices:** $50-$400 some higher. **Remarks:** Full-time maker. **Mark:** Bowles stamped or Bowles etched in script.

BOXER, BO, LEGEND FORGE, 6477 Hwy. 93 S #134, Whitefish, MT 59937, Phone: 505-799-0173
Specialties: Handmade hunting knives, Damascus hunters. Most are antler handled. Also, hand forged Damascus steel. **Patterns:** Hunters and Bowies. **Prices:** $125 to $2500 on every exceptional Damascus knives. **Mark:** The name "Legend Forge" hand engraved on every blade. **Additional:** Makes his own custom leather sheath stamped with maker stamp. His knives are used by the outdoorsman of the Smoky Mountains, North Carolina, and the Rockies of Montana and New Mexico. **Other:** Spends one-half of the year in Montana and the other part of the year in Taos New Mexico.

BOYD, FRANCIS, 1811 Prince St., Berkeley, CA 94703, Phone: 510-841-7210
Specialties: Folders and kitchen knives; Japanese swords. **Patterns:** Push-button sturdy locking folders; San Francisco-style chef's knives. **Technical:** Forges and grinds; mostly uses high-carbon steels. **Prices:** Moderate to heavy. **Remarks:** Designer. **Mark:** Name.

BOYE, DAVID, PO Box 1238, Dolan Springs, AZ 86441, Phone: 800-853-1617
Specialties: Folders, hunting and kitchen knives. Forerunner in the use of dendritic steel and dendritic cobalt for blades. **Patterns:** Boye Basics sheath knives, lockback folders, kitchen knives and hunting knives. **Technical:** Casts blades in stainless 440Cand cobalt. **Prices:** From $99 to $500. **Remarks:** Full-time maker; author of *Step-by-Step Knife making*; **Mark:** Name.

BOYER, MARK, 10515 Woodinville Dr., #17, Bothell, WA 98011, Phone: 206-487-9370
Specialties: High-tech and working/using straight knives of his design. **Patterns:** Fighters and utility/camp knives. **Technical:** Grinds 1095 and D2. Offers Kydex sheaths; heat-treats. **Prices:** $45 to $120. **Remarks:** Part-time maker; first knife sold in 1994. Doing business as Boyer Blades. **Mark:** Eagle holding two swords with name.

BOYSEN, RAYMOND A., 125 E. St. Patrick, Rapid Ciy, SD 57701, Phone: 605-341-7752
Specialties: Hunters and Bowies. **Technical:** High performance blades forged from 52100 and 5160. **Prices:** $200 and up. **Remarks:** American Bladesmith Society Journeyman Smith. **Mark:** BOYSEN. **Other:** Part-time bladesmith.

BRACK, DOUGLAS D., 119 Camino Ruiz, #71, Camirillo, CA 93012, Phone: 805-987-0490
Specialties: Working straight knives of his design. **Patterns:** Heavy-duty skinners, fighters and boots. **Technical:** Grinds 440C, ATS-34 and 5160; forges cable. **Prices:** $90 to $180; some to $300. **Remarks:** Part-time maker; first knife sold in 1984. **Mark:** tat.

BRADBURN, GARY, BRADBURN CUSTOM CUTLERY, 1714 Park Place, Wichita, KS 67203, Phone: 316-269-4273
Specialties: Specialize in clay-tempered Japanese-style knives and swords. **Patterns:** Also Bowies and fighers. **Technical:** Forge and/or grind carbon steel only. **Prices:** $150 to $1200. **Mark:** Initials GB stylized to look like Japanese character.

BRADFORD, GARRICK, 582 Guelph St., Kitchener ON, CANADA N2H-5Y4, Phone: 519-576-9863

BRADLEY, JOHN, PO Box 37, Pomona Park, FL 32181, Phone: 904-649-4739
Specialties: Fixed-blade using knives. **Patterns:** Skinners, Bowies, camp knives and Sgian Dubhs. **Technical:** Hand forged from 52100, 1095

custom knifemakers

and own Damascus. **Prices:** $125 to $500; some higher. **Remarks:** Part-time maker; first knife sold in 1988. **Mark:** Last name.

BRADLEY, DENNIS, 2410 Bradley Acres Rd., Blairsville, GA 30512, Phone: 706-745-4364
Specialties: Working straight knives and folders, some high-art. **Patterns:** Hunters, boots and daggers; slip-joints and two-blades. **Technical:** Grinds ATS-34, D2, 440C and commercial Damascus. **Prices:** $100 to $500; some to $2000. **Remarks:** Part-time maker; first knife sold in 1973. **Mark:** BRADLEY KNIVES in double heart logo.

BRADSHAW, BAILEY, PO Box 564, Diana, TX 75640, Phone: 903-968-2029
Specialties: Traditional folders and contemporary front lock folders. **Patterns:** Single or multi-blade folders, Bowies. **Technical:** Grind CPM 3V, CPM 440V, CPM 420V, Forge Damascus, 52100. **Prices:** $250 to $3000. **Remarks:** Engraves, carves and does sterling silver sheaths. **Mark:** Tori arch over initials back to back.

BRANDON, MATTHEW, 4435 Meade St., Denver, CO 80211, Phone: 303-458-0786
Specialties: Hunters, skinners, full-tang Bowies. **Prices:** $100-$250. **Remarks:** Satisfaction or full refund. **Mark:** MTB.

BRANDSEY, EDWARD P., 335 Forest Lake Dr., Milton, WI 53563, Phone: 608-868-9010
Specialties: Large Bowies. Does own scrimshaw. See Egnath's second book. **Patterns:** Hunters, fighters, Bowies and daggers, some buckskinner-styles. Native American influence on some. An occasional tanto. **Technical:** ATS-34, 440-C, 0-1, and some Damascus. Paul Boshert treating past 20 years. **Prices:** $250-$600; some to $3000. **Remarks:** Full-time maker. First knife sold in 1973. **Mark:** Initials connected - registered Wisc. Trademark since March 1983.

BRANDT, MARTIN W., 833 Kelly Blvd., Springfield, OR 97477, Phone: 541-747-5422

BRANTON, ROBERT, 4976 Seewee Rd., Awendaw, SC 29429, Phone: 843-928-3624
Specialties: Working straight knives of his design or to customer specs; throwing knives. **Patterns:** Hunters, fighters and some miniatures. **Technical:** Grinds ATS-34, A2 and 1050; forges 5160, O1. Offers hollow- or convex-grinds. **Prices:** $25 to $400. **Remarks:** Part-time maker; first knife sold in 1985. Doing business as Pro-Flyte, Inc. **Mark:** Last name; or first and last name, city, state.

BRATCHER, BRETT, 11816 County Rd. 302, Plantersville, TX 77363, Phone: 936-894-3788, Fax: (936) 894-3790
Specialties: Hunting and skinning knives. **Patterns:** Clip and Drop Point. Hand forged. **Technical:** Material 5160, D2, 1095 and Damascus. **Price:** $200 to $500. **Mark:** Bratcher.

BRAY JR., W. LOWELL, 6931 Manor Beach Rd., New Port Richey, FL 34652, Phone: 727-846-0830
Specialties: Traditional working and using straight knives and folders of his design. **Patterns:** Hunters, kitchen knives and utility knives. **Technical:** Grinds 440C and ATS34; forges high-carbon Damascus. **Prices:** $100 to $500. **Remarks:** Spare-time maker; first knife sold in 1992. **Mark:** Lowell Bray Knives in shield.

BREED, KIM, 733 Jace Dr., Clarksville, TN 37040, Phone: 931-645-9171
Specialties: High end through working folders and straight knives. **Patterns:** Hunters, fighters, daggers, Bowies. His design or customers. Likes one-of-a-kind designs. **Technical:** Makes own Mosiac and regular Damascus, but will use stainless steels. Offers filework and sculpted material. **Prices:** $150-$2000. **Remarks:** Full-time maker. First knife sold in 1990. **Mark:** Last name.

BREND, WALTER, 353 Co. Rd. 1373, Vinemont, AL 35179, Phone: 256-739-1987
Specialties: Tactical-style knives, fighters, automatics. **Technical:** Grinds D-Z and 440C blade steels, 154CM steel. **Prices:** Micarta handles, titanium handles.

BRENNAN, JUDSON, PO Box 1165, Delta Junction, AK 99737, Phone: 907-895-5153, Fax: 907-895-5404
Specialties: Period pieces. **Patterns:** All kinds of Bowies, rifle knives, daggers. **Technical:** Forges miscellaneous steels. **Prices:** Upscale, good value. **Remarks:** Muzzle-loading gunsmith; first knife sold in 1978. **Mark:** Name.

BRESHEARS, CLINT, 1261 Keats, Manhattan Beach, CA 90266, Phone: 310-372-0739, Fax: 310-372-0739
Specialties: Working straight knives and folders. **Patterns:** Hunters, Bowies and survival knives. Folders are mostly hunters. **Technical:** Grinds 440C, 154CM and ATS-34; prefers mirror finishes. **Prices:** $125 to $750; some to $1800. **Remarks:** Part-time maker; first knife sold in 1978. **Mark:** First name.

BREUER, LONNIE, PO Box 877384, Wasilla, AK 99687-7384
Specialties: Fancy working straight knives. **Patterns:** Hunters, camp knives and axes, folders and Bowies. **Technical:** Grinds 440C, AEB-L and D2; likes wire inlay, scrimshaw, decorative filing. **Prices:** $60 to $150; some to $300. **Remarks:** Part-time maker; first knife sold in 1977. **Mark:** Signature.

BRIGHTWELL, MARK, 21104 Creekside Dr., Leander, TX 78641, Phone: 512-267-4110
Specialties: Fancy and plain folders of his design. **Patterns:** Fighters, hunters and gents, some traditional. **Technical:** Hollow- or flat- grinds ATS-34, D2, custom Damascus; elaborate filework; heat-treats. Extensive choice of natural handle materials; no synthetics. **Prices:** $300 to $1500. **Remarks:** Full-time maker. **Mark:** Last name.

BRITTON, TIM, 5645 Murray Rd., Winston-Salem, NC 27106, Phone: 336-922-9582 336-922-9582, Fax: 336-923-2062
Specialties: Small and simple working knives, sgian dubhs and special tactical designs. **Technical:** Forges and grinds stainless steel. **Prices:** $110 to $600. **Remarks:** Veteran knife maker. **Mark:** Etched signature.

BROADWELL, DAVID, PO Box 4314, Wichita Falls, TX 76308, Phone: 940-692-1727, Fax: 940-692-4003
Specialties: Sculpted high-art straight and folding knives. **Patterns:** Daggers, sub-hilted fighters, folders, sculpted art knives and some Bowies. **Technical:** Grinds mostly Damascus; carves; prefers natural handle materials, including stone. Some embellishment. **Prices:** $350 to $3000; some higher. **Remarks:** Full-time maker; first knife sold in 1982. **Mark:** Stylized emblem bisecting "B"/with last name below.

BROCK, KENNETH L., PO Box 375, 207 N Skinner Rd., Allenspark, CO 80510, Phone: 303-747-2547
Specialties: Custom designs, Full-tang working knives and button lock folders of his design. **Patterns:** Hunters, miniatures and minis. **Technical:** Flat-grinds D2 and 440C; makes own sheaths; heat-treats. **Prices:** $50 to $500. **Remarks:** Full-time maker; first knife sold in 1978. **Mark:** Last name, city, state and serial number.

BROMLEY, PETER, Bromley Knives, 1408 S Bettman, Spokane, WA 99212, Phone: 509-534-4235
Specialties: Period Bowies, folder, hunting knives - all sizes and shapes. **Patterns:** Bowies, boot knives, hunters, utility, folder, working knives. Technical; High-carbon steel (1084, 1095 and 5160). Stock removal and forge. **Prices:** $85 to $750. **Remarks:** Almost full-time, first knife sold in 1987. ABS Journeyman Smith. **Mark:** Bromley, Spokane, WA.

BROOKER, DENNIS, Rt. 1, Box 12A, Derby, IA 50068, Phone: 515-533-2103
Specialties: Fancy straight knives and folders of his design. **Patterns:** Hunters, folders and boots. **Technical:** Forges and grinds. Full-time engraver and designer; instruction available. **Prices:** Moderate to upscale. **Remarks:** Part-time maker. Takes no orders; sells only completed work. **Mark:** Name.

BROOKS, BUZZ, 2345 Yosemite Dr., Los Angles, CA 90041, Phone: 323-256-2892

BROOKS, MICHAEL, 4645 52nd St .Apt. F4, Lubbock, TX 79414-3802
Specialties: Working straight knives of his design or to customer specs. **Patterns:** Tantos, swords, Bowies, hunters, skinners and boots. **Technical:** Grinds 440C, D2 and ATS-34; offers wide variety of handle materials. **Prices:** $40 to $800. **Remarks:** Part-time maker; first knife sold in 1985. **Mark:** Initials.

BROOKS, STEVE R., 1610 Dunn Ave., Walkerville, MT 59701, Phone: 406-782-5114
Specialties: Working straight knives and folders; period pieces. **Patterns:** Hunters, Bowies and camp knives; folding lockers; axes, tomahawks and buckskinner knives; swords and stilettos. **Technical:** Forges O1, Damascus and mosaic Damascus. Some knives come embellished. **Prices:** $150 to $2000. **Remarks:** Full-time maker; first knife sold in 1982. **Mark:** Lazy initials.

BROOME, THOMAS A., 1212 E. Aliak Ave., Kenai, AK 99611-8205, Phone: 907-283-9128
Specialties: Working hunters and folders **Patterns:** Traditional and custom orders. **Technical:** Grinds ATS-34, BG-42, CPM-S30V. **Prices:** $175 to $350. **Remarks:** Full-time maker; first knife sold in 1979. Doing business as Thom's Custom Knives. **Mark:** Full name, city, state. **Other:** Doing business as: Alaskan Man O; Steel Knives.

BROTHERS, ROBERT L., 989 Philpott Rd., Colville, WA 99114, Phone: 509-684-8922
Specialties: Traditional working and using straight knives and folders of his design and to customer specs. **Patterns:** Bowies, fighters and hunters. **Technical:** Grinds D2; forges Damascus. Makes own Damascus from saw steel wire rope and chain; part-time goldsmith and stone-setter.

Prices: $100 to $400; some higher. **Remarks:** Part-time maker; first knife sold in 1986. **Mark:** Initials and year made.

BROWER, MAX, 2016 Story St., Boone, IA 50036, Phone: 515-432-2938
Specialties: Working/using straight knives. **Patterns:** Bowies, hunters and boots. **Technical:** Grinds 440C and ATS-34. **Prices:** Start at $150. **Remarks:** Spare-time maker; first knife sold in 1981. **Mark:** Last name.

BROWN, TROY L., 22945 W. 867 Rd., Park Hill, OK 74451, Phone: 918-457-4128
Specialties: Working and using knives and folders. **Patterns:** Bowies, hunters, folders and scagel-style. **Technical:** Forges 5160, 52100, 1084; makes his own Damascus. Prefers stag, wood and Micarta for handles. Offers engraved bolsters and guards. **Prices:** $150 to $750. **Remarks:** Full-time maker; first knife sold in 1994. Knives. **Mark:** Troy Brown. **Other:** Doing business as Elk Creek Forge.

BROWN, ROB E., PO Box 15107, Emerald Hill 6011, Port Elizabeth, SOUTH AFRICA, Phone: 27-41-3661086, Fax: 27-41-4511731
Specialties: Contemporary-designed straight knives and period pieces. **Patterns:** Utility knives, hunters, boots, fighters and daggers. **Technical:** Grinds 440C, D2, ATS-34 and commercial Damascus. Knives mostly mirror finished; African handle materials. **Prices:** $100 to $1500. **Remarks:** Full-time maker; first knife sold in 1985. **Mark:** Name and country.

BROWN, DENNIS G., 1633 N. 197TH Pl., Shoreline, WA 98133, Phone: 206-542-3997

BROWN, HAROLD E., 3654 N.W. Hwy. 72, Arcadia, FL 34266, Phone: 863-494-7514
Specialties: Fancy and exotic working knives. **Patterns:** Folders, slip-lock, locking several kinds. **Technical:** Grinds D2, 440C and ATS-34. Embellishment available. **Prices:** $175 to $1000. **Remarks:** Part-time maker; first knife sold in 1976. **Mark:** Name and city with logo.

BROWN, JIM, 1097 Fernleigh Cove, Little Rock, AR 72210

BROWNE, RICK, 980 West 13th St., Upland, CA 91786, Phone: 909-985-1728
Specialties: Sheffield pattern pocket knives. **Patterns:** Hunters, fighters and daggers. No heavy-duty knives. **Technical:** Grinds ATS-34. **Prices:** Start at $450. **Remarks:** Part-time maker; first knife sold in 1975. **Mark:** R.E. Browne, Upland, CA.

BROWNING, STEVEN W., 3400 Harrison Rd., Benton, AR 72015, Phone: 501-316-2450

BRUNCKHORST, LYLE, Country Village, 23706 7th Ave. SE, Ste. B, Bothell, WA 98021, Phone: 425-402-3484
Specialties: Traditional working and using straight knives and folders of his design. **Patterns:** Bowies, hunters and locking folders. **Technical:** Grinds ATS-34; forges 5160 and his own Damascus. Iridescent RR spike knives. Offers scrimshaw, inlays and animal carvings in horn handles. **Prices:** $225 to $750; some to $3750. **Remarks:** Full-time maker; first knife sold in 1976. Doing business as Bronk's Knife works. **Mark:** Bucking horse.

BRUNER, RICK, 7756 Aster Lane, Jenison, MI 49428, Phone: 616-457-0403
Specialties: Sheath making.

BRUNER JR., FRED, BRUNER BLADES, E10910W Hilldale Dr., Fall Creek, WI 54742, Phone: 715-877-2496

BRUNETTA, DAVID, PO Box 4972, Laguna Beach, CA 92652, Phone: 714-497-9611
Specialties: Straights, folders and art knives. **Patterns:** Bowies, camp/hunting, folders, fighters. **Technical:** Grinds ATS-34, D2, BG42. forges O1, 52100, 5160, 1095, makes own Damascus. **Prices:** $300 to $9000. **Mark:** Circle DB logo with last name straight or curved.

BRYAN, TOM, 14822 S Gilbert Rd., Gilbert, AZ 85296, Phone: 480-812-8529
Specialties: Straight and folding knives. **Patterns:** Drop-point hunter fighters. **Technical:** ATS-34, 154CM, 440C and A2. **Prices:** $150 to $800. **Remarks:** Part-time maker; sold first knife in 1994. **Mark:** T. Bryan. **Other:** DBA as T. Bryan Knives.

BUCHMAN, BILL, 63312 South Rd., Bend, OR 97701, Phone: 503-382-8851
Specialties: Working straight knives. **Patterns:** Hunters, Bowies, fighters and boots. Makes full line of leather craft and saddle maker knives. **Technical:** Forges 440C and Sandvik 15N20. Prefers 440C for saltwater. **Prices:** $95 to $400. **Remarks:** Full-time maker; first knife sold in 1982. **Mark:** Initials or last name.

BUCHNER, BILL, PO Box 73, Idleyld Park, OR 97447, Phone: 541-498-2247
Specialties: Working straight knives, kitchen knives and high-art knives of his design. **Technical:** Uses W1, L6 and his own Damascus. Invented

"spectrum metal" for letter openers, folder handles and jewelry. Likes sculpturing and carving in Damascus. **Prices:** $40 to $3000; some higher. **Remarks:** Full-time maker; first knife sold in 1978. **Mark:** Signature.

BUCHOLZ, MARK A., PO Box 82, Holualoa, HI 96725, Phone: 808-322-4045
Specialties: Liner lock folders. **Patterns:** Hunters and fighters. **Technical:** Grinds ATS-34. **Prices:** Upscale. **Remarks:** Full-time maker; first knife sold in 1976. **Mark:** Name, city and state in buffalo skull logo or signature.

BUCKBEE, DONALD M., 243 South Jackson Trail, Grayling, MI 49738, Phone: 517-348-1386
Specialties: Working straight knives, some fancy, in standard patterns; concentrating on kitchen knives. **Patterns:** Kitchen knives, Bowies. **Technical:** Grinds D2, 440C, ATS-34. Makes ultra-lights in hunter patterns. **Prices:** $100 to $250; some to $350. **Remarks:** Part-time maker; first knife sold in 1984. **Mark:** Antlered bee—a buck bee.

BUCKNER, JIMMIE H., PO Box 162, Putney, GA 31782, Phone: 912-436-4182
Specialties: Camp knives, Bowies (one-of-a-kind), liner-lock folders, tomahawks, camp axes, neck knives for law enforcement and hide-out knives for body guards and professional people. **Patterns:** Hunters, camp knives, Bowies. **Technical:** Forges 1084, 5160 and Damascus (own), own heat treats. **Prices:** $195 to $795 and up. **Remarks:** Full-time maker; first knife sold in 1980, ABS Master Smith. **Mark:** Name over spade.

BUEBENDORF, ROBERT E., 108 Lazybrooke Rd., Monroe, CT 06468, Phone: 203-452-1769
Specialties: Traditional and fancy straight knives of his design. **Patterns:** Hand-makes and embellishes belt buckle knives. **Technical:** Forges and grinds 440C, O1, W2, 1095, his own Damascus and 154CM. **Prices:** $200 to $500. **Remarks:** Full-time maker; first knife sold in 1978. **Mark:** First and middle initials, last name and MAKER.

BULLARD, BILL, Rt. 5, Box 35, Andalusia, AL 36420, Phone: 334-222-9003
Specialties: Traditional working and using straight knives and folders of his design. **Patterns:** Hunters, slip-joint folders and utility/camp knives and folders to customer specs. **Technical:** Forges Damascus, cable. Offers filework. **Prices:** $100 to $500; some to $1500. **Remarks:** Part-time maker; first knife sold in 1974. Doing business as Five Runs Forge. **Mark:** Last name stamped on ricasso.

BULLARD, RANDALL, 7 Mesa Dr., Canyon, TX 79015, Phone: 806-655-0590
Specialties: Working/using straight knives and folders of his design or to customer specs. **Patterns:** Hunters, locking folders and slip-joint folders. **Technical:** Grinds O1, ATS-34 and 440C. Does file work. **Prices:** $125 to $300; some to $500. **Remarks:** Part-time maker; first knife sold in 1993. Doing business as Bullard Custom Knives. **Mark:** First and middle initials, last name, maker, city and state.

BULLARD, TOM, 117 MC 8068, Flippin, AR 72634, Phone: 870-453-3421
Specialties: Armadillo handle material on hunter and folders. **Patterns:** Bowies, hunters, single and 2-blade trappers, lockback folders. **Technical:** Grinds 440-C, ATS-34, 0-1, commercial Damascus. **Prices:** $150 and up. **Remarks:** Offers filework and engraving by Norvell Foster and Terry Thies. Does not make screw-together knives. **Mark:** T Bullard.

BUMP, BRUCE D., 1103 Rex Ln., Walla Walla, WA 99362, Phone: 509 522-2219
Specialties: Traditional and Mosaic Damascus. **Patterns:** Black powder pistol/knife combinations also gun/hawk. **Technical:** Enjoy the 15th-18th century "dual threat" weapons. **Prices:** $350 to $10,000. **Remarks:** American Bladesmith Society Master Smith 2003. **Mark:** Bruce D. Bump Bruce D Bump Custom Walla Walla WA.

BURAK, CHET, KNIFE SERVICES PHOTOGRAPHER, PO Box 14383, E Providence, RI 02914, Phone: 401-431-0625, Fax: 401-434-9821

BURDEN, JAMES, 405 Kelly St., Burkburnett, TX 76354

BURGER, FRED, Box 436, Munster 4278, Kwa-Zulu Natal, SOUTH AFRICA, Phone: 27 393216
Specialties: Sword canes and tactical walking sticks. **Patterns:** 440C and carbon steel blades. **Technical:** Double hollow ground and Poniard-style blades. **Prices:** $190 to $600. **Remarks:** Full-time maker with son, Barry, since 1987. **Mark:** Last name in oval pierced by a dagger. **Other:** Member South African Guild.

BURGER, PON, 12 Glenwood Ave., Woodlands, Bulawayo, Zimbabwe 75514
Specialties: Collector's items. **Patterns:** Fighters, locking folders of traditional styles, buckles. **Technical:** Scrimshaws 440C blade. Uses polished buffalo horn with brass fittings. Cased in buffalo hide book. **Prices:** $450

to $1100. **Remarks:** Full-time maker; first knife sold in 1973. Doing business as Burger Products. **Mark:** Spirit of Africa.

BURKE, BILL, 315 Courthouse Dr., Salmon, ID 83467, Phone: 208-756-3797

Specialties: Hand-forged working knives. **Patterns:** Fowler pronghorn, clip point and drop point hunters. **Technical:** Forges 52100 and 5160. Makes own Damascus from 15N20 and 1084. **Prices:** $250 to $2000. **Remarks:** Dedicated to fixed-blade high-performance knives. **Mark:** Initials connected. **Other:** Also make "Ed Fowler" miniatures.

BURKE, DAN, 22001 Ole Barn Rd., Edmond, OK 73034, Phone: 405-341-3406, Fax: 405-340-3333

Specialties: Slip joint folders. **Patterns:** Traditional folders. **Technical:** Grinds D2 and BG-42. Prefers natural handle materials; heat-treats. **Prices:** $440 to $1900. **Remarks:** Full-time maker; first knife sold in 1976. **Mark:** First initial and last name.

BURNETT, MAX, 537 Old Dug Mtn. Rd., Paris, AR 72855, Phone: 501-963-2767

Specialties: Forging with coal/charcoal; some stock removal. **Patterns:** Hunters, Bowies, camp, tactical, neck knives and kydex sheaths. **Technical:** Steels used: 1084, 1095, 52100, 5160, L6, 01 and others available. **Prices:** $50 and up for neck knives/Bowies $250 and up. **Remarks:** Full-time since March 2000. **Mark:** M.OGG and omega symbol.

BURRIS, PATRICK R., 11078 Crystal Lynn C.t, Jacksonville, FL 32226, Phone: 904-757-3938

Specialties: Traditional straight knives and locking liner folders. **Technical:** Flat grinds D-2, ATS-34, 154CM, CPM 30V, Damascus. Most knives include custom sheath. **Remarks:** Part-time maker, Charter member of Florida Knifemakers Association, Probationary Member Knifemakers Guild.

BURROWS, CHUCK, Wild Rose Trading Co, PO Box 5174, Durango, CO 81301, Phone: 970-259-8396

Specialties: Presentation knives, hawks, and sheaths based on the styles of the American frontier incorporating carving, beadwork, rawhide, braintan, and other period correct materials. Other period knives such as Scottish dirks. **Patterns:** Bowies, dags, tomahawks, war clubs, and all other 18th-19th century frontier-style edged weapons and tools. **Technical:** Carbon steel only: 5160, 1080/1084, 1095, 01, Damascus available on request. Forged knives, hawks, etc. are made in collaboration with bladesmiths: Gib Guignard (under the name of CactusRose), Dana Acker, and Mark Williams. Blades are usually forge finished and all items are given an aged, period look. **Prices:** $500 plus. **Remarks:** Full-time maker, first knife sold 1973, 40+ years experience working leather. **Mark:** A lazy eight or lazy eight with a capital T at the center. On leather either the lazy eight with T or a WRTC makers stamp.

BURROWS, STEPHEN R., 3532 Michigan, Kansas City, MO 64109, Phone: 816-921-1573

Specialties: Fantasy straight knives of his design, to customer specs and in standard patterns; period pieces. **Patterns:** Fantasy, bird and trout knives, daggers, fighters and hunters. **Technical:** Forges 5160 and 1095 high-carbon steel, O1 and his Damascus. Offers lost wax casting in bronze or silver of cross guards and pommels. **Prices:** $65 to $600; some to $2000. **Remarks:** Full-time maker; first knife sold in 1983. Doing business as Gypsy Silk. **Mark:** Etched name.

BUSFIELD, JOHN, 153 Devonshire Circle, Roanoke Rapids, NC 27870, Phone: 252-537-3949, Fax: 252-537-8704

Specialties: Investor-grade folders; high-grade working straight knives. **Patterns:** Original price-style and trailing-point interframe and sculpted-frame folders, drop-point hunters and semi-skinners. **Technical:** Grinds 154CM and ATS-34. Offers interframes, gold frames and inlays; uses jade, agate and lapis. **Prices:** $275 to $2000. **Remarks:** Full-time maker; first knife sold in 1979. **Mark:** Last name and address.

BUSSE, JERRY, 11651 Co. Rd. 12, Wauseon, OH 43567, Phone: 419-923-6471

Specialties: Working straight knives. **Patterns:** Heavy combat knives and camp knives. **Technical:** Grinds D2, A2, INFI. **Prices:** $1100 to $3500. **Remarks:** Full-time maker; first knife sold in 1983. **Mark:** Last name in logo.

BUTLER, JOHN R., 20162 6TH Ave. N.E., Shoreline, WA 98155, Phone: 206-362-3847

BUTLER, JOHN, 777 Tyre Rd., Havana, FL 32333, Phone: 850-539-5742

Specialties: Hunters, Bowies, period. **Technical:** Damascus, 52100, 5160, L6 steels. **Prices:** $80 and up. **Remarks:** Making knives since 1986. **Mark:** JB. **Other:** Journeyman (ABS).

BUTLER, BART, 822 Seventh St., Ramona, CA 92065, Phone: 760-789-6431

BYBEE, BARRY J., 795 Lock Rd. E., Cadiz, KY 42211-8615

Specialties: Working straight knives of his design. **Patterns:** Hunters, fighters, boot knives, tantos and Bowies. **Technical:** Grinds ATS-34, 440C. Likes stag and Micarta for handle materials. **Prices:** $125 to $200; some to $1000. **Remarks:** Part-time maker; first knife sold in 1968. **Mark:** Arrowhead logo with name, city and state.

BYRD, WESLEY L., 189 Countryside Dr., Evensville, TN 37332, Phone: 423-775-3826

Specialties: Hunters, fighters, Bowies, dirks, sign dubh, utility, and camp knives. **Patterns:** Wire rope, random patterns.Twists, W's, Ladder, Kite Tail. **Technical:** Uses 52100, 1084, 5160, L6, and 15n20. **Prices:** Starting at $180. **Remarks:** Prefer to work with customer for their design preferences. **Mark:** BYRD, WB<X. **Other:** ABS Journeyman Smith.

C

CABE, JERRY (BUDDY), 62 McClaren Ln., Hattieville, AR 72063, Phone: 501-354-3581

CABRERA, SERGIO B., 25711 Frampton Ave. Apt. 113, Harbor City, CA 90710

CAFFREY, EDWARD J., 2608 Central Ave. West, Great Falls, MT 59404, Phone: 406-727-9102

Specialties: One-of-a-kind, collector quality pieces, working/using knives; will accept some customer designs. **Patterns:** Folders, Bowies, hunters, fighters, camp/utility, some hawks and hatchets. **Technical:** Forges his own mosaic Damascus, 52100, 6150, 1080/1084, W-1, W-2, some cable and/or chain Damascus. Offers S30V for those who demand stainless. **Prices:** Starting at $140; typical hunters start at $350; prices for exotic mosaic Damascus pieces can range to $5000. **Remarks:** Retired military; ABS Master Smith. Full-time maker; first knife sold in 1989. **Mark:** Stamped last name with MS on straight knives. Etched last name with MS on folders.

CAIRNES JR., CARROLL B., RT. 1 Box 324, Palacios, TX 77465, Phone: 369-588-6815

CALDWELL, BILL, 255 Rebecca, West Monroe, LA 71292, Phone: 318-323-3025

Specialties: Straight knives and folders with machined bolsters and liners. **Patterns:** Fighters, Bowies, survival knives, tomahawks, razors and push knives. **Technical:** Owns and operates a very large, well-equipped blacksmith and bladesmith shop extant with six large forges and eight power hammers. **Prices:** $400 to $3500; some to $10,000. **Remarks:** Full-time maker and self-styled blacksmith; first knife sold in 1962. **Mark:** Wild Bill and Sons.

CALLAHAN, F. TERRY, PO Box 880, Boerne, TX 78006, Phone: 830-981-8274, Fax: 830-981-8279

Specialties: Custom hand-forged edged knives, collectible and functional. **Patterns:** Bowies, folders, daggers, hunters, camp knives and swords. **Technical:** Forges 5160, 1095 and his own Damascus. Offers filework and handmade sheaths. **Prices:** $125 to $2000. **Remarks:** First knife sold in 1990. **Mark:** Initials inside a keystone symbol. **Other:** ABS/Journeyman Bladesmith.

CALLAHAN, ERRETT, 2 Fredonia, Lynchburg, VA 24503

Specialties: Obsidian knives. **Patterns:** Modern-styles and Stone Age replicas. **Technical:** Flakes and knaps to order. **Prices:** $100 to $3400. **Remarks:** Part-time maker; first flint blades sold in 1974. **Mark:** Blade—engraved name, year and arrow; handle—signed edition, year and unit number.

CALVERT JR., ROBERT W. (BOB), 911 Julia, PO Box 858, Rayville, LA 71269, Phone: 318-728-4113, Fax: (318) 728-0000

Specialties: Using and hunting knives; your design or mine. Since 1990. **Patterns:** Forges own Damascus; all patterns. **Technical:** 5160, D2, 52100, 1084. Prefers natural handle material. **Prices:** $150 and up. **Remarks:** TOMB Member ABS, Journeyman Smith. **Mark:** Calvert (Block) J S.

CAMERER, CRAIG, 287 E. Main, Hettick, IL 62649, Phone: 618-778-5704

Specialties: Everyday carry knives, hunters and Bowies. **Patterns:** D-guard, historical recreations and fighters. **Technical:** Most of his knives are forged to shape. **Prices:** $100 and up. **Remarks:** Member of the ABS and PKA.

CAMERON, RON G., PO Box 183, Logandale, NV 89021, Phone: 702-398-3356

Specialties: Fancy and embellished working/using straight knives and folders of his design. **Patterns:** Bowies, hunters and utility/camp knives. **Technical:** Grinds ATS-34, 440C and Devin Thomas Damascus or his own Damascus. Does filework, fancy pins, mokume fittings. Uses exotic hardwoods, stag and Micarta for handles. **Prices:** $150-$500 some to $1000. **Remarks:** Part-time maker; first knife sold in 1994. Doing business as Cameron Handmade Knives. **Mark:** Last name, town, state or last name.

CAMERON HOUSE, 2001 Delaney Rd. Se., Salem, OR 97306, Phone: 503-585-3286
Specialties: Working straight knives. **Patterns:** Hunters, Bowies, Fighters. **Technical:** Grinds ATS-34, 530V, 154CM. **Remarks:** Part-time maker, first knife. sold in 1993. **Prices:** $150 and up. **Mark:** HOUSE.

CAMPBELL, DICK, 20000 Silver Ranch Rd., Conifer, CO 80433, Phone: 303-697-0150
Specialties: Working straight knives, period pieces. **Patterns:** Hunters, fighters, boots: 19th century Bowies. **Technical:** Grinds 440C, 154CM. **Prices:** $200 to $2500. **Remarks:** Full-time maker. First knife sold in 1975. **Mark:** Name.

CAMPBELL, COURTNAY M., PO Box 23009, Columbia, SC 29224, Phone: 803-787-0151

CAMPOS, IVAN, R.XI de Agosto, 107, Tatui, SP, BRAZIL 18270-000, Phone: 00-55-15-2518092, Fax: 00-55-15-2594368
Specialties: Brazilian handmade and antique knives.

CANDRELLA, JOE, 1219 Barness Dr., Warminster, PA 18974, Phone: 215-675-0143
Specialties: Working straight knives, some fancy. **Patterns:** Daggers, boots, Bowies. **Technical:** Grinds 440C and 154CM. **Prices:** $100 to $200; some to $1000. **Remarks:** Part-time maker; first knife sold in 1985. Does business as Franjo. **Mark:** FRANJO with knife as J.

CANNADY, DANIEL L., Box 301, Allendale, SC 29810, Phone: 803-584-2813
Specialties: Working straight knives and folders in standard patterns. **Patterns:** Drop-point hunters, Bowies, skinners, fishing knives with concave grind, steak knives and kitchen cutlery. **Technical:** Grinds D2, 440C and ATS-34. **Prices:** $65 to $325; some to $500. **Remarks:** Full-time maker; first knife sold in 1980. **Mark:** Last name above Allendale, S.C.

CANNON, RAYMOND W., PO Box 1412, Homer, AK 99603, Phone: 907-235-7779
Specialties: Fancy working knives, folders and swords of his design or to customer specs; many one-of-a-kind pieces. **Patterns:** Bowies, daggers and skinners. **Technical:** Forges and grinds O1, A6, 52100, 5160, his combinations for his own Damascus. **Remarks:** First knife sold in 1984. **Mark:** Cannon Alaska or "Hand forged by Wes Cannon".

CANNON, DAN, 9500 Leon, Dallas, TX 75217, Phone: 972-557-0268
Specialties: Damascus, hand forged. **Patterns:** Bowies, hunters, folders. **Prices:** $300. **Remarks:** Full-time maker. **Mark:** CANNON D.

CANOY, ANDREW B., 3420 Fruchey Ranch Rd., Hubbard Lake, MI 49747, Phone: 810-266-6039

CANTER, RONALD E., 96 Bon Air Circle, Jackson, TN 38305, Phone: 731-668-1780
Specialties: Traditional working knives to customer specs. **Patterns:** Beavertail skinners, Bowies, hand axes and folding lockers. **Technical:** Grinds A1, 440C and 154CM. **Prices:** $65 to $250; some $500 and higher. **Remarks:** Spare-time maker; first knife sold in 1973. **Mark:** Three last initials intertwined.

CANTRELL, KITTY D., 19720 Hwy. 78, Ramona, CA 92076, Phone: 760-788-8304

CAPDEPON, ROBERT, 829 Vatican Rd., Carencro, LA 70520, Phone: 337-896-8753, Fax: 318-896-8753
Specialties: Traditional straight knives and folders of his design. **Patterns:** Boots, hunters and locking folders. **Technical:** Grinds ATS-34, 440C and D2. Hand-rubbed finish on blades. Likes natural horn materials for handles, including ivory. Offers engraving. **Prices:** $250 to $750. **Remarks:** Full-time maker; first knife made in 1992. **Mark:** Last name.

CAPDEPON, RANDY, 553 Joli Rd., Carencro, LA 70520, Phone: 318-896-4113, Fax: 318-896-8753
Specialties: Straight knives and folders of his design. **Patterns:** Hunters and locking folders. **Technical:** Grinds ATS-34, 440C and D2. **Prices:** $200 to $600. **Remarks:** Part-time maker; first knife made in 1992. Doing business as Capdepon Knives. **Mark:** Last name.

CAREY JR., CHARLES W., 1003 Minter Rd., Griffin, GA 30223, Phone: 770-228-8994
Specialties: Working and using knives of his design and to customer specs; period pieces. **Patterns:** Fighters, hunters, utility/camp knives and forged-to-shape miniatures. **Technical:** Forges 5160, old files and cable. Offers filework; ages some of his knives. **Prices:** $35 to $400. **Remarks:** Part-time maker; first knife sold in 1991. **Mark:** Knife logo.

CARLISLE, JEFF, PO Box 282 12753 Hwy. 200, Simms, MT 59477, Phone: 406-264-5693

CARLISLE, FRANK, 5930 Hereford, Detroit, MI 48224, Phone: 313-882-8349
Specialties: Fancy/embellished and fantasy folders of his design. **Patterns:** Hunters, locking folders and swords. **Technical:** Grinds Damascus and stainless. **Prices:** $80 to $300. **Remarks:** Full-time maker; first knife sold in 1993. Doing business as Carlisle Cutlery. **Mark:** Last name.

CARLSON, KELLY, 54 S. Holt Hill, Antrim, NH 03440, Phone: 603-588-2765, Fax: 603-588-4223
Specialties: Unique folders of maker's own design. **Patterns:** One-of-a-kind, artistic folders, mostly of liner-lock design, along with interpretations of traditional designs. **Technical:** Grinds and heat treats S30V, D2, ATS34, stainless and carbon Damascus steels. Prefers hand sanded finishes and natural ivories and pearls, in conjunction with decorative accents obtained from mosaic Damascus, Damascus and various exotic materials. **Prices:** $600 to $2000. **Remarks:** Full-time maker as of 2002, first knife sold in 1975.

CARLSSON, MARC BJORN, Hansgade 31, 4000 Roskilde, DENMARK, Phone: +45 46 35 97 24, Fax: +45 33 91 17 99
Specialties: High-tech knives and folders. **Patterns:** Skinners, tantos, swords, folders and art knives. **Technical:** Grinds ATS-34, Elmax and D2. **Prices:** Start at $250. **Remarks:** Doing business as "Mememto Mori", professional jeweler and knife maker. Doing business as Metal Point. **Mark:** First name in runic letters within Viking ship.

CARNAHAN, CHARLES A., 27 George Arnold Lane, Green Spring, WV 26722, Phone: 304-492-5891
Specialties: Hand forged fixed blade knives. **Patterns:** Bowies and hunters. **Technical:** Steels used; 5160, 1095, 1085, L6 and A023-E. **Prices:** $300 - $2000. **Remarks:** Part-time maker. First knife sold in 1991. Knives all made by hand forging, no stock removal. **Mark:** Last name.

CAROLINA CUSTOM KNIVES, SEE TOMMY MCNABB

CARPENTER, RONALD W., RT. 4 Box 323, Jasper, TX 75951, Phone: 409-384-4087

CARR, TIM, 3660 Pillon Rd., Muskegon, MI 49445, Phone: 231-766-3582
Specialties: Hunters, camp knives. **Patterns:** Mine or yours. **Technical:** Hand forged 52100 and Damascus. **Prices:** $125 to $700. **Remarks:** Part-time maker. **Mark:** The letter combined from maker's initials TRC.

CARROLL, CHAD, 12182 McClelland, Grant, MI 49327, Phone: 231-834-9183
Specialties: Hunters, Bowies, folders, swords, tomahawks. **Patterns:** Fixed blades, folders. **Prices:** $100-$2000. **Remarks:** ABS Journeyman-May 2002. **Mark:** (a backward C next to a forward C, maker's initials).

CARSON, HAROLD J. "KIT", 1076 Brizendine Lane, Vine Grove, KY 40175, Phone: 270 877-6300, Fax: 270 877 6338
Specialties: Military fixed blades and art pieces. **Patterns:** Fighters, D handles, daggers, combat folders and Crosslock-styles, tactical folders, tactical fixed blades. **Technical:** Grinds Stellite 6K, Talonite, CPM steels, Damascus. **Prices:** $400 to $750; some to $5000. **Remarks:** Full-time maker; first knife sold in 1973. **Mark:** Name stamped or engraved.

CARTER, MURRAY M., 2506 Toyo Oka, Ueki Kamoto, Kumamoto, JAPAN 861-0163, Phone: 81-96-272-6759
Specialties: Traditional Japanese cutlery, utilizing San soh ko (3 layer) or Kata-ha (two layer) blade construction. Laminated neck knives, traditional Japanese etc. **Patterns:** Works from over 200 standard Japanese and North American designs. **Technical:** Forges or grinds Hitachi white steel #1, Hitachi blue super steel or Hitachi ZDP247 stainless steel exclusively. Forges own Damascus. **Prices:** $30 to $3000. **Remarks:** Full-time maker. First knife sold in 1989. Owner and designer of "Muteki" brand knives. **Mark:** Name with Japanese character on forged pieces. "Muteki" with Japanese characters on stock-removal blades.

CARTER, FRED, 5219 Deer Creek Rd., Wichita Falls, TX 76302, Phone: 904-723-4020
Specialties: High-art investor-class straight knives; some working hunters and fighters. **Patterns:** Classic daggers, Bowies; interframe, stainless and blued steel folders with gold inlay. **Technical:** Grinds a variety of steels. Uses no glue or solder. Engraves and inlays. **Prices:** Generally upscale. **Remarks:** Full-time maker. **Mark:** Signature in oval logo.

CASH, TERRY, 113 Sequoyah Cir., Canton, GA 30115, Phone: 770-345-2031
Specialties: Railroad spike knives, traditional straight knives, working/ using knives. **Patterns:** Bowies, hunters, utility, camp knives; standard, own design or to customer spec. **Technical:** Forges 5160, 1095, 52100, heat treatment, makes leather sheaths, presentation boxes and makes own Damascus. **Prices:** $125 to $800. **Remarks:** Full-time maker; first knife sold 1995. **Mark:** First initial and last name. **Other:** Doing business as Cherokee Forge.

CASHEN, KEVIN R., 5615 Tyler St., Hubbardston, MI 48845, Phone: 989-981-6780
Specialties: Working straight knives, high art pattern welded swords, traditional renaissance and ethnic pieces. **Patterns:** Hunters, Bowies, utility knives, swords, daggers. **Technical:** Forges 1095, 1084 and his own O1/L6 Damascus. **Prices:** $100 to $4000+. **Remarks:** Full-time maker; first knife sold in 1985. Doing business as Matherton Forge. **Mark:** Black letter Old English initials and Master Smith stamp.

CASTEEL, DOUGLAS, PO Box 63, Monteagle, TN 37356, Phone: 931-723-0851, Fax: 931-723-1856
Specialties: One-of-a-kind collector-class period pieces. **Patterns:** Daggers, Bowies, swords and folders. **Technical:** Grinds 440C; makes his own Damascus. Offers gold and silver castings. **Prices:** Upscale. **Remarks:** Full-time maker; first knife sold in 1982. **Mark:** Last name.

CASTEEL, DIANNA, P.O .Box 63, Monteagle, TN 37356, Phone: 931-723-0851, Fax: 931-723-1856
Specialties: Small, delicate daggers and miniatures; most knives one-of-a-kind. **Patterns:** Daggers, boot knives, fighters and miniatures. **Technical:** Grinds 440C; makes her own Damascus. **Prices:** Start at $350; miniatures start at $250. **Remarks:** Full-time maker. **Mark:** Di in script.

CASTON, DARRIEL, 3725 Duran Circle, Sacramento, CA 95821, Phone: 916-359-0613
Specialties: Investment grade jade handle folders of his design and gentleman folders. **Patterns:** Folders - slipjoints and lockback. Will be making linerlocks in the near future. **Technical:** Small gentleman folders for office and desk warriors. Grinds ATS-34, 154CM, S30V and Damascus. **Prices:** $250-$900. **Remarks:** Part-time maker; won best new maker at first show in Sept 2004. **Mark:** Etched rocket ship with "Darriel Caston" or just "Caston" on inside spring on Damascus and engraved knives.

CATOE, DAVID R., 4024 Heutte Dr., Norfolk, VA 23518, Phone: 757-480-3191
Technical: Does own forging, Damascus and heat treatments. **Price:** $200 to $500; some higher. **Remarks:** Part-time maker; trained by Dan Maragni 1985-1988; first knife sold 1989. **Mark:** Leaf of a camillia.

CAWTHORNE, CHRISTOPHER A., PO Box 604, Wrangell, AK 99929
Specialties: High-carbon steel, cable wire rope, silver wire inlay. **Patterns:** Forge welded Damascus and wire rope, random pattern. **Technical:** Hand forged, 50 lb little giant power hammer, W-2, 0-1, L6, 1095. **Prices:** $650-$2500. **Remarks:** School ABS 1985 w/bill moran, hand forged, heat treat. **Mark:** Cawthorne, forged in stamp.

CENTOFANTE, FRANK, PO Box 928, Madisonville, TN 37354-0928, Phone: 423-442-5767
Specialties: Fancy working folders. **Patterns:** Lockers and liner locks. **Technical:** Grinds ATS-34; hand-rubbed satin finish on blades. **Prices:** $600 to $1200. **Remarks:** Full-time maker; first knife sold in 1968. **Mark:** Name, city, state.

CHAFFEE, JEFF L., 14314 N. Washington St., PO Box 1, Morris, IN 47033, Phone: 812-934-6350
Specialties: Fancy working and utility folders and straight knives. **Patterns:** Fighters, dagger, hunter and locking folders. **Technical:** Grinds commercial Damascus, 440C, ATS-34, D2 and O1. Prefers natural handle materials. **Prices:** $350 to $2000. **Remarks:** Part-time maker; first knife sold in 1988. **Mark:** Last name.

CHAMBERLAIN, JOHN B., 1621 Angela St., Wenatchee, WA 98801, Phone: 509-663-6720
Specialties: Fancy working and using straight knives mainly to customer specs, though starting to make some standard patterns. **Patterns:** Hunters, Bowies and daggers. **Technical:** Grinds D2, ATS-34, M2, M4 and L6. **Prices:** $60 to $190; some to $2500. **Remarks:** Full-time maker; first knife sold in 1943. **Mark:** Name, city, state.

CHAMBERLAIN, CHARLES R., PO Box 156, Barren Springs, VA 24313-0156, Phone: 703-381-5137

CHAMBERLAIN, JON A., 15 S. Lombard, E. Wenatchee, WA 98802, Phone: 509-884-6591
Specialties: Working and kitchen knives to customer specs; exotics on special order. **Patterns:** Over 100 patterns in stock. **Technical:** Prefers ATS-34, D2, L6 and Damascus. **Prices:** Start at $50. **Remarks:** First knife sold in 1986. Doing business as Johnny Custom Knifemakers. **Mark:** Name in oval with city and state enclosing.

CHAMBERLIN, JOHN A., 11535 Our Rd., Anchorage, AK 99516, Phone: 907-346-1524, Fax: 907-562-4583
Specialties: Art and working knives. **Patterns:** Daggers and hunters; some folders. **Technical:** Grinds ATS-34, 440C, A2, D2 and Damascus. Uses Alaskan handle materials such as oosic, jade, whale jawbone, fossil ivory. **Prices:** Start at $150. **Remarks:** Does own heat treating and cryogenic deep freeze. Full-time maker; first knife sold in 1984. **Mark:** Name over English shield and dagger.

CHAMBLIN, JOEL, 960 New Hebron Church Rd., Concord, GA 30206, Phone: 770-884-9055
Specialties: Fancy and working folders. **Patterns:** Fancy locking folders, traditional, multi-blades and utility. **Technical:** Grinds ATS-34, 440V, BG-42 and commercial Damascus. Offers filework. **Prices:** Start at $300. **Remarks:** Full-time maker; first knife sold in 1989. **Mark:** Last name.

CHAMPAGNE, PAUL, 48 Brightman Rd., Mechanicville, NY 12118, Phone: 518-664-4179
Specialties: Rugged, ornate straight knives in the Japanese tradition. **Patterns:** Katanas, wakizashis, tantos and some European daggers. **Technical:** Forges and hand-finishes carbon steels and his own Damascus. Makes Tamahagane for use in traditional blades; uses traditional heat-treating techniques. **Prices:** Start at $750. **Remarks:** Has passed all traditional Japanese cutting tests. Doing business as Twilight Forge. **Mark:** Three diamonds over a stylized crown.

CHAMPION, ROBERT, 1806 Plateau Ln, Amarillo, TX 79106, Phone: 806-359-0446
Specialties: Traditional working straight knives. **Patterns:** Hunters, skinners, camp knives, Bowies, daggers. **Technical:** Grinds 440C and D2. **Prices:** $100 to $600. **Remarks:** Part-time maker; first knife sold in 1979. **Mark:** Last name with dagger logo, city and state. **Other:** Stream-line hunters.

CHAPO, WILLIAM G., 45 Wildridge Rd., Wilton, CT 06897, Phone: 203-544-9424
Specialties: Classic straight knives and folders of his design and to customer specs; period pieces. **Patterns:** Boots, Bowies and locking folders. **Technical:** Forges stainless Damascus. Offers filework. **Prices:** $750 and up. **Remarks:** Full-time maker; first knife sold in 1989. **Mark:** First and middle initials, last name, city, state.

CHARD, GORDON R., 104 S. Holiday Lane, Iola, KS 66749, Phone: 620-365-2311
Specialties: High tech folding knives in one-of-a-kind styles. **Patterns:** Liner locking folders of own design Some fixed blades. **Technical:** Clean work with attention to fit and finish. **Prices:** $150-$2000. **Remarks:** First knife sold in 1983. **Other:** Blade steel mostly ATS34 and 154CM. Also Damascus.

CHASE, ALEX, 208 E. Pennsylvania Ave., DeLand, FL 32724, Phone: 386-734-9918
Specialties: Historical steels, classic and traditional straight knives of his design and to customer specs. **Patterns:** Art, fighters and hunters. **Technical:** Forges O1-L6 Damascus, meteoric Damascus, 52100, 5160; uses fossil walrus and mastodon ivory etc. **Prices:** $150 to $1000; some to $3500. **Remarks:** Part-time maker; first knife sold in 1990. Doing business as Confederate Forge. **Mark:** Stylized initials-A.C.

CHASE, JOHN E., 217 Walnut, Aledo, TX 76008, Phone: 817-441-8331
Specialties: Straight high-tech working knives in standard patterns or to customer specs. **Patterns:** Hunters, fighters, daggers and Bowies. **Technical:** Grinds D2, 01, 440C; offers mostly satin finishes. **Prices:** Start at $235. **Remarks:** Part-time maker; first knife sold in 1974. **Mark:** Last name in logo.

CHASTAIN, WADE, Rt. 2, Box 137-A, Horse Shoe, NC 28742, Phone: 704-891-4803
Specialties: Fancy fantasy and high-art straight knives of his design; period pieces. Known for unique mounts. **Patterns:** Bowies, daggers and fighters. **Technical:** Grinds 440C, ATS-34 and O1. Engraves; offers jewelling. **Prices:** $400 to $1200; some to $2000. **Remarks:** Full-time maker; first knife sold in 1984. Doing business as The Iron Master. **Mark:** Engraved last name.

CHAUVIN, JOHN, 200 Anna St., Scott, LA 70583, Phone: 337-237-6138, Fax: 337-230-7980
Specialties: Traditional working and using straight knives of his design, to customer specs and in standard patterns. **Patterns:** Bowies, fighters, and hunters. **Technical:** Grinds ATS-34, 440C and O1 high-carbon. Paul Bos heat treating. Uses ivory, stag, oosic and stabilized Louisiana swamp maple for handle materials. Makes sheaths using alligator and ostrich. **Prices:** $200 and up. Bowies start at $500. **Remarks:** Part-time maker; first knife sold in 1995. **Mark:** Full name, city, state.

CHAUZY, ALAIN, 1 Rue de Paris, 21140 Seur-en-Auxios, FRANCE, Phone: 03-80-97-03-30, Fax: 03-80-97-34-14
Specialties: Fixed blades, folders, hunters, Bowies-scagel-style. **Technical:** Forged blades only. Steels used XC65, 07C, and own Damascus. **Prices:** Contact maker for quote. **Remarks:** Part-time maker. **Mark:** Number 2 crossed by an arrow and name.

CHAVAR, EDWARD V., 1830 Richmond Ave., Bethlehem, PA 18018, Phone: 610-865-1806
Specialties: Working straight knives to his or customer design specifications, folders, high art pieces and some forged pieces. **Patterns:** Fighters, hunters, tactical, straight and folding knives and high art straight and fold-

ing knives for collectors. **Technical:** Grinds ATS-34, 440C, L6, Damascus from various makers and uses Damascus Steel and Mokume of his own creation. **Prices:** Standard models range from $95 to $1500, custom and specialty up to $3000. **Remarks:** Full-time maker; first knife sold in 1990. **Mark:** Name, city, state or signature.

CHEATHAM, BILL, PO Box 636, Laveen, AZ 85339, Phone: 602-237-2786
Specialties: Working straight knives and folders. **Patterns:** Hunters, fighters, boots and axes; locking folders. **Technical:** Grinds 440C. **Prices:** $150 to $350; exceptional knives to $600. **Remarks:** Full-time maker; first knife sold in 1976. **Mark:** Name, city, state.

CHELQUIST, CLIFF, PO Box 91, Arroyo Grande, CA 93421, Phone: 805-489-8095
Specialties: Stylish pratical knives for the outdoorsman. **Patterns:** Trout and bird to camp knives. **Technical:** Grinds ATS-34. **Prices:** $90-$250 and up. **Remarks:** Part-time maker, first knife sold in 1983. **Mark:** Last initial.

CHERRY, FRANK J., 3412 Tiley N.E., Albuquerque, NM 87110, Phone: 505-883-8643

CHEW, LARRY, 515 Cleveland Rd., Unit A-9, Granbury, TX 76049, Phone: 817-326-0165
Specialties: High-tech folding knives. **Patterns:** Double action automatic and manual folding patterns of his design. **Technical:** CAD-designed folders utilizing his roller bearing pivot design knows as "VooDoo". Double action automatic folders with a variety of obvious and disguised release mechanisms, some with lock-outs. **Prices:** Manual folders start at $475; double action autos start at $675. **Remarks:** Made and sold first knife in 1988, first folder in 1989. Full-time maker since 1997. **Mark:** Name and location etched in blade, damascus autos marked on spring inside frame. Earliest knives stamped LC.

CHOATE, MILTON, 1665 W. County 17-1/2, Somerton, AZ 85350, Phone: 928-627-7251
Specialties: Classic working and using straight knives of his design, to customer specs and in standard patterns. **Patterns:** Bowies, hunters and utility/camp knives. **Technical:** Grinds 440C; grinds and forges 1095 and 5160. Does filework on top and guards on request. **Prices:** $150 to $600. **Remarks:** Full-time maker, first knife made in 1990. All knives come with handmade sheaths by Judy Choate. **Mark:** Knives marked "Choate".

CHRISTENSEN, JON P., 7814 Spear Dr., Shepherd, MT 59079, Phone: 406-373-0253
Specialties: Patch knives, hunter/utility knives, Bowies, tomahawks. **Technical:** All blades forged, does all own work including sheaths. Forges 0-1, 1084, 52100, 5160. Damascus from 1084/15N20. **Prices:** $170 on up. **Remarks:** ABS Journeyman Smith, first knife sold in 1999. **Mark:** First and middle initial surrounded by last initial.

CHURCHMAN, T.W., 7402 Tall Cedar, San Antonio, TX 78249, Phone: 210-690-8641
Specialties: Fancy and traditional straight knives and single blade liner locking folders. Bird/trout knives of his design and to customer specs. **Patterns:** Bird/trout knives, fillet, Bowies, daggers, fighters, boot knives, some miniatures. **Technical:** Grinds 440C and D2. Offers stainless fittings, fancy filework, exotic and stabilized woods and hand sewed lined sheaths. **Prices:** $80 to $650; some to $1500. **Remarks:** Part-time maker; first knife made n 1981 after reading "KNIVES" "81". Doing business as "Custom Knives Churchman Made". **Mark:** Last name, dagger.

CLAIBORNE, RON, 2918 Ellistown Rd., Knox, TN 37924, Phone: 615-524-2054
Specialties: Multi-blade slip joints, swords, straight knives. **Patterns:** Hunters, daggers, folders. **Technical:** Forges Damascus: mosaic, powder mosaic. Prefers bone and natural handle materials; some exotic woods. **Prices:** $125 to $2500. **Remarks:** Part-time maker; first knife sold in 1979. Doing business as Thunder Mountain Forge Claiborne Knives. **Mark:** Claiborne.

CLAIBORNE, JEFF, 1470 Roberts Rd., Franklin, IN 46131, Phone: 317-736-7443
Specialties: All one-of-a-kind by hand—no jigs or fixtures—swords, straight knives, period pieces, multi-blade slip joint folders, camp knives, hunters, fighters, ethnic swords all periods. Handle—uses stay, pearl, oosic, bone ivory, mastadon-mammoth, elephant or exotic woods. **Technical:** Forges high-carbon steel, makes Damascus, forges cable grinds, 01, 1095, 5160, 52100, L-6. **Prices:** $100 and up. **Remarks:** Part-time maker; first knife sold in 1989. **Mark:** Stylized initials in an oval.

CLARK, NATE, 484 Baird Dr., Yoncalla, OR 97499, Phone: 541-680-6077
Specialties: Automatics (Push button and hidden release) ATS-34 mirror polish or satin finish, Damascus, Pearl, Ivory, Abalone, Woods, Bone, Micarta, G-10, filework and carving and sheath knives. **Prices:** $100.-$2500. **Remarks:** Fulltime knife maker since 1996. **Mark:** Nate Clark.

CLARK, D.E. (LUCKY), 126 Woodland St., Mineral Point, PA 15942, Phone: 814-322-4725
Specialties: Working straight knives and folders to customer specs. **Patterns:** Customer designs. **Technical:** Grinds D2, 440C, 154CM. **Prices:** $100 to $200; some higher. **Remarks:** Part-time maker; first knife sold in 1975. **Mark:** Name on one side; "Lucky" on other.

CLARK, R.W., R.W. CLARK CUSTOM KNIVES, 1069 Golden Meadow, Corona, CA 92882, Phone: 909-279-3494, Fax: 909-279-4394
Specialties: Military field knives and Asian hybrids. Hand carved leather sheaths. **Patterns:** Fixed blade hunters, field utility and military. Also presentation and collector grade knives. **Technical:** First maker to use liquid metals LM1 material in knives. Other materials include S30V, O1, stainless and carbon Damascus. **Prices:** $75 to $2000. Average price $300. **Remarks:** Started knife making in 1990 full-time in 2000. **Mark:** R.W. Clark., Custom., Corona, CA in standard football shape. Also uses three Japanese characters, spelling Clark, on Asian Hybrids.

CLARK, HOWARD F., 115 35th Pl., Runnells, IA 50237, Phone: 515-966-2126
Specialties: Currently Japanese-style swords. **Patterns:** Katana. **Technical:** Forges 1086, L6, 52100 and his own all tool steel Damascus; bar stock; forged blanks. **Prices:** $500 to $3000. **Remarks:** Full-time maker; first knife sold in 1979. Doing business as Morgan Valley Forge. **Prior Mark:** Block letters and serial number on folders; anvil/initials logo on straight knives. **Current Mark:** Two character kanji "Big Ear".

CLAY, J.D., 5050 Hall Rd., Greenup, KY 41144, Phone: 606-473-6769
Specialties: Long known for cleanly finished, collector quality knives of functional design. **Patterns:** Practical hunters and locking folders. **Technical:** Grinds 440C - high mirror finishes. **Prices:** Start at $95. **Remarks:** Full-time maker; first knife sold in 1972. **Mark:** Name stamp in script on blade.

CLAY, WAYNE, Box 125B, Pelham, TN 37366, Phone: 931-467-3472, Fax: 931-467-3076
Specialties: Working straight knives and folders in standard patterns. **Patterns:** Hunters and kitchen knives; gents and hunter patterns. **Technical:** Grinds ATS-34. **Prices:** $125 to $500; some to $1000. **Remarks:** Full-time maker; first knife sold in 1978. **Mark:** Name.

CLICK, JOE, 305 Dodge St.#3, Swanton, OH 48558, Phone: 419-825-1220
Specialties: Fancy/embellished and traditional working/using straight knives of his design, to customer specs and in standard patterns. **Patterns:** Bowies, hunters and utility/camp knives. **Technical:** Grinds and forges A2, D2, 5160 and Damascus. Does fancy filework; triple temper. Uses ivory for handle material. **Prices:** $75 to $300; some to $700. **Remarks:** Doing business as Click Custom Knives. **Mark:** Full name.

COCKERHAM, LLOYD, 1717 Carolyn Ave., Denham Springs, IA 70726, Phone: 225-665-1565

COFER, RON, 188 Ozora Rd., Loganville, GA 30052
Specialties: Fancy working and using straight knives of his design. **Patterns:** Hunters, Bowies and fighters. **Technical:** Grinds 440C and ATS-34. Heat-treats. Some knives have carved stag handles or scrimshaw. Makes leather sheath for each knife and walnut and deer antler display stands for art knives. **Prices:** $125 to $250; some to $600. **Remarks:** Spare-time maker; first knife sold in 1991. **Mark:** Name, serial number.

COFFMAN, DANNY, 541 Angel Dr. S., Jacksonville, AL 36265-5787, Phone: 256-435-1619
Specialties: Straight knives and folders of his design. Now making liner locks for $650 to $1200 with natural handles and contrasting Damascus blades and bolsters. **Patterns:** Hunters, locking and slip-joint folders. **Technical:** Grinds Damascus, 440C and D2. Offers filework and engraving. **Prices:** $100 to $400; some to $800. **Remarks:** Spare-time maker; first knife sold in 1992. Doing business as Customs by Coffman. **Mark:** Last name stamped or engraved.

COHEN, N.J. (NORM), 2408 Sugarcone Rd., Baltimore, MD 21209, Phone: 410-484-3841
Specialties: Working class knives. **Patterns:** Hunters, skinners, bird knives, push daggers, boots, kitchen and practical customer designs. **Technical:** Stock removal 440C, ATS-34. Uses Micarta, Corian. Some woods in handles. **Prices:** $50 to $250. **Remarks:** Part-time maker; first knife sold in 1982. **Mark:** Etched initials or NJC MAKER.

COHEN, TERRY A., PO Box 406, Laytonville, CA 95454
Specialties: Working straight knives and folders. **Patterns:** Bowies to boot knives and locking folders; mini-boot knives. **Technical:** Grinds stainless; hand rubs; tries for good balance. **Prices:** $85 to $150; some to $325. **Remarks:** Part-time maker; first knife sold in 1983. **Mark:** TERRY KNIVES, city and state.

custom knifemakers

COIL, JIMMIE J., 2936 Asbury Pl., Owensboro, KY 42303, Phone: 270-684-7827
Specialties: Traditional working and straight knives of his design. **Patterns:** Hunters, Bowies and fighters. **Technical:** Grinds 440C, ATS-34 and D2. Blades are flat-ground with brush finish; most have tapered tang. Offers filework. **Prices:** $65 to $250; some to $750. **Remarks:** Spare-time maker; first knife sold in 1974. **Mark:** Name.

COLE, DAVE, 620 Poinsetta Dr., Satellite Beach, FL 32937, Phone: 321-773-1687
Specialties: Fixed blades and friction folders of his design or customers. **Patterns:** Utility, hunters, and Bowies. **Technical:** Grinds 01, 1095. 440C stainless Damascus; prefers natural handle materials, handmade sheaths. **Prices:** $100 and up. **Remarks:** Part-time maker, member of FKA; first knife sold in 1991. **Mark:** D Cole.

COLE, JAMES M., 505 Stonewood Blvd., Bartonville, TX 76226, Phone: 817-430-0302

COLE, WELBORN I., 3284 Inman Dr. N.E., Atlanta, GA 30319, Phone: 404-261-3977
Specialties: Traditional straight knives of his design. **Patterns:** Hunters. **Technical:** Grinds 440C, ATS-34 and D2. Good wood scales. **Prices:** NA. **Remarks:** Full-time maker; first knife sold in 1983. **Mark:** Script initials.

COLEMAN, KEITH E., 5001 Starfire Pl. N.W., Albuquerque, NM 87120-2010, Phone: 505-899-3783
Specialties: Affordable collector-grade straight knives and folders; some fancy. **Patterns:** Fighters, tantos, combat folders, gents folders and boots. **Technical:** Grinds ATS-34 and Damascus. Prefers specialty woods; offers filework. **Prices:** $150 to $700; some to $1500. **Remarks:** Full-time maker; first knife sold in 1980. **Mark:** Name, city and state.

COLLINS, HAROLD, 503 First St., West Union, OH 45693, Phone: 513-544-2982
Specialties: Traditional using straight knives and folders of his design or to customer specs. **Patterns:** Hunters, Bowies and locking folders. **Technical:** Forges and grinds 440C, ATS-34, D2, 01 and 5160. Flat-grinds standard; filework available. **Prices:** $75 to $300. **Remarks:** Full-time maker; first knife sold in 1989. **Mark:** First initial, last name.

COLLINS, LYNN M., 138 Berkley Dr., Elyria, OH 44035, Phone: 440-366-7101
Specialties: Working straight knives. **Patterns:** Field knives, boots and fighters. **Technical:** Grinds D2, 154CM and 440C. **Prices:** Start at $150. **Remarks:** Spare-time maker; first knife sold in 1980. **Mark:** Initials, asterisks.

COLTER, WADE, PO Box 2340, Colstrip, MT 59323, Phone: 406-748-4573
Specialties: Fancy and embellished straight knives, folders and swords of his design; historical and period pieces. **Patterns:** Bowies, swords and folders. **Technical:** Hand forges 52100 ball bearing steel and L6, 1090, cable and chain Damascus from 5N20 and 1084. Carves and makes sheaths. **Prices:** $250 to $3500. **Remarks:** Part-time maker; first knife sold in 1990. Doing business as "Colter's Hell" Forge. **Mark:** Initials on left side ricasso.

COLTRAIN, LARRY D., PO Box 1331, Buxton, NC 27920

COMAR, ROGER N., RT. 1 Box 485, Marion, NC 28752, Phone: 828-652-2448

COMPTON, WILLIAM E., 106 N. Sequoia Ct., Sterling, VA 20164, Phone: 703-430-2129
Specialties: Working straight knives of his design or to customer specs; some fancy knives. **Patterns:** Hunters, camp knives, Bowies and some kitchen knives. **Technical:** Also forges 5160, 1095 and make his own Damascus. **Prices:** $150 to $750, some to $1500. **Remarks:** Part-time maker, ABS Journeyman Smith. first knife sold in 1994. Doing business as Comptons Custom Knives. **Mark:** Stock removal—first and middle initials, last name, city and state. Forged first and middle initials, last name, city and state, anvil in middle.

COMUS, STEVE, PO Box 68040, Anaheim, CA 92817-9800

CONKEY, TOM, 9122 Keyser Rd., Nokesville, VA 22123, Phone: 703-791-3867
Specialties: Classic straight knives and folders of his design and to customer specs. **Patterns:** Boots, hunters and locking folders. **Technical:** Grinds ATS-34, 01 and commercial Damascus. Lockbacks have jeweled scales and locking bars with dovetailed bolsters. Folders utilize unique 2-piece bushing of his design and manufacture. Sheaths are handmade. Presentation boxes made upon request. **Prices:** $100 to $500. **Remarks:** Part-time maker; first knife sold in 1991. Collaborates with Dan Thomas. **Mark:** Last name with "handcrafted" underneath.

CONKLIN, GEORGE L., Box 902, Ft. Benton, MT 59442, Phone: 406-622-3268, Fax: 406-622-3410
Specialties: Designer and manufacturer of the "Brisket Breaker." **Patterns:** Hunters, utility/camp knives and hatchets. **Technical:** Grinds 440C, ATS-34, D2, 1095, 154CM and 5160. Offers some forging and heat-treats for others. Offers some jewelling. **Prices:** $65 to $200; some to $1000. **Remarks:** Full-time maker. Doing business as Rocky Mountain Knives. **Mark:** Last name in script.

CONLEY, BOB, 1013 Creasy Rd., Jonesboro, TN 37659, Phone: 423-753-3302
Specialties: Working straight knives and folders. **Patterns:** Lockers, two-blades, gents, hunters, traditional-styles, straight hunters. **Technical:** Grinds 440C, 154CM and ATS-34. Engraves. **Prices:** $250 to $450; some to $600. **Remarks:** Full-time maker; first knife sold in 1979. **Mark:** Full name, city, state.

CONN JR., C.T., 206 Highland Ave., Attalla, AL 35954, Phone: 205-538-7688
Specialties: Working folders, some fancy. **Patterns:** Full range of folding knives. **Technical:** Grinds O2, 440C and 154CM. **Prices:** $125 to $300; some to $600. **Remarks:** Part-time maker; first knife sold in 1982. **Mark:** Name.

CONNELL, STEVE, 217 Valley St., Adamsville, AL 35005-1852, Phone: 205-674-0440

CONNER, ALLEN L., 6399 County Rd. 305, Fulton, MO 65251, Phone: 573-642-9200

CONNOLLY, JAMES, 2486 Oro-Quincy Hwy., Oroville, CA 95966, Phone: 916-534-5363
Specialties: Classic working and using knives of his design. **Patterns:** Boots, Bowies and daggers. **Technical:** Grinds ATS-34; forges 5160; forges and grinds O1. **Prices:** $100 to $500; some to $1500. **Remarks:** Part-time maker; first knife sold in 1980. Doing business as Gold Rush Designs. **Mark:** First initial, last name, Handmade.

CONNOR, MICHAEL, Box 502, Winters, TX 79567, Phone: 915-754-5602
Specialties: Straight knives, period pieces, some folders. **Patterns:** Hunters to camp knives to traditional locking folders to Bowies. **Technical:** Forges 5160, O1, 1084 steels and his own Damascus. **Prices:** Moderate to upscale. **Remarks:** Spare-time maker; first knife sold in 1974. **Mark:** Last name, M.S. **Other:** ABS Master Smith 1983.

CONNOR, JOHN W., PO Box 12981, Odessa, TX 79768-2981, Phone: 915-362-6901

CONTI, JEFFREY D., 4640 Feigley Rd. W., Port Orchard, WA 98367, Phone: 360-405-0075
Specialties: Working straight knives. **Patterns:** Fighters and survival knives; hunters, camp knives and fishing knives. **Technical:** Grinds D2, 154CM and O1. Engraves. **Prices:** Start at $80. **Remarks:** Part-time maker; first knife sold in 1980. **Mark:** Initials, year, steel type, name and number of knife.

COOGAN, ROBERT, 1560 Craft Center Dr., Smithville, TN 37166, Phone: 615-597-6801
Specialties: One-of-a-kind knives. **Patterns:** Unique items like ooloo-style Appalachian herb knives. **Technical:** Forges; his Damascus is made from nickel steel and W1. **Prices:** Start at $100. **Remarks:** Part-time maker; first knife sold in 1979. **Mark:** Initials or last name in script.

COOK, JAMES R., 3611 Hwy. 26 W., Nashville, AR 71852, Phone: 870 845 5173
Specialties: Working straight knives and folders of his design or to customer specs. **Patterns:** Bowies, hunters and camp knives. **Technical:** Forges 1084 and high-carbon Damascus. **Prices:** $195 to $5500. **Remarks:** Part-time maker; first knife sold in 1986. **Mark:** First and middle initials, last name.

COOK, LOUISE, 475 Robinson Ln., Ozark, IL 62972, Phone: 618-777-2932
Specialties: Working and using straight knives of her design and to customer specs; period pieces. **Patterns:** Bowies, hunters and utility/camp knives. **Technical:** Forges 5160. Filework; pin work; silver wire inlay. **Prices:** Start at $50/inch. **Remarks:** Part-time maker; first knife sold in 1990. Doing business as Panther Creek Forge. **Mark:** First name and journeyman stamp on one side; panther head on the other.

COOK, MIKE, 475 Robinson Ln., Ozark, IL 62972, Phone: 618-777-2932
Specialties: Traditional working and using straight knives of his design and to customer specs. **Patterns:** Bowies, hunters and utility/camp knives. **Technical:** Forges 5160. Filework; pin work. **Prices:** Start at $50/inch. **Remarks:** Spare-time maker; first knife sold in 1991. **Mark:** First initial, last name and journeyman stamp on one side; panther head on the other.

COOK, MIKE A., 10927 Shilton Rd., Portland, MI 48875, Phone: 517-647-2518
Specialties: Fancy/embellished and period pieces of his design. **Patterns:** Daggers, fighters and hunters. **Technical:** Stone bladed knives in agate, obsidian and jasper. Scrimshaws; opal inlays. **Prices:** $60 to $300;

some to $800. **Remarks:** Part-time maker; first knife sold in 1988. Doing business as Art of Ishi. **Mark:** Initials and year.

COOMBS JR., LAMONT, 546 State Rt. 46, Bucksport, ME 04416, Phone: 207-469-3057, Fax: 207-469-3057
Specialties: Classic fancy and embellished straight knives; traditional working and using straight knives. Knives of his design and to customer specs. **Patterns:** Hunters, folders and utility/camp knives. **Technical:** Hollow- and flat-grinds ATS-34, 440C, A2, D2 and O1; grinds Damascus from other makers. **Prices:** $100 to $500; some to $3500. **Remarks:** Full-time maker; first knife sold in 1988. **Mark:** Last name on banner, hand-made underneath.

COON, RAYMOND C., 21135 S.E. Tillstrom Rd., Gresham, OR 97080, Phone: 503-658-2252
Specialties: Working straight knives in standard patterns. **Patterns:** Hunters, Bowies, daggers, boots and axes. **Technical:** Forges high-carbon steel and Damascus. **Prices:** Start at $135. **Remarks:** Full-time maker; does own leatherwork, makes own Damascus, daggers; first knife sold in 1995. **Mark:** First initial, last name.

COPELAND, THOM, 171 Country Line Rd. S., Nashville, AR 71852
Specialties: Hand forged fixed blades; hunters, Bowies and camp knives. **Mark:** Copeland. **Other:** Member of ABS and AKA (Arkansas Knifemakers Association).

COPELAND, GEORGE STEVE, 220 Pat Carr Lane, Alpine, TN 38543, Phone: 931-823-5214
Specialties: Traditional and fancy working straight knives and folders. **Patterns:** Friction folders, Congress two- and four-blade folders, button locks and one- and two-blade automatics. **Technical:** Stock removal of 440C, S300, ATS-34 and A2; heat-treats. **Prices:** $180 to $950; some higher. **Remarks:** Full-time maker; first knife sold in 1979. Doing business as Alpine Mountain Knives. **Mark:** G.S. Copeland (HANDMADE); some with four-leaf clover stamp.

COPPINS, DANIEL, 7303 Sherrard Rd., Cambridge, OH 43725, Phone: 740-439-4199
Specialties: Grinds 440 C and etching toll steels, antler, bone handles. **Patterns:** Hunters patch, neck knives, primitive, tomahawk. **Prices:** $20 and up, some to $600. **Remarks:** Sold first knife in 2002. **Mark:** DC. **Other:** Made tomahawk + knives + walking stick for country music band Confederate Railroad.

CORBY, HAROLD, 218 Brandonwood Dr., Johnson City, TN 37604, Phone: 615-926-9781
Specialties: Large fighters and Bowies; self-protection knives; art knives. Along with art knives and combat knives, Corby now has a all new automatic MO.PB1, also side lock MO LL-1 with titanium liners G-10 handles. **Patterns:** Sub-hilt fighters and hunters. **Technical:** Grinds 154CM, ATS-34 and 440C. **Prices:** $200 to $6000. **Remarks:** Full-time maker; first knife sold in 1969. Doing business as Knives by Corby. **Mark:** Last name.

CORDOVA, JOSEPH G., PO Box 977, Peralta, NM 87042, Phone: 505-869-3912
Specialties: One-of-a-kind designs, some to customer specs. **Patterns:** Fighter called the 'Gladiator', hunters, boots and cutlery. **Technical:** Forges 1095, 5160; grinds ATS-34, 440C and 154CM. **Prices:** Moderate to upscale. **Remarks:** Full-time maker; first knife sold in 1953. **Mark:** Cordova made.

CORKUM, STEVE, 34 Basehoar School Rd., Littlestown, PA 17340, Phone: 717-359-9563

CORRIGAN, DAVID P., HCR 65 Box 67, Bingham, ME 04920, Phone: 207-672-4879

COSGROVE, CHARLES G., 2314 W. Arbook Blvd., Arlington, TX 76015, Phone: 817-472-6505
Specialties: Traditional fixed or locking blade working knives. **Patterns:** Hunters, Bowies and locking folders. **Technical:** Stock removal using 440C, ATS-34 and D2; heat-treats. Makes heavy, hand-stitched sheaths. **Prices:** $250 to $2500. **Remarks:** Full-time maker; first knife sold in 1968. No longer accepting customer designs. **Mark:** First initial, last name, or full name over city and state.

COSTA, SCOTT, 409 Coventry Rd., Spicewood, TX 78669, Phone: 830-693-3431
Specialties: Working straight knives. **Patterns:** Hunters, skinners, axes, trophy sets, custom boxed steak sets, carving sets and bar sets. **Technical:** Grinds D2, ATS-34, 440 and Damascus. Heat-treats. **Prices:** $225 to $2000. **Remarks:** Full-time maker; first knife sold in 1985. **Mark:** Initials connected.

COSTELLO, DR. TIMOTHY L., 30883 Crest Forest, Farmington Hills, MI 48331, Phone: 248-592-9746

COTTRILL, JAMES I., 1776 Ransburg Ave., Columbus, OH 43223, Phone: 614-274-0020
Specialties: Working straight knives of his design. **Patterns:** Caters to the boating and hunting crowd; cutlery. **Technical:** Grinds O1, D2 and 440C. Likes filework. **Prices:** $95 to $250; some to $500. **Remarks:** Full-time maker; first knife sold in 1977. **Mark:** Name, city, state, in oval logo.

COUGHLIN, MICHAEL M., 414 Northridge Lane, Winder, GA 30680, Phone: 770-307-9509
Specialties: One-of-a-kind large folders and daily carry knives. **Remarks:** Likes customer input and involvement.

COURTNEY, ELDON, 2718 Bullinger, Wichita, KS 67204, Phone: 316-838-4053
Specialties: Working straight knives of his design. **Patterns:** Hunters, fighters and one-of-a-kinds. **Technical:** Grinds and tempers L6, 440C and spring steel. **Prices:** $100 to $500; some to $1500. **Remarks:** Full-time maker; first knife sold in 1977. **Mark:** Full name, city and state.

COURTOIS, BRYAN, 3 Lawn Avenue, Saco, ME 04072, Phone: 207-282-3977
Specialties: Working straight knives; prefers customer designs, no standard patterns. **Patterns:** Functional hunters; everyday knives. **Technical:** Grinds 440C or customer request. Hollow-grinds with a variety of finishes. Specializes in granite handles and custom skeleton knives. **Prices:** Start at $75. **Remarks:** Part-time maker; first knife sold in 1988. Doing business as Castle Knives. **Mark:** A rook chess piece machined into blade using electrical discharge process.

COUSINO, GEORGE, 7818 Norfolk, Onsted, MI 49265, Phone: 517-467-4911, Fax: 517-467-4911
Specialties: Hunters, Bowies using knives. **Patterns:** Hunters, Bowies, buckskinners, folders and daggers. **Technical:** Grinds 440C. **Prices:** $95 to $300. **Remarks:** Part-time maker; first knife sold in 1981. **Mark:** Last name.

COVER, RAYMOND A., Rt. 1, Box 194, Mineral Point, MO 63660, Phone: 573-749-3783
Specialties: High-tech working straight knives and folders in standard patterns. **Patterns:** Slip joint folders, two-bladed folders. **Technical:** Grinds D2, and ATS-34. **Prices:** $165 to $250; some to $400. **Remarks:** Part-time maker; first knife sold in 1974. **Mark:** Name.

COWLES, DON, 1026 Lawndale Dr., Royal Oak, MI 48067, Phone: 248-541-4619
Specialties: Straight, non-folding pocket knives of his design. **Patterns:** Gentlemen's pocket knives. **Technical:** Grinds ATS-34, RWL34, S30V, stainless Damascus, Talonite. Scrimshaws; pearl inlays in some handles. **Prices:** $300 to $1200. **Remarks:** Part-time maker; first knife sold in 1994. **Mark:** Full name with oak leaf.

COX, SAM, 1756 Love Springs Rd., Gaffney, SC 29341, Phone: 864-489-1892, Fax: 864-489-0403
Specialties: Classic high-art working straight knives of his design. Duck knives copyrighted. **Patterns:** Diverse. **Technical:** Grinds 154CM. **Prices:** $300 to $1400. **Remarks:** Full-time maker; first knife sold in 1983. **Mark:** Cox Call, Sam, Sam Cox, unique 2000 logo.

COX, COLIN J., 107 N. Oxford Dr., Raymore, MO 64083, Phone: 816-322-1977
Specialties: Working straight knives and folders of his design; period pieces. **Patterns:** Hunters, fighters and survival knives. Folders, two-blades, gents and hunters. **Technical:** Grinds D2, 440C, 154CM and ATS-34. **Prices:** $125 to $750; some to $4000. **Remarks:** Full-time maker; first knife sold in 1981. **Mark:** Full name, city and state.

CRAIG, ROGER L., 2815 Fairlawn Rd., Topeka, KS 66614, Phone: 785-233-9499
Specialties: Working and camp knives, some fantasy; all his design. **Patterns:** Fighters, hunter. **Technical:** Grinds 1095 and 5160. Most knives have file work. **Prices:** $50 to $250. **Remarks:** Part-time maker; first knife sold in 1991. Doing business as Craig Knives. **Mark:** Last name-Craig.

CRAIN, JACK W., PO Box 212, Granbury, TX 76048, Phone: 817-599-6414
Specialties: Fantasy and period knives; combat and survival knives. **Patterns:** One-of-a-kind art or fantasy daggers, swords and Bowies; survival knives. **Technical:** Forges Damascus; grinds stainless steel. Carves. **Prices:** $350 to $2500; some to $20,000. **Remarks:** Full-time maker; first knife sold in 1969. Designer and maker of the knives seen in the films *Dracula 2000, Executive Decision, Demolition Man, Predator I and II, Commando, Die Hard I and II, Road House, Ford Fairlane* and *Action Jackson*, and television shows *War of the Worlds, Air Wolf, Kung Fu: The Legend Cont.* and *Tales of the Crypt*. **Mark:** Stylized crane.

custom knifemakers

CRAIN, FRANK, 1127 W. Dalke, Spokane, WA 99205, Phone: 509-325-1596

CRAWFORD, PAT AND WES, 205 N. Center, West Memphis, AR 72301, Phone: 870-732-2452
 Specialties: Stainless steel Damascus. High-tech working self-defense and combat types and folders. **Patterns:** Tactical-more fancy knives now. **Technical:** Grinds ATS-34, D2 and 154CM. **Prices:** $400 to $2000. **Remarks:** Full-time maker; first knife sold in 1973. **Mark:** Last name.

CRAWLEY, BRUCE R., 16 Binbrook Dr., Croydon 3136 Victoria, AUSTRALIA
 Specialties: Folders. **Patterns:** Hunters, lockback folders and Bowies. **Technical:** Grinds 440C, ATS-34 and commercial Damascus. Offers file-work and mirror polish. **Prices:** $160 to $3500. **Remarks:** Part-time maker; first knife sold in 1990. **Mark:** Initials.

CRENSHAW, AL, Rt. 1, Box 717, Eufaula, OK 74432, Phone: 918-452-2128
 Specialties: Folders of his design and in standard patterns. **Patterns:** Hunters, locking folders, slip-joint folders, multi blade folders. **Technical:** Grinds 440C, D2 and ATS-34. Does filework on back springs and blades; offers scrimshaw on some handles. **Prices:** $150 to $300; some higher. **Remarks:** Full-time maker; first knife sold in 1981. Doing business as A. Crenshaw Knives. **Mark:** First initial, last name, Lake Eufaula, state stamped; first initial last name in rainbow; Lake Eufaula across bottom with Okla. in middle.

CROCKFORD, JACK, 1859 Harts Mill Rd., Chamblee, GA 30341, Phone: 770-457-4680
 Specialties: Lockback folders. **Patterns:** Hunters, fishing and camp knives, traditional folders. **Technical:** Grinds A2, D2, ATS-34 and 440C. Engraves and scrimshaws. **Prices:** Start at $175. **Remarks:** Part-time maker; first knife sold in 1975. **Mark:** Name.

CROSS, ROBERT, RMB 200B, Manilla Rd., Tamworth 2340, NSW AUSTRALIA, Phone: 067-618385

CROSSMAN, DANIEL C., Box 5236, Blakely Island, WA 98222, Phone: 360-375-6542

CROWDER, ROBERT, Box 1374, Thompson Falls, MT 59873, Phone: 406-827-4754
 Specialties: Traditional working knives to customer specs. **Patterns:** Hunters, Bowies, fighters and fillets. **Technical:** Grinds ATS-34, 154CM, 440C, Vascowear and commercial Damascus. **Prices:** $160 to $250; some to $2500. **Remarks:** Part-time maker; first knife sold in 1985. **Mark:** First initial, last name.

CROWELL, JAMES L., PO Box 822, Mtn. View, AR 72560, Phone: 870-746-4215
 Specialties: Bowie knives; fighters and working knives. **Patterns:** Hunters, fighters, Bowies, daggers and folders. Period pieces: War hammers, Japanese and European. **Technical:** Forges 10 series carbon steels as well as 0-1, L-6 and his own Damascus. **Prices:** $425 to $4500; some to $7500. **Remarks:** Currently part-time maker; first knife sold in 1980. Earned ABS Master Bladesmith in 1986. **Mark:** A shooting star.

CROWTHERS, MARK F., PO Box 4641, Rolling Bay, WA 98061-0641, Phone: 206-842-7501

CULPEPPER, JOHN, 2102 Spencer Ave., Monroe, LA 71201, Phone: 318-323-3636
 Specialties: Working straight knives. **Patterns:** Hunters, Bowies and camp knives in heavy-duty patterns. **Technical:** Grinds O1, D2 and 440C; hollow-grinds. **Prices:** $75 to $200; some to $300. **Remarks:** Part-time maker; first knife sold in 1970. Doing business as Pepper Knives. **Mark:** Pepper.

CULVER, STEVE, 5682 94th St., Meriden, KS 66512, Phone: 785-484-0146
 Specialties: Edged tools and weapons, collectible and functional. **Patterns:** Bowies, daggers, swords, hunters, folders and edged tools. **Technical:** Forges carbon steels and his own pattern welded steels. **Prices:** $200 to $500; some to $4000. **Remarks:** Part-time maker; first knife sold in 1989. **Mark:** Last name, J.S.

CUMMING, R.J., CUMMING KNIVES, 35 Manana Dr., Cedar Crest, NM 87008, Phone: 505-286-0509
 Specialties: Custom made Bowie knives, Plains Indians-style knife sheaths. D2, ATS34 and 1095 Damascus, exotic handles. Custom leather work, Scrimshaw and engraving. **Prices:** $225 to $750; some higher. **Remarks:** Full-time maker; first knife sold in 1978 in Denmark; mentored by late Jim Nolen. Retired US Foreign Service Officer. Member PKA, NCCKG. **Mark:** Stylized CUMMING.

CUTCHIN, ROY D., 960 Hwy. 169 S., Seale, AL 36875, Phone: 334-855-3080
 Specialties: Fancy and working folders of his design. **Patterns:** Locking folders. **Technical:** Grinds ATS-34 and commercial Damascus; uses anodized titanium. **Prices:** Start at $250. **Remarks:** Part-time maker. **Mark:** First initial, last name, city and state, number.

CUTE, THOMAS, State Rt. 90-7071, Cortland, NY 13045, Phone: 607-749-4055
 Specialties: Working straight knives. **Patterns:** Hunters, Bowies and fighters. **Technical:** Grinds O1, 440C and ATS-34. **Prices:** $100 to $1000. **Remarks:** Full-time maker; first knife sold in 1974. **Mark:** Full name.

d

DAILEY, G.E., 577 Lincoln St., Seekonk, MA 02771, Phone: 508-336-5088
 Specialties: One-of-a-kind exotic designed edged weapons. **Patterns:** Folders, daggers and swords. **Technical:** Reforges and grinds Damascus; prefers hollow-grinding. Engraves, carves, offers filework and sets stones and uses exotic gems and gold. **Prices:** Start at $1100. **Remarks:** Full-time maker. First knife sold in 1982. **Mark:** Last name or stylized initialed logo.

DAKE, MARY H., RT. 5 Box 287A, New Orleans, LA 70129, Phone: 504-254-0357

DAKE, C.M., 19759 Chef Menteur Hwy., New Orleans, LA 70129-9602, Phone: 504-254-0357, Fax: 504-254-9501
 Specialties: Fancy working folders. **Patterns:** Front-lock lockbacks, button-lock folders. **Technical:** Grinds ATS-34 and Damascus. **Prices:** $500 to $2500; some higher. **Remarks:** Full-time maker; first knife sold in 1988. Doing business as Bayou Custom Cutlery. **Mark:** Last name.

DALAND, B. MACGREGOR, RT. 5 Box 196, Harbeson, DE 19951, Phone: 302-945-2609

DALLYN, KELLY, 14695 Deerridge Dr. S.E., Calgary AB, CANADA T2J 6A8, Phone: 403-278-3056

DAMLOVAC, SAVA, 10292 Bradbury Dr., Indianapolis, IN 46231, Phone: 317-839-4952
 Specialties: Period pieces, Fantasy, Viking, Moran type all Damascus daggers. **Patterns:** Bowies, fighters, daggers, Persian-style knives. **Technical:** Uses own Damascus, some stainless, mostly hand forges. **Prices:** $150 to $2500; some higher. **Remarks:** Full-time maker; first knife sold in 1993. **Mark:** "Sava" stamped in Damascus or etched in stainless. **Other:** Specialty, Bill Moran all Damascus dagger sets, in Moran-style wood case.

D'ANDREA, JOHN, 501 Penn Estates, East Stroudsberg, PA 18301, Phone: 570-420-6050
 Specialties: Fancy working straight knives and folders with filework and distinctive leatherwork. **Patterns:** Hunters, fighters, daggers, folders and an occasional sword. **Technical:** Grinds ATS-34, 154CM, 440C and D2. **Prices:** $180 to $600; some to $1000. **Remarks:** Part-time maker; first knife sold in 1986. **Mark:** First name, last initial imposed on samurai sword.

D'ANGELO, LAURENCE, 14703 N.E. 17th Ave., Vancouver, WA 98686, Phone: 360-573-0546
 Specialties: Straight knives of his design. **Patterns:** Bowies, hunters and locking folders. **Technical:** Grinds D2, ATS-34 and 440C. Hand makes all sheaths. **Prices:** $100 to $200. **Remarks:** Full-time maker; first knife sold in 1987. **Mark:** Football logo—first and middle initials, last name, city, state, Maker.

DANIEL, TRAVIS E., 1655 Carrow Rd., Chocowinity, NC 27817, Phone: 252-940-0807
 Specialties: Traditional working straight knives of his design or to customer specs. **Patterns:** Hunters, fighters and utility/camp knives. **Technical:** Grinds ATS-34, D-2, 440-C, 154CM, forges his own Damascus. **Prices:** $90 to $1250; some to $2000. **Remarks:** Full-time maker; first knife sold in 1976. **Mark:** Carolina Custom Knives or "TED"

DANIELS, ALEX, 1416 County Rd. 415, Town Creek, AL 35672, Phone: 256-685-0943
 Specialties: Working and using straight knives and folders; period pieces, reproduction Bowies. **Patterns:** Mostly reproduction Bowies but offer full line of knives. **Technical:** Now also using BG-42 along with 440C and ATS-34. **Prices:** $200 to $2500. **Remarks:** Full-time maker; first knife sold in 1963. **Mark:** First and middle initials, last name, city and state.

DARBY, JED, 7878 E. Co. Rd. 50 N., Greensburg, IN 47240, Phone: 812-663-2696
 Specialties: Traditional working/using straight knives of his design and to customer specs. **Patterns:** Bowies, hunters and utility/camp knives. **Technical:** Grinds 440C, ATS-34 and Damascus. **Prices:** $70 to $550; some to $1000. **Remarks:** Full-time maker; first knife sold in 1992. Doing business as Darby Knives. **Mark:** Last name and year.

DARBY, RICK, 71 Nestingrock Ln., Levittown, PA 19054
Specialties: Working straight knives. **Patterns:** Boots, fighters and hunters with mirror finish. **Technical:** Grinds 440C and CPM440V. **Prices:** $125 to $300. **Remarks:** Part-time maker; first knife sold in 1974. **Mark:** First and middle initials, last name.

DARBY, DAVID T., 30652 S 533 Rd., Cookson, OK 74427, Phone: 918-457-4868

DARCEY, CHESTER L., 1608 Dominik Dr., College Station, TX 77840, Phone: 979-696-1656
Specialties: Lockback, liner lock and scale release folders. **Patterns:** Bowies, hunters and utilities. **Technical:** Stock removal on carbon and stainless steels, forge own Damascus. **Prices:** $200 to $1000. **Remarks:** Part-time maker, first knife sold in 1999. **Mark:** Last name in script.

DARPINIAN, DAVE, 15219 W. 125th, Olathe, KS 66062, Phone: 913-397-8914
Specialties: Working knives and fancy pieces to customer specs. **Patterns:** Full range of straight knives including art daggers and short swords. **Technical:** Art grinds ATS-34, 440C, 154 CM, 5160, 1095. **Prices:** $200 to $1000. **Remarks:** First knife sold in 1996, part-time maker. **Mark:** Last name.

DAVENPORT, JACK, 36842 W. Center Ave., Dade City, FL 33525, Phone: 352-521-4088
Specialties: Titanium liner lock, button-lock and release. **Patterns:** Boots and double-ground fighters. **Technical:** Grinds ATS-34, 12C27 SS and Damascus; liquid nitrogen quench; heat-treats. **Prices:** $250 to $5000. **Remarks:** Full-time maker; first knife sold in 1986. **Mark:** Last name.

DAVIDSON, EDMUND, 3345 Virginia Ave., Goshen, VA 24439, Phone: 540-997-5651
Specialties: Working straight knives; many integral patterns and upgraded models. **Patterns:** Heavy-duty skinners and camp knives. **Technical:** Grinds A2, ATS-34, BG-42, S7, 440C. **Prices:** $100 to infinity. **Remarks:** Full-time maker; first knife sold in 1986. **Mark:** Name in deer head or custom logos.

DAVIDSON, LARRY, 921 Bennett St., Cedar Hill, TX 75104, Phone: 972-291-3904

DAVIS, JOHN, 235 Lampe Rd., Selah, WA 98942, Phone: 509-697-3845, Fax: 509-697-8087
Specialties: Working and using straight knives of his own design, to customer specs and in standard patterns. **Patterns:** Boots, hunters, kitchen and utility/camp knives. **Technical:** Grinds ATS-34, 440C and commercial Damascus; makes own Damascus and mosaic Damascus. Embellishes with stabilized wood, mokume and nickel-silver. **Prices:** Start at $150. **Remarks:** Part-time maker; first knife sold in 1996. **Mark:** Name city and state on Damascus stamp initials.

DAVIS, BARRY L., 4262 U.S. 20, Castleton, NY 12033, Phone: 518-477-5036
Specialties: Collector-quality and Damascus interframe folders. **Patterns:** Traditional gentlemen's folders. **Technical:** Makes Damascus; uses only natural handle materials. **Prices:** $1000 to $2500; some to $6000. **Remarks:** Part-time maker; first knife sold in 1980. **Mark:** Initials.

DAVIS, CHARLIE, ANZA Knives, PO Box 710806, Santee, CA 92072, Phone: 619-561-9445, Fax: 619-390-6283
Specialties: Fancy and embellished working straight knives of his design. **Patterns:** Hunters, camp and utility knives. **Technical:** Grinds high-carbon files. **Prices:** $20 to $185 - custom depends. **Remarks:** Full-time maker; first knife sold in 1980. **Mark:** ANZA U.S.A. **Other:** we now offer custom.

DAVIS, JOEL, 74538 165th, Albert Lea, MN 56007, Phone: 507-377-0808
Specialties: Anything conceived by maker's imagination complete. Sole authorship. One-of-a-kind art knives, geared folding knives with various integrated opening and folding mechanisms, complex mosaic Damascus wedding bands, cowboy spurs, etc. Also sells complex mosaic Damascus barstock for other knifemakers. **Patterns:** Completely one-of-a-kind folders, daggers, axes, swords, all in high-art format. **Technical:** Forges and uses his own complex mosaic Damascus in maker-conceived patterns of "super nova" "static explosion", "static wormhole," from high-carbon bar stock of 1095, 1084, 15N20 and some nickel. Also currently experimenting heavily with mosaic mokume. **Prices:** $700-$2900, plus, currently on knives. **Remarks:** Full-time mosiac-damascus Metal Smith/Knifemaker. First knife sold in 1997. Doing business as Organic Damascus Forge. **Mark:** JOEL.

DAVIS, W.C., 19300 S. School Rd., Raymore, MO 64083, Phone: 816-331-4491
Specialties: Fancy working straight knives and folders. **Patterns:** Folding lockers and slip-joints; straight hunters, fighters and Bowies. **Technical:**

Grinds A2, ATS-34, 154, CPM T490V and CPM 530V. **Prices:** $100 to $300; some to $1000. **Remarks:** Full-time maker; first knife sold in 1972. **Mark:** Name.

DAVIS, JESSE W., 7398A Hwy. 3, Sarah, MS 38665, Phone: 662-382-7332
Specialties: Working straight knives and folders in standard patterns and to customer specs. **Patterns:** Boot knives, daggers. **Technical:** Grinds O1, A2, D2, 440C and commercial Damascus. **Prices:** $100 to $650. **Remarks:** Full-time maker; first knife sold in 1977. Former member Knife Makers Guild (in good standing). **Mark:** Name or initials.

DAVIS, JIM JR., 5129 Ridge St., Zephyrhills, FL 33541, Phone: 813-779-9213
Specialties: Presentation-grade fixed blade knives w/composite hidden tang handles. Employs a variety of ancient and contemporary ivories. **Patterns:** One-of-a-kind gents, personal, and executive knives and hunters w/ unique cam-lock pouch sheaths and display stands. **Technical:** Flat grinds ATS-34 and stainless Damascus w/most work by hand w/assorted files. **Prices:** $300 and up. **Remarks:** Full-time maker, first knives sold in 2000. **Mark:** Signature w/printed name over "HANDCRAFTED".

DAVIS, STEVE, 3370 Chatsworth Way, Powder Springs, GA 30127, Phone: 770-427-5740
Specialties: Traditional Gents and Ladies folders of his design and to customer specs. **Patterns:** Slip-joint folders, locking-liner folders, lock back folders. **Technical:** Grinds ATS-34, 440C and Damascus. Offers filework; prefers hand-rubbed finishes and natural handle materials. Uses pearl, ivory, stag and exotic woods. **Prices:** $250 to $600; some to $1500. **Remarks:** Part-time maker; first knife sold in 1988. Doing business as Custom Knives by Steve Davis. **Mark:** Name engraved on blade.

DAVIS, TERRY, Box 111, Sumpter, OR 97877, Phone: 541-894-2307
Specialties: Traditional and contemporary folders. **Patterns:** Multi-blade folders, whittlers and interframe multiblades; sunfish patterns. **Technical:** Flat-grinds ATS-34. **Prices:** $400 to $1000; some higher. **Remarks:** Full-time maker; first knife sold in 1985. **Mark:** Name in logo.

DAVIS, VERNON M., 2020 Behrens Circle, Waco, TX 76705, Phone: 254-799-7671
Specialties: Presentation-grade straight knives. **Patterns:** Bowies, daggers, boots, fighters, hunters and utility knives. **Technical:** Hollow-grinds 440C, ATS-34 and D2. Grinds an aesthetic grind line near choil. **Prices:** $125 to $550; some to $5000. **Remarks:** Part-time maker; first knife sold in 1980. **Mark:** Last name and city inside outline of state.

DAVIS, DON, 8415 Coyote Run, Loveland, CO 80537-9665, Phone: 970-669-9016, Fax: 970-669-8072
Specialties: Working straight knives in standard patterns or to customer specs. **Patterns:** Hunters, utility knives, skinners and survival knives. **Technical:** Grinds 440C, ATS-34. **Prices:** $75 to $250. **Remarks:** Full-time maker; first knife sold in 1985. **Mark:** Signature, city and state.

DAVISSON, COLE, 25939 Casa Loma Ct., Hemet, CA 92544, Phone: 909-652-8588

DAWKINS, DUDLEY L., 221 NW Broadmoor Ave., Topeka, KS 66606-1254
Specialties: Stylized old or "Dawkins Forged" with anvil in center. New Tang Stamps. **Patterns:** Straight knives. **Technical:** Mostly carbon steel; some Damascus-all knives forged. **Prices:** $125 and up. **Remarks:** All knives supplied with wood-lined sheaths. **Other:** ABS Member - sole authorship.

DAWSON, LYNN, 10A Town Plaza, Suite 303, Durango, CO 81301, Fax: 928-772-1729
Specialties: Swords, hunters, utility, and art pieces. **Patterns:** Over 25 patterns to choose from. **Technical:** Grinds 440C, ATS-34, own heat treating. **Prices:** $80 to $1000. **Remarks:** Custom work and her own designs. **Mark:** The name "Lynn" in print or script.

DAWSON, BARRY, 10A Town Plaza, Suite 303, Durango, CO 81301
Specialties: Samurai swords, combat knives, collector daggers, tactical, folding and hunting knives. **Patterns:** Offers over 60 different models. **Technical:** Grinds 440C, ATS-34, own heat-treatment. **Prices:** $75 to $1500; some to $5000. **Remarks:** Full-time maker; first knife sold in 1975. **Mark:** Last name, USA in print or last name in script.

DE MARIA JR., ANGELO, 12 Boronda Rd., Carmel Valley, CA 93924, Phone: 831-659-3381, Fax: 831-659-1315
Specialties: Damascus, fixed and folders, sheaths. **Patterns:** Mosiac and random. **Technical:** Forging 5160, 1084 and 15N20. **Prices:** $200 +. **Remarks:** Part-time maker. **Mark:** Angelo de Maria Carmel Valley, CA etch or AdM stamp.

custom knifemakers

DE VILLIERS, ANDRE AND KIRSTEN, Postnet Suite 263, Private Bag X6, Cascades 3202, SOUTH AFRICA, Phone: 27 33 4133312
Specialties: Tactical and up-market folders. **Technical:** Linerlock, buttonlocks and fixed blades. **Prices:** $300-$1200. **Remarks:** Collectors knives are artful with filework and individual specifications. **Mark:** ADV.

DEAN, HARVEY J., 3266 CR 232, Rockdale, TX 76567, Phone: 512-446-3111, Fax: 512-446-5060
Specialties: Collectible, functional knives. **Patterns:** Bowies, hunters, folders, daggers, swords, battle axes, camp and combat knives. **Technical:** Forges 1095, O1 and his Damascus. **Prices:** $350 to $10,000. **Remarks:** Full-time maker; first knife sold in 1981. **Mark:** Last name and MS.

DEBRAGA, JOSE C., 76 Rue de La Pointe, Aux Lievres Quebec, CANADA G1K 5Y3, Phone: 418-948-0105, Fax: 418-948-0105
Specialties: Art knives, fantasy pieces and working knives of his design or to customer specs. **Patterns:** Knives with sculptured or carved handles, from miniatures to full-size working knives. **Technical:** Grinds and hand-files 440C and ATS-34. A variety of steels and handle materials available. Offers lost wax casting. **Prices:** Start at $300. **Remarks:** Full-time maker; wax modeler, sculptor and knife maker; first knife sold in 1984. **Mark:** Initials in stylized script and serial number.

DEFEO, ROBERT A., 403 Lost Trail Dr., Henderson, NV 89014, Phone: 702-434-3717
Specialties: Working straight knives and period pieces. **Patterns:** Hunters, fighters, daggers and Bowies. **Technical:** Grinds ATS-34 and Damascus. **Prices:** $250 to $500; some higher. **Remarks:** Part-time maker; first knife sold in 1982. **Mark:** Last name.

DEFREEST, WILLIAM G., PO Box 573, Barnwell, SC 29812, Phone: 803-259-7883
Specialties: Working straight knives and folders. **Patterns:** Fighters, hunters and boots; locking folders and slip-joints. **Technical:** Grinds 440C, 154CM and ATS-34; clean lines and mirror finishes. **Prices:** $100 to $700. **Remarks:** Full-time maker; first knife sold in 1974. **Mark:** GORDON.

DEL RASO, PETER, 28 Mayfield Dr., Mt. Waverly, Victoria, 3149, AUSTRALIA, Phone: 613-9807 6771
Specialties: Fixed Blades, some folders, art knives. **Patterns:** Daggers, Bowies, tactical, boot, personal and working knives. **Technical:** Grinds ATS-34, commercial Damascus and any other type of steel on request. **Prices:** $100 to $1500. **Remarks:** Part-time maker, first show in 1993. **Mark:** Makers surname stamped.

DELAROSA, JIM, 202 Maccarthur Dr., Mukwonago, WI 53149, Phone: 262-363-9605
Specialties: Working straight knives and folders of his design or customer specs. **Patterns:** Hunters, skinners, fillets, utility and locking folders. **Technical:** Grinds ATS-34, 440-C, D2, 01 and commercial Damascus. **Prices:** $75 to $450; some higher. **Remarks:** Part-time maker. **Mark:** First and last name, city and state.

DELL, WOLFGANG, Am Alten Berg 9, D-73277 Owen-Teck, GERMANY, Phone: 49-7021-81802
Specialties: Fancy high-art straight of his design and to customer specs. **Patterns:** Fighters, hunters, Bowies and utility/camp knives. **Technical:** Grinds ATS-34, RWL-34, Elmax, Damascus (Fritz Schneider). Offers high gloss finish and engraving. **Prices:** $500 to $1000; some to $1600. **Remarks:** Full-time maker; first knife sold in 1992. **Mark:** Hopi hand of peace. **Other:** Member of German Knife maker Guild since 1993. Member of the Italian Knife maker Guild since 2000.

DELLANA, Starlani Int'l. Inc., 1135 Terminal Way Ste. #209, Reno, NV 89502, Phone: 775-352-4247, Fax: 775-201-0038
Specialties: Collector grade fancy/embellished high art folders and art daggers. **Patterns:** Locking folders and art daggers. **Technical:** Forges her own Damascus and W-2. Engraves, does stone setting, filework, carving and gold/platinum fabrication. Prefers exotic, high karat gold, platinum, silver, gemstone and mother-of-pearl handle materials. **Price:** Upscale. **Remarks:** Sole authorship, full-time maker, first knife sold in 1994. **Mark:** First name. **Other:** Also does one high art collaboration a year with Van Barnett. Member: Art Knife Invitational and ABS; voting member: Knifemakers Guild.

DELONG, DICK, 17561 E. Ohio Circle, Aurora, CO 80017, Phone: 303-745-2652
Specialties: Fancy working knives and fantasy pieces. **Patterns:** Hunters and small skinners. **Technical:** Grinds and files O1, D2, 440C and Damascus. Offers cocobolo and Osage orange for handles. **Prices:** Start at $50. **Remarks:** Part-time maker. **Mark:** Last name; some unmarked. **Other:** Member of Art Knife Invitational. Voting member of Knifemakers Guild. Member of ABS.

DEMENT, LARRY, PO Box 1807, Prince Fredrick, MD 20678, Phone: 410-586-9011
Specialties: Fixed blades. **Technical:** Forged and stock removal. **Prices:** $75 to $200. **Remarks:** Affordable, good feelin, quality knives. **Other:** Part-time maker.

DEMPSEY, DAVID, 103 Chadwick Dr., Macon, GA 31210, Phone: 478-474-4948
Specialties: Tactical, Utility, Working, Classic straight knives. **Patterns:** Fighters, Tantos, Hunters, Neck, Utility or Customer design. **Technical:** Grinds carbon steel and stainless including S30V. (differential heat treatment), Stainless Steels. **Prices:** Start at $150 for Neck Knives. **Remarks:** Full-time maker. First knife sold 1998. **Mark:** First and last name over knives.

DEMPSEY, GORDON S., PO Box 7497, N. Kenai, AK 99635, Phone: 907-776-8425
Specialties: Working straight knives. **Patterns:** Pattern welded Damascus and carbon steel blades. **Technical:** Pattern welded Damascus and carbon steel. **Prices:** $80 to $250. **Remarks:** Part-time maker; first knife sold in 1974. **Mark:** Name.

DENNEHY, DAN, PO Box 2F, Del Norte, CO 81132, Phone: 719-657-2545
Specialties: Working knives, fighting and military knives, throwing knives. **Patterns:** Full range of straight knives, tomahawks, buckle knives. **Technical:** Forges and grinds A2, O1 and D2. **Prices:** $200 to $500. **Remarks:** Full-time maker; first knife sold in 1942. **Mark:** First name and last initial, city, state and shamrock.

DENNING, GENO, Caveman Engineering, 135 Allenvalley Rd., Gaston, SC 29053, Phone: 803-794-6067
Specialties: Mirror finish. **Patterns:** Hunters, fighters, folders. **Technical:** ATS-34, 440V, S-30-V D-2. **Prices:** $100 and up. **Remarks:** Full-time maker since 1996. Sole income since 1999. **Mark:** Denning with year below. **Other:** A director of SCAK. South Carolina Association of Knifemakers.

DENT, DOUGLAS M., 1208 Chestnut St., S. Charleston, WV 25309, Phone: 304-768-3308
Specialties: Straight and folding sportsman's knives. **Patterns:** Hunters, boots and Bowies, interframe folders. **Technical:** Forges and grinds D2, 440C, 154CM and plain tool steels. **Prices:** $70 to $300; exceptional knives to $800. **Remarks:** Part-time maker; first knife sold in 1969. **Mark:** Last name.

DERINGER, CHRISTOPH, 625 Chemin Lower, Cookshire Quebec, CANADA J0B 1M0, Phone: 819-345-4260
Specialties: Traditional working/using straight knives and folders of his design and to customer specs. **Patterns:** Boots, hunters, folders, art knives, kitchen knives and utility/camp knives. **Technical:** Forges 5160, O1 and Damascus. Offers a variety of filework. **Prices:** Start at $250. **Remarks:** Full-time maker; first knife sold in 1989. **Mark:** Last name stamped/engraved.

DERR, HERBERT, 413 Woodland Dr., St. Albans, WV 25177, Phone: 304-727-3866
Specialties: Damascus one-of-a-kind knives, carbon steels also. **Patterns:** Birdseye, Ladder back, Mosaics. **Technical:** All styles functional as well as artistically pleasing. **Prices:** $90 to $175 carbon, Damascus $250 to $800. **Remarks:** All Damascus made by maker. **Mark:** H.K. Derr.

DETMER, PHILLIP, 14140 Bluff Rd., Breese, IL 62230, Phone: 618-526-4834
Specialties: Working knives. **Patterns:** Bowies, daggers and hunters. **Technical:** Grinds ATS-34 and D2. **Prices:** $60 to $400. **Remarks:** Part-time maker; first knife sold in 1977. **Mark:** Last name with dagger.

DI MARZO, RICHARD, 2357 Center Pl., Birmingham, AL 35205, Phone: 205-252-3331

DICKERSON, GORDON S., 152 Laurel Ln., Hohenwald, TN 38462, Phone: 931-796-1187
Specialties: Traditional working straight knives; Civil War era period pieces. **Patterns:** Bowies, hunters, tactical, camp/utility knives; some folders. **Technical:** Forges carbon steel; pattern welded and cable Damascus. **Prices:** $150 to $500; some to $3000. **Mark:** Last name. **Other:** ABS member.

DICKERSON, GAVIN, PO Box 7672, Petit 1512, SOUTH AFRICA, Phone: +27 011-965-0988, Fax: +27 011-965-0988
Specialties: Straight knives of his design or to customer specs. **Patterns:** Hunters, skinners, fighters and Bowies. **Technical:** Hollow-grinds D2, 440C, ATS-34, 12C27 and Damascus upon request. Prefers natural handle materials; offers synthetic handle materials. **Prices:** $190 to $2500. **Remarks:** Part-time maker; first knife sold in 1982. **Mark:** Name in full.

DICKISON, SCOTT S., Fisher Circle, Portsmouth, RI 02871, Phone: 401-419-4175
Specialties: Working and using straight knives and locking folders of his design and automatics. **Patterns:** Trout knives, fishing and hunting knives. **Technical:** Forges and grinds commercial Damascus and D2, O1. Uses natural handle materials. **Prices:** $400 to $750; some higher. **Remarks:** Part-time maker; first knife sold in 1989. **Mark:** Stylized initials.

DICRISTOFANO, ANTHONY P., PO Box 2369, Northlake, IL 60164, Phone: 847-845-9598
Specialties: Japanese-style swords. **Patterns:** Katana, Wakizashi, Otanto, Kozuka. **Technical:** Tradition and some modern steels. All clay tempered and traditionally hand polished using Japanese wet stones. **Remarks:** Part-time maker. **Prices:** Varied, available on request. **Mark:** Blade tang signed in "Masatoni" Japanese.

DIEBEL, CHUCK, PO Box 13, Broussard, LA 70516-0013

DIETZ, HOWARD, 421 Range Rd., New Braunfels, TX 78132, Phone: 830-885-4662
Specialties: Lock-back folders, working straight knives. **Patterns:** Folding hunters, high-grade pocket knives. ATS-34, 440C, CPM 440V, D2 and stainless Damascus. **Prices:** $300 to $1000. **Remarks:** Full-time gun and knife maker; first knife sold in 1995. **Mark:** Name, city, and state.

DIETZEL, BILL, PO Box 1613, Middleburg, FL 32068, Phone: 904-282-1091
Specialties: Forged straight knives and folders. **Patterns:** His interpretations. **Technical:** Forges his Damascus and other steels. **Prices:** Middle ranges. **Remarks:** Likes natural materials; uses titanium in folder liners. **Mark:** Name. **Other:** Master Smith (1997).

DIGANGI, JOSEPH M., Box 950, Santa Cruz, NM 87567, Phone: 505-753-6414, Fax: 505-753-8144
Specialties: Kitchen and table cutlery. **Patterns:** French chef's knives, carving sets, steak knife sets, some camp knives and hunters. Holds patents and trademarks for "System II" kitchen cutlery set. **Technical:** Grinds ATS-34. **Prices:** $150 to $595; some to $1200. **Remarks:** Full-time maker; first knife sold in 1983. **Mark:** DiGangi Designs.

DILL, DAVE, 7404 NW 30th St., Bethany, OK 73008, Phone: 405-789-0750
Specialties: Folders of his design. **Patterns:** Various patterns. **Technical:** Hand-grinds 440C, ATS-34. Offers engraving and filework on all folders. **Prices:** Starting at $450. **Remarks:** Full-time maker; first knife sold in 1987. **Mark:** First initial, last name.

DILL, ROBERT, 1812 Van Buren, Loveland, CO 80538, Phone: 970-667-5144, Fax: 970-667-5144
Specialties: Fancy and working knives of his design. **Patterns:** Hunters, Bowies and fighters. **Technical:** Grinds 440C and D2. **Prices:** $100 to $800. **Remarks:** Full-time maker; first knife sold in 1984. **Mark:** Logo stamped into blade.

DILLUVIO, FRANK J., 13611 Joyce Dr., Warren, MI 48093, Phone: 810-775-1216
Specialties: Traditional working straight knives, some high-tech. **Patterns:** Hunters, Bowies, fishing knives, sub-hilts, liner lock folders and miniatures. **Technical:** Grinds D2, 440C, CPM; works for precision fits—no solder. **Prices:** $95 to $450; some to $800. **Remarks:** Full-time maker; first knife sold in 1984. **Mark:** Name and state.

DION, GREG, 3032 S. Jackson St., Oxnard, CA 93033, Phone: 805-483-1781
Specialties: Working straight knives, some fancy. Welcomes special orders. **Patterns:** Hunters, fighters, camp knives, Bowies and tantos. **Technical:** Grinds ATS-34, 154CM and 440C. **Prices:** $85 to $300; some to $600. **Remarks:** Part-time maker; first knife sold in 1985. **Mark:** Name.

DIOTTE, JEFF, Diotte Knives, 159 Laurier Dr., LaSalle Ontario, CANADA N9J 1L4, Phone: 519-978-2764

DIPPOLD, AL, 90 Damascus Ln., Perryville, MO 63775, Phone: 573-547-1119
Specialties: Fancy one-of-a-kind locking folders. **Patterns:** Locking folders. **Technical:** Forges and grinds mosaic and pattern welded Damascus. Offers filework on all folders. **Prices:** $500 to $3500; some higher. **Remarks:** Full-time maker; first knife sold in 1980. **Mark:** Last name in logo inside of liner.

DISKIN, MATT, PO Box 653, Freeland, WA 98249, Phone: 360-730-0451
Specialties: Damascus autos. **Patterns:** Dirks and daggers. **Technical:** Forges mosaic Damascus using 15N20, 1084, 02, 06, L6; pure nickel. **Prices:** Start at $500. Remarks; Full-time maker. **Mark:** Last name.

DIXON JR., IRA E., PO Box 2581, Ventura, CA 93002-2581, Phone: 805-659-5867
Specialties: Utilitarian straight knives of his design. **Patterns:** Camp, hunters, boot, fighters. **Technical:** Grinds ATS-34, 440C, D2, 5160.

Prices: $150 to $400. **Remarks:** Part-time maker; first knife sold in 1993. **Mark:** First name, Handmade.

DODD, ROBERT F., 4340 E Canyon Dr., Camp Verde, AZ 86322, Phone: 928-567-3333
Specialties: Useable fixed blade hunter/skinners, some Bowies and collectables. **Patterns:** Drop point. **Technical:** ATS-34 stainless and Damascus. **Prices:** $300 and up. **Remarks:** Hand tooled leather sheaths, users and collectables. **Mark:** R. F. Dodd, Camp Verde AZ.

DOGGETT, BOB, 1310 Vinetree Rd., Brandon, FL 33510, Phone: 813-786-9057
Specialties: Clean, functional working knives. **Patterns:** Classic-styled hunter, fighter and utility fixed blades; liner locking folders. **Technical:** Uses stainless steel and commercial Damascus, 416 stainless for bolsters and hardware, hand-rubbed satin finish, top quality handle materials and titanium liners on folders Uses a variety of modern stainless steels and commercial Damascus. **Prices:** Start at $175. **Remarks:** Part-time maker; specializes in web design for knife makers. **Mark:** Last name.

DOIRON, DONALD, 6 Chemin Petit Lac Des Ced, Messines PQ, CANADA JOX-2JO, Phone: 819-465-2489

DOLAN, ROBERT L., 220—B Naalae Rd., Kula, HI 96790, Phone: 808-878-6406
Specialties: Working straight knives in standard patterns, his designs or to customer specs. **Patterns:** Fixed blades and potter's tools, ceramic saws. **Technical:** Grinds O1, D2, 440C and ATS-34. Heat-treats and engraves. **Prices:** Start at $75. **Remarks:** Full-time tool and knife maker; first knife sold in 1985. **Mark:** Last name, USA.

DOLE, ROGER, DOLE CUSTOM KNIFE WORKS, PO Box 323, Buckley, WA 98321, Phone: 253-862-6770
Specialties: Folding knives. They include slip joint, lock back and locking liner type knives. Most have integral bolster and liners. The locking liner knives have a removable titanium side lock that is machined into the integral liner, they are also available with a split liner lock. **Technical:** Makes ATS-34, 440-C and BG-42 stainless steel. Has in stock or available all types of natural and synthetic handle materials. Uses 416, 303, and 304 stainless steel, 7075-T6 aluminum and titanium for the guards on the fixed blade knives and integral liners on the folding knives. The locking liner lock mechanisms are made from 6AL4V titanium. Uses the stock removal method to fabricate all of the blades produced. The blades are ground on a 2 X 72 inch belt grinder. Not a bladesmith. **Patterns:** 51 working designs for fixed blade knives. They include small bird and trout knives to skinning axes. Most are working designs. All come with hand crafted leather sheath Kydex sheaths; can be special ordered. **Remarks:** First knife sold in 1975.

DOMINY, CHUCK, PO Box 593, Colleyville, TX 76034, Phone: 817-498-4527
Specialties: Titanium liner lock folders. **Patterns:** Hunters, utility/camp knives and liner lock folders. **Technical:** Grinds 440C and ATS-34. **Prices:** $250 to $3000. **Remarks:** Full-time maker; first knife sold in 1976. **Mark:** Last name.

DOOLITTLE, MIKE, 13 Denise Ct., Novato, CA 94947, Phone: 415-897-3246
Specialties: Working straight knives in standard patterns. **Patterns:** Hunters and fishing knives. **Technical:** Grinds 440C, 154CM and ATS-34. **Prices:** $125 to $200; some to $750. **Remarks:** Part-time maker; first knife sold in 1981. **Mark:** Name, city and state.

DORNELES, LUCIANO OLIVERIRA, Rua 15 De Novembro 2222, Nova Petropolis, RS, BRAZIL 95150-000, Phone: 011-55-54-303-303-90
Specialties: Traditional "true" Brazilian-style working knives and to customer specs. **Patterns:** Brazilian hunters, utility and camp knives, Bowies, Dirk. A master at the making of the true "Faca Campeira Gaucha," the true camp knife of the famous Brazilian Gauchos. A Dorneles knife is 100% hand-forged with sledge hammers only. Can makes spectacular Damascus hunters/daggers. **Technical:** Forges only 52100 and his own Damascus, can put silver wire inlay on customer design handles on special orders; uses only natural handle materials. **Prices:** $250 to $1000. **Mark:** Symbol with L. Dorneles.

DOTSON, TRACY, 1280 Hwy. C-4A, Baker, FL 32531, Phone: 850-537-2407
Specialties: Folding fighters and small folders. **Patterns:** Liner lock and lockback folders. **Technical:** Hollow-grinds ATS-34 and commercial Damascus. **Prices:** Start at $250. **Remarks:** Part-time maker; first knife sold in 1995. **Mark:** Last name.

DOUGLAS, JOHN J., 506 Powell Rd., Lynch Station, VA 24571, Phone: 804-369-7196
Specialties: Fancy and traditional straight knives and folders of his design and to customer specs. **Patterns:** Locking folders, swords and sgian dubhs. **Technical:** Grinds 440C stainless, ATS-34 stainless and customer's choice. Offers newly designed non-pivot uni-lock folders. Prefers

custom knifemakers

highly polished finish. **Prices:** $160 to $1400. **Remarks:** Full-time maker; first knife sold in 1975. Doing business as Douglas Keltic. **Mark:** Stylized initial. Folders are numbered; customs are dated.

DOURSIN, GERARD, Chemin des Croutoules, F 84210, Pernes les Fontaines, FRANCE
 Specialties: Period pieces. **Patterns:** Liner locks and daggers. **Technical:** Forges mosaic Damascus. **Prices:** $600 to $4000. **Remarks:** First knife sold in 1983. **Mark:** First initial, last name and I stop the lion.

DOUSSOT, LAURENT, 6262 De La Roche, Montreal, Quebec, CANADA H2H 1W9, Phone: 516-270-6992, Fax: 516-722-1641
 Specialties: Fancy and embellished folders and fantasy knives. **Patterns:** Fighters and locking folders. **Technical:** Grinds ATS-34 and commercial Damascus. Scale carvings on all knives; most bolsters are carved titanium. **Prices:** $350 to $3000. **Remarks:** Part-time maker; first knife was sold in 1992. **Mark:** Stylized initials inside circle.

DOWELL, T.M., 139 NW St. Helen's Pl., Bend, OR 97701, Phone: 541-382-8924
 Specialties: Integral construction in hunting knives. **Patterns:** Limited to featherweights, lightweights, integral hilt and caps. **Technical:** Grinds D-2, BG-42 and Vasco wear. **Prices:** $185 and up. **Remarks:** Full-time maker; first knife sold in 1967. **Mark:** Initials logo.

DOWNIE, JAMES T., 10076 Estate Dr., Port Franks, Ont., CANADA NOM 2LO, Phone: 519-243-1488, Fax: 519-243-1487
 Specialties: Serviceable straight knives and folders; period pieces. **Patterns:** Hunters, Bowies, camp knives and miniatures. **Technical:** Grinds D2, 440C and ATS-34, Damasteel, stainless steel Damascus. **Prices:** $100 to $500; some higher. **Remarks:** Full-time maker, first knife sold in 1978. **Mark:** Signature of first and middle initials, last name.

DOWNING, TOM, 2675 12th St., Cuyahoga Falls, OH 44223, Phone: 330-923-7464
 Specialties: Working straight knives; period pieces. **Patterns:** Hunters, fighters and tantos. **Technical:** Grinds 440C, ATs-34 and CPM-T-440V. Prefers natural handle materials. **Prices:** $150 to $900, some to $1500. **Remarks:** Part-time maker; first knife sold in 1979. **Mark:** First and middle initials, last name.

DOWNING, LARRY, 12268 Hwy. 181N, Bremen, KY 42325, Phone: 270-525-3523, Fax: 270-525-3372
 Specialties: Working straight knives and folders. **Patterns:** From mini-knives to daggers, folding lockers to interframes. **Technical:** Forges and grinds 154CM, ATS-34 and his own Damascus. **Prices:** $150 to $750; some higher. **Remarks:** Part-time maker; first knife sold in 1979. **Mark:** Name in arrowhead.

DOWNS, JAMES F., 35 Sunset Rd., Londonderry, OH 45647, Phone: 740-887-2099
 Specialties: Working straight knives of his design or to customer specs. **Patterns:** Folders, Bowies, boot, hunters, utility. **Technical:** Grinds 440C and other steels. Prefers mastodon ivory, all pearls, stabilized wood and elephant ivory. **Prices:** $75 to $1200. **Remarks:** Full-time maker; first knife sold in 1980. Brochures $2. **Mark:** Last name.

DOX, JAN, Zwanebloemlaan 27, B 2900 Schoten, BELGIUM, Phone: 32 3 658 77 43
 Specialties: Working/using knives, from kitchen to battlefield. **Patterns:** Own designs, some based on traditional ethnic patterns (Scots, Celtic, Scandinavian and Japanese) or to customer specs. **Technical:** Grinds D2/A2 and stainless, forges carbon steels, convex edges. Handles: Wrapped in modern or traditional patterns, resin impregnated if desired. Natural or synthetic materials, some carved. **Prices:** Start at 25 to 50 Euro (USD) and up. **Remarks:** Spare-time maker, first knife sold 2001. **Mark:** Name or stylized initials.

DOZIER, BOB, PO Box 1941, Springdale, AR 72765, Phone: 888-823-0023/479-756-0023, Fax: 479-756-9139
 Specialties: Using knives (fixed blades and folders). **Patterns:** Some fine collector-grade knives. **Technical:** Uses D2. Prefers Micarta handle material. **Prices:** Using knives: $145 to $595. **Remarks:** Full-time maker; first knife sold in 1965. **Mark:** State, made, last name in a circle (for fixed blades); Last name with arrow through 'D' and year over name (for folders). **Other:** Also sells a semi-handmade line of fixed blade with mark; state, knives, last name in circle.

DRAPER, MIKE, #10 Creek Dr., Riverton, WY 82501, Phone: 307-856-6807
 Specialties: Hand-forged working straight knives, folders. **Patterns:** Hunters, Bowies and camp knives, tactical survival. **Technical:** Grinds 530V and Damascus. **Prices:** Starting at $250+. **Remarks:** Full-time maker; first knife sold in 1996. **Mark:** Initials M.J.D. or name, city and state.

DRAPER, AUDRA, #10 Creek Dr., Riverton, WY 82501, Phone: 307-856-6807 or 307-851-0426 cell
 Specialties: One-of-a-kind straight and folding knives. Also pendants, earring and bracelets of Damascus. **Patterns:** Design custom knives,

using, Bowies, and mini's. **Technical:** Forge Damascus; heat-treats all knives. **Prices:** Vary depending on item. **Remarks:** Full-time maker; master bladesmith in the ABS. Member of the PKA; first knife sold in 1995. **Mark:** Audra.

DREW, GERALD, 2 Glenn Cable, Asheville, NC 28805, Phone: 828-299-7821
 Specialties: Blade ATS-34 5 1/2". Handle spalted Maple. 10" OAL. Straight knives. **Patterns:** Hunters, camp knives, some Bowies and tactical. **Technical:** ATS-34 preferred. **Price:** $110 to $200. **Mark:** GL DREW.

DRISCOLL, MARK, 4115 Avoyer Pl., La Mesa, CA 91941, Phone: 619-670-0695
 Specialties: High-art, period pieces and working/using knives of his design or to customer specs; some fancy. **Patterns:** Swords, Bowies, Fighters, daggers, hunters and primitive (mountain man-styles). **Technical:** Forges 52100, 5160, O1, L6, 1095, and maker his own Damascus and mokume; also does multiple quench heat treating. Uses exotic hardwoods, ivory and horn, offers fancy file work, carving, scrimshaws. **Prices:** $150 to $550; some to $1500. **Remarks:** Part-time maker; first knife sold in 1986. Doing business as Mountain Man Knives. **Mark:** Double "M".

DRISKILL, BERYL, PO Box 187, Braggadocio, MO 63826, Phone: 573-757-6262
 Specialties: Fancy working knives. **Patterns:** Hunting knives, fighters, Bowies, boots, daggers and lockback folders. **Technical:** Grinds ATS-34. **Prices:** Start at $200. **Remarks:** Part-time maker; first knife sold in 1984. **Mark:** Name.

DROST, MICHAEL B., Rt. 2, Box 49, French Creek, WV 26218, Phone: 304-472-7901
 Specialties: Working/using straight knives and folders of all designs. **Patterns:** Hunters, locking folders and utility/camp knives. **Technical:** Grinds ATS-34, D2 and CPM-T-440V. Offers dove-tailed bolsters and spacers, filework and scrimshaw. **Prices:** $125 to $400; some to $740. **Remarks:** Full-time maker; first knife sold in 1990. Doing business as Drost Custom Knives. **Mark:** Name, city and state.

DROST, JASON D., Rt. 2, Box 49, French Creek, WV 26218, Phone: 304-472-7901
 Specialties: Working/using straight knives of his design. **Patterns:** Hunters and utility/camp knives. **Technical:** Grinds 154CM and D2. **Prices:** $125 to $5000. **Remarks:** Spare-time maker; first knife sold in 1995. **Mark:** First and middle initials, last name, maker, city and state.

DUBLIN, DENNIS, 728 Stanley St., Box 986, Enderby, BC, CANADA V0E 1V0, Phone: 604-838-6753
 Specialties: Working straight knives and folders, plain or fancy. **Patterns:** Hunters and Bowies, locking hunters, combination knives/axes. **Technical:** Forges and grinds high-carbon steels. **Prices:** $100 to $400; some higher. **Remarks:** Full-time maker; first knife sold in 1970. **Mark:** Name.

DUFF, BILL, 14380 Ghost Rider Dr., Reno, NV 89511, Phone: 775-851-9331
 Specialties: Straight knives and folders, some fancy. **Patterns:** Hunters, folders and miniatures. **Technical:** Grinds 440-C and commercial Damascus. **Prices:** $200-$1000 some higher. **Remarks:** First knife some in 1976. **Mark:** Bill Duff, city and state.

DUFOUR, ARTHUR J., 8120 De Armoun Rd., Anchorage, AK 99516, Phone: 907-345-1701
 Specialties: Working straight knives from standard patterns. **Patterns:** Hunters, Bowies, camp and fishing knives—grinded thin and pointed. **Technical:** Grinds 440C, ATS-34, AEB-L. Tempers 57-58R; hollow-grinds. **Prices:** $135; some to $250. **Remarks:** Part-time maker; first knife sold in 1970. **Mark:** Prospector logo.

DUGAN, BRAD M., 422 A Cribbage Ln., San Marcos, CA 92069, Phone: 760-752-4417

DUGGER, DAVE, 2504 West 51, Westwood, KS 66205, Phone: 913-831-2382
 Specialties: Working straight knives; fantasy pieces. **Patterns:** Hunters, boots and daggers in one-of-a-kind styles. **Technical:** Grinds D2, 440C and 154CM. **Prices:** $75 to $350; some to $1200. **Remarks:** Part-time maker; first knife sold in 1979. Not currently accepting orders. Doing business as Dog Knives. **Mark:** DOG.

DUNKERLEY, RICK, PO Box 582, Seeley Lake, MT 59868, Phone: 406-677-5496
 Specialties: Mosaic Damascus folders and carbon steel utility knives. **Patterns:** One-of-a-kind folders, standard hunters and utility designs. **Technical:** Forges 52100, Damascus and mosaic Damascus. Prefers natural handle materials. **Prices:** $200 and up. **Remarks:** Full-time maker; first knife sold in 1984, ABS Master Smith. Doing business as Dunkerley Custom Knives. **Mark:** Dunkerley, MS.

DUNN, STEVE, 376 Biggerstaff Rd., Smiths Grove, KY 42171, Phone: 270-563-9830
Specialties: Working and using straight knives of his design; period pieces. Patterns: Hunters, skinners, Bowies, fighters, camp knives, folders, swords and battle axes. Technical: Forges his Damascus, O1, 5160, L6 and 1095. Prices: Moderate to upscale. Remarks: Full-time maker; first knife sold in 1990. Mark: Last name and MS.

DUNN, CHARLES K., 17740 GA Hwy. 116, Shiloh, GA 31826, Phone: 706-846-2666
Specialties: Fancy and working straight knives and folders of his design and to customer specs. Patterns: Bowies, hunters and locking folders. Technical: Grinds 440C and ATS-34. Engraves; filework offered. Prices: $75 to $300. Remarks: Part-time maker; first knife sold in 1988. Mark: First initial, last name, city, state.

DURAN, JERRY T., PO Box 80692, Albuquerque, NM 87198-0692, Phone: 505-873-4676
Specialties: Tactical folders, Bowies, fighters, liner locks and hunters. Patterns: Folders, Bowies, hunters and tactical knives. Technical: Forges own Damascus and forges carbon steel. Prices: Moderate to upscale. Remarks: Full-time maker; first knife sold in 1978. Mark: Initials in elk rack logo.

DURHAM, KENNETH, BUZZARD ROOST FORGE, 10495 White Pike, Cherokee, AL 35616, Phone: 256-359-4287
Specialties: Bowies, dirks, hunters. Patterns: Traditional patterns. Technical: Forges 1095, 5160, 52100 and makes own Damascus. Prices: $85 to $1600. Remarks: Began making knives about 1995. Received journeyman stamp 1999. Mark: Bull's head with Ken Durham above and Cherokee AL below.

DURIO, FRED, 144 Gulino St., Opelousas, LA 70570, Phone: 337-948-4831
Specialties: Folders. Patterns: Liner locks; plain and fancy. Technical: Makes own Damascus. Prices: Moderate to upscale. Remarks: Full-time maker. Mark: Last name-Durio.

DUVALL, LARRY E., Rt. 3, Gallatin, MO 64640, Phone: 816-663-2742
Specialties: Fancy working straight knives and folders. Patterns: Hunters to swords, minis to Bowies; locking folders. Technical: Grinds D2, 440C and 154CM. Prices: $150 to $350; some to $2000. Remarks: Part-time maker; first knife sold in 1980. Mark: Name and address in logo.

DUVALL, FRED, 10715 Hwy. 190, Benton, AR 72015, Phone: 501-778-9360
Specialties: Working straight knives and folders. Patterns: Locking folders, slip joints, hunters, fighters and Bowies. Technical: Grinds D2 and CPM440V; forges 5160. Prices: $100 to $400; some to $800. Remarks: Part-time maker; first knife sold in 1973. Mark: Last name.

DYER, DAVID, 4531 Hunters Glen, Granbury, TX 76048, Phone: 817-573-1198
Specialties: Working skinners and early period knives. Patterns: Customer designs, his own patterns. Technical: Coal forged blades; 5160 and 52100 steels. Prices: $150 for neck-knives and small (3" to 3-1/2"). To $600 for large blades and specialty blades. Mark: Last name DYER electro etched. Other: Grinds D-2, 1095, L-6.

DYESS, EDDIE, 1005 Hamilton, Roswell, NM 88201, Phone: 505-623-5599
Specialties: Working and using straight knives in standard patterns. Patterns: Hunters and fighters. Technical: Grinds 440C, 154CM and D2 on request. Prices: $85 to $135; some to $250. Remarks: Spare-time maker; first knife sold in 1980. Mark: Last name.

DYRNOE, PER, Sydskraenten 10, Tulstrup, DK 3400 Hilleroed, DENMARK, Phone: +45 42287041
Specialties: Hand-crafted knives with zirconia ceramic blades. Patterns: Hunters, skinners, Norwegian-style tolle knives, most in animal-like ergonomic shapes. Technical: Handles of exotic hardwood, horn, fossil ivory, etc. Norwegian-style sheaths. Prices: Start at $500. Remarks: Part-time maker in cooperation with Hans J. Henriksen; first knife sold in 1993. Mark: Initial logo.

e

EAKER, ALLEN L., 416 Clinton Ave., Dept KI, Paris, IL 61944, Phone: 217-466-5160
Specialties: Traditional straight knives and folders of his design. Patterns: Hunters, locking folders and slip-joint folders. Technical: Grinds 440C; inlays. Prices: $125 to $325; some to $500. Remarks: Spare-time maker; first knife sold in 1994. Mark: Initials in tankard logo stamped on tang, serial number on back side.

EALY, DELBERT, PO Box 121, Indian River, MI 49749, Phone: 231-238-4705

EASLER JR., RUSSELL O., PO Box 301, Woodruff, SC 29388, Phone: 864-476-7830
Specialties: Working straight knives and folders. Patterns: Hunters, tantos and boots; locking folders and interframes. Technical: Grinds 440C, 154CM and ATS-34. Prices: $100 to $350; some to $800. Remarks: Part-time maker; first knife sold in 1973. Mark: Name or name with bear logo.

EATON, AL, PO Box 43, Clayton, CA 94517, Phone: 925-672-5351
Specialties: One-of-a-kind high-art knives and fantasy knives of his design, full size and miniature. Patterns: Hunters, fighters, daggers. Technical: Grinds 440C, 154CM and ATS-34; ivory and metal carving. Prices: $125 to $3000; some to $5000. Remarks: Full-time maker; first knife sold in 1977. Mark: Full name, city and state.

EATON, RICK, 9944 McCranie St., Shepherd, MT 59079 3126
Specialties: Interframe folders and one-hand-opening side locks. Patterns: Bowies, daggers, fighters and folders. Technical: Grinds 154CM, ATS-34, 440C and other maker's Damascus. Offers high-quality hand engraving, Bulino and gold inlay. Prices: Upscale. Remarks: Full-time maker; first knife sold in 1982. Mark: Full name or full name and address.

EBISU, HIDESAKU, 3-39-7 KOI OSAKO NISHI KU, Hiroshima City, JAPAN 733 0816

ECHOLS, ROGER, 46 Channing Rd., Nashville, AR 71852-8588, Phone: 870-451-9089
Specialties: Liner locks, auto-scale release, lock backs. Patterns: My own or yours. Technical: Autos. Prices: $500 to $1700. Remarks: Likes to use pearl, ivory and Damascus the most. Mark: Name. Other: Made first knife in 1984. Remarks: Part-time maker; tool and die maker by trade.

EDDY, HUGH E., 211 E Oak St., Caldwell, ID 83605, Phone: 208-459-0536

EDEN, THOMAS, PO Box 57, Cranbury, NJ 08512, Phone: 609-371-0774
Patterns: Fixed blade, working patterns, hand forged. Technical: Damascus. Mark: Eden (script). Remarks: ABS Smith.

EDGE, TOMMY, PO Box 156, Cash, AR 72421, Phone: 501-477-5210
Specialties: Fancy/embellished working knives of his design. Patterns: Bowies, hunters and utility/camping knives. Technical: Grinds 440C, ATS-34 and D2. Makes own cable Damascus; offers filework. Prices: $70 to $250; some to $1500. Remarks: Part-time maker; first knife sold in 1993. Mark: Stamped first initial, last name and stenciled name, city and state in oval shape.

EDWARDS, LYNN, 778 CR B91, W. Columbia, TX 77486, Phone: 979-345-4080, Fax: 979-345-3472
Specialties: Traditional working and using straight knives of his design and to customer specs. Patterns: Bowies, hunters and utility/camp knives. Technical: Forges 5168 and O1; forges and grinds D2. Triple-hardens on request; offers silver wire inlay, stone inlays and spacers, filework. Prices: $100 to $395; some to $800. Remarks: Part-time maker; first knife sold in 1988. Doing business as EandE Emporium. Mark: Last name in script.

EDWARDS, FAIN E., PO Box 280, Topton, NC 28781, Phone: 828-321-3127

EDWARDS, MITCH, 303 New Salem Rd., Glasgow, KY 42141, Phone: 270-651-9257
Specialties: Period pieces. Patterns: Neck knives, camp, rifleman and Bowie knives. Technical: All hand forged, forges own Damascus 01, 1084, 1095, L-6, 15N20. Prices: $200 to $1000. Remarks: Journeyman Smith. Mark: Broken heart.

EHRENBERGER, DANIEL ROBERT, 6192 Hwy 168, Shelbyville, MO 63469, Phone: 573-633-2010
Specialties: Affordable working/using straight knives of his design and to custom specs. Patterns: 10" western Bowie, fighters, hunting and skinning knives. Technical: Forges 1085, 1095, his own Damascus and cable Damascus. Prices: $80 to $500. Remarks: Full-time maker, first knife sold 1994. Mark: Ehrenberger JS.

EKLUND, MAIHKEL, Föne 1111, S-820 41 Farila, SWEDEN
Specialties: Collector-grade working straight knives. Patterns: Hunters, Bowies and fighters. Technical: Grinds ATS-34, Uddeholm and Dama steel. Engraves and scrimshaws. Prices: $150 to $700. Remarks: Full-time maker; first knife sold in 1983. Mark: Initials or name.

ELDER JR., PERRY B., 1321 Garretsburg Rd., Clarksville, TN 37042-2516, Phone: 931-647-9416
Specialties: Hunters, combat Bowies bird and trout. Technical: High-carbon steel and Damascus blades. Prices: $250 and up depending on blade desired. Mark: ELDER.

custom knifemakers

ELDRIDGE, ALLAN, 7731 Four Winds Dr., Ft Worth, TX 76133, Phone: 817-370-7778
Specialties: Fancy classic straight knives in standard patterns. **Patterns:** Hunters, Bowies, fighters, folders and miniatures. **Technical:** Grinds O1 and Damascus. Engraves silver-wire inlays, pearl inlays, scrimshaws and offers filework. **Prices:** $50 to $500; some to $1200. **Remarks:** Spare-time maker; first knife sold in 1965. **Mark:** Initials.

ELISHEWITZ, ALLEN, PO Box 3059, Canyon Lake, TX 78133, Phone: 830-899-5356
Specialties: Collectible high-tech working straight knives and folders of his design. **Patterns:** Working, utility and tactical knives. **Technical:** Grinds 154CM and stainless steel Damascus. All designs drafted and field-tested. **Prices:** $400 to $600. **Remarks:** Full-time maker; first knife sold in 1989. **Mark:** Last name with a Japanese crane.

ELKINS, R. VAN, PO Box 156, Bonita, LA 71223, Phone: 318-823-2124, Fax: 318-283-6802
Specialties: High-art Bowies, fighters, folders and period daggers; all one-of-a-kind pieces. **Patterns:** Welcomes customer designs. **Technical:** Forges his own Damascus in several patterns, O1 and 5160. **Prices:** $250 to $2800. **Remarks:** First knife sold in 1984. **Mark:** Last name.

ELLEFSON, JOEL, PO Box 1016, 310 S. 1st St., Manhattan, MT 59741, Phone: 406-284-3111
Specialties: Working straight knives, fancy daggers and one-of-a-kinds. **Patterns:** Hunters, daggers and some folders. **Technical:** Grinds A2, 440C and ATS-34. Makes own mokume in bronze, brass, silver and shibuishi; makes brass/steel blades. **Prices:** $75 to $500; some to $2000. **Remarks:** Part-time maker; first knife sold in 1978. **Mark:** Stylized last initial.

ELLERBE, W.B., 3871 Osceola Rd., Geneva, FL 32732, Phone: 407-349-5818
Specialties: Period and primitive knives and sheaths. **Patterns:** Bowies to patch knives, some tomahawks. **Technical:** Grinds Sheffield O1 and files. **Prices:** Start at $35. **Remarks:** Full-time maker; first knife sold in 1971. Doing business as Cypress Bend Custom Knives. **Mark:** Last name or initials.

ELLIOTT, JERRY, 4507 Kanawha Ave., Charleston, WV 25304, Phone: 304-925-5045
Specialties: Classic and traditional straight knives and folders of his design and to customer specs. **Patterns:** Hunters, locking folders and Bowies. **Technical:** Grinds ATS-34, 154CM, O1, D2 and T-440-V. All guards silver-soldered; bolsters are pinned on straight knives, spot-welded on folders. **Prices:** $80 to $265; some to $1000. **Remarks:** Full-time maker; first knife sold in 1972. **Mark:** First and middle initials, last name, knife maker, city, state.

ELLIOTT, MARCUS, Pen Dinas, Wyddfydd Rd., Great Orme, Llandudno Gwynedd, GREAT BRITAIN LL30 2QL, Phone: 01492-872747
Specialties: Fancy working knives. **Patterns:** Boots and small hunters. **Technical:** Grinds O1, 440C and ATS-34. **Prices:** $160 to $250. **Remarks:** Spare-time maker; first knife sold in 1981. Makes only a few knives each year. **Mark:** First name, middle initial, last name, knife maker, city, state.

ELLIS, WILLY B., WILLY B CUSTOM STICKS and PICKS, 10 Cutler Rd., Litchfield, NH 03052, Phone: 603-880-9722, Fax: SAME
Specialties: One-of-a-kind high art and fantasy knives of his design. Occasional customs full size and miniatures. **Patterns:** Bowies, fighters, hunters and others. **Technical:** Grinds 440C, ATS-34, 1095, carbon Damascus, ivory bone, stone and metal carving. **Prices:** $175-$15,000. **Remarks:** Full-time maker, first knife made in 1973.Probationary member Knifemakers Guild. **Mark:** Willy B. or WB"S C etched or carved. **Other:** Jewel setting inlays.

ELLIS, DAVE/ABS MASTERSMITH, 380 South Melrose Dr. #407, Vista, CA 92083, Phone: 760-643-4032 Eves: 760-945-7177
Specialties: Bowies, utility and combat knives. **Patterns:** Using knives to art quality pieces. **Technical:** Forges 5160, L-6, 52100, cable and his own Damascus steels. **Prices:** $300 to $4000. **Remarks:** Part-time maker. California's first ABS Master Smith. **Mark:** Dagger-Rose with name and M.S. mark.

ELLIS, WILLIAM DEAN, 8875 N. Barton, Fresno, CA 93720, Phone: 209-299-0303
Specialties: Classic and fancy knives of his design. **Patterns:** Boots, fighters and utility knives. **Technical:** Grinds ATS-34, D2 and Damascus. Offers tapered tangs and six patterns of filework; tooled multi-colored sheaths. **Prices:** $180 to $350; some to $1300. **Remarks:** Part-time maker; first knife sold in 1991. Doing business as Billy's Blades. **Mark:** "B" in a five-point star next to "Billy," city and state within a rounded-corner rectangle.

ELROD, ROGER R., 58 Dale Ave., Enterprise, AL 36330, Phone: 334-347-1863

EMBRETSEN, KAJ, FALUVAGEN 67, S-82821 Edsbyn, SWEDEN, Phone: 46-271-21057, Fax: 46-271-22961
Specialties: High quality folders. **Patterns:** Scandinavian-style knives. **Technical:** Forges Damascus. Uses only his blades; natural materials. **Prices:** Upscale. **Remarks:** Full-time maker. **Mark:** Name.

EMERSON, ERNEST R., PO Box 4180, Torrance, CA 90510-4180, Phone: 310-212-7455
Specialties: High-tech folders and combat fighters. **Patterns:** Fighters, liner lock combat folders and SPECWAR combat knives. **Technical:** Grinds 154CM and Damascus. Makes folders with titanium fittings, liners and locks. Chisel grind specialist. **Prices:** $550 to $850; some to $10,000. **Remarks:** Full-time maker; first knife sold in 1983. **Mark:** Last name and Specwar knives.

ENCE, JIM, 145 S 200 East, Richfield, UT 84701, Phone: 435-896-6206
Specialties: High-art period pieces (spec in California knives) art knives. **Patterns:** Art, boot knives, fighters, Bowies and occasional folders. **Technical:** Grinds 440C for polish and beauty boys'; makes own Damascus. **Prices:** Upscale. **Remarks:** Full-time maker; first knife sold in 1977. Does own engraving, gold work and stone work. **Mark:** Ence, usually engraved. **Other:** Guild member since 1977. Founding member of the AKI.

ENGLAND, VIRGIL, 1340 Birchwood St., Anchorage, AK 99508, Phone: 907-274-9494
Specialties: Edged weapons and equipage, one-of-a-kind only. **Patterns:** Axes, swords, lances and body armor. **Technical:** Forges and grinds as pieces dictate. Offers stainless and Damascus. **Prices:** Upscale. **Remarks:** A veteran knife maker. No commissions. **Mark:** Stylized initials.

ENGLE, WILLIAM, 16608 Oak Ridge Rd., Boonville, MO 65233, Phone: 816-882-6277
Specialties: Traditional working and using straight knives of his design. **Patterns:** Hunters, Bowies and fighters. **Technical:** Grinds 440C, ATS-34 and 154 CM. **Prices:** $250 to $500; some higher. **Remarks:** Part-time maker; first knife sold in 1982. All knives come with certificate of authenticity. **Mark:** Last name in block lettering.

ENGLEBRETSON, GEORGE, 1209 NW 49th St., Oklahoma City, OK 73118, Phone: 405-840-4784
Specialties: Working straight knives. **Patterns:** Hunters and Bowies. **Technical:** Grinds A2, D2, 440C and ATS-34. **Prices:** Start at $150. **Remarks:** Full-time maker; first knife sold in 1967. **Mark:** "By George," name and city.

ENGLISH, JIM, 14586 Olive Vista Dr., Jamul, CA 91935, Phone: 619-669-0833
Specialties: Traditional working straight knives to customer specs. **Patterns:** Hunters, Bowies, fighters, tantos, daggers, boot and utility/camp knives. **Technical:** Grinds 440C, ATS-34, commercial Damascus and customer choice. **Prices:** $130 to $350. **Remarks:** Part-time maker; first knife sold in 1985. In addition to custom line, also does business as Mountain Home Knives. **Mark:** Double "A," Double "J" logo.

ENNIS, RAY, 1220S 775E, Ogden, UT 84404, Phone: 800-410-7603, Fax: 501-621-2683

ENOS III, THOMAS M., 12302 State Rd. 535, Orlando, FL 32836, Phone: 407-239-6205
Specialties: Heavy-duty working straight knives; unusual designs. **Patterns:** Swords, machetes, daggers, skinners, filleting, period pieces. **Technical:** Grinds 440C, D2, 154CM. **Prices:** $75 to $1500. **Remarks:** Full-time maker; first knife sold in 1972. **Mark:** Name in knife logo and year, type of steel and serial number. **Other:** No longer accepting custom requests. Will be making his own designs. Send SASE for listing of items for sale.

ENTIN, ROBERT, 127 Pembroke St. 1, Boston, MA 02118

EPTING, RICHARD, 4021 Cody Dr., College Station, TX 77845, Phone: 979-690-6496
Specialties: Folders and working straight knives. **Patterns:** Hunters, Bowies, and locking folders. **Technical:** Forges high-carbon steel and his own Damascus. **Prices:** $200 to $800; some to $1800. **Remarks:** Part-time maker; first knife sold 1996. **Mark:** Name in arch logo.

ERICKSON, L.M., PO Box 132, Liberty, UT 84310, Phone: 801-745-2026
Specialties: Straight knives; period pieces. **Patterns:** Bowies, fighters, boots and hunters. **Technical:** Grinds 440C, 154CM and commercial Damascus. **Prices:** $200 to $900; some to $5000. **Remarks:** Part-time maker; first knife sold in 1981. **Mark:** Name, city, state.

ERICKSON, WALTER E., 22280 Shelton Tr., Atlanta, MI 49709, Phone: 989-785-5262
Specialties: Unusual survival knives and high-tech working knives. **Patterns:** Butterflies, hunters, tantos. **Technical:** Grinds ATS-34 or customer

choice. **Prices:** $150 to $500; some to $1500. **Remarks:** Full-time maker; first knife sold in 1981. **Mark:** Last name in depressed area on blade.

ERIKSEN, JAMES THORLIEF, dba VIKING KNIVES, 3830 Dividend Dr., Garland, TX 75042, Phone: 972-494-3667, Fax: 972-235-4932

Specialties: Heavy-duty working and using straight knives and folders utilizing traditional, Viking original and customer specification patterns. Some high-tech and fancy/embellished knives available. **Patterns:** Bowies, hunters, skinners, boot and belt knives, utility/camp knives, fighters, daggers, locking folders, slip-joint folders and kitchen knives. **Technical:** Hollow-grinds 440C, D2, ASP-23, ATS-34, 154CM, Vascowear. **Prices:** $150 to $300; some to $600. **Remarks:** Full-time maker; first knife sold in 1985. Doing business as Viking Knives. For a color catalog showing 50 different models, mail $5 to above address. **Mark:** VIKING or VIKING USA for export.

ESSEGIAN, RICHARD, 7387 E. Tulare St., Fresno, CA 93727, Phone: 309-255-5950

Specialties: Fancy working knives of his design; art knives. **Patterns:** Bowies and some small hunters. **Technical:** Grinds A2, D2, 440C and 154CM. Engraves and inlays. **Prices:** Start at $600. **Remarks:** Part-time maker; first knife sold in 1986. **Mark:** Last name, city and state.

ETZLER, JOHN, 11200 N. Island, Grafton, OH 44044, Phone: 440-748-2460

Specialties: High-art and fantasy straight knives and folders of his design and to customer specs. **Patterns:** Folders, daggers, fighters, utility knives. **Technical:** Forges and grinds nickel Damascus and tool steel; grinds stainless steels. Prefers exotic, natural materials. **Prices:** $250 to $1200; some to $6500. **Remarks:** Full-time maker; first knife sold in 1992. **Mark:** Name or initials.

EVANS, CARLTON, PO Box 815, Aledo, TX 76008, Phone: 817-441-1363

Specialties: In high end and working liner locks, slip-joint sull and narrow tang knives. **Patterns:** Working, hunting and fighters. **Technical:** Use the stock removal method. The materials used are of the highest quality. **Prices:** Starts at $350. **Remarks:** Part-time knifemaker. Probationary member in knifemakers' guild.

EVANS, BRUCE A., 409 CR 1371, Booneville, MS 38829, Phone: 662-720-0193

Specialties: Forges blades. **Patterns:** Hunters, Bowies, or will work with customer. **Technical:** 5160, cable Damascus, pattern welded Damascus. **Prices:** $200 and up. **Mark:** Bruce A. Evans Same with JS on reverse of blade.

EVANS, VINCENT K. AND GRACE, 6301 Apache Trail, Show Low, AZ 85901, Phone: 928-537-9123

Specialties: Period pieces; swords. **Patterns:** Scottish, Viking, central Asian. **Technical:** Forges 5160 and his own Damascus. **Prices:** $300 to $2000; some to $8000. **Remarks:** Full-time maker; first knife sold in 1983. **Mark:** Last initial with fish logo.

EVANS, RONALD B., 209 Hoffer St., Middleton, PA 17057-2723, Phone: 717-944-5464

EWING, JOHN H., 3276 Dutch Valley Rd., Clinton, TN 37716, Phone: 615-457-5757

Specialties: Working straight knives, hunters, camp knives. **Patterns:** Hunters. **Technical:** Grinds 440, Forges 5160 52100; prefers forging. **Prices:** $150 to $2000. **Remarks:** Part-time maker; first knife sold in 1985. **Mark:** First initial, last name, some embellishing done on knives.

f

FAGAN, JAMES A., 109 S 17 Ave., Lake Worth, FL 33460, Phone: 561-585-9349

FANT JR., GEORGE, 1983 CR 3214, Atlanta, TX 75551-6515, Phone: (903) 846-2938

FARID R., MEHR, 8 Sidney Close, Tunbridge Wells, Kent, ENGLAND TN2 5QQ, Phone: 011-44-1892 520345

Specialties: High-tech fixed blades and titanium folders. **Patterns:** Chisel ground liner lock and integral mechanism folders. **Technical:** Grinds 440C, CPM-T-440V, CPM-420V, CPM-15V, CPMS125V, and T-1 high speed steel and Vasco-max alloy and tool steel. **Prices:** $550 to $15,000. **Remarks:** Full-time maker; first knife sold in 1991. **Mark:** First name and country.

FARR, DAN, 285 Glen Ellyn Way, Rochester, NY 14618, Phone: 585-721-1388

Specialties: Hunting, camping, fighting and utility. **Patterns:** Fixed blades. **Technical:** Forged or stock removal. **Prices:** $150-$750.

FASSIO, MELVIN G., 420 Tyler Way, Lolo, MT 59847, Phone: 406-273-9143

Specialties: Working folders to customer specs. **Patterns:** Locking folders, hunters and traditional-style knives. **Technical:** Grinds 440C. **Prices:** $125 to $350. **Remarks:** Part-time maker; first knife sold in 1975. **Mark:** Name and city, dove logo.

FAUCHEAUX, HOWARD J., PO Box 206, Loreauville, LA 70552, Phone: 318-229-6467

Specialties: Working straight knives and folders; period pieces. Also a hatchet with capping knife in the handle. **Patterns:** Traditional locking folders, hunters, fighters and Bowies. **Technical:** Forges W2, 1095 and his own Damascus; stock removal D2. **Prices:** Start at $200. **Remarks:** Full-time maker; first knife sold in 1969. **Mark:** Last name.

FAUST, DICK, 624 Kings Hwy. N, Rochester, NY 14617, Phone: 585-544-1948

Specialties: High-performance working straight knives. **Patterns:** Hunters and utility/camp knives. **Technical:** Hollow grinds ATS-34 and 154CM full tang. Exotic woods, stag and Micarta handles. Provides a custom leather sheath with each knife. **Prices:** From $100 to $500, some higher. **Remarks:** Full-time maker. **Mark:** Signature.

FAUST, JOACHIM, Kirchgasse 10, 95497 Goldkronach, GERMANY

FECAS, STEPHEN J., 1312 Shadow Lane, Anderson, SC 29625, Phone: 864-287-4834, Fax: 864-287-4834

Specialties: Front release lock backs, liner locks. Folders only. **Patterns:** Gents folders. **Technical:** Grinds ATS-34, Damascus-Ivories and pearl handles. **Prices:** $650 to $1200. **Remarks:** Full-time maker since 1980. First knife sold in 1977. **Mark:** Last name signature. **Other:** All knives hand finished to 1500 grit.

FEIGIN, B., Liir Corp, 3037 Holly Mill Run, Marietta, GA 30062, Phone: 770-579-1631, Fax: 770-579-1199

FELIX, ALEXANDER, PO Box 4036, Torrance, CA 90510, Phone: 310-320-1836

Specialties: Straight working knives, fancy ethnic designs. **Patterns:** Hunters, Bowies, daggers, period pieces. **Technical:** Forges carbon steel and Damascus; forged stainless and titanium jewelry, gold and silver casting. **Prices:** $110 and up. **Remarks:** Jeweler, ABS Journeyman Smith. **Mark:** Last name.

FELLOWS, MIKE, PO Box 166, Velddrie 7365, SOUTH AFRICA, Phone: 27 82 960 3868

Specialties: Miniatures, art knives, subhilt fighters and folders. **Patterns:** Original designs and client's specs. **Technical:** Uses own Damascus (L6 and nickel). **Other:** All knives carry strong, reliable thru-tang handles screwed and bonded together. Uses only indigenous material for handles, i.e., various hard woods, selected horns, ivory, warthog tusk, hippo tooth, etc. Love to carve animal heads; favorite-Roses. **Mark:** "Shin" letter from Hebrew alphabet in front of Hebrew word "Karat". **Prices:** R800 – R5500 (approximately $100 to $700).

FERDINAND, DON, PO Box 1564, Shady Cove, OR 97539-1564, Phone: 503-560-3355

Specialties: One-of-a-kind working knives and period pieces; all tool steel Damascus. **Patterns:** Bowies, push knives and fishing knives. **Technical:** Forges high-carbon alloy steels L6, D2; makes his own Damascus. Exotic handle materials offered. **Prices:** $100 to $500. **Remarks:** Full-time maker since 1980. Does business as Wyvern. **Mark:** Initials connected.

FERGUSON, JIM, 32131 Via Bande, Temecula, CA 92592, Phone: 909-719-1552

Specialties: Nickel Damascus - Bowies - Daggers - Push Blades. **Patterns:** All styles. **Technical:** Forges Damascus and sells in U.S. and Canada. **Prices:** $120 to $5000. **Remarks:** 1200 Sq. Ft. commercial shop - 75 ton press **Mark:** Jim Ferguson over push blade. Also make swords, battle axes and utilities.

FERGUSON, JIM, PO Box 764, San Angelo, TX 76902, Phone: 915-651-6656

Specialties: Straight working knives and folders. **Patterns:** Working belt knives, hunters, Bowies and some folders. **Technical:** Grinds ATS-34, D2 and Vascowear. Flat-grinds hunting knives. **Prices:** $200 to $600; some to $1000. **Remarks:** Full-time maker; first knife sold in 1987. **Mark:** First and middle initials, last name.

FERGUSON, LEE, 1993 Madison 7580, Hindsville, AR 72738, Phone: 479-443-0084

Specialties: Straight working knives and folders, some fancy. **Patterns:** Hunters, daggers, swords, locking folders and slip-joints. **Technical:** Grinds D2, 440C and ATS-34; heat-treats. **Prices:** $50 to $600; some to $4000. **Remarks:** Full-time maker; first knife sold in 1977. **Mark:** Full name.

custom knifemakers

FERRARA, THOMAS, 122 Madison Dr., Naples, FL 33942, Phone: 813-597-3363, Fax: 813-597-3363
Specialties: High-art, traditional and working straight knives and folders of all designs. Patterns: Boots, Bowies, daggers, fighters and hunters. Technical: Grinds 440C, D2 and ATS-34; heat-treats. Prices: $100 to $700; some to $1300. Remarks: Part-time maker; first knife sold in 1983. Mark: Last name.

FERRIER, GREGORY K., 3119 Simpson Dr., Rapid City, SD 57702, Phone: 605-342-9280

FERRIS, BILL, 186 Thornton Dr., Palm Beach Garden, FL 33418

FERRY, TOM, 16005 SE 322nd St., Auburn, WA 98092, Phone: 253-939-4468
Specialties: Damascus, fixed blades and folders. Patterns: Folders Damascus, and fixed blades. Technical: Specialize in Damascus and timascus TM (Titanium Damascus). Prices: $400 to $2000. Remarks: Name Tom Ferry DBA: Soos Creek Ironworks. Mark: Combined T and F in a circle and/or last name on folders. Other: Co-developer of Timascus TM (Titanium Damascus).

FIKES, JIMMY L., PO Box 3457, Jasper, AL 35502, Phone: 205-387-9302, Fax: 205-221-1980
Specialties: High-art working knives; artifact knives; using knives with cord-wrapped handles; swords and combat weapons. Patterns: Axes to buckskinners, camp knives to miniatures, tantos to tomahawks; spring less folders. Technical: Forges W2, O1 and his own Damascus. Prices: $135 to $3000; exceptional knives to $7000. Remarks: Full-time maker. Mark: Stylized initials.

FILIPPOU, IOANNIS-MINAS, 7 KRINIS STR NEA SMYRNI, ATHENS 17122, GREECE, Phone: (1) 935-2093

FINCH, RICKY D., 2446 HWY 191, West Liberty, KY 41472, Phone: 606-743-7151
Specialties: Traditional working/using straight knives of his design or to customer spec. Patterns: Hunters, skinners and utility/camp knives. Technical: Grinds 440C and ATS-34, hand rubbed stain finish, use Micarta, stabilized wood - natural and exotic. Prices: $55 to $175; some $250. Remarks: Part-time maker, first knife made 1994. Doing business as Finch Knives. Mark: Last name inside outline of state of Kentucky.

FIORINI, BILL, E2371 Axlen Rd., DeSoto, WI 54624, Phone: 608-780-5898
Specialties: Fancy working knives. Patterns: Hunters, boots, Japanese-style knives and kitchen/utility knives and folders. Technical: Forges own Damascus, mosaic and mokune-gane. Prices: Full range. Remarks: Full-time metal smith researching pattern materials. Mark: Orchid crest with name KOKA in Japanese.

FISHER, THEO (TED), 8115 Modoc Lane, Montague, CA 96064, Phone: 916-459-3804
Specialties: Moderately priced working knives in carbon steel. Patterns: Hunters, fighters, kitchen and buckskinner knives, Damascus miniatures. Technical: Grinds ATS-34, L6 and 440C. Prices: $65 to $165; exceptional knives to $300. Remarks: First knife sold in 1981. Mark: Name in banner logo.

FISHER, JAY, 1405 Edwards, Clouis, NM 88101, Phone: 505-763-2268, Fax: 505-463-2346
Specialties: High-art, ancient and exact working and using straight knives of his design and client's designs. Military working and commemoratives. Patterns: Hunters, daggers, folding knives, museum pieces and high-art sculptures. Technical: Grinds 440C, ATS-34, 01and D2. Prolific maker of stone-handled knives and swords. Prices: $250 to $50,000; some higher. Remarks: Full-time maker; first knife sold in 1980. Mark: Very fine— JaFisher—Quality Custom Knives. Other: High resolution etching, computer and manual engraving.

FISK, JERRY, 10095 Hwy. 278 W, Nashville, AR 71852, Phone: 870-845-4456
Specialties: Edged weapons, collectible and functional. Patterns: Bowies, daggers, swords, hunters, camp knives and others. Technical: Forges carbon steels and his own pattern welded steels. Prices: $250 to $15,000. Remarks: National living treasure. Mark: Name, MS.

FISTER, JIM, PO Box 307, Simpsonville, KY 40067
Specialties: One-of-a-kind collectibles and period pieces. Patterns: Bowies, camp knives, hunters, buckskinners, and daggers. Technical: Forges, 1085, 5160, 52100, his own Damascus, pattern and turkish. Prices: $150 to $2500. Remarks: Part-time maker; first knife sold 1982. Mark: Name and MS.

FITCH, JOHN S., 45 Halbrook Rd., Clinton, AR 72031-8910, Phone: 501-893-2020

FITZGERALD, DENNIS M., 4219 Alverado Dr., Fort Wayne, IN 46816-2847, Phone: 219-447-1081
Specialties: One-of-a-kind collectibles and period pieces. Patterns: Skinners, fighters, camp and utility knives; period pieces. Technical:

Forges 1085, 1095, L6, 5160, 52100, his own pattern and Turkish Damascus. Prices: $100 to $500. Remarks: Part-time maker; first knife sold in 1985. Doing business as The Ringing Circle. Mark: Name and circle logo.

FLINT, ROBERT, 2902 Aspen, Anchorage, AK 99517, Phone: 907-243-6706
Specialties: Working straight knives and folders. Patterns: Utility, hunters, fighters and gents. Technical: Grinds ATS-34, BG-42, D2 and Damascus. Prices: $150 and up. Remarks: Part-time maker, first knife sold in 1998. Mark: Last name; stylized initials.

FLORES, HENRY, 1000 Kiely Blvd #115, Santa Clara, CA 95051-4819, Phone: 408-246-0491

FLOURNOY, JOE, 5750 Lisbon Rd., El Dorado, AR 71730, Phone: 870-863-7208
Specialties: Working straight knives and folders. Patterns: Hunters, Bowies, camp knives, folders and daggers. Technical: Forges only high-carbon steel, steel cable and his own Damascus. Prices: $350 Plus. Remarks: First knife sold in 1977. Mark: Last name and MS in script.

FOGARIZZU, BOITEDDU, via Crispi, 6, 07016 Pattada, ITALY
Specialties: Traditional Italian straight knives and folders. Patterns: Collectible folders. Technical: forges and grinds 12C27, ATS-34 and his Damascus. Prices: $200 to $3000. Remarks: Full-time maker; first knife sold in 1958. Mark: Full name and registered logo.

FOGG, DON, 40 Alma Rd., Jasper, AL 35501-8813, Phone: 205-483-0822
Specialties: Swords, daggers, Bowies and hunting knives. Patterns: Collectible folders. Technical: Hand-forged high-carbon and Damascus steel. Prices: $200 to $5000. Remarks: Full-time maker; first knife sold in 1976. Mark: 24K gold cherry blossom.

FONTENOT, GERALD J., 901 Maple Ave., Mamou, LA 70554, Phone: 318-468-3180

FORREST, BRIAN, FORREST KNIVES, PO Box 203, Descanso, CA 91916, Phone: 619-445-6343
Specialties: Working straight knives, some fancy made to customer order. Patterns: Traditional patterns, Bowies, hunters, skinners and daggers. Technical: Grinds 440C, files and rasps. Prices: $125 and up. Remarks: Member of California Knifemakers Association. Full-time maker. First knife sold in 1971. Mark: Forrest USA.

FORSTALL, AL, 38379 Aunt Massey Rd., Pearl River, LA 70452, Phone: 504-863-2930
Specialties: Traditional working and using straight knives of his design or to customer specs. Patterns: Fighters, hunters and utility/camp knives. Technical: Grinds ATS-34, 440C, commercial Damascus and others upon request. Prices: $75 to $250. Remarks: Spare-time maker; first knife sold in 1991. Mark: Fleur-di-lis with name.

FORTHOFER, PETE, 5535 Hwy. 93S, Whitefish, MT 59937, Phone: 406-862-2674
Specialties: Interframes with checkered wood inlays; working straight knives. Patterns: Interframe folders and traditional-style knives; hunters, fighters and Bowies. Technical: Grinds D2, 440C, 154CM and ATS-34. Prices: $350 to $2500; some to $1500. Remarks: Part-time maker; full-time gunsmith. First knife sold in 1979. Mark: Name and logo.

FORTUNE PRODUCTS, INC., 205 Hickory Creek Rd., Marble Falls, TX 78654, Phone: 830-693-6111, Fax: 830-693-6394
Specialties: Knife sharpeners.

FOSTER, BURT, 23697 Archery Range Rd., Bristol, VA 24202, Phone: 276-669-0121
Specialties: Working straight knives, Laminated blades, and some art knives of his design. Patterns: Bowies, hunters, daggers. Technical: Forges 52100, W-2 and own Damascus. Does own heat treating. Remarks: ABS Journeyman Smith. Full-time maker, believes in sole authorship. Mark: Signed "BF" initials.

FOSTER, R.L. (BOB), 745 Glendale Blvd., Mansfield, OH 44907, Phone: 419-756-6294

FOSTER, NORVELL C., 619 Holmgreen Rd., San Antonio, TX 78220, Phone: 210-333-1675
Specialties: Engraving; ivory handle carving. Patterns: American-large and small scroll-oak leaf and acorns. Prices: $25 to $400. Mark: N.C. Foster - S.A., TX and current year.

FOSTER, RONNIE E., 95 Riverview Rd., Morrilton, AR 72110, Phone: 501-354-5389
Specialties: Working, using knives, some period pieces, work with customer specs. Patterns: Hunters, fighters, Bowies, liner-lock folders, camp knives. Technical: Forge-5160, 1084, 01, 15N20-makes own Damascus. Prices: $200 (start). Remarks: Part-time maker. First knife sold 1994. Mark: Ronnie Foster MS.

FOSTER, TIMOTHY L., 723 Sweet Gum Acres Rd., El Dorado, AR 71730, Phone: 870-863-6188

FOSTER, AL, 118 Woodway Dr., Magnolia, TX 77355, Phone: 936-372-9297
Specialties: Straight knives and folders. Patterns: Hunting, fishing, folders and Bowies. Technical: Grinds 440-C, ATS-34 and D2. Prices: $100 to $1000. Remarks: Full-time maker; first knife sold in 1981. Mark: Scorpion logo and name.

FOWLER, RICKY AND SUSAN, FOWLER CUSTOM KNIVES, 18535-B Co. Rd. 45, Robertsdale, AL 36567, Phone: 251-550-6169
Specialties: Traditional working/using straight knives of his design or to customer specifications. Patterns: Skinners, fighters, tantos, Bowies and utility/camp knives. Technical: Grinds O1, exclusively. Prices: Start at $150. Remarks: Full-time maker; first knife sold in 1994. Doing business as Fowler Custom Knives. Mark: Last name tang stamped and serial numbered.

FOWLER, JERRY, 610 FM 1660 N., Hutto, TX 78634, Phone: 512-846-2860
Specialties: Using straight knives of his design. Patterns: A variety of hunting and camp knives, combat knives. Custom designs considered. Technical: Forges 5160, his own Damascus and cable Damascus. Makes sheaths. Prefers natural handle materials. Prices: Start at $150. Remarks: Part-time maker; first knife sold in 1986. Doing business as Fowler Forge Knife works. Mark: First initial, last name, date and J.S.

FOWLER, ED A., Willow Bow Ranch, PO Box 1519, Riverton, WY 82501, Phone: 307-856-9815
Specialties: High-performance working and using straight knives. Patterns: Hunter, camp, bird, and trout knives and Bowies. New model, the gentleman's Pronghorn. Technical: Low temperature forged 52100 from virgin 5 1/2 round bars, multiple quench heat treating, engraves all knives, all handles domestic sheep horn processed and aged at least 5 years. Makes heavy duty hand-stitched waxed harness leather pouch type sheathes. Prices: $800-$7000. Remarks: Full-time maker. First knife sold in 1962. Mark: Initials connected.

FOWLER, CHARLES R., 226 National Forest Rd. 48, Ft McCoy, FL 32134-9624, Phone: 904-467-3215

FOX, JACK L., 7085 Canelo Hills Dr., Citrus Heights, CA 95610, Phone: 916-723-8647
Specialties: Traditional working/using straight knives of all designs. Patterns: Hunters, utility/camp knives and bird/fish knives. Technical: Grinds ATS-34, 440C and D2. Prices: $125 to $225; some to $350. Remarks: Spare-time maker; first knife sold in 1985. Doing business as Fox Knives. Mark: Stylized fox head.

FOX, PAUL, 4721 Rock Barn Rd., Claremont, NC 28610, Phone: 828-459-2000, Fax: 828-459-9200
Specialties: Hi-Tech. Patterns: Naibsek, Otnat, and Zorro (tactical) knives. Technical: Grinds ATS-34, 440C and D2. Prices: $500. Remarks: Spare-time maker; first knife sold in 1985. Doing business as Fox Knives. Mark: Laser engraved.

FOX, WENDELL, 1480 S 39th St., Springfield, OR 97478, Phone: 541-747-2126
Specialties: Large camping knives and friction folders of his design and to customer specs. One-of-a-kind prices. Patterns: Hunters, locking folders, slip-joint folders and utility/camp knives. Technical: Forges and grinds high-carbon steel only. Prices: $200 and up. Remarks: Full-time maker; first knife sold in 1952. Mark: Stamped name or logo. Other: All one-of-a-kind pieces. Specializing in early American.

FRALEY, D.B., 1355 Fairbanks Ct., Dixon, CA 95620, Phone: 707-678-0393
Specialties: Traditional working/using straight knives and folders of his design and in standard patterns. Patterns: Fighters, hunters, utility/camp knives. Technical: Grinds ATS-34. Offers hand-stitched sheaths. Prices: Start at $100. Remarks: Part-time maker; first knife sold in 1990. Mark: First and middle initials, last name over buffalo.

FRAMSKI, WALTER P., 24 Rek Ln., Prospect, CT 06712, Phone: 203-758-5634

FRANCE, DAN, Box 218, Cawood, KY 40815, Phone: 606-573-6104
Specialties: Traditional working and using straight knives of his design. Patterns: Hunters, Bowies and utility/camp knives. Technical: Forges and grinds O1, 5160 and L6. Prices: $35 to $125; some to $350. Remarks: Spare-time maker; first knife sold in 1985. Mark: First name.

FRANCIS, VANCE, 2612 Alpine Blvd., Alpine, CA 91901, Phone: 619-445-0979
Specialties: Working straight knives. Patterns: Bowies and utility knives. Technical: Uses ATS-34, A2, D2 and Damascus; differentially tempers

large blades. Prices: $175 to $600. Remarks: Part-time maker. Mark: First name, last name, city and state under feather in oval.

FRANCIS, JOHN D., FRANCIS KNIVES, 18 Miami St., Ft. Loramie, OH 45845, Phone: 937-295-3941
Specialties: Utility and hunting-style fixed bladed knives of ATS-34 steel; micarta, exotic woods, and other types of handle materials. Prices: $100-$150 range. Remarks: Exceptional quality and a vague at factory prices. Mark: Francis-Ft. Loramie, OH stamped on tang.

FRANK, HEINRICH H., 13868 NW Keleka Pl., Seal Rock, OR 97376, Phone: 541-563-3041, Fax: 541-563-3041
Specialties: High-art investor-class folders, handmade and engraved. Patterns: Folding daggers, hunter-size folders and gents. Technical: Grinds 07 and O1. Prices: $4800 to $16,000. Remarks: Full-time maker; first knife sold in 1965. Doing business as H.H. Frank Knives. Mark: Name, address and date.

FRANKL, JOHN M., 12 Holden St., Cambridge, MA 02138, Phone: 617-547-0359
Specialties: Hand forged tool steel and Damascus. Patterns: Camp knives, Bowies, hunters and fighters. Technical: Forge own Damascus, 5160 and V 1084. Prices: $150-$1000. Mark: Last name "Frankl" on ricasso.

FRANKLIN, MIKE, 9878 Big Run Rd., Aberdeen, OH 45101, Phone: 937-549-2598
Specialties: High-tech tactical folders. Patterns: Tactical folders. Technical: Grinds CPM-T-440V, 440-C, ATS-34; titanium liners and bolsters; carbon fiber scales. Uses radical grinds and severe serrations. Prices: $275 to $600. Remarks: Full-time maker; first knife sold in 1969. Mark: Stylized boar with HAWG.

FRAPS, JOHN R., 3810 Wyandotte Tr., Indianpolis, IN 46240-3422, Phone: 317-849-9419, Fax: 317-842-2224
Specialties: Working and Collector Grade liner lock and slip joint folders. Patterns: One-of-a kind linerlocks and traditional slip joints. Technical: Flat and hollow grinds ATS-34, Damascus, Talonite, CPM S30V, 154Cm, Stellite 6K; hand rubbed or mirror finish. Prices: $200 to $1500, some higher. Remarks: Full-time maker; first knife sold in 1997. Mark: Cougar Creek Knives and/or name.

FRAZIER, RON, 2107 Urbine Rd., Powhatan, VA 23139, Phone: 804-794-8561
Specialties: Classy working knives of his design; some high-art straight knives. Patterns: Wide assortment of straight knives, including miniatures and push knives. Technical: Grinds 440C; offers satin, mirror or sand finishes. Prices: $85 to $700; some to $3000. Remarks: Full-time maker; first knife sold in 1976. Mark: Name in arch logo.

FRED, REED WYLE, 3149 X S., Sacramento, CA 95817, Phone: 916-739-0237
Specialties: Working using straight knives of his design. Patterns: Hunting and camp knives. Technical: Forges any 10 series, old files and carbon steels. Offers initialing upon request; prefers natural handle materials. Prices: $30 to $300; some to $300. Remarks: Part-time maker; first knife sold in 1994. Doing business as R.W. Fred Knife maker. Mark: Engraved first and last initials.

FREDERICK, AARON, 1213 Liberty Rd., West Liberty, KY 41472, Phone: 606-743-3399

FREEMAN, JOHN, 160 Concession St., Cambridge, Ont., CANADA N1R 2H7, Phone: 519-740-2767, Fax: 519-740-2785
Specialties: Kitchen knives, outdoor knives, sharpeners and folders. Patterns: Hunters, skinners, utilities, backpackers. Technical: Flat ground 440C. Prices: Start at $135 and up. Remarks: Full-time maker; first knife sold in 1985. Mark: Last name, country.

FREER, RALPH, 114 12th St., Seal Beach, CA 90740, Phone: 562-493-4925, Fax: same
Specialties: Exotic knives, liner locks, folding daggers, fixed blades. Patterns: All original. Technical: Lots of Damascus, ivory, pearl, jeweled, thumb studs, carving ATS-34, 420V, 530V. Prices: $400-$2500 and up. Mark: Freer in German-style text, also Freer shield.

FREILING, ALBERT J., 3700 Niner Rd., Finksburg, MD 21048, Phone: 301-795-2880
Specialties: Working straight knives and folders; some period pieces. Patterns: Boots, Bowies, survival knives and tomahawks in 4130 and 440C; some locking folders and interframes; ball-bearing folders. Technical: Grinds O1, 440C and 154CM. Prices: $100 to $300; some to $500. Remarks: Part-time maker; first knife sold in 1966. Mark: Initials connected.

FREY, STEVE, 19103 131st Drive SE, Snohomish, WA 98296, Phone: 360-668-7351
Remarks: Custom crafted knives-all styles.

custom knifemakers

FREY JR., W. FREDERICK, 305 Walnut St., Milton, PA 17847, Phone: 570-742-9576
Specialties: Working straight knives and folders, some fancy. **Patterns:** Wide range—boot knives to tomahawks. **Technical:** Grinds A2, O1 and D2; hand finishes only. **Prices:** $55 to $170; some to $600. **Remarks:** Spare-time maker; first knife sold in 1983. **Mark:** Last name in script.

FRIEDLY, DENNIS E., 12 Cottontail Ln. - E, Cody, WY 82414, Phone: 307-527-6811
Specialties: Fancy working straight knives and daggers, lock back folders and liner locks. **Patterns:** Hunters, fighters, short swords, minis and miniatures; new line of full-tang hunters/boots. **Technical:** Grinds 440C, commercial Damascus, mosaic Damascus and ATS-34 blades; prefers hidden tangs. **Prices:** $135 to $900; some to $2500. **Remarks:** Full-time maker; first knife sold in 1972. **Mark:** Name, city, state.

FRIGAULT, RICK, 3584 Rapidsview Dr., Niagara Falls ON, CANADA L2G 6C4, Phone: 905-295-6695
Specialties: Fixed blades. **Patterns:** Hunting, tactical and large Bowies. **Technical:** Grinds ATS-34, 440-C, D-2, CPMS30V, CPMS60V, CPMS90V, BG42 and Damascus. Use G-10, Micarta, ivory, antler, ironwood and other stabilized woods for carbon fiber handle material. Makes leather sheaths by hand. Tactical blades include a Concealex sheath made by "On Scene Tactical". **Remarks:** Sold first knife in 1997. Member of Canadian Knifemakers Guild. **Mark:** RFRIGAULT.

FRITZ, JESSE, 900 S. 13th St., Slaton, TX 79364, Phone: 806-828-5083, Fax: 915-530-0508
Specialties: Working and using straight knives in standard patterns. **Patterns:** Hunters, utility/camp knives and skinners with gut hook. **Technical:** Grinds 440C, O1 and 1095. Fline-napped steel design, blued blades, filework and machine jewelling. Inlays handles with turquoise, coral and mother-of-pearl. Makes sheaths. **Prices:** $85 to $275; some to $500. **Mark:** Crossed half ovals: handmade on top, last name in middle, city and state on bottom.

FRIZZELL, TED, 14056 Low Gap Rd., West Fork, AR 72774, Phone: 501-839-2516
Specialties: Swords, axes and self-defense weapons. **Patterns:** Small skeleton knives to large swords. **Technical:** Grinds 5160 almost exclusively—1/4" to 1/2"— bars some O1 and A2 on request. All knives come with Kydex sheaths. **Prices:** $45 to $1200. **Remarks:** Full-time maker; first knife sold in 1984. Doing business as Mineral Mountain Hatchet Works. Wholesale orders welcome. **Mark:** A circle with line in the middle; MM and HW within the circle.

FRONEFIELD, DANIEL, 137 Catherine Dr., Hampton Cove, AL 35763-9732, Phone: 256-536-7827
Specialties: Fixed and folding knives featuring meteorites and other exotic materials. **Patterns:** San-mai Damascus, custom Damascus. **Prices:** $500 to $3000.

FROST, DEWAYNE, 1016 Van Buren Rd., Barnesville, GA 30204, Phone: 770-358-1426
Specialties: Working straight knives and period knives. **Patterns:** Hunters, Bowies and utility knives. **Technical:** Forges own Damascus, cable, etc. as well as stock removal. **Prices:** $150-$500. **Remarks:** Part-time maker ABS Journeyman Smith. **Mark:** Liberty Hill Forge Dewayne Frost w/liberty bell.

FRUHMANN, LUDWIG, Stegerwaldstr 8, 84489 Burghausen, GERMANY
Specialties: High-tech and working straight knives of his design. **Patterns:** Hunters, fighters and boots. **Technical:** Grinds ATS-34, CPM-T-440V and Schneider Damascus. Prefers natural handle materials. **Prices:** $200 to $1500. **Remarks:** Spare-time maker; first knife sold in 1990. **Mark:** First initial and last name.

FUEGEN, LARRY, 617 N. Coulter Circle, Prescott, AZ 86303, Phone: 928-776-8777
Specialties: High-art folders and classic and working straight knives. **Patterns:** Forged scroll folders, lockback folders and classic straight knives. **Technical:** Forges 5160, 1095 and his own Damascus. Works in exotic leather; offers elaborate filework and carving; likes natural handle materials, now offers own engraving. **Prices:** $575 to $9000. **Remarks:** Full-time maker; first knife sold in 1975. **Mark:** Initials connected. Other: Sole authorship on all knives.

FUJIKAWA, SHUN, Sawa 1157 Kaizuka, Osaka 597 0062, JAPAN, Phone: 81-724-23-4032, Fax: 81-726-23-9229
Specialties: Folders of his design and to customer specs. **Patterns:** Locking folders. **Technical:** Grinds his own steel. **Prices:** $450 to $2500; some to $3000. **Remarks:** Part-time maker.

FUJISAKA, STANLEY, 45-004 Holowai St., Kaneohe, HI 96744, Phone: 808-247-0017
Specialties: Fancy working straight knives and folders. **Patterns:** Hunters, boots, personal knives, daggers, collectible art knives. **Technical:** Grinds 440C, 154CM and ATS-34; clean lines, inlays. **Prices:** $150 to $1200; some to $3000. **Remarks:** Full-time maker; first knife sold in 1984. **Mark:** Name, city, state.

FUKUTA, TAK, 38-Umeagae-cho, Seki-City, Gifu-Pref, JAPAN, Phone: 0575-22-0264
Specialties: Bench-made fancy straight knives and folders. **Patterns:** Sheffield-type folders, Bowies and fighters. **Technical:** Grinds commercial Damascus. **Prices:** Start at $300. **Remarks:** Full-time maker. **Mark:** Name in knife logo.

FULLER, JACK A., 7103 Stretch Ct., New Market, MD 21774, Phone: 301-798-0119
Specialties: Straight working knives of his design and to customer specs. **Patterns:** Fighters, camp knives, hunters, tomahawks and art knives. **Technical:** Forges 5160, O1, W2 and his own Damascus. Does silver wire inlay and own leather work, wood lined sheaths for big camp knives. **Prices:** $300 to $850. **Remarks:** Part-time maker. Master Smith in ABS; first knife sold in 1979. **Mark:** Fuller's Forge, MS.

FULLER, BRUCE A., 1305 Airhart Dr., Baytown, TX 77520, Phone: 713-427-1848
Specialties: One-of-a-kind working/using straight knives and folders of his designs. **Patterns:** Bowies, hunters, folders, and utility/camp knives. **Technical:** Forges high-carbon steel and his own Damascus. Prefers El Solo Mesquite and natural materials. Offers filework. **Prices:** $200 to $500; some to $1800. **Remarks:** Spare-time maker; first knife sold in 1991. Doing business as Fullco Forge. **Mark:** Fullco, M.S.

FULTON, MICKEY, 406 S Shasta St., Willows, CA 95988, Phone: 530-934-5780
Specialties: Working straight knives and folders of his design. **Patterns:** Hunters, Bowies, lockback folders and steak knife sets. **Technical:** Hand-filed, sanded, buffed ATS-34, 440C and A2. **Prices:** $65 to $600; some to $1200. **Remarks:** Full-time maker; first knife sold in 1979. **Mark:** Signature.

g

GADBERRY, EMMET, 82 Purple Plum Dr., Hattieville, AR 72063, Phone: 501-354-4842

GADDY, GARY LEE, 205 Ridgewood Lane, Washington, NC 27889, Phone: 252-946-4359
Specialties: Working/using straight knives of his design; period pieces. **Patterns:** Bowies, hunters, utility/camp knives. **Technical:** Grinds ATS-34, 01; forges 1095 **Prices:** $100 to $225; some to $400. **Remarks:** Spare-time maker; first knife sold in 1991. **Mark:** Quarter moon logo.

GAETA, ROBERTO, Rua Shikazu Myai 80, 05351 Sao Paulo, BRAZIL, Phone: 11-37684626
Specialties: Wide range of using knives. **Patterns:** Brazilian and North American hunting and fighting knives. **Technical:** Grinds stainless steel; likes natural handle materials. **Prices:** $100 to $250; some to $500. **Remarks:** Full-time maker; first knife sold in 1979. **Mark:** BOB'G.

GAETA, ANGELO, R. Saldanha Marinho, 1295 Centro Jau, SP-17201-310, BRAZIL, Phone: 0146-224543, Fax: 0146-224543
Specialties: Straight using knives to customer specs. **Patterns:** Hunters, fighting, daggers, belt push dagger. **Technical:** Grinds D6, ATS-34 and 440C stainless. titanium nitride golden finish upon request. **Prices:** $60 to $300. **Remarks:** Full-time maker; first knife sold in 1992. **Mark:** First initial, last name.

GAGSTAETTER, PETER, Nibelungenschmiede, Bergstrasse 2, 9306 Freidorf Tg, SWITZERLAND

GAINES, BUDDY, GAINES KNIVES, 155 Red Hill Rd., Commerce, GA 30530
Specialties: Collectible and working folders and straight knives. **Patterns:** Folders, hunters, Bowies, tactical knives. **Technical:** Forges own Damascus, grinds ATS-34, D2, commercial Damascus. Prefers mother-of-pearl and stag. **Prices:** Start at $200. **Remarks:** Part-time maker, sold first knife in 1985. **Mark:** Last name

GAINEY, HAL, 904 Bucklevel Rd., Greenwood, SC 29649, Phone: 864-223-0225
Specialties: Traditional working and using straight knives and folders. **Patterns:** Hunters, slip-joint folders and utility/camp knives. **Technical:** Hollow-grinds ATS-34 and D2; makes sheaths. **Prices:** $95 to $145; some to $500. **Remarks:** Full-time maker; first knife sold in 1975. **Mark:** Eagle head and last name.

GALLAGHER, BARRY, 135 Park St., Lewistown, MT 59457, Phone: 406-538-7056
Specialties: One-of-a-kind Damascus folders. **Patterns:** Folders - utility to high art, some straight knives - hunter, Bowies, and art pieces. **Technical:** Forges own mosaic Damascus and carbon steel, some stainless.

Prices: $400 to $5000+. **Remarks:** Full-time maker; first knife sold in 1993. Doing business as Gallagher Custom Knives. **Mark:** Last name.

GALLAGHER, SEAN, 24828 114th PL SE, Monroe, WA 98272-7685

GAMBLE, ROGER, 2801 65 Way N., St. Petersburg, FL 33710, Phone: 727-384-1470
Specialties: Traditional working/using straight knives and folders of his design. **Patterns:** Liner locks and hunters. **Technical:** Grinds ATS-34 and Damascus. **Prices:** $150 to $2000. **Remarks:** Part-time maker; first knife sold in 1982. Doing business as Gamble Knives. **Mark:** First name in a fan of cards over last name.

GAMBLE, FRANK, 3872 Dunbar Pl., Fremont, CA 94536, Phone: 510-797-7970
Specialties: Fantasy and high-art straight knives and folders of his design. **Patterns:** Daggers, fighters, hunters and special locking folders. **Technical:** Grinds 440C and ATS-34; forges Damascus. Inlays; offers jewelling. Prices $150 to $10,000. **Remarks:** Full-time maker; first knife sold in 1976. **Mark:** First initial, last name.

GANSTER, JEAN-PIERRE, 18, Rue du Vieil Hopital, F-67000 Strasbourg, FRANCE, Phone: (0033) 388 32 65 61, Fax: (0033) 388 32 52 79
Specialties: Fancy and high-art miniatures of his design and to customer specs. **Patterns:** Bowies, daggers, fighters, hunters, locking folders and miniatures. **Technical:** Forges and grinds stainless Damascus, ATS-34, gold and silver. **Prices:** $100 to $380; some to $2500. **Remarks:** Part-time maker; first knife sold in 1972. **Mark:** Stylized first initials.

GARCIA, MARIO EIRAS, R. Edmundo Scanapieco, 300 Caxingui, Sao Paulo SP-05516-070, BRAZIL, Fax: 011-37214528
Specialties: Fantasy knives of his design; one-of-a-kind only. **Patterns:** Fighters, daggers, boots and two-bladed knives. **Technical:** Forges car leaf springs. Uses only natural handle material. **Prices:** $100 to $200. **Remarks:** Part-time maker; first knife sold in 1976. **Mark:** Two "B"s, one opposite the other.

GARDNER, ROB, 3381 E Rd., Loxahatchee, FL 33470, Phone: 561-784-4994
Specialties: High-art working and using knives of his design and to customer specs. **Patterns:** Daggers, hunters and ethnic-patterned knives. **Technical:** Forges Damascus, L6 and 10-series steels. Engraves and inlays. Handles and fittings may be carved. **Prices:** $175 to $500; some to $2500. **Remarks:** Full-time maker; artist blacksmith, first knife sold in 1987. Knives made by custom order only. **Mark:** Engraved or stamped initials.

GARNER, LARRY W., 13069 FM 14, Tyler, TX 75706, Phone: 903-597-6045
Specialties: Fixed blade hunters and Bowies. **Patterns:** My designs or yours. **Technical:** Hand forges 5160. **Prices:** $200 to $500. **Remarks:** Apprentice bladesmith. **Mark:** Last name.

GARNER JR., WILLIAM O., 2803 East DeSoto St., Pensacola, FL 32503, Phone: 850-438-2009
Specialties: Working straight and art knives. **Patterns:** Hunters and folders. **Technical:** Grinds 440C and ATS-34 steels. **Prices:** $235 to $600. **Remarks:** Full-time maker; first knife sold in 1985. **Mark:** First and last name in oval logo or last name.

GARRITY, TIMOTHY P., 217 S Grandview Blvd., Waukesha, WI 53188, Phone: 414-785-1803

GARVOCK, MARK W., RR 1, Balderson, Ontario, CANADA K1G 1A0, Phone: 613-833-2545, Fax: 613-833-2208
Specialties: Hunters, Bowies, Japanese, daggers and swords. **Patterns:** Cable Damascus, random pattern welded or to suit. **Technical:** Forged blades; hi-carbon. **Prices:** $250 to $900. **Remarks:** Also CKG member and ABS member. **Mark:** Big G with M in middle. **Other:** Shipping and taxes extra.

GASTON, RON, 330 Gaston Dr., Woodruff, SC 29388, Phone: 803-433-0807, Fax: 803-433-9958
Specialties: Working period pieces. **Patterns:** Hunters, fighters, tantos, boots and a variety of other straight knives; single-blade slip-joint folders. **Technical:** Grinds ATS-34. Hand-rubbed satin finish is standard. **Prices:** $200 to $600; some to $1000. **Remarks:** Full-time maker; first knife sold in 1980. **Mark:** Ron Gaston, Woodruff SC.

GATHERWOOD, ROB SPROKHOLT AND DENISE, Werkendelslaan 108, 1851VE Heiloo, Nederland Europe, Phone: 0031-72-5336097
Specialties: One-of-a-kind stiff knives. Top materials collector grade made to use. Oiled realwood handles, intarsia mostly wood. Characteristic one row of massive silver pins or tubes. **Patterns:** Outdoor knives (hunting, sailing, hiking), Bowies, Mans Surviving Companions MSC, big tantos. **Technical:** Stockremoval grinder; flat, hollow or confex steel; 440, RWL-34, ATS-34 powder steel Damascener, D-2, stiff knives, mostly full tang,

home made mokume-gane. **Prices:** Starts at Euro 260. **Remarks:** Part-time knifemaker. Writer of first Dutch knifemaking book. **Mark:** Gatherwood in an elipse etched in the blade or stamped in an intarsia of silver in the spine. **Other:** Wife is his co-worker and goldsmith. Do everything themselves. Supply shop for knife enthusiastics. First knife sold in 2000.

GAUDETTE, LINDEN L., 5 Hitchcock Rd., Wilbraham, MA 01095, Phone: 413-596-4896
Specialties: Traditional working knives in standard patterns. **Patterns:** Broad-bladed hunters, Bowies and camp knives; wood carver knives; locking folders. **Technical:** Grinds ATS-34, 440C and 154CM. **Prices:** $150 to $400; some higher. **Remarks:** Full-time maker; first knife sold in 1975. **Mark:** Last name in Gothic logo; used to be initials in circle.

GAULT, CLAY, #1225 PR 7022, Lexington, TX 78947, Phone: 979-773-3305
Specialties: Classic straight and folding hunting knives and multi-blade folders of his design. **Patterns:** Folders and hunting knives. **Technical:** Grinds BX-NSM 174 steel, custom rolled from billets to his specifications. Uses exotic leathers for sheaths, and fine natural materials for all knives. **Prices:** $325 to $600; some higher. **Remarks:** Full-time maker; first knife sold in 1970. **Mark:** Name or name with cattle brand.

GEDRAITIS, CHARLES J., GEDRAITIS HAND CRAFTED KNIVES, 82 Campbell St., Rutland, MA 01543, Phone: 508-886-0221
Specialties: Folding gend knives of maker's own design. **Patterns:** Lots of filework and embellishment. **Technical:** Grinds commercial Damascus and D-2. Stock removal some forging. **Prices:** $200-$2000. **Mark:** 3 scallop shells with an initial in each one.

GEISLER, GARY R., PO Box 294, Clarksville, OH 45113, Phone: 937-383-4055
Specialties: Period Bowies and such; flat ground. **Patterns:** Working knives usually modeled close after an existing antique. **Technical:** Flat grinds 440C, A2 and ATS-34. **Prices:** $300 and up. **Remarks:** Part-time maker; first knife sold in 1982. **Mark:** G.R. Geisler Maker; usually in script on reverse side because I'm left-handed.

GENSKE, JAY, 283 Doty St., Fond du Lac, WI 54935, Phone: 920-921-8019/Cell Phone 920-579-0144
Specialties: Working/using knives and period pieces of his design and to customer specs. **Patterns:** Bowies, fighters, hunters. **Technical:** Grinds ATS-34 and 440C, 01 and 1095 forges and grinds Damascus and 1095. Offers custom-tooled sheaths, scabbards and hand carved handles. **Prices:** $95 to $500; some to $1000. **Remarks:** Full-time maker; first knife sold in 1985. Doing business as Genske Knives. **Mark:** Stamped or engraved last name.

GEORGE, HARRY, 3137 Old Camp Long Rd., Aiken, SC 29805, Phone: 803-649-1963
Specialties: Working straight knives of his design or to customer specs. **Patterns:** Hunters, skinners and utility knives. **Technical:** Grinds ATS-34. Prefers natural handle materials, hollow-grinds and mirror finishes. **Prices:** Start at $70. **Remarks:** Part-time maker; first knife sold in 1985. Trained under George Herron. Member SCAK. Member Knifemakers Guild. **Mark:** Name, city, state.

GEORGE, LES, 1703 Payne, Wichita, KS 67203, Phone: 316-267-0736
Specialties: Classic, traditional and working/using straight knives of his design and to customer specs. **Patterns:** Fighters, hunters, swords and miniatures. **Technical:** Grinds D2; forges 5160 and Damascus. Uses mosaic handle pins and his own mokume-gane. **Prices:** $35 to $200; some to $800. **Remarks:** No orders taken at this time due to enlistment in the U.S. Marine Corps.; first knife sold in 1992. Doing business as George Custom Knives. **Mark:** Last name or initials stacked.

GEORGE, TOM, 550 Aldbury Dr., Henderson, NV 89014
Specialties: Working straight knives, display knives and folders of his design. **Patterns:** Hunters, Bowies, daggers and buckskinners and folders. **Technical:** Uses D2, 440C, ATS-34 and 154CM. **Prices:** $250 to $10,000. **Remarks:** Custom orders 'not' accepted. Full-time maker. **Mark:** Tom George maker.

GEPNER, DON, 2615 E. Tecumseh, Norman, OK 73071, Phone: 405-364-2750
Specialties: Traditional working and using straight knives of his design. **Patterns:** Bowies and daggers. **Technical:** Forges his Damascus, 1095 and 5160. **Prices:** $100 to $400; some to $1000. **Remarks:** Spare-time maker; first knife sold in 1991. Has been forging since 1954; first edged weapon made at 9 years old. **Mark:** Last initial.

GERNER, THOMAS, 939 German Rd., Glentui RD, Oxford, NEW ZEALAND 8253
Specialties: Forged working knives; plain steel and pattern welded. **Patterns:** Tries most patterns heard or read about. **Technical:** 5160, L6, 01, 52100 steels; Australian hardwood handles. **Prices:** $160 and up.

custom knifemakers

Remarks: Achieved ABS Master Smith rating in 2001. **Mark:** Like a standing arrow and a leaning cross, T.G. in the Runic (Viking) alphabet.

GERUS, GERRY, PO Box 2295, G.P.O. Cairns, Qld. 4870, AUSTRALIA 070-341451, Phone: 019 617935
Specialties: Fancy working and using straight knives of his design. **Patterns:** Hunters, Bowies and fighters. **Technical:** Uses 440C, ATS-34 and commercial Damascus. **Prices:** $275 to $600; some to $1200. **Remarks:** Part-time maker; first knife sold in 1988. **Mark:** Last name; or last name, Hand Made, city, country.

GEVEDON, HANNERS (HANK), 1410 John Cash Rd., Crab Orchard, KY 40419-9770
Specialties: Traditional working and using straight knives. **Patterns:** Hunters, swords, utility and camp knives. **Technical:** Forges and grinds his own Damascus, 5160 and L6. Cast aluminum handles. **Prices:** $50 to $250; some to $400. **Remarks:** Part-time maker; first knife sold in 1983. **Mark:** Initials and LBF tang stamp.

GIAGU, SALVATORE AND DEROMA MARIA ROSARIA, Via V. Emanuele 64, 07016 Pattada (SS), ITALY, Phone: 079-755918, Fax: 079-755918
Specialties: Using and collecting traditional and new folders from Sardegna. **Patterns:** Folding, hunting, utility, skinners and kitchen knives. **Technical:** Forges ATS-34, 440, D2 and Damascus. **Prices:** $200 to $2000; some higher. **Mark:** First initial, last name and name of town and muflon's head.

GIBERT, PEDRO, Gutierrez 5189, 5603 Rama Caida, San Rafael Mendoza, ARGENTINA, Phone: 02627 441138
Specialties: Hand forges: Stock removal and integral. High quality artistic knives of his design and to customer specifications. **Patterns:** Country (Argentine gaucho-style), knives, folders, Bowies, daggers, hunters. Others upon request. **Technical:** Blade: Bohler k110 Austrian steel (high resistance to waste). Handles: (Natural materials) ivory elephant, killer whale, hippo, walrus tooth, deer antler, goat, ram, buffalo horn, bone, rhea, goat, sheep, cow, exotic woods (South America native woods) hand carved and engraved guards and blades. Stainless steel guards, finely polished: semi-matte or shiny finish. Sheaths: Raw or tanned leather, hand-stitched; rawhide or cotton yarn embroidered. Box: One wood piece, hand carved. Wooden hinges and locks. **Prices:** $400 and up. **Remarks:** Full-time maker. Supply contractors. **Mark:** Logo and last name. Buyer's initials upon request.

GIBO, GEORGE, PO Box 4304, Hilo, HI 96720, Phone: 808-987-7002
Specialties: Straight knives and folders. **Patterns:** Hunters, bird and trout, utility, gentlemen and tactical knives. **Technical:** Grinds ATS-34, BG-42, Talonite, Stainless Steel Damascus. **Prices:** $250 to $1000. **Remarks:** Spare-time maker; first knife sold in 1995. **Mark:** Name, city and state around Hawaiian "Shaka" sign.

GIBSON SR., JAMES HOOT, 90 Park Place Ave., Bunnell, FL 32110, Phone: 904-437-4383
Specialties: Bowies, folders, daggers, and hunters. **Patterns:** Most all. **Technical:** ATS-440C hand cut and grind. **Prices:** $1250 to $3000. **Remarks:** 100% handmade. **Mark:** Hoot.

GILBERT, CHANTAL, 291 Rue Christophe-Colomb est. #105, Quebec City Quebec, CANADA G1K 3T1, Phone: 418-525-6961, Fax: 418-525-4666
Specialties: Straight art knives that may resemble creatures, often with wings, shells and antennae, always with a beak of some sort, fixed blades in a feminine style. **Technical:** ATS-34 and Damascus. Handle materials usually silver that she forms to shape via special molds and a press; ebony and fossil ivory. **Prices:** Range from $500-$4000. **Other:** Often embellishes her art knives with rubies, meteorite, 18k gold and similar elements.

GILBREATH, RANDALL, 55 Crauswell Rd., Dora, AL 35062, Phone: 205-648-3902
Specialties: Damascus folders and fighters. **Patterns:** Folders and fixed blades. **Technical:** Forges Damascus and high-carbon; stock removal stainless steel. **Prices:** $300 to $1500. **Remarks:** Full-time maker; first knife sold in 1979. **Mark:** Name in ribbon.

GILJEVIC, BRANKO, 35 Hayley Crescent, Queanbeyan 2620, N.S.W., AUSTRALIA 0262977613
Specialties: Classic working straight knives and folders of his design. **Patterns:** Hunters, Bowies, skinners and locking folders. **Technical:** Grinds 440C. Offers acid etching, scrimshaw and leather carving. **Prices:** $150 to $1500. **Remarks:** Part-time maker; first knife sold in 1987. Doing business as Sambar Custom Knives. **Mark:** Company name in logo.

GITTINGER, RAYMOND, 6940 S Rt. 100, Tiffin, OH 44883, Phone: 419-397-2517

GLOVER, WARREN D., dba BUBBA KNIVES, PO Box 475, Cleveland, GA 30528, Phone: 706-865-3998, Fax: 706-348-7176
Specialties: Traditional and custom working and using straight knives of his design and to customer request. **Patterns:** Hunters, skinners, bird and fish, utility and kitchen knives. **Technical:** Grinds 440, ATS-34 and stainless steel Damascus. **Prices:** $75 to $400 and up. **Remarks:** Part-time maker; sold first knife in 1995. **Mark:** Bubba, year, name, state.

GLOVER, RON, 7702 Misty Springs Ct., Mason, OH 45040, Phone: 513-398-7857
Specialties: High-tech working straight knives and folders. **Patterns:** Hunters to Bowies; some interchangeable blade models; unique locking mechanisms. **Technical:** Grinds 440C, 154CM; buys Damascus. **Prices:** $70 to $500; some to $800. **Remarks:** Part-time maker; first knife sold in 1981. **Mark:** Name in script.

GODDARD, WAYNE, 473 Durham Ave., Eugene, OR 97404, Phone: 541-689-8098
Specialties: Working/using straight knives and folders. **Patterns:** Hunters and folders. **Technical:** Works exclusively with wire Damascus and his own-pattern welded material. **Prices:** $250 to $4000. **Remarks:** Full-time maker; first knife sold in 1963. Three-year backlog on orders. **Mark:** Blocked initials on forged blades; regular capital initials on stock removal.

GOERS, BRUCE, 3423 Royal Ct. S., Lakeland, FL 33813, Phone: 941-646-0984
Specialties: Fancy working and using straight knives of his design and to customer specs. **Patterns:** Hunters, fighters, Bowies and fantasy knives. **Technical:** Grinds ATS-34, some Damascus. **Prices:** $195 to $600; some to $1300. **Remarks:** Part-time maker; first knife sold in 1990. Doing business as Vulture Cutlery. **Mark:** Buzzard with initials.

GOERTZ, PAUL S., 201 Union Ave. SE, #207, Renton, WA 98059, Phone: 425-228-9501
Specialties: Working straight knives of his design and to customer specs. **Patterns:** Hunters, skinners, camp, bird and fish knives, camp axes, some Bowies, fighters and boots. **Technical:** Grinds ATS-34, BG42, and CPM420V. **Prices:** $75 to $500. **Remarks:** Full-time maker; first knife sold in 1985. **Mark:** Signature.

GOFOURTH, JIM, 3776 Aliso Cyn Rd., Santa Paula, CA 93060, Phone: 805-659-3814
Specialties: Period pieces and working knives. **Patterns:** Bowies, locking folders, patent lockers and others. **Technical:** Grinds A2 and 154CM. **Prices:** Moderate. **Remarks:** Spare-time maker. **Mark:** Initials interconnected.

GOGUEN, SCOTT, 166 Goguen Rd., Newport, NC 28570, Phone: 252-393-6013
Specialties: Classic and traditional working knives. **Patterns:** Kitchen, camp, hunters, Bowies. **Technical:** Forges high-carbon steel and own Damascus. Offers clay tempering and cord wrapped handles. **Prices:** $85 to $1500. **Remarks:** Spare-time maker; first knife sold in 1988. **Mark:** Last name or name in Japanese characters.

GOLDBERG, DAVID, 1120 Blyth Ct., Blue Bell, PA 19422, Phone: 215-654-7117
Specialties: Japanese-style designs, will work with special themes in Japanese Genre. **Patterns:** Kozuka, Tanto, Wakazashi, Katana, Tachi, Sword canes, Yari and Naginata. **Technical:** Forges his own Damascus and makes his own handmade steel from straw ash, iron, carbon and clay. Uses traditional materials, carves fittings handles and cases. Hardens all blades in traditional Japanese clay differential technique. **Remarks:** Full-time maker; first knife sold in 1987. **Mark:** Name (kinzan) in Japanese Kanji on Tang under handle. **Other:** Japanese swordsmanship teacher (jaido) and Japanese self-defense teach (aikido).

GOLDING, ROBIN, PO Box 267, Lathrop, CA 95330, Phone: 209-982-0839
Specialties: Working straight knives of his design. **Patterns:** Survival knives, Bowie extractions, camp knives, dive knives and skinners. **Technical:** Grinds 440C, 154CM and ATS-34. **Prices:** $95 to $250; some to $500. **Remarks:** Full-time maker; first knife sold in 1985. Up to 1-1/2 year waiting period on orders. **Mark:** Signature of last name.

GOLTZ, WARREN L., 802 4th Ave. E., Ada, MN 56510, Phone: 218-784-7721
Specialties: Fancy working knives in standard patterns. **Patterns:** Hunters, Bowies and camp knives. **Technical:** Grinds 440C and ATS-34. **Prices:** $120 to $595; some to $950. **Remarks:** Part-time maker; first knife sold in 1984. **Mark:** Last name.

GONZALEZ, LEONARDO WILLIAMS, Ituzaingo 473, Maldonado, CP 20000, URUGUAY, Phone: 598 4222 1617, Fax: 598 4222 1617

Specialties: Classic high-art and fantasy straight knives; traditional working and using knives of his design, in standard patterns or to customer specs. **Patterns:** Hunters, Bowies, daggers, fighters, boots, swords and utility/camp knives. **Technical:** Forges and grinds high-carbon and stainless Bohler steels. **Prices:** $100 to $2500. **Remarks:** Full-time maker; first knife sold in 1985. **Mark:** Willy, whale, R.O.U.

GOO, TAI, 5920 W Windy Lou Ln., Tucson, AZ 85742, Phone: 520-744-9777

Specialties: High art, neo-tribal, bush and fantasy. **Technical:** hand forges, does own heat treating, makes own Damascus. **Prices:** $150-$500 some to $10,000. **Remarks:** Full-time maker; first knife sold in 1978. **Mark:** Chiseled signature.

GOODE, BRIAN, 104 Cider Dr., Shelby, NC 28152, Phone: 704-484-9020

Specialties: Flat ground working knives with etched/antique finish or hand rubbed. **Patterns:** Field, camp, hunters, skinners, survival, maker's design or yours. Currently full tang only with supplied leather sheath. Kydex can be outsourced if desired. **Technical:** 0-1, 1095, or similar high-carbon ground flatstock. Stock removal and differential heat treat preferred. Will offer handforged with the same differential heat treat method in future. Etched antique/etched satin working finish preferred. Micarta and hardwoods for strength. **Prices:** $85-$350. **Remarks:** Part-time maker and full-time knife lover. First knife sold in 2004. **Mark:** B. Goode with NC separated by a feather.

GOODE, BEAR, PO Box 6474, Navajo Dam, NM 87419, Phone: 505-632-8184

Specialties: Working/using straight knives of his design and in standard patterns. **Patterns:** Bowies, hunters and utility/camp knives. **Technical:** Grinds 440C, ATS-34, 154-CM; forges and grinds 1095, 5160 and other steels on request; uses Damascus. **Prices:** $60 to $225; some to $500 and up. **Remarks:** Part-time maker; first knife sold in 1993. Doing business as Bear Knives. **Mark:** First and last name with a three-toed paw print.

GOODLING, RODNEY W., 6640 Old Harrisburg Rd., York Springs, PA 17372

GORDON, LARRY B., 23555 Newell Cir. W, Farmington Hills, MI 48336, Phone: 248-477-5483

GORENFLO, GABE, 9145 Sullivan Rd, Baton Rouge, LA 70818, Phone: 504-261-5868

GORENFLO, JAMES T. (JT), 9145 Sullivan Rd., Baton Rouge, LA 70818, Phone: 225-261-5868

Specialties: Traditional working and using straight knives of his design. **Patterns:** Bowies, hunters and utility/camp knives. **Technical:** Forges 5160, 1095, 52100 and his own Damascus. **Prices:** Start at $200. **Remarks:** Part-time maker; first knife sold in 1992. **Mark:** Last name or initials, J.S. on reverse.

GOTTAGE, JUDY, 43227 Brooks Dr., Clinton Twp., MI 48038-5323, Phone: 810-286-7275

Specialties: Custom folders of her design or to customer specs. **Patterns:** Interframes or integral. **Technical:** Stock removal. **Prices:** $300 to $3000. **Remarks:** Full-time maker; first knife sold in 1980. **Mark:** Full name, maker in script.

GOTTAGE, DANTE, 43227 Brooks Dr., Clinton Twp., MI 48038-5323, Phone: 810-286-7275

Specialties: Working knives of his design or to customer specs. **Patterns:** Large and small skinners, fighters, Bowies and fillet knives. **Technical:** Grinds O1, 440C and 154CM and ATS-34. **Prices:** $150 to $600. **Remarks:** Part-time maker; first knife sold in 1975. **Mark:** Full name in script letters.

GOTTSCHALK, GREGORY J., 12 First St. (Ft. Pitt), Carnegie, PA 15106, Phone: 412-279-6692

Specialties: Fancy working straight knives and folders to customer specs. **Patterns:** Hunters to tantos, locking folders to minis. **Technical:** Grinds 440C, 154CM, ATS-34. Now making own Damascus. Most knives have mirror finishes. **Prices:** Start at $150. **Remarks:** Part-time maker; first knife sold in 1977. **Mark:** Full name in crescent.

GOUKER, GARY B., PO Box 955, Sitka, AK 99835, Phone: 907-747-3476

Specialties: Hunting knives for hard use. **Patterns:** Skinners, semi-skinners, and such. **Technical:** Likes natural materials, inlays, stainless steel. **Prices:** Moderate. **Remarks:** New Alaskan maker. **Mark:** Name.

GOYTIA, ENRIQUE, 2120 E Paisano Ste. 276, El Paso, TX 79905

GRAFFEO, ANTHONY I., 100 Riess Place, Chalmette, LA 70043, Phone: 504-277-1428

Specialties: Traditional working and using straight knives of his design, to customer specs and in standard patterns. **Patterns:** Hunters, utility/camp knives and fishing knives. **Technical:** Hollow- and flat-grinds ATS-34, 440C and 154CM. Handle materials include Pakkawood, Micarta and sambar stag. **Prices:** $65 to $100; some to $250. **Remarks:** Part-time maker; first knife sold in 1991. Doing business as Knives by: Graf. **Mark:** First and middle initials, last name city, state, Maker.

GRAHAM, GORDON, Rt. 3 Box 207, New Boston, TX 75570, Phone: 903-628-6337

GRANGER, PAUL J., 2820 St. Charles Ln., Kennesaw, GA 30144, Phone: 770-426-6298

Specialties: Working straight knives of his own design and a few folders. **Patterns:** 2.75" - 4.0" work knives, skinners, tactical knives and Bowies from 5"-9". **Technical:** Forges 52100 and 5160 and his own carbon steel Damascus. Offers filework. **Prices:** $95-$400. **Remarks:** Part-time maker since 1997. Sold first knife in 1997. Doing business as Granger Knives and Pale Horse Fighters. **Mark:** "Granger" or "Palehorse Fighters". **Other:** Member of ABS and OBG.

GRAVELINE, PASCAL AND ISABELLE, 38, Rue de Kerbrezillic, 29350 Moelan-sur-Mer, FRANCE, Phone: 33 2 98 39 73 33, Fax: 33 2 98 39 73 33

Specialties: French replicas from the 17th, 18th and 19th centuries. **Patterns:** Traditional folders and multi-blade pocket knives; traveling knives, fruit knives and fork sets; puzzle knives and friend's knives; rivet less knives. **Technical:** Grind 12C27, ATS-34, Damascus and carbon steel. **Prices:** $500 to $5000; some to $2000. **Remarks:** Full-time makers; first knife sold in 1992. **Mark:** Last name over head of ram.

GRAY, DANIEL, GRAY KNIVES, 686 Main Rd., Brownville, ME 04414, Phone: 207-965-2191

Specialties: Straight knives, Fantasy, folders, automatics and traditional of his own design. **Patterns:** Automatics, fighters, hunters. **Technical:** Grind 01, 154CM and D2. **Prices:** From $155 to $750. **Remarks:** Full-time maker; first knife sold in 1974. **Mark:** Gray Knives.

GRAY, BOB, 8206 N. Lucia Court, Spokane, WA 99208, Phone: 509-468-3924

Specialties: Straight working knives of his own design or to customer specs. **Patterns:** Hunter, fillet and carving knives. **Technical:** Forges 5160, L6 and some 52100; grinds 440C. **Prices:** $100 to $600. **Remarks:** Part-time knife maker; first knife sold in 1991. Doing business as Hi-Land Knives. **Mark:** HI-L.

GREBE, GORDON S., PO Box 296, Anchor Point, AK 99556-0296, Phone: 907-235-8242

Specialties: Working straight knives and folders, some fancy. **Patterns:** Tantos, Bowies, boot fighter sets, locking folders. **Technical:** Grinds stainless steels; likes 1/4" inch stock and glass-bead finishes. **Prices:** $75 to $250; some to $2000. **Remarks:** Full-time maker; first knife sold in 1968. **Mark:** Initials in lightning logo.

GRECO, JOHN, 100 Mattie Jones Rd., Greensburg, KY 42743, Phone: 270-932-3335, Fax: 270-932-2225

Specialties: Limited edition knives and swords. **Patterns:** Tactical, fighters, camp knives, short swords. **Technical:** Stock removal carbon steel. **Prices:** Affordable. **Remarks:** Full-time maker since1986. First knife sold in 1979. **Mark:** Greco and steroc w/mo mark. **Other:** Do custom limited edition knives for other designers complete with their logo.

GREEN, RUSS, 6013 Briercrest Ave., Lakewood, CA 90713, Phone: 562-867-2305

Specialties: Sheaths and using knives. **Technical:** Knives 440C, ATS-34, 5160, 01, cable Damascus. **Prices:** Knives-$135 to $850; sheaths- $30 to $200. **Mark:** Russ Green and year.

GREEN, MARK, 1523 S Main St. PO Box 20, Graysville, AL 35073, Phone: 205-647-9353

GREEN, BILL, 706 Bradfield, Garland, TX 75042, Phone: 972-272-4748

Specialties: High-art and working straight knives and folders of his design and to customer specs. **Patterns:** Bowies, hunters, kitchen knives and locking folders. **Technical:** Grinds ATS-34, D2 and 440V. Hand-tooled custom sheaths. **Prices:** $70 to $350; some to $750. **Remarks:** Part-time maker; first knife sold in 1990. **Mark:** Last name.

GREEN, WILLIAM (BILL), 46 Warren Rd., View Bank Vic., AUSTRALIA 3084, Fax: 03-9459-1529

Specialties: Traditional high-tech straight knives and folders. **Patterns:** Japanese-influenced designs, hunters, Bowies, folders and miniatures. **Technical:** Forges O1, D2 and his own Damascus. Offers lost wax castings for bolsters and pommels. Likes natural handle materials, gems, sil-

custom knifemakers

ver and gold. **Prices:** $400 to $750; some to $1200. **Remarks:** Full-time maker. **Mark:** Initials.

GREENAWAY, DON, 3325 Dinsmore Tr., Fayetteville, AR 72704, Phone: 501-521-0323

GREENE, DAVID, 570 Malcom Rd., Covington, GA 30209, Phone: 770-784-0657
　Specialties: Straight working using knives. **Patterns:** Hunters. **Technical:** Forges mosaic and twist Damascus. Prefers stag and desert iron-wood for handle material.

GREENE, CHRIS, 707 Cherry Lane, Shelby, NC 28150, Phone: 704-434-5620

GREENE, STEVE, DUNN KNIVES INC., PO Box 204, Rossville, KS 66533, Phone: 785-584-6856, Fax: 785-584-6856

GREENFIELD, G.O., 2605 15th St. #522, Everett, WA 98201, Phone: 425-258-1551
　Specialties: High-tech and working straight knives and folders of his design. **Patterns:** Boots, daggers, hunters and one-of-a-kinds. **Technical:** Grinds ATS-34, D2, 440C and T-440V. Makes sheaths for each knife. **Prices:** $100 to $800; some to $5000. **Remarks:** Part-time maker; first knife sold in 1978. **Mark:** Springfield®, serial number.

GREGORY, MICHAEL, 211 Calhoun Rd., Belton, SC 29627, Phone: 864-338-8898
　Specialties: Working straight knives and folders. **Patterns:** Hunters, tantos, locking folders and slip-joints, boots and fighters. **Technical:** Grinds 440C, 154CM and ATS-34; mirror finishes. **Prices:** $95 to $200; some to $1000. **Remarks:** Part-time maker; first knife sold in 1980. **Mark:** Name, city in logo.

GREINER, RICHARD, 1073 E. County Rd. 32, Green Springs, OH 44836

GREISS, JOCKL, Herrenwald 15, D 77773 Schenkenzell, GERMANY, Phone: +49 7836 95 71 69 or +49 7836 95 55 76
　Specialties: Classic and working using straight knives of his design. **Patterns:** Bowies, daggers and hunters. **Technical:** Uses only Jerry Rados Damascus. All knives are one-of-a-kind made by hand; no machines are used. **Prices:** $700 to $2000; some to $3000. **Remarks:** Full-time maker; first knife sold in 1984. **Mark:** An "X" with a long vertical line through it.

GREY, PIET, PO Box 363, Naboomspruit 0560, SOUTH AFRICA, Phone: 014-743-3613
　Specialties: Fancy working and using straight knives of his design. **Patterns:** Fighters, hunters and utility/camp knives. **Technical:** Grinds ATS-34 and AEB-L; forges and grinds Damascus. Solder less fitting of guards. Engraves and scrimshaws. **Prices:** $125 to $750; some to $1500. **Remarks:** Part-time maker; first knife sold in 1970. **Mark:** Last name.

GRIFFIN, RENDON AND MARK, 9706 Cedardale, Houston, TX 77055, Phone: 713-468-0436
　Specialties: Working folders and automatics of their designs. **Patterns:** Standard lockers and slip-joints. **Technical:** Most blade steels; stock removal. **Prices:** Start at $350. **Remarks:** Rendon's first knife sold in 1966; Mark's in 1974. **Mark:** Last name logo.

GRIFFIN, THOMAS J., 591 Quevli Ave., Windom, MN 56101, Phone: 507-831-1089
　Specialties: Period pieces and fantasy straight knives of his design. **Patterns:** Daggers and swords. **Technical:** Forges 1095, 52100 and L6. Most blades are his own Damascus; turned fittings and wire-wrapped grips. **Prices:** $250 to $800; some to $2000. **Remarks:** Full-time maker; first knife sold in 1991. Doing business as Griffin Knives. **Mark:** Last name etched.

GRIFFIN JR., HOWARD A., 14299 SW 31st Ct., Davie, FL 33330, Phone: 305-474-5406
　Specialties: Working straight knives and folders. **Patterns:** Hunters, Bowies, locking folders with his own push-button lock design. **Technical:** Grinds 440C. **Prices:** $100 to $200; some to $500. **Remarks:** Part-time maker; first knife sold in 1983. **Mark:** Initials.

GRIFFITH, LYNN, 5103 S Sheridan Rd. #402, Tulsa, OK 74145-7627, Phone: 918-366-8303
　Specialties: Flat ground, full tang tactical knives. **Patterns:** Neck and multi-carry knives, drop and clip points, tantos and Wharncliffes. **Technical:** Grinds ATS34 and Talonite. **Prices:** $125 to $400; some to $700. **Remarks:** Full-time knife maker; first knife sold in 1987. **Mark:** Last name over year made.

GROSPITCH, ERNIE, 18440 Amityville Dr., Orlando, FL 32820, Phone: 407-568-5438
　Specialties: Bowies, hunting, fishing, kitchen, lockback folders, leather craft. **Patterns:** His design or customer's. **Technical:** Stock removal using most available steels. **Prices:** $140 and up. **Remarks:** Full-time maker, sold first knife in 1990. Mark: Etched name/maker city and state.

GROSS, W.W., 109 Dylan Scott Dr., Archdale, NC 27263-3858
　Specialties: Working knives. **Patterns:** Hunters, boots, fighters. **Technical:** Grinds. **Prices:** Moderate. **Remarks:** Full-time maker. **Mark:** Name.

GROSSMAN, STEWART, 24 Water St., #419, Clinton, MA 01510, Phone: 508-365-2291; 800-mysword
　Specialties: Miniatures and full-size knives and swords. **Patterns:** One-of-a-kind miniatures—jewelry, replicas—and wire-wrapped figures. Full-size art, fantasy and combat knives, daggers and modular systems. **Technical:** Forges and grinds most metals and Damascus. Uses gems, crystals, electronics and motorized mechanisms. **Prices:** $20 to $300; some to $4500 and higher. **Remarks:** Full-time maker; first knife sold in 1985. **Mark:** G1.

GROSSMAN, SCOTT, RAZORBACK KNIVES, PO Box 815, Forest Hill, MD 21050, Phone: 410-452-8456
　Specialties: Heavy duty knives for big game hunting and survival. **Patterns:** Drop point hunters, semi-skinners and spear point hunters. **Technical:** Grinds D-2, convex grind, gear pattern filework standard around full tang handles. **Price:** $175-$300. **Remarks:** Part-time maker does business as Razorback Knives. **Mark:** First and last initials and year.

GRUSSENMEYER, PAUL G., 310 Kresson Rd., Cherry Hill, NJ 08034, Phone: 856-428-1088
　Specialties: Assembling fancy and fantasy straight knives with his own carved handles. **Patterns:** Bowies, daggers, folders, swords, hunters and miniatures. **Technical:** Uses forged steel and Damascus, stock removal and knapped obsidian blades. **Prices:** $250 to $4000. **Remarks:** Spare-time maker; first knife sold in 1991. **Mark:** First and last initial hooked together on handle.

GUARNERA, ANTHONY R., 42034 Quail Creek Dr., Quartzhill, CA 93536, Phone: 661-722-4032
　Patterns: Hunters, camp, Bowies, kitchen, fighter knives. **Technical:** Forged and stock removal. **Prices:** $100 and up.

GUESS, RAYMOND L., 7214 Salineville Rd. NE, Mechanicstown, OH 44651, Phone: 330-738-2793
　Specialties: Working straight knives and folders of his design or to customer specs. **Patterns:** Hunters, Bowies, fillet knives, steak and paring knife sets. **Technical:** Grinds 440C. Offers silver inlay work and mirror finishes. Custom-made leather sheath for each knife. **Prices:** $65 to $850; some to $700. **Remarks:** Spare-time maker; first knife sold in 1985. **Mark:** First initial, last name.

GUIDRY, BRUCE, 24550 Adams Ave., Murrieta, CA 92562, Phone: 909-677-2384

GUIGNARD, GIB, Box 3413, Quartzsite, AZ 85359, Phone: 928-927-4831
　Specialties: Rustic finish on primitive Bowies with stag or ironwood handles and turquoise inlay. **Patterns:** Very large in 5160 and ATS-34 - Small and med. size hunting knives in ATS-34. **Technical:** Forges 5160 and grind ATS-34. **Prices:** $100 to $1000. **Remarks:** Full-time maker first knife sold in 1989. Doing business as Cactus Forge. Also do collaborations with Chuck Burrows of Wild Rose Trading Co. these collaborations are done under the name of Cactus Rose. **Mark:** Last name or G+ on period pieces and primitive.

GUNDERSEN, D.F. "DOC", 5811 S Siesta Lane, Tempe, AZ 85283
　Specialties: Small and medium belt knives, sword canes/staffs, kitchen cutlery, slip joint folders, throwers. **Patterns:** Utility, hunters, fighters and sailors' knives. **Technical:** Both forged and stock removal knives available in a variety of steels. Unique carvings available on many items. **Prices:** $65 to $250. **Remarks:** Full-time maker; first knife sold in 1988. Doing business as L and H Knife Works. **Mark:** LandH Knife Works.

GUNN, NELSON L., 77 Blake Rd., Epping, NH 03042, Phone: 603-679-5119
　Specialties: Classic and working/using straight knives of his design. **Patterns:** Bowies, fighters and hunters. **Technical:** Grinds O1 and 440C. Carved stag handles with turquoise inlays. **Prices:** $125 to $300; some to $700. **Remarks:** Part-time maker; first knife sold in 1996. Doing business as Nelson's Custom Knives. **Mark:** First and last initial.

GUNTER, BRAD, 13 Imnaha Rd., Tijeras, NM 87059, Phone: 505-281-8080

GURGANUS, MELVIN H., 2553 N.C. 45 South, Colerain, NC 27924, Phone: 252-356-4831, Fax: 252-356-4650
　Specialties: High-tech working folders. **Patterns:** Leaf-lock and back-lock designs, bolstered and interframe. **Technical:** D2 and 440C; Heat-treats, carves and offers lost wax casting. **Prices:** $300 to $3000. **Remarks:** Part-time maker; first knife sold in 1983. **Mark:** First initial, last name and maker.

GURGANUS, CAROL, 2553 N.C. 45 South, Colerain, NC 27924, Phone: 252-356-4831, Fax: 252-356-4650
   Specialties: Working and using straight knives. **Patterns:** Fighters, hunters and kitchen knives. **Technical:** Grinds D2, ATS-34 and Damascus steel. Uses stag, and exotic wood handles. **Prices:** $100 to $300. **Remarks:** Part-time maker; first knife sold in 1992. **Mark:** Female symbol, last name, city, state.

GUTHRIE, GEORGE B., 1912 Puett Chapel Rd., Bassemer City, NC 28016, Phone: 704-629-3031
   Specialties: Working knives of his design or to customer specs. **Patterns:** Hunters, boots, fighters, locking folders and slip-joints in traditional styles. **Technical:** Grinds D2, 440C and 154CM. **Prices:** $105 to $300; some to $450. **Remarks:** Part-time maker; first knife sold in 1978. **Mark:** Name in state.

h

HAGEN, PHILIP L., PO Box 58, Pelican Rapids, MN 56572, Phone: 218-863-8503
   Specialties: High-tech working straight knives and folders. **Patterns:** Defense-related straight knives; wide variety of folders. **Technical:** Scale release autos-boloter release autos. **Prices:** $100 to $800; some to $3000. **Remarks:** Part-time maker; first knife sold in 1975. **Mark:** DOC HAGEN in shield, knife, banner logo; or DOC.

HAGGERTY, GEORGE S., PO Box 88, Jacksonville, VT 05342, Phone: 802-368-7437
   Specialties: Working straight knives and folders. **Patterns:** Hunters, claws, camp and fishing knives, locking folders and backpackers. **Technical:** Forges and grinds W2, 440C and 154CM. **Prices:** $85 to $300. **Remarks:** Part-time maker; first knife sold in 1981. **Mark:** Initials or last name.

HAGUE, GEOFF, The Malt House, Hollow Ln., Wilton Marlborough, Wiltshire, ENGLAND SN8 3SR, Phone: (+44) 01672-870212, Fax: (+44) 01672 870212
   Specialties: Fixed blade and folding knives. **Patterns:** Locking and friction folders, hunters and small knives. **Technical:** Grinds ATS-34, RWL34 and Damascus; others by agreement. **Prices:** Start at $200. **Remarks:** Full-time maker. **Mark:** Last name. **Other:** British voting member of the Knife Makers Guild.

HAINES, JEFF, HAINES CUSTOM KNIVES, 302 N. Mill St., Wauzeka, WI 53826, Phone: 608-875-5002
   Patterns: Hunters, skinners, camp knives, customer designs welcome. **Technical:** Forges 1095, 5160, and Damascus, grinds A2. **Prices:** $40 and up. **Remarks:** Part-time maker since 1995. **Mark:** Last name.

HALL, JEFF, PO Box 435, Los Alamitos, CA 90720, Phone: 562-594-4740
   Specialties: Collectible and working folders of his design. **Technical:** Grinds S30V, ATS-34, and various makers' Damascus. **Patterns:** Fighters, gentleman's, hunters and utility knives. **Prices:** $300 to $500; some to $1000. **Remarks:** Full-time maker. First knife sold 1998. **Mark:** Last name.

HALLIGAN, ED, 14 Meadow Way, Sharpsburg, GA 30277, Phone: 770-251-7720, Fax: 770-251-7720
   Specialties: Working straight knives and folders, some fancy. **Patterns:** Liner locks, hunters, skinners, boots, fighters and swords. **Technical:** Grinds ATS-34; forges 5160; makes cable and pattern Damascus. **Prices:** $160 to $2500. **Remarks:** Full-time maker; first knife sold in 1985. Doing business as Halligan Knives. **Mark:** Last name, city, state and USA.

HAMLET JR., JOHNNY, 300 Billington, Clute, TX 77531, Phone: 409-265-6929
   Specialties: Working straight knives and folders. **Patterns:** Hunters, fighters, fillet and kitchen knives, locking folders. Likes upswept knives and trailing-points. **Technical:** Grinds 440C, D2, ATS-34. Makes sheaths. **Prices:** $55 to $225; some to $500. **Remarks:** Part-time maker; first knife sold in 1988. **Mark:** Hamlet's Handmade in script.

HAMMOND, JIM, PO Box 486, Arab, AL 35016, Phone: 256-586-4151, Fax: 256-586-0170
   Specialties: High-tech fighters and folders. **Patterns:** Proven-design fighters. **Technical:** Grinds 440C, 440V, ATS-34 and other specialty steels. **Prices:** $385 to $1200; some to $8500. **Remarks:** Full-time maker; first knife sold in 1977. Designer for Columbia River Knife and Tool. **Mark:** Full name, city, state in shield logo.

HANCOCK, TIM, 10805 N. 83rd St., Scottsdale, AZ 85260, Phone: 480-998-8849
   Specialties: High-art and working straight knives and folders of his design and to customer preferences. **Patterns:** Bowies, fighters, daggers, tantos, swords, folders. **Technical:** Forges Damascus and 52100; grinds ATS-34. Makes Damascus. Silver-wire inlays; offers carved fittings and file work.

Prices: $500 to $10,000. **Remarks:** Full-time maker; first knife sold in 1988. **Mark:** Last name or heart. **Other:** Master Smith ABS.

HAND, BILL, PO Box 773, 1103 W. 7th St., Spearman, TX 79081, Phone: 806-659-2967, Fax: 806-659-5117
   Specialties: Traditional working and using straight knives and folders of his design or to customer specs. **Patterns:** Hunters, Bowies, folders and fighters. **Technical:** Forges 5160, 52100 and Damascus. **Prices:** Start at $150. **Remarks:** Part-time maker; Journeyman Smith. Current delivery time 12 to 16 months. **Mark:** Stylized hand.

HANKINS, R., 9920 S Rural Rd. #10859, Tempe, AZ 85284, Phone: 480-940-0559
   Specialties: Completely hand-made tactical, practical and custom Bowie knives. **Technical:** Use Damascus, ATS-34 and 440C stainless steel for blades. Stock removal method of grinding. Handle material varies from ivory, stag to Micarta, depending on application and appearance. **Remarks:** Part-time maker applying for Knifemakers Guild Int'l membership in June 2001.

HANSEN, LONNIE, PO Box 4956, Spanaway, WA 98387, Phone: 253-847-4632
   Specialties: Working straight knives of his design. **Patterns:** Tomahawks, tantos, hunters, filet. **Technical:** Forges 1086, 52100, grinds 440V, BG-42. **Prices:** Starting at $300. **Remarks:** Part-time maker since 1989. **Mark:** First initial and last name. Also first and last initial.

HANSEN, ROBERT W., 35701 University Ave. N.E., Cambridge, MN 55008, Phone: 612-689-3242
   Specialties: Working straight knives, folders and integrals. **Patterns:** From hunters to minis, camp knives to miniatures; folding lockers and slip-joints in original styles. **Technical:** Grinds O1, 440C and 154CM; likes file-work. **Prices:** $75 to $175; some to $550. **Remarks:** Part-time maker; first knife sold in 1983. **Mark:** Fish with last initial inside.

HANSON III, DON L., PO Box 13, Success, MO 65570-0013, Phone: 573-674-3045
   Specialties: One-of-a-kind Damascus folders. **Patterns:** Small, fancy pocket knives, large folding fighters. **Technical:** Forges own Damascus, file work and carving. **Prices:** $800 and up. **Remarks:** Full-time maker, first knife sold in 1984. **Mark:** Sunfish.

HARA, KOUJI, 292-2 Ohsugi, Seki-City, Gifu-Pref. 501-32, JAPAN, Phone: 0575-24-7569, Fax: 0575-24-7569
   Specialties: High-tech and working straight knives of his design; some folders. **Patterns:** Hunters, locking folders and utility/camp knives. **Technical:** Grinds Cowry X, Cowry Y and ATS-34. Prefers high mirror polish; pearl handle inlay. **Prices:** $80 to $500; some to $1000. **Remarks:** Full-time maker; first knife sold in 1980. Doing business as Knife House "Hara". **Mark:** First initial, last name in fish.

HARDY, SCOTT, 639 Myrtle Ave., Placerville, CA 95667, Phone: 530-622-5780
   Specialties: Traditional working and using straight knives of his design. **Patterns:** Most anything with an edge. **Technical:** Forges carbon steels. Japanese stone polish. Offers mirror finish; differentially tempers. **Prices:** $100 to $1000. **Remarks:** Part-time maker; first knife sold in 1982. **Mark:** First initial, last name and Handmade with bird logo.

HARDY, DOUGLAS E., 114 Cypress Rd., Franklin, GA 30217, Phone: 706-675-6305

HARILDSTAD, MATT, 18627 68 Ave., Edmonton, AB, T5T 2M8, CANADA, Phone: 780-481-3165
   Specialties: Working knives, fancy fighting knives, kitchen cutlery, letter openers. **Patterns:** Full range of straight knives in classic patterns. **Technical:** Grinds ATS-34, 440C, commercial Damascus and some high-carbon. **Prices:** $120 to $500 (U.S.). **Remarks:** Part-time maker, first knife sold in 1997. **Mark:** Name, city, province.

HARKINS, J.A., PO Box 218, Conner, MT 59827, Phone: 406-821-1060
   Specialties: Investment grade folders. **Patterns:** flush buttons, lockers. **Technical:** Grinds ATS-34. Engraves; offers gem work. **Prices:** Start at $550. **Remarks:** Full-time maker and engraver; first knife sold in 1988. **Mark:** First and middle initials, last name.

HARLEY, RICHARD, 348 Deerfield Dr., Bristol, TN 37620, Phone: 423-878-5368/423-571-0638
   Specialties: Hunting knives, Bowies, friction folders, one-of-a-kind. **Technical:** Forges 1084, S160, 52100, Lg. **Prices:** $150-$1000. **Mark:** Pine tree with name.

HARLEY, LARRY W., 348 Deerfield Dr., Bristol, TN 37620, Phone: 423-878-5368 (shop)/Cell 423-571-0638, Fax: 276-466-6771
   Specialties: One-of-a-kind Persian in one-of-a-kind Damascus. Working knives, period pieces. **Technical:** Forges and grinds ATS-34, 440c, L6, 15, 20, 1084, and 52100. **Patterns:** Full range of straight knives, toma-

custom knifemakers

hawks, razors, buck skinners and hog spears. **Prices:** $200 and up. **Mark:** Pine tree.

HARM, PAUL W., 818 Young Rd., Attica, MI 48412, Phone: 810-724-5582
Specialties: Early American working knives. **Patterns:** Hunters, skinners, patch knives, fighters, folders. **Technical:** Forges and grinds 1084, 01, 52100 and own Damascus. **Prices:** $75 to $1000. **Remarks:** First knife sold in 1990. **Mark:** Connected initials.

HARMON, JAY, 462 Victoria Rd., Woodstock, GA 30189, Phone: 770-928-2734
Specialties: Working straight knives and folders of his design or to customer specs; collector-grade pieces. **Patterns:** Bowies, daggers, fighters, boots, hunters and folders. **Technical:** Grinds 440C, 440V, ATS-34, D2 1095 and Damascus; heat-treats; makes own mokume. **Prices:** Start at $185. **Remarks:** Part-time maker; first knife sold in 1984. **Mark:** Last name.

HARRINGTON, ROGER, 3 Beech Farm Cottages, Bugsell Ln., East Sussex, ENGLAND TN 32 5 EN, Phone: 44 0 1580 882194
Specialties: Working knives to his or customer's designs, flat saber Norwegian-style grinds on full tang knives. **Technical:** Grinds 01, D2, Damascus. **Prices:** $100-$500. **Remarks:** First knife made by hand in 1997 whilst traveling around the world. **Mark:** Bison with bison written under.

HARRIS, CASS, 19855 Fraiser Hill Ln., Bluemont, VA 20135, Phone: 540-554-8774
Prices: $160 to $500.

HARRIS, JEFFERY A., 705 Olive St. Ste. 325, St. Louis, MO 63101, Phone: 314-241-2442
Remarks: Purveyor and collector of handmade knives.

HARRIS, JAY, 991 Johnson St., Redwood City, CA 94061, Phone: 415-366-6077
Specialties: Traditional high-tech straight knives and folders of his design. **Patterns:** Daggers, fighters and locking folders. **Technical:** Uses 440C, ATS-34 and CPM. **Prices:** $250 to $850. **Remarks:** Spare-time maker; first knife sold in 1980.

HARRIS, JOHN, 14131 Calle Vista, Riverside, CA 92508, Phone: 909-653-2755
Specialties: Hunters, Daggers, Bowies, Bird and Trout, period pieces, Damascus and carbon steel knives, forged and stock removal. **Prices:** $200-$1000.

HARRIS, RALPH DEWEY, 2607 Bell Shoals Rd., Brandon, FL 33511, Phone: 813-681-5293, Fax: 813-654-8175
Specialties: Collector quality interframe folders. **Patterns:** High tech locking folders of his own design with various mechanisms. **Technical:** Grinds 440C, ATS-34 and commercial Damascus. Offers various frame materials including 416ss, and titanium; file worked frames and his own engraving. **Prices:** $400 to $3000. **Remarks:** Full-time maker; first knife sold in 1978. **Mark:** Last name, or name and city.

HARRISON, JIM (SEAMUS), 721 Fairington View Dr., St. Louis, MO 63129, Phone: 314-894-2525
Specialties: Gent's locking liner folders. Compact straight blades for hunting, backpacking and canoeing. **Patterns:** Fixed blade preference for modified Wharncliffes. These patterns developed in BWCAW and Quetico. **Technical:** Grinds 440C, "D-2", talonite, S-30V and pattern welded. Heat treats. **Prices:** Straight blades $225-$400; folders $300-$500. **Remarks:** Likes knives to be carry friendly. **Mark:** Seamus.

HARSEY, WILLIAM H., 82710 N. Howe Ln., Creswell, OR 97426, Phone: 519-895-4941
Specialties: High-tech kitchen and outdoor knives. **Patterns:** Folding hunters, trout and bird folders; straight hunters, camp knives and axes. **Technical:** Grinds; etches. **Prices:** $125 to $300; some to $1500. Folders start at $350. **Remarks:** Full-time maker; first knife sold in 1979. **Mark:** Full name, state, U.S.A.

HART, BILL, 647 Cedar Dr., Pasadena, MD 21122, Phone: 410-255-4981
Specialties: Fur-trade era working straight knives and folders. **Patterns:** Springbuck folders, skinners, Bowies and patch knives. **Technical:** Forges and stock removes 1095 and 5160 wire Damascus. **Prices:** $100 to $600. **Remarks:** Part-time maker; first knife sold in 1986. **Mark:** Name.

HARTMAN, ARLAN (LANNY), 340 Ruddiman, N. Muskegon, MI 49445, Phone: 231-744-3635
Specialties: Working straight knives and folders. **Patterns:** Drop-point hunters, coil spring lockers, slip-joints. **Technical:** Flat-grinds D2, 440C and ATS-34. **Prices:** $300 to $2000. **Remarks:** Part-time maker; first knife sold in 1982. **Mark:** Last name.

HARTSFIELD, PHILL, PO Box 1637, Newport Beach, CA 92659-0637, Phone: 949-722-9792 and 714-636-7633
Specialties: Heavy-duty working and using straight knives. **Patterns:** Fighters, swords and survival knives, most in Japanese profile. **Technical:** Grinds A2. **Prices:** $350 to $20,000. **Remarks:** Full-time maker; first knife sold about 1976. Doing business as A Cut Above. **Mark:** Initials, chiseled character plus register mark. **Other:** Color catalog $10.

HARVEY, KEVIN, HEAVIN FORGE, PO Box 768, Belfast 1100, SOUTH AFRICA, Phone: 27-13-253-0914
Specialties: Large knives of presentation quality and creative art knives. **Patterns:** Fixed blades of Bowie, dagger and fighter-styles, occasionally folders. **Technical:** Stock removal of stainless and forging of carbon steel and own Damascus. Indigenous African handle materials preferred. Stacked file worked handles. Ostrich, bull frog, fish, crocodile and snake leathers used on unique sheaths. Surface texturing and heat coloring of materials. Often collaborate with wife, Heather (ABS MS) under the logo "Heavin". **Prices:** $500-$5000 average $1500. **Remarks:** Full-time maker and knifemaking instructor. Master bladesmith with ABS. First knife sold in 1984. **Mark:** First name and surname - oval with "M S" in the middle.

HARVEY, MAX, 14 Bass Rd., Bull Creek, Perth 6155, WESTERN AUSTRALIA, Phone: 09-332-7585
Specialties: Daggers, Bowies, fighters and fantasy knives. **Patterns:** Hunters, Bowies, tantos and skinners. **Technical:** Hollow-and flat-grinds 440C, ATS-34, 154CM and Damascus. Offers gem work. **Prices:** $250 to $4000. **Remarks:** Part-time maker; first knife sold in 1981. **Mark:** First and middle initials, last name.

HARVEY, HEATHER, HEAVIN FORGE, PO Box 768, Belfast 1100, SOUTH AFRICA, Phone: 27-13-253-0914
Specialties: Integral hand forged knives, traditional African weapons, primitive folders and by-gone forged-styles. **Patterns:** All forged knives, war axes, spears, arrows, forks, spoons, and swords. **Technical:** Own carbon Damascus and mokume. Also forges stainless, brass, copper and titanium. Traditional forging and heat-treatment methods used. **Prices:** $300-$5000, average $1000. **Remarks:** Full-time maker and knifemaking instructor. Master bladesmith with ABS. First Damascus sold in 1995, first knife sold in 1998. Often collaborate with husband, Kevin (ABS MS) using the logo Heavin". **Mark:** First name and sur name - oval shape with "M S' in middle.

HASLINGER, THOMAS, 164 Fairview Dr. SE, Calgary AB, CANADA T2H 1B3, Phone: 403-253-9628
Specialties: One-of-a-kind using, working and art knives HCK signature sweeping grind liners. Differential heat treated stainless steel. **Patterns:** No fixed patterns, likes to work with customers on design. **Technical:** Grinds Various specialty alloys, including Damascus, High end satin finish. Prefers natural handle materials e.g. ancient ivory stag, pearl, abalone, stone and exotic woods. Does inlay work with stone, some sterling silver, niobium and gold wire work. Custom sheaths using matching woods or hand stitched with unique leather like sturgeon, Nile perch or carp. Offers engraving. **Prices:** Starting at $150. **Remarks:** Full-time maker; first knife sold in 1994. Doing business as Haslinger Custom Knives. **Mark:** Two marks used, high end work uses stylized initials, other uses elk antler with Thomas Haslinger, Canada, Handcrafted above.

HATCH, KEN, PO Box 203, Dinosaur, CO 81610
Specialties: Indian and early trade knives. **Patterns:** Buckskinners and period Bowies. **Technical:** Forges and grinds 1095, O1, W2, ATS-34. Prefers natural handle materials. **Prices:** $85 to $400. **Remarks:** Part-time maker, custom leather and bead work; first knife sold in 1977. **Mark:** Last name or dragonfly stamp.

HAWES, CHUCK, HAWES FORGE, PO Box 176, Weldon, IL 61882, Phone: 217-736-2479
Specialties: 95% of all work in own Damascus. **Patterns:** Slip-joints liner locks, hunters, Bowie's, swords, anything in between. **Technical:** Forges everything, uses all high-carbon steels, no stainless. **Prices:** $150-$4000. **Remarks:** Like to do custom orders, his style or yours. Sells Damascus. **Mark:** Small football shape. Chuck Hawes maker Weldon,IL. **Other:** Full-time maker sine 1995.

HAWK, GRANT AND GAVIN, Box 401, Idaho City, ID 83631, Phone: 208-392-4911
Specialties: Large folders with unique locking systems D.O.G. lock, toad lock. **Technical:** Grinds ATS-34, titanium folder parts. **Prices:** $450 and up. **Remarks:** Full-time maker. **Mark:** First initials and last names.

HAWK, JACK L., Rt. 1, Box 771, Ceres, VA 24318, Phone: 703-624-3878
Specialties: Fancy and embellished working and using straight knives of his design or to customer specs. **Patterns:** Hunters, Bowies and daggers. **Technical:** Hollow-grinds 440C, ATS-34 and D2; likes bone and ivory handles. **Prices:** $75 to $1200. **Remarks:** Full-time maker; first knife sold in 1982. **Mark:** Full name and initials.

HAWK, JOEY K., Rt. 1, Box 196, Ceres, VA 24318, Phone: 703-624-3282
Specialties: Working straight knives, some fancy. Welcomes customer designs. **Patterns:** Hunters, fighters, daggers, Bowies and miniatures. **Technical:** Grinds 440C or customer preference. Offers some knives with jewelling. **Prices:** $100 to $250; some to $500. **Remarks:** Part-time maker; first knife sold in 1983. **Mark:** First and middle initials, last name stamped.

HAWKINS, RADE, 110 Buckeye Rd., Fayetteville, GA 30214, Phone: 770-964-1177, Fax: 770-306-2877
Specialties: Exotic steels, custom designs, one-of-a-kind knives. **Patterns:** All styles. **Technical:** Grinds CPM10V, CPM440V, Vascomax C-350, and Damascus. **Prices:** Start at $190. **Remarks:** Full-time maker; first knife sold in 1972. **Mark:** Rade Hawkins Custom Knives.

HAWKINS, BUDDY, PO Box 5969, Texarkana, TX 75505-5969, Phone: 903-838-7917

HAYES, SCOTTY, Texarkana College, 2500 N Robinson Rd., Tesarkana, TX 75501, Phone: 903-838-4541, ext. 3236, Fax: 903-832-5030
Specialties: ABS School of Bladesmithing.

HAYES, DOLORES, PO Box 41405, Los Angeles, CA 90041, Phone: 213-258-9923
Specialties: High-art working and using straight knives of her design. **Patterns:** Art knives and miniatures. **Technical:** Grinds 440C, stainless AEB, commercial Damascus and ATS-34. **Prices:** $50 to $500; some to $2000. **Remarks:** Spare-time maker; first knife sold in 1978. **Mark:** Last name.

HAYES, WALLY, 1026 Old Montreal Rd., Orleans, Ont., CANADA K4A-3N2, Phone: 613-824-9520
Specialties: Classic and fancy straight knives and folders. **Patterns:** Daggers, Bowies, fighters, tantos. **Technical:** Forges own Damascus and O1; engraves. **Prices:** $150 to $14,000. **Mark:** Last name, M.S. and serial number.

HAYNES, JERRY, 6902 Teton Ridge, San Antonio, TX 78233, Phone: 210-599-2928
Specialties: Working straight knives and folders of his design, also historical blades. **Patterns:** Hunters, skinners, carving knives, fighters, renaissance daggers, locking folders and kitchen knives. **Technical:** Grinds ATS-34, CPM, Stellite 6K, D2 and acquired Damascus. Prefers exotic handle materials. Has B.A. in design. Studied with R. Buckminster Fuller. **Prices:** $200 to $1200. **Remarks:** Part-time maker - will go full-time after retirement in 2007. First knife sold in 1953. **Mark:** Arrowhead and last name.

HAYNIE, CHARLES, 125 Cherry Lane, Toccoa, GA 30577, Phone: 706-886-8665

HAYS, MARK, Hays Handmade Knives, 1008 Kavanagh Dr., Austin, TX 78748, Phone: 512-292-4410
Specialties: Working straight knives and folders. Patterns inspired by Randall and Stone. **Patterns:** Bowies, hunters and slip-joint folders. **Technical:** 440C stock removal. Repairs and restores Stone knives. **Prices:** Start at $200. **Remarks:** Part-time maker, brochure available, with Stone knives 1974-1983, 1990-1991. **Mark:** First initial, last name, state and serial number.

HAZEN, MARK, 9600 Surrey Rd., Charlotte, NC 28227, Phone: 704-573-0904, Fax: 704-573-0052
Specialties: Working/using straight knives of his design and to customer specs. **Patterns:** Hunters/skinners, fillet, utility/camp, fighters, short swords. **Technical:** Grinds 154 CM, ATS-34, 440C. **Prices:** $75 to $450; some to $1500. **Remarks:** Part-time maker. First knife sold 1982. **Mark:** Name with cross in it, stamped in blade.

HEADRICK, GARY, 122 Wilson Blvd., Juane Les Pins, FRANCE 06160, Phone: 04 93 61 25 15
Specialties: Hi-tech folders with natural furnishings. **Patterns:** Damascus and Mokumes. **Prices:** $500 to $2000. **Remarks:** Full-time maker for last 5 years. **Mark:** G/P in a circle. **Other:** 8 years active.

HEARN, TERRY L., Rt. 14 Box 7676, Lufkin, TX 75904, Phone: 936-632-5045

HEASMAN, H.G., 28 St. Mary's Rd., Llandudno, N. Wales U.K. LL302UB, Phone: (UK)0492-876351
Specialties: Miniatures. **Patterns:** Bowies, daggers and swords. **Technical:** Files from stock high-carbon and stainless steel. **Prices:** $400 to $600. **Remarks:** Part-time maker; first knife sold in 1975. Doing business as Reduced Reality. **Mark:** NA.

HEATH, WILLIAM, PO Box 131, Bondville, IL 61815, Phone: 217-863-2576
Specialties: Classic and working straight knives, folders. **Patterns:** Hunters and Bowies liner lock folders. **Technical:** Grinds ATS-34, 440C, 154CM, Damascus, handle materials micarta, woods to exotic materials

snake skins cobra, rattle snake, African flower snake. Does own heat treating. **Prices:** $75 to $300 some $1000. **Remarks:** Full-time maker. First knife sold in 1979. **Mark:** W. D. HEATH.

HEDRICK, DON, 131 Beechwood Hills, Newport News, VA 23608, Phone: 757-877-8100
Specialties: Working straight knives; period pieces and fantasy knives. **Patterns:** Hunters, boots, Bowies and miniatures. **Technical:** Grinds 440C and commercial Damascus. Also makes micro-mini Randall replicas. **Prices:** $150 to $550; some to $1200. **Remarks:** Part-time maker; first knife sold in 1982. **Mark:** First initial, last name in oval logo.

HEFLIN, CHRISTOPHER M., 6013 Jocely Hollow Rd., Nashville, TN 37205, Phone: 615-352-3909

HEGWALD, J.L., 1106 Charles, Humboldt, KS 66748, Phone: 316-473-3523
Specialties: Working straight knives, some fancy. **Patterns:** Makes Bowies, miniatures. **Technical:** Forges or grinds O1, L6, 440C; mixes materials in handles. **Prices:** $35 to $200; some higher. **Remarks:** Part-time maker; first knife sold in 1983. **Mark:** First and middle initials.

HEHN, RICHARD KARL, Lehnmuehler Str. 1, 55444 Dorrebach, GERMANY, Phone: 06724 3152
Specialties: High-tech, full integral working knives. **Patterns:** Hunters, fighters and daggers. **Technical:** Grinds CPM T-440V, CPM T-420V, forges his own stainless Damascus. **Prices:** $1000 to $10,000. **Remarks:** Full-time maker; first knife sold in 1963. **Mark:** Runic last initial in logo.

HEINZ, JOHN, 611 Cafferty Rd., Upper Black Eddy, PA 18972, Phone: 610-847-8535

HEITLER, HENRY, 8106 N Albany, Tampa, FL 33604, Phone: 813-933-1645
Specialties: Traditional working and using straight knives of his design and to customer specs. **Patterns:** Fighters, hunters, utility/camp knives and fillet knives. **Technical:** Flat-grinds ATS-34; offers tapered tangs. **Prices:** $135 to $450; some to $600. **Remarks:** Part-time maker; first knife sold in 1990. **Mark:** First initial, last name, city, state circling double H's.

HELSCHER, JOHN W., 2645 Highway 1, Washington, IA 52353, Phone: 319-653-7310

HELTON, ROY, Helton Knives, 2941 Comstock St., San Diego, CA 92111, Phone: 858-277-5024

HEMBROOK, RON, HEMBROOK KNIVES, PO Box 201, Neosho, WI 53059, Phone: 920-625-3607
Specialties: Hunters, working knives. **Technical:** Grinds ATS34, 440C, 01 and Damascus. **Prices:** $125 to $750, some to $1000. **Remarks:** First knife sold in 1980. **Mark:** Hembrook plus a serial number. Part-time maker, makes hunters, daggers, Bowies, folders and miniatures.

HEMPERLEY, GLEN, 13322 Country Run Rd., Willis, TX 77318, Phone: 281-350-0283
Specialties: Specializes in hunting knives, does fixed and folding knives.

HENDRICKS, SAMUEL J., 2162 Van Buren Rd., Maurertown, VA 22644, Phone: 703-436-3305
Specialties: Integral hunters and skinners of thin design. **Patterns:** Boots, hunters and locking folders. **Technical:** Grinds ATS-34, 440C and D2. Integral liners and bolsters of N-S and 7075 T6 aircraft aluminum. Does leatherwork. **Prices:** $50 to $250; some to $500. **Remarks:** Full-time maker; first knife sold in 1992. **Mark:** First and middle initials, last name, city and state in football-style logo.

HENDRICKSON, E. JAY, 4204 Ballenger Creek Pike, Frederick, MD 21703, Phone: 301-663-6923
Specialties: Classic collectors and working straight knives of his design. **Patterns:** Bowies, Kukri's, camp, hunters, and fighters. **Technical:** Forges 06, 1084, 5160, 52100, D2, L6 and W2; makes Damascus; offers silver wire inlay. Moran-styles on order. **Prices:** $400 to $5000. **Remarks:** Full-time maker; first knife sold in 1975. **Mark:** Last name, M.S.

HENDRICKSON, SHAWN, 2327 Kaetzel Rd., Knoxville, MD 21758, Phone: 301-432-4306
Specialties: Hunting knives. **Patterns:** Clip points, drop points and trailing point hunters. **Technical:** Forges 5160, 1084 and L6. **Prices:** $175 to $400.

HENDRIX, WAYNE, 9636 Burton's Ferry Hwy., Allendale, SC 29810, Phone: 803-584-3825, Fax: 803-584-3825
Specialties: Working/using knives of his design. **Patterns:** Hunters and fillet knives. **Technical:** Grinds ATS-34, D2 and 440C. **Prices:** $55 to $300. **Remarks:** Full-time maker; first knife sold in 1985. **Mark:** Last name.

HENDRIX, JERRY, HENDRIX CUSTOM KNIVES, 175 Skyland Dr. Ext., Clinton, SC 29325, Phone: 864-833-2659
Specialties: Traditional working straight knives of all designs. **Patterns:** Hunters, utility, boot, bird and fishing. **Technical:** grinds ATS-34 and

custom knifemakers

HENDRIX—HILL

440C. **Prices:** $85-$275. **Remarks:** Full-time maker. **Mark:** Full name in shape of knife. **Other:** Hand stitched, waxed leather sheaths.

HENNICKE, METALLGESTALTUNG, Wassegasse 4, 55578 Wallertheim, GERMANY, Phone: 0049 6732 930414, Fax: 0049 6732 930415
Specialties: All kinds of knives folder with titanium leiner and inlaid springs. **Patterns:** Huntingknives, Bowies, kukris, swords, daggers, camp knives. **Technical:** Forge damststeels mostly wild pattern and sanmai pattern to get strong blades. **Prices:** 400 Euro till 3000 Euro swords about 3000 to 6000 Euro. **Mark:** Is an Mamuth walking out of the ricasso to the blade ore an UH in a circle.

HENRIKSEN, HANS J., Birkegaardsvej 24, DK 3200 Helsinge, DENMARK, Fax: 45 4879 4899
Specialties: Zirconia ceramic blades. **Patterns:** Customer designs. **Technical:** Slip-cast zirconia-water mix in plaster mould; offers hidden or full tang. **Prices:** White blades start at $10cm; colored +50 percent. **Remarks:** Part-time maker; first ceramic blade sold in 1989. **Mark:** Initial logo.

HENSLEY, WAYNE, PO Box 904, Conyers, GA 30012, Phone: 770-483-8938
Specialties: Period pieces and fancy working knives. **Patterns:** Boots to Bowies, locking folders to miniatures. Large variety of straight knives. **Technical:** Grinds ATS34, 440C, D2 and commercial Damascus. **Prices:** $85 and up. **Remarks:** Full-time maker; first knife sold in 1974. **Mark:** Last name.

HERBST, PETER, Komotauer Strasse 26, 91207 Lauf a.d. Pegn., GERMANY, Phone: 09123-13315, Fax: 09123-13379
Specialties: Working/using knives and folders of his design. **Patterns:** Hunters, fighters and daggers; interframe and integral. **Technical:** Grinds CPM-T-440V, UHB-Elmax, ATS-34 and stainless Damascus. **Prices:** $300 to $3000; some to $8000. **Remarks:** Full-time maker; first knife sold in 1981. **Mark:** First initial, last name.

HERMAN, TIM, 7721 Foster, Overland Park, KS 66204, Phone: 913-649-3860, Fax: 913-649-0603
Specialties: Investment-grade folders of his design; interframes and bolster frames. **Patterns:** Interframes and new designs in carved stainless. **Technical:** Grinds ATS-34 and damasteel Damascus. Engraves and gold inlays with pearl, jade, lapis and Australian opal. **Prices:** $1000 to $15,000. **Remarks:** Full-time maker; first knife sold in 1978. **Mark:** Etched signature.

HERNDON, WM. R. "BILL", 32520 Michigan St., Acton, CA 93510, Phone: 661-269-5860
Specialties: Straight knives, plain and fancy. **Technical:** Carbon steel (white and blued), Damascus, stainless steels. **Prices:** Start at $120. **Remarks:** Full-time maker; first knife sold in 1976. **Mark:** Signature and/or helm logo.

HERRING, MORRIS, Box 85, 721 W Line St., Dyer, AR 72935, Phone: 501-997-8861

HERRON, GEORGE, 474 Antonio Way, Springfield, SC 29146, Phone: 803-258-3914
Specialties: High-tech working and using straight knives; some folders. **Patterns:** Hunters, fighters, boots in personal styles. **Technical:** Grinds 154CM, ATS-34. **Prices:** $150 to $1000; some to $2000. **Remarks:** Full-time maker; first knife sold in 1963. About 12 year back log. Not excepting orders. No catalog. **Mark:** Last name in script.

HESSER, DAVID, PO Box 1079, Dripping Springs, TX 78620, Phone: 512-894-0100
Specialties: High-art daggers and fantasy knives of his design; court weapons of the Renaissance. **Patterns:** Daggers, swords, axes, miniatures and sheath knives. **Technical:** Forges 1065, 1095, O1, D2 and recycled tool steel. Offers custom lapidary work and stone-setting, stone handles and custom hardwood scabbards. **Prices:** $95 to $500; some to $6000. **Remarks:** Full-time maker; first knife sold in 1989. Doing business as Exotic Blades. **Mark:** Last name, year.

HETHCOAT, DON, Box 1764, Clovis, NM 88101, Phone: 505-762-5721
Specialties: Liner lock-locking and multi-blade folders **Patterns:** Hunters, Bowies. **Technical:** Grinds stainless; forges Damascus. **Prices:** Moderate to upscale. **Remarks:** Full-time maker; first knife sold in 1969. **Mark:** Last name on all.

HIBBEN, GIL, PO Box 13, LaGrange, KY 40031, Phone: 502-222-1397, Fax: 502-222-2676
Specialties: Working knives and fantasy pieces to customer specs. **Patterns:** Full range of straight knives, including swords, axes and miniatures; some locking folders. **Technical:** Grinds ATS-34, 440C and 154CM. **Prices:** $300 to $2000; some to $10,000. **Remarks:** Full-time maker; first knife sold in 1957. Maker and designer of *Rambo III* knife; made swords for movie *Marked for Death* and throwing knife for movie *Under Seige*;

made belt buckle knife and knives for movie *Perfect Weapon*; made knives featured in movie *Star Trek the Next Generation* Star Trek Nemesis 1990 inductee cutlery hall of fame; designer for United Cutlery. Official klingon armourer for Star Trek, over 34 movies and TV productions. **Mark:** Hibben Knives. City and state, or signature.

HIBBEN, WESTLEY G., 14101 Sunview Dr., Anchorage, AK 99515
Specialties: Working straight knives of his design or to customer specs. **Patterns:** Hunters, fighters, daggers, combat knives and some fantasy pieces. **Technical:** Grinds 440C mostly. Filework available. **Prices:** $200 to $400; some to $3000. **Remarks:** Part-time maker; first knife sold in 1988. **Mark:** Signature.

HIBBEN, JOLEEN, PO Box 172, LaGrange, KY 40031, Phone: 502-222-0983
Specialties: Miniature straight knives of her design; period pieces. **Patterns:** Hunters, axes and fantasy knives. **Technical:** Grinds Damascus, 1095 tool steel and stainless 440C or ATS-34. Uses wood, ivory, bone, feathers and claws on/for handles. **Prices:** $60 to $200. **Remarks:** Sparetime maker; first knife sold in 1991. **Mark:** Initials or first name.

HIBBEN, DARYL, PO Box 172, LaGrange, KY 40031-0172, Phone: 502-222-0983
Specialties: Working straight knives, some fancy to customer specs. **Patterns:** Hunters, fighters, Bowies, short sword, art and fantasy. **Technical:** Grinds 440C, ATS-34, 154CM, Damascus; prefers hollow-grinds. **Prices:** $175 to $3000. **Remarks:** Full-time maker; first knife sold in 1979. **Mark:** Etched full name in script.

HIGGINS, J.P. DR., ART KNIVES BY, 120 N Pheasant Run, Coupeville, WA 98239, Phone: 360-678-9269, Fax: 360-678-9269
Specialties: Since 2003 Dr. J.P. Higgins and Tom Sterling have created a unique collaboration of one-of-a-kind, ultra-quality art knives with percussion or pressured flaked stone blades and creatively sculpted handles. Their knives are often highly influenced by the traditions of Japanese netsuke and unique fusions of cultures, reflecting stylistically integrated choices of exotic hardwoods, fossil ivories and semi-precious materials, contrasting inlays and polychromed and pyrographed details. **Prices:** $300-$900. **Remarks:** Limited output ensures highest quality artwork and exceptional levels of craftsmanship. **Mark:** Signatures Sterling and Higgins.

HIGH, TOM, 5474 S. 112.8 Rd., Alamosa, CO 81101, Phone: 719-589-2108
Specialties: Hunters, some fancy. **Patterns:** Drop-points in several shapes; some semi-skinners. Knives designed by and for top outfitters and guides. **Technical:** Grinds ATS-34; likes hollow-grinds, mirror finishes; prefers scrim able handles. **Prices:** $175 to $8000. **Remarks:** Full-time maker; first knife sold in 1965. Limited edition wildlife series knives. **Mark:** Initials connected; arrow through last name.

HILKER, THOMAS N., PO Box 409, Williams, OR 97544, Phone: 541-846-6461
Specialties: Traditional working straight knives and folders. **Patterns:** Folding skinner in two sizes, Bowies, fork and knife sets, camp knives and interchangeable. **Technical:** Grinds D2, 440C and ATS-34. Heat-treats. **Prices:** $50 to $350; some to $400. Doing business as Thunderbolt Artisans. Only limited production models available; not currently taking orders. **Remarks:** Full-time maker; first knife sold in 1983. **Mark:** Last name.

HILL, HOWARD E., 111 Mission Lane, Polson, MT 59860, Phone: 406-883-3405, Fax: 406-883-3486
Specialties: Autos, complete new design, legal in Montana (with permit). **Patterns:** Bowies, daggers, skinners and lockback folders. **Technical:** Grinds 440C; uses micro and satin finish. **Prices:** $150 to $1000. **Remarks:** Full-time maker; first knife sold in 1981. **Mark:** Persuader.

HILL, STEVE E., 40 Rand Pond Rd., Goshen, NH 03752, Phone: 603-863-4762, Fax: 603-863-4762
Specialties: Fancy manual and automatic liner lock folders, some working grade. **Patterns:** Classic to cool folding and fixed blade designs. **Technical:** Grinds Damascus and occasional 440C, D2. Prefers natural handle materials; offers elaborate filework, carving, and inlays. **Prices:** $375 to $5000; some higher. **Remarks:** Full-time maker; first knife sold in 1978. **Mark:** First initial, last name and handmade. (4400, D2). Damascus folders: mark inside handle. **Other:** Google search: Steve Hill custom knives.

HILL, RICK, 20 Nassau, Maryville, IL 62062-5618, Phone: 618-288-4370
Specialties: Working knives and period pieces to customer specs. **Patterns:** Hunters, locking folders, fighters and daggers. **Technical:** Grinds D2, 440C and 154CM; forges his own Damascus. **Prices:** $75 to $500; some to $3000. **Remarks:** Part-time maker; first knife sold in 1983. **Mark:** Full name in hill shape logo.

HILLMAN, CHARLES, 225 Waldoboro Rd., Friendship, ME 04547, Phone: 207-832-4634
Specialties: Working knives of his own or custom design. Heavy Scagel influence. Patterns: Hunters, fishing, camp and general utility. Occasional folders. Technical: Grinds D2 and 440C. File work, blade and handle carving, engraving. Natural handle materials-antler, bone, leather, wood, horn. Sheaths made to order. Prices: $60 to $500. Remarks: Part-time maker; first knife sold 1986. Mark: Last name in oak leaf.

HINDERER, RICK, 5423 Kister Rd., Wooster, OH 44691, Phone: 216-263-0962
Specialties: Working knives to one-of-a-kind Damascus straight knives and folders. Patterns: All. Technical: Grinds ATS-34 and D2; forges O1, W2 and his own nickel Damascus steel. Prices: $50 to $3200. Remarks: Part-time maker; first knife sold in 1988. Doing business as Mustang Forge. Mark: Initials or first initial, last name.

HINK III, LES, 1599 Aptos Lane, Stockton, CA 95206, Phone: 209-547-1292
Specialties: Working straight knives and traditional folders in standard patterns or to customer specs. Patterns: Hunting and utility/camp knives; others on request. Technical: Grinds carbon and stainless steels. Prices: $80 to $200; some higher. Remarks: Part-time maker; first knife sold in 1980. Mark: Last name, or last name 3.

HINMAN, TED, 183 Highland Ave., Watertown, MA 02472

HINSON AND SON, R., 2419 Edgewood Rd., Columbus, GA 31906, Phone: 706-327-6801
Specialties: Working straight knives and folders. Patterns: Locking folders, liner locks, combat knives and swords. Technical: Grinds 440C and commercial Damascus. Prices: $100 to $350; some to $1500. Remarks: Part-time maker; first knife sold in 1983. Son Bob is co-worker. Mark: HINSON, city and state.

HINTZ, GERALD M., 5402 Sahara Ct., Helena, MT 59602, Phone: 406-458-5412
Specialties: Fancy, high-art, working/using knives of his design. Patterns: Bowies, hunters, daggers, fish fillet and utility/camp knives. Technical: Forges ATS-34, 440C and D2. Animal art in horn handles or in the blade. Prices: $75 to $400; some to $1000. Remarks: Part-time maker; first knife sold in 1980. Doing business as Big Joe's Custom Knives. Will take custom orders. Mark: F.S. or W.S. with first and middle initials and last name.

HIRAYAMA, HARUMI, 4-5-13 Kitamachi, Warabi City, Saitama Pref. 335-0001, JAPAN, Phone: 048-443-2248, Fax: 048-443-2248
Specialties: High-tech working knives of her design. Patterns: Locking folders, interframes, straight gents and slip-joints. Technical: Grinds 440C or equivalent; uses natural handle materials and gold. Prices: Start at $700. Remarks: Part-time maker; first knife sold in 1985. Mark: First initial, last name.

HIROTO, FUJIHARA, , 2-34-7 Koioosako Nishi-ku Hiroshima-city, Hiroshima, JAPAN, Phone: 082-271-8389

HITCHMOUGH, HOWARD, 95 Old Street Rd., Peterborough, NH 03458-1637, Phone: 603-924-9646, Fax: 603-924-9595
Specialties: High class folding knives. Technical: Lockback folders, liner locks, pocket knives. Technical: Uses ATS-34, stainless Damascus, titanium, gold and gemstones. Prefers hand-rubbed finishes and natural handle materials. Prices: $850 to $3500; some to $4500. Remarks: Full-time maker; first knife sold in 1967. Mark: Last name.

HOBART, GENE, 100 Shedd Rd., Windsor, NY 13865, Phone: 607-655-1345

HOCKENBARY, WARREN E., 1806 Vallecito Dr., San Pedro, CA 90732

HOCKENSMITH, DAN, 33514 CR 77, Crook, CO 80726, Phone: 970-886-3404
Specialties: Traditional working and using straight knives of his design. Patterns: Hunters, Bowies, folders and utility/camp knives. Technical: Uses his Damascus, 5160, carbon steel, 52100 steel and 1084 steel. Hand forged. Prices: $250 to $1500; some to $1000. Remarks: Part-time maker; first knife sold in 1987. Mark: Last name or stylized "D" with H inside.

HODGE, J.B., 1100 Woodmont Ave. SE, Huntsville, AL 35801, Phone: 205-536-8388
Specialties: Fancy working folders. Patterns: Slip-joints. Technical: Grinds 154CM and ATS-34. Prices: Start at $175. Remarks: Part-time maker; first knife sold in 1978. Not currently taking orders. Mark: Name, city and state.

HODGE III, JOHN, 422 S. 15th St., Palatka, FL 32177, Phone: 904-328-3897
Specialties: Fancy straight knives and folders. Patterns: Various. Technical: Pattern-welded Damascus—"Southern-style." Prices: To $1000. Remarks: Part-time maker; first knife sold in 1981. Mark: JH3 logo.

HODGSON, RICHARD J., 9081 Tahoe Lane, Boulder, CO 80301, Phone: 303-666-9460
Specialties: Straight knives and folders in standard patterns. Patterns: High-tech knives in various patterns. Technical: Grinds 440C, AEB-L and CPM. Prices: $850 to $2200. Remarks: Part-time maker. Mark: None.

HOEL, STEVE, PO Box 283, Pine, AZ 85544, Phone: 602-476-4278
Specialties: Investor-class folders, straight knives and period pieces of his design. Patterns: Folding interframes lockers and slip-joints; straight Bowies, boots and daggers. Technical: Grinds 154CM, ATS-34 and commercial Damascus. Prices: $600 to $1200; some to $7500. Remarks: Full-time maker. Mark: Initial logo with name and address.

HOFER, LOUIS, GEN DEL, Rose Prairie BC, CANADA V0C 2H0, Phone: 250-630-2513

HOFFMAN, KEVIN L., 28 Hopeland Dr., Savannah, GA 31419, Phone: 407 207-2643, Fax: 407 207-2643
Specialties: Distinctive folders and fixed blades. Patterns: Titanium frame lock folders. Technical: Sculpted guards and fittings cast in sterling silver and 14k gold. Grinds ATS-34, Damascus. Makes kydex sheaths for his fixed blade working knives. Prices: $400 and up. Remarks: Full-time maker since 1981. Mark: KLH.

HOFFMANN, UWE H., PO Box 60114, Vancouver, BC, CANADA V5W 4B5, Phone: 604-572-7320 (after 5 p.m.)
Specialties: High-tech working knives, folders and fantasy knives of his design or to customer specs. Patterns: Hunters, fishing knives, combat and survival knives, folders and diver's knives. Technical: Grinds 440C, ATS-34, D2 and commercial Damascus. Prices: $95 to $900; some to $2000 and higher. Remarks: Full-time maker; first knife sold in 1985. Mark: Hoffmann Handmade Knives.

HOGAN, THOMAS R., 2802 S. Heritage Ave., Boise, ID 83709, Phone: 208-362-7848

HOGSTROM, ANDERS T., Granvagen 2, 135 52 Tyreso, SWEDEN, Phone: 46 8 798 5802
Specialties: Short and long daggers, fighters and swords For select pieces makes wooden display boxes. Patterns: Daggers, fighters, short knives and swords and an occasional sword. Technical: Grinds 1050 High Carbon, Damascus and stanless, forges own Damasus on occasion. Does clay tempering and uses exotic hardwoods. Prices: Start at $500. Marks: Last name in various typefaces.

HOKE, THOMAS M., 3103 Smith Ln., LaGrange, KY 40031, Phone: 502-222-0350
Specialties: Working/using knives, straight knives. Own designs and customer specs. Patterns: Daggers, Bowies, hunters, fighters, short swords. Technical: Grind 440C, Damascus and ATS-34. Filework on all knives. Tooling on sheaths (custom fit on all knives). Any handle material - mostly exotic. Prices: $100 to $700; some to $1500. Remarks: Full-time maker, first knife sold in 1986. Mark: Dragon on banner which says T.M. Hoke.

HOLBROOK, H.L., PO Box 483, Sandy Hook, KY 41171, Phone: 606-738-9922 home/606-738-6842 Shop
Specialties: Traditional working using straight knives and folders of his design, to customer specs and in standard patterns. Stablized wood. Patterns: Hunters, folders. Technical: Grinds 440C, ATS-34 and D2. Blades have hand-rubbed satin finish. Uses exotic woods, stag and Micarta. Hand-sewn sheath with each straight knife. Prices: $90 to $270; some to $400. Remarks: Part-time maker; first knife sold in 1983. Doing business as Holbrook knives. Mark: Name, city, state.

HOLDEN, LARRY, PO Box 2017, Ridgecrest, CA 93555, Phone: 760-375-7955
Specialties: Sculptured high art, fantasy, and classical fixed blade knives of his design. Patterns: Sculptured art knives, fantasy, Bowies, bustier, traditional or non traditional. Will work with customer on designs. Technical: Hand grinds modern steels, Boye dendritic blanks, Damascus. Sculpts integrated blade, handle, and sheath designs. Mastodon ivory, natural, and exotic materials. Casts in precious metals. Prices: $300 and up. Remarks: Full-time maker, first complete knife sold 1995. Mark: Dragon logo followed by makers name and city.

HOLDER, D'ALTON, 7148 W. Country Gables Dr., Peoria, AZ 85381, Phone: 623-878-3064, Fax: 623-878-3964
Specialties: Deluxe working knives and high-art hunters. Patterns: Drop-point hunters, fighters, Bowies. Technical: Grinds 440C and 154CM; uses amber and other materials in combination on stick tangs. Prices: $300 to $1000; some to $2000. Remarks: Full-time maker; first knife sold in 1966. Mark: D'HOLDER, city and state.

custom knifemakers

HOLLAND, JOHN H., 1580 Nassau St., Titusville, FL 32780, Phone: 321-267-4378
Specialties: Traditional and fancy working/using straight knives and folders of his design, to customer specs and in standard patterns. **Patterns:** Hunters, and slip-joint folders. **Technical:** Grinds 440V and 440C. Offers engraving. **Prices:** $200 to $500; some to $1000. **Remarks:** Part-time maker; first knife sold in 1988. doing business as Holland Knives. **Mark:** First and last name, city, state.

HOLLAR, BOB, 701 2nd Ave. SW, Great Falls, MT 59404, Phone: 406-268-8252
Specialties: Working/using straight knives and folders of his design and to customer specs; period pieces. **Patterns:** Fighters, hunters, liners and back lock folders. **Technical:** Forges 52100, 5160, 15N20 and 1084 (Damascus)*. **Prices:** $225 to $650; some to $1500. **Remarks:** Full-time maker. Doing business as Goshawk Knives. **Mark:** Goshawk stamped. **Other:** *Burled woods, stag, ivory; all stabilized material for handles.

HOLLOWAY, PAUL, 714 Burksdale Rd., Norfolk, VA 23518, Phone: 804-588-7071
Specialties: Working straight knives and folders to customer specs. **Patterns:** Lockers and slip-joints; fighters and boots; fishing and push knives, from swords to miniatures. **Technical:** Grinds A2, D2, 154CM, 440C and ATS-34. **Prices:** $125 to $400; some to $1200. **Remarks:** Part-time maker; first knife sold in 1981. **Mark:** Last name, or last name and city in logo.

HOLMES, ROBERT, 1431 S Eugene St., Baton Rouge, LA 70808-1043, Phone: 504-291-4864
Specialties: Using straight knives and folders of his design or to customer specs. **Patterns:** Bowies, utility hunters, camp knives, skinners, slip-joint and lock-back folders. **Technical:** Forges 1065, 1095 and L6. Makes his own Damascus and cable Damascus. Offers clay tempering. **Prices:** $150 to $1500. **Remarks:** Part-time maker; first knife sold in 1988. **Mark:** DOC HOLMES, or anvil logo with last initial inside.

HORN, DES, 5 Wenlock Rd., NEWLANDS, 7700 Cape Town, SOUTH AFRICA, Phone: 27 21 671 5795, Fax: 27 21 671 5795
Specialties: Folding knives. **Patterns:** Ball release side lock mechanism and interframe automatics. **Technical:** Prefers working in totally stainless materials. **Prices:** $400 to $2000. **Remarks:** Enjoys working in gold, titanium, meteorite, pearl and mammoth. **Mark:** Des Horn.

HORN, JESS, 2526 Lansdown Rd., Eugene, OR 97404, Phone: 541-463-1510
Specialties: Investor-class working folders; period pieces; collectibles. **Patterns:** High-tech design and finish in folders; liner locks, traditional slip-joints and featherweight models. **Technical:** Grinds ATS-34, 154CM. **Prices:** Start at $1000. **Remarks:** Full-time maker; first knife sold in 1968. **Mark:** Full name or last name.

HORNE, GRACE, 182 Crimicar Ln., Sheffield Britian, UNITED KINGDOM S10 4EJ
Specialties: Knives of own design including kitchen and utility knives for people with reduced hand use. **Technical:** Working at Sheffield Hallam University researching innovative, contemporary Damascus steels using non-traditional methods of manufacture. **Remarks:** Spare-time maker/full-time researcher. **Mark:** 'gH' and 'Sheffield'.

HORTON, SCOT, PO Box 451, Buhl, ID 83316, Phone: 208-543-4222
Specialties: Traditional working stiff knives and folders. **Patterns:** Hunters, skinners, utility and show knives. **Technical:** Grinds ATS-34. Uses stag, abalone and exotic woods. **Prices:** $200 to $2500. **Remarks:** First knife sold in 1990. **Mark:** Full name in arch underlined with arrow, city, state.

HOSSOM, JERRY, 3585 Schilling Ridge, Duluth, GA 30096, Phone: 770-449-7809
Specialties: Working straight knives of his own design. **Patterns:** Fighters, combat knives, modern Bowies and daggers, modern swords, concealment knives for military and LE uses. **Technical:** Grinds 154CM, S30V, CPM-3V and stainless Damascus. Uses natural and synthetic handle materials. **Prices:** $250-1500, some higher. **Remarks:** Full-time maker since 1997. First knife sold in 1983. **Mark:** First initial and last name, includes city and state since 2002.

HOUSE, LAWRENCE, 932 Eastview Dr., Canyon Lake, TX 78133, Phone: 830-899-6932

HOUSE, GARY, 2851 Pierce Rd., Ephrata, WA 98823, Phone: 509-754-3272
Specialties: Mosaic Damascus bar stock. **Patterns:** Unlimited, SW Indian designs, geometric patterns, using 1084, 15N20 and some nickel. **Prices:** $50 per inch and up. **Remarks:** Some of the finest and most unique patterns available.

HOWARD, DURVYN M., 4220 McLain St. S., Hokes Bluff, AL 35903, Phone: 256-492-5720
Specialties: Collectible upscale folders; one of kinds, gentlemen's folders. Multiple patents. **Patterns:** Conceptual designs; each unique and different. **Technical:** Uses natural and exotic materials and precious metals. **Prices:** $5000 to $25,000. **Remarks:** Full-time maker; by commission or available work. **Mark:** Howard: new for 2000; Howard in Garamond Narrow "etched". **Other:** Work displayed at select shows, K.G. Show etc.

HOWE, TORI, 13000 E Stampede Rd., Athol, ID 83801

HOWELL, TED, 1294 Wilson Rd., Wetumpka, AL 36092, Phone: 205-569-2281, Fax: 205-569-1764
Specialties: Working/using straight knives and folders of his design; period pieces. **Patterns:** Bowies, fighters, hunters. **Technical:** Forges 5160, 1085 and cable. Offers light engraving and scrimshaw; filework. **Prices:** $75 to $250; some to $450. **Remarks:** Part-time maker; first knife sold in 1991. Doing business as Howell Co. **Mark:** Last name, Slapout AL.

HOWELL, JASON G., 213 Buffalo Trl., Lake Jackson, TX 77566, Phone: 979-297-9454
Specialties: Fixed blades and liner lock folders. Makes own Damascus. **Patterns:** Clip and drop point. **Prices:** $150 to $750. **Remarks:** Likes making Mosaic Damascus out of the ordinary stuff. Member of TX Knifemakers and Collectors Association; apprentice in ABS; working towards Journeyman Stamp. **Mark:** Name, city, state.

HOWELL, LEN, 550 Lee Rd. 169, Opelika, AL 36804, Phone: 334-749-1942
Specialties: Traditional and working knives of his design and to customer specs. **Patterns:** Buckskinner, hunters and utility/camp knives. **Technical:** Forges cable Damascus, 1085 and 5160; makes own Damascus. **Mark:** Engraved last name.

HOWELL, ROBERT L., Box 1617, Kilgore, TX 75663, Phone: 903-986-4364
Specialties: Straight knives and folders of his design. **Patterns:** Hunters and locking folders. **Technical:** Grinds D2 and ATS-34; forges and grinds Damascus. **Prices:** $75 to $200; some to $2500. **Remarks:** Part-time maker; first knife sold in 1978. Doing business as Howell Knives. **Mark:** Last name.

HOWSER, JOHN C., 54 Bell Ln., Frankfort, KY 40601, Phone: 502-875-3678
Specialties: Slip joint folders (old patterns-multi blades). **Patterns:** traditional slip joint folders, lockbacks, hunters and fillet knives. **Technical:** ATS-34 standard steel, will use D-2, 440V-hand rubbed satin finish natural materials. **Prices:** $100-$400 some to $500. **Remarks:** Full-time maker; first knife sold in 1974. **Mark:** Signature or stamp.

HOY, KEN, 54744 Pinchot Dr., North Fork, CA 93643, Phone: 209-877-7805

HRISOULAS, JIM, 330 S. Decatur Ave., Suite 109, Las Vegas, NV 89107, Phone: 702-566-8551
Specialties: Working straight knives; period pieces. **Patterns:** Swords, daggers and sgian dubhs. **Technical:** Double-edged differential heat treating. **Prices:** $85 to $175; some to $600 and higher. **Remarks:** Full-time maker; first knife sold in 1973. Author of *The Complete Bladesmith*, *The Pattern Welded Blade* and *The Master Bladesmith*. Doing business as Salamander Armory. **Mark:** 8R logo and sword and salamander.

HUCKABEE, DALE, 254 Hwy 260, Maylene, AL 35114, Phone: 205-664-2544
Specialties: Fixed blade hunter and Bowies of his design. **Technical:** Steel used: 5160, 1095, 1084 and some Damascus. **Prices:** Starting at $150 and up, depending on materials used. **Remarks:** Hand forged. Journeyman Smith. **Mark:** Stamped Huckabee J.S. **Other:** Part-time maker.

HUDSON, ANTHONY B., PO Box 368, Amanda, OH 43102, Phone: 740-969-4200
Specialties: Hunting knives, fighters, survival. **Remarks:** ABS Journeyman Smith. **Mark:** A.B. HUDSON.

HUDSON, ROB, 340 Roush Rd., Northumberland, PA 17857, Phone: 570-473-9588
Specialties: Custom hunters, Bowies, daggers, tantos, custom orders. **Technical:** Grinds ATS-34, stainless, Damascus, hollow grinds or flat. Filework, finger grooves. Engraving and scrimshaw available. **Prices:** $200 to $700. **Remarks:** Full-time maker. Does business as Rob's Custom Knives. **Mark:** Capital R, Capital H in script.

HUDSON, C. ROBBIN, 22280 Frazier Rd., Rock Hall, MD 21661, Phone: 410-639-7273
Specialties: High-art working knives. **Patterns:** Hunters, Bowies, fighters and kitchen knives. **Technical:** Forges W2, nickel steel, pure nickel steel, composite and mosaic Damascus; makes knives one-at-a-time. **Prices:** 500 to $1200; some to $5000. **Remarks:** Full-time maker; first knife sold in 1970. **Mark:** Last name and MS.

HUDSON, ROBERT, 3802 Black Cricket Ct., Humble, TX 77396, Phone: 713-454-7207
Specialties: Working straight knives of his design. **Patterns:** Bowies, hunters, skinners, fighters and utility knives. **Technical:** Grinds D2, 440C, 154CM and commercial Damascus. **Prices:** $85 to $350; some to $1500. **Remarks:** Part-time maker; first knife sold in 1980. **Mark:** Full name, handmade, city and state.

HUGHES, DAN, 13743 Persimmon Blvd., West Palm Beach, FL 33411
Specialties: Working straight knives to customer specs. **Patterns:** Hunters, fighters, fillet knives. **Technical:** Grinds 440C and ATS-34. **Prices:** $55 to $175; some to $300. **Remarks:** Part-time maker; first knife sold in 1984. **Mark:** Initials.

HUGHES, ED, 280 1/2 Holly Lane, Grand Junction, CO 81503, Phone: 970-243-8547
Specialties: Working and art folders. **Patterns:** Buys Damascus. **Technical:** Grinds stainless steels. Engraves. **Prices:** $300 and up. **Remarks:** Full-time maker; first knife sold in 1978. **Mark:** Name or initials.

HUGHES, DARYLE, 10979 Leonard, Nunica, MI 49448, Phone: 616-837-6623
Specialties: Working knives. **Patterns:** Buckskinners, hunters, camp knives, kitchen and fishing knives. **Technical:** Forges and grinds W2, O1 and D2. **Prices:** $40 to $100; some to $400. **Remarks:** Part-time maker; first knife sold in 1979. **Mark:** Name and city in logo.

HUGHES, LAWRENCE, 207 W. Crestway, Plainview, TX 79072, Phone: 806-293-5406
Specialties: Working and display knives. **Patterns:** Bowies, daggers, hunters, buckskinners. **Technical:** Grinds D2, 440C and 154CM. **Prices:** $125 to $300; some to $2000. **Remarks:** Full-time maker; first knife sold in 1979. **Mark:** Name with buffalo skull in center.

HUGHES, BILL, 110 Royale Dr., Texarkana, TX 75503, Phone: 903- 838-0134

HULETT, STEVE, 115 Yellowstone Ave., West Yellowstone, MT 59758, Phone: 406-646-4116
Specialties: Classic, working/using knives, straight knives, folders. Your design, custom specs. **Patterns:** Utility/camp knives, hunters, and liner lock folders. **Technical:** Grinds 440C stainless steel, O1 Carbon, 1095. Shop is retail and knife shop—people watch their knives being made. We do everything in house—"all but smelt the ore, or tan the hide." **Prices:** $125 to $7000. **Remarks:** Full-time maker; first knife sold in 1994. **Mark:** Seldom seen knives/West Yellowstone Montana.

HULL, MICHAEL J., 1330 Hermits Circle, Cottonwood, AZ 86326, Phone: 928-634-2871
Specialties: Period pieces and working knives. **Patterns:** Hunters, fighters, Bowies, camp and Mediterranean knives, etc. **Technical:** Grinds 440C, ATS-34 and BG42 and S30V. **Prices:** $125 to $750; some to $1000. **Remarks:** Full-time maker; first knife sold in 1983. **Mark:** Name, city, state.

HULSEY, HOYT, 379 Shiloh, Attalla, AL 35954, Phone: 256-538-6765
Specialties: Traditional working straight knives and folders of his design. **Patterns:** Hunters and utility/camp knives. **Technical:** Grinds 440C, ATS-34, O1 and A2. **Prices:** $75 to $250. **Remarks:** Part-time maker; first knife sold in 1989. **Mark:** Hoyt Hulsey Attalla AL.

HUME, DON, , 2731 Tramway Cir. NE, Albuquerque, NM 87122, Phone: 505-796-9451

HUMENICK, ROY, PO Box 55, Rescue, CA 95672
Specialties: Multiblade folders. **Patterns:** Original folder and fixed blade designs, also traditional patterns. **Technical:** Grinds premium steels and Damascus. **Prices:** $350 and up; some to $1500. **Remarks:** First knife sold in 1984. **Mark:** Last name in ARC.

HUMPHREYS, JOEL, 3260 Palmer Rd., Bowling Green, FL 33834-9801, Phone: 863-773-0439
Specialties: Traditional working/using straight knives and folders of his design and in standard patterns. **Patterns:** Hunters, folders and utility/ camp knives. **Technical:** Grinds ATS-34, D2, 440C. All knives have tapered tangs, mitered bolster/handle joints, handles of horn or bone fitted sheaths. **Prices:** $135 to $225; some to $350. **Remarks:** Part-time maker; first knife sold in 1990. Doing business as Sovereign Knives. **Mark:** First name or "H" pierced by arrow.

HUNT, MAURICE, 2492 N. 800 E, Winter: 2925 Argyle Rd. Venice FL 34293, Avon, IN 46123, Phone: 317 272-2669/Winter: 941-493-4027, Fax: 317 272-2159
Patterns: Bowies, hunters, fighters. **Prices:** $200 to $800. **Remarks:** Part-time maker. **Other:** Journeyman Smith.

HUNTER, HYRUM, 285 N. 300 W, PO Box 179, Aurora, UT 84620, Phone: 435-529-7244
Specialties: Working straight knives of his design or to customer specs. **Patterns:** Drop and clip, fighters dagger, some folders. **Technical:** Forged from two piece Damascus. **Prices:** Prices are adjusted according to size, complexity and material used. **Remarks:** Will consider any design you have. Part-time maker; first knife sold in 1990. **Mark:** Initials encircled with first initial and last name and city, then state. Some patterns are numbered.

HUNTER, RICHARD D., 7230 NW 200th Ter., Alachua, FL 32615, Phone: 386-462-3150
Specialties: Traditional working/using knives of his design or customer suggestions; filework. **Patterns:** Folders of various types, Bowies, hunters, daggers. **Technical:** Traditional blacksmith; hand forges high-carbon steel (5160, 1084, 52100) and makes own Damascus; grinds 440C and ATS34. **Prices:** $200 and up. **Remarks:** Part-time maker; first knife sold in 1992. **Mark:** Last name in capital letters.

HURST, JEFF, PO Box 247, Rutledge, TN 37861, Phone: 865-828-5729
Specialties: Working straight knives and folders of his design. **Patterns:** Tomahawks, hunters, boots, folders and fighters. **Technical:** Forges W2, O1 and his own Damascus. Makes mokume. **Prices:** $175 to $350; some to $500. **Remarks:** Full-time maker; first knife sold in 1984. Doing business as Buzzard's Knob Forge. **Mark:** Last name; partnered knives are marked with Newman L. Smith, handle artisan, and SH in script.

HURST, COLE, 1583 Tedford, E. Wenatchee, WA 98802, Phone: 509-884-9206
Specialties: Fantasy, high-art and traditional straight knives. **Patterns:** Bowies, daggers and hunters. **Technical:** Blades are made of stone; handles are made of stone, wood or ivory and embellished with fancy woods, ivory or antlers. **Prices:** $100 to $300; some to $2000. **Remarks:** Spare-time maker; first knife sold in 1985. **Mark:** Name and year.

HURT, WILLIAM R., 9222 Oak Tree Cir., Frederick, MD 21701, Phone: 301-898-7143
Specialties: Traditional and working/using straight knives. **Patterns:** Bowies, hunters, fighters and utility knives. **Technical:** Forges 5160, O1 and O6; makes own Damascus. Offers silver wire inlay. **Prices:** $200 to $600; some higher. **Remarks:** Full-time maker; first knife sold in 1989. **Mark:** First and middle initials, last name.

HUSIAK, MYRON, PO Box 238, Altona 3018, Victoria, AUSTRALIA, Phone: 03-315-6752
Specialties: Straight knives and folders of his design or to customer specs. **Patterns:** Hunters, fighters, lock-back folders, skinners and boots. **Technical:** forges and grinds his own Damascus, 440C and ATS-34. **Prices:** $200 to $900. **Remarks:** Part-time maker; first knife sold in 1974. **Mark:** First initial, last name in logo and serial number.

HUTCHESON, JOHN, SURSUM KNIFE WORKS, 1237 Brown's Ferry Rd., Chattanooga, TN 37419, Phone: 423-667-6193
Specialties: Straight working knives, hunters. **Patterns:** Customer designs, hunting, speciality working knives. **Technical:** Grinds D2, S7, 01 and 5160, ATS34 on request. **Prices:** $100-$300, some to $600. **Remarks:** First knife sold 1985, also produces a mid-tech line. **Mark:** Family crest boar's head over 3 arrows. **Other:** Doing business as Sursum Knife Works.

HYDE, JIMMY, 5094 Stagecoach Rd., Ellenwood, GA 30049, Phone: 404-968-1951, Fax: 404-209-1741
Specialties: Working straight knives of any design; period pieces. **Patterns:** Bowies, hunters and utility knives. **Technical:** Grinds 440C; forges 5160, 1095 and O1. Makes his own Damascus and cable Damascus. **Prices:** $150 to $600. **Remarks:** Part-time maker; first knife sold in 1978. **Mark:** First initial, last name.

HYTOVICK, JOE "HY", 14872 SW 111th St., Dunnellon, FL 34432, Phone: 800-749-5339
Specialties: Straight, Folder and Miniature. **Technical:** Blades from Wootz, Damascus and Alloy steel. **Prices:** To $5000. **Mark:** HY.

i

IKOMA, FLAVIO YUJI, R. MANOEL R. TEIXEIRA, 108, 108, Centro Presidente Prudente, SP-19031-220, BRAZIL, Phone: 0182-22-0115
Specialties: Straight knives and folders of all designs. **Patterns:** Fighters, hunters, Bowies, swords, folders, skinners, utility and defense knives. **Technical:** Grinds and forges D6, 440C, high-carbon steels and Damascus. **Prices:** $60 to $350; some to $3300. **Remarks:** Full-time maker; first knife sold in 1991. All stainless steel blades are ultra sub-zero quenched. **Mark:** Ikoma Knives beside eagle.

IMBODEN II, HOWARD L., 620 Deauville Dr., Dayton, OH 45429, Phone: 513-439-1536
   Specialties: One-of-a-kind hunting, flint, steel and art knives. **Technical:** Forges and grinds stainless, high-carbon and Damascus. Uses obsidian, cast sterling silver, 14K and 18K gold guards. Carves ivory animals and more. **Prices:** $65 to $25,000. **Remarks:** Full-time maker; first knife sold in 1986. Doing business as Hill Originals. **Mark:** First and last initials, II.

IMEL, BILLY MACE, 1616 Bundy Ave., New Castle, IN 47362, Phone: 765-529-1651
   Specialties: High-art working knives, period pieces and personal cutlery. **Patterns:** Daggers, fighters, hunters; locking folders and slip-joints with interframes. **Technical:** Grinds D2, 440C and 154CM. **Prices:** $300 to $2000; some to $6000. **Remarks:** Part-time maker; first knife sold in 1973. **Mark:** Name in monogram.

INMAN III, PAUL R., 3120 B Blake Ave #224, Glenwood Springs, CO 81601, Phone: 970-963-5951
   Specialties: Bowies in the Moran-style. **Prices:** $300-$1000.

IRIE, MICHAEL L., MIKE IRIE HANDCRAFT, 1606 Auburn Dr., Colorado Springs, CO 80909, Phone: 719-572-5330
   Specialties: Working fixed blade knives and handcrafted blades for the do-it-yourselfer. **Patterns:** Twenty standard designs along with custom. **Technical:** Blades are ATS-34, BG-43, 440C with some outside Damascus. **Prices:** Fixed blades $95 and up, blade work $45 and up. **Remarks:** Formerly dba Wood, Irie and Co. with Barry Wood. Full-time maker since 1991. **Mark:** Name.

IRON WOLF FORGE, SEE NELSON, KEN

ISAO, OHBUCHI, 702-1 Nouso Yame-City, Fukuoka, JAPAN, Phone: 0943-23-4439

ISGRO, JEFFERY, 1516 First St., West Babylon, NY 11704, Phone: 631-587-7516
   Specialties: File work, glass beading, kydex, leather. **Patterns:** Tactical use knives, skinners, capers, Bowies, camp, hunters. **Technical:** ATS-34, 440C and D2. **Price:** $120 to $600. **Remarks:** Part-time maker. **Mark:** First name, last name, Long Island, NY.

ISHIHARA, HANK, 86-18 Motomachi, Sakura City, Chiba Pref., JAPAN, Phone: 043-485-3208, Fax: 043-485-3208
   Specialties: Fantasy working straight knives and folders of his design. **Patterns:** Boots, Bowies, daggers, fighters, hunters, fishing, locking folders and utility camp knives. **Technical:** Grinds ATS-34, 440C, D2, 440V, CV-134, COS25 and Damascus. Engraves. **Prices:** $250 to $1000; some to $10,000. **Remarks:** Full-time maker; first knife sold in 1987. **Mark:** HANK.

j

JACKS, JIM, 344 S. Hollenbeck Ave., Covina, CA 91723-2513, Phone: 626-331-5665
   Specialties: Working straight knives in standard patterns. **Patterns:** Bowies, hunters, fighters, fishing and camp knives, miniatures. **Technical:** Grinds Stellite 6K, 440C and ATS-34. **Prices:** Start at $100. **Remarks:** Spare-time maker; first knife sold in 1980. **Mark:** Initials in diamond logo.

JACKSON, DAVID, 214 Oleander Ave., Lemoore, CA 93245, Phone: 559-925-8547
   Specialties: Forged steel. **Patterns:** Hunters, camp knives, Bowies. **Prices:** $150 and up. **Mark:** G.D. Jackson - Maker - Lemoore CA.

JACKSON, CHARLTON R., 6811 Leyland Dr., San Antonio, TX 78239, Phone: 210-601-5112

JACKSON, JIM, 7 Donnington Close, Chapel Row Bucklebury RG7 6PU, ENGLAND, Phone: 011-89-712743, Fax: 011-89-710495
   Specialties: Large Bowies, concentrating on form and balance; collector quality Damascus daggers. **Patterns:** With fancy filework and engraving available. **Technical:** Forges O1, 5160 and CS70 and 15N20 Damascus. **Prices:** From $1000. **Remarks:** Part-time maker. **Mark:** Jackson England with in a circle M.S. **Other:** All knives come with a custom tooled leather swivel sheath or exotic materials.

JAKSIK JR., MICHAEL, 427 Marschall Creek Rd., Fredericksburg, TX 78624, Phone: 830-997-1119
   Mark: MJ or M. Jaksik.

JANIGA, MATTHEW A., 2090 Church Rd., Hummelstown, PA 17036-9796, Phone: 717-533-5916
   Specialties: Period pieces, swords, daggers. **Patterns:** Daggers, fighters and swords. **Technical:** Forges and Damascus. Does own heat treating. Forges own pattern-welded steel. **Prices:** $100 - $1000; some to $5000. **Remarks:** Spare-time maker; first knife sold in 1991. **Mark:** Interwoven initials.

JARVIS, PAUL M., 30 Chalk St., Cambridge, MA 02139, Phone: 617-547-4355 or 617-666-9090
   Specialties: High-art knives and period pieces of his design. **Patterns:** Japanese and Mid-Eastern knives. **Technical:** Grinds Myer Damascus, ATS-34, D2 and O1. Specializes in height-relief Japanese-style carving. Works with silver, gold and gems. **Prices:** $200 to $17,000. **Remarks:** Part-time maker; first knife sold in 1978.

JEAN, GERRY, 25B Cliffside Dr., Manchester, CT 06040, Phone: 860-649-6449
   Specialties: Historic replicas. **Patterns:** Survival and camp knives. **Technical:** Grinds A2, 440C and 154CM. Handle slabs applied in unique tongue-and-groove method. **Prices:** $125 to $250; some to $1000. **Remarks:** Spare-time maker; first knife sold in 1973. **Mark:** Initials and serial number.

JEFFRIES, ROBERT W., Route 2, Box 227, Red House, WV 25168, Phone: 304-586-9780
   Specialties: Straight knives and folders. **Patterns:** Hunters, skinners and folders. **Technical:** Uses 440C, ATS-34; makes his own Damascus. **Prices:** Moderate. **Remarks:** Part-time maker; first knife sold in 1988. **Mark:** NA.

JENSEN, JOHN LEWIS, dba MAGNUS DESIGN STUDIO, PO Box 60547, Pasadena, CA 91116, Phone: 626-449-1148, Fax: 626-449-1148
   Specialties: Designer and fabricator of modern, unique, elegant, innovative, original, one-of-a-kind, hand crafted, custom ornamental edged weaponry. Combines skill, precision, distinction and the finest materials, geared toward the discriminating art collector. **Patterns:** Folding knives and fixed blades, daggers, fighters and swords. **Technical:** High embellishment, BFA 96 Rhode Island School of Design: Jewelry and metalsmithing. Grinds 440C, ATS-34, Damascus. Works with custom made Damascus to his specs. Uses gold, silver, gemstones, pearl, titanium, fossil mastodon and walrus ivories. Carving, file work, soldering, deep etches Damascus, engraving, layers, bevels, blood grooves Also forges his own Damascus. **Prices:** Start at $3500. **Remarks:** Available on a first come basis and via commission based on his designs Knifemakers guild voting member and ABS apprenticesmith and member of the Society of North American Goldsmiths. **Mark:** Maltese cross/butterfly shield.

JENSEN JR., CARL A., 1130 Colfax St., Blair, NE 68008, Phone: 402-426-3353
   Specialties: Working knives of his design; some customer designs. **Patterns:** Hunters, fighters, boots and Bowies. **Technical:** Grinds A2, D2, O1, 440C, 5160 and ATS-34; recycles old files, leaf springs; heat-treats. **Prices:** $35 to $350. **Remarks:** Part-time maker; first knife sold in 1980. **Mark:** Stamp "BEAR'S CUTLERY" or etch of letters "BEAR" forming silhouette of a Bear.

JERNIGAN, STEVE, 3082 Tunnel Rd., Milton, FL 32571, Phone: 850-994-0802, Fax: 850-994-0802
   Specialties: Investor-class folders and various theme pieces. **Patterns:** Array of models and sizes in side plate locking interframes and conventional liner construction. **Technical:** Grinds ATS-34, CPM-T-440V and Damascus. Inlays mokume (and minerals) in blades and sculpts marble cases. **Prices:** $650 to $1800; some to $6000. **Remarks:** Full-time maker; first knife sold in 1982. Takes orders for folders only. **Mark:** Last name.

JOBIN, JACQUES, 46 St. Dominique, Levis Quebec, CANADA G6V 2M7, Phone: 418-833-0283, Fax: 418-833-8378
   Specialties: Fancy and working straight knives and folders; miniatures. **Patterns:** Minis, fantasy knives, fighters and some hunters. **Technical:** ATS-34, some Damascus and titanium. Likes native snake wood. Heat-treats. **Prices:** Start at $250. **Remarks:** Full-time maker; first knife sold in 1986. **Mark:** Signature on blade.

JOEHNK, BERND, Posadowskystrasse 22, 24148 Kiel, GERMANY, Phone: 0431-7297705, Fax: 0431-7297705
   Specialties: One-of-a-kind fancy/embellished and traditional straight knives of his design and from customer drawing. **Patterns:** Daggers, fighters, hunters and letter openers. **Technical:** Grinds and file 440C, ATS-34, powder metal orgical, commercial Damascus and various stainless and corrosion-resistant steels. **Prices:** Upscale. **Remarks:** Likes filework. Leather sheaths. Offers engraving. Part-time maker; first knife sold in1990. **Other:** Doing business as metal design kiel. All knives made by hand. **Mark:** From 2005 full name and city, with certificate.

JOHANNING CUSTOM KNIVES, TOM, 1735 Apex Rd., Sarasota, FL 34240 9386, Phone: 941-371-2104, Fax: 941-378-9427
   Specialties: Survival knives. **Prices:** $375-$775.

JOHANSSON, ANDERS, Konstvartarevagen 9, S-772 40 Grangesberg, SWEDEN, Phone: 46 240 23204, Fax: +46 21 358778
   Specialties: Scandinavian traditional and modern straight knives. **Patterns:** Hunters, fighters and fantasy knives. **Technical:** Grinds stainless

steel and makes own Damascus. Prefers water buffalo and mammoth for handle material. **Prices:** Start at $100. **Remarks:** Spare-time maker; first knife sold in 1994. Works together with scrimshander Viveca Sahlin. **Mark:** Stylized initials.

JOHNS, ROB, 1423 S. Second, Enid, OK 73701, Phone: 405-242-2707

Specialties: Classic and fantasy straight knives of his design or to customer specs; fighters for use at Medieval fairs. **Patterns:** Bowies, daggers and swords. **Technical:** Forges and grinds 440C, D2 and 5160. Handles of nylon, walnut or wire-wrap. **Prices:** $150 to $350; some to $2500. **Remarks:** Full-time maker; first knife sold in 1980. **Mark:** Medieval Customs, initials.

JOHNSON, RUFFIN, 215 LaFonda Dr., Houston, TX 77060, Phone: 281-448-4407

Specialties: Working straight knives and folders. **Patterns:** Hunters, fighters and locking folders. **Technical:** Grinds 440C and 154CM; hidden tangs and fancy handles. **Prices:** $200 to $400; some to $1095. **Remarks:** Full-time maker; first knife sold in 1972. **Mark:** Wolf head logo and signature.

JOHNSON, RANDY, 2575 E. Canal Dr., Turlock, CA 95380, Phone: 209-632-5401

Specialties: Folders. **Patterns:** Locking folders. **Technical:** Grinds Damascus. **Prices:** $200 to $400. **Remarks:** Spare-time maker; first knife sold in 1989. Doing business as Puedo Knifeworks. **Mark:** PUEDO.

JOHNSON, HAROLD "HARRY" C., 98 Penn St., Trion, GA 30753-1520

Specialties: Working straight knives. **Patterns:** Mostly hunters and large Bowies. **Technical:** Grinds popular steels. Offers leatherwork, sheaths and cases. **Prices:** $125 to $2000; some higher. **Remarks:** Part-time maker; first knife sold in 1973. **Mark:** First initial, last name, city, state. **Other:** Also makes wood and leather cases for knives and guns.

JOHNSON, GORDEN W., 5426 Sweetbriar, Houston, TX 77017, Phone: 713-645-8990

Specialties: Working knives and period pieces. **Patterns:** Hunters, boots and Bowies. **Technical:** Flat-grinds 440C; most knives have narrow tang. **Prices:** $90 to $450. **Remarks:** Full-time maker; first knife sold in 1974. **Mark:** Name, city, state.

JOHNSON, DURRELL CARMON, PO Box 594, Sparr, FL 32192, Phone: 352-622-5498

Specialties: Old-fashioned working straight knives and folders of his design or to customer specs. **Patterns:** Bowies, hunters, fighters, daggers, camp knives and Damascus miniatures. **Technical:** Forges 5160, his own Damascus, W2, wrought iron, nickel and horseshoe rasps. Offers filework. **Prices:** $100 to $2000. **Remarks:** Full-time maker and blacksmith; first knife sold in 1957. **Mark:** Middle name.

JOHNSON, C.E. GENE, 5648 Redwood Ave., Portage, IN 46368, Phone: 219-762-5461

Specialties: Lock-back folders and sprinters of his design or to customer specs. **Patterns:** Hunters, Bowies, survival lock-back folders. **Technical:** Grinds D2, 440C, A18, O1, Damascus; likes filework. **Prices:** $100 to $2000. **Remarks:** Full-time maker; first knife sold in 1975. **Mark:** "Gene" city, state and serial number.

JOHNSON, R.B., Box 11, Clearwater, MN 55320, Phone: 320-558-6128

Specialties: Liner Locks with Titanium - Mosaic Damascus. **Patterns:** Liner lock folders, skeleton hunters, frontier Bowies. **Technical:** Damascus, Mosaic Damascus, A-2, O-1, 1095. **Prices:** $200 and up. **Remarks:** Full-time maker since 1973. Not accepting orders. **Mark:** R B Johnson (signature).

JOHNSON, JOHN R., 5535 Bob Smith Ave., Plant City, FL 33565, Phone: 813-986-4478

Specialties: Hand forged and stock removal. **Technical:** High tec. Folders. **Mark:** J.R. Johnson Plant City, FL.

JOHNSON, STEVEN R., 202 E. 200 N., PO Box 5, Manti, UT 84642, Phone: 435-835-7941

Specialties: Investor-class working knives. **Patterns:** Hunters, fighters, boots and folders of locking liner variety. **Technical:** Grinds ATS-34, 440-C, RWL-34. **Prices:** $500 to $5000. **Remarks:** Full-time maker; first knife sold in 1972. **Mark:** Name, city, state and optional signature mark.

JOHNSON, RICHARD, W165 N10196 Wagon Trail, Germantown, WI 53022, Phone: 262-251-5772

Specialties: Custom knives and knife repair.

JOHNSON, RYAN M., 7320 Foster Hixson Cemetery Rd., Hixson, TN 37343, Phone: 615-842-9323

Specialties: Working and using straight knives of his design and to customer specs. **Patterns:** Bowies, hunters and utility/camp knives. **Techni-**

cal: Forges 5160, Damascus and files. Prices; $70 to $400; some to $800. **Remarks:** Full-time maker; first knife sold in 1986. **Mark:** Sledge-hammer with halo.

JOHNSON, DAVID A., 1791 Defeated Creek Rd., Pleasant Shade, TN 37145, Phone: 615-774-3596

JOHNSTON, DR. ROBT., PO Box 9887, 1 Lomb Mem Dr., Rochester, NY 14623

JOKERST, CHARLES, 9312 Spaulding, Omaha, NE 68134, Phone: 402-571-2536

Specialties: Working knives in standard patterns. **Patterns:** Hunters, fighters and pocketknives. **Technical:** Grinds 440C, ATS-34. **Prices:** $90 to $170. **Remarks:** Spare-time maker; first knife sold in 1984. **Mark:** Early work marked RCJ; current work marked with last name and city.

JONES, BARRY M. AND PHILLIP G., 221 North Ave., Danville, VA 24540, Phone: 804-793-5282

Specialties: Working and using straight knives and folders of their design and to customer specs; combat and self-defense knives. **Patterns:** Bowies, fighters, daggers, swords, hunters and liner lock folders. **Technical:** Grinds 440C, ATS-34 and D2; flat-grinds only. All blades hand polished. **Prices:** $100 to $1000, some higher. **Remarks:** Part-time makers; first knife sold in 1989. **Mark:** Jones Knives, city, state.

JONES, FRANKLIN (FRANK) W., 6030 Old Dominion Rd., Columbus, GA 31909, Phone: 706-563-6051

Specialties: Traditional/working/tactical/period straight knives of his or your design. **Patterns:** Liner lock folders. Hunters, skinners, utility/camp, Bowies, fighters, kitchen, carving sets. **Technical:** Forges all straight knives using 5160, 01, 52100, 1085 and 1095. **Prices:** $150 to $1000. **Remarks:** Full-time, American Bladesmith Society Journeyman Smith. **Mark:** F.W. Jones, Columbus, GA.

JONES, BOB, 6219 Aztec NE, Albuquerque, NM 87110, Phone: 505-881-4472

Specialties: Fancy working knives of his design. **Patterns:** Mountain man/buckskinner-type knives; multi-blade folders, locking folders, and slip-joints. **Technical:** Grinds A2, O1, 1095 and commercial Damascus; uses no stainless steel. Engraves. **Prices:** $100 to $500; some to $1500. **Remarks:** Full-time maker; first knife sold in 1960. **Mark:** Initials on fixed blades; initials encircled on folders.

JONES, CHARLES ANTHONY, 36 Broadgate Close, Bellaire Barnstaple, No. Devon E31 4AL, ENGLAND, Phone: 0271-75328

Specialties: Working straight knives. **Patterns:** Simple hunters, fighters and utility knives. **Technical:** Grinds 440C, O1 and D2; filework offered. Engraves. **Prices:** $100 to $500; engraving higher. **Remarks:** Spare-time maker; first knife sold in 1987. **Mark:** Tony engraved.

JONES, ROGER MUDBONE, GREENMAN WORKSHOP, PO Box 367, Waverly, OH 45690, Phone: 740-947-5684

Specialties: Working in cutlery to suit working woodsman and fine collector. **Patterns:** Bowies, hunters, folders, hatchets in both period and modern style, scale miniatures a specialty. **Technical:** All cutlery hand forged to shape with traditional methods; multiple quench and draws, limited Damascus production hand carves wildlife and historic themes in stag/antler/ivory, full line of functional and high art leather. All work sole authorship. **Prices:** $50-$5000 **Remarks:** Full-time maker/first knife sold in 1979. **Mark:** Stamped R. Jones hand made or hand engraved sig. W/ Bowie knife mark.

JONES, JOHN A., 779 SW 131 HWY, Holden, MO 64040, Phone: 816-850-4318

Specialties: Working, using knives. Hunters, skinners and fighters. **Technical:** Grinds D2, 01, 440C, 1095. Prefers forging; creates own Damascus. File working on most blades. **Prices:** $50 to $500. **Remarks:** Part-time maker; first knife sold in 1996. Doing business as Old John Knives. **Mark:** OLD JOHN and serial number.

JONES, CURTIS J., 39909 176th St. E., Palmdale, CA 93591, Phone: 805-264-2753

Specialties: Big Bowies, daggers, his own style of hunters. **Patterns:** Bowies, daggers, hunters, swords, boots and miniatures. **Technical:** Grinds 440C, ATS-34 and D2. Fitted guards only; does not solder. Heat-treats. Custom sheaths-hand-tooled and stitched. **Prices:** $125 to $1500; some to $3000. **Remarks:** Full-time maker; first knife sold in 1975. Mail orders accepted. **Mark:** Stylized initials on either side of three triangles interconnected.

JONES, JOHN, 12 Schooner Circuit, Manly West, QLD 4179, AUSTRALIA, Phone: 07-339-33390

Specialties: Straight knives and folders. **Patterns:** Working hunters, folding lockbacks, fancy daggers and miniatures. **Technical:** Grinds 440C, O1 and L6. **Prices:** $180 to $1200; some to $2000. **Remarks:** Part-time maker; first knife sold in 1986. **Mark:** Jones.

custom knifemakers

JONES, ENOCH, 7278 Moss Ln., Warrenton, VA 20187, Phone: 540-341-0292
Specialties: Fancy working straight knives. **Patterns:** Hunters, fighters, boots and Bowies. **Technical:** Forges and grinds O1, W2, 440C and Damascus. **Prices:** $100 to $350; some to $1000. **Remarks:** Part-time maker; first knife sold in 1982. **Mark:** First name.

JORGENSEN, GERD, Jernbanegata 8, N-3262 Larvik, NORWAY, Phone: (+47) 33 18 66 06, Fax: (+47) 33 18 66 06
Specialties: Scandinavian-styles hunters, working/using straight knives of maker's design, flint knives. **Patterns:** Mild modifications of traditional Scandinavian patterns, hunters, camp knives and fighters/tactical. **Technical:** Grinds Sandvik 12C27, forges own blades collaborates with other Scandinavian blacksmiths. Buys Damascus blades. **Prices:** $100 to $400. **Remarks:** Part-time maker; first knife sold in 1990. **Mark:** First name or initials.

JURGENS, JOHN, 3650 Emerald St. Apt. Y-1, Torrence, CA 90503, Phone: 310-542-3985

JUSTICE, SHANE, 425 South Brooks St., Sheridan, WY 82801, Phone: 307-673-4432
Specialties: Fixed blade working knives. **Patterns:** Hunters, skinners and camp knives. Other designs produced on a limited basis. **Technical:** Hand forged 5160 and 52100. **Remarks:** Part-time maker. Sole author. **Mark:** Cross over a Crescent.

k

K B S, KNIVES, RSD 181, North Castlemaine, Vic 3450, AUSTRALIA, Phone: 0011 61 3 54 705864, Fax: 0011 61 3 54 706233
Specialties: Bowies, daggers and miniatures. **Patterns:** Art daggers, traditional Bowies, fancy folders and miniatures. **Technical:** Hollow or flat grind, most steels. **Prices:** $200 to $600+. **Remarks:** Full-time maker; first knife sold in 1983. **Mark:** Initials and address in Southern Cross motif.

KACZOR, TOM, 375 Wharncliffe Rd. N., Upper London, Ont., CANADA N6G 1E4, Phone: 519-645-7640

KADASAH, AHMED BIN, PO Box 1969, Jeddah 21441, SAUDI ARABIA, Phone: (26) 913-0082

KAGAWA, KOICHI, 1556 Horiyamashita, Hatano-Shi, Kanagawa, JAPAN
Specialties: Fancy high-tech straight knives and folders to customer specs. **Patterns:** Hunters, locking folders and slip-joints. **Technical:** Uses 440C and ATS-34. **Prices:** $500 to $2000; some to $20,000. **Remarks:** Part-time maker; first knife sold in 1986. **Mark:** First initial, last name-YOKOHAMA.

KAIN, CHARLES, KAIN DESIGNS, 5412 N College Ave., Indianapolis, IN 46220
Specialties: Damascus Art Pieces. **Patterns:** Any. **Remarks:** Specialize in unique art pieces. **Mark:** Kain and signed stamp for unique pieces.

KAJIN, AL, PO Box 1047, Forsyth, MT 59327, Phone: 406-356-2442
Specialties: Damascus, utility knives, working knives; make his own Damascus. **Patterns:** All types. **Technical:** Maker since 1989; ABS member. **Prices:** $175 and up. **Remarks:** Like to work with customer on design. **Mark:** AK on forged blades. Stylized Kajin in outline of Montana for stock removal knives.

KALFAYAN, EDWARD N., 410 Channing, Ferndale, MI 48220, Phone: 248-548-4882
Specialties: Working straight knives and lockback folders; some art and fantasy pieces. **Patterns:** Bowies, toothpicks, fighters, daggers, swords and hunters. **Technical:** Grinds ATS-34, 440C, O1, 5160 and Damascus. **Prices:** $150 to $5000. **Remarks:** Full-time maker; first knife sold in 1973. **Mark:** Last name.

KALUZA, WERNER, Lochnerstr. 32, 90441 Nurnberg, GERMANY, Phone: 0911 666047
Specialties: Fancy high-art straight knives of his design. **Patterns:** Boots and ladies knives. **Technical:** Grinds ATS-34, CPM-T-440V and Schneider Damascus. Engraving available. **Prices:** NA. **Remarks:** Part-time maker. **Mark:** First initial and last name.

KANDA, MICHIO, 7-32-5 Shinzutumi-cho, Shunan-shi, Yamaguchi 7460033, JAPAN, Phone: 0834-62-1910, Fax: 011-81-83462-1910
Specialties: Fantasy knives of his design. **Patterns:** Animal knives. **Technical:** Grinds ATS-34. **Prices:** $300 to $3000. **Remarks:** Full-time maker; first knife sold in 1985. Doing business as Shusui Kanda. **Mark:** Last name inside "M".

KANKI, IWAO, 14-25 3-CHOME FUKUI MIKI, Hydugo, JAPAN 673-0433, Phone: 07948-3-2555
Specialties: Plane, knife. **Prices:** Not determined yet. **Mark:** Chiyozuru Sadahide. **Other:** Masters of traditional crafts designated by the Minister of International Trade and Industry (Japan).

KANSEI, MATSUNO, 109-8 Uenomachi Nishikaiden, Gitu-city, JAPAN 501-1168, Phone: 81-58-234-8643
Specialties: Folders of original design. **Patterns:** Liner lock folder. **Technical:** Grinds VG-10, Damascus. **Prices:** $350-$2000. **Remarks:** Full-time maker. First knife sold in 1993. **Mark:** Name.

KANTER, MICHAEL, ADAM MICHAEL KNIVES, 14550 West Honey Ln., New Berlin, WI 53151, Phone: 262-860-1136
Specialties: Fixed Blades and liner Lock Folders. **Patterns:** Drop Point hunters, and Bowies. **Technical:** My own Damascus, BG42, ATS34 and CPMS60V. **Prices:** $200-$1000. **Mark:** Adam Michael over wavy line. **Other:** Ivory, Mamoth Ivory, stabilized woods, and pearl handles.

KARP, BOB, PO Box 47304, Phoenix, AZ 85068, Phone: 602 870-1234, Fax: 602 331-0283

KATO, SHINICHI, 3233-27-5-410 Kikko Taikogane, Moriyama-ku Nagoya, JAPAN 463-0004, Phone: 81-52-736-6032
Specialties: Flat grind and hand finish. **Patterns:** Bowie, fighter. Hunting knife. **Technical:** Flat grind ATS-34. **Prices:** $100-$1500. **Remarks:** Part-time maker. First knife sold in 1995. **Mark:** Name.

KATO, KIYOSHI, 4-6-4 Himonya Meguro-ku, Tokyo 152, JAPAN
Specialties: Swords, Damascus knives, working knives and paper knives. **Patterns:** Traditional swords, hunters, Bowies and daggers. **Technical:** Forges his own Damascus and carbon steel. Grinds ATS-34. **Prices:** $260 to $700; some to $4000. **Remarks:** Full-time maker. **Mark:** First initial, last name.

KATSUMARO, SHISHIDO, 2-6-11 Kamiseno Aki-ku, Hiroshima, JAPAN, Phone: 090-3634-9054, Fax: 082-227-4438

KAUFFMAN, DAVE, 120 Clark Creek Loop, Montana City, MT 59634, Phone: 406-442-9328
Specialties: Field grade and exhibition grade hunting knives and ultra light folders. **Patterns:** Fighters, Bowies and drop-point hunters. **Technical:** ATS-34 and Damascus. **Prices:** $60 to $1200. **Remarks:** Full-time maker; first knife sold in 1989. On the cover of Knives '94. **Mark:** First and last name, city and state.

KAUFMAN, SCOTT, 302 Green Meadows Cr., Anderson, SC 29624, Phone: 864-231-9201
Specialties: Classic and working/using straight knives in standard patterns. **Patterns:** Fighters, hunters and utility/camp knives. Technical Grinds ATS-34, 440C, O1. **Prices:** $100 to $500. **Remarks:** Part-time maker; first knife sold in 1987. **Mark:** Kaufman Knives with Bible in middle.

KAWASAKI, AKIHISA, 11-8-9 Chome Minamiamachi, Suzurandai Kita-Ku, Kobe, JAPAN, Phone: 078-593-0418, Fax: 078-593-0418
Specialties: Working/using knives of his design. **Patterns:** Hunters, kit camp knives. **Technical:** Forges and grinds Molybdenum Panadium. Grinds ATS-34 and stainless steel. Uses Chinese Quince wood, desert ironwood and cow leather. **Prices:** $300 to $800; some to $1000. **Remarks:** Full-time maker. **Mark:** A.K.

KAY, J. WALLACE, 332 Slab Bridge Rd., Liberty, SC 29657

KAZSUK, DAVID, PO Box 39, Perris, CA 92572-0039, Phone: 909-780-2288
Specialties: Hand forged. **Prices:** $150+. **Mark:** Last name.

KEARNEY, JAROD, 7200 Townsend Forest Ct., Brown Summit, NC 27214, Phone: 336-656-4617

KEESLAR, STEVEN C., 115 Lane 216, Hamilton, IN 46742, Phone: 260-488-3161
Specialties: Traditional working/using straight knives of his design and to customer specs. **Patterns:** Bowies, hunters, utility/camp knives. **Technical:** Forges 5160, files 52100 Damascus. **Prices:** $100 to $600; some to $1500. **Remarks:** Part-time maker; first knife sold in 1976. ABS members. **Mark:** Fox lead in flames over Steven C Keeslar.

KEESLAR, JOSEPH F., 391 Radio Rd., Almo, KY 42020, Phone: 270-753-7919, Fax: 270-753-7919
Specialties: Classic and contemporary Bowies, combat, hunters, daggers and folders. **Patterns:** Decorative filework, engraving and custom leather sheaths available. **Technical:** Forges 5160, 52100 and his own Damascus steel. **Prices:** $300 to $3000. **Remarks:** Full-time maker; first knife sold in 1976. **Mark:** First and middle initials, last name in hammer, knife and anvil logo, M.S. **Other:** ABS Master Smith.

KEETON, WILLIAM L., 6095 Rehobeth Rd. SE, Laconia, IN 47135-9550, Phone: 812-969-2836
Specialties: Plain and fancy working knives. **Patterns:** Hunters and fighters; locking folders and slip-joints. Names patterns after Kentucky Derby

winners. **Technical:** Grinds D2, ATS-34, 440C, 440V and 154CM; mirror and satin finishes. **Prices:** $95 to $2000. **Remarks:** Full-time maker; first knife sold in 1971. **Mark:** Logo of key.

KEHIAYAN, ALFREDO, Cuzco 1455, Ing. Maschwitz, CP B1623GXU Buenos Aires, ARGENTINA, Phone: 03488-4-42212
  Specialties: Functional straight knives. **Patterns:** Utility knives, skinners, hunters and boots. **Technical:** Forges and grinds SAE 52.100, SAE 6180, SAE 9260, SAE 5160, 440C and ATS-34, titanium with nitride. All blades mirror-polished; makes leather sheath and wood cases. **Prices:** $70 to $800; some to $6000. **Remarks:** Full-time maker; first knife sold in 1983. **Mark:** Name. **Other:** Some knives are satin finish (utility knives).

KEIDEL, GENE W. AND SCOTT J., 4661 105th Ave. SW, Dickinson, ND 58601
  Specialties: Fancy/embellished and working/using straight knives of his design. **Patterns:** Bowies, hunters and miniatures. **Technical:** Grind 440C and O1 tool steel. Offer scrimshaw and filework. **Prices:** $95 to $500. **Remarks:** Full-time makers; first knife sold in 1990. Doing business as Keidel Knives. **Mark:** Last name.

KEISUKE, GOTOH, 105 Cosumo-City Otozu 202 Ohita-city, Ohita, JAPAN, Phone: 097-523-0750

KELLEY, THOMAS P., 4711 E Ashler Hill Dr., Cave Creek, AZ 85331, Phone: 480-488-3101

KELLEY, GARY, 17485 SW Pheasant Lane, Aloha, OR 97006, Phone: 503-649-7867
  Specialties: Primitive knives and blades. **Patterns:** Fur trade era rifleman's knives, fur trade, cowboy action, hunting knives. **Technical:** Hand-forges and precision investment casts. **Prices:** $35 to $125. **Remarks:** Family business, reproduction blades. Doing business as Reproduction Blades. **Mark:** Fir tree logo.

KELLOGG, BRIAN R., 19048 Smith Creek Rd., New Market, VA 22844, Phone: 540-740-4292
  Specialties: Fancy and working straight knives of his design and to customer specs. **Patterns:** Fighters, hunters and utility/camp knives. **Technical:** Grinds 440C, D2 and A2. Offers filework and fancy pin and cable pin work. Prefers natural handle materials. **Prices:** $75 to $225; some to $350. **Remarks:** Part-time maker; first knife sold in 1983. **Mark:** Last name.

KELLY, LANCE, 1723 Willow Oak Dr., Edgewater, FL 32132, Phone: 904-423-4933
  Specialties: Investor-class straight knives and folders. **Patterns:** Kelly-style in contemporary outlines. **Technical:** Grinds O1, D2 and 440C; engraves; inlays gold and silver. **Prices:** $600 to $3500. **Remarks:** Full-time engraver and knife maker; first knife sold in 1975. **Mark:** Last name.

KELSO, JIM, 577 Collar Hill Rd., Worcester, VT 05682, Phone: 802-229-4254, Fax: 802-229-0595
  Specialties: Fancy high-art straight knives and folders that mix Eastern and Western influences. Only uses own designs, but accepts suggestions for themes. **Patterns:** Daggers, swords and locking folders. **Technical:** Grinds only custom Damascus. Works with top Damascus Blade Smiths. **Prices:** $3000 to $8000; some to $15,000. **Remarks:** Full-time maker; first knife sold in 1980. **Mark:** Stylized initials.

KENNEDY JR., BILL, PO Box 850431, Yukon, OK 73085, Phone: 405-354-9150
  Specialties: Working straight knives. **Patterns:** Hunters, fighters, minis and fishing knives. **Technical:** Grinds D2, 440C and Damascus. **Prices:** $80 and higher. **Remarks:** Part-time maker; first knife sold in 1980. **Mark:** Last name and year made.

KERBY, MARLIN W., Rt. 1, Box114D, Brashear, TX 75420, Phone: 903-485-6201

KERN, R. W., 20824 Texas Trail W, San Antonio, TX 78257-1602, Phone: 210-698-2549
  Specialties: Damascus, straight and folders. **Patterns:** Hunters, Bowies and folders. **Technical:** Grinds ATS-34, 440C and BG42. Forge own Damascus. **Prices:** $200 and up. **Remarks:** First knives 1980; retired; work as time permits. **Mark:** Outline of Alamo with kern over outline. **Other:** Member ABS, Texas Knifemaker and Collectors Association.

KESSLER, RALPH A., PO Box 61, Fountain Inn, SC 29644-0061
  Specialties: Traditional-style knives. **Patterns:** Folders, hunters, fighters, Bowies and kitchen knives. **Technical:** Grinds D2, O1, A2 and ATS-34. Forges 1090 and 1095. **Prices:** $100 to $500. **Remarks:** Part-time maker; first knife sold in 1982. **Mark:** Last name or initials with last name.

KEYES, DAN, 6688 King St., Chino, CA 91710, Phone: 909-628-8329

KHALSA, JOT SINGH, 368 Village St., Millis, MA 02054, Phone: 508-376-8162, Fax: 508-376-8081
  Specialties: Liner locks, one-of-a-kind daggers, swords, and kirpans (Sikh daggers) all original designs. **Technical:** Forges own Damascus,

uses others high quality Damascus including stainless, and grinds stainless steels. Uses natural handle materials frequently unusual minerals. Pieces are frequently engraved and more recently carved. **Prices:** Start at $700.

KHARLAMOV, YURI, Oboronnay 46, 2, Tula, 300007, RUSSIA
  Specialties: Classic, fancy and traditional knives of his design. **Patterns:** Daggers and hunters. **Technical:** Forges only Damascus with nickel. Uses natural handle materials; engraves on metal, carves on nut-tree; silver and pearl inlays. **Prices:** $600 to $2380; some to $4000. **Remarks:** Full-time maker; first knife sold in 1988. **Mark:** Initials.

KI, SHIVA, 5222 Ritterman Ave., Baton Rouge, LA 70805, Phone: 225-356-7274
  Specialties: Fancy working straight knives and folders to customer specs. **Patterns:** Emphasis on personal defense knives, martial arts weapons. **Technical:** Forges and grinds; makes own Damascus; prefers natural handle materials. **Prices:** $135 to $850; some to $1800. **Remarks:** Full-time maker; first knife sold in 1981. **Mark:** Name with logo.

KIEFER, TONY, 112 Chateaugay Dr., Pataskala, OH 43062, Phone: 740-927-6910
  Specialties: Traditional working and using straight knives in standard patterns. **Patterns:** Bowies, fighters and hunters. **Technical:** Grinds 440C and D2; forges D2. Flat-grinds Bowies; hollow-grinds drop-point and trailing-point hunters. **Prices:** $95 to $140; some to $200. **Remarks:** Spare-time maker; first knife sold in 1988. **Mark:** Last name.

KILBY, KEITH, 1902 29th St., Cody, WY 82414, Phone: 307-587-2732
  Specialties: Works with all designs. **Patterns:** Mostly Bowies, camp knives and hunters of his design. **Technical:** Forges 52100, 5160, 1095, Damascus and mosaic Damascus. **Prices:** $250 to $3500. **Remarks:** Part-time maker; first knife sold in 1974. Doing business as Foxwood Forge. **Mark:** Name.

KIMBERLEY, RICHARD L., 86-B Arroyd Hondo Rd., Santa Fe, NM 87508, Phone: 505-820-2727
  Specialties: Fixed-blade and period knives. **Technical:** O1, 52100, 9260 steels. **Remarks:** Member ABS. **Mark:** "By D. KIMBERLEY SANTA FE NM". **Other:** Marketed under "Kimberleys of Santa Fe".

KIMSEY, KEVIN, 198 Cass White Rd. N.W., Cartersville, GA 30121, Phone: 770-387-0779 and 770-655-8879
  Specialties: Tactical fixed blades and folders. **Patterns:** Fighters, folders, hunters and utility knives. **Technical:** Grinds 440C, ATS-34 and D2 carbon. **Prices:** $100 to $400; some to $600. **Remarks:** Three-time "Blade" award winner, Knife maker since 1983. **Mark:** Rafter and stylized KK.

KING, FRED, 430 Grassdale Rd., Cartersville, GA 30120, Phone: 770-382-8478
  Specialties: Fancy and embellished working straight knives and folders. **Patterns:** Hunters, Bowies and fighters. **Technical:** Grinds ATS-34 and D2; forges 5160 and Damascus. Offers filework. **Prices:** $100 to $3500. **Remarks:** Spare-time maker; first knife sold in 1984. **Mark:** Kings Edge.

KING, BILL, 14830 Shaw Rd., Tampa, FL 33625, Phone: 813-961-3455
  Specialties: Folders, lockbacks, liner locks and stud openers. **Patterns:** Wide varieties; folders. **Technical:** ATS-34 and some Damascus; single and double grinds. Offers filework and jewel embellishment; nickel-silver Damascus and mokume bolsters. **Prices:** $150 to $475; some to $850. **Remarks:** Full-time maker; first knife sold in 1976. All titanium fitting on liner-locks; screw or rivet construction on lock-backs. **Mark:** Last name in crown.

KING, HERMAN, PO Box 122, Millington, TN 38083, Phone: 901-876-3062

KING, JASON M., Box 151, Eskridge, KS 66423, Phone: 785-449-2638
  Specialties: Working and using straight knives of his design and sometimes to customer specs. Some slip joint and lockback folders. **Patterns:** Hunters, Bowies, tacticals, fighters; some miniatures. **Technical:** Grinds D2, 440C and other Damascus. **Prices:** $75 to $200; some up to $500. **Remarks:** Full-time maker since 2000. First knife sold in 1998. **Mark:** JMK. **Other:** Likes to use height quality stabilized wood.

KING JR., HARVEY G., Box 184, Eskridge, KS 66423-0184, Phone: 785-449-2487
  Specialties: Traditional working and using straight knives of his design and to customer specs. **Patterns:** Hunters, Bowies and fillet knives. **Technical:** Grinds O1, A2 and D2. Prefers natural handle materials; offers leatherwork. **Prices:** Start at $70. **Remarks:** 3/4-time maker; first knife sold in 1988. **Mark:** Name and serial number based on steel used, year made and number of knives made that year.

custom knifemakers

KINKADE, JACOB, 197 Rd. 154, Carpenter, WY 82054, Phone: 307-649-2446
Specialties: Working/using knives of his design or to customer specs; some miniature swords, daggers and battle axes. **Patterns:** Hunters, daggers, boots; some miniatures. **Technical:** Grinds carbon and stainless and commercial Damascus. Prefers natural handle material. **Prices:** Start at $30. **Remarks:** Part-time maker; first knife sold in 1990. **Mark:** Connected initials or none.

KINKER, MIKE, 8755 E County Rd. 50 N, Greensburg, IN 47240, Phone: 812-663-5277, Fax: 812-662-8131
Specialties: Working/using knives, Straight knives. Starting to make folders. Your design. **Patterns:** Boots, daggers, hunters, skinners, hatchets. **Technical:** Grind 440C and ATS34, others if required. Damascus, dovetail bolsters, jeweled blade. **Prices:** $125 to 375; some to $1000. **Remarks:** Part-time maker; first knife sold in 1991. Doing business as Kinker Knives. **Mark:** Kinker and Kinker plus year.

KINNIKIN, TODD, Eureka Forge, 8356 John McKeever Rd., House Springs, MO 63051, Phone: 314-938-6248
Specialties: Mosaic Damascus. **Patterns:** Hunters, fighters, folders and automatics. **Technical:** Forges own mosaic Damascus with tool steel Damascus edge. Prefers natural, fossil and artifact handle materials. **Prices:** $400 to $2400. **Remarks:** Full-time maker; first knife sold in 1994. **Mark:** Initials connected.

KIOUS, JOE, 1015 Ridge Pointe Rd., Kerrville, TX 78028, Phone: 830-367-2277, Fax: 830-367-2286
Specialties: Investment-quality interframe and bolstered folders. **Patterns:** Folder specialist - all types. **Technical:** Both stainless and non stainless Damascus. **Prices:** $450 to $3000; some to $10,000. **Remarks:** Full-time maker; first knife sold in 1969. **Mark:** Last name, city and state or last name only.

KIRK, RAY, PO Box 1445, Tahlequah, OK 74465, Phone: 918-456-1519
Specialties: Using knives with natural handles. **Patterns:** Neck knives and small hunters and skinners. **Technical:** Uses 52100 and 15N20 for Damascus. Some stock removal. **Prices:** $65 to $800. **Remarks:** Started forging in 1989; makes own Damascus. Has some 52100 and Damascus in custom flat bar 512E3 for sale **Mark:** Stamped "Raker" on blade.

KITSMILLER, JERRY, 67277 Las Vegas Dr., Montrose, CO 81401, Phone: 970-249-4290
Specialties: Working straight knives in standard patterns. **Patterns:** Hunters, boots. **Technical:** Grinds ATS-34 and 440C only. **Prices:** $75 to $200; some to $300. **Remarks:** Spare-time maker; first knife sold in 1984. **Mark:** JandS Knives.

KNICKMEYER, HANK, 6300 Crosscreek, Cedar Hill, MO 63016, Phone: 314-285-3210
Specialties: Complex mosaic Damascus constructions. **Patterns:** Fixed blades, swords, folders and automatics. **Technical:** Mosaic Damascus with all tool steel Damascus edges. **Prices:** $500 to $2000; some $3000 and higher. **Remarks:** Part-time maker; first knife sold in 1989. Doing business as Dutch Creek Forge and Foundry. **Mark:** Initials connected.

KNICKMEYER, KURT, 6344 Crosscreek, Cedar Hill, MO 63016, Phone: 314-274-0481

KNIGHT, JASON, 110 Paradie Pond Ln., Harleyville, SC 29448, Phone: 843-452-1163
Specialties: Bowies. **Patterns:** Bowies and anything from history or his own design. **Technical:** 1084, 5160, 01, 52102, Damascus/forged blades. **Prices:** $200 and up. **Remarks:** Bladesmith. **Mark:** KNIGHT.

KNIPSCHIELD, TERRY, 808 12th Ave. NE, Rochester, MN 55906, Phone: 507-288-7829
Specialties: Working straight and some folding knives in standard patterns. **Patterns:** Lockback and slip-joint knives. **Technical:** Grinds ATS-34. **Prices:** $55 to $350; some to $600. **Remarks:** Part-time maker; first knife sold in 1986. Doing business as Knip Custom Knives. **Mark:** KNIP in Old English with shield logo.

KNIPSTEIN, R.C. (JOE), 731 N. Fielder, Arlington, TX 76012, Phone: 817-265-0573;817-265-2021, Fax: 817-265-3410
Specialties: Traditional pattern folders along with custom designs. **Patterns:** Hunters, Bowies, fighters, utility knives. **Technical:** Grinds 440C, D2, 154CM and ATS-34. Natural handle materials and full tangs are standard. **Prices:** Start at $300. **Remarks:** Part-time maker; first knife sold in 1989. **Mark:** Last name.

KNOTT, STEVE, KNOTT KNIVES, PO Box 963, Rincon, GA 31326, Phone: 912-754-4326
Technical: Uses ATS-34/440C and some commercial Damascus, single and double grinds with mirror or satin finishes. **Patters:** Hunters, boot knives, Bowies, and tantos, slip joint and lock-back folders. Uses a wide variety of handle materials to include ironwood, coca-bola and colored stabilized wood, also horn, bone and ivory upon customer request. **Remarks:** First knife sold in 1991. Part-time maker.

KNUTH, JOSEPH E., 3307 Lookout Dr., Rockford, IL 61109, Phone: 815-874-9597
Specialties: High-art working straight knives of his design or to customer specs. **Patterns:** Daggers, fighters and swords. **Technical:** Grinds 440C, ATS-34 and D2. **Prices:** $150 to $1500; some to $15,000. **Remarks:** Full-time maker; first knife sold in 1989. **Mark:** Initials on bolster face.

KOHLS, JERRY, N4725 Oak Rd., Princeton, WI 54968, Phone: 920-295-3648
Specialties: Working knives and period pieces. **Patterns:** Hunters-boots and Bowies - your designs or mine. **Technical:** Grinds, ATS-34 440c 154CM and 1095 and commercial Damascus. **Remarks:** Part-time maker. **Mark:** Last name.

KOJETIN, W., 20 Bapaume Rd., Delville, Germiston 1401, SOUTH AFRICA, Phone: 27118733305/mobile 27836256208
Specialties: High-art and working straight knives of all designs. **Patterns:** Daggers, hunters and his own Man hunter Bowie. **Technical:** Grinds D2 and ATS-34; forges and grinds 440B/C. Offers "wrap-around" pava and abalone handles, scrolled wood or ivory, stacked filework and setting of faceted semi-precious stones. **Prices:** $185 to $600; some to $11,000. **Remarks:** Spare-time maker; first knife sold in 1962. **Mark:** Billy K.

KOLITZ, ROBERT, W9342 Canary Rd., Beaver Dam, WI 53916, Phone: 920-887-1287
Specialties: Working straight knives to customer specs. **Patterns:** Bowies, hunters, bird and trout knives, boots. **Technical:** Grinds O1, 440C; commercial Damascus. **Prices:** $50 to $100; some to $500. **Remarks:** Spare-time maker; first knife sold in 1979. **Mark:** Last initial.

KOMMER, RUSS, 9211 Abbott Loop Rd., Anchorage, AK 99507, Phone: 907-346-3339
Specialties: Working straight knives with the outdoorsman in mind. **Patterns:** Hunters, semi-skinners, fighters, folders and utility knives, art knives. **Technical:** Hollow-grinds ATS-34, 440C and 440V. **Prices:** $125 to $850; some to $3000. **Remarks:** Full-time maker; first knife sold in 1995. **Mark:** Bear paw—full name, city and state or full name and state.

KOPP, TODD M., PO Box 3474, Apache Jct., AZ 85217, Phone: 480-983-6143
Specialties: Classic and traditional straight knives. Fluted handled daggers. **Patterns:** Bowies, boots, daggers, fighters, hunters, swords and folders. **Technical:** Grinds 5160, 440C, ATS-34. All Damascus steels, or customers choice. Some engraving and filework. **Prices:** $200 to $1200; some to $4000. **Remarks:** Part-time maker; first knife sold in 1989. **Mark:** Last name in old english, some others name, city and state.

KOSTER, STEVEN C., 16261 Gentry Ln., Hunting Beach, CA 92647, Phone: 714-840-8621
Specialties: Bowies, daggers, skinners, camp knives. **Technical:** Use 5160, 52100, 1084, 1095 steels. **Prices:** $200 to $1000. **Remarks:** Wood and leather sheaths with silver furniture. **Mark:** Koster squeezed between lines. **Other:** ABS journeyman 2003.

KOVAR, EUGENE, 2626 W. 98th St., Evergreen Park, IL 60642, Phone: 708-636-3724
Specialties: One-of-a-kind miniature knives only. **Patterns:** Fancy to fantasy miniature knives; knife pendants and tie tacks. **Technical:** Files and grinds nails, nickel-silver and sterling silver. **Prices:** $5 to $35; some to $100. **Mark:** GK.

KOYAMA, CAPTAIN BUNSHICHI, 3-23 Shirako-cho, Nakamura-ku, Nagoya City 453-0817, JAPAN, Phone: 052-461-7070
Specialties: Innovative folding knife. **Patterns:** General purpose one hand. **Technical:** Grinds ATS-34 and Damascus. **Prices:** $400 to $900; some to $1500. **Remarks:** Part-time maker; first knife sold in 1994. **Mark:** Captain B. Koyama and the shoulder straps of CAPTAIN.

KRAFT, ELMER, 1358 Meadowlark Lane, Big Arm, MT 59910, Phone: 406-849-5086, Fax: 406-883-3056
Specialties: Traditional working/using straight knives of all designs. **Patterns:** Fighters, hunters, utility/camp knives. **Technical:** Grinds 440C, D2. Custom makes sheaths. **Prices:** $125 to $350; some to $500. **Remarks:** Part-time maker; first knife sold in 1984. **Mark:** Last name.

KRAFT, STEVE, 315 S.E. 6th, Abilene, KS 67410, Phone: 785-263-1411
Specialties: Folders, lockbacks, scale release auto, push button auto. **Patterns:** Hunters, boot knives and folders. **Technical:** Grinds ATS-34, Damascus; uses titanium, pearl, ivory etc. **Prices:** $500 to $2500. **Remarks:** Part-time maker; first knife sold in 1984. **Mark:** Kraft.

KRANNING, TERRY L., 548 W Wyeth St, Pocatello, ID 83204, Phone: 208-234-1812
Specialties: Miniature and full-size fantasy and working knives of his design. **Patterns:** Miniatures and some mini straight knives including

razors, tomahawks, hunters, Bowies and fighters. **Technical:** Grinds 1095, 440C, commercial Damascus and nickel-silver. Uses exotic materials like meteorite. **Prices:** $40 to $150. **Remarks:** Part-time maker; first knife sold in 1978. **Mark:** Last initial or full initials in eagle head logo.

KRAPP, DENNY, 1826 Windsor Oak Dr., Apopka, FL 32703, Phone: 407-880-7115
Specialties: Fantasy and working straight knives of his design. **Patterns:** Hunters, fighters and utility/camp knives. **Technical:** Grinds ATS-34 and 440C. **Prices:** $85 to $300; some to $800. **Remarks:** Spare-time maker; first knife sold in 1988. **Mark:** Last name.

KRAUSE, ROY W., 22412 Corteville, St. Clair Shores, MI 48081, Phone: 810-296-3995, Fax: 810-296-2663
Specialties: Military and law enforcement/Japanese-style knives and swords. **Patterns:** Combat and back-up, Bowies, fighters, boot knives, daggers, tantos, wakazashis and katanas. **Technical:** Grinds ATS-34, A2, D2, 1045, O1 and commercial Damascus; differentially hardened Japanese-style blades. **Prices:** Moderate to upscale. **Remarks:** Full-time maker. **Mark:** Last name on traditional knives; initials in Japanese characters on Japanese-style knives.

KRAVITT, CHRIS, Treestump Leather, HC 31, Box 6484, Ellsworth, ME 04605-9320, Phone: 207-584-3000, Fax: 207-584-3000

KREH, LEFTY, 210 Wichersham Way, "Cockeysville", MD 21030

KREIBICH, DONALD L., 1638 Commonwealth Circle, Reno, NV 89503, Phone: 775-746-0533
Specialties: Working straight knives in standard patterns. **Patterns:** Bowies, boots and daggers; camp and fishing knives. **Technical:** Grinds 440C, 154CM and ATS-34; likes integrals. **Prices:** $100 to $200; some to $500. **Remarks:** Part-time maker; first knife sold in 1980. **Mark:** First and middle initials, last name.

KRESSLER, D.F., Schloss Odetzhausen, Schlossberg 1-85235, Odetzhausen, GERMANY, Phone: 08134-998 7290, Fax: 08134-998 7290
Specialties: High-tech Integral and Interframe knives. **Patterns:** Hunters, fighters, daggers. **Technical:** Grinds new state-of-the-art steels; prefers natural handle materials. **Prices:** Upscale. **Mark:** Name in logo.

KRETSINGER JR., PHILIP W., 17536 Bakersville Rd., Boonsboro, MD 21713, Phone: 301-432-6771
Specialties: Fancy and traditional period pieces. **Patterns:** Hunters, Bowies, camp knives, daggers, carvers, fighters. **Technical:** Forges W2, 5160 and his own Damascus. **Prices:** Start at $200. **Remarks:** Full-time knife maker. **Mark:** Name.

KUBAIKO, HANK, 10765 Northvale, Beach City, OH 44608, Phone: 330-359-2418
Specialties: Reproduce antique Bowies. Distal tapering and clay zone tempering. **Patterns:** Bowies, fighters, fishing knives, kitchen cutlery, lockers, slip-joints, camp knives, axes and miniatures. Also makes American, European and traditional samurai swords and daggers. **Technical:** Grinds 440C, ATS-34 and D2; will use CPM-T-440C at extra cost. **Prices:** Moderate. **Remarks:** Full-time maker. Allow three months for sword order fulfillment. **Mark:** Alaskan Maid and name. **Other:** 25th year as a knife maker. Will be making 25 serial numbered knives-folder (liner-locks).

KUBASEK, JOHN A., 74 Northhampton St., Easthampton, MA 01027, Phone: 413-532-3288
Specialties: Left- and right-handed liner lock folders of his design or to customer specs Also new knives made with Ripcord patent. **Patterns:** Fighters, tantos, drop points, survival knives, neck knives and belt buckle knives. **Technical:** Grinds ATS-34 and Damascus. **Prices:** $395 to $1500. **Remarks:** Part-time maker; first knife sold in 1985. **Mark:** Name and address etched.

I

LADD, JIMMIE LEE, 1120 Helen, Deer Park, TX 77536, Phone: 713-479-7186
Specialties: Working straight knives. **Patterns:** Hunters, skinners and utility knives. **Technical:** Grinds 440C and D2. **Prices:** $75 to $225. **Remarks:** First knife sold in 1979. **Mark:** First and middle initials, last name.

LADD, JIM S., 1120 Helen, Deer Park, TX 77536, Phone: 713-479-7286
Specialties: Working knives and period pieces. **Patterns:** Hunters, boots and Bowies plus other straight knives. **Technical:** Grinds D2, 440C and 154CM. **Prices:** $125 to $225; some to $550. **Remarks:** Part-time maker; first knife sold in 1965. Doing business as The Tinker. **Mark:** First and middle initials, last name.

LAGRANGE, FANIE, 12 Canary Crescent, Table View 7441, South Africa, Phone: 27 21 55 76 805
Specialties: African-influenced styles in folders and fixed blades. **Patterns:** All original patterns with many one-of-a-kinds. **Technical:** Mostly stock removal in 12c27, ATS-34, stainless Damascus. **Prices:** $350-$3000. **Remarks:** Professional maker. S A Guild Member 13 years. **Mark:** Name over spear.

LAINSON, TONY, 114 Park Ave., Council Bluffs, IA 51503, Phone: 712-322-5222
Specialties: Working straight knives, liner locking folders. **Technical:** Grinds 154CM, ATS-34, 440C buys Damascus. Handle materials include Micarta, carbon fiber G-10 ivory pearl and bone. **Prices:** $95 to $600. **Remarks:** Part-time maker; first knife sold in 1987. **Mark:** Name and state.

LAIRSON SR., JERRY, H C 68 Box 970, Ringold, OK 74754, Phone: 580-876-3426
Specialties: Fighters and hunters. **Patterns:** Damascus, random, raindrop, ladder, twist and others. **Technical:** All knives hammer forged. **Prices:** Carbon steel $400 and up; Damascus $600 and up. **Remarks:** Makes any style knife but prefer fighters and hunters.

LAKE, RON, 3360 Bendix Ave., Eugene, OR 97401, Phone: 541-484-2683
Specialties: High-tech working knives; inventor of the modern interframe folder. **Patterns:** Hunters, boots, etc.; locking folders. **Technical:** Grinds 154CM and ATS-34. Patented interframe with special lock release tab. **Prices:** $2200 to $3000; some higher. **Remarks:** Full-time maker; first knife sold in 1966. **Mark:** Last name.

LALA, PAULO RICARDO P. AND LALA, ROBERTO P., R. Daniel Martins, 636, Centro, Presidente Prudente, SP-19031-260, BRAZIL, Phone: 0182-210125
Specialties: Straight knives and folders of all designs to customer specs. **Patterns:** Bowies, daggers fighters, hunters and utility knives. **Technical:** Grinds and forges D6, 440C, high-carbon steels and Damascus. **Prices:** $60 to $400; some higher. **Remarks:** Full-time makers; first knife sold in 1991. All stainless steel blades are ultra sub-zero quenched. **Mark:** Sword carved on top of anvil under KORTH.

LAMB, CURTIS J., 3336 Louisiana Ter., Ottawa, KS 66067-8996, Phone: 785-242-6657

LAMBERT, JARRELL D., 2321 FM 2982, Granado, TX 77962, Phone: 512-771-3744
Specialties: Traditional working and using straight knives of his design and to customer specs. **Patterns:** Bowies, hunters, tantos and utility/camp knives. **Technical:** Grinds ATS-34; forges W2 and his own Damascus. Makes own sheaths. **Prices:** $80 to $600; some to $1000. **Remarks:** Part-time maker; first knife sold in 1982. **Mark:** Etched first and middle initials, last name; or stamped last name.

LAMEY, ROBERT M., 15800 Lamey Dr., Biloxi, MS 39532, Phone: 228-396-9066, Fax: 228-396-9022
Specialties: Bowies, fighters, hard use knives. **Patterns:** Bowies, fighters, hunters and camp knives. **Technical:** Forged and stock removal. **Prices:** $125 to $350. **Remarks:** Lifetime reconditioning; will build to customer designs, specializing in hard use, affordable knives. **Mark:** LAMEY.

LAMPREY, MIKE, 32 Pathfield, Great Torrington, Devon EX38 7BX, ENGLAND, Phone: 01805 601331
Specialties: High-tech locking folders of his design. **Patterns:** Side lock folders. **Technical:** Grinds ATS-34, Dendritic 440C, PM stainless Damascus. Linerless handle shells in titanium. Belt clips in ATS-34. **Prices:** $300 to $750; some to $1000. **Remarks:** Part-time maker; first knife sold in 1982. **Mark:** Signature or Celtic knot.

LAMPSON, FRANK G., 3215 Saddle Bag Circle, Rimrock, AZ 86335, Phone: 928-567-7395
Specialties: Working folders; one-of-a-kinds. **Patterns:** Folders, hunters, utility knives, fillet knives and Bowies. **Technical:** Grinds ATS-34, 440C and 154CM. **Prices:** $100 to $750; some to $3500. **Remarks:** Full-time maker; first knife sold in 1971. **Mark:** Name in fish logo.

LANCASTER, C.G., No 2 Schoonwinkel St., Parys, Free State, SOUTH AFRICA, Phone: 0568112090
Specialties: High-tech working and using knives of his design and to customer specs. **Patterns:** Hunters, locking folders and utility/camp knives. **Technical:** Grinds Sandvik 12C27, 440C and D2. Offers anodized titanium bolsters. **Prices:** $450 to $750; some to $1500. **Remarks:** Part-time maker; first knife sold in 1990. **Mark:** Etched logo.

LANCE, BILL, PO Box 4427, Eagle River, AK 99577, Phone: 907-694-1487
Specialties: Ooloos and working straight knives; limited issue sets. **Patterns:** Several ooloo patterns, drop-point skinners. **Technical:** Uses ATS-34, Vascomax 350; ivory, horn and high-class wood handles. **Prices:** $85 to $300; art sets to $3000. **Remarks:** First knife sold in 1981. **Mark:** Last name over a lance.

custom knifemakers

LANDERS, JOHN, 758 Welcome Rd., Newnan, GA 30263, Phone: 404-253-5719
Specialties: High-art working straight knives and folders of his design. **Patterns:** hunters, fighters and slip-joint folders. **Technical:** Grinds 440C, ATS-34, 154CM and commercial Damascus. **Prices:** $85 to $250; some to $500. **Remarks:** Part-time maker; first knife sold in 1989. **Mark:** Last name.

LANE, BEN, 4802 Massie St., North Little Rock, AR 72218, Phone: 501-753-8238
Specialties: Fancy straight knives of his design and to customer specs; period pieces. **Patterns:** Bowies, hunters, utility/camp knives. **Technical:** Grinds D2 and 154CM; forges and grinds 1095. Offers intricate handle work including inlays and spacers. **Prices:** $120 to $450; some to $5000. **Remarks:** Part-time maker; first knife sold in 1989. **Mark:** Full name, city, state.

LANER, DEAN, 1480 Fourth St., Susanville, CA 96130, Phone: 530-310-1917
Specialties: Fancy working fixed blades, of his design, will do custom orders. **Patterns:** Hunters, fighters, combat, fishing, Bowies, utility, and kitchen knives. **Technical:** Grinds 154-CM, ATS-34, D-2, buys Damascus. Does mostly hallow grinding, some flat grinds. Uses Micata, mastodon ivory, hippo ivory, exotic woods. Loves ding spacer work on stick tang knives. A leather or kydes sheath comes with every knife. Life-time warrantee and free sharpening also. **Remarks:** Pat-time maker, first knife sold in 1993. **Prices:** $150 to $1000. **Mark:** LANER CUSTOM KNIVES over D nest to a tree.

LANG, BUD, 265 S Anita Dr. Ste. 20, Orange, CA 92868-3310, Phone: 714-939-9991

LANG, KURT, 4908 S. Wildwood Dr., McHenry, IL 60050, Phone: 708-516-4649
Specialties: High-art working knives. **Patterns:** Bowies, utilitarian-type knives with rough finishes. **Technical:** Forges welded steel in European and Japanese-styles. **Prices:** Moderate to upscale. **Remarks:** Part-time maker. **Mark:** "Crazy Eye" logo.

LANGLEY, GENE H., 1022 N. Price Rd., Florence, SC 29506, Phone: 843-669-3150
Specialties: Working knives in standard patterns. **Patterns:** Hunters, boots, fighters, locking folders and slip-joints. **Technical:** Grinds 440C, 154CM and ATS-34. **Prices:** $125 to $450; some to $1000. **Remarks:** Part-time maker; first knife sold in 1979. **Mark:** Name.

LANKTON, SCOTT, 8065 Jackson Rd. R-11, Ann Arbor, MI 48103, Phone: 313-426-3735
Specialties: Pattern welded swords, krisses and Viking period pieces. **Patterns:** One-of-a-kind. **Technical:** Forges W2, L6 nickel and other steels. **Prices:** $600 to $12,000. **Remarks:** Part-time bladesmith, full-time smith; first knife sold in 1976. **Mark:** Last name logo.

LAPEN, CHARLES, Box 529, W. Brookfield, MA 01585
Specialties: Chefs knives for the culinary artist. **Patterns:** camp knives, Japanese-style swords and wood working tools, hunters. **Technical:** Forges 1075, car spring and his own Damascus. Favors narrow and Japanese tangs. **Prices:** $200 to $400; some to $2000. **Remarks:** Part-time maker; first knife sold in 1972. **Mark:** Last name.

LAPLANTE, BRETT, 4545 CR412, McKinney, TX 75071, Phone: 972-838-9191
Specialties: Working straight knives and folders to customer specs. **Patterns:** Survival knives, Bowies, skinners, hunters. **Technical:** Grinds D2 and 440C. Heat-treats. **Prices:** $175 to $600. **Remarks:** Part-time maker; first knife sold in 1987. **Mark:** Last name in Canadian maple leaf logo.

LARAMIE, MARK, 181 Woodland St., Fitchburg, MA 01420, Phone: 978-353-6979
Specialties: Fancy and working folders and straight knives. **Patterns:** Locking folders, hunters. **Technical:** Grinds 440c, ATS-34, and commercial Damascus. **Prices:** $100 to $1500. **Remarks:** part-time maker; first knife sold in 2000. **Mark:** name, city, state or initials.

LARGIN, KELGIN KNIVES, PO Box 151, Metamora, IN 47030, Phone: 765-969-5012
Specialties: Meteorite knife blades. **Prices:** $100 to $8000. **Mark:** KELGIN or K.C. LARGIN.

LARSON, RICHARD, 549 E. Hawkeye Ave., Turlock, CA 95380, Phone: 209-668-1615
Specialties: Traditional working/using straight knives in standard patterns. **Patterns:** Bowies, hunters and utility/camp knives. **Technical:** Grinds ATS-34, 440C, and 154CM. Engraves and scrimshaws holsters and handles. Hand-sews sheaths with tooling. **Prices:** $150 to $300; some to $1000. **Remarks:** Part-time maker; first knife sold in 1986. Doing business as Larson Knives. **Mark:** Knife logo spelling last name.

LARY, ED, 651 Rangeline Rd., Mosinee, WI 54455, Phone: 715-693-3940
Specialties: Upscale hunters and art knives. **Patterns:** Hunters, fighters, period pieces. **Technical:** Grinds all steels, heat treats, fancy file work. **Prices:** Upscale. **Remarks:** Since 1974. **Mark:** Lary.

LAURENT, KERMIT, 1812 Acadia Dr., LaPlace, LA 70068, Phone: 504-652-5629
Specialties: Traditional and working straight knives and folders of his design. **Patterns:** Bowies, hunters, utilities and folders. **Technical:** Forges own Damascus, plus uses most tool steels and stainless. Specializes in altering cable patterns. Uses stabilized handle materials, especially select exotic woods. **Prices:** $100 to $2500; some to $50,000. **Remarks:** Full-time maker; first knife sold in 1982. Doing business as Kermit's Knife Works. Favorite material is meteorite Damascus **Mark:** First name.

LAWRENCE, ALTON, 201 W Stillwell, De Queen, AR 71832, Phone: 870-642-7643, Fax: 870-642-4023
Specialties: Classic straight knives and folders to customer specs. **Patterns:** Bowies, hunters, folders and utility/camp knives. **Technical:** Forges 5160, 1095, 1084, Damascus and railroad spikes. **Prices:** Start at $100. **Remarks:** Part-time maker; first knife sold in 1988. **Mark:** Last name inside fish symbol.

LAY, L.J., 602 Mimosa Dr., Burkburnett, TX 76354, Phone: 817-569-1329
Specialties: Working straight knives in standard patterns; some period pieces. **Patterns:** Drop-point hunters, Bowies and fighters. **Technical:** Grinds ATS-34 to mirror finish; likes Micarta handles. **Prices:** Moderate. **Remarks:** Full-time maker; first knife sold in 1985. **Mark:** Name or name with ram head and city or stamp L J Lay.

LAY, R.J. (BOB), Box 122, Falkland BC, CANADA V0E 1W0, Phone: 250-379-2265, Fax: SAME
Specialties: Traditional-styled, fancy straight knifes of his design. Specializing in hunters. **Patterns:** Bowies, fighters and hunters. **Technical:** Grinds 440C, ATS-34, 530V, forges and grinds tool steels. Uses exotic handle and spacer material. File cut, prefers narrow tang. Sheaths available. **Price:** $200 to $500, some to $5000. **Remarks:** Full-time maker, first knife sold in 1976. Doing business as Lay's Custom Knives. **Mark:** Signature acid etched.

LEACH, MIKE J., 5377 W. Grand Blanc Rd., Swartz Creek, MI 48473, Phone: 810-655-4850
Specialties: Fancy working knives. **Patterns:** Hunters, fighters, Bowies and heavy-duty knives; slip-joint folders and integral straight patterns. **Technical:** Grinds D2, 440C and 154CM; buys Damascus. **Prices:** Start at $150. **Remarks:** Full-time maker; first knife sold in 1952. **Mark:** First initial, last name.

LEAVITT JR., EARL F., Pleasant Cove Rd., Box 306, E. Boothbay, ME 04544, Phone: 207-633-3210
Specialties: 1500-1870 working straight knives and fighters; pole arms. **Patterns:** Historically significant knives, classic/modern custom designs. **Technical:** Flat-grinds O1; heat-treats. Filework available. **Prices:** $90 to $350; some to $1000. **Remarks:** Full-time maker; first knife sold in 1981. Doing business as Old Colony Manufactory. **Mark:** Initials in oval.

LEBATARD, PAUL M., 14700 Old River Rd., Vancleave, MS 39565, Phone: 228-826-4137, Fax: 228-826-2933
Specialties: Sound working knives; lightweight folder; practical tactical knives. **Patterns:** Hunters, trout and bird knives, fish fillet knives, kitchen knives, Bowies, one and two blade folders, plus a new line of tactical sheath knives. **Technical:** Grinds ATS-34, D-2, CPM 3-V, and commercial Damascus; forges and grinds 52100. Machines folder frames from aircraft aluminum. **Prices:** $50 to $650. **Remarks:** Part-time maker; celebrating 30 years of knifemaking; first knife made in 1974. Offers knife repair, restoration and sharpening. **Mark:** Stamped last name or etched logo of last name, city, and state. **Other:** All knives are serial numbered and registered in the name of the original purchaser.

LEBER, HEINZ, Box 446, Hudson's Hope, BC, CANADA V0C 1V0, Phone: 250-783-5304
Specialties: Working straight knives of his design. **Patterns:** 20 models, form capers to Bowies. **Technical:** Hollow-grinds D2 and M2 steel; mirror-finishes and full tang only. Likes moose, elk, stone sheep for handles. **Prices:** $175 to $1000. **Remarks:** Full-time maker; first knife sold in 1975. **Mark:** Initials connected.

LEBLANC, JOHN, Rt. 2, Box 22950, Winnsboro, TX 75494, Phone: 903-629-7745

LECK, DAL, Box 1054, Hayden, CO 81639, Phone: 970-276-3663
Specialties: Classic, traditional and working knives of his design and in standard patterns; period pieces. **Patterns:** Boots, daggers, fighters, hunters and push daggers. **Technical:** Forges O1 and 5160; makes his own Damascus. **Prices:** $175 to $700; some to $1500. **Remarks:** Part-

time maker; first knife sold in 1990. Doing business as The Moonlight Smithy. **Mark:** Stamped: hammer and anvil with initials.

LEE, RANDY, PO Box 1873, St. Johns, AZ 85936, Phone: 928-337-2594, Fax: 928-337-5002
 Specialties: Traditional working and using straight knives of his design. **Patterns:** Bowies, fighters, hunters, daggers and professional throwing knives. **Technical:** Grinds ATS-34, 440C and D2. Offers sheaths. **Prices:** $235 to $1500; some to $800. **Remarks:** Part-time maker; first knife sold in 1979. **Mark:** Full name, city, state.

LELAND, STEVE, 2300 Sir Francis Drake Blvd., Fairfax, CA 94930-1118, Phone: 415-457-0318, Fax: 415-457-0995
 Specialties: Traditional and working straight knives and folders of his design. **Patterns:** Hunters, fighters, Bowies, chets. **Technical:** Grinds O1, ATS-34 and 440C. Does own heat treat. Makes nickel silver sheaths. **Prices:** $150 to $750; some to $1500. **Remarks:** Part-time maker; first knife sold in 1987. Doing business as Leland Handmade Knives. **Mark:** Last name.

LEMCKE, JIM L., 10649 Haddington Ste 180, Houston, TX 77043, Phone: 888-461-8632, Fax: 713-461-8221
 Specialties: Large supply of custom ground and factory finished blades; knife kits; leather sheaths; in-house heat treating and cryogenic tempering; exotic handle material (wood, ivory, oosik, horn, stabilized woods); machines and supplies for knife making; polishing and finishing supplies; heat treat ovens; etching equipment; bar, sheet and rod material (brass, stainless steel, nickel silver); titanium sheet material. Catalog. $4.

LEONARD, RANDY JOE, 188 Newton Rd., Sarepta, LA 71071, Phone: 318-994-2712

LEONE, NICK, 9 Georgetown, Pontoon Beach, IL 62040, Phone: 618-797-1179
 Specialties: Working straight knives and art daggers. **Patterns:** Bowies, skinners, hunters, camp/utility, fighters, daggers and primitive knives. **Technical:** Forges 5160, W2, O1, 1098, 52100 and his own Damascus. **Prices:** t$100 to $1000; some to $3500. **Remarks:** Full-time maker; first knife sold in 1987. Doing business as Anvil Head Forge. **Mark:** Last name, NL, AHF.

LEPORE, MICHAEL J., 66 Woodcutters Dr., Bethany, CT 06524, Phone: 203-393-3823
 Specialties: One-of-a-kind designs to customer specs; mostly handmade. **Patterns:** Fancy working straight knives and folders. **Technical:** Forges and grinds W2, W1 and O1; prefers natural handle materials. **Prices:** Start at $350. **Remarks:** Spare-time maker; first knife sold in 1984. **Mark:** Last name.

LERCH, MATTHEW, N88 W23462 North Lisbon Rd., Sussex, WI 53089, Phone: 262-246-6362
 Specialties: Gentlemen's folders. **Patterns:** Interframe and integral folders; lock backs, slip-joints, side locks, button locks and liner locks. **Technical:** Grinds ATS-34, 1095, 440 and Damascus. Offers filework and embellished bolsters. **Prices:** $400 to $6000. **Remarks:** Part-time maker; first knife sold in 1995. **Mark:** Last name.

LEVENGOOD, BILL, 15011 Otto Rd., Tampa, FL 33624, Phone: 813-961-5688
 Specialties: Working straight knives and folders. **Patterns:** Hunters, Bowies, folders and collector pieces. **Technical:** Grinds ATS-34, BG-42 and Damascus. **Prices:** $175 to $1500. **Remarks:** Part-time maker; first knife sold in 1983. **Mark:** Last name, city, state.

LEVERETT, KEN, PO Box 696, Lithia, FL 33547, Phone: 813-689-8578
 Specialties: High-tech and working straight knives and folders of his design and to customer specs. **Patterns:** Bowies, hunters and locking folders. **Technical:** Grinds ATS-34, Damascus. **Prices:** $100 to $350; some to $1500. **Remarks:** Part-time maker; first knife sold in 1991. **Mark:** Name, city, state.

LEVIN, JACK, 7216 Bay Pkwy., Brooklyn, NY 11204, Phone: 718-232-8574
 Specialties: Highly embellished collector knives.

LEVINE, BOB, 101 Westwood Dr., Tullahoma, TN 37388, Phone: 931-454-9943
 Specialties: Working left- and right-handed Liner Lock® folders. **Patterns:** Hunters and folders. **Technical:** Grinds ATS-34, 440C, D2, O1 and some Damascus; hollow and some flat grinds. Uses sheep horn, fossil ivory, Micarta and exotic woods. Provides custom leather sheath with each fixed knife. **Prices:** $125 to $500; some higher. **Remarks:** Full-time maker; first knife sold in 1984. Voting member Knife Makers Guild. **Mark:** Name and logo.

LEWIS, STEVE, Knife Dealer, PO Box 9056, Woodland Park, CO 80866, Phone: 719-686-1120 or 888-685-2322
 Specialties: Buy, sell, trade and consign W. F. Moran and other fine custom-made knives. Mail order and major shows.

LEWIS, MIKE, 21 Pleasant Hill Dr., DeBary, FL 32713, Phone: 386-753-0936
 Specialties: Traditional straight knives. **Patterns:** Swords and daggers. **Technical:** Grinds 440C, ATS-34 and 5160. Frequently uses cast bronze and cast nickel guards and pommels. **Prices:** $100 to $750. **Remarks:** Part-time maker; first knife sold in 1988. **Mark:** Dragon Steel and serial number.

LEWIS, TOM R., 1613 Standpipe Rd., Carlsbad, NM 88220, Phone: 505-885-3616
 Specialties: Traditional working straight knives and pocketknives. **Patterns:** Outdoor knives, hunting knives and Bowies and pocketknives. **Technical:** Grinds ATS-34 forges 5168 and 01. Makes wire, pattern welded and chainsaw Damascus. **Prices:** $100 to $900. **Remarks:** Part-time maker; first knife sold in 1980. Doing business as TR Lewis Handmade Knives. **Mark:** Lewis family crest.

LEWIS, BILL, PO Box 63, Riverside, IA 52327, Phone: 319-629-5574
 Specialties: Folders of all kins including those made from one-piece of white tail antler with or without the crown. **Patterns:** Hunters, folding hunters, fillet, Bowies, push daggers, etc. **Prices:** $20 to $200. **Remarks:** Full-time maker; first knife sold in 1978. **Mark:** W.E.L.

LEWIS, K.J., 374 Cook Rd., Lugoff, SC 29078, Phone: 803-438-4343

LICATA, STEVEN, LICATA CUSTOM KNIVES, 142 Orchard St., Garfield, NJ 07026, Phone: 973-341-4288
 Prices: $200-$25,000.

LIEBENBERG, ANDRE, 8 Hilma Rd., Bordeauxrandburg 2196, SOUTH AFRICA, Phone: 011-787-2303
 Specialties: High-art straight knives of his design. **Patterns:** Daggers, fighters and swords. **Technical:** Grinds 440C and 12C27. **Prices:** $250 to $500; some $4000 and higher. Giraffe bone handles with semi-precious stones. **Remarks:** Spare-time maker; first knife sold in 1990. **Mark:** Initials.

LIEGEY, KENNETH R., 132 Carney Dr., Millwood, WV 25262, Phone: 304-273-9545
 Specialties: Traditional working/using straight knives of his design and to customer specs. **Patterns:** Hunters, utility/camp knives, miniatures. **Technical:** Grinds 440C. **Prices:** $75 to $150; some to $300. **Remarks:** Spare-time maker; first knife sold in 1977. **Mark:** First and middle initials, last name.

LIGHTFOOT, GREG, RR #2, Kitscoty AB, CANADA T0B 2P0, Phone: 780-846-2812
 Specialties: Stainless steel and Damascus. **Patterns:** Boots, fighters and locking folders. **Technical:** Grinds BG-42, 440C, D2, CPM steels, Stellite 6K. Offers engraving. **Prices:** $250 to $500; some to $850. **Remarks:** Full-time maker; first knife sold in 1988. Doing business as Lightfoot Knives. **Mark:** Shark with Lightfoot Knives below.

LIKARICH, STEVE, PO Box 961, Colfax, CA 95713, Phone: 530-346-8480
 Specialties: Fancy working knives; art knives of his design. **Patterns:** Hunters, fighters and art knives of his design. **Technical:** Grinds ATS-34, 154CM and 440C; likes high polishes and filework. **Prices:** $200 to $2000; some higher. **Remarks:** Full-time maker; first knife sold in 1987. **Mark:** Name.

LINDSAY, CHRIS A., 1324 N.E. Locksley Dr., Bend, OR 97701, Phone: 541-389-3875
 Specialties: Working knives in standard patterns. **Patterns:** Hunters and camp knives. **Technical:** Hollow- and flat-grinds 440C and ATS-34; offers brushed finishes, tapered tangs. **Prices:** $75 to $160; knife kits $60 to $80. **Remarks:** Part-time maker; first knife sold in 1980. **Mark:** Last name, town and state in oval.

LINKLATER, STEVE, 8 Cossar Dr., Aurora, Ont., CANADA L4G 3N8, Phone: 905-727-8929
 Specialties: Traditional working/using straight knives and folders of his design. **Patterns:** Fighters, hunters and locking folders. **Technical:** Grinds ATS-34, 440V and D2. **Prices:** $125 to $350; some to $600. **Remarks:** Part-time maker; first knife sold in 1987. Doing business as Links Knives. **Mark:** LINKS.

LISTER JR., WELDON E., 9140 Sailfish Dr., Boerne, TX 78006, Phone: 210-981-2210
 Specialties: One-of-a-kind fancy and embellished folders. **Patterns:** Locking and slip-joint folders. **Technical:** Commercial Damascus and O1. All knives embellished. Engraves, inlays, carves and scrimshaws. **Prices:** Upscale. **Remarks:** Spare-time maker; first knife sold in 1991. **Mark:** Last name.

custom knifemakers

LITTLE, LARRY, 1A Cranberry Ln., Spencer, MA 01562, Phone: 508-885-2301
Specialties: Working straight knives of his design or to customer specs. Likes Scagel-style. **Patterns:** Hunters, fighters…can grind other patterns. **Technical:** Grinds L6 and O1, most have file work. Prefers natural handle material especially antler. Uses nickel silver. Makes own heavy duty leather sheath. **Prices:** start at $100. **Remarks:** Part-time maker. First knife sold in 1985. Offers knife repairs. **Mark:** Last name.

LITTLE, GUY A., 486 W Lincoln Ave., Oakhurst, NJ 07755

LITTLE, GARY M., HC84 Box 10301, PO Box 156, Broadbent, OR 97414, Phone: 503-572-2656
Specialties: Fancy working knives. **Patterns:** Hunters, tantos, Bowies, axes and buckskinners; locking folders and interframes. **Technical:** Forges and grinds O1, L6, 1095; makes his own Damascus; bronze fittings. **Prices:** $85 to $300; some to $2500. **Remarks:** Full-time maker; first knife sold in 1979. Doing business as Conklin Meadows Forge. **Mark:** Name, city and state.

LITTLE, JIMMY L., PO Box 871652, Wasilla, AK 99687, Phone: 907-373-7831
Specialties: Working straight knives; fancy period pieces. **Patterns:** Bowies, bush swords and camp knives. **Technical:** Grinds 440C, 154CM and ATS-34. **Prices:** $100 to $1000. **Remarks:** Full-time maker; first knife sold in 1984. **Mark:** First and middle initials, last name.

LIVELY, TIM AND MARIAN, PO Box 8784 CRB, Tucson, AZ 85738
Specialties: Multi-cultural primitive knives of their design on speculation. **Patterns:** Neo-tribal one-of-a-kinds. **Technical:** Hand forges using ancient techniques; hammer finish. **Prices:** Moderate. **Remarks:** Full-time makers; first knife sold in 1974. **Mark:** Last name.

LIVESAY, NEWT, 3306 S. Dogwood St., Siloam Springs, AR 72761, Phone: 479-549-3356, Fax: 479-549-3357
Specialties: Combat utility knives, hunting knives, titanium knives, swords, axes, KYDWX sheaths for knives and pistols, custom orders.

LIVINGSTON, ROBERT C., PO Box 6, Murphy, NC 28906, Phone: 704-837-4155
Specialties: Art letter openers to working straight knives. **Patterns:** Minis to machetes. **Technical:** Forges and grinds most steels. **Prices:** Start at $20. **Remarks:** Full-time maker; first knife sold in 1988. Doing business as Mystik Knife works. **Mark:** MYSTIK.

LOCKE, KEITH, PMB 141, 7120 Rufe Snow Dr. Ste. 106, Watauga, TX 76148-1867, Phone: 817-514-7272
Technical: Forges carbon steel and handcrafts sheaths for his knives. **Remarks:** Sold first knife in 1996.

LOCKETT, LOWELL C., 66653 Gunderson Rd., North Bend, OR 97459-9210, Phone: 541-756-1614
Specialties: Traditional and working/using knives. **Patterns:** Bowies, hunters, utility/camp knives. **Technical:** Forges 5160, 1095, 1084, 02, L6. Makes own guards and sheaths. **Prices:** Start at $90. **Remarks:** Full-time maker. **Mark:** L C lockett (on side of blade) ABS Journeyman Smith, member OKCA.

LOCKETT, STERLING, 527 E. Amherst Dr., Burbank, CA 91504, Phone: 818-846-5799
Specialties: Working straight knives and folders to customer specs. **Patterns:** Hunters and fighters. **Technical:** Grinds. **Prices:** Moderate. **Remarks:** Spare-time maker. **Mark:** Name, city with hearts.

LOERCHNER, WOLFGANG, WOLFE FINE KNIVES, PO Box 255, Bayfield, Ont., CANADA N0M 1G0, Phone: 519-565-2196
Specialties: Traditional straight knives, mostly ornate. **Patterns:** Small swords, daggers and stilettos; locking folders and miniatures. **Technical:** Grinds D2, 440C and 154CM; all knives hand-filed and flat-ground. **Prices:** $300 to $5000; some to $10,000. **Remarks:** Part-time maker; first knife sold in 1983. Doing business as Wolfe Fine Knives. **Mark:** WOLFE.

LONEWOLF, J. AGUIRRE, 481 Hwy 105, Demorest, GA 30535, Phone: 706-754-4660, Fax: 706-754-8470
Specialties: High-art working and using straight knives of his design. **Patterns:** Bowies, hunters, utility/camp knives and fine steel blades. **Technical:** Forges Damascus and high-carbon steel. Most knives have hand-carved moose antler handles. **Prices:** $55 to $500; some to $2000. **Remarks:** Full-time maker; first knife sold in 1980. Doing business as Lonewolf Trading Post. **Mark:** Stamp.

LONG, GLENN A., 10090 SW 186th Ave., Dunnellon, FL 34432, Phone: 352-489-4272
Specialties: Classic working and using straight knives of his design and to customer specs. **Patterns:** Hunters, Bowies, utility. **Technical:** Grinds 440C D2 and 440V. **Prices:** $85 to $300; some to $800. **Remarks:** Part-time maker; first knife sold in 1990. **Mark:** Last name inside diamond.

LONGWORTH, DAVE, 1811 SR 774, Hamersville, OH 45130, Phone: 513-876-3637
Specialties: High-tech working knives. **Patterns:** Locking folders, hunters, fighters and elaborate daggers. **Technical:** Grinds O1, ATS-34, 440C; buys Damascus. **Prices:** $125 to $600; some higher. **Remarks:** Part-time maker; first knife sold in 1980. **Mark:** Last name.

LOOS, HENRY C., 210 Ingraham, New Hyde Park, NY 11040, Phone: 516-354-1943
Specialties: Miniature fancy knives and period pieces of his design. **Patterns:** Bowies, daggers and swords. **Technical:** Grinds O1 and 440C. Uses sterling, 18K, rubies and emeralds. All knives come with handmade hardwood cases. **Prices:** $90 to $195; some to $250. **Remarks:** Spare-time maker; first knife sold in 1990. **Mark:** Script last initial.

LORO, GENE, 2457 State Route 93 NE, Crooksville, OH 43731, Phone: 740-982-4521, Fax: 740-982-1249
Specialties: Hand forged knives. **Patterns:** Damascus, Random, Ladder, Twist, etc. **Technical:** ABS Journeyman Smith. **Prices:** $200 and up. **Remarks:** Loro and hand forged by Gene Loro. **Mark:** Loro. Retired engineer.

LOTT-SINCLAIR, SHERRY, 112 E Main St., Campbellsville, KY 42718, Phone: 270-465-0577
Specialties: One-of-a-kind, usually carved handles. **Patterns:** Art. **Technical:** Carbon steel, stock removal. Prices: Moderate. **Mark:** Sherry Sinclair. **Other:** First knife sold in 1994.

LOVE, ED, 19443 Mill Oak, San Antonio, TX 78258, Phone: 210-497-1021
Specialties: Hunting, working knives and some art pieces. **Technical:** Grinds ATS-34, and 440C. **Prices:** $150 and up. **Remarks:** Part-time maker. First knife sold in 1980. **Mark:** Name in a weeping heart.

LOVELESS, R.W., PO Box 7836, Riverside, CA 92503, Phone: 909-689-7800
Specialties: Working knives, fighters and hunters of his design. **Patterns:** Contemporary hunters, fighters and boots. **Technical:** Grinds 154CM and ATS-34. **Prices:** $850 to $4950. **Remarks:** Full-time maker since 1969. **Mark:** Name in logo.

LOVESTRAND, SCHUYLER, 1136 19th St. SW, Vero Beach, FL 32962, Phone: 561-778-0282, Fax: 561-466-1126
Specialties: Fancy working straight knives of his design and to customer specs; unusual fossil ivories. **Patterns:** Hunters, fighters, Bowies and fishing knives. **Technical:** Grinds stainless steel. **Prices:** $275 and up. **Remarks:** Part-time maker; first knife sold in 1982. **Mark:** Name in logo.

LOZIER, DON, 5394 SE 168th Ave., Ocklawaha, FL 32179, Phone: 352-625-3576
Specialties: Fancy and working straight knives of his design and in standard patterns. **Patterns:** Daggers, fighters, boot knives, and hunters. **Technical:** Grinds ATS-34, 440C and Damascus. Most pieces are highly embellished by notable artisans. Taking limited number of orders per annum. **Prices:** Start at $250; most are $1250 to $3000; some to $12,000. **Remarks:** Full-time maker. **Mark:** Name.

LUCHAK, BOB, 15705 Woodforest Blvd., Channelview, TX 77530, Phone: 281-452-1779
Specialties: Presentation knives; start of The Survivor series. **Patterns:** Skinners, Bowies, camp axes, steak knife sets and fillet knives. **Technical:** Grinds 440C. Offers electronic etching; filework. **Prices:** $50 to $1500. **Remarks:** Full-time maker; first knife sold in 1983. Doing business as Teddybear Knives. **Mark:** Full name, city and state with Teddybear logo.

LUCHINI, BOB, 1220 Dana Ave., Palo Alto, CA 94301, Phone: 650-321-8095

LUCIE, JAMES R., 4191 E. Fruitport Rd., Fruitport, MI 49415, Phone: 231-865-6390, Fax: 231-865-3170
Specialties: Hand-forges William Scagel-style knives. **Patterns:** Authentic scagel-style knives and miniatures. **Technical:** Forges 5160, 52100 and 1084 and forges his own pattern welded Damascus steel. **Prices:** Start at $750. **Remarks:** Full-time maker; first knife sold in 1975. Believes in sole authorship of his work. ABS Journeyman Smith. **Mark:** Scagel Kris with maker's name and address.

LUCKETT, BILL, 108 Amantes Ln., Weatherford, TX 76088, Phone: 817-613-9412
Specialties: Uniquely patterned robust straight knives. **Patterns:** Fighters, Bowies, hunters. **Technical:** Grinds 440C and commercial Damascus; makes heavy knives with deep grinding. **Prices:** $275 to $1000; some to $2000. **Remarks:** Part-time maker; first knife sold in 1975. **Mark:** Last name over Bowie logo.

LUDWIG, RICHARD O., 57-63 65 St., Maspeth, NY 11378, Phone: 718-497-5969
Specialties: Traditional working/using knives. **Patterns:** Boots, hunters and utility/camp knives folders. Technical Grinds 440C, ATS-34 and

BG42. File work on guards and handles; silver spacers. Offers scrimshaw. **Prices:** $325 to $400; some to $2000. **Remarks:** Full-time maker. **Mark:** Stamped first initial, last name, state.

LUI, RONALD M., 4042 Harding Ave., Honolulu, HI 96816, Phone: 808-734-7746
Specialties: Working straight knives and folders in standard patterns. **Patterns:** Hunters, boots and liner locks. **Technical:** Grinds 440C and ATS-34. **Prices:** $100 to $700. **Remarks:** Spare-time maker; first knife sold in 1988. **Mark:** Initials connected.

LUM, ROBERT W., 901 Travis Ave., Eugene, OR 97404, Phone: 541-688-2737
Specialties: High-art working knives of his design. **Patterns:** Hunters, fighters, tantos and folders. **Technical:** Grinds 440C, 154CM and ATS-34; plans to forge soon. **Prices:** $175 to $500; some to $800. **Remarks:** Full-time maker; first knife sold in 1976. **Mark:** Chop with last name underneath.

LUMAN, JAMES R., Clear Creek Trail, Anaconda, MT 59711, Phone: 406-560-1461
Specialties: San Mai and composite end patterns. **Patterns:** Pool and eye Spirograph southwest composite patterns. **Technical:** All patterns with blued steel; all made by him. **Prices:** $200 to $800. **Mark:** Stock blade removal. Pattern welded steel. Bottom ricasso JRL.

LUNDSTROM, JAN-AKE, Mastmostigen 8, 66010 Dals-Langed, SWEDEN, Phone: 0531-40270
Specialties: Viking swords, axes and knives in cooperation with handle makers. **Patterns:** All traditional-styles, especially swords and inlaid blades. **Technical:** Forges his own Damascus and laminated steel. **Prices:** $200 to $1000. **Remarks:** Full-time maker; first knife sold in 1985; collaborates with museums. **Mark:** Runic.

LUNN, LARRY A., PO Box 48931, St. Petersburg, FL 33743, Phone: 727-345-7455
Specialties: Fancy folders and double action autos; some straight blades. **Patterns:** All types; his own designs. **Technical:** Stock removal; commercial Damascus. **Prices:** $125 and up. **Remarks:** File work inlays and exotic materials. **Mark:** Name in script.

LUNN, GAIL, PO Box 48931, St. Petersburg, FL 33743, Phone: 727-345-7455
Specialties: Fancy folders and double action autos, some straight blades. **Patterns:** One-of-a-kind - All types. **Technical:** Stock removal - Hand made. **Prices:** $300 and up. **Remarks:** Fancy file work, exotic materials, inlays, stone etc. **Mark:** Name in script.

LUPOLE, JAMIE G., KUMA KNIVES, 285 Main St., Kirkwood, NY 13795, Phone: 607-775-9368
Specialties: Working and collector grade fixed blades, ethnic-styled blades. **Patterns:** Fighters, Bowies, tacticals, hunters, camp, utility, personal carry knives, some swords. **Technical:** Forges and grinds 10XX series and other high-carbon steels, grinds ATS-34 and 440C, will use just about every handle material available. **Prices:** $80 - $500 and up. **Remarks:** Part-time maker since 1999. **Marks:** "KUMA" hot stamped, name, city and state-etched, or "Daiguma saku" in kanji.

LUTZ, GREG, 127 Crescent Rd., Greenwood, SC 29646, Phone: 864-229-7340
Specialties: Working and using knives and period pieces of his design and to customer specs. **Patterns:** Fighters, hunters and swords. **Technical:** Forges 1095 and O1; grinds ATS-34. Differentially heat-treats forged blades; uses cryogenic treatment on ATS-34. **Prices:** $50 to $350; some to $1200. **Remarks:** Part-time maker; first knife sold in 1986. Doing business as Scorpion Forge. **Mark:** First initial, last name.

LYLE III, ERNEST L., LYLE KNIVES, PO Box 1755, Chiefland, FL 32644, Phone: 352-490-6693
Specialties: Fancy period pieces; one-of-a-kind and limited editions. **Patterns:** Arabian/Persian influenced fighters, military knives, Bowies and Roman short swords; several styles of hunters. **Technical:** Grinds 440C, D2 and 154 CM. Engraves. **Prices:** Upscale. **Remarks:** Full-time maker; first knife sold in 1972. **Mark:** Last name in capital letters - LYLE over a much smaller Chief land.

LYTTLE, BRIAN, Box 5697, High River, AB, CANADA T1V 1M7, Phone: 403-558-3638
Specialties: Fancy working straight knives and folders; art knives. **Patterns:** Bowies, daggers, dirks, Sgian Dubhs, folders, dress knives. **Technical:** Forges Damascus steel; engraving; scrimshaw; heat-treating; classes. **Prices:** $200 to $1000; some to $5000. **Remarks:** Full-time maker; first knife sold in 1983. **Mark:** Last name, country.

m

MACDONALD, JOHN, 9 David Dr., Raymond, NH 03077, Phone: 603-895-0918
Specialties: Working/using straight knives of his design and to customer specs. **Patterns:** Japanese cutlery, Bowies, hunters and working knives. **Technical:** Grinds O1, L6 and ATS-34. Swords have matching handles and scabbards with Japanese flair. **Prices:** $70 to $250; some to $500. **Remarks:** Part-time maker; first knife sold in 1988. Wood/glass-topped custom cases. Doing business as Mac the Knife. **Mark:** Initials.

MACDONALD, DAVID, 2824 Hwy 47, Los Lunas, NM 87031, Phone: 505-866-5866

MACKIE, JOHN, 13653 Lanning, Whittier, CA 90605, Phone: 562-945-6104
Specialties: Forged. **Patterns:** Bowie and camp knives. **Technical:** Attended ABS Bladesmith School. **Prices:** $75 to $500. **Mark:** JSM in a triangle.

MACKRILL, STEPHEN, PO Box 1580, Pinegowrie 2123, Johannesburg, SOUTH AFRICA, Phone: 27-11-886-2893, Fax: 27-11-334-6230
Specialties: Art fancy, historical, collectors and corporate gifts cutlery. **Patterns:** Fighters, hunters, camp, custom lock back and liner lock folders. **Technical:** N690, 12C27, ATS-34, silver and gold inlay on handles; wooden and silver sheaths. **Prices:** $330 and upwards. **Remarks:** First knife sold in 1978. **Mark:** Oval with first initial, last name, "Maker" country of origin.

MADISON II, BILLY D., 2295 Tyler Rd., Remlap, AL 35133, Phone: 205-680-6722
Specialties: Traditional working and using straight knives and folders of his design or yours. **Patterns:** Hunters, locking folders, utility/camp knives, and fighters. **Technical:** Grinds 440C, ATS-34, D2 and BG-42; forges some high-carbons. Prefers natural handle material. Ivory, bone, exotic woods and horns. **Prices:** $250 to $500 depending on knife. My mirror finish has to be seen to aff. **Remarks:** Limited part-time maker (disabled machinist); first knife sold in 1978. Had first knife returned a folder needed buff! Horn re-epoxied. **Mark:** Last name and year. Offers sheaths. **Other:** Wife makes sheaths. All knives have unconditional lifetime warranty. Never had a knife returned in 27 years.

MADRULLI, MME JOELLE, RESIDENCE STE CATHERINE B1, Salon De Provence, FRANCE 13330

MAE, TAKAO, 1-119, 1-4 Uenohigashi, Toyonaka, Osaka, JAPAN 560-0013, Phone: 81-6-6852-2758, Fax: 81-6-6481-1649
Remarks: Distinction stylish in art-forged blades, with lacquered ergonomic handles.

MAESTRI, PETER A., S11251 Fairview Rd., Spring Green, WI 53588, Phone: 608-546-4481
Specialties: Working straight knives in standard patterns. **Patterns:** Camp and fishing knives, utility green-river-styled. **Technical:** Grinds 440C, 154CM and 440A. **Prices:** $15 to $45; some to $150. **Remarks:** Full-time maker; first knife sold in 1981. Provides professional cutler service to professional cutters. **Mark:** CARISOLO, MAESTRI BROS., or signature.

MAGEE, JIM, 319 N 12th, Salina, KS 67401, Phone: 785-820-8535
Specialties: Working and fancy folding knives. **Patterns:** Liner locking folders, favorite is his Persian. **Technical:** Grinds ATS34, George woth Damascus, titanium. Liners Prefer mother-of-pearl handles. **Prices:** Start at $225 to $1200. **Remarks:** Part-time maker, first knife sold in 2001. Purveyor since 1982. Currently President of the Professional Knifemakers Assn. **Mark:** Last name.

MAHOMEDY, A. R., PO Box 76280, Marble Ray KZN, 4035, SOUTH AFRICA, Phone: +27 31 577 1451
Specialties: Daggers, fighters, elegant folders, hunters, utilities and to customers specific designs. Personally prefer to work to Commissions, Collector and Presentation. Grade quality in liaison with (internationally recognized) engravers and embellishers. Working steels: ATS34, 440C (N690), 440A, sandvik 12 C 27, Damasteel and Damascus all currently via the stock removal method. Exotic stabilized woods, beautiful indigenous woods, giraffe bone, buffalo, kudu, sheep horns, elephant, hippo, whale, ivory, mother-of-pearl, G10, micarta, dymondwood etc. **Prices:** Starting from $350 to $2000. **Remarks:** Part-time maker, first show, two knives sold to same collector in 1995. Following year won show award for best bird and trout knife notice category. Presently submitting 5 knives for evaluation and membership to SA knifemakers guild. **Mark:** LOGO of initials A R M crowned with a "MINARET".

custom knifemakers

MAIENKNECHT, STANLEY, 38648 S.R. 800, Sardis, OH 43946

MAINES, JAY, SUNRISE RIVER CUSTOM KNIVES, 5584 266th St., Wyoming, MN 55092, Phone: 651-462-5301
Specialties: Heavy duty working, classic and traditional fixed blades. Some high-tech and fancy embellished knives available. **Patterns:** Hunters, skinners, Bowies, Tantos, fillet, fighters, daggers, boot and cutlery sets. **Technical:** Hollow ground, stock removal blades of 440C, ATS34 and CPM S-90V. Prefers natural handle materials, exotic hard woods, and stag, rams and buffalo horns. Offers dovetailed bolsters in brass, stainless steel and nickel silver. Custom sheaths from matching wood or hand-stitched from heavy duty water buffalo hide. **Prices:** Moderate to up-scale. **Remarks:** Part-time maker; first knife sold in 1992. Color brochure available upon request. Doing business as Sunrise River Custom Knives. **Mark:** Full name under a Rising Sun logo. **Other:** Offers fixed blade knives repair and handle conversions.

MAISEY, ALAN, PO Box 197, Vincentia 2540, NSW AUSTRALIA, Phone: 2-4443 7829
Specialties: Daggers, especially krisses; period pieces. **Technical:** Offers knives and finished blades in Damascus and nickel Damascus. **Prices:** $75 to $2000; some higher. **Remarks:** Part-time maker; provides complete restoration service for krisses. Trained by a Javanese Kris Smith. **Mark:** None, triangle in a box, or three peaks.

MAJER, MIKE, 50 Palmetto Bay Rd., Hilton Head, SC 29928, Phone: 843-681-3483

MAKOTO, KUNITOMO, 3-3-18 Imazu-cho Fukuyama-city, Hiroshima, JAPAN, Phone: 084-933-5874

MALABY, RAYMOND J., 835 Calhoun Ave., Juneau, AK 99801, Phone: 907-586-6981

MALLETT, JOHN, 760 E Francis St. #N, Ontario, CA 91761, Phone: 800-532-3336/ 909-923-4116, Fax: 909-923-9932
Specialties: Complete line of 3/M, Norton and Hermes belts for grinding and polishing 24-2000 grit; also hard core, Bader and Burr King grinders. Baldor motors and buffers. ATS-34, 440C, BG42 and 416 stainless steel.

MALLOY, JOE, 1039 Schwabe St., Freeland, PA 18224, Phone: 570-636-2781
Specialties: Working straight knives and lock back folders—plain and fancy—of his design. **Patterns:** Hunters, utility, Bowie, survival knives, folders. **Technical:** Grinds ATS-34, 440C, D2 and A2 and Damascus. Makes own leather and kyder sheaths. **Prices:** $100 to $1800. **Remarks:** Part-time maker; first knife sold in 1982. **Mark:** First and middle initials, last name, city and state.

MANABE, MICHAEL K., 3659 Tomahawk Lane, San Diego, CA 92117, Phone: 619-483-2416
Specialties: Classic and high-art straight knives of his design or to customer specs. **Patterns:** Bowies, fighters, hunters, utility/camp knives; all knives one-of-a-kind. **Technical:** Forges and grinds 52100, 5160 and 1095. Does multiple quenching for distinctive temper lines. Each blade triple-tempered. **Prices:** Start at $200. **Remarks:** Part-time maker; first knife sold in 1994. **Mark:** First and middle initials, last name and J.S. on other side.

MANEKER, KENNETH, RR 2, Galiano Island, B.C., CANADA V0N 1P0, Phone: 604-539-2084
Specialties: Working straight knives; period pieces. **Patterns:** Camp knives and hunters; French chef knives. **Technical:** Grinds 440C, 154CM and Vascowear. **Prices:** $50 to $200; some to $300. **Remarks:** Part-time maker; first knife sold in 1981. Doing business as Water Mountain Knives. **Mark:** Japanese Kanji of initials, plus glyph.

MANKEL, KENNETH, 7836 Cannonsburg Rd., Cannonsburg, MI 49317, Phone: 616-874-6955

MANLEY, DAVID W., 3270 Six Mile Hwy., Central, SC 29630, Phone: 864-654-1125
Specialties: Working straight knives of his design or to custom specs. **Patterns:** Hunters, boot and fighters. **Technical:** Grinds 440C and ATS34. **Prices:** $60 to $250. **Remarks:** Part-time maker; first knife sold in 1994. **Mark:** First initial, last name, year and serial number.

MANN, TIM, BLADEWORKS, PO Box 1196, Honokaa, HI 96727, Phone: 808-775-0949, Fax: 808-775-0949
Specialties: Hand-forged knives and swords. **Patterns:** Bowies, Tantos, pesh kabz, daggers. **Technical:** Use 5160, 1050, 1075, 1095 and ATS-34 steels, cable Damascus. **Prices:** $200 to $800. **Remarks:** Just learning to forge Damascus. **Mark:** None yet.

MANN, MICHAEL L., IDAHO KNIFE WORKS, PO Box 144, Spirit Lake, ID 83869, Phone: 509 994-9394
Specialties: Good working blades-historical reproduction, modern or custom design. **Patterns:** Cowboy Bowies, Mountain Man period blades, old-style folders, designer and maker of "The Cliff Knife", hunter and hook knives, hand ax, fish fillet and kitchen knives. **Technical:** High-carbon

steel blades-hand forged 5160 or grind L6 tool steel. **Prices:** $100 to $630+. **Remarks:** Made first knife in 1965. Full-time making knives as Idaho Knife Works since 1986. Functional as well as collectible. Each knife truly unique! **Mark:** Four mountain peaks are his initials MM.

MARAGNI, DAN, RD 1, Box 106, Georgetown, NY 13072, Phone: 315-662-7490
Specialties: Heavy-duty working knives, some investor class. **Patterns:** Hunters, fighters and camp knives, some Scottish types. **Technical:** Forges W2 and his own Damascus; toughness and edge-holding a high priority. **Prices:** $125 to $1000. **Remarks:** Full-time maker; first knife sold in 1975. **Mark:** Celtic initials in circle.

MARKLEY, KEN, 7651 Cabin Creek Lane, Sparta, IL 62286, Phone: 618-443-5284
Specialties: Traditional working and using knives of his design and to customer specs. **Patterns:** Hunters, fighters and utility/camp knives. **Technical:** Forges 5160, 1095 and L6; makes his own Damascus; does file work. **Prices:** $150 to $800; some to $2000. **Remarks:** Part-time maker; first knife sold in 1991. Doing business as Cabin Creek Forge. **Mark:** Last name, JS.

MARKS, CHRIS, Rt. 2 Box 527, Ava, MO 65608, Phone: 417-683-1065
Specialties: Mosaic Damascus. **Patterns:** Too numerous to list - ever changing. **Technical:** W1, W2, 1095, 203E, Nickel 200. **Prices:** $20 and up. **Mark:** Anvil with name in center.

MARLOWE, CHARLES, 10822 Poppleton Ave., Omaha, NE 68144, Phone: 402-933-5065
Specialties: Folding knives and balisong. **Patterns:** Tactical pattern folders. **Technical:** Grind ATS-34, S30V, others on request. **Prices:** Start at $310. **Remarks:** First knife sold in 1993. Full-time since 1999. **Mark:** MARLOWE.

MARLOWE, DONALD, 2554 Oakland Rd., Dover, PA 17315, Phone: 717-764-6055
Specialties: Working straight knives in standard patterns. **Patterns:** Bowies, fighters, boots and utility knives. **Technical:** Grinds D2 and 440C. **Prices:** $120 to $525. **Remarks:** Spare-time maker; first knife sold in 1977. **Mark:** Last name.

MARSHALL, STEPHEN R., 975 Harkreader Rd., Mt. Juliet, TN 37122

MARSHALL, GLENN, PO Box 1099, 1117 Hofmann St., Mason, TX 76856, Phone: 915-347-6207
Specialties: Working knives and period pieces. **Patterns:** Straight and folding hunters, fighters and camp knives. **Technical:** Steel used 440C, D2, CPM and 440V. **Prices:** $90 and up according to options. **Remarks:** Full-time maker; first knife sold in 1932. **Mark:** First initial, last name, city and state with anvil logo.

MARTIN, MICHAEL W., Box 572, Jefferson St., Beckville, TX 75631, Phone: 903-678-2161
Specialties: Classic working/using straight knives of his design and in standard patterns. **Patterns:** Hunters. **Technical:** Grinds ATS-34, 440C, O1 and A2. Bead blasted, Parkerized, high polish and satin finishes. Sheaths are handmade. Also hand forges cable Damascus. **Prices:** $145 to $230. **Remarks:** Part-time maker; first knife sold in 1995. Doing business as Michael W. Martin Knives. **Mark:** Name and city, state in arch.

MARTIN, BRUCE E., Rt. 6, Box 164-B, Prescott, AR 71857, Phone: 501-887-2023
Specialties: Fancy working straight knives of his design. **Patterns:** Bowies, camp knives, skinners and fighters. **Technical:** Forges 5160, 1095 and his own Damascus. Uses natural handle materials; filework available. **Prices:** $75 to $350; some to $500. **Remarks:** Full-time maker; first knife sold in 1979. **Mark:** Name in arch.

MARTIN, JIM, 1120 S. Cadiz Ct., Oxnard, CA 93035, Phone: 805-985-9849
Specialties: Fancy and working/using folders of his design. **Patterns:** Automatics, locking folders and miniatures. **Technical:** Grinds 440C, AEB-L, 304SS and Damascus. **Prices:** $350 to $700; some to $1500. **Remarks:** Full-time maker; first knife sold in 1992. Doing business as Jim Martin Custom Knives.

MARTIN, ROBB, 7 Victoria St., Elmira, Ontario, CANADA N3B 1R9

MARTIN, RANDALL J., 51 Bramblewood St, Bridgewater, MA 02324, Phone: 860-347-1161
Specialties: High-performance using knives. **Patterns:** Neck knives, tactical liner locks, survival, utility and Japanese knives. **Technical:** Grinds BG42, CPMM4, D2 and A2; aerospace composite materials; carbon fiber sheaths. **Prices:** Start at $150. **Remarks:** Part-time maker; first knife sold in 1976. Doing business as Martinsite Knives. **Mark:** First and middle initials, last name.

MARTIN, PETER, 28220 N. Lake Dr., Waterford, WI 53185, Phone: 262-895-2815
Specialties: Fancy, fantasy and working straight knives and folders of his design and in standard patterns. **Patterns:** Bowies, fighters, hunters, locking folders and liner locks. **Technical:** Forges own Mosaic Damascus, powdered steel and his own Damascus. Prefers natural handle material; offers file work and carved handles. **Prices:** Moderate. **Remarks:** Part-time maker; first knife sold in 1988. Doing business as Martin Custom Products. Uses only natural handle materials. **Mark:** Martin Knives.

MARTIN, JOHN ALEXANDER, 821 N Grand Ave., Okmulgee, OK 74447, Phone: 918-758-1099
Specialties: Inlaid and engraved handles. **Patterns:** Bowies, fighters, hunters and traditional patterns. **Technical:** Forges 5160, 1084, and his own Damascus. **Prices:** Start at $185. **Remarks:** Part-time maker. **Mark:** Initials or two initials and last name with JS.

MARTIN, GENE, PO Box 396, Williams, OR 97544, Phone: 541-846-6755
Specialties: Straight knives and folders. **Patterns:** Fighters, hunters, skinners, boot knives, spring back and lock back folders. **Technical:** Grinds ATS-34, 440C, Damascus and 154CM. Forges; makes own Damascus; scrimshaws. **Prices:** $150-$2500. **Remarks:** Full-time maker; first knife sold in 1993. Doing business as Provision Forge. **Mark:** Name and/or crossed staff and sword.

MARTIN, TONY, 108 S. Main St., PO Box 324, Arcadia, MO 63621, Phone: 573-546-2254
Specialties: Specializes in historical designs. Puko, etc.

MARTIN, WALTER E., 570 Cedar Flat Rd., Williams, OR 97544, Phone: 541-846-6755

MARTIN, HAL W., 781 Hwy. 95, Morrilton, AR 72110, Phone: 501-354-1682

MARZITELLI, PETER, 19929 35A Ave., Langley, BC, CANADA V3A 2R1, Phone: 604-532-8899
Specialties: Specializes in unique functional knife shapes and designs using natural and synthetic handle materials. **Patterns:** Mostly folders, some daggers and art knives. **Technical:** Grinds ATS-34, S/S Damascus and others. **Prices:** $220 to $1000 (average $375). **Remarks:** Full-time maker; first knife sold in 1984. **Mark:** Stylized logo reads "Marz."

MASON, BILL, 1114 St. Louis, #33, Excelsior Springs, MO 64024, Phone: 816-637-7335
Specialties: Combat knives; some folders. **Patterns:** Fighters to match knife types in book *Cold Steel*. **Technical:** Grinds O1, 440C and ATS-34. **Prices:** $115 to $250; some to $350. **Remarks:** Spare-time maker; first knife sold in 1979. **Mark:** Initials connected.

MASSEY, AL, Box 14, Site 15, RR#2, Mount Uniacke, Nova Scotia, CANADA B0N 1Z0, Phone: 902-866-4754
Specialties: Working knives and period pieces. **Patterns:** Swords and daggers of Celtic to medieval design, Bowies. **Technical:** Forges 5160, 1084 and 1095. Makes own Damascus. **Prices:** $100 to $400, some to $900. **Remarks:** Part-time maker, first blade sold in 1988. **Mark:** Initials and JS on Ricasso.

MASSEY, ROGER, 4928 Union Rd., Texarkana, AR 71854, Phone: 870-779-1018
Specialties: Traditional and working straight knives and folders of his design and to customer specs. **Patterns:** Bowies, hunters, daggers and utility knives. **Technical:** Forges 1084 and 52100, makes his own Damascus. Offers filework and silver wire inlay in handles. **Prices:** $200 to $1500; some to $2500. **Remarks:** Part-time maker; first knife sold in 1991. **Mark:** Last name, M.S.

MASSEY, RON, 61638 El Reposo St., Joshua Tree, CA 92252, Phone: 760-366-9239 after 5 p.m., Fax: 763-366-4620
Specialties: Classic, traditional, fancy/embellished, high art, period pieces, working/using knives, straight knives, folders, and automatics. Your design, customer specs, about 175 standard patterns. **Patterns:** Automatics, hunters and fighters. All folders are side-locking folders. Unless requested as lock books slip joint he specializes in custom designs. **Technical:** ATS-34, 440C, D-2 upon request. Engraving, filework, scrimshaw, most of the exotic handle materials. All aspects are performed by maker: inlay work in pearls or stone, handmade Pem' work. **Prices:** $110 to $2500; some to $6000. **Remarks:** Part-time maker; first knife sold in 1976.

MATA, LEONARD, 3583 Arruza St., San Diego, CA 92154, Phone: 619-690-6935

MATHEWS, CHARLIE AND HARRY, TWIN BLADES, 121 Mt Pisgah Church Rd., Statesboro, GA 30458, Phone: 912-865-9098
Specialties: Working straight knives. **Patterns:** Hunters, fighters, Bowies and period pieces. **Technical:** Grinds D2, BG42, CPMS30V, CPM3V, ATS-34 and commercial Damascus; handmade sheaths some with exotic leather, file work. **Prices:** Starting at $125. **Remarks:** Twin brothers mak-ing knives full-time under the label of Twin Blades. Charter members Georgia Custom Knifemaker's Guild. **Mark:** Twin Blades over crossed knives, reverse side steel type.

MATSUSAKI, TAKESHI, MATSUSAKI KNIVES, 151 Ono-Cho Sasebo-shi, Nagasaki, JAPAN, Phone: 0956-47-2938
Specialties: Working and collector grade front look and slip joint. **Patterns:** Sheffield type folders. **Technical:** Grinds ATS-34 k-120. **Price:** $250-$1000, some to $8000. **Remarks:** Part-time maker, first knife sold in 1990. **Mark:** Name and initials.

MAXEN, MICK, 2 Huggins Welham Green, "Hatfield, Herts", UNITED KINGDOM AL97LR, Phone: 01707 261213
Specialties: Damascus and Mosaic. **Patterns:** Medieval-style daggers and Bowies. **Technical:** Forges CS75 and 15N20 / nickel Damascus. **Mark:** Last name with axe above.

MAXFIELD, LYNN, 382 Colonial Ave., Layton, UT 84041, Phone: 801-544-4176
Specialties: Sporting knives, some fancy. **Patterns:** Hunters, fishing, fillet, special purpose: some locking folders. **Technical:** Grinds 440-C, ATS-34, 154-CM, D2, CPM-S60V, S90V, 530V, CPM-3, Talonite, and Damascus. **Prices:** $125 to $400; some to $900. **Remarks:** Part-time maker; first knife sold in 1979. **Mark:** Name, city and state.

MAXWELL, DON, 3164 N. Marks, Suite 122, Fresno, CA 93722, Phone: 559-497-8441
Specialties: Fancy working and using straight knives of his design. **Patterns:** Hunters, fighters, utility/camp knives, liner lock folders and fantasy knives. **Technical:** Grinds 440C, ATS-34, D2 and commercial Damascus. **Prices:** $250 to $1000; some to $2500. **Remarks:** Full-time maker; first knife sold in 1987. **Mark:** Last name, city, state or last name only.

MAYNARD, LARRY JOE, PO Box 493, Crab Orchard, WV 25827
Specialties: Fancy and fantasy straight knives. **Patterns:** Big knives; a Bowie with a full false edge; fighting knives. **Technical:** Grinds standard steels. **Prices:** $350 to $500; some to $1000. **Remarks:** Full-time maker; first knife sold in 1986. **Mark:** Middle and last initials.

MAYNARD, WILLIAM N., 2677 John Smith Rd., Fayetteville, NC 28306, Phone: 910-425-1615
Specialties: Traditional and working straight knives of all designs. **Patterns:** Combat, Bowies, fighters, hunters and utility knives. **Technical:** Grinds 440C, ATS-34 and commercial Damascus. Offers fancy filework; handmade sheaths. **Prices:** $100 to $300; some to $750. **Remarks:** Full-time maker; first knife sold in 1988. **Mark:** Last name.

MAYO JR., TOM, 67-420 Alahaka St., Waialua, HI 96791, Phone: 808-637-6560
Specialties: Presentation grade working knives. **Patterns:** Combat knives, hunters, Bowies and folders. **Technical:** Uses BG-42 and 440V (ATS-34 and 440C upon request). **Prices:** Start at $250. **Remarks:** Part-time maker; first knife sold in 1983. **Mark:** Volcano logo with name and state.

MAYVILLE, OSCAR L., 2130 E. County Rd. 910S., Marengo, IN 47140, Phone: 812-338-3103
Specialties: Working straight knives; period pieces. **Patterns:** Kitchen cutlery, Bowies, camp knives and hunters. **Technical:** Grinds A2, O1 and 440C. **Prices:** $50 to $350; some to $500. **Remarks:** Full-time maker; first knife sold in 1984. **Mark:** Initials over knife logo.

MCABEE, WILLIAM, 27275 Norton Grade, Colfax, CA 95713, Phone: 530-389-8163
Specialties: Working/using knives. **Patterns:** Fighters, Bowies, Hunters. **Technical:** Grinds ATS-34. **Prices:** $75 to $200; some to $350. **Remarks:** Part-time maker; first knife sold in 1990. **Mark:** Stylized WM stamped.

MCCALLEN JR., HOWARD H., 110 Anchor Dr., So Seaside Park, NJ 08752

MCCARLEY, JOHN, 4165 Harney Rd., Taneytown, MD 21787
Specialties: Working straight knives; period pieces. **Patterns:** Hunters, Bowies, camp knives, miniatures, throwing knives. **Technical:** Forges W2, O1 and his own Damascus. **Prices:** $150 to $300; some to $1000. **Remarks:** Part-time maker; first knife sold in 1977. **Mark:** Initials in script.

MCCARTY, HARRY, 1479 Indian Ridge Rd., Blaine, TN 37709
Specialties: Period pieces. **Patterns:** Trade knives, Bowies, 18th and 19th century folders and hunting swords. **Technical:** Forges and grinds high-carbon steel. **Prices:** $75 to $1300. **Remarks:** Full-time maker; first knife sold in 1977. **Mark:** Stylized initials inside a shamrock. **Other:** Doing business as Indian Ridge Forge.

MCCLURE, JOE AND SANDY 3052 Isim Road, Norman, OK 73026, Phone: 405-321-3614.
Specialties: Hammer forged rustic hunters. **Prices:** $175 to $350. **Remarks:** All knives come with brain tanned deer leather sheath. **Mark:** My name is SAS.

custom knifemakers

MCCLURE, JERRY 3052 Isim Road, Norman, OK 73026, 405-321-3614. **Specialties:** Makes a line of folding knives. All have his jewel balde movement, and damasteel stainless Damascus. **Prices:** $600 to $900. **Remarks:** He also makes a variety of hunting knives. **Mark:** Jmcclure (in an arch).

MCCLURE, MICHAEL, 803 17th Ave., Menlo Park, CA 94025, Phone: 650-323-2596 **Specialties:** Working/using straight knives of his design and to customer specs. **Patterns:** Bowies, hunters, skinners, utility/camp, tantos, fillets and boot knives. **Technical:** Forges high-carbon and Damascus; also grinds stainless, all grades. **Prices:** Start at $100. **Remarks:** Part-time maker; first knife sold in 1991. **Mark:** Mike McClure. **Other:** ABS Journeyman Smith.

MCCONNELL, CHARLES R., 158 Genteel Ridge, Wellsburg, WV 26070, Phone: 304-737-2015 **Specialties:** Working straight knives. **Patterns:** Hunters, Bowies, daggers, minis and push knives. **Technical:** Grinds 440C and 154CM; likes full tangs. **Prices:** $65 to $325; some to $800. **Remarks:** Part-time maker; first knife sold in 1977. **Mark:** Name.

MCCONNELL JR., LOYD A., 1710 Rosewood, Odessa, TX 79761, Phone: 915-363-8344 **Specialties:** Working straight knives and folders, some fancy. **Patterns:** Hunters, boots, Bowies, locking folders and slip-joints. **Technical:** Grinds CPM Steels, ATS-34 and BG-42 and commercial Damascus. **Prices:** $175 to $900; some to $10,000. **Remarks:** Full-time maker; first knife sold in 1975. Doing business as Cactus Custom Knives. Markets product knives under name: Lone Star Knives. **Mark:** Name, city and state in cactus logo.

MCCORNOCK, CRAIG, MCC MTN OUTFITTERS, 4775 Rte. 212, Willow, NY 12495, Phone: 914-679-9758

MCCOUN, MARK, 14212 Pine Dr., DeWitt, VA 23840, Phone: 804-469-7631 **Specialties:** Working/using straight knives of his design and in standard patterns; custom miniatures. **Patterns:** Locking liners, integrals. **Technical:** Grinds Damascus, ATS-34 and 440C. **Prices:** $150 to $500. **Remarks:** Part-time maker; first knife sold in 1989. **Mark:** Name, city and state.

MCCRACKIN, KEVIN, 3720 Hess Rd., House Spings, MO 63051, Phone: 636-677-6066

MCCRACKIN AND SON, V.J., 3720 Hess Rd., House Springs, MO 63051, Phone: 636-677-6066 **Specialties:** Working straight knives in standard patterns. **Patterns:** Hunters, Bowies and camp knives. **Technical:** Forges L6, 5160, his own Damascus, cable Damascus. **Prices:** $125 to $700; some to $1500. **Remarks:** Part-time maker; first knife sold in 1983. Son Kevin helps make the knives. **Mark:** Last name, M.S.

MCCULLOUGH, JERRY, 274 West Pettibone Rd., Georgiana, AL 36033, Phone: 334-382-7644 **Specialties:** Standard patterns or custom designs. **Technical:** Forge and grind scrap-tool and Damascus steels. Use natural handle materials and turquoise trim on some. Filework on others. **Prices:** $65 to $250 and up. **Remarks:** Part-time maker. **Mark:** Initials (JM) combined.

MCDERMOTT, MICHAEL, 151 Hwy F, Defiance, MO 63341, Phone: 314-798-2077

MCDONALD, RICH, 4590 Kirk Rd., Columbiana, OH 44408, Phone: 330-482-0007, Fax: 330-482-0007 **Specialties:** Traditional working/using and art knives of his design. **Patterns:** Bowies, hunters, folders, primitives and tomahawks. **Technical:** Forges 5160, 1084, 1095, 52100 and his own Damascus. Fancy filework. **Prices:** $200 to $1500. **Remarks:** Full-time maker; first knife sold in 1994. **Mark:** First and last initials connected.

MCDONALD, ROBERT J., 14730 61 Court N., Loxahatchee, FL 33470, Phone: 561-790-1470 **Specialties:** Traditional working straight knives to customer specs. **Patterns:** Fighters, swords and folders. **Technical:** Grinds 440C, ATS-34 and forges own Damascus. **Prices:** $150 to $1000. **Remarks:** Part-time maker; first knife sold in 1988. **Mark:** Electro-etched name.

MCDONALD, W.J. "JERRY", 7173 Wickshire Cove E., Germantown, TN 38138, Phone: 901-756-9924 **Specialties:** Classic and working/using straight knives of his design and in standard patterns. **Patterns:** Bowies, hunters kitchen and traditional spring back pocket knives. **Technical:** Grinds ATS-34, 154CM, D2, 440V, BG42 and 440C. **Prices:** $125 to $1000. **Remarks:** Full-time maker; first knife sold in 1989. **Mark:** First and middle initials, last name, maker, city and state. Some of his knives are stamped McDonald in script.

MCDONALD, ROBIN J., 6509 E Jeffrey Dr., Fayetteville, NC 28314 **Specialties:** Working knives of maker's design. **Patterns:** Bowies, hunters, camp knives and fighters. **Technical:** Forges primarily 5160. **Prices:** $100 to $500. **Remarks:** Part-time maker; first knife sold in 1999. **Mark:** Initials RJM.

MCFALL, KEN, PO Box 458, Lakeside, AZ 85929, Phone: 928-537-2026, Fax: 928-537-8066 **Specialties:** Fancy working straight knives and some folders. **Patterns:** Daggers, boots, tantos, Bowies; some miniatures. **Technical:** Grinds D2, ATS-34 and 440C. Forges his own Damascus. **Prices:** $200 to $1200. **Remarks:** Part-time maker; first knife sold in 1984. **Mark:** Name, city and state.

MCFARLIN, ERIC E., PO Box 2188, Kodiak, AK 99615, Phone: 907-486-4799 **Specialties:** Working knives of his design. **Patterns:** Bowies, skinners, camp knives and hunters. **Technical:** Flat and convex grinds 440C, A2 and AEB-L. **Prices:** Start at $200. **Remarks:** Part-time maker; first knife sold in 1989. **Mark:** Name and city in rectangular logo.

MCFARLIN, J.W., 3331 Pocohantas Dr., Lake Havasu City, AZ 86404, Phone: 928-855-8095, Fax: 928-855-8095 **Technical:** Flat grinds, D2, ATS-34, 440C, Thomas and Peterson Damascus. **Remarks:** From working knives to investment. Customer designs always welcome. 100% hand made. **Prices:** $150 to $3000. **Mark:** Hand written in the blade.

MCGILL, JOHN, PO Box 302, Blairsville, GA 30512, Phone: 404-745-4686 **Specialties:** Working knives. **Patterns:** Traditional patterns; camp knives. **Technical:** Forges L6 and 9260; makes Damascus. **Prices:** $50 to $250; some to $500. **Remarks:** Full-time maker; first knife sold in 1982. **Mark:** XYLO.

MCGOWAN, FRANK E., 12629 Howard Lodge Dr., Sykesville, MD 21784, Phone: 410-489-4323 **Specialties:** Fancy working knives and folders to customer specs. **Patterns:** Survivor knives, fighters, fishing knives, folders and hunters. **Technical:** Grinds and forges O1, 440C, 5160, ATS-34, 52100, or customer choice. **Prices:** $100 to $1000; some more. **Remarks:** Full-time maker; first knife sold in 1986. **Mark:** Last name.

MCGRATH, PATRICK T., 8343 Kenyon Ave., Westchester, CA 90045, Phone: 310-338-8764

MCGRODER, PATRICK J., 5725 Chapin Rd., Madison, OH 44057, Phone: 216-298-3405, Fax: 216-298-3405 **Specialties:** Traditional working/using knives of his design. **Patterns:** Bowies, hunters and utility/camp knives. **Technical:** Grinds ATS-34, D2 and customer requests. Does reverse etching; heat-treats; prefers natural handle materials; custom made sheath with each knife. **Prices:** $125 to $250. **Remarks:** Part-time maker. **Mark:** First and middle initials, last name, maker, city and state.

MCGUANE IV, THOMAS F., 410 South 3rd Ave., Bozeman, MT 59715, Phone: 406-586-0248 **Specialties:** Multi metal inlaid knives of handmade steel. **Patterns:** Lock back and liner lock folders, fancy straight knives. **Technical:** 1084/1SN20 Damascus and Mosaic steel by maker. **Prices:** $1000 and up. **Mark:** Surname or name and city, state.

MCHENRY, WILLIAM JAMES, Box 67, Wyoming, RI 02898, Phone: 401-539-8353 **Specialties:** Fancy high-tech folders of his design. **Patterns:** Locking folders with various mechanisms. **Technical:** One-of-a-kind only, no duplicates. Inventor of the Axis Lock. Most pieces disassemble and feature top-shelf materials including gold, silver and gems. **Prices:** Upscale. **Remarks:** Full-time maker; first knife sold in 1988. Former goldsmith. **Mark:** Last name or first and last initials.

MCINTOSH, DAVID L., PO Box 948, Haines, AK 99827, Phone: 907-766-3673 **Specialties:** Working straight knives and folders of all designs. **Patterns:** All styles, except swords. **Technical:** Grinds ATS-34 and top name maker Damascus. Engraves; offers tooling on sheaths. Uses fossil ivory. **Prices:** $60 to $800; some to $2000. **Remarks:** Full-time maker; first knife sold in 1984. **Mark:** Last name, serial number, steel type, city and state.

MCKENZIE, DAVID BRIAN, 2311 B Ida Rd., Campbell River B, CANADA V9W-4V7

MCKIERNAN, STAN, 205 E. Park St., Vandalia, MO 63382, Phone: 573-594-6135 **Specialties:** Self-sheathed knives and miniatures. **Patterns:** Daggers, ethnic designs and individual styles. **Technical:** Grinds Damascus and 440C. **Prices:** $200-$500, some to $1500. **Mark:** "River's Bend" inside two concentric circles.

MCLENDON, HUBERT W., 125 Thomas Rd., Waco, GA 30182, Phone: 770-574-9796
Specialties: Using knives; his design or customer's. **Patterns:** Bowies and hunters. **Technical:** Hand ground or forged ATS-34, 440C and D2. **Prices:** $100 to $300. **Remarks:** First knife sold in 1978. **Mark:** McLendon or Mc.

MCLUIN, TOM, 36 Fourth St., Dracut, MA 01826, Phone: 978-957-4899
Specialties: Working straight knives and folders of his design. **Patterns:** Boots, hunters and folders. **Technical:** Grinds ATS-34, 440C, O1 and Damascus; makes his own mokume. **Prices:** $100 to $400; some to $700. **Remarks:** Part-time maker; first knife sold in 1991. **Mark:** Last name.

MCLURKIN, ANDREW, 2112 Windy Woods Dr., Raleigh, NC 27607, Phone: 919-834-4693
Specialties: Collector grade folders, working folders, fixed blades, and miniatures. Knives made to order and to his design. **Patterns:** Locking liner and lock back folders, hunter, working and tactical designs. **Technical:** Using patterned Damascus, Mosaic Damascus, ATS-34, BG-42, and CPM steels. Prefers natural handle materials such as pearl, ancient ivory and stabilized wood. Also using synthetic materials such as carbon fiber, titanium, and G10. **Prices:** $250 and up. **Mark:** Last name. Mark is often on inside of folders.

MCMANUS, DANNY, 413 Fairhaven Drive., Taylors, SC 29687, Phone: 864-268-9849, Fax: 864-268-9699
Specialties: High-tech and traditional working/using straight knives of his design, to customer specs and in standard patterns. **Patterns:** Boots, Bowies, fighters, hunters and utility/camp knives. **Technical:** Forges stainless steel Damascus; grinds ATS-34. Offers engraving and scrimshaw. **Prices:** $300 to $2000; some to $3000. **Remarks:** Full-time maker; first knife sold in 1997. Doing business as Stamascus KnifeWorks Corp. **Mark:** Stamascus.

MCNABB, TOMMY, CAROLINA CUSTOM KNIVES, 4015 Brownsboro Rd., Winston-Salem, NC 27106, Phone: 336-924-6053, Fax: 336-924-4854

MCNEIL, JIMMY, 1175 Mt. Moriah Rd., Memphis, TN 38117, Phone: 901-544-0710 or 901-683-8133
Specialties: Fancy high-art straight knives of his design. **Patterns:** Bowies, daggers and swords. **Technical:** Grinds O1 and Damascus. Engraves, carves and inlays. **Prices:** $50 to $300; some to $2000. **Remarks:** Spare-time maker; first knife sold in 1993. Doing business as McNeil's Minerals and Knives. **Mark:** Crossed mining picks and serial number.

MCRAE, J. MICHAEL, 6100 Lake Rd, Mint Hill, NC 28227, Phone: 704-545-2929
Specialties: Scottish dirks and sgian dubhs. **Patterns:** Traditional blade styles with traditional and slightly non-traditional handle treatments. **Technical:** Forges 1095, 5160 and his own Damascus. Prefers Stag and exotic hardwoods for handles, many intricately carved. **Prices:** Starting at $125, some to $3500. **Remarks:** Journeyman Smith in ABS, member of North Carolina Custom Knifemakers Guild and ABANA. Full-time maker, first knife sold in 1982. Doing business as Scotia Metalwork. **Mark:** Last name underlined with a claymore.

MEERDINK, KURT, 120 Split Rock Dr., Barryville, NY 12719, Phone: 845-557-0783
Specialties: Working straight knives. **Patterns:** Hunters, Bowies, tactical and neck knives. **Technical:** Grinds ATS34, 440C, D2, Damascus. **Prices:** $95 to $1100. **Remarks:** Full-time maker, first knife sold in 1994. **Mark:** Meerdink Maker, Rio NY.

MEIER, DARYL, 75 Forge Rd., Carbondale, IL 62901, Phone: 618-549-3234
Specialties: One-of-a-kind knives and swords. **Patterns:** Collaborates on blades. **Technical:** Forges his own Damascus, W1 and A203E, 440C, 431, nickel 200 and clad steel. **Prices:** $250 to $450; some to $6000. **Remarks:** Full-time smith and researcher since 1974; first knife sold in 1974. **Mark:** Name or circle/arrow symbol or SHAWNEE.

MELIN, GORDON C., 11259 Gladhill Rd Unit 4, Whittier, CA 90604, Phone: 562-946-5753

MELLARD, J. R., 17006 Highland Canyon Dr., Houston, TX 77095, Phone: 281-550-9464

MELOY, SEAN, 7148 Rosemary Lane, Lemon Grove, CA 91945-2105, Phone: 619-465-7173
Specialties: Traditional working straight knives of his design. **Patterns:** Bowies, fighters and utility/camp knives. **Technical:** Grinds 440C, ATS-34 and D2. **Prices:** $125 to $300. **Remarks:** Part-time maker; first knife sold in 1985. **Mark:** Broz Knives.

MENSCH, LARRY C., 578 Madison Ave., Milton, PA 17847, Phone: 570-742-9554
Specialties: Custom orders. **Patterns:** Bowies, daggers, hunters, tantos, short swords and miniatures. **Technical:** Grinds ATS-34, carbon and stainless steel Damascus; blade grinds hollow, flat and slack. Filework; bending guards and fluting handles with finger grooves. Offers engraving and scrimshaw. **Prices:** $200 and up. **Remarks:** Full-time maker; first knife sold in 1993. Doing business as Larry's Knife Shop. **Mark:** Connected capital "L" and small "m" in script.

MERCER, MIKE, 149 N. Waynesville Rd., Lebanon, OH 45036, Phone: 513-932-2837
Specialties: Jeweled gold and ivory daggers; multi-blade folders. **Patterns:** 1-1/4" folders, hunters, axes, replicas. **Technical:** Uses O1 Damascus and mokume. **Prices:** $150 to $1500. **Remarks:** Full-time maker since 1991. **Mark:** Last name in script.

MERCHANT, TED, 7 Old Garrett Ct., White Hall, MD 21161, Phone: 410-343-0380
Specialties: Traditional and classic working knives. **Patterns:** Bowies, hunters, camp knives, fighters, daggers and skinners. **Technical:** Forges W2 and 5160; makes own Damascus. Makes handles with wood, stag, horn, silver and gem stone inlay; fancy filework. **Prices:** $125 to $600; some to $1500. **Remarks:** Full-time maker; first knife sold in 1985. **Mark:** Last name.

MERZ III, ROBERT L., 1447 Winding Canyon, Katy, TX 77493, Phone: 281-391-2897
Specialties: Working straight knives and folders, some fancy, of his design. **Patterns:** Hunters, skinners, fighters and camp knives. **Technical:** Flat-grinds 440C, 154CM, ATS-34, 440V and commercial Damascus. **Prices:** $150 to $450; some to $600. **Remarks:** Part-time maker; first knife sold in 1974. **Mark:** MERZ KNIVES, city and state, or last name in oval.

MESHEJIAN, MARDI, 33 Elm Dr., E. Northport, NY 11731, Phone: 631-757-4541
Specialties: One-of-a-kind fantasy and high-art straight knives of his design. **Patterns:** Swords, daggers, finger knives and other edged weapons. **Technical:** Forged Damascus and Chain Damascus. **Prices:** $150 to $2500; some to $3000. **Remarks:** Full-time maker; first knife sold in 1996. Doing business as Tooth and Nail Metalworks. **Mark:** Stamped Etched stylized "M".

MESSER, DAVID T., 134 S. Torrence St., Dayton, OH 45403-2044, Phone: 513-228-6561
Specialties: Fantasy period pieces, straight and folding, of his design. **Patterns:** Bowies, daggers and swords. **Technical:** Grinds 440C, O1, 06 and commercial Damascus. Likes fancy guards and exotic handle materials. **Prices:** $100 to $225; some to $375. **Remarks:** Spare-time maker; first knife sold in 1991. **Mark:** Name stamp.

METHENY, H.A. "WHITEY", 7750 Waterford Dr., Spotsylvania, VA 22553, Phone: 703-582-3228
Specialties: Working and using straight knives of his design and to customer specs. **Patterns:** Hunters and kitchen knives. **Technical:** Grinds 440C and ATS-34. Offers filework; tooled custom sheaths. **Prices:** $200 to $350. **Remarks:** Spare-time maker; first knife sold in 1990. **Mark:** Initials/full name football logo.

METZ, GREG T., c/o James Ranch HC 83, Cascade, ID 83611, Phone: 208-382-4336
Specialties: Hunting and utility knives. **Prices:** $300 and up. **Remarks:** Natural handle materials; hand forged blades; 1084 and 1095. **Mark:** METZ (last name).

MICHINAKA, TOSHIAKI, I-679 Koyamacho-nishi, Totton-shi, Tottori 680-0947, JAPAN, Phone: 0857-28-5911

MICHO, KANDA, 7-32-5 Shinzutsumi-cho Shinnanyo-city, Yamaguchi, JAPAN, Phone: 0834-62-1910

MICKLEY, TRACY, 42112 Kerns Dr., North Mankato, MN 56003, Phone: 507-947-3760
Specialties: Working and collectable straight knives using mammoth ivory or burl woods, liner lock folders. **Patterns:** Custom and classic hunters, utility, fighters and Bowies. **Technical:** Grinding 154-CM, BG-42 forging 01 and 52100. **Prices:** Starting at $250 **Remarks:** Part-time since 1999. **Mark:** Last name.

MILFORD, BRIAN A., RD 2 Box 294, Knox, PA 16232, Phone: 814-797-2595, Fax: 814-226-4351
Specialties: Traditional and working/using straight knives of his design or to customer specs. **Patterns:** Fighters, hunters and utility/camp knives. **Technical:** Forges Damascus and 52100; grinds 440C. **Prices:** $50 to $300; some to $750. **Remarks:** Part-time maker; first knife sold in 1991. Doing business as BAM Forge. **Mark:** Full name or initials.

custom knifemakers

MILITANO, TOM, CUSTOM KNIVES, 77 Jason Rd., Jacksonville, AL 36265-6655, Phone: 256-435-7132
Specialties: Fixed blade, one-of-a-kind knives. **Patterns:** Bowies, fighters, hunters and tactical knives. **Technical:** Grinds 440C, ATS-34, A2, and Damascus. Hollow grinds, flat grinds, and decorative filework. **Prices:** $150 plus. **Remarks:** Part-time maker. **Mark:** Name, city and state in oval with maker in the center. Sold first knives in the mid to late 1980s. Memberships: founding member-New England Custom Knife Association, Flint River Knife Club.

MILLARD, FRED G., 27627 Kopezyk Ln., Richland Center, WI 53581, Phone: 608-647-5376
Specialties: Working/using straight knives of his design or to customer specs. **Patterns:** Bowies, hunters, utility/camp knives, kitchen/steak knives. **Technical:** Grinds ATS-34, O1, D2 and 440C. Makes sheaths. **Prices:** $110 to $300. **Remarks:** Full-time maker; first knife sold in 1993. Doing business as Millard Knives. **Mark:** Mallard duck in flight with serial number.

MILLER, DON, 1604 Harrodsburg Rd., Lexington, KY 40503, Phone: 606-276-3299

MILLER, HANFORD J., Box 97, Cowdrey, CO 80434, Phone: 970-723-4708
Specialties: Working knives in Moran-style; period pieces. **Patterns:** Bowies, fighters, camp knives and other large straight knives. **Technical:** Forges W2, 1095, 5160 and his own Damascus; differential tempers; offers wire inlay. **Prices:** $300 to $800; some to $3000. **Remarks:** Full-time maker; first knife sold in 1968. **Mark:** Initials or name within Bowie logo.

MILLER, JAMES P., 9024 Goeller Rd., RR 2, Box 28, Fairbank, IA 50629, Phone: 319-635-2294
Specialties: All tool steel Damascus; working knives and period pieces. **Patterns:** Hunters, Bowies, camp knives and daggers. **Technical:** Forges and grinds 1095, 52100, 440C and his own Damascus. **Prices:** $100 to $350; some to $1500. **Remarks:** Full-time maker; first knife sold in 1970. **Mark:** First and middle initials, last name with knife logo.

MILLER, M.A., 11625 Community Center Dr., Northglenn, CO 80233, Phone: 303-280-3816
Specialties: Using knives for hunting. 3-1/2"-4" Loveless drop-point. Made to customer specs. **Patterns:** Skinners and camp knives. **Technical:** Grinds 440C, D2, O1 and ATS-34 Damascus miniatures. **Prices:** $225 to $275; miniatures $75. **Remarks:** Part-time maker; first knife sold in 1988. **Mark:** Last name stamped in block letters or first and middle initials, last name, maker, city and state with triangles on either side etched.

MILLER, MICHAEL E., 1400 Skyview Dr., El Reno, OK 73036, Phone: 405-422-3602
Specialties: Traditional working/using knives of his design. **Patterns:** Bowies, hunters and kitchen knives. **Technical:** Grinds ATS-34, CPM 440V; forges Damascus and cable Damascus and 52100. Prefers scrimshaw, fancy pins, basket weave and embellished sheaths. **Prices:** $80 to $300; some to $500. **Remarks:** Part-time maker; first knife sold in 1984. Doing business as Miller Custom Knives. **Mark:** First and middle initials, last name, maker, city and state.

MILLER, MICHAEL K., 28510 Santiam Hwy., Sweet Home, OR 97386, Phone: 541-367-4927
Specialties: Specializes in kitchen cutlery of his design or made to customer specs. **Patterns:** Hunters, utility/camp knives and kitchen cutlery. **Technical:** Grinds ATS-34, AEBL and 440-C. Wife does scrimshaw as well. Makes custom sheaths and holsters. **Prices:** $200. **Remarks:** Full-time maker; first knife sold in 1989. **Mark:** MandM Kustom Krafts.

MILLER, R.D., 10526 Estate Lane, Dallas, TX 75238, Phone: 214-348-3496
Specialties: One-of-a-kind collector-grade knives. **Patterns:** Boots, hunters, Bowies, camp and utility knives, fishing and bird knives, miniatures. **Technical:** Grinds a variety of steels to include O1, D2, 440C, 154CM and 1095. **Prices:** $65 to $300; some to $900. **Remarks:** Full-time maker; first knife sold in 1984. **Mark:** R.D. Custom Knives with date or bow and arrow logo.

MILLER, RICK, 516 Kanaul Rd., Rockwood, PA 15557, Phone: 814-926-2059
Specialties: Working/using straight knives of his design and in standard patterns. **Patterns:** Bowies, daggers, hunters and friction folders. **Technical:** Grinds L6. Forges 5160, L6 and Damascus. Patterns for Damascus are random, twist, rose or ladder. **Prices:** $75 to $250; some to $400. **Remarks:** Part-time maker; first knife sold in 1982. **Mark:** Script stamp "R.D.M.".

MILLER, RONALD T., 12922 127th Ave. N., Largo, FL 34644, Phone: 813-595-0378 (after 5 p.m.)
Specialties: Working straight knives in standard patterns. **Patterns:** Combat knives, camp knives, kitchen cutlery, fillet knives, locking folders and butterflies. **Technical:** Grinds D2, 440C and ATS-34; offers brass inlays and scrimshaw. **Prices:** $45 to $325; some to $750. **Remarks:** Part-time maker; first knife sold in 1984. **Mark:** Name, city and state in palm tree logo.

MILLER, BOB, 7659 Fine Oaks Pl., Oakville, MO 63129, Phone: 314-846-8934
Specialties: Mosaic Damascus; collector using straight knives and folders. **Patterns:** Hunters, Bowies, utility/camp knives, daggers. **Technical:** Forges own Damascus, mosaic-Damascus and 52100. **Prices:** $125 to $500. **Remarks:** Part-time maker; first knife sold in 1983. **Mark:** First and middle initials and last name, or initials.

MILLS, MICHAEL, 5604 Lanham Station Rd., Lanham, MD 20706-2531, Phone: 301-459-7226
Specialties: Working knives, Hunters, Skinners, Utility and Bowies. **Technical:** Forge 5160 Differential Heat-Treats. **Prices:** $200 and up. **Remarks:** Part-time maker, ABS Journeyman. **Mark:** Last name in script.

MILLS, LOUIS G., 9450 Waters Rd., Ann Arbor, MI 48103, Phone: 734-668-1839
Specialties: High-art Japanese-style period pieces. **Patterns:** Traditional tantos, daggers and swords. **Technical:** Makes steel from iron; makes his own Damascus by traditional Japanese techniques. **Prices:** $900 to $2000; some to $8000. **Remarks:** Spare-time maker. **Mark:** Yasutomo in Japanese Kanji.

MINK, DAN, PO Box 861, 196 Sage Circle, Crystal Beach, FL 34681, Phone: 727-786-5408
Specialties: Traditional and working knives of his design. **Patterns:** Bowies, fighters, folders and hunters. **Technical:** Grinds ATS-34, 440C and D2. Blades and tanges embellished with fancy filework. Uses natural and rare handle materials. **Prices:** $125 to $450. **Remarks:** Part-time maker; first knife sold in 1985. **Mark:** Name and star encircled by custom made, city, state.

MINNICK, JIM, 144 North 7th St., Middletown, IN 47356, Phone: 765-354-4108
Specialties: Lever-lock folding art knives, liner-locks. **Patterns:** Stilettos, Persian and one-of-a-kind folders. **Technical:** Grinds and carves Damascus, stainless, and high-carbon. **Prices:** $950 to $7000. **Remarks:** Part-time maker; first knife sold in 1976. **Mark:** Minnick and JMJ. **Other:** Husband and wife team.

MIRABILE, DAVID, 1715 Glacier Ave., Juneau, AK 99801, Phone: 907-463-3404
Specialties: Elegant edged weapons. **Patterns:** Fighters, Bowies, claws, tklinget daggers, executive desk knives. **Technical:** Forged high-carbon steels, his own Damascus; uses ancient walrus ivory and prehistoric bone extensively, very rarely uses wood. **Prices:** $350 to $7000. **Remarks:** Full-time maker. Knives sold through art gallery in Juneau, AK. **Mark:** Last name etched or engraved.

MITCHELL, JAMES A., PO Box 4646, Columbus, GA 31904, Phone: 404-322-8582
Specialties: Fancy working knives. **Patterns:** Hunters, fighters, Bowies and locking folders. **Technical:** Grinds D2, 440C and commercial Damascus. **Prices:** $100 to $400; some to $900. **Remarks:** Part-time maker; first knife sold in 1976. Sells knives in sets. **Mark:** Signature and city.

MITCHELL, MAX, DEAN AND BEN, 3803 V.F.W. Rd., Leesville, LA 71440, Phone: 318-239-6416
Specialties: Hatchet and knife sets with folder and belt and holster all match. **Patterns:** Hunters, 200 L6 steel. **Technical:** L6 steel; soft back, hand edge. **Prices:** $300 to $500. **Remarks:** Part-time makers; first knife sold in 1965. Custom orders only; no stock. **Mark:** First names.

MITCHELL, WM. DEAN, PO Box 2, Warren, TX 77664, Phone: 409-547-2213
Specialties: Classic and period knives. **Patterns:** Bowies, hunters, daggers and swords. **Technical:** Forged carbon steel and Damascus 52100, 1095, 5160; makes pattern, composite and mosaic Damascus; offers filework. Makes wooden display cases. **Prices:** Mid-scale. **Remarks:** Hobbist maker since 1986. First knife sold in 1986.D.B.A. The Thicket Smithy. **Mark:** Full name with anvil, MS.

MITSUYUKI, ROSS, 94-1071 Kepakepa St, C-3, Waipahu, HAWAII 96797, Phone: 808-671-3335, Fax: 808-671-3335
Specialties: Working straight knives and folders. **Patterns:** Hunting, fighters, utility knives and boot knives. **Technical:** 440C, BG-42, ATS-34, 530V, and Damascus. **Prices:** $100-$500. **Remarks:** Spare-time maker, first knife sold in 1998. **Mark:** Name, state, Hawaiian sea turtle.

MIVILLE-DESCHENES, ALAIN, 1952 Charles A, Parent, QC, CANADA G2B 4B2, Phone: 418-845-0950
Specialties: Working knives of his design or to customer specs and art knives. **Patterns:** Bowies, skinner, hunter, utility, camp knives, fighters, art knives. **Technical:** Grinds ATS-34, 440C, CPM S30V, 0-1, etc. **Prices:** $175 to $500; some higher. **Remarks:** Part-time maker; first knife sold in 2001. **Mark:** Logo (small hand) and initials (AMD).

MIZE, RICHARD, FOX CREEK FORGE, 2038 Fox Creek Rd., Lawrenceburg, KY 40342, Phone: 502-859-0602
Specialties: Forges spring steel, 5160, 10xx steels, natural handle materials. **Patterns:** Traditional working knives, period flavor Bowies, rifle knives. **Technical:** Does own heat treating, differential temper. **Prices:** $100 to $400. **Remarks:** Strongly advocates sole authorship. **Mark:** Initial M hot stamped.

MOMCILOVIC, GUNNAR, Nordlysv, 16, Waipahu, NORWAY, Phone: 0111-47-3287-3586

MONCUS, MICHAEL STEVEN, 1803 US 19 N, Smithville, GA 31787, Phone: 912-846-2408

MONK, NATHAN P., 1304 4th Ave. SE, Cullman, AL 35055, Phone: 205-737-0463
Specialties: Traditional working and using straight knives of his design and to customer specs; fancy knives. **Patterns:** Bowies, daggers, fighters, hunters, utility/camp knives, bird knives and one-of-a-kinds. **Technical:** Grinds ATS-34, 440C and A2. **Prices:** $50 to $175. **Remarks:** Spare-time maker; first knife sold in 1990. **Mark:** First and middle initials, last name, city, state.

MONTANO, GUS A., 11217 Westonhill Dr., San Diego, CA 92126-1447, Phone: 619-273-5357
Specialties: Traditional working/using straight knives of his design. **Patterns:** Boots, Bowies and fighters. **Technical:** Grinds 1095 and 5160; grinds and forges cable. Double or triple hardened and triple drawn; hand-rubbed finish. Prefers natural handle materials. **Prices:** $200 to $400; some to $600. **Remarks:** Spare-time maker; first knife sold in 1997. **Mark:** First initial and last name.

MONTEIRO, VICTOR, 31, Rue D'Opprebais, 1360 Maleves Ste Marie, BELGIUM, Phone: 010 88 0441
Specialties: Working and fancy straight knives, folders and integrals of his design. **Patterns:** Fighters, hunters and kitchen knives. **Technical:** Grinds ATS-34, 440C, D2, Damasteel and other CPH's and commercial Damascus, embellishment, filework and domed pins. **Prices:** $300 to $1000, some higher. **Remarks:** Part-time maker; first knife sold in 1989. **Mark:** Logo with initials connected.

MONTJOY, CLAUDE, 706 Indian Creek Rd., Clinton, SC 29325, Phone: 864-697-6160
Specialties: Folders, slip joint, lock, lock liner and inter frame. **Patterns:** Hunters, boots, fighters, some art knives and folders. **Technical:** Grinds ATS-34 and Damascus. Offers inlaid handle scales. **Prices:** $100 to $500. **Remarks:** Full-time maker; first knife sold in 1982. **Mark:** Montjoy. **Other:** Custom orders, no catalog.

MOORE, TED, 340 E Willow St., Elizabethtown, PA 17022, Phone: 717-367-3939
Specialties: Damascus folders, cigar cutters. **Patterns:** Locking folders and slip joint. **Technical:** Grinds Damascus, high-carbon and stainless; also ATS34 and D2. **Prices:** $250 to $1500. **Remarks:** Part-time maker; first knife sold 1993. **Mark:** Moore U.S.A.

MOORE, MARVE, HC 89 Box 393, Willow, AK 99688, Phone: 907-232-0478
Specialties: Fixed blades forged and stock removal. **Patterns:** Gunter, skinners, fighter, short swords. **Technical:** 100% of his work is done by hand. **Prices:** $100 - $500. **Remarks:** Also makes his own sheaths. **Mark:** -MM-.

MOORE, MICHAEL ROBERT, 61 Beauliew St., Lowell, MA 01850, Phone: 978-459-2163, Fax: 978-441-1819

MOORE, JAMES B., 1707 N. Gillis, Ft. Stockton, TX 79735, Phone: 915-336-2113
Specialties: Classic working straight knives and folders of his design. **Patterns:** Hunters, Bowies, daggers, fighters, boots, utility/camp knives, locking folders and slip-joint folders. **Technical:** Grinds 440C, ATS-34, D2, L6, CPM and commercial Damascus. **Prices:** $85 to $700; exceptional knives to $1500. **Remarks:** Full-time maker; first knife sold in 1972. **Mark:** Name, city and state.

MORAN JR., WM. F., PO Box 68, Braddock Heights, MD 21714, Phone: 301-371-7543
Specialties: High-art working knives of his design. **Patterns:** Fighters, camp knives, Bowies, daggers, axes, tomahawks, push knives and miniatures. **Technical:** Forges W2, 5160 and his own Damascus; puts silver wire inlay on most handles; uses only natural handle materials. **Prices:** $400 to $7500; some to $9000. **Remarks:** Full-time maker. **Mark:** W. F. Moran Jr. Master Smith MS.

MORETT, DONALD, 116 Woodcrest Dr., Lancaster, PA 17602-1300, Phone: 717-746-4888

MORGAN, JEFF, 9200 Arnaz Way, Santee, CA 92071, Phone: 619-448-8430
Specialties: Fancy working straight knives. **Patterns:** Hunters, fighters, boots, miniatures. **Technical:** Grinds D2, 440C and ATS-34; likes exotic handles. **Prices:** $60 to $300; some to $800. **Remarks:** Full-time maker; first knife sold in 1977. **Mark:** Initials connected.

MORGAN, TOM, 14689 Ellett Rd., Beloit, OH 44609, Phone: 330-537-2023
Specialties: Working straight knives and period pieces. **Patterns:** Hunters, boots and presentation tomahawks. **Technical:** Grinds O1, 440C and 154CM. **Prices:** Knives, $65 to $200; tomahawks, $100 to $325. **Remarks:** Full-time maker; first knife sold in 1977. **Mark:** Last name and type of steel used.

MORRIS, DARRELL PRICE, 92 Union, St. Plymouth, Devon, ENGLAND PL1 3EZ, Phone: 0752 223546
Specialties: Traditional Japanese knives, Bowies and high-art knives. **Technical:** Nickel Damascus and mokamame. **Prices:** $1000 to $4000. **Remarks:** Part-time maker; first knife sold in 1990. **Mark:** Initials and Japanese name—Kuni Shigae.

MORRIS, C.H., 1590 Old Salem Rd., Frisco City, AL 36445, Phone: 334-575-7425
Specialties: Liner lock folders. **Patterns:** Interframe liner locks. **Technical:** Grinds 440C and ATS-34. **Prices:** Start at $350. **Remarks:** Full-time maker; first knife sold in 1973. Doing business as Custom Knives. **Mark:** First and middle initials, last name.

MORRIS, ERIC, 306 Ewart Ave., Beckley, WV 25801, Phone: 304-253-3951

MORTENSON, ED, 2742 Hwy. 93 N, Darby, MT 59829, Phone: 406-821-3146, Fax: 406-821-3146
Specialties: Period pieces and working/using straight knives of his design, to customer specs and in standard patterns. **Patterns:** Bowies, hunters and kitchen knives. **Technical:** Grinds ATS-34, 5160 and 1095. Sheath combinations - flashlight/knife, hatchet/knife, etc. **Prices:** $60 to $140; some to $300. **Remarks:** Full-time maker; first knife sold in 1993. Doing business as The Blade Lair. **Mark:** M with attached O.

MOSES, STEVEN, 1610 W Hemlock Way, Santa Ana, CA 92704

MOSIER, RICHARD, 52 Dapplegran Ln., Rollings Hills Est, CA 90274

MOSIER, JOSHUA J., SPRING CREEK KNIFE WORKS, PO Box 442/802 6th St., Edgar, NE 68935
Specialties: Working straight and folding knives of his designs with customer specs. **Patterns:** Hunters, utilities, locking liner folders, kitchen and camp knives. **Technical:** Forges and grinds 5160, W2, L6, simple carbon steels and his own Damascus, uses some antique materials, provides a history of the materials used in each knife. **Prices:** $55 and up. **Remarks:** Part-time maker, sold first knife in 1986. **Mark:** SCKW.

MOSSER, GARY E., 11827 NE 102nd Place, Kirkland, WA 98033-5170, Phone: 425-827-2279
Specialties: Working knives. **Patterns:** Hunters, skinners, camp knives, some art knives. **Technical:** Stock removal method; prefers ATS-34. **Prices:** $100 to $250; special orders and art knives are higher. **Remarks:** Part-time maker; first knife sold in 1976. **Mark:** Name.

MOULTON, DUSTY, 135 Hillview Lane, Loudon, TN 37774, Phone: 865-408-9779
Specialties: Fancy and working straight knives. **Patterns:** Hunters, fighters, fantasy and miniatures. **Technical:** Grinds ATS-34 and Damascus. **Prices:** $300 to $2000. **Remarks:** Full-time maker; first knife sold in 1991. **Mark:** Last name. **Other:** Now doing engraving on own knives as well as other makers.

MOUNT, DON, 4574 Little Finch Ln., Las Vegas, NV 89115, Phone: 702-531-2925
Specialties: High-tech working and using straight knives of his design. **Patterns:** Bowies, fighters and utility/camp knives. **Technical:** Uses 440C and ATS-34. **Prices:** $150 to $300; some to $1000. **Remarks:** Part-time maker; first knife sold in 1985. **Mark:** Name below a woodpecker.

MOUNTAIN HOME KNIVES, PO Box 167, Jamul, CA 91935, Phone: 619-669-0833
Specialties: High-quality working straight knives. **Patterns:** Hunters, fighters, skinners, tantos, utility and fillet knives, Bowies and san-mai Damascus Bowies. **Technical:** Hollow-grind 440C by hand. Feature linen Micarta handles, nickel-silver handle bolts and handmade sheaths. **Prices:** $65 to $270. **Remarks:** Company owned by Jim English. **Mark:** Mountain Home Knives.

MOYER, RUSS, HC 36 Box 57C, Havre, MT 59501, Phone: 406-395-4423
Specialties: Working knives to customer specs. **Patterns:** Hunters, Bowies and survival knives. **Technical:** Forges W2. **Prices:** $150 to $350. **Remarks:** Part-time maker; first knife sold in 1976. **Mark:** Initials in logo.

MULLER, JODY AND PAT, PO Box 35, Pittsburg, MO 65724, Phone: 417-852-4306/417-752-3260
Specialties: Hand engraving, carving and inlays, fancy folders. One-of-a-kind personal carry knives with billfold cases, cleavers. **Patterns:** One-of-

custom knifemakers

a-kind fixed blades and folders in all styles. **Technical:** Forges patterned Damascus. **Prices:** $200 and up. **Remarks:** Son and father team of part-time makers. Jody made first knife at age 12. Now does fine hand-engraving, carving and inlay. **Mark:** Muller Forge in script. **Other:** Cross reference Muller Forge.

MULLIN, STEVE, 500 Snowberry Lane, Sandpoint, ID 83864, Phone: 208-263-7492
Specialties: Damascus period pieces and folders. **Patterns:** Full range of folders, hunters and Bowies. **Technical:** Forges and grinds O1, D2, 154CM and his own Damascus. Engraves. **Prices:** $100 to $2000. **Remarks:** Full-time maker; first knife sold in 1975. Sells line of using knives under Pack River Knife Co. **Mark:** Full name, city and state.

MUNROE, DERYK C., PO Box 3454, Bozeman, MT 59772

MURRAY, BILL, 1632 Rio Mayo, Green Valley, AZ 85614

MURSKI, RAY, 12129 Captiva Ct., Reston, VA 22091-1204, Phone: 703-264-1102
Specialties: Fancy working/using folders of his design. **Patterns:** Hunters, slip-joint folders and utility/camp knives. **Technical:** Grinds CPM-3V **Prices:** $125-$500. **Remarks:** Spare-time maker; first knife sold in 1996. **Mark:** Etched name with serial number under name.

MYERS, PAUL, 644 Maurice St., Wood River, IL 62095, Phone: 618-258-1707
Specialties: Fancy working straight knives and folders. **Patterns:** Full range of folders, straight hunters and Bowies; tie tacks; knife and fork sets. **Technical:** Grinds D2, 440C, ATS-34 and 154CM. **Prices:** $100 to $350; some to $3000. **Remarks:** Full-time maker; first knife sold in 1974. **Mark:** Initials with setting sun on front; name and number on back.

n

NATEN, GREG, 1804 Shamrock Way, Bakersfield, CA 93304-3921
Specialties: Fancy and working/using folders of his design. **Patterns:** Fighters, hunters and locking folders. **Technical:** Grinds 440C, ATS-34 and CPM440V. Heat-treats; prefers desert ironwood, stag and mother-of-pearl. Designs and sews leather sheaths for straight knives. **Prices:** $175 to $600; some to $950. **Remarks:** Spare-time maker; first knife sold in 1992. **Mark:** Last name above battle-ax, handmade.

NAVAGATO, ANGELO, 5 Commercial Apt 2, Camp Hill, PA 17011

NEALEY, IVAN F. (FRANK), Anderson Dam Rd., Box 65, HC #87, Mt. Home, ID 83647, Phone: 208-587-4060
Specialties: Working straight knives in standard patterns. **Patterns:** Hunters, skinners and utility knives. **Technical:** Grinds D2, 440C and 154CM. **Prices:** $90 to $135; some higher. **Remarks:** Part-time maker; first knife sold in 1975. **Mark:** Name.

NEALY, BUD, 1439 Poplar Valley Rd., Stroudsburg, PA 18360, Phone: 570-402-1018, Fax: 570-402-1019
Specialties: Original design concealment knives with designer multi-concealment sheath system. **Patterns:** Concealment knives, boots, combat and collector pieces. **Technical:** Grinds ATS-34; uses Damascus. **Prices:** $200 to $2500. **Remarks:** Full-time maker; first knife sold in 1980. **Mark:** Name, city, state or signature.

NEDVED, DAN, 206 Park Dr., Kalispell, MT 59901, Phone: 406-752-5060
Specialties: Slip joint folders, liner locks, straight knives. **Patterns:** Mostly traditional or modern blend with traditional lines. **Technical:** Grinds ATS34, 440C, 1095 and uses other makers Damascus. **Prices:** $95 and up. Mostly in the $150 to $200 range. **Remarks:** Part-time maker, averages 2 a month. **Mark:** Dan Nedved or Nedved with serial # on opposite side.

NEELY, GREG, 5419 Pine St., Bellaire, TX 77401, Phone: 713-991-2677
Specialties: Traditional patterns and his own patterns for work and/or collecting. **Patterns:** Hunters, Bowies and utility/camp knives. **Technical:** Forges own Damascus, 1084, 5160 and some tool steels. Differentially tempers. **Prices:** $225 to $1200. **Remarks:** Part-time maker; first knife sold in 1987. **Mark:** Last name or interlocked initials, MS.

NEILSON, J., RR 2 Box 16, Wyalusing, PA 18853, Phone: 570-746-4944
Specialties: Working and collectable fixed blade knives. **Patterns:** Hunter/fighters, Bowies, neck knives and daggers. **Technical:** Flat grinds, 1084, 5160, maker's own Damascus and occasionally 440C. **Prices:** $150-$800. **Remarks:** Full-time maker, first knife sold in 2000. Doing business as Neilson's Mountain Hollow. **Mark:** J. Neilson. **Other:** Each knife comes with a sheath by Tess.

NELSON, KEN, 11059 Hwy 73, Pittsville, WI 54466, Phone: 715-884-6448
Specialties: Working straight knives, period pieces. **Patterns:** Utility, hunters, dirks, daggers, throwers, hawks, axes, swords, and pole arms. **Technical:** Forges 5160, 52100, W2, 10xx, L6, and own Damascus. Multiple and differential heat treating. **Prices:** $50 to $350, some to $3000. **Remarks:** Part-time maker. First knife sold in 1995. Doing business as Iron Wolf Forge. Member of ABS. **Mark:** Stylized wolf paw print.

NELSON, DR. CARL, 2500 N Robison Rd., Texarkana, TX 75501

NELSON, TOM, PO Box 2298, Wilropark 1731, Gauteng, SOUTH AFRICA

NELSON, BOB, 21 Glen Rd., Sparta, NJ 07871

NETO JR., NELSON AND DE CARVALHO, HENRIQUE M., R. Joao Margarido, No. 20-V, Guerra, Braganca Paulista, SP-12900-000, BRAZIL, Phone: 011-7843-6889, Fax: 011-7843-6889
Specialties: Straight knives and folders. **Patterns:** Bowies, katanas, jambyias and others. **Technical:** Forges high-carbon steels. **Prices:** $70 to $3000. **Remarks:** Full-time makers; first knife sold in 1990. **Mark:** HandN.

NEUHAEUSLER, ERWIN, Heiligenangerstrasse 15, 86179 Augsburg, GERMANY, Phone: 0821/81 49 97
Specialties: Using straight knives of his design. **Patterns:** Hunters, boots, Bowies. **Technical:** Grinds ATS-34, RWL-34 and Damascus. **Prices:** $200 to $750. **Remarks:** Spare-time maker; first knife sold in 1991. **Mark:** Etched logo, last name and city.

NEVLING, MARK, BURR OAK KNIVES, PO Box 9, Hume, IL 61932, Phone: 217-887-2522
Specialties: Straight knives and folders of his own design. **Patterns:** Hunters, fighters, Bowies, folders, and small executive knives. **Technical:** Convex grinds, Forges, uses only high-carbon and Damascus. **Prices:** $200 - $2000. **Remarks:** Full-time maker, first knife sold 1988.

NEWCOMB, CORBIN, 628 Woodland Ave., Moberly, MO 65270, Phone: 660-263-4639
Specialties: Working straight knives and folders; period pieces. **Patterns:** Hunters, axes, Bowies, buckskinned blades and boots. **Technical:** Hollow-grinds D2, 440C and 154CM; prefers natural handle materials. Makes own Damascus; offers cable Damascus. **Prices:** $100 to $500. **Remarks:** Full-time maker; first knife sold in 1982. Doing business as Corbin Knives. **Mark:** First name and serial number.

NEWHALL, TOM, 3602 E 42nd Stravenue, Tucson, AZ 85713, Phone: 520-721-0562

NEWTON, RON, 223 Ridge Ln., London, AR 72847, Phone: 479-293-3001
Specialties: Mosaic Damascus folders with accelerated actions. **Patterns:** One-of-a-kind. **Technical:** 1084-15N20 steels used in his mosaic Damascus steels. **Prices:** $1000 to $5000. **Remarks:** Also making antique Bowie repros and various fixed blades. **Mark:** All capital letters in NEWTON "Western Invitation" font.

NEWTON, LARRY, 1758 Pronghorn Ct., Jacksonville, FL 32225, Phone: 904-221-2340, Fax: 904-220-4098
Specialties: Traditional and slender high-grade gentlemen's automatic folders, locking liner type tactical, and working straight knives. **Patterns:** Front release locking folders, interframes, hunters, and skinners. **Technical:** Grinds Damascus, ATS-34, 440C and D2. **Prices:** Folders start at $350, straights start at $150. **Remarks:** Spare-time maker; first knife sold in 1989. **Mark:** Last name.

NICHOLSON, R. KENT, PO Box 204, Phoenix, MD 21131, Phone: 410-323-6925
Specialties: Large using knives. **Patterns:** Bowies and camp knives in the Moran-style. **Technical:** Forges W2, 9260, 5160; makes Damascus. **Prices:** $150 to $995. **Remarks:** Part-time maker; first knife sold in 1984. **Mark:** Name.

NIELSON, JEFF V., PO Box 365, Monroe, UT 84754, Phone: 801-527-4242
Specialties: Classic knives of his design and to customer specs. **Patterns:** Fighters, hunters, locking folders; miniatures. **Technical:** Grinds 440C stainless and Damascus. **Prices:** $100 to $1200. **Remarks:** Part-time maker; first knife sold in 1991. **Mark:** Name, location.

NIEMUTH, TROY, 3143 North Ave., Sheboygan, WI 53083, Phone: 414-452-2927
Specialties: Period pieces and working/using straight knives of his design and to customer specs. **Patterns:** Hunters and utility/camp knives. **Technical:** Grinds 440C, 1095 and A2. **Prices:** $85 to $350; some to $500. **Remarks:** Full-time maker; first knife sold in 1995. **Mark:** Etched last name.

NILSSON, JOHNNY WALKER, Tingsstigen 11, SE-133 33 Arvidsjaur, SWEDEN, Phone: 46-960-130-48
Specialties: High-end hand-carved and engraved Sami-style horn knives. **Patterns:** Nordic and Scandinavian-styles. **Technical:** Grinds carbon and Damascus steels himself as of 2003. Uses Damascus forged to specification by Conny Persson, Kaj Embretsen, Mattias Styrefors. **Prices:** $650-$2500. **Remarks:** Nordic (five countries) champion of horn knives for many years. Yearly award in his name in future Nordic Championships. Inspired by the 10,000-year-old Sami culture, he combines traditional designs and techniques with his own innovations. Handles in Arctic burls and reindeer horn, bark dye, bark and pewter spacers. Engraved horn sheaths with wood and horn inlays, 3D inlays, cutouts and filework. Full-time maker since 1988. **Mark:** JN.

NISHIUCHI, MELVIN S., 6121 Forest Park Dr., Las Vegas, NV 89156, Phone: 702-438-2327
Specialties: Collectable quality using/working knives. **Patterns:** Locking liner folders, fighters, hunters and fancy personal knives. **Technical:** Grinds ATS-34 and Devin Thomas Damascus; prefers semi-precious stone and exotic natural handle materials. **Prices:** $375-$2000. **Remarks:** Part-time maker; first knife sold in 1985. **Mark:** Circle with a line above it.

NIX, ROBERT T., 4194 Cadillac, Wayne, MI 48184, Phone: 734-729-6468
Specialties: Hunters, skinners, art, Bowie, camp/survival/boot folders. Most are file worked. Custom leather work available also, mainly sheaths/ overlays, inlays, tooling, combinations of material/leather, micarta, wood, kydex, nylon. **Technical:** Stock removal, ATS-34, stainless Damascus, 440C, 420V, 440V, BG42, D2, 01, carbon Damascus. Every blade gets Rockwelled. Likes the natural handle materials best, but will use anything available; ivory, bone, horn, pearl, stabilized woods, micarta. **Prices:** Knives from $125 to $2500. Sheaths from $40 to $400. **Remarks:** Part-time maker, first knife sold in 1993. Make each piece as if it were for me. **Mark:** R.T. Nix in script or Nix in bold face.

NOLEN, R.D. AND STEVE, 1110 Lakeshore Dr., Estes Park, CO 80517-7113, Phone: 970-586-5814, Fax: 970-586-8827
Specialties: Working knives; display pieces. **Patterns:** Wide variety of straight knives, butterflies and buckles. **Technical:** Grind D2, 440C and 154CM. Offer filework; make exotic handles. **Prices:** $150 to $800; some higher. **Remarks:** Full-time makers; first knife sold in 1968. Steve is third generation maker. **Mark:** NK in oval logo.

NORDELL, INGEMAR, Skarpå 2103, 82041 Färila, SWEDEN, Phone: 0651-23347
Specialties: Classic working and using straight knives. **Patterns:** Hunters, Bowies and fighters. **Technical:** Forges and grinds ATS-34, D2 and Sandvik. **Prices:** $120 to $1500. **Remarks:** Part-time maker; first knife sold in 1985. **Mark:** Initials or name.

NOREN, DOUGLAS E., 14676 Boom Rd., Springlake, MI 49456, Phone: 616-842-4247
Specialties: Hand forged blades, custom built and made to order. Hand file work, carving and casting. Stag and stacked handles. Replicas of Scagel and Joseph Rogers. Hand tooled custom made sheaths. **Technical:** 5160, 52100 and 1084 steel. **Prices:** Start at $250. **Remarks:** Sole authorship, works in all mediums, ABS journey man msn., all knives come with a custom hand-tooled sheath. Also makes anvils. **Other:** Enjoy the challenge and meeting people.

NORFLEET, ROSS W., 3947 Tanbark Rd., Richmond, VA 23235, Phone: 804-276-4169
Specialties: Classic, traditional and working/using knives of his design or in standard patterns. **Patterns:** Hunters and folders. **Technical:** Hollow-grinds 440C and ATS-34. **Prices:** $150 to $550. **Remarks:** Part-time maker; first knife sold in 1992. **Mark:** Last name.

NORRIS, DON, 8710 N Hollybrook, Tucson, AZ 85742, Phone: 520-744-2494
Specialties: Classic and traditional working/using straight knives and folders of his design, or to customer specs etc. **Patterns:** Bowies, daggers, fighters, hunters and utility/camp knives. **Technical:** Grinds and forges Damascus; grinds ATS-34 and 440C. Cast sterling guards and bolsters on Bowies. **Prices:** $350 to $2000, some to $3500. **Remarks:** Full-time maker; first knife sold in 1990. Doing business as Norris Custom Knives. **Mark:** Last name.

NORTON, DON, 7517 Mountain Quail Dr., Las Vegas, NV 89131, Phone: 702-648-5036
Specialties: Fancy and plain straight knives. **Patterns:** Hunters, small Bowies, tantos, boot knives, fillets. **Technical:** Prefers 440C, Micarta, exotic woods and other natural handle materials. Hollow-grinds all knives except fillet knives. **Prices:** $185 to $2800; average is $200. **Remarks:** Full-time maker; first knife sold in 1980. **Mark:** Full name, Hsi Shuai, city, state.

NOTT, RON P., PO Box 281, Summerdale, PA 17093, Phone: 717-732-2763
Specialties: High-art folders and some straight knives. **Patterns:** Scale release folders. **Technical:** Grinds ATS-34, 416 and nickel-silver. Engraves, inlays gold. **Prices:** $250 to $3000. **Remarks:** Full-time maker; first knife sold in 1993. Doing business as Knives By Nott, customer engraving. **Mark:** First initial, last name and serial number.

NOWLAND, RICK, 3677 E Bonnie Rd., Waltonville, IL 62894, Phone: 618-279-3170
Specialties: Fancy single blade slip joints and trappers using Damascus and Mokume. **Patterns:** Uses several Remington patterns and also his own designs. **Technical:** Uses ATS-34, 440C; forges his own Damascus; makes Mokume. **Prices:** Start at $200. **Remarks:** Part-time maker; first knife sold in 1986. **Mark:** Last name.

NUNN, GREGORY, HC64 Box 2107, Castle Valley, UT 84532, Phone: 435-259-8607
Specialties: High-art working and using knives of his design; new edition knife with handle made from anatomized dinosaur bone - first ever made. **Patterns:** Flaked stone knives. **Technical:** Uses gem-quality agates, jaspers and obsidians for blades. **Prices:** $250 to $2300. **Remarks:** Full-time maker; first knife sold in 1989. **Mark:** Name, knife and edition numbers, year made.

O

OBENAUF, MIKE, 355 Sandy Ln., Vine Grove, KY 40175, Phone: 270-828-4138/270-877-6300
Specialties: Tactical and gentleman's type folders, tactical fixed blades. **Technical:** Grinds CPM Steels, Damascus, etc. **Prices:** $275 and up. **Remarks:** Full-time maker since 2000. First knife sold in 2000. **Mark:** OBENAUF engraved or stamped.

OBRIEN, GEORGE, 22511 Tullis Trails Ct., Katy, TX 77494-8265

OCHS, CHARLES F., 124 Emerald Lane, Largo, FL 33771, Phone: 727-536-3827, Fax: 727-536-3827
Specialties: Working knives; period pieces. **Patterns:** Hunters, fighters, Bowies, buck skinners and folders. **Technical:** Forges 52100, 5160 and his own Damascus. **Prices:** $150 to $1800; some to $2500. **Remarks:** Full-time maker; first knife sold in 1978. **Mark:** OX Forge.

O'DELL, CLYDE, 176 Ouachita 404, Camden, AR 71701, Phone: 870-574-2754
Specialties: Working knives. **Patterns:** Hunters, camp knives, Bowies, daggers, tomahawks. **Technical:** Forges 5160 and 1084. **Prices:** Starting at $175. **Remarks:** Spare-time maker. **Mark:** Last name.

ODGEN, RANDY W., 10822 Sage Orchard, Houston, TX 77089, Phone: 713-481-3601

ODOM, VIC, PO Box 572, North, SC 29112, Phone: 803-247-5614
Specialties: Forged knives and tomahawks; stock removal knives. **Patterns:** Hunters, Bowies. **Prices:** $50 and up. **Mark:** Steel stamp "ODOM" and etched "Odom Forge North, SC" plus a serial number.

OGDEN, BILL, OGDEN KNIVES, PO Box 52, Avis AVIS, PA 17721, Phone: 570-753-5568
Specialties: One-of-a-kind, liner-lock folders, hunters, skinners, minis. **Technical:** Grinds ATS-34, 440-C, D2, 52100, Damascus, natural and unnatural handle materials, hand-stitched custom sheaths. **Prices:** $50 and up. **Remarks:** Part-time maker since 1992. **Marks:** Last name or "OK" stamp (Ogden Knives).

OGLETREE JR., BEN R., 2815 Israel Rd., Livingston, TX 77351, Phone: 409-327-8315
Specialties: Working/using straight knives of his design. **Patterns:** Hunters, kitchen and utility/camp knives. **Technical:** Grinds ATS-34, W1 and 1075; heat-treats. **Prices:** $200 to $400. **Remarks:** Part-time maker; first knife sold in 1955. **Mark:** Last name, city and state in oval with a tree on either side.

O'HARE, SEAN, PO Box 374, Fort Simpson, NT, CANADA X0E 0N0, Phone: 867-695-2619
Specialties: Fixed blade hunters and tactical knives. **Patterns:** Neck knives to larger hunter and tactical knives. **Technical:** Stock removal, full and hidden tang knives. **Prices:** $115 USD to $300 USD. **Remarks:** Strives to balance aesthetics, functionality and durability. **Mark:** 1st is "OHARE KNIVES", 2nd is "NWT CANADA".

OLIVE, MICHAEL E., HC 78 Box 442, Leslie, AR 72645, Phone: 870-363-4452

custom knifemakers

OLIVER, TODD D., RR5 Box 659, Spencer, IN 47460, Phone: 812-829-1762
Specialties: Damascus hunters and daggers. High-carbon as well. **Patterns:** Ladder, twist random. **Technical:** Sole author of all his blades. **Prices:** $350 and up. **Remarks:** Learned bladesmithing from Jim Batson at the ABS school and Damascus from Billy Merritt in Indiana. **Mark:** T.D. Oliver Spencer IN. **Other:** Two crossed swords and a battle ax.

OLLER, VINCE, dba OMEGA TACTICAL RESOURCES, LLC, PO Box 835072, Miami, FL 33283-5072
Specialties: Custom and production knives; firearm & CQC training; adventure gear and electronics; firearms accessories.

OLOFSON, CHRIS, 29 KNIVES, 1 Kendall SQ Bldg. 600, Cambridge, MA 02139, Phone: 617-492-0451

OLSON, DARROLD E., PO Box 1539, Springfield, OR 97477, Phone: 541-726-8300/541-914-7238
Specialties: Straight knives and folders of his design and to customer specs. **Patterns:** Hunters, liner locks and locking folders. **Technical:** Grinds 440C, ATS-34 and 154CM. Uses anodized titanium; sheaths wet-molded. **Prices:** $150 to $350. **Remarks:** Part-time maker; first knife sold in 1989. **Mark:** Etched logo, year, type of steel and name.

OLSON, WAYNE C., 890 Royal Ridge Dr., Bailey, CO 80421, Phone: 303-816-9486
Specialties: High-tech working knives. **Patterns:** Hunters to folding lockers; some integral designs. **Technical:** Grinds 440C, 154CM and ATS-34; likes hand-finishes; precision-fits stainless steel fittings—no solder, no nickel silver. **Prices:** $275 to $600; some to $3000. **Remarks:** Part-time maker; first knife sold in 1979. **Mark:** Name, maker.

OLSON, ROD, Box 5973, High River, AB, CANADA T1V 1P6, Phone: 403-652-2744, Fax: 403-646-5838
Specialties: Lockback folders with gold toothpicks. **Patterns:** Locking folders. **Technical:** Grinds ATS-34 blades and spring - filework- 14kt bolsters and liners. **Prices:** Mid range. **Remarks:** Part-time maker; first knife sold in 1979. **Mark:** Last name on blade.

OLSZEWSKI, STEPHEN, 1820 Harkney Hill Rd., Coventry, RI 02816, Phone: 401-397-4774
Specialties: Lock back, liner locks, automatics (art knives). **Patterns:** One-of-a-kind art knives specializing in figurals. **Technical:** Damascus steel, titanium file worked liners, fossil ivory and pearl. **Prices:** $1800 to $6500. **Remarks:** Will custom build to your specifications. **Other:** Quality work with guarantee. **Mark:** SCO inside fish symbol. Also "Olszewski".

O'MALLEY, DANIEL, 4338 Evanston Ave. N, Seattle, WA 98103, Phone: 206-527-0315
Specialties: Custom chef's knives. **Remarks:** Making knives since 1997.

ONION, KENNETH J., 47-501 Hui Kelu St., Kaneohe, HI 96744, Phone: 808-239-1300, Fax: 429-4840 (cell)
Specialties: Mostly folders featuring "speed safe", some fixed blades and miscellany. **Patterns:** Hybrid, art, fighter, utility. **Technical:** S-30X, BG-42, cowey Y, Damascus. **Prices:** $500 to $15,000. **Remarks:** Full-time maker; designer, first knife sold in 1991. **Mark:** Name and state.

ORTEGA, BEN M., 165 Dug Rd., Wyoming, PA 18644, Phone: 717-696-3234

ORTON, RICH, 3625 Fleming St., Riverside, CA 92509, Phone: 909-685-3019
Specialties: Collectible folders, using and collectible straight knives. **Patterns:** Wharncliffe, gents, tactical, boot, neck knives, bird and trout, hunters, camp, Bowie. **Technical:** Grinds ATS-34, Jim Fergeson Damascus titanium liners, bolsters, anodize, lots of filework, jigged and picked bone, giraffe bone. Scrimshaw on some. **Prices:** Folders $300 to $600; straight $100 to $750. **Remarks:** Full-time maker; first knife sold in 1992. Doing business as Orton Knife Works. Now making folders. **Mark:** Rich Orton (maker) Riverside, CA.

OSBORNE, WARREN, 215 Edgefield, Waxahachie, TX 75165, Phone: 972-935-0899, Fax: 972-937-9004
Specialties: Investment grade collectible, interframes, one-of-a-kinds; unique locking mechanisms. **Patterns:** Folders; bolstered and interframes; conventional lockers, front lockers and back lockers; some slip-joints; some high-art pieces; fighters. **Technical:** Grinds ATS-34, 440 and 154; some Damascus and CPM400V. **Prices:** $400 to $2000; some to $4000. Interframes $650 to $1500. **Remarks:** Full-time maker; first knife sold in 1980. **Mark:** Last name in boomerang logo.

OSBORNE, DONALD H., 5840 N McCall, Clovis, CA 93611, Phone: 559-299-9483, Fax: 559-298-1751
Specialties: Traditional working using straight knives and folder of his design. **Patterns:** Working straight knives, Bowies, hunters, camp knives and folders. **Technical:** Forges carbon steels and makes Damascus. Grinds ATS-34, 154CM, and 440C. **Prices:** $150 and up. **Remarks:** Part-time maker. **Mark:** Last name logo and J.S.

OSTERMAN, DANIEL E., 1644 W. 10th, Junction City, OR 97448, Phone: 541-998-1503
Specialties: One-third scale copies of period pieces, museum class miniatures. **Patterns:** Antique Bowies. **Technical:** Grinds all cutlery grade steels, engraves, etches, inlays and overlays. **Remarks:** Full-time maker; first miniature knife sold in 1975. **Mark:** Initials.

OTT, FRED, 1257 Rancho Durango Rd., Durango, CO 81303, Phone: 970-375-9669
Patterns: Bowies, camp knives and hunters. **Technical:** Forges 1084 Damascus **Prices:** $150 to $800. **Remarks:** Full-time maker. **Mark:** Last name.

OVEREYNDER, T.R., 1800 S. Davis Dr., Arlington, TX 76013, Phone: 817-277-4812, Fax: 817-277-4812
Specialties: Highly finished collector-grade knives. **Patterns:** Fighters, Bowies, daggers, locking folders, slip-joints and 90 percent collector-grade interframe folders. **Technical:** Grinds D2, BG-42, S-60V, S-30V, 154CM, vendor supplied Damascus. Has been making titanium-frame folders since 1977. **Prices:** $500 to $1500; some to $7000. **Remarks:** Full-time maker; first knife sold in 1977. Doing business as TRO Knives. **Mark:** T.R. OVEREYNDER KNIVES, city and state.

OWENS, DONALD, 2274 Lucille Ln., Melbourne, FL 32935, Phone: 321-254-9765

OWENS, JOHN, 14500 CR 270, Nathrop, CO 81236, Phone: 719-395-0870
Specialties: Hunters. **Prices:** $175 to $235; some to $650. **Remarks:** Spare-time maker. **Mark:** Last name.

OWNBY, JOHN C., 3316 Springbridge Ln., Plano, TX 75025
Specialties: Hunters, utility/camp knives. **Patterns:** Hunters, locking folders and utility/camp knives. **Technical:** 440C, D2 and ATS-34. All blades are flat ground. Prefers natural materials for handles—exotic woods, horn and antler. **Prices:** $150 to $350; some to $500. **Remarks:** Part-time maker; first knife sold in 1993. **Mark:** Name, city, state. **Other:** Doing business as John C. Ownby Handmade Knives.

OYSTER, LOWELL R., 543 Grant Rd., Corinth, ME 04427, Phone: 207-884-8663
Specialties: Traditional and original designed multi-blade slip-joint folders. **Patterns:** Hunters, minis, camp and fishing knives. **Technical:** Grinds O1; heat-treats. **Prices:** $55 to $450; some to $750. **Remarks:** Full-time maker; first knife sold in 1981. **Mark:** A scallop shell.

p

PACHI, FRANCESCO, Via Pometta, 1, 17046 Sassello (SV), ITALY, Phone: 019 720086, Fax: 019 720086
Specialties: Folders and straight knives of his design. **Patterns:** Utility, hunters and skinners. **Technical:** Grinds RWL-34, CPM S30V and Damascus. **Prices:** $800 to $3500. **Remarks:** Full-time maker; first knife sold in 1991. **Mark:** Logo with last name.

PACKARD, BOB, PO Box 311, Elverta, CA 95626, Phone: 916-991-5218
Specialties: Traditional working/using straight knives of his design and to customer specs. **Patterns:** Hunters, fishing knives, utility/camp knives. **Technical:** Grinds ATS-34, 440C; Forges 52100, 5168 and cable Damascus. **Prices:** $75 to $225. **Mark:** Engraved name and year.

PADGETT JR., EDWIN L., 340 Vauxhall St., New London, CT 06320-3838, Phone: 860-443-2938
Specialties: Skinners and working knives of any design. **Patterns:** Straight and folding knives. **Technical:** Grinds ATS-34 or any tool steel upon request. **Prices:** $50 to $300. **Mark:** Name.

PADILLA, GARY, PO Box 6928, Auburn, CA 95604, Phone: 530-888-6992
Specialties: Native American influenced working and using straight knives of his design. **Patterns:** Hunters, kitchen knives, utility/camp knives and obsidian ceremonial knives. **Technical:** Grinds 440C, ATS-34, O1 and Damascus. **Prices:** Generally $100-$200. **Remarks:** Part-time maker; first knife sold in 1977. Doing business as Bighorn Knifeworks. **Mark:** Stylized initials or name over company name.

PAGE, REGINALD, 6587 Groveland Hill Rd., Groveland, NY 14462, Phone: 716-243-1643
Specialties: High-art straight knives and one-of-a-kind folders of his design. **Patterns:** Hunters, locking folders and slip-joint folders. **Technical:** Forges O1, 5160 and his own Damascus. Prefers natural handle materials but will work with Micarta. **Remarks:** Spare-time maker; first knife sold in 1985. **Mark:** First initial, last name.

PAGE, LARRY, 1200 Mackey Scott Rd., Aiken, SC 29801-7620, Phone: 803-648-0001
Specialties: Working knives of his design. **Patterns:** Hunters, boots and fighters. **Technical:** Grinds ATS-34. **Prices:** Start at $85. **Remarks:** Part-time maker; first knife sold in 1983. **Mark:** Name, city and state in oval.

PALAZZO, TOM, 207-30 Jordon Dr., Bayside, NY 11360, Phone: 718-352-2170
Specialties: Fixed blades, custom sheaths, neck knives. **Patterns:** No fixed patterns. **Prices:** $150 and up.

PALMER, TAYLOR, TAYLOR-MADE SCENIC KNIVES INC., Box 97, Blanding, UT 84511, Phone: 435-678-2523
Specialties: Bronze carvings inside of blade area. **Prices:** $250 and up. **Mark:** Taylor Palmer Utah.

PANAK, PAUL S., 9000 Stanhope Kellogsville Rd., Kinsman, OH 44428, Phone: 330-876-8473
Specialties: Italian-styled knives. **Patterns:** Vintage-styled Italians, fighting folders and high art gothic-styles all with various mechanisms. **Technical:** Grinds ATS-34, 154 CM, 440C and Damascus. **Prices:** $800-$3000. **Remarks:** Full-time maker, first knife sold in 1998. **Mark:** "Burn".

PANKIEWICZ, PHILIP R., RFD #1, Waterman Rd., Lebanon, CT 06249
Specialties: Working straight knives. **Patterns:** Hunters, daggers, minis and fishing knives. **Technical:** Grinds D2, 440C and 154CM. **Prices:** $60 to $125; some to $250. **Remarks:** Spare-time maker; first knife sold in 1975. **Mark:** First initial in star.

PARDUE, MELVIN M., Rt. 1, Box 130, Repton, AL 36475, Phone: 334-248-2447
Specialties: Folders, collectable, combat, utility and tactical. **Patterns:** Lockback, liner lock, pushbutton; all blade and handle patterns. **Technical:** Grinds 154-CM, 440-C, 12-C-27. Forges Mokume and Damascus. Uses Titanium. **Prices:** $400 to $1600. **Remarks:** Full-time maker; Guild member, ABS member, AFC member. **Mark:** Mel Pardue or Pardue. **Other:** First knife made 1957; first knife sold professionally 1974.

PARDUE, JOE, PO Box 693, Spurger, TX 77660, Phone: 409-429-7074, Fax: 409-429-5657

PARKER, ROBERT NELSON, 5223 Wilhelm Rd. N.W., Rapid City, MI 49676, Fax: 248-545-8211
Specialties: Traditional working and using straight knives of his design. **Patterns:** Hunters, fighters, utility/camp knives; some Bowies. **Technical:** Grinds ATS-34;GB-42, forges 01, 530V, 5160, L6 hollow and flat grinds, full and hidden tangs. Hand-stitched leather sheaths. **Prices:** $225 to $500; some to $1000. **Remarks:** Full-time maker; first knife sold in 1986. **Mark:** Full name.

PARKER, CLIFF, 6350 Tulip Dr., Zephyrhills, FL 33544, Phone: 813-973-1682
Specialties: Damascus gent knives. **Patterns:** Locking liners, some straight knives. **Technical:** Mostly use 1095, 1084, 15N20, 203E and powdered steel. **Prices:** $300 to $1500. **Remarks:** Making own Damascus and specializing in mosaics; first knife sold in 1996. **Mark:** CP. **Other:** Full-time beginning in 2000.

PARKER, J.E., 11 Domenica Cir., Clarion, PA 16214, Phone: 814-226-4837
Specialties: Fancy/embellished, traditional and working straight knives of his design and to customer specs. Engraving and scrimshaw by the best in the business. **Patterns:** Bowies, hunters and liner lock folders. **Technical:** Grinds 440C, 440V, ATS-34 and nickel Damascus. Prefers mastodon, oosik, amber and malachite handle material. **Prices:** $75 to $5200. **Remarks:** Full-time maker; first knife sold in 1991. Doing business as Custom Knife. **Mark:** J E Parker and Clarion PA stamped or etched in blade.

PARKS, BLANE C., 15908 Crest Dr., Woodbridge, VA 22191, Phone: 703-221-4680
Specialties: Knives of his design. **Patterns:** Boots, Bowies, daggers, fighters, hunters, kitchen knives, locking and slip-joint folders, utility/camp knives, letter openers and friction folders. **Technical:** Grinds ATS-34, 440C, D2 and other carbon steels. Offers filework, silver wire inlay and wooden sheaths. **Prices:** Start at $250 and up. **Remarks:** Part-time maker; first knife sold in 1993. Doing business as B.C. Parks Knives. **Mark:** First and middle initials, last name.

PARKS, JOHN, 3539 Galilee Church Rd., Jefferson, GA 30549, Phone: 706-367-4916
Specialties: Traditional working and using straight knives of his design. **Patterns:** Trout knives, hunters and integral bolsters. **Technical:** Forges 1095 and 5168. **Prices:** $175 to $450; some to $650. **Remarks:** Part-time maker; first knife sold in 1989. **Mark:** Initials.

PARLER, THOMAS O., 11 Franklin St., Charleston, SC 29401, Phone: 803-723-9433

PARRISH, ROBERT, 271 Allman Hill Rd., Weaverville, NC 28787, Phone: 828-645-2864
Specialties: Heavy-duty working knives of his design or to customer specs. **Patterns:** Survival and duty knives; hunters and fighters. **Techni-**

cal: Grinds 440C, D2, O1 and commercial Damascus. **Prices:** $200 to $300; some to $6000. **Remarks:** Part-time maker; first knife sold in 1970. **Mark:** Initials connected, sometimes with city and state.

PARRISH III, GORDON A., 940 Lakloey Dr., North Pole, AK 99705, Phone: 907-488-0357
Specialties: Classic and high-art straight knives of his design and to customer specs. Working and using knives. **Patterns:** Bowies and hunters. **Technical:** Grinds tool steel and ATS-34. Uses mostly Alaskan handle materials. **Prices:** $150 to $1000. **Remarks:** Spare-time maker; first knife sold in 1980. **Mark:** Last name, state.

PARSONS, MICHAEL R., MCKEE KNIVES, 7042 McFarland Rd., Indianapolis, IN 46227, Phone: 317-784-7943
Specialties: Hand-forged fixed-blade knives, all fancy but all are useable knives. **Patterns:** Engraves, carves, wire inlay, and leather work. All knives one-of-a-kind. **Technical:** Blades forged from files, all work hand done. **Prices:** $350-$2000. **Mark:** McKee.

PASSMORE, JIMMY D., 316 SE Elm, Hoxie, AR 72433, Phone: 870-886-1922

PATRICK, BOB, 12642 24A Ave., S. Surrey, B.C., CANADA V4A 8H9, Phone: 604-538-6214, Fax: 604-888-2683
Specialties: Presentation pieces of his design only. **Patterns:** Bowies, push daggers, art pieces. **Technical:** D2, 5160, Damascus. **Prices:** Fair. **Remarks:** Full-time maker; first knife sold in 1987. Doing business as Crescent Knife Works. **Mark:** Logo with name and province or Crescent Knife Works.

PATRICK, PEGGY, PO Box 127, Brasstown, NC 28902, Phone: 828-837-7627
Specialties: Authentic period and Indian sheaths, braintan, rawhide, beads and quill work. **Technical:** Does own braintan, rawhide; uses only natural dyes for quills, old color beads.

PATRICK, CHUCK, PO Box 127, Brasstown, NC 28902, Phone: 828-837-7627
Specialties: Period pieces. **Patterns:** Hunters, daggers, tomahawks, pre-Civil War folders. **Technical:** Forges hardware, his own cable and Damascus, available in fancy pattern and mosaic. **Prices:** $150 to $1000; some higher. **Remarks:** Full-time maker. **Mark:** Hand-engraved name or flying owl.

PATRICK, WILLARD C., PO Box 5716, Helena,, MT 59604, Phone: 406-458-6552
Specialties: Working straight knives and one-of-a-kind art knives of his design or to customer specs. **Patterns:** Hunters, Bowies, fish, patch and kitchen knives. **Technical:** Grinds ATS-34, 1095, O1, A2 and Damascus. **Prices:** $85 to $350; some to $600. **Remarks:** Full-time maker; first knife sold in 1989. Doing business as Wil-A-Mar Cutlery. **Mark:** Shield with last name and a dagger.

PATTAY, RUDY, 510 E. Harrison St., Long Beach, NY 11561, Phone: 516-431-0847
Specialties: Fancy and working straight knives of his design. **Patterns:** Bowies, hunters, utility/camp knives. **Technical:** Hollow-grinds ATS-34, 440C, O1. Offers commercial Damascus, stainless steel soldered guards; fabricates guard and butt cap on lathe and milling machine. Heat-treats. Prefers synthetic handle materials. Offers hand-sewn sheaths. **Prices:** $100 to $350; some to $500. **Remarks:** Part-time maker; first knife sold in 1990. **Mark:** First initial, last name in sorcerer logo.

PATTERSON, PAT, Box 246, Barksdale, TX 78828, Phone: 830-234-3586
Specialties: Traditional fixed blades and liner lock folders. **Patterns:** Hunters and folders. **Technical:** Grinds 440C, ATS-34, D2, 01 and Damascus. **Prices:** $250 to $1000. **Remarks:** Full-time maker. First knife sold in 1991. **Mark:** Name and city.

PATTON, DICK AND ROB, 6803 View Ln., Nampa, ID 83687, Phone: 208-468-4123
Specialties: Custom Damascus, hand forged, fighting knives-Bowie and tactical. **Patterns:** Mini Bowie, Merlin Fighter, Mandrita Fighting Bowie. **Prices:** $100 to $2000.

PAULO, FERNANDES R., Raposo Tavares, No. 213, Lencois Paulista, 18680, Sao Paulo, BRAZIL, Phone: 014-263-4281
Specialties: An apprentice of Jose Alberto Paschoarelli, his designs are heavily based on the later designs. **Technical:** Grinds tool steels and stainless steels. Part-time knife maker. **Prices:** Start from $100. **Mark:** P.R.F.

PAWLOWSKI, JOHN R., 804 Iron Gate Ct., Newport News, VA 23602, Phone: 757-890-9098
Specialties: Traditional working and using straight knives and folders. **Patterns:** Hunters, Bowies, fighters and camp knives. **Technical:** Stock removal, grinds 440C, ATS34, 154CM and buys Damascus. **Prices:** $150 to $500, some higher. **Remarks:** Part-time maker, first knife sold in 1983. **Mark:** Early mark, name over attacking Eagle and Alaska. Current mark, name over attacking Eagle and Virginia.

PEAGLER, RUSS, PO Box 1314, Moncks Corner, SC 29461, Phone: 803-761-1008
Specialties: Traditional working straight knives of his design and to customer specs. **Patterns:** Hunters, fighters, boots. **Technical:** Hollow-grinds 440C, ATS-34 and O1; uses Damascus steel. Prefers bone handles. **Prices:** $85 to $300; some to $500. **Remarks:** Spare-time maker; first knife sold in 1983. **Mark:** Initials.

PEASE, W.D., 657 Cassidy Pike, Ewing, KY 41039, Phone: 606-845-0387
Specialties: Display-quality working folders. **Patterns:** Fighters, tantos and boots; locking folders and interframes. **Technical:** Grinds ATS-34 and commercial Damascus; has own side-release lock system. **Prices:** $500 to $1000; some to $3000. **Remarks:** Full-time maker; first knife sold in 1970. **Mark** First and middle initials, last name and state. W. D. Pease Kentucky.

PEELE, BRYAN, 219 Ferry St., PO Box 1363, Thompson Falls, MT 59873, Phone: 406-827-4633
Specialties: Fancy working and using knives of his design. **Patterns:** Hunters, Bowies and fighters. **Technical:** Grinds 440C, ATS-34, D2, O1 and commercial Damascus. **Prices:** $110 to $300; some to $900. **Remarks:** Part-time maker; first knife sold in 1985. **Mark:** The Elk Rack, full name, city, state.

PENDLETON, LLOYD, 24581 Shake Ridge Rd., Volcano, CA 95689, Phone: 209-296-3353, Fax: 209-296-3353
Specialties: Contemporary working knives in standard patterns. **Patterns:** Hunters, fighters and boots. **Technical:** Grinds 154CM and ATS-34; mirror finishes. **Prices:** $400 to $725; some to $2500. **Remarks:** Full-time maker; first knife sold in 1973. **Mark:** First initial, last name logo, city and state.

PENDRAY, ALFRED H., 13950 NE 20th St., Williston, FL 32696, Phone: 352-528-6124
Specialties: Working straight knives and folders; period pieces. **Patterns:** Fighters and hunters, axes, camp knives and tomahawks. **Technical:** Forges Wootz steel; makes his own Damascus; makes traditional knives from old files and rasps. **Prices:** $125 to $1000; some to $3500. **Remarks:** Part-time maker; first knife sold in 1954. **Mark:** Last initial in horseshoe logo.

PENFOLD, MICK, PENFOLD CUSTOM KNIVES, 5 Highview Close, Tremar, Cornwall PL14 5SJ, ENGLAND, Phone: 01579-345783
Specialties: Hunters, fighters, Bowies. **Technical:** Grinds 440C, ATS34, and Damascus. **Prices:** $150-$1200. **Remarks:** Full-time maker. First knives sold in 1999. **Mark:** Last names.

PENNINGTON, C.A., 163 Kainga Rd., Kainga Christchurch 8009, NEW ZEALAND, Phone: 03-3237292
Specialties: Classic working and collectors knives. Folders a specialty. **Patterns:** Classical styling for hunters and collectors. **Technical:** Forges his own all tool steel Damascus. Grinds D2 when requested. **Prices:** $240 to $2000. **Remarks:** Full-time maker; first knife sold in 1988. **Mark:** Name, country. **Other:** Color brochure $3.

PEPIOT, STEPHAN, 73 Cornwall Blvd., Winnipeg, Man., CANADA R3J-1E9, Phone: 204-888-1499
Specialties: Working straight knives in standard patterns. **Patterns:** Hunters and camp knives. **Technical:** Grinds 440C and industrial hack-saw blades. **Prices:** $75 to $125. **Remarks:** Spare-time maker; first knife sold in 1982. Not currently taking orders. **Mark:** PEP.

PERRY, JOHN, 9 South Harrell Rd., Mayflower, AR 72106, Phone: 501-470-3043
Specialties: Investment grade and working folders; some straight knives. **Patterns:** Front and rear lock folders, liner locks and hunters. **Technical:** Grinds CPM440V, D2 and making own Damascus. Offers filework. **Prices:** $375 to $950; some to $2500. **Remarks:** Part-time maker; first knife sold in 1990. Doing business as Perry Custom Knives. **Mark:** Initials or last name in high relief set in a diamond shape.

PERRY, CHRIS, 1654 W. Birch, Fresno, CA 93711, Phone: 209-498-2342
Specialties: Traditional working/using straight knives of his design. **Patterns:** Boots, hunters and utility/camp knives. **Technical:** Grinds ATS-34 and 416 ss fittings. **Prices:** $190 to $225. **Remarks:** Spare-time maker. **Mark:** Name above city and state.

PERRY, JOHNNY, PO Box 4666, Spartanburg, SC 29305-4666, Phone: 803-578-3533

PERRY, JIM, Hope Star, PO Box 648, Hope, AR 71801

PERSSON, CONNY, PL 588, 820 50 Loos, SWEDEN, Phone: +46 657 10305, Fax: +46 657 413 435
Specialties: Mosaic Damascus. **Patterns:** Mosaic Damascus. **Technical:** Straight knives and folders. **Prices:** $1000 and up. **Mark:** C. Persson.

PETEAN, FRANCISCO AND MAURICIO, R. Dr.Carlos de Carvalho Rosa, 52, Centro, Birigui, SP-16200-000, BRAZIL, Phone: 0186-424786
Specialties: Classic knives to customer specs. **Patterns:** Bowies, boots, fighters, hunters and utility knives. **Technical:** Grinds D6, 440C and high-carbon steels. Prefers natural handle material. **Prices:** $70 to $500. **Remarks:** Full-time maker; first knife sold in 1985. **Mark:** Last name, hand made.

PETERSEN, DAN L., 10610 SW 81st, Auburn, KS 66402, Phone: 785-256-2640
Specialties: Period pieces and forged integral hilts on hunters and fighters. **Patterns:** Texas-style Bowies, boots and hunters in high-carbon and Damascus steel. **Technical:** Austempers forged high-carbon blades. **Prices:** $200 to $3000. **Remarks:** First knife sold in 1978. **Mark:** Stylized initials, MS.

PETERSON, KAREN, THE PEN AND THE SWORD LTD., PO Box 290741, Brooklyn, NY 11229-0741, Phone: 718-382-4847, Fax: 718-376-5745

PETERSON, ELDON G., 260 Haugen Heights Rd., Whitefish, MT 59937, Phone: 406-862-2204
Specialties: Fancy and working folders, any size. **Patterns:** Lockback interframes, integral bolster folders, liner locks, and two-blades. **Technical:** Grinds 440C and ATS-34. Offers gold inlay work, gem stone inlays and engraving. **Prices:** $285 to $5000. **Remarks:** Full-time maker; first knife sold in 1974. **Mark:** Name, city and state.

PETERSON, CHRIS, Box 143, 2175 W. Rockyford, Salina, UT 84654, Phone: 801-529-7194
Specialties: Working straight knives of his design. **Patterns:** Large fighters, boots, hunters and some display pieces. **Technical:** Forges O1 and meteor. Makes and sells his own Damascus. Engraves, scrimshaws and inlays. **Prices:** $150 to $600; some to $1500. **Remarks:** Full-time maker; first knife sold in 1986. **Mark:** A drop in a circle with a line through it.

PETERSON, LLOYD (PETE) C., 64 Halbrook Rd., Clinton, AR 72031, Phone: 501-893-0000
Specialties: Miniatures, and mosaic folders. **Prices:** $250 and up. **Remarks:** Lead time is 6-8 months. **Mark:** Pete.

PFANENSTIEL, DAN, 1824 Lafayette Ave., Modesto, CA 95355, Phone: 209-575-5937
Specialties: Japanese tanto, swords. One-of-a-kind knives. **Technical:** Forges simple carbon steels, some Damascus. **Prices:** $200-$1000. **Mark:** Circle with wave inside.

PHILIPPE, D. A., PO Box 306, Cornish, NH 03746, Phone: 603-543-0662
Specialties: Traditional working straight knives. **Patterns:** Hunters, trout and bird, camp knives etc. **Technical:** Grinds ATS-34, 440c, A-2, Damascus, flat and hollow ground. Exotic woods and antler handles. Brass, nickel silver and stainless components. **Prices:** $125 - $800. **Remarks:** Full-time maker, first knife sold in 1984. **Mark:** First initial, last name.

PHILLIPS, JIM, PO Box 168, Williamstown, NJ 08094, Phone: 609-567-0695

PHILLIPS, RANDY, 759 E. Francis St., Ontario, CA 91761, Phone: 909-923-4381
Specialties: Hunters, collector-grade liner locks and high-art daggers. **Technical:** Grinds D2, 440C and 154CM; embellishes. **Prices:** Start at $200. **Remarks:** Part-time maker; first knife sold in 1981. Not currently taking orders. **Mark:** Name, city and state in eagle head.

PHILLIPS, DENNIS, 16411 West Bennet Rd., Independence, LA 70443, Phone: 985-878-8275
Specialties: Specializes in fixed blade military combat tacticals.

PHILLIPS, SCOTT C., 671 California Rd., Gouverneur, NY 13642, Phone: 315-287-1280
Specialties: Sheaths in leather. Fixed blade hunters, boot knives, Bowies, buck skinners (hand forged and stock removal). **Technical:** 440C, 5160, 1095 and 52100. **Prices:** Start at $125. **Remarks:** Part-time maker; first knife sold in 1993. **Mark:** Before "2000" as above after S Mangus.

PICKENS, SELBERT, Rt. 1, Box 216, Liberty, WV 25124, Phone: 304-586-2190
Specialties: Using knives. **Patterns:** Standard sporting knives. **Technical:** Stainless steels; stock removal method. **Prices:** Moderate. **Remarks:** Part-time maker. **Mark:** Name.

PIENAAR, CONRAD, 19A Milner Rd., Bloemfontein 9300, SOUTH AFRICA, Phone: 051 436 4180, Fax: 051 436 7400
Specialties: Fancy working and using straight knives and folders of his design, to customer specs and in standard patterns. **Patterns:** Hunters, locking folders, cleavers, kitchen and utility/camp knives. **Technical:** Grinds 12C27, D2 and ATS-34. Uses some Damascus. Scrimshaws; inlays gold. Knives come with wooden box and custom-made leather sheath. **Prices:** $300 to $1000. **Remarks:** Part-time maker; first knife sold

in 1981. Doing business as C.P. Knife maker. **Mark:** Initials and serial number. **Other:** Makes slip joint folders and liner locking folders.

PIERCE, HAROLD L., 106 Lyndon Lane, Louisville, KY 40222, Phone: 502-429-5136
Specialties: Working straight knives, some fancy. **Patterns:** Big fighters and Bowies. **Technical:** Grinds D2, 440C, 154CM; likes sub-hilts. **Prices:** $150 to $450; some to $1200. **Remarks:** Full-time maker; first knife sold in 1982. **Mark:** Last name with knife through the last initial.

PIERCE, RANDALL, 903 Wyndam, Arlington, TX 76017, Phone: 817-468-0138

PIERGALLINI, DANIEL E., 4011 N. Forbes Rd., Plant City, FL 33565, Phone: 813-754-3908
Specialties: Traditional and fancy straight knives and folders of his design or to customer's specs. **Patterns:** Hunters, fighters, three-fingered skinners, fillet, working and camp knives. **Technical:** Grinds 440C, O1, D2, ATS-34, some Damascus; forges his own mokume. Uses natural handle material. **Prices:** $250-$600; some to $1600. **Remarks:** Part-time maker; sold first knife in 1994. **Mark:** Last name, city, state or last name in script.

PIESNER, DEAN, 2633 Herrgott Rd., St. Clements ON, CANADA N0B 2M0, Phone: 519-699-4319, Fax: 519-699-5452
Specialties: Classic and period pieces of his design and to customer specs. **Patterns:** Bowies, skinners, fighters and swords. **Technical:** Forges 5160, 52100, steel Damascus and nickel-steel Damascus. Makes own mokume gane with copper, brass and nickel silver. Silver wire inlays in wood. **Prices:** Start at $150. **Remarks:** Full-time maker; first knife sold in 1990. **Mark:** First initial, last name, JS.

PIOREK, JAMES S., PO Box 335, Rexford, MT 59930, Phone: 406-889-5510
Specialties: True custom and semi-custom production (SCP), specialized concealment blades; advanced sheaths and tailored body harnessing systems. **Patterns:** Tactical/personal defense fighters, swords, utility and custom patterns. **Technical:** Grinds A2 and Talonite®; heat-treats. Sheaths: Kydex or Kydex-lined leather laminated or Kydex-lined with Rigger Coat™. Exotic materials available. **Prices:** $50 to $10,000. **Remarks:** Full-time maker. Doing business as Blade Rigger L.L.C. **Mark:** For true custom: Initials with abstract cutting edge and for SCP: Blade Rigger. **Other:** Martial artist and unique defense industry tools and equipment.

PITMAN, DAVID, PO Drawer 2566, Williston, ND 58802, Phone: 701-572-3325

PITT, DAVID F., 6812 Digger Pine Ln., Anderson, CA 96007, Phone: 530-357-2393
Specialties: Fixed blade, hunters and hatchets. Flat ground mirror finish. **Patterns:** Hatchets with gut hook, small gut hooks, guards, bolsters or guard less. **Technical:** Grinds A2, 440C, 154CM, ATS-34, D2. **Prices:** $150 to $750. **Remarks:** Guild member since 1982. **Mark:** Bear paw with name David F. Pitt.

PLUNKETT, RICHARD, 29 Kirk Rd., West Cornwall, CT 06796, Phone: 860-672-3419; Toll free: 888-KNIVES-8
Specialties: Traditional, fancy folders and straight knives of his design. **Patterns:** Slip-joint folders and small straight knives. **Technical:** Grinds O1 and stainless steel. Offers many different file patterns. **Prices:** $150 to $450. **Remarks:** Full-time maker; first knife sold in 1994. **Mark:** Signature and date under handle scales.

POLK, CLIFTON, 4625 Webber Creek Rd, Van Buren, AR 72956, Phone: 479-474-3828
Specialties: Fancy working folders. **Patterns:** Locking folders slip joints. **Technical:** Straight knives techical and automatic and two bladers. **Prices:** $200-$3000. **Mark:** Polk.

POLK, RUSTY, 5900 Wildwood Dr., Van Buren, AR 72956, Phone: 479-410-3661
Specialties: Skinner's, hunter's, Bowie's, fighter's and forging working knives fancy Damascus, hunting, Bowies, fighters daggers, boot knives and survival knives. **Patterns:** Drop point, and forge to shape. **Technical:** ATS-34, 440C, Damascus, D2, 51/60, 1084, 15N20, Damascus and do all his forging. **Prices:** $200-$1000. **Remarks:** R. Polk all hand made. **Mark:** R. Polk.

POLKOWSKI, AL, 8 Cathy Ct., Chester, NJ 07930, Phone: 908-879-6030
Specialties: High-tech straight knives and folders for adventurers and professionals. **Patterns:** Fighters, side-lock folders, boots and concealment knives. **Technical:** Grinds D2 and ATS-34; features satin and bead-blast finishes; Kydex sheaths. **Prices:** Start at $100. **Remarks:** Full-time maker; first knife sold in 1985. **Mark:** Full name, Handmade.

POLLOCK, WALLACE J., 806 Russet Vly Dr., Cedar Park, TX 78613
Specialties: Using knives, skinner, hunter, fighting, camp knives. **Patterns:** Use his own patterns or your. Traditional hunters, daggers, fighters, camp knives. **Technical:** Grinds ATS-34, D-2, BG-42, makes own Dam-

ascus, D-2, 0-1, ATS-34, prefer D-2, handles exotic wood, horn, bone, ivory. **Remarks:** Full-time maker, sold first knife 1973. **Prices:** $250 to $2500. **Mark:** Last name, maker, city/state.

POLZIEN, DON, 1912 Inler Suite-L, Lubbock, TX 79407, Phone: 806-791-0766
Specialties: Traditional Japanese-style blades; restores antique Japanese swords, scabbards and fittings. **Patterns:** Hunters, fighters, one-of-a-kind art knives. **Technical:** 1045-1050 carbon steels, 440C, D2, ATS-34, standard and cable Damascus. **Prices:** $150 to $2500. **Remarks:** Full-time maker. First knife sold in 1990. **Mark:** Oriental characters inside square border.

PONZIO, DOUG, 3212 93rd St., Pleasant Prairie, WI 53158, Phone: 262-694-3188
Specialties: Damascus - Gem stone handles. **Mark:** P.F.

POOLE, STEVE L., 200 Flintlock Trail, Stockbridge, GA 30281, Phone: 770-474-9154
Specialties: Traditional working and using straight knives and folders of his design, to customer specs and in standard patterns. **Patterns:** Bowies, fighters, hunters, utility and locking folders. **Technical:** Grinds ATS-34 and 440V; buys Damascus. Heat-treats; offers leatherwork. **Prices:** $85 to $350; some to $800. **Remarks:** Spare-time maker; first knife sold in 1991. **Mark:** Stylized first and last initials.

POOLE, MARVIN O., PO Box 552, Commerce, GA 30529, Phone: 803-225-5970
Specialties: Traditional working/using straight knives and folders of his design and in standard patterns. **Patterns:** Bowies, fighters, hunters, locking folders, bird and trout knives. **Technical:** Grinds 440C, D2, ATS-34. **Prices:** $50 to $150; some to $750. **Remarks:** Part-time maker; first knife sold in 1980. **Mark:** Last name, year, serial number.

POSKOCIL, HELMUT, Oskar Czeijastrasse 2, A-3340 Waidhofen/Ybbs, AUSTRIA, Phone: 0043-7442-54519, Fax: 0043-7442-54519
Specialties: High-art and classic straight knives and folders of his design. **Patterns:** Bowies, daggers, hunters and locking folders. **Technical:** Grinds ATS-34 and stainless and carbon Damascus. Hardwoods, fossil ivory, horn and amber for handle material; silver wire and gold inlays; silver butt caps. Offers engraving and scrimshaw. **Prices:** $350 to $850; some to $3500. **Remarks:** Part-time maker; first knife sold in 1991. **Mark:** Name.

POSNER, BARRY E., 12501 Chandler Blvd., Suite 104, N. Hollywood, CA 91607, Phone: 818-752-8005, Fax: 818-752-8006
Specialties: Working/using straight knives. **Patterns:** Hunters, kitchen and utility/camp knives. **Technical:** Grinds ATS-34; forges 1095 and nickel. **Prices:** $95 to $400. **Remarks:** Part-time maker; first knife sold in 1987. Doing business as Posner Knives. Supplier of finished mosaic handle pin stock. **Mark:** First and middle initials, last name.

POTIER, TIMOTHY F., PO Box 711, Oberlin, LA 70655, Phone: 337-639-2229
Specialties: Classic working and using straight knives to customer specs; some collectible. **Patterns:** Hunters, Bowies, utility/camp knives and belt axes. **Technical:** Forges carbon steel and his own Damascus; offers filework. **Prices:** $300 to $1800; some to $4000. **Remarks:** Part-time maker; first knife sold in 1981. **Mark:** Last name, MS.

POTOCKI, ROGER, Route 1, Box 333A, Goreville, IL 62939, Phone: 618-995-9502

POTTER, FRANK, 25 Renfrew Ave., Middletown, RI 02842, Phone: 401-846-5352
Specialties: Autos. **Patterns:** Liner lock; his own design. **Technical:** Damascus bolters and blades; ivory and pearl. **Prices:** $1000 to $3000. **Remarks:** Full-time maker, first knife sold 1996. **Mark:** Frank Potter.

POTTER, BILLY, 6280 Virginia Rd., Nashport, OH 43830, Phone: 740-454-7412, Fax: 740-319-1751
Specialties: Working straight knives; his design or to customers patterns. **Patterns:** Bowie, fighters, utilities, skinners, hunters, folding lock blade, miniatures and tomahawks. **Technical:** Grinds and forges, carbon steel, L-6, 0-1, 1095, 5160, 1084 and 52000. Grinds 440C stainless. Forges own Damascus. Handles: prefers exotic hardwood, curly and birdseye maples. Bone, ivory, antler, pearl and horn. Some scrimshaw. **Prices:** Start at $100 up to $800. **Remarks:** Part-time maker; first knife sold 1996. **Mark:** Last name.

POWELL, JAMES, 2500 North Robinson Rd., Texarkana, TX 75501

POWELL, ROBERT CLARK, PO Box 321, 93 Gose Rd., Smarr, GA 31086, Phone: 478-994-5418
Specialties: Composite bar Damascus blades. **Patterns:** Art knives, hunters, combat, tomahawks. **Patterns:** Hand forge all blades. **Prices:** $300 and up. **Remarks:** Member ABS. **Mark:** Powell.

POYTHRESS, JOHN, PO Box 585, 625 Freedom St., Swainsboro, GA 30401, Phone: 478-237-9233 day/478-237-9478 night
Specialties: Traditional working and using straight knives of his design or to customer specs. **Patterns:** Hunters, liner lock folders, dagger, tanto. **Technical:** Uses 440C, ATS-34 and D2. **Prices:** $150 and up. **Remarks:** Part-time maker; first knife sold in 1983. Member N.C. Customer Knife-maker's Guild. **Other:** Also current president of the newly formed GA Custom Knifemakers Guild. **Mark:** Poythress.

PRATER, MIKE, PRATER AND COMPANY, 81 Sanford Ln., Flintstone, GA 30725
Specialties: Customizing factory knives. **Patterns:** Buck knives, case knives, hen and rooster knives. **Technical:** Manufacture of mica pearl. **Prices:** Varied. **Remarks:** First knife sold in 1980. **Mark:** Mica pearl.

PRESSBURGER, RAMON, 59 Driftway Rd., Howell, NJ 07731, Phone: 732-363-0816
Specialties: BG-42. Only knife maker in U.S.A. that has complete line of affordable hunting knives made from BG-42. **Patterns:** All types hunting styles. **Technical:** Uses all steels; main steels are D-2 and BG-42. **Prices:** $75 to $500. **Remarks:** Full-time maker; has been making hunting knives for 30 years. **Mark:** NA. **Other:** Makes knives to your patterning.

PRICE, TIMMY, PO Box 906, Blairsville, GA 30514, Phone: 706-745-5111

PRIMOS, TERRY, 932 Francis Dr., Shreveport, LA 71118, Phone: 318-686-6625
Specialties: Traditional forged straight knives. **Patterns:** Hunters, Bowies, camp knives, and fighters. **Technical:** Forges primarily 1084 and 5160; also forges Damascus. **Prices:** $250 to $600. **Remarks:** Full-time maker; first knife sold in 1993. **Mark:** Last name.

PRITCHARD, RON, 613 Crawford Ave., Dixon, IL 61021, Phone: 815-284-6005
Specialties: Plain and fancy working knives. **Patterns:** Variety of straight knives, locking folders, interframes and miniatures. **Technical:** Grinds 440C, 154CM and commercial Damascus. **Prices:** $100 to $200; some to $1500. **Remarks:** Part-time maker; first knife sold in 1979. **Mark:** Name and city.

PROVENZANO, JOSEPH D., 3024 Ivy Place, Chalmette, LA 70043, Phone: 504-279-3154
Specialties: Working straight knives and folders in standard patterns. **Patterns:** Hunters, Bowies, folders, camp and fishing knives. **Technical:** Grinds ATS-34, 440C, 154CM, CPM 4400V, CPM420V and Damascus. Hollow-grinds hunters. **Prices:** $110 to $300; some to $1000. **Remarks:** Part-time maker; first knife sold in 1980. **Mark:** Joe-Pro.

PRYOR, STEPHEN L., HC Rt. 1, Box 1445, Boss, MO 65440, Phone: 573-626-4838, Fax: same
Specialties: Working and fancy straight knives, some to customer specs. **Patterns:** Bowies, hunting/fishing, utility/camp, fantasy/art. **Technical:** Grinds 440C, ATS34, 1085, some Damascus, and does filework. Stag and exotic hardwood handles. **Prices:** $250 and up. **Remarks:** Full-time maker; first knife sold in 1991. **Mark:** Stylized first initial and last name over city and state.

PUDDU, SALVATORE, Via Lago Bunnari, 11 Localita Flumini, Quartu s Elena (CA), ITALY 09046
Specialties: Collector-quality folders, straight. **Patterns:** Multi blade, folders, automatics. **Technical:** Grinds ATS-34 and 440 C. **Prices:** Start $400 to $2500. **Remarks:** Full-time maker. **Mark:** Name.

PUGH, VERNON, 701-525 3RD Ave. N, Saskatoon SK, CANADA S7K 2J6, Phone: 306-652-9274

PUGH, JIM, PO Box 711, Azle, TX 76020, Phone: 817-444-2679, Fax: 817-444-5455
Specialties: Fancy/embellished limited editions by request. **Patterns:** 5- to 7-inch Bowies, wildlife art pieces, hunters, daggers and fighters; some commemoratives. **Technical:** Multi color transplanting in solid 18K gold, fine gems; grinds 440C and ATS-34. Offers engraving, fancy file etching and leather sheaths for wildlife art pieces. Ivory and coco bolo handle material on limited editions. Designs animal head butt caps and paws or bear claw guards; sterling silver heads and guards. **Prices:** $60,000 to $80,000 each in the Big Five 2000 edition. **Remarks:** Full-time maker; first knife sold in 1970. **Mark:** Pugh (old English).

PULIS, VLADIMIR, Horna Ves 43/B/25, 96 701 Kremnica, SLOVAKIA, Phone: 00427-45-6757274
Specialties: Fancy and high-art straight knives of his design. **Patterns:** Daggers and hunters. **Technical:** Forges Damascus steel. All work done

by hand. **Prices:** $250 to $3000; some to $10,000. **Remarks:** Full-time maker; first knife sold in 1990. **Mark:** Initials in sixtagon.

PULLIAM, MORRIS C., 560 Jeptha Knob Rd., Shelbyville, KY 40065, Phone: 502-633-2261
Specialties: Working knives; classic Bowies. Cherokee River pattern Damascus. **Patterns:** Bowies, hunters, and tomahawks. **Technical:** Forges L6, W2, 1095, Damascus and bar 320 layer Damascus. **Prices:** $165 to $1200. **Remarks:** Full-time maker; first knife sold in 1974. Makes knives for Native American festivals. Doing business as Knob Hill Forge. Member of Piqua Sept Shawnee of Ohio. **Mark:** Small and large - Pulliam. **Other:** As a member of a state tribe,is an American Indian artist and craftsman by federal law.

PURSLEY, AARON, 8885 Coal Mine Rd., Big Sandy, MT 59520, Phone: 406-378-3200
Specialties: Fancy working knives. **Patterns:** Locking folders, straight hunters and daggers, personal wedding knives and letter openers. **Technical:** Grinds O1 and 440C; engraves. **Prices:** $900 to $2500; some to $1500. **Remarks:** Full-time maker; first knife sold in 1975. **Mark:** Initials connected with year.

PURVIS, BOB AND ELLEN, 2416 N Loretta Dr., Tucson, AZ 85716, Phone: 520-795-8290
Specialties: Hunter, skinners, Bowies, using knives, gentlemen's folders and collectible knives. **Technical:** Grinds ATS-34, 440C, Damascus, Dama steel, heat-treats and cryogenically quenches. We do gold-plating, salt bluing, scrimshawing, filework and fashion hand made leather sheaths. Materials used for handles include exotic woods, mammoth ivory, mother-of-pearl, G-10 and micarta. **Prices:** $165 to $800. **Remarks:** Knifemaker since retirement in 1984. Selling them since 1993. **Mark:** Script or print R.E. Purvis ~ Tucson, AZ or last name only.

PUTNAM, DONALD S., 590 Wolcott Hill Rd., Wethersfield, CT 06109, Phone: 203-563-9718, Fax: 203-563-9718
Specialties: Working knives for the hunter and fisherman. **Patterns:** His design or to customer specs. **Technical:** Uses stock removal method, O1, W2, D2, ATS-34, 154CM, 440C and CPM REX 20; stainless steel Damascus on request. **Prices:** NA. **Remarks:** Full-time maker; first knife sold in 1985. **Mark:** Last name with a knife outline.

q

QUAKENBUSH, THOMAS C., 2426 Butler Rd., Ft Wayne, IN 46808, Phone: 219-483-0749

QUARTON, BARR, PO Box 4335, McCall, ID 83638, Phone: 208-634-3641
Specialties: Plain and fancy working knives; period pieces. **Patterns:** Hunters, tantos and swords. **Technical:** Forges and grinds 154CM, ATS-34 and his own Damascus. **Prices:** $180 to $450; some to $4500. **Remarks:** Part-time maker; first knife sold in 1978. Doing business as Barr Custom Knives. **Mark:** First name with bear logo.

QUATTLEBAUM, CRAIG, 2 Ridgewood Ln., Searcy, AR 72143
Specialties: Traditional straight knives and one-of-a-kind knives of his design; period pieces. **Patterns:** Bowies and fighters. **Technical:** Forges 5168, 52100 and own Damascus. **Prices:** $100 to $1200. **Remarks:** Part-time maker; first knife sold in 1988. **Mark:** Stylized initials.

QUICK, MIKE, 23 Locust Ave., Kearny, NJ 07032, Phone: 201-991-6580
Specialties: Traditional working/using straight knives. **Patterns:** Bowies. **Technical:** 440C and ATS-34 for blades; Micarta, wood and stag for handles.

r

R. BOYES KNIVES, N81 W16140 Robin Hood Dr., Menomonee Falls, WI 53051, Phone: 262-255-7341
Specialties: Hunters, working knives. **Technical:** Grinds ATS-34, 440C, 01 tool steel and Damascus. **Prices:** $60 to $700. **Remarks:** First knife sold in 1998. Tom Boyes changed to R. Boyes Knives.

RACHLIN, LESLIE S., 1200 W. Church St., Elmira, NY 14905, Phone: 607-733-6889
Specialties: Classic and working/using straight knives and folders of his design. **Patterns:** Hunters, locking folders and utility/camp knives. **Technical:** Grinds 440C and Damascus. **Prices:** $110 to $200; some to $450. **Remarks:** Spare-time maker; first knife sold in 1989. Doing business as Tinkermade Knives. **Mark:** Stamped initials or Tinkermade, city and state.

RADOS, JERRY F., 7523 E 5000 N Rd., Grant Park, IL 60940, Phone: 815-472-3350, Fax: 815-472-3944
Specialties: Deluxe period pieces. **Patterns:** Hunters, fighters, locking folders, daggers and camp knives. **Technical:** Forges and grinds his own Damascus which he sells commercially; makes pattern-welded Turkish Damascus. **Prices:** Start at $900. **Remarks:** Full-time maker; first knife sold in 1981. **Mark:** Last name.

RAGSDALE, JAMES D., 3002 Arabian Woods Dr., Lithonia, GA 30038, Phone: 770-482-6739
Specialties: Fancy and embellished working knives of his design or to customer specs. **Patterns:** Hunters, folders and fighters. **Technical:** Grinds 440C, ATS-34 and A2. **Prices:** $150 and up. **Remarks:** Full-time maker; first knife sold in 1984. **Mark:** Fish symbol with name above, town below.

RAINVILLE, RICHARD, 126 Cockle Hill Rd., Salem, CT 06420, Phone: 860-859-2776
Specialties: Traditional working straight knives. **Patterns:** Outdoor knives, including fishing knives. **Technical:** L6, 400C, ATS-34. **Prices:** $100 to $800. **Remarks:** Full-time maker; first knife sold in 1982. **Mark:** Name, city, state in oval logo.

RALEY, R. WAYNE, 825 Poplar Acres Rd., Collierville, TN 38017, Phone: 901-853-2026

RALPH, DARREL, BRIAR KNIVES, 4185 S St. Rt. 605, Galena, OH 43021, Phone: 740-965-9970
Specialties: Fancy, high-art, high-tech, collectible straight knives and folders of his design and to customer specs; unique mechanisms, some disassemble. **Patterns:** Daggers, fighters and swords. **Technical:** Forges his own Damascus, nickel and high-carbon. Uses mokume and Damascus; mosaics and special patterns. Engraves and heat-treats. Prefers pearl, ivory and abalone handle material; uses stones and jewels. **Prices:** $250 to six figures. **Remarks:** Full-time maker; first knife sold in 1987. Doing business as Briar Knives. **Mark:** DDR.

RAMEY, MARSHALL F., PO Box 2589, West Helena, AR 72390, Phone: 501-572-7436, Fax: 501-572-6245
Specialties: Traditional working knives. **Patterns:** Designs military combat knives; makes butterfly folders, camp knives and miniatures. **Technical:** Grinds D2 and 440C. **Prices:** $100 to $500. **Remarks:** Full-time maker; first knife sold in 1978. **Mark:** Name with ram's head.

RAMEY, LARRY, 1315 Porter Morris Rd., Chapmansboro, TN 37035-5120, Phone: 615-307-4233
Specialties: Titanium knives. **Technical:** Pictures taken by Hawkinson Photography.

RAMSEY, RICHARD A., 8525 Trout Farm Rd., Neosho, MO 64850, Phone: 417-451-1493
Specialties: Drop point hunters. **Patterns:** Various Damascus. **Prices:** $125-$1500. **Mark:** RR double R also last name-RAMSEY.

RANDALL JR., JAMES W., 11606 Keith Hall Rd., Keithville, LA 71047, Phone: 318-925-6480, Fax: 318-925-1709
Specialties: Collectible and functional knives. **Patterns:** Bowies, hunters, daggers, swords, folders and combat knives. **Technical:** Forges 5160, 1084, 01 and his Damascus. **Prices:** $400 to $8000. **Remarks:** Part-time. First knive sold in 1998. **Mark:** J.W Randall M.S.

RANDALL MADE KNIVES, PO Box 1988, Orlando, FL 32802, Phone: 407-855-8075, Fax: 407-855-9054
Specialties: Working straight knives. **Patterns:** Hunters, fighters and Bowies. **Technical:** Forges and grinds O1 and 440B. **Prices:** $65 to $250; some to $450. **Remarks:** Full-time maker; first knife sold in 1937. **Mark:** Randall, city and state in scimitar logo.

RANDOW, RALPH, 4214 Blalock Rd., Pineville, LA 71360, Phone: 318-640-3369

RANKL, CHRISTIAN, Possenhofenerstr. 33, 81476 Munchen, GERMANY, Phone: 0049 01 71 3 66 26 79, Fax: 0049 8975967265
Specialties: Tail-lock knives. **Patterns:** Fighters, hunters and locking folders. **Technical:** Grinds ATS-34, D2, CPM1440V, RWL 34 also stainless Damascus. **Prices:** $450 to $950; some to $2000. **Remarks:** Full-time maker; first knife sold in 1989. **Mark:** Electrochemical etching on blade.

RAPP, STEVEN J., 7273 South 245 East, Midvale, UT 84047, Phone: 801-567-9553
Specialties: Gold quartz; mosaic handles. **Patterns:** Daggers, Bowies, fighters and San Francisco knives. **Technical:** Hollow- and flat-grinds 440C and Damascus. **Prices:** Start at $500. **Remarks:** Full-time maker; first knife sold in 1981. **Mark:** Name and state.

RAPPAZZO, RICHARD, 142 Dunsbach Ferry Rd., Cohoes, NY 12047, Phone: 518-783-6843
Specialties: Damascus locking folders and straight knives. **Patterns:** Folders, dirks, fighters and tantos in original and traditional designs. **Technical:** Hand-forges all blades; specializes in Damascus; uses only natural handle materials. **Prices:** $400 to $1500. **Remarks:** Part-time maker; first knife sold in 1985. **Mark:** Name, date, serial number.

RARDON, ARCHIE F., 1589 SE Price Dr., Polo, MO 64671, Phone: 660-354-2330
Specialties: Working knives. **Patterns:** Hunters, Bowies and miniatures. **Technical:** Grinds O1, D2, 440C, ATS-34, cable and Damascus. **Prices:** $50 to $500. **Remarks:** Part-time maker. **Mark:** Boar hog.

RARDON, A.D., 1589 SE Price Dr., Polo, MO 64671, Phone: 660-354-2330
Specialties: Folders, miniatures. **Patterns:** Hunters, buck skinners, Bowies, miniatures and daggers. **Technical:** Grinds O1, D2, 440C and ATS-34. **Prices:** $150 to $2000; some higher. **Remarks:** Full-time maker; first knife sold in 1954. **Mark:** Fox logo.

RAY, ALAN W., PO Box 479, Lovelady, TX 75851, Phone: 936-636-2350, Fax: 936-636-2931
Specialties: Working straight knives of his design. **Patterns:** Hunters, camp knives, steak knives and carving sets. **Technical:** Forges L6 and 5160 for straight knives; grinds D2 and 440C for folders and kitchen cutlery. **Prices:** $200 to $1000. **Remarks:** Full-time maker; first knife sold in 1979. **Mark:** Stylized initials.

REBELLO, INDIAN GEORGE, 358 Elm St., New Bedford, MA 02740-3837, Phone: 508-999-7090
Specialties: One-of-a-kind fighters and Bowies. **Patterns:** To customer's specs, hunters and utilities. **Technical:** Forges his own Damascus, 5160, 52100, 1084, 1095, cable and O-1. Grinds S30V, ATS-34, 154CM, 440C, D2 and A2. Makes own Mokume. **Prices:** Starting at $250. **Remarks:** Full-time maker, first knife sold in 1991. Doing business as Indian George's Knives. President and founding father of the New England Custom Knives Association. **Mark:** Indian George's Knives.

RED, VERNON, 2020 Benton Cove, Conway, AR 72032, Phone: 501-450-7284
Specialties: Custom design straight knives or folders of your design or mine. Love one-of-a-kind. **Patterns:** Hunters, fighters, Bowies, fillet, folders and lock-blades. **Technical:** Hollow Grind or flat grind; use 440C, D-2, ATS-34, Damascus. **Prices:** $150 and up. **Remarks:** Made first skinner in 1982, first lock blade folder in 1992. Make about 50/50. Part-time maker; first knife sold in 1992. Do scrimshaw on ivory and micarta. **Mark:** Last name. **Other:** Member of (AKA) Arkansas Knives Assoc., attend annual show in Feb. at Little Rock, AR. Custom Made Knives by Vernon Red.

REDDIEX, BILL, 27 Galway Ave., Palmerston North, NEW ZEALAND, Phone: 06-357-0383, Fax: 06-358-2910
Specialties: Collector-grade working straight knives. **Patterns:** Traditional-style Bowies and drop-point hunters. **Technical:** Grinds 440C, D2 and O1; offers variety of grinds and finishes. **Prices:** $130 to $750. **Remarks:** Full-time maker; first knife sold in 1980. **Mark:** Last name around kiwi bird logo.

REED, DAVE, Box 132, Brimfield, MA 01010, Phone: 413-245-3661
Specialties: Traditional styles. Makes knives from chains, rasps, gears, etc. **Patterns:** Bush swords, hunters, working minis, camp and utility knives. **Technical:** Forges 1075 and his own Damascus. **Prices:** Start at $50. **Remarks:** Part-time maker; first knife sold in 1970. **Mark:** Initials.

REED, JOHN M., 257 Navajo Dr., Oak Hill, FL 32759, Phone: 386-345-4763
Specialties: Hunter, utility, some survival knives. **Patterns:** Trailing Point, and drop point sheath knives. **Technical:** ATS-34, rockwell 60 exotic wood or natural material handles. **Prices:** $135-$300. Depending on handle material. **Remarks:** Likes the stock removal method. "Old Fashioned trainling point blades". **Mark:** "Reed" acid etched on left side of blade. **Other:** Hand made and sewn leather sheaths.

REEVE, CHRIS, 11624 W. President Dr., Ste. B, Boise, ID 83713, Phone: 208-375-0367, Fax: 208-375-0368
Specialties: Originator and designer of the One Piece range of fixed blade utility knives and of the Sebenza Integral Lock folding knives made by Chris Reeve Knives. Currently makes only one or two pieces per year himself. **Patterns:** Art folders and fixed blades; one-of-a-kind. **Technical:** Grinds specialty stainless steels, Damascus and other materials to his own design. **Prices:** $1000 and upwards. **Remarks:** Full-time in knife business; first knife sold in 1982. **Mark:** Signature and date.

REGGIO JR., SIDNEY J., PO Box 851, Sun, LA 70463, Phone: 504-886-5886
Specialties: Miniature classic and fancy straight knives of his design or in standard patterns. **Patterns:** Fighters, hunters and utility/camp knives. **Technical:** Grinds 440C, ATS-34 and commercial Damascus. Engraves;

custom knifemakers

scrimshaws; offers filework. Hollow grinds most blades. Prefers natural handle material. Offers handmade sheaths. **Prices:** $85 to $250; some to $500. **Remarks:** Part-time maker; first knife sold in 1988. Doing business as Sterling Workshop. **Mark:** Initials.

REPKE, MIKE, 4191 N. Euclid Ave., Bay City, MI 48706, Phone: 517-684-3111
Specialties: Traditional working and using straight knives of their design or to customer specs; classic knives; display knives. **Patterns:** Hunters, Bowies, skinners, fighters boots, axes and swords. **Technical:** Grind 440C. Offer variety of handle materials. **Prices:** $99 to $1500. **Remarks:** Full-time makers. Doing business as Black Forest Blades. **Mark:** Knife logo.

REVERDY, PIERRE, 5 Rue de L'egalite', 26100 Romans, FRANCE, Phone: 334 75 05 10 15, Fax: 334 75 02 28 40
Specialties: Art knives; legend pieces. **Patterns:** Daggers, Bowies, hunters and other large patterns. **Technical:** Forges his Damascus and "poetique Damascus"; works with his own EDM machine to create any kind of pattern inside the steel with his own touch. **Prices:** $2000 and up. **Remarks:** Full-time maker; first knife sold in 1986. Nicole (wife) collaborates with enamels. **Mark:** Initials connected.

REVISHVILI, ZAZA, 2102 Linden Ave., Madison, WI 53704, Phone: 608-243-7927
Specialties: Fancy/embellished and high-art straight knives and folders of his design. **Patterns:** Daggers, swords and locking folders. **Technical:** Uses Damascus; silver filigree, silver inlay in wood; enameling. **Prices:** $1000 to $9000; some to $15,000. **Remarks:** Full-time maker; first knife sold in 1987. **Mark:** Initials, city.

REXROAT, KIRK, 527 Sweetwater Circle, Box 224, Wright, WY 82732, Phone: 307-464-0166
Specialties: Using and collectible straight knives and folders of his design or to customer specs. **Patterns:** Bowies, hunters, folders. **Technical:** Forges Damascus patterns, mosaic and 52100. **Prices:** $400 and up. **Remarks:** Part-time maker, Master Smith in the ABS; first knife sold in 1984. Doing business as Rexroat Knives. **Mark:** Last name.

REYNOLDS, DAVE, Rt. 2, Box 36, Harrisville, WV 26362, Phone: 304-643-2889
Specialties: Working straight knives of his design. **Patterns:** Bowies, kitchen and utility knives. **Technical:** Grinds and forges L6, 1095 and 440C. Heat-treats. **Prices:** $50 to $85; some to $175. **Remarks:** Full-time maker; first knife sold in 1980. Doing business as Terra-Gladius Knives. **Mark:** Mark on special orders only; serial number on all knives.

REYNOLDS, JOHN C., #2 Andover, HC77, Gillette, WY 82716, Phone: 307-682-6076
Specialties: Working knives, some fancy. **Patterns:** Hunters, Bowies, tomahawks and buck skinners; some folders. **Technical:** Grinds D2, ATS34, 440C and forges own Damascus and Knifes now. Scrimshaws. **Prices:** $200 to $3000. **Remarks:** Spare-time maker; first knife sold in 1969. **Mark:** On ground blades JC Reynolds Gillette,WY, on forged blades, initials make the mark-JCR.

RHO, NESTOR LORENZO, Primera Junta 589, (6000) Junin, Buenos Aires, ARGENTINA, Phone: (02362) 15670686
Specialties: Classic and fancy straight knives of his design. **Patterns:** Bowies, fighters and hunters. **Technical:** Grinds 420C, 440C and 1050. Offers semi-precious stones on handles, acid etching on blades and blade engraving. **Prices:** $60 to $300 some to $1200. **Remarks:** Full-time maker; first knife sold in 1975. **Mark:** Name.

RHODES, JAMES D., 205 Woodpoint Ave., Hagerstown, MD 21740, Phone: 301-739-2657
Specialties: Traditional working and using straight knives of his design. **Patterns:** Bowies, fighters, hunters and kitchen knives. **Technical:** Forges 5160, 1085, and 9260; makes own Damascus. Hard edges, soft backs, dead soft tangs. Heat-treats. **Prices:** $150 to $350. **Remarks:** Part-time maker. **Mark:** Last name, JS.

RICARDO ROMANO, BERNARDES, Ruai Coronel Rennò, 1261, Itajuba MG, BRAZIL 37500, Phone: 0055-2135-622-5896
Specialties: Hunters, fighters, Bowies. **Technical:** Grinds blades of stainless and tools steels. **Patterns:** Hunters. **Prices:** $100 to $700. **Mark:** Romano.

RICE, STEPHEN E., 11043 C Oak Spur Ct., St. Louis, MO 63146, Phone: 314-432-2025

RICHARD, RON, 4875 Calaveras Ave., Fremont, CA 94538, Phone: 510-796-9767
Specialties: High-tech working straight knives of his design. **Patterns:** Bowies, swords and locking folders. **Technical:** Forges and grinds ATS-34, 154CM and 440V. All folders have dead-bolt button locks. **Prices:** $650 to $850; some to $1400. **Remarks:** Full-time maker; first knife sold in 1968. **Mark:** Full name.

RICHARDS JR., ALVIN C., 2889 Shields Ln., Fortuna, CA 95540-3241, Phone: 707-725-2526
Specialties: Fixed blade Damascus. One-of-a-kind. **Patterns:** Hunters, fighters. **Prices:** $125 to $500. **Remarks:** Like to work with customers on a truly custom knife. **Mark:** A C Richards or ACR.

RICHARDSON JR., PERCY, PO Box 973, Hemphill, TX 75948, Phone: 409-787-2279
Specialties: Traditional and working straight knives and folders in standard patterns and to customer specs. **Patterns:** Bowies, daggers, hunters, automatics, locking folders, slip-joints and utility/camp knives. **Technical:** Grinds ATS-34, 440C and D2. **Prices:** $125 to $600; some to $1800. **Remarks:** Full-time maker; first knife sold in 1990. Doing business as Lone Star Custom Knives. **Mark:** Lone Star with last name across it.

RICHTER, JOHN C., 932 Bowling Green Trail, Chesapeake, VA 23320
Specialties: Hand-forged knives in original patterns. **Patterns:** Hunters, fighters, utility knives and other belt knives, folders, swords. **Technical:** Hand-forges high-carbon and his own Damascus; makes mokume gane. **Prices:** $75 to $1500. **Remarks:** Part-time maker. **Mark:** Richter Forge.

RICHTER, SCOTT, 516 E. 2nd St., S. Boston, MA 02127, Phone: 617-269-4855
Specialties: Traditional working/using folders. **Patterns:** Locking folders, swords and kitchen knives. **Technical:** Grinds ATS-34, 5160 and A2. High-tech materials. **Prices:** $150 to $650; some to $1500. **Remarks:** Full-time maker; first knife sold in 1991. Doing business as Richter Made. **Mark:** Last name, Made.

RICKE, DAVE, 1209 Adams, West Bend, WI 53090, Phone: 262-334-5739
Specialties: Working knives; period pieces. **Patterns:** Hunters, boots, Bowies; locking folders and slip-joints. **Technical:** Grinds ATS-34, A2, 440C and 154CM. **Prices:** $125-$1600. **Remarks:** Full-time maker; first knife sold in 1976. **Mark:** Last name.

RIDER, DAVID M., PO Box 5946, Eugene, OR 97405-0911, Phone: 541-343-8747

RIEPE, RICHARD A., 17604 E 296 St., Harrisonville, MO 64701

RIETVELD, BERTIE, PO Box 53, Magaliesburg 1791, SOUTH AFRICA, Phone: +2714 577 1294, Fax: 014 577 1294
Specialties: Damascus, Persian, art daggers, button-lock folders. **Patterns:** Mostly one-ofs. **Technical:** Work only in own stainless Damascus and other exotics. **Prices:** $500 to $8000. **Remarks:** First knife made in 1979. Past chairman of SA Knifemakers Guild. Member SA Knifemakers Guild and Knifemakers Guild (U.S.A.). Also a member of the Italian Guild. **Mark:** Elephant with last name.

RIGNEY JR., WILLIE, 191 Colson Dr., Bronston, KY 42518, Phone: 606-679-4227
Specialties: High-tech period pieces and fancy working knives. **Patterns:** Fighters, boots, daggers and push knives. **Technical:** Grinds 440C and 154CM; buys Damascus. Most knives are embellished. **Prices:** $150 to $1500; some to $10,000. **Remarks:** Full-time maker; first knife sold in 1978. **Mark:** First initial, last name.

RINALDI, T.H., RINALDI CUSTOM BLADES, PO Box 718, Winchester, CA 92596, Phone: 909-926-5422
Technical: Grinds S30V, 3V, A2 and talonite fixed blades. **Prices:** $175-600. **Remarks:** Tactical and utility for the most part.

RINKES, SIEGFRIED, Am Sportpl 2, D 91459, Markterlbach, GERMANY

RIZZI, RUSSELL J., 37 March Rd., Ashfield, MA 01330, Phone: 413-625-2842
Specialties: Fancy working and using straight knives and folders of his design or to customer specs. **Patterns:** Hunters, locking folders and fighters. **Technical:** Grinds 440C, D2 and commercial Damascus. **Prices:** $150 to $750; some to $2500. **Remarks:** Part-time maker; first knife sold in 1990. **Mark:** Last name, Ashfield, MA.

ROATH, DEAN, 3050 Winnipeg Dr., Baton Rouge, LA 70819, Phone: 225-272-5562
Specialties: Classic working knives; focusing on fillet knives for salt water fishermen. **Patterns:** Hunters, filets, canoe/trail, and boating/sailing knives. **Technical:** Grinds 440C. **Prices:** $85 to $500; some to $1500. **Remarks:** Part-time maker; first knife sold in 1978. **Mark:** Name, city and state.

ROBBINS, HOWARD P., 1407 S. 217th Ave., Elkhorn, NE 68022, Phone: 402-289-4121
Specialties: High-tech working knives with clean designs, some fancy. **Patterns:** Folders, hunters and camp knives. **Technical:** Grinds 440C. Heat-treats; likes mirror finishes. Offers leatherwork. **Prices:** $100 to $500; some to $1000. **Remarks:** Full-time maker; first knife sold in 1982. **Mark:** Name, city and state.

ROBERTS, E. RAY, 191 Nursery Rd., Monticello, FL 32344, Phone: 850-997-4403
Specialties: High-Carbon Damascus knives and tomahawks.

ROBERTS, MIKE, 601 Oakwood Dr., Clinton, MS 39056-4332, Phone: 601-924-3154

ROBERTS, MICHAEL, 601 Oakwood Dr., Clinton, MS 39056, Phone: 601-924-3154; Pager 601-978-8180
Specialties: Working and using knives in standard patterns and to customer specs. **Patterns:** Hunters, Bowies, tomahawks and fighters. **Technical:** Forges 5160, O1, 1095 and his own Damascus. Uses only natural handle materials. **Prices:** $145 to $500; some to $1100. **Remarks:** Part-time maker; first knife sold in 1988. **Mark:** Last name or first and last name in Celtic script.

ROBERTS, GEORGE A., PO Box 31228, 211 Main St., Whitehorse, YT, CANADA Y1A 5P7, Phone: 867-667-7099, Fax: 867-667-7099
Specialties: Mastadon ivory, fossil walrus ivory handled knives, scrimshawed or carved. **Patterns:** Side lockers, fancy bird and trout knives, hunters, fillet blades. **Technical:** Grinds stainless Damascus, all surgical steels. **Prices:** Up to $3500 U.S. **Remarks:** Full-time maker; first knives sold in 1986. Doing business as Bandit Blades. **Mark:** Bandit Yukon with pick and shovel crossed. **Other:** Most recent works have gold nuggets in fossilized Mastodon ivory. Something new using mosaic pins in mokume bolster and in mosaic Damascus, it creates a new look.

ROBERTS, CHUCK, PO Box 7174, Golden, CO 80403, Phone: 303-642-0512
Specialties: Sheffield Bowies; historic-styles only. **Patterns:** Bowies and California knives. **Technical:** Grinds 440C, 5160 and ATS-34. Handles made of stag, ivory or mother-of-pearl. **Prices:** Start at $750. **Remarks:** Full-time maker. **Mark:** Last initial or last name.

ROBERTS, JACK, 10811 Sagebluff Dr., Houston, TX 77089, Phone: 218-481-1784
Specialties: Hunting knives and folders, offers scrimshaw by wife Barbara. **Patterns:** Drop point hunters and liner lock folders. **Technical:** Grinds 440-C, offers file work, texturing, natural handle materials and micarta. **Prices:** $200 to $800 some higher. **Remarks:** Part-time maker, sold first knife in 1965. **Mark:** Name, city, state.

ROBERTSON, LEO D., 3728 Pleasant Lake Dr., Indianpolis, IN 46227, Phone: 317-882-9899
Specialties: Hunting and folders. **Patterns:** Hunting, fillet, Bowie, utility, folders and tantos. **Technical:** Uses ATS-34, 154CM, 440C, 1095, D2 and Damascus steels. **Prices:** Fixed knives $75 to $350, folders $350 to $600. **Remarks:** Handles made with stag, wildwoods, laminates, mother-of-pearl. **Mark:** Logo with full name in oval around logo. **Other:** Made first knife in 1990. Member of American bladesmith society.

ROBINSON, ROBERT W., 1569 N. Finley Pt., Polson, MT 59860, Phone: 406-887-2259, Fax: 406-887-2259
Specialties: High-art straight knives, folders and automatics of his design. **Patterns:** Hunters and locking knives. **Technical:** Grinds ATS-34, 154CM and 440V. Inlays pearl and gold; engraves sheep horn and ivory. **Prices:** $150 to $500; some to $2000. **Remarks:** Full-time maker; first knife sold in 1983. Doing business as Robbie Knife. **Mark:** Name on left side of blade.

ROBINSON, CHUCK, Sea Robin Forge, 1423 Third Ave., Picayune, MS 39466, Phone: 601-798-0060
Specialties: Deluxe period pieces and working / using knives of his design and to customer specs. **Patterns:** Bowies, fighters, hunters, folders, utility knives and original designs. **Technical:** Forges own Damascus, 52100, 01, L6 and 1070 thru 1095. **Prices:** Start At $225. **Remarks:** First knife 1958. Recently transitioned to full-time maker. **Mark:** Fish logo, anchor and initials C.R.

ROBINSON, CHARLES (DICKIE), PO Box 221, Vega, TX 79092, Phone: 806-267-2629
Specialties: Classic and working/using knives. **Patterns:** Bowies, daggers, fighters, hunters and camp knives. **Technical:** Forges O1, 5160, 52100 and his own Damascus. **Prices:** $350 to $850; some to $5000. **Remarks:** Part-time maker; first knife sold in 1988. Doing business as Robinson Knives. ABS Master Smith. **Mark:** Robinson MS.

ROBINSON III, REX R., 10531 Poe St., Leesburg, FL 34788, Phone: 352-787-4587
Specialties: One-of-a-kind high-art automatics of his design. **Patterns:** Automatics, liner locks and lock back folders. **Technical:** Uses tool steel and stainless Damascus and mokume; flat grinds. Hand carves folders.

Prices: $1800 to $7500. **Remarks:** First knife sold in 1988. **Mark:** First name inside oval.

ROCHFORD, MICHAEL R., PO Box 577, Dresser, WI 54009, Phone: 715-755-3520
Specialties: Working straight knives and folders. Classic Bowies and Moran traditional. **Patterns:** Bowies, fighters, hunters: slip-joint, locking and liner lock folders. **Technical:** Grinds ATS-34, 440C, 154CM and D-2; forges W2, 5160, and his own Damascus. Offers metal and metal and leather sheaths. Filework and wire inlay. **Prices:** $150 to $1000; some to $2000. **Remarks:** Part-time maker; first knife sold in 1984. **Mark:** Name.

RODEBAUGH, JAMES L., 9374 Joshua Rd., Oak Hills, CA 92345

RODEWALD, GARY, 447 Grouse Ct., Hamilton, MT 59840, Phone: 406-363-2192
Specialties: Bowies of his design as inspired from his torical pieces. **Patterns:** Hunters, Bowies and camp/combat. Forges 5160 1084 and his own Damascus of 1084, 15N20, field grade hunters AT-34 - 440C, 440V, and BG42. **Prices:** $200-$1500 **Remarks:** Sole author on knives - sheaths done by saddle maker. **Mark:** Rodewald.

RODKEY, DAN, 18336 Ozark Dr., Hudson, FL 34667, Phone: 727-863-8264
Specialties: Traditional straight knives of his design and in standard patterns. **Patterns:** Boots, fighters and hunters. **Technical:** Grinds 440C, D2 and ATS-34. **Prices:** Start at $200. **Remarks:** Full-time maker; first knife sold in 1985. Doing business as Rodkey Knives. **Mark:** Etched logo on blade.

ROE JR., FRED D., 4005 Granada Dr., Huntsville, AL 35802, Phone: 205-881-6847
Specialties: Highly finished working knives of his design; period pieces. **Patterns:** Hunters, fighters and survival knives; locking folders; specialty designs like divers' knives. **Technical:** Grinds 154CM, ATS-34 and Damascus. Field-tests all blades. **Prices:** $125 to $250; some to $2000. **Remarks:** Part-time maker; first knife sold in 1980. **Mark:** Last name.

ROGERS, RODNEY, 602 Osceola St., Wildwood, FL 34785, Phone: 352-748-6114
Specialties: Traditional straight knives and folders. **Patterns:** Fighters, hunters, skinners. **Technical:** Flat-grinds ATS-34 and Damascus. Prefers natural materials. **Prices:** $150 to $1400. **Remarks:** Full-time maker; first knife sold in 1986. **Mark:** Last name, Handmade.

ROGERS, RICHARD, PO Box 769, Magdalena, NM 87825, Phone: 505-854-2567
Specialties: Sheffield-style folders and multi-blade folders. **Patterns:** Folders: various traditional patterns. One-of-a-kind fixed blades. Fixed blades: Bowies, daggers, hunters, utility knives. **Technical:** Mainly use ATS-34 and prefer natural handle materials. **Prices:** $400 and up. **Mark:** Last name.

ROGERS, CHARLES W., Rt. 1 Box 1552, Douglas, TX 75943, Phone: 409-326-4496

ROGERS JR., ROBERT P., 3979 South Main St., Acworth, GA 30101, Phone: 404-974-9982
Specialties: Traditional working knives. **Patterns:** Hunters, 4-inch trailing-points. **Technical:** Grinds D2, 154CM and ATS-34; likes ironwood and ivory Micarta. **Prices:** $125 to $175. **Remarks:** Spare-time maker; first knife sold in 1975. **Mark:** Name.

ROGHMANS, MARK, 607 Virginia Ave., LaGrange, GA 30240, Phone: 706-885-1273
Specialties: Classic and traditional knives of his design. **Patterns:** Bowies, daggers and fighters. **Technical:** Grinds ATS-34, D2 and 440C. **Prices:** $250 to $500. **Remarks:** Part-time maker; first knife sold in 1984. Doing business as LaGrange Knife. **Mark:** Last name and/or LaGrange Knife.

ROHN, FRED, 7675 W Happy Hill Rd., Coeur d'Alene, ID 83814, Phone: 208-667-0774
Specialties: Hunters, boot knives, custom patterns. **Patterns:** Drop points, double edge etc. **Technical:** Grinds 440 or 154CM. **Prices:** $85 and up. **Remarks:** Part-time maker. **Mark:** Logo on blade; serial numbered.

ROLLERT, STEVE, PO Box 65, Keensburg, CO 80643-0065, Phone: 303-732-4858
Specialties: Highly finished working knives. **Patterns:** Variety of straight knives; locking folders and slip-joints. **Technical:** Forges and grinds W2, 1095, ATS-34 and his pattern-welded, cable Damascus and nickel Damascus. **Prices:** $300 to $1000; some to $3000. **Remarks:** Full-time maker; first knife sold in 1980. Doing business as Dove Knives. **Mark:** Last name in script.

ROLLICK, WALTER D., 2001 Cochran Rd., Maryville, TN 37803, Phone: 423-681-6105

RONZIO, N. JACK, PO Box 248, Fruita, CO 81521, Phone: 970-858-0921

ROSA, PEDRO GULLHERME TELES, R. das Magnolias, 45 CECAP Presidente Prudente, SP-19065-410, BRAZIL, Phone: 0182-271769
Specialties: Using straight knives and folders to customer specs; some high-art. **Patterns:** Fighters, Bowies and daggers. **Technical:** Grinds and forges D6, 440C, high-carbon steels and Damascus. **Prices:** $60 to $400. **Remarks:** Full-time maker; first knife sold in 1991. **Mark:** A hammer over "Hammer."

ROSE, DEREK W., 14 Willow Wood Rd., Gallipolis, OH 45631, Phone: 740-446-4627

ROSENFELD, BOB, 955 Freeman Johnson Rd., Hoschton, GA 30548, Phone: 770-867-2647
Specialties: Fancy and embellished working/using straight knives of his design and in standard patterns. **Patterns:** Daggers, hunters and utility/camp knives. **Technical:** Forges 52100, A203E, 1095 and L6 Damascus. Offers engraving. **Prices:** $125 to $650; some to $1000. **Remarks:** Full-time maker; first knife sold in 1984. Also makes folders; ABS journeyman. **Mark:** Last name or full name, Knifemaker.

ROSS, TIM, 3239 Oliver Rd., RR #17, Thunder Bay, ONT, CANADA P7B 6C2, Phone: 807-935-2667
Specialties: Fancy working knives of his design. **Patterns:** Fishing and hunting knives, Bowies, daggers and miniatures. **Technical:** Uses D2, Stellite 6K and 440C; forges 52100 and Damascus. Makes antler handles and sheaths; has supply of whale teeth and moose antlers for trade. Prefers natural materials only. Wife Katherine scrimshaws. **Prices:** $100 to $350; some to $2100. **Remarks:** Part-time maker; first knife sold in 1975. **Mark:** Last name stamped on tang.

ROSS, GREGG, 4556 Wenhart Rd., Lake Worth, FL 33463, Phone: 407-439-4681
Specialties: Working/using straight knives. **Patterns:** Bowies, hunters and utility/camp knives. **Technical:** Forges and grinds ATS-34, Damascus and cable Damascus. Uses decorative pins. **Prices:** $125 to $250; some to $400. **Remarks:** Part-time maker; first knife sold in 1992. **Mark:** Name, city and state.

ROSS, STEPHEN, 534 Remington Dr., Evanston, WY 82930, Phone: 307-789-7104
Specialties: One-of-a-kind collector-grade classic and contemporary straight knives and folders of his design and to customer specs; some fantasy pieces. **Patterns:** Combat and survival knives, hunters, boots and folders. **Technical:** Grinds stainless; forges spring and tool steel. Engraves, scrimshaws. Makes leather sheaths. **Prices:** $160 to $3000. **Remarks:** Part-time-time maker; first knife sold in 1971. **Mark:** Last name in modified Roman; sometimes in script.

ROSS, D.L., 27 Kinsman St., Dunedin, NEW ZEALAND, Phone: 64 3 464 0239, Fax: 64 3 464 0239
Specialties: Working straight knives of his design. **Patterns:** Hunters, various others. **Technical:** Grinds 440C. **Prices:** $100 to $450; some to $700 NZ dollars. **Remarks:** Part-time maker; first knife sold in 1988. **Mark:** Dave Ross, Maker, city and country.

ROSSDEUTSCHER, ROBERT N., 133 S Vail Ave., Arlington Heights, IL 60005, Phone: 847-577-0404
Specialties: Frontier-style and historically inspired knives. **Patterns:** Trade knives, Bowies, camp knives and hunting knives. **Technical:** Most knives are hand forged, a few are stock removal. **Prices:** $85 to $600. **Remarks:** Journeyman Smith of the American Bladesmith Society and Neo-Tribal Metalsmiths. **Mark:** Back-to-back "R's", one upside down and backwards, one right side up and forward in an oval. Sometimes with name, town and state; depending on knife style.

ROTELLA, RICHARD A., 643—75th St., Niagara Falls, NY 14304
Specialties: Working knives of his design. **Patterns:** Various fishing, hunting and utility knives; folders. **Technical:** Grinds ATS-34. Prefers hand-rubbed finishes. **Prices:** $65 to $450; some to $900. **Remarks:** Spare-time maker; first knife sold in 1977. Not taking orders at this time; only sells locally. **Mark:** Name and city in stylized waterfall logo.

ROULIN, CHARLES, 113 B Rt. de Soral, 1233 Geneva, SWITZERLAND, Phone: 022-757-4479, Fax: 022-757-4479
Specialties: Fancy high-art straight knives and folders of his design. **Patterns:** Bowies, locking folders, slip-joint folders and miniatures. **Technical:** Grinds 440C, ATS-34 and D2. Engraves; carves nature scenes and detailed animals in steel, ivory, on handles and blades. **Prices:** $500 to $3000; some to $10,000. **Remarks:** Full-time maker; first knife sold in 1988. **Mark:** Symbol of fish with name or name engraved.

ROWE, STEWART G., 8-18 Coreen Court, Mt. Crosby, Brisbane 4306, AUSTRALIA, Phone: Ph: 073-201-0906, Fax: 073-201-2406
Specialties: Designer knives, reproduction of ancient weaponry, traditional Japanese tantos and edged tools. **Patterns:** "Shark"—blade range. **Technical:** Forges W1, W2, D2; creates own Tamahagne steel and composite pattern-welded billets. Gold, silver and ivory fittings available. **Prices:** $300 to $11,000. **Remarks:** Full-time maker; first knife sold in 1981. Doing business as Stewart Rowe Productions Pty Ltd.

ROWE, FRED, BETHEL RIDGE FORGE, 3199 Roberts Rd., Amesville, OH 45711, Phone: 866-325-2164
Specialties: Damascus and carbon steel sheath knives. **Patterns:** Bowies, hunters, fillet small kokris. **Technical:** My own Damascus, 52100, 0-P, L-6, 1095 carbon steels. **Prices:** $150-$800. **Remarks:** All blades are clay hardened. **Mark:** Bethel Ridge Forge.

ROZAS, CLARK D., 1436 W "G" St., Wilmington, CA 90744, Phone: 310-518-0488
Specialties: Hand forged blades. **Patterns:** Pig stickers, toad stabbers, whackers, choppers. **Technical:** Damascus, 52100, 1095, 1084, 5160. **Prices:** $200 to $600. **Remarks:** ABS member; part-time maker since 1995. **Mark:** Name over dagger.

RUANA KNIFE WORKS, Box 520, Bonner, MT 59823, Phone: 406-258-5368
Specialties: Working knives and period pieces. **Patterns:** Variety of straight knives. **Technical:** Forges 5160 chrome alloy for Bowies and 1095. **Prices:** $145 and up. **Remarks:** Full-time maker; first knife sold in 1938. Currently making knife honoring the lewis and clark expedition. **Mark:** Name.

RUPERT, BOB, 301 Harshaville Rd., Clinton, PA 15026, Phone: 724-573-4569
Specialties: Wrought period pieces with natural elements. **Patterns:** Elegant straight blades - friction folders. **Technical:** Forges colonial 7; 1095; 5160; diffuse mokume-gane and form Damascus. **Prices:** $150 to $1500; some higher. **Remarks:** Part-time maker; first knife sold in 1980. Evening hours studio since 1980. **Mark:** R etched in Old English. **Other:** Likes simplicity that disassembles.

RUPLE, WILLIAM H., PO Box 370, Charlotte, TX 78011, Phone: 830-277-1371
Specialties: Multi-blade folders, slip joints, some lock backs. **Patterns:** Like to reproduce old patterns. **Technical:** Grinds 440C, ATS-34, D2 and commercial Damascus. Offers filework on back springs and liners. **Prices:** $300 to $500; some to $1000. **Remarks:** Full-time maker; first knife sold in 1988. **Mark:** Ruple.

RUSS, RON, 5351 NE 160th Ave., Williston, FL 32696, Phone: 352-528-2603
Specialties: Damascus and Mokume. **Patterns:** Ladder, rain drop and butterfly. **Technical:** Most knives, including Damascus, are forged from 52100-E. **Prices:** $65 to $2500. **Mark:** Russ.

RUSSELL, MICK, 4 Rossini Rd., Pari Park, Port Elizabeth 6070, SOUTH AFRICA
Specialties: Art knives. **Patterns:** Working and collectible bird, trout and hunting knives, defense knives and folders. **Technical:** Grinds D2, 440C, ATS-34 and Damascus. Offers mirror or satin finishes. **Prices:** Start at $100. **Remarks:** Full-time maker; first knife sold in 1986. **Mark:** Stylized rhino incorporating initials.

RUSSELL, TOM, 6500 New Liberty Rd., Jacksonville, AL 36265, Phone: 205-492-7866
Specialties: Straight working knives of his design or to customer specs. **Patterns:** Hunters, folders, fighters, skinners, Bowies and utility knives. **Technical:** Grinds D2, 440C and ATS-34; offers filework. **Prices:** $75 to $225. **Remarks:** Part-time maker; first knife sold in 1987. Full-time tool and die maker. **Mark:** Last name with tulip stamp.

RUTH, MICHAEL G, 3101 New Boston Rd., Texarkana, TX 75501, Phone: 903-832-7166

RYAN, C.O., 902-A Old Wormley Creek Rd., Yorktown, VA 23692, Phone: 757-898-7797
Specialties: Working/using knives. **Patterns:** Hunters, kitchen knives, locking folders. **Technical:** Grinds 440C and ATS-34. **Prices:** $45 to $130; some to $450. **Remarks:** Part-time maker; first knife sold in 1980. **Mark:** Name-C.O. Ryan.

RYBAR JR., RAYMOND B., 726 W Lynwood St., Phoenix, AZ 85007, Phone: 605-523-0201
Specialties: Fancy/embellished, high-art and traditional working using straight knives and folders of his design and in standard patterns; period pieces. **Patterns:** Daggers, fighters and swords. **Technical:** Forges Damascus. All blades have etched biblical scripture or biblical significance. **Prices:** $120 to $1200; some to $4500. **Remarks:** Full-time maker; first

knife sold in 1972. Doing business as **Stone Church Forge. Mark:** Last name or business name.

RYBERG, GOTE, Faltgatan 2, S-562 00 Norrahammar, SWEDEN, Phone: 4636-61678

RYDBOM, JEFF, PO Box 548, Annandale, MN 55302, Phone: 320-274-9639
Specialties: Ring knives. **Patterns:** Hunters, fighters, Bowie and camp knives. **Technical:** Straight grinds 01, A2, 1566 and 5150 steels. **Prices:** $150-$1000. **Remarks:** No pinning of guards or pommels. All silver brazed. **Mark:** Capital "C" with J R inside.

RYDER, BEN M., PO Box 133, Copperhill, TN 37317, Phone: 615-496-2750
Specialties: Working/using straight knives of his design and to customer specs. **Patterns:** Fighters, hunters, utility/camp knives. **Technical:** Grinds 440C, ATS-34, D2, commercial Damascus. **Prices:** $75 to $400. **Remarks:** Part-time maker; first knife sold in 1992. **Mark:** Full name in double butterfly logo.

RYUICHI, KUKI, 504-7 Tokorozawa-shinmachi Tokorozawa-city, Saitama, JAPAN, Phone: 042-943-3451

RZEWNICKI, GERALD, 8833 S Massbach Rd., Elizabeth, IL 61028-9714, Phone: 815-598-3239

S

SAINDON, R. BILL, 233 Rand Pond Rd., Goshen, NH 03752, Phone: 603-863-1874
Specialties: Collector-quality folders of his design or to customer specs. **Patterns:** Latch release, liner lock and lockback folders. **Technical:** Offers limited amount of own Damascus; also uses Damas makers steel. Prefers natural handle material, gold and gems. **Prices:** $500 to $4000. **Remarks:** Full-time maker; first knife sold in 1981. Doing business as Daynia Forge. **Mark:** Sun logo or engraved surname.

ST. CLAIR, THOMAS K., 12608 Fingerboard Rd., Monrovia, MD 21770, Phone: 301-482-0264

ST. AMOUR, MURRAY, RR 3, 222 Dicks Rd., Pembroke ON, CANADA K8A 6W4, Phone: 613-735-1061
Specialties: Working fixed blades. **Patterns:** Hunters, fish, fighters, Bowies and utility knives. **Technical:** Grinds ATS-34, 154-CM, CPM-440V and Damascus. **Prices:** $75 and up. **Remarks:** Full-time maker; sold first knife in 1992. **Mark:** Last name over Canada.

ST. CYR, H. RED, 1218 N Cary Ave., Wilmington, CA 90744, Phone: 310-518-9525

SAKAKIBARA, MASAKI, 20-8 Sakuragaoka, 2-Chome Setagaya-ku, Tokyo 156-0054, JAPAN, Phone: 81-3-3420-0375

SAKMAR, MIKE, 1451 Clovelly Ave., Rochester, MI 48307, Phone: 248-852-6775, Fax: 248-852-8544
Specialties: Mokume in various patterns and alloy combinations. **Patterns:** Bowies, fighters, hunters and integrals. **Technical:** Grinds ATS-34, Damascus and high-carbon tool steels. Uses mostly natural handle materials—elephant ivory, walrus ivory, stag, wildwood, oosic, etc. Makes mokume for resale. **Prices:** $250 to $2500; some to $4000. **Remarks:** Part-time maker; first knife sold in 1990. **Mark:** Last name. **Other:** Supplier of Mokume.

SALLEY, JOHN D., 3965 Frederick-Ginghamsburg Rd., Tipp City, OH 45371, Phone: 937-698-4588, Fax: 937-698-4131
Specialties: Fancy working knives and art pieces. **Patterns:** Hunters, fighters, daggers and some swords. **Technical:** Grinds ATS-34, 12C27 and W2; buys Damascus. **Prices:** $85 to $1000; some to $6000. **Remarks:** Part-time maker; first knife sold in 1979. **Mark:** First initial, last name.

SAMPSON, LYNN, 381 Deakins Rd., Jonesborough, TN 37659, Phone: 423-348-8373
Specialties: Highly finished working knives, mostly folders. **Patterns:** Locking folders, slip-joints, interframes and two-blades. **Technical:** Grinds D2, 440C and ATS-34; offers extensive filework. **Prices:** Start at $300. **Remarks:** Full-time maker; first knife sold in 1982. **Mark:** Name and city in logo.

SANDBERG, RONALD B., 24784 Shadowwood Ln., Browntown, MI 48134, Phone: 734-671-6866
Specialties: Good looking and functional hunting knives, filework, mixing of handle materials. **Patterns:** Hunters, skinners and Bowies. **Prices:** $120 and up. **Mark:** R.B. Sandberg.

SANDERS, A.A., 3850 72 Ave. NE, Norman, OK 73071, Phone: 405-364-8660
Specialties: Working straight knives and folders. **Patterns:** Hunters, fighters, daggers and Bowies. **Technical:** Forges his own Damascus; offers stock removal with ATS-34, 440C, A2, D2, O1, 5160 and 1095.

Prices: $85 to $1500. **Remarks:** Full-time maker; first knife sold in 1985. Formerly known as Athern Forge. **Mark:** Name.

SANDERS, BILL, 335 Bauer Ave., PO Box 957, Mancos, CO 81328, Phone: 970-533-7223
Specialties: Working straight knives, some fancy and some fantasy, of his design. **Patterns:** Hunters, boots, utility knives, using belt knives. **Technical:** Grinds 440C, ATS-34 and commercial Damascus. Provides wide variety of handle materials. **Prices:** $170 to $350; some to $800. **Remarks:** Full-time maker. Formerly of Timberline knives. **Mark:** Name, city and state.

SANDERS, MICHAEL M., PO Box 1106, Ponchatoula, LA 70454, Phone: 225-294-3601
Specialties: Working straight knives and folders, some deluxe. **Patterns:** Hunters, fighters, Bowies, daggers, large folders and deluxe Damascus miniatures. **Technical:** Grinds O1, D2, 440C, ATS-34 and Damascus. **Prices:** $75 to $650; some higher. **Remarks:** Full-time maker; first knife sold in 1967. **Mark:** Name and state.

SANDERSON, RAY, 4403 Uplands Way, Yakima, WA 98908, Phone: 509-965-0128
Specialties: One-of-a-kind Buck knives; traditional working straight knives and folders of his design. **Patterns:** Bowies, hunters and fighters. **Technical:** Grinds 440C and ATS-34. **Prices:** $200 to $750. **Remarks:** Part-time maker; first knife sold in 1984. **Mark:** Sanderson Knives in shape of Bowie.

SANDLIN, LARRY, 4580 Sunday Dr., Adamsville, AL 35005, Phone: 205-674-1816
Specialties: High-art straight knives of his design. **Patterns:** Boots, daggers, hunters and fighters. **Technical:** Forges 1095, L6, O1, carbon steel and Damascus. **Prices:** $200 to $1500; some to $5000. **Remarks:** Part-time maker; first knife sold in 1990. **Mark:** Chiseled last name in Japanese.

SANDS, SCOTT, 2 Lindis Ln., New Brighton, Christchurch 9, NEW ZEALAND
Specialties: Classic working and fantasy swords. **Patterns:** Fantasy, medieval, celtic, viking, katana, some daggers. **Technical:** Forges own Damascus; 1080 and L6; 5160 and L6; 01 and L6. All hand-polished, does own heat-treating, forges non-Damascus on request. **Prices:** $1500 to $15,000+. **Remarks:** Full-time maker; first blade sold in 1996. **Mark:** Stylized S.

SARVIS, RANDALL J., 110 West Park Ave., Fort Pierre, SD 57532, Phone: 605-223-2772

SASS, GARY N., 23 Baker Ave., Hermitage, PA 16148, Phone: 724-342-7833
Specialties: Working straight knives of his design or to customer specifications. **Patterns:** Hunters, fighters, utility knives, push daggers. **Technical:** Grinds 440C, ATS-34 and Damascus. Uses exotic wood, buffalo horn, warthog tusk and semi-precious stones. **Prices:** $50-$250, some higher. **Remarks:** Part-time maker. First knife sold in 2003. **Mark:** Initials G.S. formed into a diamond shape.

SAUER, CHARLES, CUSTOM SAUER KNIVES LLC, 1079 1/2 Hodgson Rd., Columbia Falls, MT 59912-9027, Phone: 406-257-9310, Fax: 775-213-9883
Specialties: Hand forges his own steel, makes Damascus, and does all of his own heat treating to insure quality. He also make Damascus for gunmakers-scope rings, floorplate, grip cap. **Patterns:** 3D and W's.

SAWBY, SCOTT, 480 Snowberry Ln., Sandpoint, ID 83864, Phone: 208-263-4171
Specialties: Folders, working and fancy. **Patterns:** Locking folders, patent locking systems and interframes. **Technical:** Grinds D2, 440C, 154CM, CPM-T-440V and ATS-34. **Prices:** $500 to $1500. **Remarks:** Full-time maker; first knife sold in 1974. Engraving by wife Marian. **Mark:** Last name, city and state.

SCARROW, WIL, c/o LandW Mail Service, 919 E Hermosa Dr., San Gabriel, CA 91775, Phone: 626-286-6069
Specialties: Carving knives, also working straight knives in standard patterns or to customer specs. **Patterns:** Carving, fishing, hunting, skinning, utility, swords and Bowies. **Technical:** Forges and grinds: A2, L6, W1, D2, 5160, 1095, 440C, AEB-L, ATS-34 and others on request. Offers some filework. **Prices:** $105 to $850; some higher. Prices include sheath (carver's $40 and up). **Remarks:** Spare-time maker; first knife sold in 1983. Two to eight month construction time on custom orders. Doing business as Scarrow's Custom Stuff and Gold Hill Knife works (in Oregon). **Mark:** SC with arrow and date/year made. **Other:** Carving knives available at the 'Wild Duck' Woodcarvers Supply. Contact at duckstore@aol.com.

SCHALLER, ANTHONY BRETT, 5609 Flint Ct. NW, Albuquerque, NM 87120, Phone: 505-899-0155
Specialties: Straight knives and locking-liner folders of his design and in standard patterns. **Patterns:** Boots, fighters, utility knives and folders.

custom knifemakers

Technical: Grinds ATS-34, BG42 and stainless Damascus. Offers filework, hand-rubbed finishes and full and narrow tangs. Prefers exotic woods or Micarta for handle materials, G-10 and carbon fiber to handle materials. **Prices:** $60 to $350; some to $500. **Remarks:** Part-time maker; first knife sold in 1990. **Mark:** A.B. Schaller - Albuquerque NM - handmade.

SCHEID, MAGGIE, 124 Van Stallen St., Rochester, NY 14621-3557
Specialties: Simple working straight knives. **Patterns:** Kitchen and utility knives; some miniatures. **Technical:** Forges 5160 high-carbon steel. **Prices:** $100 to $200. **Remarks:** Part-time maker; first knife sold in 1986. **Mark:** Full name.

SCHEMPP, MARTIN, PO Box 1181, 5430 Baird Springs Rd. N.W., Ephrata, WA 98823, Phone: 509-754-2963, Fax: 509-754-3212
Specialties: Fantasy and traditional straight knives of his design, to customer specs and in standard patterns; Paleolithic-styles. **Patterns:** Fighters and Paleolithic designs. **Technical:** Uses opal, Mexican rainbow and obsidian. Offers scrimshaw. **Prices:** $15 to $100; some to $250. **Remarks:** Spare-time maker; first knife sold in 1995. **Mark:** Initials and date.

SCHEMPP, ED, PO Box 1181, Ephrata, WA 98823, Phone: 509-754-2963, Fax: 509-754-3212
Specialties: Mosaic Damascus and unique folder designs. **Patterns:** Primarily folders. **Technical:** Grinds CPM440V; forges many patterns of mosaic using powdered steel. **Prices:** $100 to $400; some to $2000. **Remarks:** Part-time maker; first knife sold in 1991. Doing business as Ed Schempp Knives. **Mark:** Ed Schempp Knives over five heads of wheat, city and state.

SCHEPERS, GEORGE B., PO Box 395, Shelton, NE 68876-0395
Specialties: Fancy period pieces of his design. **Patterns:** Bowies, swords, tomahawks; locking folders and miniatures. **Technical:** Grinds W1, W2 and his own Damascus; etches. **Prices:** $125 to $600; some higher. **Remarks:** Full-time maker; first knife sold in 1981. **Mark:** Schep.

SCHEURER, ALFREDO E. FAES, Av. Rincon de los Arcos 104, Col. Bosque Res. del Sur, C.P. 16010, MEXICO, Phone: 5676 47 63
Specialties: Fancy and fantasy knives of his design. **Patterns:** Daggers. **Technical:** Grinds stainless steel; casts and grinds silver. Sets stones in silver. **Prices:** $2000 to $3000. **Remarks:** Spare-time maker; first knife sold in 1989. **Mark:** Symbol.

SCHILLING, ELLEN, 95 Line Rd., Hamilton Square, NJ 08690, Phone: 609-448-0483

SCHIPPNICK, JIM, PO Box 326, Sanborn, NY 14132, Phone: 716-731-3715
Specialties: Nordic, early American, rustic. **Mark:** Runic R. **Remarks:** Also import Nordic knives from Norway, Sweden and Finland.

SCHIRMER, MIKE, 312 E 6th St., Rosalia, WA 99170-9506, Phone: 208-523-3249
Specialties: Working straight knives of his design or to customer specs; mostly hunters and personal knives. **Patterns:** Hunters, camp, kitchen, Bowies and fighters. **Technical:** Grinds O1, D2, A2 and Damascus and Talonite. **Prices:** Start at $150. **Remarks:** Full-time maker; first knife sold in 1992. Doing business as Ruby Mountain Knives. **Mark:** Name or name and location.

SCHLOMER, JAMES E., 2543 Wyatt Pl., Kissimmee, FL 34741, Phone: 407-348-8044
Specialties: Working and show straight knives. **Patterns:** Hunters, Bowies and skinners. **Technical:** Stock removal method, 440C. Scrimshaws; carves sambar stag handles. Works on corean and Micarta. **Prices:** $150 to $750. **Remarks:** Full-time maker. **Mark:** Name and steel number.

SCHLUETER, DAVID, PO Box 463, Syracuse, NY 13209, Phone: 315-485-0829
Specialties: Japanese-style swords, handmade fittings, leather wraps. **Patterns:** Kozuka to Tach, blades with bo-hi and o-kissaki. **Technical:** Sole author, forges and grinds, high-carbon steels. Blades are tempered after clay-coated and water-quenched heat treatment. All fittings are handmade. **Prices:** $800 to $5000 plus. **Remarks:** Full-time maker, doing business as Odd Frog Forge. **Mark:** Full name and date.

SCHMIDT, RICK, PO Box 1318, Whitefish, MT 59937, Phone: 406-862-6471, Fax: 406-862-6078
Specialties: Traditional working and using straight knives and folders of his design and to customer specs. **Patterns:** Fighters, hunters, cutlery and utility knives. **Technical:** Flat-grinds D2 and ATS-34. Custom leather sheaths. **Prices:** $120 to $250; some to $1900. **Remarks:** Full-time maker; first knife sold in 1975. **Mark:** Stylized initials.

SCHMITZ, RAYMOND E., PO Box 1787, Valley Center, CA 92082, Phone: 760-749-4318

SCHMOKER, RANDY, SPIRIT OF THE HAMMER, HC 63 Box 1085, Slana, AK 99586, Phone: 907-822-3371
Specialties: Hand carved, natural materials, mastodon ivory, moose antler. **Patterns:** Hunter, skinner, Bowie, fighter, artistic collectables. **Technical:** Hand forged. **Prices:** $300 to $600. **Remarks:** 01 tool steel, 1095, 5160, 52100. **Mark:** Sheep with an S. **Other:** Custom sheaths, display stands.

SCHNEIDER, CRAIG M., 5380 N Amity Rd., Claremont, IL 62421, Phone: 217-377-5715
Specialties: Straight knives of his own design. **Patterns:** Bowies, hunters and miniatures. **Technical:** Forged high-carbon steel and Damascus. Flat grind and differential heat treatment use a wide selection of handle, guard and bolster material also offer leather sheaths. **Prices:** $85 to $2500. **Remarks:** Part-time maker; first knife sold in 1985. **Mark:** Stylized initials.

SCHNEIDER, KARL A., 209 N. Brownleaf Rd., Newark, DE 19713, Phone: 302-737-0277
Specialties: Traditional working and using straight knives of his design. **Patterns:** Hunters, kitchen and fillet knives. **Technical:** Grinds ATS-34. Shapes handles to fit hands; uses Micarta, Pakkawood and exotic woods. Makes hand-stitched leather cases. **Prices:** $95 to $225. **Remarks:** Part-time maker; first knife sold in 1984-85. **Mark:** Name, address; also name in shape of fish.

SCHOEMAN, CORRIE, Box 28596, Danhof 9310, SOUTH AFRICA, Phone: 027 51 4363528 Cell: 027 82-3750789
Specialties: High-tech folders of his design or to customer's specs. **Patterns:** Linerlock folders and automatics. **Technical:** ATS-34, Damascus or stainless Damascus with titanium frames; prefers exotic materials for handles. **Prices:** $500 to $2000. **Remarks:** Full-time maker; first knife sold in 1984. **Mark:** Logo in knife shape engraved on inside of back bar. **Other:** All folders come with filed liners and back and jewled inserts.

SCHOENFELD, MATTHEW A., RR #1, Galiano Island, B.C., CANADA V0N 1P0, Phone: 250-539-2806
Specialties: Working knives of his design. **Patterns:** Kitchen cutlery, camp knives, hunters. **Technical:** Grinds 440C. **Prices:** $85 to $500. **Remarks:** Part-time maker; first knife sold in 1978. **Mark:** Signature, Galiano Is. B.C., and date.

SCHOENINGH, MIKE, 49850 Miller Rd, North Powder, OR 97867, Phone: 541-856-3239

SCHOLL, TIM, 1389 Langdon Rd., Angier, NC 27501, Phone: 910-897-2051
Specialties: Fancy and working/using straight knives and folders of his design and to customer specs. **Patterns:** tomahawks, swords, tantos, hunters and fantasy knives. **Technical:** Grinds ATS-34 and D2; forges carbon and tool steel and Damascus. Offers filework, engraving and scrimshaw. **Prices:** $110; some to $4000. **Remarks:** Part-time maker; first knife sold in 1990. Doing business as Tim Scholl Custom Knives. **Mark:** S pierced by arrow.

SCHRADER, ROBERT, 55532 Gross De, Bend, OR 97707, Phone: 541-598-7301
Specialties: Hunting, utility, Bowie. **Patterns:** Fixed blade. **Prices:** $150-$600.

SCHRAP, ROBERT G., CUSTOM LEATHER KNIFE SHEATH CO., 7024 W. Wells St., Wauwatosa, WI 53213-3717, Phone: 414-771-6472, Fax: 414-479-9765
Specialties: Leatherwork. **Prices:** $35 to $100. **Mark:** Schrap in oval.

SCHROEN, KARL, 4042 Bones Rd., Sebastopol, CA 95472, Phone: 707-823-4057, Fax: 707-823-2914
Specialties: Using knives made to fit. **Patterns:** Sgian dubhs, carving sets, wood-carving knives, fishing knives, kitchen knives and new cleaver design. **Technical:** Forges A2, ATS-34,D2 and L-6 cruwear S30V 590V. **Prices:** $150 to $6000. **Remarks:** Full-time maker; first knife sold in 1968. Author of *The Hand Forged Knife.* **Mark:** Last name.

SCHULTZ, ROBERT W., PO Box 70, Cocolalla, ID 83813-0070

SCHWARZER, STEPHEN, PO Box 4, Pomona Park, FL 32181, Phone: 386-649-5026, Fax: 386-649-8585
Specialties: Mosaic Damascus and picture mosaic in folding knives. **Patterns:** Folders, axes and buckskinner knives. **Technical:** Specializes in picture mosaic Damascus and powder metal mosaic work. Sole authorship; all work including carving done in-house. Most blades have file work and carving. **Prices:** $1500 to $5000, some higher; carbon steel and primitive knives much less. **Remarks:** Full-time maker; first knife sold in 1976, considered by many to be one of the top mosaic Damascus specialists in the world. Mosaic Master level work. **Mark:** Schwarzer + anvil.

SCIMIO, BILL, HC 01 Box 24A, Spruce Creek, PA 16683, Phone: 814-632-3751

SCOFIELD, EVERETT, 2873 Glass Mill Rd., Chickamauga, GA 30707, Phone: 706-375-2790
Specialties: Historic and fantasy miniatures. **Patterns:** All patterns. **Technical:** Uses only the finest tool steels and other materials. Uses only natural, precious and semi-precious materials. **Prices:** $100 to $1500. **Remarks:** Full-time maker; first knife sold in 1971. Doing business as Three Crowns Cutlery. **Mark:** Three Crowns logo.

SCORDIA, PAOLO, Via Terralba 143, 00050 Torrimpietra, Roma, ITALY, Phone: 06-61697231
Specialties: Working and fantasy knives of his own design. **Patterns:** Any pattern. **Technical:** Forges own Damascus, welds own Mokume and grinds ATS-34, etc. use hardwoods and Micarta for handles, brass and nickel-silver for fittings. Makes sheaths. **Prices:** $100 to $1000. **Remarks:** Part-time maker; first knife sold in 1988. **Mark:** Initials with sun and moon logo.

SCOTT, AL, 2245 Harper Valley Rd., Harper, TX 78631, Phone: 830-864-4182
Specialties: High-art straight knives of his design. **Patterns:** Daggers, swords, early European, Middle East and Japanese knives. **Technical:** Uses ATS-34, 440C and Damascus. Hand engraves; does file work cuts filigree in the blade; offers ivory carving and precious metal inlay. **Remarks:** Full-time maker; first knife sold in 1994. Doing business as Al Scott Maker of Fine Blade Art. **Mark:** Name engraved in old English, sometime inlaid in 24K gold.

SCROGGS, JAMES A., 108 Murray Hill Dr., Warrensburg, MO 64093, Phone: 660-747-2568
Specialties: Straight knives, prefers light weight. **Patterns:** Hunters, hide-outs, and fighters. **Technical:** Grinds 5160, 01, and 52-100. Prefers handles of walnut in English, bastonge, American black Also uses myrtle, maple, Osage orange. **Prices:** $200-$1000. **Remarks:** 1st knife sold in 1985. Part-time maker, no orders taken. **Mark:** SCROGGS in block or script.

SCULLEY, PETER E., 340 Sunset Dr., Rising Fawn, GA 30738, Phone: 706-398-0169

SEARS, MICK, 1697 Peach Orchard Rd. #302, Sumter, SC 29154, Phone: 803-499-5074
Specialties: Scots and confederate reproductions; Bowies and fighters. **Patterns:** Bowies, fighters. **Technical:** Grinds 440C and 1095. **Prices:** $50 to $150; some to $300. **Remarks:** Part-time maker; first knife sold in 1975. Doing business as Mick's Custom Knives. **Mark:** First name.

SELENT, CHUCK, PO Box 1207, Bonners Ferry, ID 83805-1207, Phone: 208-267-5807
Specialties: Period, art and fantasy miniatures; exotics; one-of-a-kinds. **Patterns:** Swords, daggers and others. **Technical:** Works in Damascus, meteorite, 440C and tool steel. Offers scrimshaw. Offers his own casting and leatherwork; uses jewelry techniques. Makes display cases for miniatures. **Prices:** $75 to $400. **Remarks:** Part-time maker; first knife sold in 1990. **Mark:** Last name and bear paw print logo scrimshawed on handles or leatherwork.

SELF, ERNIE, 950 O'Neill Ranch Rd., Dripping Springs, TX 78620-9760, Phone: 512-858-7133
Specialties: Traditional and working straight knives and folders of his design and in standard patterns. **Patterns:** Hunters, locking folders and slip-joints. **Technical:** Grinds 440C, D2, 440V, ATS-34 and Damascus. Offers fancy filework. **Prices:** $125 to $500; some to $1500. **Remarks:** Full-time maker; first knife sold in 1982. **Mark:** In oval shape - Ernie Self Maker Dripping Springs TX. **Other:** Also customizes Buck 110's and 112's folding hunters.

SELLEVOLD, HARALD, S.Kleivesmau:2, PO Box 4134, N5834 Bergen, NORWAY, Phone: 55-310682
Specialties: Norwegian-styles; collaborates with other Norse craftsmen. **Patterns:** Distinctive ferrules and other mild modifications of traditional patterns; Bowies and friction folders. **Technical:** Buys Damascus blades; blacksmiths his own blades. Semi-gemstones used in handles; gemstone inlay. **Prices:** $350 to $2000. **Remarks:** Full-time maker; first knife sold in 1980. **Mark:** Name and country in logo.

SELZAM, FRANK, Martin Reinhard Str 23, 97631, Bad Koenigshofen, GERMANY, Phone: 09761-5980
Specialties: Hunters, working knives to customers specs, hand tooled and stitched leather sheaths large stock of wood and German stag horn. **Patterns:** Mostly own design. **Technical:** Forged blades, own Damascus, also stock removal stainless. **Prices:** $250 - $1500. **Remark:** First knife sold in 1978. **Mark:** Last name stamped.

SENTZ, MARK C., 4084 Baptist Rd., Taneytown, MD 21787, Phone: 410-756-2018
Specialties: Fancy straight working knives of his design. **Patterns:** Hunters, fighters, folders and utility/camp knives. **Technical:** Forges 1085, 1095, 5160, 5155 and his Damascus. Most knives come with wood-lined leather sheath or wooden presentation sheath. **Prices:** Start at $275. **Remarks:** Full-time maker; first knife sold in 1989. Doing business as M. Charles Sentz Gunsmithing, Inc. **Mark:** Last name.

SERAFEN, STEVEN E., 24 Genesee St., New Berlin, NY 13411, Phone: 607-847-6903
Specialties: Traditional working/using straight knives of his design and to customer specs. **Patterns:** Bowies, fighters, hunters. **Technical:** Grinds ATS-34, 440C, high-carbon steel. **Prices:** $175 to $600; some to $1200. **Remarks:** Part-time maker; first knife sold in 1990. **Mark:** First and middle initial, last name in script.

SERVEN, JIM, PO Box 1, Fostoria, MI 48435, Phone: 517-795-2255
Specialties: Highly finished unique folders. **Patterns:** Fancy working folders, axes, miniatures and razors; some straight knives. **Technical:** Grinds 440C; forges his own Damascus. **Prices:** $150 to $800; some to $1500. **Remarks:** Full-time maker; first knife sold in 1971. **Mark:** Name in map logo.

SEVEY CUSTOM KNIFE, 94595 Chandler Rd., Gold Beach, OR 97444, Phone: 541-247-2649
Specialties: Fixed blade hunters. **Patterns:** Drop point, trailing paint, clip paint, full tang, hidden tang. **Technical:** D-2, and ATS-34 blades, stock removal. Heat treatment by Paul Bos. **Prices:** $225 and up depending on overall length and grip material. **Mark:** Sevey Custom Knife.

SFREDDO, RODRITO MENEZES, Rua 15 De Novembro 2222, Nova Petropolis, RS, BRASIL 95150-000, Phone: 011-55-54-303-303-90
Specialties: Traditional Brazilian-style working and high-art knives of his design. **Patterns:** Fighters, Bowies, utility and camp knives, classic Mediterranean Dirk. Welcome customer design. **Technical:** Forges only with sledge hammers (no power hammer here) 100% to shape in 52100 and his own Damascus. Makes own sheaths in the true traditional Brazilian-style. **Remark:** Full-time maker. **Prices:** $250 to $1100 for his elaborate Mediterranean Dirk. Uses only natural handle materials. Considered by many to be Brazil's best bladesmith.

SHADLEY, EUGENE W., 26315 Norway Dr., Bovey, MN 55709, Phone: 218-245-3820, Fax: 218-245-1639
Specialties: Classic multi-blade folders. **Patterns:** Whittlers, stockman, sowbelly, congress, trapper, etc. **Technical:** Grinds ATS-34, 416 frames. **Prices:** Start at $300. **Remarks:** Full-time maker; first knife sold in 1985. Doing business as Shadley Knives. **Mark:** Last name.

SHADMOT, BOAZ, MOSHAV PARAN D N, Arava, ISRAEL 86835

SHARRIGAN, MUDD, 111 Bradford Rd., Wiscasset, ME 04578-4457, Phone: 207-882-9820, Fax: 207-882-9835
Specialties: Custom designs; repair straight knives, custom leather sheaths. **Patterns:** Daggers, fighters, hunters, buckskinner, Indian crooked knives and seamen working knives; traditional Scandinavian-styles. **Technical:** Forges 1095, 52100, 5160, W2, O1. Laminates 1095 and mild steel. **Prices:** $50 to $325; some to $1200. **Remarks:** Full-time maker; first knife sold in 1982. **Mark:** First name and swallow tail carving.

SHAVER II, JAMES R., 1529 Spider Ridge Rd., Parkersburg, WV 26104, Phone: 304-422-2692
Specialties: Hunting and working straight knives in carbon and Damascus steel. **Patterns:** Bowies and daggers in Damascus and carbon steels. **Technical:** Forges 5160 carbon and Damascus in O101018 mild steel and pvee nickel. **Prices:** $85 to $225; some to $750. **Remarks:** Part-time maker; sold first knife in 1998. Believes in sole authorship. **Mark:** Last name.

SHEEHY, THOMAS J., 4131 NE 24th Ave., Portland, OR 97211-6411, Phone: 503-493-2843
Specialties: Hunting knives and ULUs. **Patterns:** Own or customer designs. **Technical:** 1095/01 and ATS-34 steel. **Prices:** $35 to $200. **Remarks:** Do own heat treating; forged or ground blades. **Mark:** Name.

SHEETS, STEVEN WILLIAM, 6 Stonehouse Rd, Mendham, NJ 07945, Phone: 201-543-5882

SHIFFER, STEVE, PO Box 582, Leakesville, MS 39451, Phone: 601-394-4425
Specialties: Bowies, Fighters, Hard use knives. **Patterns:** Fighters, Hunters, Combat/Utility knives Walker pattern liner lock knives. Allen pattern scale and bolster release autos. **Technical:** Most work forged, stainless stock removal. Make own Damascus. O-1 and 5160 most used also 1084, 440c, 154cm, s30v. **Prices:** $125-$1000. **Remarks:** First knife sold in

custom knifemakers

2000, all heat treatment done by myself. Doing business as Choctaw Plantation Forge. **Mark:** Hot mark sunrise over creek.

SHIKAYAMA, TOSHIAKI, 259-2 Suka Yoshikawa City, Saitama 342-0057, JAPAN, Phone: 04-89-81-6605, Fax: 04-89-81-6605
Specialties: Folders in standard patterns. **Patterns:** Locking and multi-blade folders. **Technical:** Grinds ATS, carbon steel, high speed steel. **Prices:** $400 to $2500; $4500 with engraving. **Remarks:** Full-time maker; first knife sold in 1952. **Mark:** First initial, last name.

SHINOSKY, ANDY, 3117 Meanderwood Dr., Canfield, OH 44406, Phone: 330-702-0299
Specialties: Collectible fancy folders and interframes. **Patterns:** Drop points, trailing points and daggers. **Technical:** Grinds ATS-34 and Damascus. Prefers natural handle materials. **Prices:** Start at $450. **Remarks:** Part-time maker; first knife sold in 1992. **Mark:** Name or bent folder logo.

SHIPLEY, STEVEN A., 800 Campbell Rd. Ste 137, Richardson, TX 75081, Phone: 972-644-7981, Fax: 972-644-7985
Specialties: Hunters, skinners and traditional straight knives. **Technical:** Hand grinds ATS-34, 440C and Damascus steels. Each knife is custom sheathed by his son, Dan. **Prices:** $175 to $2000. **Remarks:** Part-time maker; like smooth lines and unusual handle materials. **Mark:** S A Shipley.

SHOEBOTHAM, HEATHER, HEATHER'S BLACKSMITH SHOP, POB 768, Belfast 1100, SOUTH AFRICA, Phone: +27 11 496 1600, Fax: +27 11 835 2932
Specialties: All steel hand forged knives of her own design. **Patterns:** Traditional African weapons, friction folders and by-gone forged styles. **Technical:** Own Damascus, specializing in drive chain and steel wire rope, Meteorite, 420 and Mokume. Also using forged brass, copper and titanium fittings. All work hand-forged using a traditional coal fire. Differential heat-treatment used. **Prices:** $150 to $3000. **Remarks:** Full-time practicing blacksmith and furrier and part-time bladesmith. First Damascus sold in 1995. First knife sold in 1998. Member of ABS. **Mark:** Knives: Rearing unicorn in horseshoe surrounded with first name. Damascus: Sold under "Damsel Damascus".

SHOEMAKER, CARROLL, 380 Yellowtown Rd., Northup, OH 45658, Phone: 740-446-6695
Specialties: Working/using straight knives of his design. **Patterns:** Hunters, utility/camp and early American backwoodsmen knives. **Technical:** Grinds ATS-34; forges old files, O1 and 1095. Uses some Damascus; offers scrimshaw and engraving. **Prices:** $100 to $175; some to $350. **Remarks:** Spare-time maker; first knife sold in 1977. **Mark:** Name and city or connected initials.

SHOEMAKER, SCOTT, 316 S. Main St., Miamisburg, OH 45342, Phone: 513-859-1935
Specialties: Twisted, wire-wrapped handles on swords, fighters and fantasy blades; new line of seven models with quick-draw, multi-carry Kydex sheaths. **Patterns:** Bowies, boots and one-of-a-kinds in his design or to customer specs. **Technical:** Grinds A6 and ATS-34; buys Damascus. Hand satin finish is standard. **Prices:** $100 to $1500; swords to $8000. **Remarks:** Part-time maker; first knife sold in 1984. **Mark:** Angel wings with last initial, or last name.

SHOGER, MARK O., 14780 SW Osprey Dr., Suite 345, Beaverton, OR 97007, Phone: 503-579-2495
Specialties: Working and using straight knives and folders of his design; fancy and embellished knives. **Patterns:** Hunters, Bowies, daggers and locking folders. **Technical:** Forges O1, W2 and his own pattern-welded Damascus. **Remarks:** Spare-time maker. **Mark:** Last name or stamped last initial over anvil.

SHORE, JOHN I., ALASKA KNIFEMAKER, 2901 Sheldon Jackson St., Anchorage, AK 99508, Phone: 907-272-2253
Specialties: Working straight knives, hatchets, and folders. **Patterns:** Hunters, skinners, Bowies, fighters, working using knives. **Technical:** Prefer use exotic steels, grinds CPM's, Damasteel, RWL34, BG42, D2 and some ATS34. Prefers exotic hardwoods, stabilized materials, Micarta, and Pearl. **Prices:** Start at $200. **Remarks:** Full-time maker; first knife sold in 1985. **Mark:** Name in script, Anchorage, AK.

SHOSTLE, BEN, 1121 Burlington, Muncie, IN 47302, Phone: 765-282-9073, Fax: 765-282-5270
Specialties: Fancy high-art straight knives of his design. **Patterns:** Bowies, daggers and fighters. **Technical:** Uses 440C, ATS-34 and commercial Damascus. All knives and engraved. **Prices:** $900 to $3200; some to $4000. **Remarks:** Full-time maker; first knife sold in 1987. Doing business as The Gun Room (T.G.R.). **Mark:** Last name.

SHOSTLE, BEN, 1121 Burlington, Muncie, IN 47302, Phone: 765-282-9073, Fax: 765-282-5270
Specialties: Fancy high-art straight knives of his design. **Patterns:** Bowies, daggers and fighters. **Technical:** Uses 440C, ATS-34 and commercial

Damascus. All knives and engraved. **Prices:** $900 to $3200; some to $4000. **Remarks:** Full-time maker; first knife sold in 1987. Doing business as The Gun Room (T.G.R.). **Mark:** Last name.

SIBERT, SHANE, PO Box 241, Gladstone, OR 97027, Phone: 503-650-2082
Specialties: Advanced tactical fixed blade and folding knives. **Patterns:** Fighters, lightweight backpacking, survival, diving, kitchen knives, one-of-a-kind combat daggers. **Technical:** Hollow grinds CPM S30V stainless steel. G-10 handles attached with flared titanium tubing. Kydex sheaths. **Prices:** $150 to $500; some one-of-a-kind pieces to $1000. **Remarks:** Full-time maker; first knife sold in 1994. **Mark:** Last name.

SIGMAN, CORBET R., Rt. 1, Box 260, Liberty, WV 25124, Phone: 304-586-9131
Specialties: Collectible working straight knives and folders. **Patterns:** Hunters, fighters, boots, camp knives and exotics such as sgian dubhs—distinctly Sigman lines; folders. **Technical:** Grinds D2, 154CM, plain carbon tool steel and ATS-34. **Prices:** $60 to $800; some to $4000. **Remarks:** Full-time maker; first knife sold in 1970. **Mark:** Name or initials.

SIGMAN, JAMES P., 10391 Church Rd., North Adams, MI 49262, Phone: 517-523-3028
Specialties: High-tech working knives of his design. **Patterns:** Daggers, hunters, fighters and folders. **Technical:** Forges and grinds L6, O1, W2 and his Damascus. **Prices:** $150 to $750. **Remarks:** Part-time maker; first knife sold in 1982. **Mark:** Sig or Sig Forge.

SIMMONS, H.R., 1100 Bay City Rd., Aurora, NC 27806, Phone: 252-322-5969
Specialties: Working/using straight knives of his design. **Patterns:** Fighters, hunters and utility/camp knives. **Technical:** Forges and grinds Damascus and L6; grinds ATS-34. **Prices:** $150 to $250; some to $400. **Remarks:** Part-time maker; first knife sold in 1987. Doing business as HRS Custom Knives, Royal Forge and Trading Company. **Mark:** Initials.

SIMONELLA, GIANLUIGI, 15, via Rosa Brustolo, 33085 Maniago, ITALY, Phone: 01139-427-730350
Specialties: Traditional and classic folding and working/using knives of his design and to customer specs. **Patterns:** Bowies, fighters, hunters, utility/camp knives. **Technical:** Forges ATS-34, D2, 440C. **Prices:** $250 to $400; some to $1000. **Remarks:** Full-time maker; first knife sold in 1988. **Mark:** Wilson.

SIMONICH, ROB, PO Box 278, Clancy, MT 59634, Phone: 406-933-8274
Specialties: Working knives in standard patterns. **Patterns:** Hunters, combat knives, Bowies and small fancy knives. **Technical:** Grinds D2, ATS-34 and 440C; forges own cable Damascus. Offers filework on most knives. **Prices:** $75 to $300; some to $1000. **Remarks:** Spare-time maker; first knife sold in 1984. Not currently taking orders. **Mark:** Last name in buffalo logo.

SIMONS, BILL, 6217 Michael Ln., Lakeland, FL 33811, Phone: 863-646-3783
Specialties: Working folders. **Patterns:** Locking folders, liner locks, hunters, slip joints most patterns; some straight camp knives. **Technical:** Grinds D2, ATS-34 and O1. **Prices:** Start at $100. **Remarks:** Full-time maker; first knife sold in 1970. **Mark:** Last name.

SIMS, BOB, PO Box 772, Meridian, TX 76665, Phone: 254-435-6240
Specialties: Traditional working straight knives and folders in standard patterns; banana/sheep foot blade combinations in trapper patterns. **Patterns:** Locking folders, slip-joint folders and hunters. **Technical:** Grinds D2, ATS-34 and O1. Offers filework on some knives. **Prices:** $150 to $275; some to $600. **Remarks:** Part-time maker; first knife sold in 1975. **Mark:** The division sign.

SINCLAIR, J.E., 520 Francis Rd., Pittsburgh, PA 15239, Phone: 412-793-5778
Specialties: Fancy hunters and fighters, liner locking folders. **Patterns:** Fighters, hunters and folders. **Technical:** Flat-grinds and hollow grind, prefers hand rubbed satin finish. Uses natural handle materials. **Prices:** $185 to $800. **Remarks:** Part-time maker; first knife sold in 1995. **Mark:** First and middle initials, last name and maker.

SINYARD, CLESTON S., 27522 Burkhardt Dr., Elberta, AL 36530, Phone: 334-987-1361
Specialties: Working straight knives and folders of his design. **Patterns:** Hunters, buckskinners, Bowies, daggers, fighters and all-Damascus folders. **Technical:** Makes Damascus from 440C, stainless steels, D2 and regular high-carbon steel; forges "forefinger pad" into hunters and skinners. **Prices:** In Damascus $450 to $1500; some $2500. **Remarks:** Full-time maker; first knife sold in 1980. Doing business as Nimo Forge. **Mark:** Last name, U.S.A. in anvil.

SISEMORE, CHARLES RUSSEL, RR 2 Box 329AL, Mena, AR 71953, Phone: 918-383-1360

SISKA, JIM, 6 Highland Ave., Westfield, MA 01085, Phone: 413-568-9787, Fax: 413-568-6341

Specialties: Traditional working straight knives and folders. **Patterns:** Hunters, fighters, Bowies and one-of-a-kinds; folders. **Technical:** Grinds D2 and ATS-34; buys Damascus. Likes exotic woods. **Prices:** $195 to $2500. **Remarks:** Part-time maker; first knife sold in 1983. **Mark:** Last name in Old English.

SJOSTRAND, KEVIN, 1541 S. Cain St., Visalia, CA 93292, Phone: 209-625-5254

Specialties: Traditional and working/using straight knives and folders of his design or to customer specs. **Patterns:** Bowies, hunters, utility/camp knives, lockback, springbuck and liner lock folders. **Technical:** Grinds ATS-34, 440C and 1095. Prefers high polished blades and full tang. Natural and stabilized hardwoods, Micarta and stag handle material. **Prices:** $75 to $300. **Remarks:** Part-time maker; first knife sold in 1992. Doing business as Black Oak Blades. **Mark:** Oak tree, Black Oak Blades, name, or just last name.

SKIFF, STEVEN, SKIFF MADE BLADES, PO Box 537, Broadalbin, NY 12025, Phone: 518-883-4875

Specialties: Custom using/collector grade straight blades and liner lock folders of maker's design or customer specifications. **Patterns:** Hunters, utility/camp knives - tactical/fancy art folders **Prices:** $180-$395 some to $325 and up. **Technical:** Stock removal hollow ground ATS-34, 154 CM, S30V, and tool steel. Damascus-Devon Thomas, Robert Eggerling, Mike Norris and Delbert Ealy. Nickel silver and stainless in-house heat treating. Handle materials man made and natural woods (stabilized). Horn shells sheaths for straight blades sews own leather and uses sheaths by "Tree-Stump Leather". **Remarks:** First knife sold 1997. Started making folders in 2000. **Mark:** SKIFF on blade of straight blades and in inside of backspacer on folders.

SKOW, H. A. "TEX", TEX CUSTOM KNIVES, 3534 Gravel Springs Rd., Senatobia, MS 38668, Phone: 662-301-1568

Specialties: One-of-a-kind daggers, Bowies, boot knives and hunters. **Patterns:** Different Damascus patterns (By Bob Eggerling). **Technical:** 440C, 58, 60 Rockwell hardness. Engraving by Joe Mason. **Prices:** Negotiable. **Remarks:** 30 hunters 10 collector knives per year. **Mark:** TEX.

SLEE, FRED, 9 John St., Morganville, NJ 07751, Phone: 908-591-9047

Specialties: Working straight knives, some fancy, to customer specs. **Patterns:** Hunters, fighters, boots, fancy daggers and folders. **Technical:** Grinds D2, 440C and ATS-34. **Prices:** $285 to $1100. **Remarks:** Part-time maker; first knife sold in 1980. **Mark:** Last name in old English.

SLOAN, SHANE, 4226 FM 61, Newcastle, TX 76372, Phone: 940-846-3290

Specialties: Collector-grade straight knives and folders. **Patterns:** Uses stainless Damascus, ATS-34 and 12-C-27. Bowies, lockers, slip-joints, fancy folders, fighters and period pieces. **Technical:** Grinds D2 and ATS-34. Uses rare natural handle materials. Prefers hand-rubbed satin finish. **Prices:** $250 to $6500. **Remarks:** Full-time maker; first knife sold in 1985. **Mark:** Name and city.

SLOBODIAN, SCOTT, 4101 River Ridge Dr., PO Box 1498, San Andreas, CA 95249, Phone: 209-286-1980, Fax: 209-286-1982

Specialties: Japanese-style knives and swords, period pieces, fantasy pieces and miniatures. **Patterns:** Small kweikens, tantos, wakazashis, katanas, traditional samurai swords. **Technical:** Flat-grinds 1050, commercial Damascus. **Prices:** $800 to $3500; some to $7500. **Remarks:** Full-time maker; first knife sold in 1987. **Mark:** Blade signed in Japanese characters and various scripts.

SMALE, CHARLES J., 509 Grove Ave., Waukegan, IL 60085, Phone: 847-244-8013

SMALL, ED, Rt. 1, Box 178-A, Keyser, WV 26726, Phone: 304-298-4254

Specialties: Working knives of his design; period pieces. **Patterns:** Hunters, daggers, buckskinners and camp knives; likes one-of-a-kinds. **Technical:** Forges and grinds W2, L6 and his own Damascus. **Prices:** $150 to $1500. **Remarks:** Full-time maker; first knife sold in 1978. Doing business as Iron Mountain Forge Works. **Mark:** Script initials connected.

SMALLWOOD, WAYNE, 146 Poplar Dr., Kalispell, MT 59901

SMART, STEVE, 907 Park Row Cir., McKinney, TX 75070-3847, Phone: 214-837-4216, Fax: 214-837-4111

Specialties: Working/using straight knives and folders of his design, to customer specs and in standard patterns. **Patterns:** Bowies, hunters, kitchen knives, locking folders, utility/camp, fishing and bird knives. **Technical:** Grinds ATS-34, D2, 440C and O1. Prefers mirror polish or satin finish; hollow-grinds all blades. All knives come with sheath. Offers some

filework. **Prices:** $95 to $225; some to $500. **Remarks:** Spare-time maker; first knife sold in 1983. **Mark:** Name, Custom, city and state in oval.

SMART, STEATEN, 15815 Acorn Cir., Tavares, FL 32778, Phone: 352-343-8423

SMIT, GLENN, 627 Cindy Ct., Aberdeen, MD 21001, Phone: 410-272-2959

Specialties: Working and using straight and folding knives of his design or to customer specs. Customizes and repairs all types of cutlery. Exclusive maker of Dave Murphy Style knives. **Patterns:** Hunters, Bowies, daggers, fighters, utility/camp, folders, kitchen knives and miniatures, Murphy combat, C.H.A.I.K., Little 88 and Tiny 90-styles. **Technical:** Grinds 440C, ATS-34, O1, A2 also grinds 6AL4V titanium allox for blades. Reforges commercial Damascus and makes own Damascus, cast aluminum handles. **Prices:** Miniatures start at $20; full-size knives start at $40. **Remarks:** Spare-time maker; first knife sold in 1986. Doing business as Wolf's Knives. **Mark:** G.P. SMIT, with year on reverse side, Wolf's knives-Murphy's way with date.

SMITH, RICK, BEAR BONE KNIVES, 1843 W Evans Creek Rd., Rogue River, OR 97537, Phone: 541-582-4144

Specialties: Classic, historical-style Bowies for re-enactors and custom sheaths. **Patterns:** Historical-style Bowies, varied contemporary knife styles. **Technical:** Made by stock removal method; also forge weld tricable Damascus blades. Do own heat treating and tempering using an even heat digital kiln. Preferred steels are ATS-34, 154CM, 5160, D-2, 1095 and 01 tool and various carbon Damascus. **Prices:** $250 to $1000. **Remarks:** Full-time maker since 1997 Now forging random pattern Damascus up to 600 layers. Discontinued using BG42 steel. Serial numbers now appear under log. Damascus knives are not given a serial number. Official business name is Bear Bone Knives. **Mark:** "Bear Bone" over initials "R S" (separated by downward arrow) on blade; initials R S (separated by downward arrow) within a 3/8" circle; 2 shooting stars and a Bowie. Serial numbers appear on ricasso area of blade unless otherwise requested.

SMITH, J.D., 69 Highland, Roxbury, MA 02119, Phone: 617-989-0723

Specialties: Fighters, Bowies, Persian, locking folders and swords. **Patterns:** Bowies, fighters and locking folders. **Technical:** Forges and grinds D2, his Damascus, O1, 52100 etc. and wootz-pattern hammer steel. **Prices:** $500 to $2000; some to $5000. **Remarks:** Full-time maker; first knife sold in 1987. Doing business as Hammersmith. **Mark:** Last initial alone or in cartouche.

SMITH, D. NOEL, 12018 NE Lonetree Ct., Poulsbo, WA 98370, Phone: 360-697-6992

Specialties: Fantasy art knives of his own design or to standard patterns. **Patterns:** Daggers, hunters and art knives. **Technical:** Grinds O1, D2, 440C stainless and Damascus. Offers natural and synthetic carved handles, engraved and acid etched blades, sculptured guards, butt caps and bases. **Prices:** Start at $250. **Remarks:** Full-time maker; first knife sold in 1990. Doing business as Minds' Eye Metal master. **Mark:** Signature.

SMITH, JOHN M., 3450 E Beguelin Rd., Centralia, IL 62801, Phone: 618-249-6444, Fax: 618-249-6444

Specialties: Traditional work knives, art knives. **Patterns:** daggers, Bowies, folders. **Technical:** Forges Damascus and hi-carbon. Also uses stainless. **Prices:** $250 to $2500. **Remarks:** Full-time maker; first knife sold in 1980. **Mark:** Etched signature or logo.

SMITH, JOHN W., 1322 Cow Branch Rd., West Liberty, KY 41472, Phone: 606-743-3599

Specialties: Fancy and working locking folders of his design or to customer specs. **Patterns:** Interframes, traditional and daggers. **Technical:** Grinds 530V and his own Damascus. Offers gold inlay, engraving with gold inlay, hand-fitted mosaic pearl inlay and filework. Prefers hand-rubbed finish. Pearl and ivory available. **Prices:** Utility pieces $375-$650. Art knives $1200 to $10,000 **Remarks:** Full-time maker. **Mark:** Initials engraved inside diamond.

SMITH, JOSH, Box 753, Frenchtown, MT 59834, Phone: 406-626-5775

Specialties: Mosaic, Damascus, liner lock folders, Bowies, fighters, etc. **Patterns:** Bowies, designs and folders. **Technical:** Advanced Mosaic and Damascus. **Prices:** $450-$3000. **Mark:** JOSH. **Other:** ABS Master Smith.

SMITH, MICHAEL J., 1418 Saddle Gold Ct., Brandon, FL 33511, Phone: 813-431-3790

Specialties: Fancy high art folders of his design. **Patterns:** Locking locks and automatics. **Technical:** Uses ATS-34, non-stainless and stainless Damascus; hand carves folders, prefers ivory and pearl. Hand-rubbed satin finish. Liners are 6AL4V titanium. **Prices:** $500 to $3000. **Remarks:** Full-time maker; first knife sold in 1989. **Mark:** Name, city, state.

custom knifemakers

SMITH, NEWMAN L., 676 Glades Rd., Shop #3, Gatlinburg, TN 37738, Phone: 423-436-3322
   Specialties: Collector-grade and working knives. **Patterns:** Hunters, slip-joint and lock-back folders, some miniatures. **Technical:** Grinds O1 and ATS-34; makes fancy sheaths. **Prices:** $110 to $450; some to $1000. **Remarks:** Full-time maker; first knife sold in 1984. Partners part-time to handle Damascus blades by Jeff Hurst; marks these with SH connected. **Mark:** First and middle initials, last name.

SMITH, RAYMOND L., 217 Red Chalk Rd., Erin, NY 14838, Phone: 607-795-5257
   Specialties: Working/using straight knives and folders to customer specs and in standard patterns; perios pieces. **Patterns:** Bowies, hunters, skip-joints. **Technical:** Forges 5160, 52100, 1018 Damascus and wire cable Damascus. Filework. **Prices:** $75 to $750; estimates for custom orders. **Remarks:** Part-time maker; first knife sold in 1991. ABS Master Smith. Doing business as The Anvils Edge. **Mark:** Initials in script.

SMITH, LENARD C., PO Box D68, Valley Cottage, NY 10989, Phone: 914-268-7359

SMITH, GREGORY H., 8607 Coddington Ct., Louisville, KY 40299, Phone: 502-491-7439
   Specialties: Traditional working straight knives and fantasy knives to customer specs. **Patterns:** Fighters and modified Bowies; camp knives and swords. **Technical:** Grinds O1, 440C and commercial Damascus bars. **Prices:** $55 to $300. **Remarks:** Part-time maker; first knife sold in 1985. **Mark:** JAGED, plus signature.

SMITH JR., JAMES B. "RED", Rt. 2, Box 1525, Morven, GA 31638, Phone: 912-775-2844
   Specialties: Folders. **Patterns:** Rotating rear-lock folders. **Technical:** Grinds ATS-34, D2 and Vascomax 350. **Prices:** Start at $350. **Remarks:** Full-time maker; first knife sold in 1985. **Mark:** GA RED in cowboy hat.

SMOCK, TIMOTHY E., 1105 N Sherwood Dr., Marion, IN 46952, Phone: 765-664-0123

SMOKER, RAY, 113 Church Rd., Searcy, AR 72143, Phone: 501-796-2712
   Specialties: Working/using fixed blades of his design only. **Patterns:** Hunters, skinners, utility/camp and flat-ground knives. **Technical:** Forges his own Damascus and 52100; makes sheaths. Uses improved multiple edge quench he developed. **Prices:** $140 to $200; price includes sheath. **Remarks:** Full-time maker; first knife sold in 1992. **Mark:** Last name.

SNARE, MICHAEL, 3352 E. Mescal St., Phoenix, AZ 85028

SNELL, JERRY L., 235 Woodsong Dr., Fayetteville, GA 30214, Phone: 770-461-0586
   Specialties: Working straight knives of his design and in standard patterns. **Patterns:** Hunters, boots, fighters, daggers and a few folders. **Technical:** Grinds 440C, ATS-34; buys Damascus. **Prices:** $175 to $1000. **Remarks:** Part-time maker. **Mark:** Last name, or name, city and state.

SNODY, MIKE, 7169 Silk Hope Rd., Liberty, NC 27298, Phone: 888-393-9534
   Specialties: High performance straight knives in traditional and Japanese-styles. **Patterns:** Skinners, hunters, tactical, Kwaiken andTantos. **Technical:** Grinds BG-42, ATS-34, 440C and A-2. Offers full or tapered tangs, upgraded handle materials such as fossil ivory, coral and exotic woods. Traditional diamond wrap over stingray on Japanese-style knives. Sheaths available in leather or Kydex. **Prices:** $100 to $1000. **Remarks:** Part-time maker; first knife sold in 1999. **Mark:** Name over knife maker.

SNOW, BILL, 4824 18th Ave., Columbus, GA 31904, Phone: 706-576-4390
   Specialties: Traditional working/using straight knives and folders of his design and to customer specs. Offers engraving and scrimshaw. **Patterns:** Bowies, fighters, hunters and folders. **Technical:** Grinds ATS-34, 440V, 440C, 420V, CPM350, BG42, A2, D2, 5160, 52100 and O1; forges if needed. Cryogenically quenches all steels; inlaid handles; some integrals; leather or Kydex sheaths. **Prices:** $125 to $700; some to $3500. **Remarks:** Now also have 530V, 10V and 3V steels in use. Full-time maker; first knife sold in 1958. Doing business as Tipi Knife works. **Mark:** Old English scroll "S" inside a tipi.

SNYDER, MICHAEL TOM, PO Box 522, Zionsville, IN 46077-0522, Phone: 317-873-6807

SOLOMON, MARVIN, 23750 Cold Springs Rd., Paron, AR 72122, Phone: 501-821-3170, Fax: 501-821-6541
   Specialties: Traditional working and using straight knives of his design and to customer specs also lock back 7 liner lock folders. **Patterns:** Single blade folders. **Technical:** Forges 5160, 1095, O1 and random Damascus. **Prices:** $125 to $1000. **Remarks:** Part-time maker; first knife sold in 1990. Doing business as Cold Springs Forge. **Mark:** Last name.

SONNTAG, DOUGLAS W., 906 N 39 ST, Nixa, MO 65714, Phone: 417-693-1640, Fax: 417-582-1392
   Specialties: Working knives; art knives. **Patterns:** Hunters, boots, straight working knives; Bowies, some folders, camp/axe sets. **Technical:** Grinds D-2, ATS-34, forges own Damascus; does own heat treating. **Prices:** $175 to $500; some higher. **Remarks:** Part-time maker; first knife sold in 1986. **Mark:** Etched name in arch.

SONTHEIMER, G. DOUGLAS, 12604 Bridgeton Dr., Potomac, MD 20854, Phone: 301-948-5227
   Specialties: Fixed blade knives. **Patterns:** Whitetail deer, backpackers, camp, claws, filet, fighters. **Technical:** Hollow Grinds. **Price:** $325 and up. **Remarks:** Spare-time maker; first knife sold in 1976. **Mark:** LORD.

SOPPERA, ARTHUR, "Pilatusblick", Oberer Schmidberg, CH-9631 Ulisbach, SWITZERLAND, Phone: 71-988 47 57, Fax: 71-988 23 27
   Specialties: High-art, high-tech knives of his design. **Patterns:** Mostly locking folders, some straight knives. **Technical:** Grinds ATS-34 and commercial Damascus. Folders have button lock of his own design; some are fancy folders in jeweler's fashion. Also makes jewelry with integrated small knives. **Prices:** $200 to $1000; some $2000 and higher. **Remarks:** Full-time maker; first knife sold in 1986. **Mark:** Stylized initials, name, country.

SORNBERGER, JIM, 25126 Overland Dr., Volcano, CA 95689, Phone: 209-295-7819
   Specialties: Classic San Francisco-style knives. Collectible straight knives. **Patterns:** Forges 1095-1084/15W2. Makes own Damascus and powder metal. Fighters, daggers, Bowies; miniatures; hunters, custom canes, liner locks folders. **Technical:** Grinds 440C, 154CM and ATS-34; engraves, carves and embellishes. **Prices:** $500 to $14,000 in gold with gold quartz inlays. **Remarks:** Full-time maker; first knife sold in 1970. **Mark:** First initial, last name, city and state.

SOWELL, BILL, 100 Loraine Forest Ct., Macon, GA 31210, Phone: 478- 994-9863
   Specialties: Antique reproduction Bowies, forging Bowies, hunters, fighters, and most others. Also folders. **Technical:** Makes own Damascus, using 1084/15N20, also making own designs in powder metals, forges 5160-1095-1084, and other carbon steels, grinds ATS34. **Prices:** Starting at $150 and up. **Remarks:** Part-time maker. Sold first knife in 1998. **Mark:** Iron Horse Knives; Iron Horse Forge. **Other:** Does own leather work.

SPARKS, BERNARD, PO Box 73, Dingle, ID 83233, Phone: 208-847-1883
   Specialties: Maker engraved, working and art knives. Straight knives and folders of his own design. **Patterns:** Locking inner-frame folders, hunters, fighters, one-of-a-kind art knives. **Technical:** Grinds 530V steel, 440-C, 154CM, ATS-34, D-2 and forges by special order; triple temper, cryogenic soak. Mirror or hand finish. New Liquid metal steel. **Prices:** $300 to $2000. **Remarks:** Full-time maker, first knife sold in 1967. **Mark:** Last name over state with a knife logo on each end of name. Prior 1980, stamp of last name.

SPICKLER, GREGORY NOBLE, 5614 Mose Cir., Sharpsburg, MD 21782, Phone: 301-432-2746

SPINALE, RICHARD, 4021 Canterbury Ct., Lorain, OH 44053, Phone: 440-282-1565
   Specialties: High-art working knives of his design. **Patterns:** Hunters, fighters, daggers and locking folders. **Technical:** Grinds 440C, ATS-34 and 07; engraves. Offers gold bolsters and other deluxe treatments. **Prices:** $300 to $1000; some to $3000. **Remarks:** Spare-time maker; first knife sold in 1976. **Mark:** Name, address, year and model number.

SPIVEY, JEFFERSON, 9244 W. Wilshire, Yukon, OK 73099, Phone: 405-721-4442
   Specialties: The Saber tooth: a combination hatchet, saw and knife. **Patterns:** Built for the wilderness, all are one-of-a-kind. **Technical:** Grinds chromemoly steel. The saw tooth spine curves with a double row of biangular teeth. **Prices:** Start at $300. **Remarks:** First knife sold in 1977. The above Saber tooth knives are no longer in production as of Jan 1 2004. **Mark:** Name and serial number.

SPRAGG, WAYNE E., PO Box 508, 1314 3675 East Rd., Ashton, ID 83420
   Specialties: Working straight knives, some fancy. **Patterns:** Folders. **Technical:** Forges carbon steel and makes Damascus. **Prices:** $110 to $400; some higher. **Remarks:** All stainless heat-treated by Paul Bos. Carbon steel in shop heat treat. **Mark:** Name, city and state with bucking horse logo.

SPROUSE, TERRY, 1633 Newfound Rd., Asheville, NC 28806, Phone: 704-683-3400
   Specialties: Traditional and working straight knives of his design. **Patterns:** Bowies and hunters. **Technical:** Grinds ATS-34, 440C and D2. Makes sheaths. **Prices:** $85 to $125; some to $225. **Remarks:** Part-time maker; first knife sold in 1989. **Mark:** NA.

STAFFORD, RICHARD, 104 Marcia Ct., Warner Robins, GA 31088, Phone: 912-923-6372
Specialties: High-tech straight knives and some folders. **Patterns:** Hunters in several patterns, fighters, boots, camp knives, combat knives and period pieces. **Technical:** Grinds ATS-34 and 440C; satin finish is standard. **Prices:** Starting at $75. **Remarks:** Part-time maker; first knife sold in 1983. **Mark:** Last name.

STALCUP, EDDIE, PO Box 2200, Gallup, New Mexico 87305, Phone: 505-863-3107
Specialties: Working and fancy hunters, bird and trout. Special custom orders. **Patterns:** Drop point hunters, locking liner and multi blade folders. **Technical:** ATS-34. **Prices:** $150 - $500. **Mark:** E.F. Stalcup, Gallup, NM. **Other:** Scrimshaw, Exotic handle material, wet formed sheaths. Membership Arizona Knife Collectors Association.

STANCER, CHUCK, 62 Hidden Ranch Rd. NW, Calgary AB, CANADA T3A 5S5, Phone: 403-295-7370

STANLEY, JOHN, 604 Elm St., Crossett, AR 71635, Phone: 970-304-3005
Specialties: Hand forged fixed blades with engraving and carving. **Patterns:** Scottish dirks, skeans and fantasy blades. **Technical:** Forge high-carbon steel, own Damascus. Prices $70 to $500. **Remarks:** All work is sole authorship. **Mark:** Varies. **Other:** Offer engraving and carving services on other knives and handles.

STAPEL, CHUCK, Box 1617, Glendale, CA 91209, Phone: 213-66-KNIFE, Fax: 213-669-1577
Specialties: Working knives of his design. **Patterns:** Variety of straight knives tantos, hunters, folders and utility knives. **Technical:** Grinds D2, 440C and AEB-L. **Prices:** $185 to $12,000. **Remarks:** Full-time maker; first knife sold in 1974. **Mark:** Last name or last name, U.S.A.

STAPLETON, WILLIAM E., BUFFALO 'B' FORGE, 5425 Country Ln., Merritt Island, FL 32953
Specialties: Classic and traditional knives of his design and customer spec. **Patterns:** Hunters and using knives. **Technical:** Forges, 01 and L-6 Damascus, cable Damascus and 5160; stock removal on request. **Prices:** $150 to $1000. **Remarks:** Part-time maker, first knife sold 1990. Doing business as Buffalo "B" Forge. **Mark:** Anvil with S initial in center of anvil.

STAPLETON, WILLIAM E., 5425 Country Ln., Merritt Island, FL 32953, Phone: 407-452-8946

STECK, VAN R., 260 W Dogwood Ave., Orange City, FL 32763, Phone: 386-775-7303
Specialties: Neck knives, hunters, fighters, Bowies and Japanese swords. **Technical:** Uses ATS-34, D-2, Damascus, A-2. Grinds hollow and distal taper. Handle materials titanium, ebony, coco-bolo, ironwood. **Prices:** $75-$600.

STEFFEN, CHUCK, 504 Dogwood Ave. NW, St. Michael, MN, Phone: 763-497-6315
Specialties: Custom hunting knives, fixed blades folders. Specializing in exotic materials. Damascus excellent fit form and finishes.

STEGALL, KEITH, 2101 W. 32nd, Anchorage, AK 99517, Phone: 907-276-6002
Specialties: Traditional working straight knives. **Patterns:** Most patterns. **Technical:** Grinds 440C and 154CM. **Prices:** $100 to $300. **Remarks:** Spare-time maker; first knife sold in 1987. **Mark:** Name and state with anchor.

STEGNER, WILBUR G., 9242 173rd Ave. SW, Rochester, WA 98579, Phone: 360-273-0937
Specialties: Working/using straight knives and folders of his design. **Patterns:** Hunters and locking folders. **Technical:** Grinds ATS-34 and other tool steels. Quenches, tempers and hardness tests each blade. **Prices:** $100 to $1000; some to $5000. **Remarks:** Full-time maker; first knife sold in 1979. **Other:** Google search key words-"STEGNER KNIVES". **Mark:** First and middle initials, last name in bar over shield logo.

STEIGER, MONTE L., Box 186, Genesee, ID 83832, Phone: 208-285-1769
Specialties: Traditional working/using straight knives of all designs. **Patterns:** Hunters, utility/camp knives, filet and chefs. **Technical:** Grinds 1095, O1, 440C, ATS-34. Handles of stacked leather, natural wood, Micarta or Pakkawood. Each knife comes with right- or left-handed sheath. **Prices:** $70 to $220. **Remarks:** Spare-time maker; first knife sold in 1988. **Mark:** First initial, last name, city and state.

STEIGERWALT, KEN, PO Box 172, Orangeville, PA 17859, Phone: 717-683-5156
Specialties: Fancy classic folders of his design. **Patterns:** Folders, button locks and rear locks. **Technical:** Grinds ATS-34, 440C and commercial Damascus. Experiments with unique filework. **Prices:** $200 to $600; some to $1500. **Remarks:** Full-time maker; first knife sold in 1981. **Mark:** Initials.

STEINAU, JURGEN, Julius-Hart Strasse 44, Berlin 0-1162, GERMANY, Phone: 372-6452512, Fax: 372-645-2512
Specialties: Fantasy and high-art straight knives of his design. **Patterns:** Boots, daggers and switch-blade folders. **Technical:** Grinds 440B, 2379 and X90 Cr.Mo.V. 78. **Prices:** $1500 to $2500; some to $3500. **Remarks:** Full-time maker; first knife sold in 1984. **Mark:** Symbol, plus year, month day and serial number.

STEINBERG, AL, 5244 Duenas, Laguna Woods, CA 92653, Phone: 949-951-2889
Specialties: Fancy working straight knives to customer specs. **Patterns:** Hunters, Bowies, fishing, camp knives, push knives and high end kitchen knives. **Technical:** Grinds O1, 440C and 154CM. **Prices:** $60 to $2500. **Remarks:** Full-time maker; first knife sold in 1972. **Mark:** Signature, city and state.

STEINBRECHER, MARK W., 4725 Locust Ave., Glenview, IL 60025, Phone: 847-298-5721
Specialties: Working and fancy folders. **Patterns:** Daggers, pocket knives, fighters and gents of his own design or to customer specs. **Technical:** Hollow grinds ATS-34, O-1 other makers Damascus. Uses natural handle materials: stag, ivories, mother-of-pearl. File work and some inlays. **Prices:** $500 to $1200, some to $2500. **Remarks:** Part-time maker, first folder sold in 1989. **Mark:** Name etched or handwritten on ATS-34; stamped on Damascus.

STEKETEE, CRAIG A., 871 N. Hwy. 60, Billings, MO 65610, Phone: 417-744-2770
Specialties: Classic and working straight knives and swords of his design. **Patterns:** Bowies, hunters, and Japanese-style swords. **Technical:** Forges his own Damascus; bronze, silver and Damascus fittings, offers filework. Prefers exotic and natural handle materials. **Prices:** $200 to $4000. **Remarks:** Full-time maker. **Mark:** STEK.

STEPHAN, DANIEL, 2201 S. Miller Rd., Valrico, FL 33594, Phone: 813-684-2781

STERLING, MURRAY, 693 Round Peak Church Rd., Mount Airy, NC 27030, Phone: 336-352-5110, Fax: Fax: 336-352-5105
Specialties: Single and dual blade folders. Interframes and integral dovetail frames. **Technical:** Grinds ATS-34 or Damascus by Mike Norris and/or Devin Thomas. **Prices:** $300 and up. **Remarks:** Full-time maker; first knife sold in 1991. **Mark:** Last name stamped.

STEVENS, BARRY B., 901 Amherst, Cridersville, OH 45806, Phone: 419-221-2446
Specialties: Small fancy folders of his design and to customer specs; mini-hunters and fighters. **Patterns:** Fighters, hunters, liner locks, lockback and bolster release folders. **Technical:** Grinds ATS-34, 440C, Damascus and SS Damascus. Prefers hand-rubbed finishes and natural handle materials-horn, ivory, pearls, exotic woods. **Prices:** $300 to $1000; some to $2500. **Remarks:** Part-time maker; first knife sold in 1991. Doing business as Bare Knives. **Mark:** First and middle initials, last name.

STEWART, EDWARD L., 4297 Audrain Rd. 335, Mexico, MO 65265, Phone: 573-581-3883
Specialties: Fixed blades, working knives some art. **Patterns:** Hunters, Bowies, Utility/camp knives. **Technical:** Forging 1095-W-2-l-6-52100 makes own Damascus. **Prices:** $85-$500. **Remarks:** Part-time maker first knife sold in 1993. **Mark:** First and last initials-last name.

STIMPS, JASON M., 374 S Shaffer St., Orange, CA 92866, Phone: 714-744-5866

STIPES, DWIGHT, 2651 SW Buena Vista Dr., Palm City, FL 34990, Phone: 772-597-0550
Specialties: Traditional and working straight knives in standard patterns. **Patterns:** Boots, Bowies, daggers, hunters and fighters. **Technical:** Grinds 440C, D2 and D3 tool steel. Handles of natural materials, animal, bone or horn. **Prices:** $75 to $150. **Remarks:** Full-time maker; first knife sold in 1972. **Mark:** Stipes.

STOCKWELL, WALTER, 368 San Carlos Ave., Redwood City, CA 94061, Phone: 650-363-6069
Specialties: Scottish dirks,sgian dubhs. **Patterns:** All knives one-of-a-kind. **Technical:** Grinds ATS-34, forges 5160, 52100, L6. **Prices:** $125 - $500. **Remarks:** Part-time maker since 1992; graduate of ABS bladesmithing school. **Mark:** Shooting star over "STOCKWELL". Pre-2000, "WKS".

STODDARD'S, INC., COPLEY PLACE, 100 Huntington Ave., Boston, MA 02116, Phone: 617-536-8688, Fax: 617-536-8689
Specialties: Cutlery (kitchen, pocket knives, Randall-made Knives, custom knives, scissors, and manicure tools), binoculars, low vision aids, personal care items (hair brushes, manicure sets, mirrors).

STODDART, W.B. BILL, 917 Smiley, Forest Park, OH 45240, Phone: 513-851-1543
Specialties: Sportsmen's working knives and multi-blade folders. **Patterns:** Hunters, camp and fish knives; multi-blade reproductions of old

standards. **Technical:** Grinds A2, 440C and ATS-34; makes sheaths to match handle materials. **Prices:** $80 to $300; some to $850. **Remarks:** Part-time maker; first knife sold in 1976. **Mark:** Name, Cincinnati, state.

STOKES, ED, 22614 Cardinal Dr., Hockley, TX 77447, Phone: 713-351-1319
Specialties: Working straight knives and folders of all designs. **Patterns:** Boots, Bowies, daggers, fighters, hunters and miniatures. **Technical:** Grinds ATS-34, 440C and D2. Offers decorative butt caps, tapered spacers on handles and finger grooves, nickel-silver inlays, hand-made sheaths. **Prices:** $185 to $290; some to $350. **Remarks:** Full-time maker; first knife sold in 1973. **Mark:** First and last name, Custom Knives with Apache logo.

STONE, JERRY, PO Box 1027, Lytle, TX 78052, Phone: 512-772-4502
Specialties: Traditional working and using folders of his design and to customer specs; fancy knives. **Patterns:** Fighters, hunters, locking folders and slip-joints. **Technical:** Grinds 440C and ATS-34. Offers filework. **Prices:** $125 to $375; some to $700. **Remarks:** Full-time maker; first knife sold in 1973. **Mark:** Initials.

STORCH, ED, R.R. 4 Mannville, Alberta T0B 2W0, CANADA, Phone: 780-763-2214
Specialties: Working knives, fancy fighting knives, kitchen cutlery and art knives.Knife making classes. **Patterns:** Working patterns, Bowies and folders. **Technical:** Forges his own Damascus. Grinds ATS-34. Builds friction folders. Salt heat treating. **Prices:** $45 to $750 (US). **Remarks:** Part-time maker; first knife sold in 1984. Hosts annual northwest canadian knifemakers symposium 60 to 80 knife makers and families. **Mark:** Last name.

STORMER, BOB, 10 Karabair Rd., St. Peters, MO 63376, Phone: 636-441-6807
Specialties: Straight knives - Using collector grade. **Patterns:** Bowies, skinners, hunters, camp knives. **Technical:** Forges 5160, 1095. **Prices:** $150-$400. **Remarks:** Part-time maker ABS Journeyman Smith 2001. **Mark:** Setting sun/Fall trees/Initials.

STOUT, CHARLES, RT3 178 Stout Rd., Gillham, AR 71841, Phone: 870-386-5521

STOUT, JOHNNY, 1205 Forest Trail, New Braunfels, TX 78132, Phone: 830-606-4067
Specialties: Folders, some fixed blades. Working knives, some fancy. **Patterns:** Hunters, tactical, Bowies, automatics, liner locks and slip-joints. **Technical:** Grinds stainless and carbon steels; forges own Damascus. **Prices:** $450 to $895; some to $3500. **Remarks:** Full-time maker; first knife sold in 1983. **Mark:** Name and city in logo with serial number. **Other:** Hosts semi-annual Guadalupe forge hammer-in and knifemakers rendezvous.

STOVER, HOWARD, 100 Palmetto Dr. Apt. 7, Pasadena, CA 91105, Phone: 765-452-3928

STOVER, TERRY "LEE", 1809 N. 300 E., Kokomo, IN 46901, Phone: 765-452-3928
Specialties: Damascus folders with filework; Damascus Bowies of his design or to customer specs. **Patterns:** Lockback folders and Sheffield-style knives. **Technical:** Forges 1095, Damascus using O2, 203E or O2, pure nickel. Makes mokume. Uses only natural handle material. **Prices:** $300 to $1700; some to $2000. **Remarks:** Part-time maker; first knife sold in 1984. **Mark:** First and middle initials, last name in knife logo; Damascus blades marked in Old English.

STRAIGHT, DON, PO Box 12, Points, WV 25437, Phone: 304-492-5471
Specialties: Traditional working straight knives of his design. **Patterns:** Hunters, Bowies and fighters. **Technical:** Grinds 440C, ATS-34 and D2. **Prices:** $75 to $125; some to $225. **Remarks:** Spare-time maker; first knife sold in 1978. **Mark:** Last name.

STRAIGHT, KENNETH J., 11311 103 Lane N., Largo, FL 33773, Phone: 813-397-9817

STRANDE, POUL, Soster Svenstrup Byvej 16, Dastrup 4130 Viby Sj., DENMARK, Phone: 46 19 43 05, Fax: 46 19 53 19
Specialties: Classic fantasy working knives; Damasceret blade, Nikkel Damasceret blade, Lamineret - Lamineret blade with Nikkel. **Patterns:** Bowies, daggers, fighters, hunters and swords. **Technical:** Uses carbon steel and 15C20 steel. **Prices:** NA. **Remarks:** Full-time maker; first knife sold in 1985. **Mark:** First and last initials.

STRICKLAND, DALE, 1440 E. Thompson View, Monroe, UT 84754, Phone: 435-896-8362
Specialties: Traditional and working straight knives and folders of his design and to customer specs. **Patterns:** Hunters, folders, miniatures and utility knives. **Technical:** Grinds Damascus and 440C. **Prices:** $120 to

$350; some to $500. **Remarks:** Part-time maker; first knife sold in 1991. **Mark:** Oval stamp of name, Maker.

STRIDER, MICK, STRIDER KNIVES, 120 N Pacific Unit L-7, San Marcos, CA 92069, Phone: 760-471-8275, Fax: 503-218-7069

STRONG, SCOTT, 2138 Oxmoor Dr., Beavercreek, OH 45431, Phone: 937-426-9290
Specialties: Working knives, some deluxe. **Patterns:** Hunters, fighters, survival and military-style knives, art knives. **Technical:** Forges and grinds O1, A2, D2, 440C and ATS-34. Uses no solder; most knives disassemble. **Prices:** $75 to $450; some to $1500. **Remarks:** Spare-time maker; first knife sold in 1983. **Mark:** Strong Knives.

STROYAN, ERIC, Box 218, Dalton, PA 18414, Phone: 717-563-2603
Specialties: Classic and working/using straight knives and folders of his design. **Patterns:** Hunters, locking folders, slip-joints. **Technical:** Forges Damascus; grinds ATS-34, D2. **Prices:** $200 to $600; some to $2000. **Remarks:** Part-time maker; first knife sold in 1968. **Mark:** Signature or initials stamp.

STUART, STEVE, Box 168, Gores Landing, Ont., CANADA K0K 2E0, Phone: 905-342-5617
Specialties: Straight knives. **Patterns:** Tantos, fighters, skinners, file and rasp knives. **Technical:** Uses 440C, files, Micarta and natural handle materials. **Prices:** $60 to $400. **Remarks:** Part-time maker. **Mark:** Interlocking SS with last name.

SUEDMEIER, HARLAN, RFD 2, Box 299D, Nebraska City, NE 68410, Phone: 402-873-4372
Specialties: Working straight knives. **Patterns:** Hunters, fighters and Bowies. **Technical:** Grinds ATS-34 and 440C; forges 52100. **Prices:** Start at $75. **Remarks:** Part-time maker; first knife sold in 1982. Not currently taking orders. **Mark:** First initial, last name.

SUGIHARA, KEIDOH, 4-16-1 Kamori-Cho, Kishiwada City, Osaka, F596-0042, JAPAN, Fax: 0724-44-2677
Specialties: High-tech working straight knives and folders of his design. **Patterns:** Bowies, hunters, fighters, fishing, boots, some pocket knives and liner-lock folders. **Technical:** Grinds ATS-34, COS-25, buys Damascus and high-carbon steels. **Prices** $60 to $4000. **Remarks:** Full-time maker, first knife sold in 1980. **Mark:** Initial logo with fish design.

SUGIYAMA, EDDY K., 2361 Nagayu Naoirimachi Naoirigun, Ohita, JAPAN, Phone: 0974-75-2050
Specialties: One of kind, exotic-style knives. **Patterns:** Working, utility and miniatures. **Technical:** CT rind, ATS-34 and D2. **Prices:** $400-$1200. **Remarks:** Full-time maker. **Mark:** Name or cedar mark.

SUMMERS, ARTHUR L., 1310 Hess Rd., Concord, NC 28025, Phone: 704-795-2863
Specialties: Collector-grade knives in drop points, clip points or straight blades. **Patterns:** Hunters, Bowies and personal knives. **Technical:** Grinds 440C, ATS-34, D2 and Damascus. **Prices:** $150 to $650; some to $2000. **Remarks:** Full-time maker; first knife sold in 1987. **Mark:** Last name and serial number.

SUMMERS, DAN, 2675 NY Rt. 11, Whitney Pt., NY 13862, Phone: 607-692-2391
Specialties: Period knives and tomahawks. **Technical:** All hand forging. **Prices:** Most $100 to $400.

SUMMERS, DENNIS K., 827 E. Cecil St., Springfield, OH 45503, Phone: 513-324-0624
Specialties: Working/using knives. **Patterns:** Fighters and personal knives. **Technical:** Grinds 440C, A2 and D2. Makes drop and clip point. **Prices:** $75 to $200. **Remarks:** Part-time maker; first knife sold in 1995. **Mark:** First and middle initials, last name, serial number.

SUNDERLAND, RICHARD, Av Infraganti 23, Col Lazaro Cardenas, Puerto Escondido Oaxaca, Mexico 71980, Phone: 011 52 94 582 1451
Specialties: Personal and hunting knives with carved handles in oosic and ivory. **Patterns:** Hunters, Bowies, daggers, camp and personal knives. **Technical:** Grinds 440C, ATS-34 and O1. Handle materials of rosewoods, fossil mammoth ivory and oosic. **Prices:** $150 to $1000. **Remarks:** Part-time maker; first knife sold in 1983. Doing business as Sun Knife Co. **Mark:** SUN.

SUTTON, S. RUSSELL, 4900 Cypress Shores Dr., New Bern, NC 28562, Phone: 252-637-3963
Specialties: Straight knives and folders to customer specs and in standard patterns. **Patterns:** Boots, hunters, interframes, slip joints and locking liners. **Technical:** Grinds ATS-34, 440C and stainless Damascus. **Prices:** $185 to $650; some to $950. **Remarks:** Full-time maker; first knife sold in 1992. **Mark:** Etched last name.

SWEAZA, DENNIS, 4052 Hwy 321 E, Austin, AR 72007, Phone: 501-941-1886

SWEDER, JORAM, TILARU METALSMITHING, PO Box 4175, Ocala, FL 34470, Phone: 352-546-4438
  Specialties: Hand forged one-of-a-kind and custom pieces. **Prices:** $100 and up.

SWEENEY, COLTIN D., 1216 S 3 St. W, Missoula, MT 59801, Phone: 406-721-6782

SWYHART, ART, 509 Main St., PO Box 267, Klickitat, WA 98628, Phone: 509-369-3451
  Specialties: Traditional working and using knives of his design. **Patterns:** Bowies, hunters and utility/camp knives. **Technical:** Forges 52100, 5160 and Damascus 1084 mixed with either 15N20 or 0186. Blades differentially heat-treated with visible temper line. **Prices:** $75 to $250; some to $350. **Remarks:** Part-time maker; first knife sold in 1983. **Mark:** First name, last initial in script.

SYMONDS, ALBERTO E., Rambla M Gandhi 485, Apt 901, Montevideo 11300, URUGUAY, Phone: 011 598 2 7103201, Fax: 011 598 5608207
  Specialties: All sorts-including puukos, nice sheaths, leather and wood. **Prices:** $140 to $900. **Mark:** AESH and year (2004).

SYSLO, CHUCK, 3418 South 116 Ave., Omaha, NE 68144, Phone: 402-333-0647
  Specialties: High-tech working straight knives. **Patterns:** Hunters, daggers and survival knives; locking folders. **Technical:** Flat-grinds D2, 440C and 154CM; hand polishes only. **Prices:** $175 to $500; some to $3000. **Remarks:** Part-time maker; first knife sold in 1978. **Mark:** CISCO in logo.

SZAREK, MARK G., 94 Oakwood Ave., Revere, MA 02151, Phone: 781-289-7102
  Specialties: Classic period working and using straight knives and tools. **Patterns:** Hunting knives, American and Japanese woodworking tools. **Technical:** Forges 5160, 1050, Damascus; differentially hardens blades with fireclay. **Prices:** $50 to $750. **Remarks:** Part-time maker; first knife sold in 1989. **Mark:** Last name. **Other:** Produces Japanese alloys for sword fittings and accessories. Custom builds knife presentation boxes and cabinets.

SZILASKI, JOSEPH, 29 Carroll Dr., Wappingers Falls, NY 12590, Phone: 845-297-5397
  Specialties: Straight knives, folders and tomahawks of his design, to customer specs and in standard patterns. Many pieces are one-of-a-kind. **Patterns:** Bowies, daggers, fighters, hunters, art knives and early American-styles. **Technical:** Forges A2, D2, O1 and Damascus. **Prices:** $450 to $4000; some to $10,000. **Remarks:** Full-time maker; first knife sold in 1990. **Mark:** Snake logo. **Other:** ABS Master Smith and voting member KMG.

t

TAKAHASHI, KAORU, 2506 TOYO OKA YADO UEKI, Kamoto Kumamoto, JAPAN 861-01, Phone: (8196) 272-6759

TAKAHASHI, MASAO, 39-3 Sekine-machi, Maebashi-shi, Gunma 371 0047, JAPAN, Phone: 81 27 234 2223, Fax: 81 27 234 2223
  Specialties: Working straight knives. **Patterns:** Daggers, fighters, hunters, fishing knives, boots. **Technical:** Grinds ATS-34 and Damascus. **Prices:** $350 to $1000 and up. **Remarks:** Full-time maker; first knife sold in 1982. **Mark:** M. Takahashi.

TALLY, GRANT, 26961 James Ave., Flat Rock, MI 48134, Phone: 734-789-8961
  Specialties: Straight knives and folders of his design. **Patterns:** Bowies, daggers, fighters. **Technical:** Grinds ATS-34, 440C and D2. Offers filework. **Prices:** $250 to $1000. **Remarks:** Part-time maker; first knife sold in 1985. Doing business as Tally Knives. **Mark:** Tally (last name).

TAMBOLI, MICHAEL, 12447 N. 49 Ave., Glendale, AZ 85304, Phone: 602-978-4308
  Specialties: Miniatures, some full size. **Patterns:** Miniature hunting knives to fantasy art knives. **Technical:** Grinds 440C, 154CM and Damascus. **Prices:** $75 to $500; some to $1000. **Remarks:** Part-time maker; first knife sold in 1978. **Mark:** Initials or last name, city and state.

TASMAN, KERLEY, 9 Avignon Retreat, Pt. Kennedy, 6172, Western Australia, AUSTRALIA, Phone: 61 8 9593 0554, Fax: 61 8 9593 0554
  Specialties: Knife/harness/sheath systems for elite military personnel and body guards. **Patterns:** Utility/tactical knives, hunters small game and presentation grade knives. **Technical:** ATS-34 and 440C, Damascus, flat and hollow grids. **Prices:** US $200 to $1800. **Remarks:** Will take presentation

grade commissions. **Mark:** Makers Initials. **Other:** Multi award winning maker and custom jeweler.

TAY, LARRY C-G., Siglap PO Box 315, Singapore 9145, SINGAPORE, Phone: 65-2419421, Fax: 65-2434879
  Specialties: Push knives, working and using straight knives and folders of his design; Marble's Safety Knife with stained or albino Asian buffalo horn and bone or rosewood handles. **Patterns:** Fighters and utility/camp knives. **Technical:** Forges and grinds D2, truck leaf springs. **Prices:** $200 to $1000. **Remarks:** Spare-time maker; first knife sold in 1957. **Mark:** LDA/LAKELL, from 1999 initials L.T.

TAYLOR, SCOTT, 18124 B LaSalle Ave., Gardena, CA 90248, Phone: 310-538-8104
  Specialties: Hand forged fixed blade knives. **Patterns:** Bowies, daggers, hunters, period pieces. **Technical:** Carbon steels, Damascus, gold and silver fabrication and castings. **Prices:** $400 and up. **Remarks:** ABS Master Smith, jeweler, one-of-a-kind pieces. **Mark:** Celtic triangle knot and/or name.

TAYLOR, SHANE, 18 Broken Bow Ln., Miles City, MT 59301, Phone: 406-232-7175
  Specialties: One-of-a-kind fancy Damascus straight knives and folders. **Patterns:** Bowies, folders and fighters. **Technical:** Forges own mosaic and pattern welded Damascus. **Prices:** $450 and up. **Remarks:** ABS Master Smith, full-time maker; first knife sold in 1982. **Mark:** First name.

TAYLOR, C. GRAY, 560 Poteat Ln., Fall Branch, TN 37656, Phone: 423-348-8304
  Specialties: High-art display knives; period pieces. **Patterns:** Fighters, Bowies, daggers, locking folders and interframes. **Technical:** Grinds 440C, 154CM and ATS-34. **Prices:** $350 and up. **Remarks:** Full-time maker; first knife sold in 1975. **Mark:** Name, city and state.

TAYLOR, BILLY, 10 Temple Rd., Petal, MS 39465, Phone: 601-544-0041
  Specialties: Straight knives of his design. **Patterns:** Bowies, skinners, hunters and utility knives. **Technical:** Flat-grinds 440C, ATS-34 and 154CM. **Prices:** $60 to $300. **Remarks:** Part-time maker; first knife sold in 1991. **Mark:** Full name, city and state.

TERAUCHI, TOSHIYUKI, 7649-13 219-11 Yoshida, Fujita-Cho Gobo-Shi, JAPAN

TERRILL, STEPHEN, 21363 Rd. 196, Lindsay, CA 93247, Phone: 559-562-1966
  Specialties: Deluxe working straight knives and folders. **Patterns:** Fighters, tantos, boots, locking folders and axes; traditional oriental patterns. **Technical:** Forges 1095, 5160, Damascus, stock removal ATS-34. **Prices:** $250-$1000, some $8000 **Remarks:** Full-time maker; first knife sold in 1972. **Mark:** Name, city, state in logo.

TERZUOLA, ROBERT, 3933 Agua Fria St., Santa Fe, NM 87501, Phone: 505-473-1002, Fax: 505-438-8018
  Specialties: Working folders of his design; period pieces. **Patterns:** High-tech utility, defense and gentleman's pieces. **Technical:** Grinds 154CM and CPM S30V. Offers titanium, carbon fiber and G10 composite for side-lock folders and tactical folders. **Prices:** $400 to $1200. **Remarks:** Full-time maker; first knife sold in 1980. **Mark:** Mayan dragon head, name.

THAYER, DANNY O., 8908S 100W, Romney, IN 47981, Phone: 765-538-3105
  Specialties: Hunters, fighters, Bowies. **Prices:** $250 and up.

THEIS, TERRY, 21452 FM 2093, Harper, TX 78631, Phone: 830-864-4438
  Specialties: All European and American engraving styles. **Prices:** $200 to $2000. **Remarks:** Engraver only.

THEUNS PRINSLOO KNIVES, PO Box 2263, Bethlehem, 9700, SOUTH AFRICA, Phone: 27 58 3037111, Fax: same
  Specialties: Fancy folders. **Technical:** Own Damascus and Mokume. **Prices:** $450-$1500.

THEVENOT, JEAN-PAUL, 16 Rue De La Prefecture, Dijon, FRANCE 21000

THIE, BRIAN, 11987 Sperry Rd., Sperry, IA 52650, Phone: 319-985-2276
  Specialties: Working using knives from basic to fancy. **Patterns:** Hunters, fighters, camp and folders. **Technical:** Forges blades and own Damascus. **Prices:** $100 and up. **Remarks:** Member of ABS, part-time maker. Sole author of blades including forging, heat treat, engraving and sheath making. **Mark:** Last name, anvil with last name initial inside, serial number all hand engraved into the blade.

THILL, JIM, 10242 Bear Run, Missoula, MT 59803, Phone: 406-251-5475
  Specialties: Traditional and working/using knives of his design. **Patterns:** Fighters, hunters and utility/camp knives. **Technical:** Grinds D2 and ATS-34; forges 10-95-85, 52100, 5160, 10 series, reg. Damascus-

custom knifemakers

mosaic. Offers hand cut sheaths with rawhide lace. **Prices:** $145 to $350; some to $1250. **Remarks:** Full-time maker; first knife sold in 1962. **Mark:** Running bear in triangle.

THOMAS, KIM, PO Box 531, Seville, OH 44273, Phone: 330-769-9906
Specialties: Fancy and traditional straight knives of his design and to customer specs; period pieces. **Patterns:** Boots, daggers, fighters, swords. **Technical:** Forges own Damascus from 5160, 1010 and nickel. **Prices:** $135 to $1500; some to $3000. **Remarks:** Part-time maker; first knife sold in 1986. Doing business as Thomas Iron Works. **Mark:** KT.

THOMAS, ROCKY, 1716 Waterside Blvd., Moncks Corner, SC 29461, Phone: 843-761-7761
Specialties: Traditional working and using straight knives in standard patterns. **Patterns:** Hunters and utility/camp knives. **Technical:** Grinds 440C, ATS-34 and commercial Damascus. **Prices:** $85 to $150. **Remarks:** Spare-time maker; first knife sold in 1986. **Mark:** First name in script and/or block.

THOMAS, DEVIN, 90 N. 5th St., Panaca, NV 89042, Phone: 775-728-4363
Specialties: Traditional straight knives and folders in standard patterns. **Patterns:** Bowies, fighters, hunters. **Technical:** Forges stainless Damascus, nickel and 1095. Uses, makes and sells Mokume with brass, copper and nickel-silver. **Prices:** $300 to $1200. **Remarks:** Full-time maker; first knife sold in 1979. **Mark:** First and last name, city and state with anvil, or first name only.

THOMAS, DAVID E., 8502 Hwy 91, Lillian, AL 36549, Phone: 251-961-7574
Specialties: Bowies and hunters. **Technical:** Hand forged blades in 5160, 1095 and own Damascus. **Prices:** $400 and up. **Mark:** Stylized DT, maker's last name, serial number.

THOMAS, BOB G., RR 1 Box 121, Thebes, IL 62990-9718

THOMPSON, LLOYD, PO Box 1664, Pagosa Springs, CO 81147, Phone: 970-264-5837
Specialties: Working and collectible straight knives and folders of his design. **Patterns:** Straight blades, lock back folders and slip joint folders. **Technical:** Hollow-grinds ATS-34, D2 and O1. Uses sambar stag and exotic woods. **Prices:** $150 to upscale. **Remarks:** Full-time maker; first knife sold in 1985. Doing business as Trapper Creek Knife Co. **Remarks:** Offers three-day knife-making classes. **Mark:** Name.

THOMPSON, LEON, 45723 S.W. Saddleback Dr., Gaston, OR 97119, Phone: 503-357-2573
Specialties: Working knives. **Patterns:** Locking folders, slip-joints and liner locks. **Technical:** Grinds ATS-34, D2 and 440C. **Prices:** $200 to $600. **Remarks:** Full-time maker; first knife sold in 1976. **Mark:** First and middle initials, last name, city and state.

THOMPSON, TOMMY, 4015 NE Hassalo, Portland, OR 97232-2607, Phone: 503-235-5762
Specialties: Fancy and working knives; mostly liner-lock folders. **Patterns:** Fighters, hunters and liner locks. **Technical:** Grinds D2, ATS-34, CPM440V and T15. Handles are either hardwood inlaid with wood banding and stone or shell, or made of agate, jasper, petrified woods, etc. **Prices:** $75 to $500; some to $1000. **Remarks:** Part-time maker; first knife sold in 1987. Doing business as Stone Birds. **Mark:** First and last name, city and state. **Other:** Knife making temporarily stopped due to family obligations.

THOMPSON, KENNETH, 4887 Glenwhite Dr., Duluth, GA 30136, Phone: 770-446-6730
Specialties: Traditional working and using knives of his design. **Patterns:** Hunters, Bowies and utility/camp knives. **Technical:** Forges 5168, O1, 1095 and 52100. **Prices:** $75 to $1500; some to $2500. **Remarks:** Part-time maker; first knife sold in 1990. **Mark:** P/W; or name, P/W, city and state.

THOMSEN, LOYD W., HCR-46, Box 19, Oelrichs, SD 57763, Phone: 605-535-6162
Specialties: High-art and traditional working/using straight knives and presentation pieces of his design and to customer specs; period pieces. Hand carved animals in crown of stag on handles and carved display stands. **Patterns:** Bowies, hunters, daggers and utility/camp knives. **Technical:** Forges and grinds 1095HC, 1084, L6, 15N20, 440C stainless steel, nickel 200; special restoration process on period pieces. Makes sheaths. Uses natural materials for handles. **Prices:** $350 to $1000. **Remarks:** Full-time maker; first knife sold in 1995. Doing business as Horsehead Creek Knives. **Mark:** Initials and last name over a horse's head.

THOUROT, MICHAEL W., T-814 Co. Rd. 11, Napoleon, OH 43545, Phone: 419-533-6832, Fax: 419-533-3516
Specialties: Working straight knives to customer specs. Designed two-handled skinning ax and limited edition engraved knife and art print set.

Patterns: Fishing and fillet knives, Bowies, tantos and hunters. **Technical:** Grinds O1, D2, 440C and Damascus. **Prices:** $200 to $5000. **Remarks:** Part-time maker; first knife sold in 1968. **Mark:** Initials.

THUESEN, ED, 21211 Knolle Rd., Damon, TX 77430, Phone: 979-553-1211, Fax: 979-553-1211
Specialties: Working straight knives. **Patterns:** Hunters, fighters and survival knives. **Technical:** Grinds D2, 440C, ATS-34 and Vascowear. **Prices:** $150 to $275; some to $600. **Remarks:** Part-time maker; first knife sold in 1979. Runs knife maker supply business. **Mark:** Last name in script.

TICHBOURNE, GEORGE, 7035 Maxwell Rd. #5, Mississauga, Ont., CANADA L5S 1R5, Phone: 905-670-0200
Specialties: Traditional working and using knives as well as unique collectibles. **Patterns:** Bowies, hunters, outdoor, kitchen, integrals, art, military, Scottish dirks, folders, kosher knives. **Technical:** Stock removal 440C, Stellite 6K, stainless Damascus, liquid metal. Handle materials include mammoth, meteorite, mother-of-pearl, Precious gems, Mosiac, Abalone, Stag, Micarta, Exotic High Resin Woods and Corian scrimshawed by George. Leather sheaths are hand stitched and tooled by George as well as the silver adornments for the Dirk Sheaths. **Prices:** $60 U.S. up to $5000 U.S. **Remarks:** Full-time maker with his OWN STORE. First knife sold in 1990. **Mark:** Full name over Maple Leaf.

TIENSVOLD, JASON, PO Box 795, Rushville, NE 69360, Phone: 308-327-2046
Specialties: Working and using straight knives of his design; period pieces. Gentlemans folders, art folders. **Patterns:** Hunters, skinners, Bowies, fighters, daggers, linder locks. **Technical:** Forges own Damascus using 15N20 and 1084, nickle, custom file work. **Prices:** $200 to $4000. **Remarks:** Full-time maker, first knife sold in 1994; doing business under Tiensvold Custom Knives. **Mark:** Tiensvold USA Handmade in a circle.

TIENSVOLD, ALAN L., PO Box 355, Rushville, NE 69360, Phone: 308-327-2046
Specialties: Working knives, tomahawks and period pieces, high end Damascus knives. **Patterns:** Random, ladder, twist and many more. **Technical:** Hand forged blades, we forge our own Damascus. **Prices:** Working knives start at $300. **Remarks:** Feceived journeyman rating with the ABS in 2002. **Mark:** Tiensvold hand made U.S.A. on left side, JS on right. **Other:** Does own engraving and fine work.

TIGHE, BRIAN, RR 1, Ridgeville, Ont, CANADA L0S 1M0, Phone: 905-892-2734, Fax: 905-892-2734
Specialties: High tech tactical folders. **Patterns:** Boots, daggers, locking and slip-joint folders. **Technical:** CPM 440V and CPM 420V. Prefers natural handle material inlay; hand finishes. **Prices:** $450 to $2000. **Remarks:** Part-time maker; first knife sold in 1989. **Mark:** Etched signature.

TILL, CALVIN E. AND RUTH, 211 Chaping, Chadron, NE 69337
Specialties: Straight knives, hunters, Bowies; no folders **Patterns:** Training point, drop point hunters, Bowies. **Technical:** ATS-34 sub zero quench RC-59, 61. **Prices:** $700 to $1200. **Remarks:** Sells only the absolute best knives they can make. **Mark:** RC Till. The R is for Ruth. **Other:** Manufactures every part in their knives.

TILTON, JOHN, 24041 HWY 383, Iowa, LA 70647, Phone: 337-582-6785
Specialties: Camp knives and skinners. **Technical:** All forged blades. **Prices:** $125 and up. **Mark:** Initials J.E.T. **Other:** ABS Journeyman Smith.

TINDERA, GEORGE, BURNING RIVER FORGE, 751 Hadcock Rd., Brunswick, OH 44212-2648, Phone: 330-220-6212
Specialties: Straight knives; his designs. **Patterns:** Personal knives; classic Bowies and fighters. **Technical:** Hand-forged high-carbon; his own cable and pattern welded Damascus. **Prices:** $100 to $400. **Remarks:** Spare-time maker; sold first knife in 1995. **Other:** Natural handle materials.

TINGLE, DENNIS P., 19390 E Clinton Rd., Jackson, CA 95642, Phone: 209-223-4586
Specialties: Fixed-blade hunting, using knives w/guards and natural handle materials.

TIPPETTS, COLTEN, PO Box 1436, Ketchum, ID 83340, Phone: 208-578-1690
Specialties: Fancy and working straight knives and fancy locking folders of his own design or to customer specifications. **Patterns:** Hunters and skinners, fighters and utility. **Technical:** Grinds BG-42, high-carbon 1095 and Damascus. **Prices:** $200 to $1000. **Remarks:** Part-time maker; first knife sold in 1996. **Mark:** Fused initials.

TODD, RICHARD C., RR 1, Chambersburg, IL 62323, Phone: 217-327-4380
Specialties: Multi blade folders and silver sheaths. **Patterns:** Blacksmithing and tool making. **Mark:** RT with letter R crossing the T.

TOICH, NEVIO, Via Pisacane 9, Rettorgole di Caldogna, Vincenza, ITALY 36030, Phone: 0444-985065, Fax: 0444-301254
Specialties: Working/using straight knives of his design or to customer specs. **Patterns:** Bowies, hunters, skinners and utility/camp knives. **Technical:** Grinds 440C, D2 and ATS-34. Hollow-grinds all blades and uses mirror polish. Offers hand-sewn sheaths. Uses wood and horn. **Prices:** $120 to $300; some to $450. **Remarks:** Spare-time maker; first knife sold in 1989. Doing business as Custom Toich. **Mark:** Initials and model number punched.

TOKAR, DANIEL, Box 1776, Shepherdstown, WV 25443
Specialties: Working knives; period pieces. **Patterns:** Hunters, camp knives, buckskinners, axes, swords and battle gear. **Technical:** Forges L6, 1095 and his Damascus; makes mokume, Japanese alloys and bronze daggers; restores old edged weapons. **Prices:** $25 to $800; some to $3000. **Remarks:** Part-time maker; first knife sold in 1979. Doing business as The Willow Forge. **Mark:** Arrow over rune and date.

TOLLEFSON,, BARRY A., 177 Blackfoot Trail, Gunnison, CO 81230-9720, Phone: 970-641-0752
Specialties: Working straight knives, some fancy. **Patterns:** Hunters, skinners, fighters and camp knives. **Technical:** Grinds 440C, ATS-34 and D2. Likes mirror-finishes; offers some fancy filework. Handles made from elk, deer and exotic hardwoods. **Prices:** $75 to $300; some higher. **Remarks:** Part-time maker; first knife sold in 1990. **Mark:** Stylized initials.

TOMBERLIN, BRION R., ANVIL TOP CUSTOM KNIVES, 825 W Timberdell, Norman, OK 73072, Phone: 405-202-6832
Specialties: Hand forged blades, working pieces, standard classic patterns, some swords, and customer designs. **Patterns:** Bowies, hunters, fighters, Persian and eastern-styles. Likes Japanese blades. **Technical:** Forge 1050,1075,1084,1095,5160, some forged stainless, also do some stock removal in stainless. **Prices:** Start at $150 up to $800 or higher for swords and custom pieces. **Remarks:** Part-time maker, first knife sold in 1984, member America Bladesmith Society, member Japanese Sword Society. **Mark:** "BRION" on forged blades, :ATCK" on stock removal, stainless ad early forged blades. **Other:** Prefer natural handle materials, hand rubbed finishes. Like temperlines.

TOMES, P.J., 594 High Peak Ln., Shipman, VA 22971, Phone: 804-263-8662
Specialties: Scagel reproductions. **Patterns:** Front-lock folders. **Technical:** Forges 52100. **Prices:** $150 to $750. **Mark:** Last name, USA, MS, stamped in forged blades.

TOMEY, KATHLEEN, 146 Buford Pl., Macon, GA 31204, Phone: 478-746-8454
Specialties: Working hunters, skinners, daily users in fixed blades, plain and embellished. Tactical neck and tanto. Bowies. **Technical:** Grinds 01, ATS-34, flat or hollow grind, filework, satin and mirror polish finishes. High quality sheaths with tooling. Kydex with tactical. **Prices:** $150 to $500. **Remarks:** Almost full-time maker. **Mark:** Last name in diamond.

TOMPKINS, DAN, PO Box 398, Peotone, IL 60468, Phone: 708-258-3620
Specialties: Working knives, some deluxe, some folders. **Patterns:** Hunters, boots, daggers and push knives. **Technical:** Grinds D2, 440C, ATS-34 and 154CM. **Prices:** $85 to $150; some to $400. **Remarks:** Part-time maker; first knife sold in 1975. **Mark:** Last name, city, state.

TONER, ROGER, 531 Lightfoot Place, Pickering, Ont., CANADA L1V 5Z8, Phone: 905-420-5555
Specialties: Exotic Sword canes. **Patterns:** Bowies, daggers and fighters. **Technical:** Grinds 440C, D2 and Damascus. Scrimshaws and engraves. Silver cast pommels and guards in animal shapes; twisted silver wire inlays. Uses semi-precious stones. **Prices:** $200 to $2000; some to $3000. **Remarks:** Part-time maker; first knife sold in 1982. **Mark:** Last name.

TOPLISS, M.W. "IKE", 1668 Hermosa Ct., Montrose, CO 81401, Phone: 970-249-4703
Specialties: Working/using straight knives of his design and to customer specs. **Patterns:** Boots, hunters, utility/camp knives. **Technical:** Prefers ATS-34. Other steels available on request. Likes stabilized wood, natural hardwoods, antler and Micarta. **Prices:** $175 to $300; some to $800. **Remarks:** Part-time maker; first knife sold in 1984. **Mark:** Name, city, state.

TORGESON, SAMUEL L., 25 Alpine Ln., Sedona, AZ 86336-6809

TOSHIFUMI, KURAMOTO, 3435 Higashioda Asakura-gun, Fukuoka, JAPAN, Phone: 0946-42-4470

TOWELL, DWIGHT L., 2375 Towell Rd., Midvale, ID 83645, Phone: 208-355-2419
Specialties: Solid, elegant working knives; art knives. **Patterns:** Hunters, Bowies, daggers; folders in several weights. **Technical:** Grinds 154CM;

some engraving. **Prices:** $250 to $800; some $3500 and higher. **Remarks:** Part-time maker; first knife sold in 1970. **Mark:** Last name.

TOWNSEND, ALLEN MARK, 6 Pine Trail, Texarkana, AR 71854, Phone: 870-772-8945

TRACY, BUD, 495 Flanders Rd., Reno, NV 8951-4784

TREIBER, LEON, PO Box 342, Ingram, TX 78025, Phone: 830-367-2246
Specialties: Folders of his design and to customer specs. **Patterns:** Locking folders. **Technical:** Grinds CPM-T-440V, D2, 440C, Damascus, 420v and ats34. **Prices:** $250 to $1500. **Remarks:** Part-time maker; first knife sold in 1992. Doing business as Treiber Knives. **Mark:** First initial, last name, city, state.

TREML, GLENN, RR #14, Site 11-10, Thunder Bay, Ont., CANADA P7B 5E5, Phone: 807-767-1977
Specialties: Working straight knives of his design and to customer specs. **Patterns:** Hunters, kitchen knives and double-edged survival knives. **Technical** Grinds 440C, ATS-34 and O1; stock removal method. Uses various woods and Micarta for handle material. **Prices:** $60 to $400; some higher. **Mark:** Stamped last name.

TRINDLE, BARRY, 1660 Ironwood Trail, Earlham, IA 50072-8611, Phone: 515-462-1237
Specialties: Engraved folders. **Patterns:** Mostly small folders, classical-styles and pocket knives. **Technical:** 440 only. Engraves. Handles of wood or mineral material. **Prices:** Start at $1000. **Mark:** Name on tang.

TRISLER, KENNETH W., 6256 Federal 80, Rayville, LA 71269, Phone: 318-728-5541

TRITZ, JEAN JOSE, Schopstrasse 23, 20255 Hamburg, GERMANY, Phone: 040-49 78 21
Specialties: Scandinavian knives, Japanese kitchen knives, friction folders, swords. **Patterns:** Puukkos, Tollekniven, Hocho, friction folders, swords. **Technical:** Forges tool steels, carbon steels, 52100 Damascus Mokume, San Maj. **Prices:** $200 to $2000; some higher. **Remarks:** Full-time maker; first knife sold in 1989. **Mark:** Initials in monogram. **Other:** Does own leatherwork, prefers natural materials. Sole authorship. Speaks French, German, English, Norwegian.

TRUDEL, PAUL, 525 Braydon Ave., Ottawa ON, CANADA K1G 0W7
Remarks: Part-time knife maker.

TRUJILLO, ALBERT M.B., 2035 Wasmer Cir., Bosque Farms, NM 87068, Phone: 505-869-0428
Specialties: Working/using straight knives of his design or to customer specs. **Patterns:** Hunters, skinners, fighters, working/using knives. File work offered. **Technical:** Grinds ATS34, D2, 440C. Tapers tangs, all blades cryogenically treated. **Prices:** $75 to $500. **Remarks:** Part-time maker; first knife sold in 1997. **Mark:** First and last name under logo.

TRUJILLO, THOMAS A., 3001 Tanglewood Dr., Anchorage, AK 99517, Phone: 907-243-6093
Specialties: High-end art knives. **Patterns:** Hunters, Bowies, daggers and locking folders. **Technical:** Grinds to customer choice, including rock and commercial Damascus. Inlays jewels and carves handles. **Prices:** $150 to $900; some to $6000. **Remarks:** Full-time maker; first knife sold in 1976. Doing business as Alaska Knife and Service Co. **Mark:** Alaska Knife and/or Thomas Anthony.

TRUJILLO, ADAM, 3001 Tanglewood Dr., Anchorage, AK 99517, Phone: 907-243-6093
Specialties: Working/using straight knives of his design. **Patterns:** Hunters and utility/camp knives. **Technical:** Grinds 440C, ATS-34 and O1; ice tempers blades. Sheaths are dipped in wax and oil base. **Prices:** $200 to $500; some to $1000. **Remarks:** Spare-time maker; first knife sold in 1995. Doing business as Alaska Knife and Service Co. **Mark:** NA.

TRUJILLO, MIRANDA, 3001 Tanglewood Dr.., Anchorage, AK 99517, Phone: 907-243-6093
Specialties: Working/using straight knives of her design. **Patterns:** Hunters and utility/camp knives. **Technical:** Grinds ATS-34 and 440C. Sheaths are water resistant. **Prices:** $145 to $400; some to $600. **Remarks:** Spare-time maker; first knife sold in 1989. Doing business as Alaska Knife and Service Co. **Mark:** NA.

TSCHAGER, REINHARD, Piazza Parrocchia 7, I-39100 Bolzano, ITALY, Phone: 0471-970642, Fax: 0471-970642
Specialties: Classic, high-art, collector-grade straight knives of his design. **Patterns:** Hunters. **Technical:** Grinds ATS-34, D2 and Damascus. Oval pins. Gold inlay. Offers engraving. **Prices:** $500 to $1200; some to $4000. **Remarks:** Spare-time maker; first knife sold in 1979. **Mark:** Gold inlay stamped with initials.

custom knifemakers

TURCOTTE, LARRY, 1707 Evergreen, Pampa, TX 79065, Phone: 806-665-9369, 806-669-0435
Specialties: Fancy and working/using knives of his design and to customer specs. **Patterns:** Hunters, kitchen knives, utility/camp knives. **Technical:** Grinds 440C, D2, ATS-34. Engraves, scrimshaws, silver inlays. **Prices:** $150 to $350; some to $1000. **Remarks:** Part-time maker; first knife sold in 1977. Doing business as Knives by Turcotte. **Mark:** Last name.

TURECEK, JIM, 12 Elliott Rd., Ansonia, CT 06401, Phone: 203-734-8406
Specialties: Exotic folders, art knives and some miniatures. **Patterns:** Trout and bird knives with split bamboo handles and one-of-a-kind folders. **Technical:** Grinds and forges stainless and carbon Damascus. **Prices:** $750 to $1500; some to $3000. **Remarks:** Full-time maker; first knife sold in 1983. **Mark:** Last initial in script, or last name.

TURNBULL, RALPH A., 14464 Linden Dr., Spring Hill, FL 34609, Phone: 352-688-7089
Specialties: Fancy folders. **Patterns:** Primarily gents pocket knives. **Technical:** Wire EDM work on bolsters. **Prices:** $300 and up. **Remarks:** Full-time maker; first knife sold in 1973. **Mark:** Signature or initials.

TURNER, KEVIN, 17 Hunt Ave., Montrose, NY 10548, Phone: 914-739-0535
Specialties: Working straight knives of his design and to customer specs; period pieces. **Patterns:** Daggers, fighters and utility knives. **Technical:** Forges 5160 and 52100. **Prices:** $90 to $500. **Remarks:** Part-time maker; first knife sold in 1991. **Mark:** Acid-etched signed last name and year.

TYCER, ART, 23820 N Cold Springs Rd., Paron, AR 72122, Phone: 501-821-4487
Specialties: Fancy working/using straight knives of his design, to customer specs and standard patterns. **Patterns:** Boots, Bowies, daggers, fighters, hunters, kitchen and utility knives. **Technical:** Grinds ATS-34, 440C and a variety of carbon steels. Uses exotic woods with spacer material, stag and water buffalo. Offers filework. **Prices:** $125 and up depending on size and embellishments. **Remarks:** Making and using his own Damascus and other Damascus also. **Mark:** Flying "T" over first initial inside an oval. **Other:** Full-time maker.

TYSER, ROSS, 1015 Hardee Court, Spartanburg, SC 29303, Phone: 864-585-7616
Specialties: Traditional working and using straight knives and folders of his design and in standard patterns. **Patterns:** Bowies, hunters and slip-joint folders. **Technical:** Grinds 440C and commercial Damascus. Mosaic pins; stone inlay. Does filework and scrimshaw. Offers engraving and cutwork and some inlay on sheaths. **Prices:** $45 to $125; some to $400. **Remarks:** Part-time maker; first knife sold in 1995. Doing business as RT Custom Knives. **Mark:** Stylized initials.

U

UCHIDA, CHIMATA, 977-2 Oaza Naga Shisui Ki, Kumamoto, JAPAN 861-1204

UEKAMA, NOBUYUKI, 3-2-8-302 Ochiai, Tama City, Tokyo, JAPAN

V

VAGNINO, MICHAEL, PO Box 67, Visalia, CA 93279, Phone: 559-528-2800
Specialties: Working and fancy straight knives and folders of his design and to customer specs. **Patterns:** Hunters, Bowies, camp, kitchen and folders: locking liners, slip-joint, lock-back and double-action autos. **Technical:** Forges 52100, A2, 1084 and 15N20 Damascus and grinds stainless. **Prices:** $275 to $2000 plus. **Remarks:** Full-time maker, ABS Master Smith. **Mark:** Logo, last name.

VAIL, DAVE, 554 Sloop Point Rd., Hampstead, NC 28443, Phone: 910-270-4456
Specialties: Working/using straight knives of his own design or to the customer's specs. **Patterns:** Hunters/skinners, utility, fillet, Bowies. **Technical:** Grinds ATS-34, 440c, 154 CM and 1095 carbon steel. **Prices:** $90-$450. **Remarks:** Part-time maker. Member of NC Custom Knifemakers Guild. **Mark:** Etched oval with "Dave Vail Hampstead NC" inside.

VALLOTTON, THOMAS, 621 Fawn Ridge Dr., Oakland, OR 97462, Phone: 541-459-2216
Specialties: Custom autos. **Patterns:** Tactical, fancy. **Technical:** File work, uses Damascus, uses Spectrum Metal. **Prices:** From $350 to $700. **Remarks:** Full-time maker. **Mark:** T and a V mingled. **Other:** Maker of Protégé 3 canoe.

VALLOTTON, SHAWN, 621 Fawn Ridge Dr., Oakland, OR 97462, Phone: 503-459-2216
Specialties: Left-hand knives. **Patterns:** All styles. **Technical:** Grinds 440C, ATS-34 and Damascus. Uses titanium. Prefers bead-blasted or anodized finishes. **Prices:** $250 to $1400. **Remarks:** Full-time maker. **Mark:** Name and specialty.

VALLOTTON, RAINY D., 1295 Wolf Valley Dr., Umpqua, OR 97486, Phone: 541-459-0465
Specialties: Folders, one-handed openers and art pieces. **Patterns:** All patterns. **Technical:** Stock removal all steels; uses titanium liners and bolsters; uses all finishes. **Prices:** $350 to $3500. **Remarks:** Full-time maker. **Mark:** Name.

VALLOTTON, BUTCH AND AREY, 621 Fawn Ridge Dr., Oakland, OR 97462, Phone: 541-459-2216, Fax: 541-459-7473
Specialties: Quick opening knives w/complicated mechanisms. **Patterns:** Tactical, fancy, working, and some art knives. **Technical:** Grinds all steels, uses others' Damascus. Uses Spectrum Metal. **Prices:** From $350 to $4500. **Remarks:** Full-time maker since 1984; first knife sold in 1981. **Mark:** Name w/viper head in the "V". **Other:** Co/designer, Appelgate Fairbarn folding w/Bill Harsey.

VALOIS, A. DANIEL, 3552 W. Lizard Ck. Rd., Lehighton, PA 18235, Phone: 717-386-3636
Specialties: Big working knives; various sized lock-back folders with new safety releases. **Patterns:** Fighters in survival packs, sturdy working knives, belt buckle knives, military-style knives, swords. **Technical:** Forges and grinds A2, O1 and 440C; likes full tangs. **Prices:** $65 to $240; some to $600. **Remarks:** Full-time maker; first knife sold in 1969. **Mark:** Anvil logo with last name inside.

VAN CLEVE, STEVE, Box 372, Sutton, AK 99674, Phone: 907-745-3038

VAN DE MANAKKER, THIJS, Koolweg 34, 5759 px Helenaveen, HOLLAND, Phone: 0493539369
Specialties: Classic high-art knives. **Patterns:** Swords, utility/camp knives and period pieces. **Technical:** Forges soft iron, carbon steel and Bloomery Iron. Makes own Damascus, Bloomery Iron and patterns. **Prices:** $20 to $2000; some higher. **Remarks:** Full-time maker; first knife sold in 1969. **Mark:** Stylized "V".

VAN DEN ELSEN, GERT, Purcelldreef 83, 5012 AJ Tilburg, NETHERLANDS, Phone: 013-4563200
Specialties: Fancy, working/using, miniatures and integral straight knives of the maker's design or to customer specs. **Patterns:** Bowies, fighters, hunters and Japanese-style blades. **Technical:** Grinds ATS-34 and 440C; forges Damascus. Offers filework, differentially tempered blades and some mokume-gane fittings. **Prices:** $350 to $1000; some to $4000. **Remarks:** Part-time maker; first knife sold in 1982. Doing business as G-E Knives. **Mark:** Initials GE in lozenge shape.

VAN EIZENGA, JERRY W., 14227 Cleveland, Nunica, MI 49448, Phone: 616-842-2699
Specialties: Hand forged blades, Scagel patterns and other styles. **Patterns:** Camp, hunting, bird, trout, folders, axes, miniatures. **Technical:** 5160, 52100, 1084. **Prices:** Start at $250. **Remarks:** Part-time maker, sole author of knife and sheath. **Mark:** Interconnecting letters spelling VAN, city and state. **Other:** First knife made early 1970s. ABS member who believes in the beauty of simplicity.

VAN ELDIK, FRANS, Ho Flaan 3, 3632BT Loenen, NETHERLANDS, Phone: 0031 294 233 095, Fax: 0031 294 233 095
Specialties: Fancy collector-grade straight knives and folders of his design. **Patterns:** Hunters, fighters, boots and folders. **Technical:** Forges and grinds D2, 154CM, ATS-34 and stainless Damascus. **Prices:** Start at $225. **Remarks:** Spare-time maker; first knife sold in 1979. Knivemaker 25 years. **Mark:** Lion with name and Amsterdam.

VAN RIJSWIJK, AAD, AVR KNIVES, Arij Koplaan 16B, 3132 AA Vlaardingen, THE NETHERLANDS, Phone: +31 10 2343227, Fax: +31 10 2343648
Specialties: High-art interframe folders of his design and in shaving sets. **Patterns:** Hunters and locking folders. **Technical:** Uses semi-precious stones, mammoth, ivory, walrus ivory, iron wood. **Prices:** $550 to $3800. **Remarks:** Full-time maker; first knife sold in 1993. **Mark:** NA.

VAN RIPER, JAMES N., PO Box 7045, Citrus Heights, CA 95621-7045, Phone: 916-721-0892

VANDERFORD, CARL G., Rt. 9, Box 238B, Columbia, TN 38401, Phone: 615-381-1488
Specialties: Traditional working straight knives and folders of his design. **Patterns:** Hunters, Bowies and locking folders. **Technical:** Forges and grinds 440C, O1 and wire Damascus. **Prices:** $60 to $125. **Remarks:** Part-time maker; first knife sold in 1987. **Mark:** Last name.

VANDEVENTER, TERRY L., 3274 Davis Rd., Terry, MS 39170-9750, Phone: 601-371-7414
Specialties: Camp knives, Bowies, friction folders. **Technical:** 1095, 1084, L-6, Damascus and Mokume; natural handles. **Prices:** $250 to $1200. **Remarks:** Sole author; makes everything here. **Mark:** T L Vandeventer (with silhouette of snake), handcrafted knives. **Other:** Part-time since 1994. ABS Journeyman Smith.

VANHOY, ED AND TANYA, 24255 N Fork River Rd., Abingdon, VA 24210, Phone: 276-944-4885
Specialties: Traditional and working/using straight knives of his design, make folders. **Patterns:** Fighters, straight knives, folders, hunters and art knives. **Technical:** Grinds ATS-34 and 440V; offers D2. Offers filework, engraves, acid etching, mosaic pins, decorative bolsters and custom fitted English bridle leather sheaths. **Prices:** $250 to $3000. **Remarks:** Full-time maker; first knife sold in 1977. Wife also engraves. Doing business as Van Hoy Custom Knives. **Mark:** Acid etched last name.

VASQUEZ, JOHNNY DAVID, 1552 7th St., Wyandotte, MI 48192, Phone: 734-281-2455

VAUGHAN, IAN, 351 Doe Run Rd., Manheim, PA 17545-9368, Phone: 717-665-6949

VEATCH, RICHARD, 2580 N. 35th Pl., Springfield, OR 97477, Phone: 541-747-3910
Specialties: Traditional working and using straight knives of his design and in standard patterns; period pieces. **Patterns:** Daggers, hunters, swords, utility/camp knives and minis. **Technical:** Forges and grinds his own Damascus; uses L6 and O1. Prefers natural handle materials; offers leatherwork. **Prices:** $50 to $300; some to $500. **Remarks:** Full-time maker; first knife sold in 1991. **Mark:** Stylized initials.

VEIT, MICHAEL, 3289 E. Fifth Rd., LaSalle, IL 61301, Phone: 815-223-3538
Specialties: Damascus folders. **Technical:** Engraver-Sole author. **Prices:** $2500 to $6500. **Remarks:** Part-time maker; first knife sold in 1985. **Mark:** Name in script.

VELARDE, RICARDO, 7240 N Greefield Dr., Park City, UT 84098, Phone: 435-940-1378/Cell 801-360-1413/801-361-0204
Specialties: Investment grade integrals and interframs. **Patterns:** Boots, fighters and hunters; hollow grind. **Technical:** BG on Integrals. **Prices:** $850 to $4500. **Remarks:** First knife sold in 1992. **Mark:** First initial, last name on blade; city, state, U.S.A. at bottom of tang.

VENSILD, HENRIK, Gl Estrup, Randersvei 4, DK-8963 Auning, DENMARK, Phone: +45 86 48 44 48
Specialties: Classic and traditional working and using knives of his design; Scandinavian influence. **Patterns:** hunters and using knives. **Technical:** Forges Damascus. Hand makes handles, sheaths and blades. **Prices:** $350 to $1000. **Remarks:** Part-time maker; first knife sold in 1967. **Mark:** Initials.

VIALLON, HENRI, Les Belins, 63300 Thiers, FRANCE, Phone: 04-73-80-24-03, Fax: 04 73-51-02-02
Specialties: Folders and complex Damascus **Patterns:** My draws. **Technical:** Forge **Prices:** $1000-$5000. **Mark:** H. Viallon.

VIELE, H.J., 88 Lexington Ave., Westwood, NJ 07675, Phone: 201-666-2906
Specialties: Folding knives of distinctive shapes. **Patterns:** High-tech folders. **Technical:** Grinds 440C and ATS-34. **Prices:** Start at $475. **Remarks:** Full-time maker; first knife sold in 1973. **Mark:** Last name with stylized throwing star.

VIKING KNIVES (SEE JAMES THORLIEF ERIKSEN)

VILAR, RICARDO AUGUSTO FERREIRA, Rua Alemada Dos Jasmins, NO 243, Parque Petropolis, Mairipora Sao Paulo, BRASIL 07600-000, Phone: 011-55-11-44-85-43-46
Specialties: Traditional Brazilian-style working knives of the Sao Paulo state. **Patterns:** Fighters, hunters, utility, and camp knives, welcome customer design. Specialize in the "true" Brazilian camp knife "Soracabana". **Technical:** Forges only with sledge hammer to 100% shape in 5160 and 52100 and his own Damascus steels. Makes own sheaths in the "true" traditional "Paulista"-style of the state of Sao Paulo. **Remark:** Full-time maker. **Prices:** $250 to $600. Uses only natural handle materials. **Mark:** Special designed signature styled name R. Vilar.

VILLA, LUIZ, R. Com. Miguel Calfat, 398 Itaim Bibi, Sao Paulo, SP-04537-081, BRAZIL, Phone: 011-8290649
Specialties: One-of-a-kind straight knives and jewel knives of all designs. **Patterns:** Bowies, hunters, utility/camp knives and jewel knives. **Technical:** Grinds D6, Damascus and 440C; forges 5160. Prefers natural handle material. **Prices:** $70 to $200. **Remarks:** Part-time maker; first knife sold in 1990. **Mark:** Last name and serial number.

VILLAR, RICARDO, Al. dos Jasmins, 243, Mairipora, S.P. 07600-000, BRAZIL, Phone: 011-4851649
Specialties: Straight working knives to customer specs. **Patterns:** Bowies, fighters and utility/camp knives. **Technical:** Grinds D6, ATS-34 and 440C stainless. **Prices:** $80 to $200. **Remarks:** Part-time maker; first knife sold in 1993. **Mark:** Percor over sword and circle.

VISTE, JAMES, Edgewize Forge, 13401 Mt Elliot, Detroit, MI 48212, Phone: 313-664-7455
Mark: EWF touch mark.

VISTNES, TOR, N-6930 Svelgen, NORWAY, Phone: 047-57795572
Specialties: Traditional and working knives of his design. **Patterns:** Hunters and utility knives. **Technical:** Grinds Uddeholm Elmax. Handles made of rear burls of different Nordic stabilized woods. **Prices:** $300 to $1100. **Remarks:** Part-time maker; first knife sold in 1988. **Mark:** Etched name and deer head.

VITALE, MACE, 925 Rt 80, Guilford, CT 06437, Phone: 203-457-5591
Specialties: Hand forged blades. **Patterns:** Hunters, utility, chef, Bowies and fighters. **Technical:** 5160, 1095, 1084, L-6. Hand forged and finished. **Prices:** $50 to $500. **Remarks:** Full-time maker; first knife sold 2001. **Mark:** MACE.

VOGT, DONALD J., 9007 Hogans Bend, Tampa, FL 33647, Phone: 813 973-3245
Specialties: Art knives, folders, automatics, large fixed blades. **Technical:** Uses Damascus steels for blade and bolsters, filework, hand carving on blade bolsters and handles. Other materials used - jewels, gold, stainless steel, mokume. Prefers to use natural handle materials. **Prices:** $800 to $7000. **Remarks:** Part-time maker; first knife sold in 1997. **Mark:** Last name.

VOGT, PATRIK, KUNGSVAGEN 83, S-30270 Halmstad, SWEDEN, Phone: 46-35-30977
Specialties: Working straight knives. **Patterns:** Bowies, hunters and fighters. **Technical:** Forges carbon steel and own Damascus. **Prices:** From $100. **Remarks:** Not currently making knives. **Mark:** Initials or last name.

VOORHIES, LES, 14511 Lk. Mazaska Tr., Faribault, MN 55021, Phone: 507-332-0736
Specialties: Steels. **Technical:** ATS-34 Damascus. **Prices:** $75-$450.

VOSS, BEN, 362 Clark St., Galesburg, IL 61401, Phone: 309-342-6994
Specialties: Fancy working knives of his design. **Patterns:** Bowies, fighters, hunters, boots and folders. **Technical:** Grinds 440C, ATS-34 and D2. **Prices:** $35 to $1200. **Remarks:** Part-time maker; first knife sold in 1986. **Mark:** Name, city and state.

VOTAW, DAVID P., Box 327, Pioneer, OH 43554, Phone: 419-737-2774
Specialties: Working knives; period pieces. **Patterns:** Hunters, Bowies, camp knives, buckskinners and tomahawks. **Technical:** Grinds O1 and D2. **Prices:** $100 to $200; some to $500. **Remarks:** Part-time maker; took over for the late W.K. Kneubuhler. Doing business as W-K Knives. **Mark:** WK with V inside anvil.

VOWELL, DONALD J., 815 Berry Dr., Mayfield, KY 42066, Phone: 270-247-2157

VUNK, ROBERT, 3166 Breckenridge Dr., Colorado Springs, CO 80906, Phone: 719-576-5505
Specialties: Working knives, some fancy; period pieces. **Patterns:** Variety of tantos, fillet knives, kitchen knives, camp knives and folders. **Technical:** Grinds O1, 440C and ATS-34; provides mountings, cases, stands. **Prices:** $55 to $1300. **Remarks:** Part-time maker; first knife sold in 1985. Doing business as RV Knives. **Mark:** Initials.

W

WADA, YASUTAKA, Fujinokidai 2-6-22, Nara City, Nara prefect 631-0044, JAPAN, Phone: 0742 46-0689
Specialties: Fancy and embellished one-of-a-kind straight knives of his design. **Patterns:** Bowies, daggers and hunters. **Technical:** Grinds ATS-34, Cowry X and Cowry X L-30 laminate. **Prices:** $400 to $2500; some higher. **Remarks:** Part-time maker; first knife sold in 1990. **Mark:** Owl eyes with initial and last name underneath.

WAGAMAN, JOHN K., 107 E Railroad St., Selma, NC 27576, Phone: 919-965-9659, Fax: 919-965-9901
Specialties: Fancy working knives. **Patterns:** Bowies, miniatures, hunters, fighters and boots. **Technical:** Grinds D2, 440C, 154CM and commercial Damascus; inlays mother-of-pearl. **Prices:** $110 to $2000. **Remarks:** Part-time maker; first knife sold in 1975. **Mark:** Last name.

custom knifemakers

WAHLSTER, MARK DAVID, 1404 N. Second St., Silverton, OR 97381, Phone: 503-873-3775
Specialties: Automatics, antique and high-tech folders in standard patterns and to customer specs. **Patterns:** Hunters, fillets and combat knives. **Technical:** Flat grinds 440C, ATS-34, D2 and Damascus. Uses titanium in folders. **Prices:** $100 to $1000. **Remarks:** Full-time maker; first knife sold in 1981. **Mark:** Name, city and state or last name.

WALDROP, MARK, 14562 SE 1st Ave. Rd., Summerfield, FL 34491, Phone: 352-347-9034
Specialties: Period pieces. **Patterns:** Bowies and daggers. **Technical:** Uses stock removal. Engraves. **Prices:** Moderate to upscale. **Remarks:** Part-time maker; first knife sold in 1978. **Mark:** Last name.

WALKER, JOHN W., 10620 Moss Branch Rd., Bon Aqua, TN 37025, Phone: 931-670-4754
Specialties: Straight knives, daggers and folders; sterling rings, 14K gold wire wrap; some stone setting. **Patterns:** Hunters, boot knives, others. **Technical:** Grinds 440C, ATS-34, L6, etc. Buys Damascus. **Prices:** $150 to $500 some to $1500. **Remarks:** Part-time maker; first knife sold in 1982. **Mark:** Hohenzollern Eagle with name, or last name.

WALKER, BILL, 431 Walker Rd., Stevensville, MD 21666, Phone: 410-643-5041

WALKER, DON, 3236 Halls Chapel Rd., Burnsville, NC 28714, Phone: 828-675-9716

WALKER, MICHAEL L., PO Box 1924, Rancho de Taos, NM 87571, Phone: 505-737-3086, Fax: 505-751-0284
Specialties: Innovative knife designs and locking systems; Titanium and SS furniture and art. **Patterns:** Folders from utility grade to museum quality art; others upon request. **Technical:** State-of-the-art materials: titanium, stainless Damascus, gold, etc. **Prices:** $3500 and above. **Remarks:** Designer/MetalCrafts; Full-time professional knife maker since 1980; Four U.S. Patents. Invented Liner Lock® and was awarded Registered U.S. Trademark No. 1,585,333. **Mark:** Early mark MW, Walker's Lockers by M.L. Walker; current M.L. Walker or Michael Walker.

WALKER, JIM, 22 Walker Lane, Morrilton, AR 72110, Phone: 501-354-3175
Specialties: Period pieces and working/using knives of his design and to customer specs. **Patterns:** Bowies, fighters, hunters, camp knives. **Technical:** Forges 5160, O1, L6, 52100, 1084, 1095. **Prices:** Start at $375. **Remarks:** Full-time maker; first knife sold in 1993. **Mark:** Three arrows with last name/MS.

WALKER, GEORGE A., PO Box 3272, 483 Aspen Hills, Alpine, WY 83128-0272, Phone: 307-883-2372, Fax: 307-883-2372
Specialties: Deluxe working knives. **Patterns:** Hunters, boots, fighters, Bowies and folders. **Technical:** Forges his own Damascus and cable; engraves, carves, scrimshaws. Makes sheaths. **Prices:** $125 to $750; some to $1000. **Remarks:** Full-time maker; first knife sold in 1979. Partners with wife. **Mark:** Name, city and state.

WALKER III, JOHN WADE, 2595 HWY 1647, Paintlick, KY 40461, Phone: 606-792-3498

WALLACE, ROGER L., 4902 Collins Lane, Tampa, FL 33603, Phone: 813-239-3261
Specialties: Working straight knives, Bowies and camp knives to customer specs. **Patterns:** Hunters, skinners and utility knives. **Technical:** Forges high-carbon steel. **Prices:** Start at $75. **Remarks:** Part-time maker; first knife sold in 1985. **Mark:** First initial, last name.

WALLINGFORD JR., CHARLES W., 9024 US 42, Union, KY 41091, Phone: 859-384-4141
Specialties: 18th and 19th century styles - Patch knives, Rifleman knives. **Technical:** 1084 and 5160 forged blades. **Prices:** $125 to $300. **Mark:** CW.

WALTERS, A.F., PO Box 523, 275 Crawley Rd., TyTy, GA 31795, Phone: 229-528-6207
Specialties: Working knives, some to customer specs. **Patterns:** Locking folders, straight hunters, fishing and survival knives. **Technical:** Grinds D2, 154CM and 13C26. **Prices:** Start at $200. **Remarks:** Part-time maker. Label: "The jewel knife" **Mark:** "J" in diamond and knife logo.

WARD, J.J., 7501 S.R. 220, Waverly, OH 45690, Phone: 614-947-5328
Specialties: Traditional and working/using straight knives and folders of his design. **Patterns:** Hunters and locking folders. **Technical:** Grinds ATS-34, 440C and Damascus. Offers handmade sheaths. **Prices:** $125 to $250; some to $500. **Remarks:** Spare-time maker; first knife sold in 1980. **Mark:** Etched name.

WARD, RON, 1363 Nicholas Dr., Loveland, OH 45140, Phone: 513-722-0602
Specialties: Classic working and using straight knives, fantasy knives. **Patterns:** Bowies, hunter, fighters, and utility/camp knives. **Technical:** Grinds 440C, 154CM, ATS-34, uses composite and natural handle materials, makes sheaths. **Prices:** $50-$500. **Remarks:** Part-time maker, first knife sold in 1992. Doing business as Ron Ward Blades, Loveland OH. **Mark:** Ron Ward Blades.

WARD, W.C., 817 Glenn St., Clinton, TN 37716, Phone: 615-457-3568
Specialties: Working straight knives; period pieces. **Patterns:** Hunters, Bowies, swords and kitchen cutlery. **Technical:** Grinds O1. **Prices:** $85 to $150; some to $500. **Remarks:** Part-time maker; first knife sold in 1969. He styled the Tennessee Knife Maker. **Mark:** TKM.

WARD, CHUCK, 1010 E. North St., Benton, AR 72015, Phone: 501-778-4329
Specialties: Traditional working and using straight knives and folders of his design. **Technical:** Grinds 440C, D2, A2, ATS34 and O1; uses natural and composite handle materials. **Prices:** $90 to $400, some higher. **Remarks:** Part-time maker; first knife sold in 1990. **Mark:** First initial, last name.

WARD, KEN, 5122 Lake Shastina Blvd., Weed, CA 96094, Phone: 530-938-9720
Specialties: Working knives, some to customer specs. **Patterns:** Straight and folding hunters, axes, Bowies, buckskinners and miniatures. **Technical:** Grinds ATS-34, Damascus and Stellite 6K. **Prices:** $100 to $700. **Remarks:** Part-time maker; first knife sold in 1977. **Mark:** Name.

WARDELL, MICK, 20, Clovelly Rd., Bideford, N Devon EX39 3BU, ENGLAND, Phone: 01237 475312, Fax: 01237 475312
Specialties: Folders of his design. **Patterns:** Locking and slip-joint folders, Bowies. **Technical:** Grinds stainless Damascus and RWL34. Heat-treats. **Prices:** $200 to $2000. **Remarks:** Full-time maker; first knife sold in 1986. **Mark:** M. Wardell - England.

WARDEN, ROY A., 275 Tanglewood Rd., Union, MO 63084, Phone: 314-583-8813
Specialties: Complex mosaic designs of "EDM wired figures" and " Stack up" patterns and "Lazer Cut" and "Torch cut" and "Sawed" patterns combined. **Patterns:** Mostly "all mosaic" folders, automatics, fixed blades. **Technical:** Mosaic Damascus with all tool steel edges. **Prices:** $500 to $2000 and up. **Remarks:** Part-time maker; first knife sold in 1987. **Mark:** WARDEN stamped or initials connected.

WARE, TOMMY, PO Box 488, Datil, NM 87821, Phone: 505-772-5817
Specialties: Traditional working and using straight knives, folders and automatics of his design and to customer specs. **Patterns:** Hunters, automatics and locking folders. **Technical:** Grinds ATS-34, 440C and D2. Offers engraving and scrimshaw. **Prices:** $275 to $575; some to $1000. **Remarks:** Full-time maker; first knife sold in 1990. Doing business as Wano Knives. **Mark:** Last name inside oval, business name above, city and state below, year on side.

WARENSKI, BUSTER, PO Box 214, Richfield, UT 84701, Phone: 435-896-5319
Specialties: Investor-class straight knives. **Patterns:** Daggers, swords. **Technical:** Grinds, engraves and inlays; offers surface treatments. All engraved by Julie Warenski. **Prices:** Upscale. **Remarks:** Full-time maker. **Mark:** Warenski (hand engraved on blade).

WARREN, DANIEL, 571 Lovejoy Rd., Canton, NC 28716, Phone: 828-648-7351
Specialties: Using knives. **Patterns:** Drop point hunters. **Prices:** $200 to $500. **Mark:** Warren-Bethel NC.

WARREN, AL, 1423 Sante Fe Circle, Roseville, CA 95678, Phone: 916-784-3217/Cell Phone 916-257-5904
Specialties: Working straight knives and folders, some fancy. **Patterns:** Hunters, Bowies, daggers, sword, fillets, fighters and kitchen knives. **Technical:** Grinds D2, ATS-34 and 440C, 440V. **Prices:** $110 to $1100 some to $3700. **Remarks:** Part-time maker; first knife sold in 1978. **Mark:** First and middle initials, last name.

WARREN (SEE DELLANA), DELLANA

WARTHER, DALE, 331 Karl Ave., Dover, OH 44622, Phone: 216-343-7513
Specialties: Working knives; period pieces. **Patterns:** Kitchen cutlery, daggers, hunters and some folders. **Technical:** Forges and grinds O1, D2 and 440C. **Prices:** $250 to $7000. **Remarks:** Full-time maker; first knife sold in 1967. Takes orders only at shows or by personal interviews at his shop. **Mark:** Warther Originals.

WASHBURN, ARTHUR D., ADW CUSTOM KNIVES, 10 Hinman St/POB 625, Pioche, NV 89043, Phone: 775-962-5463
Specialties: Locking liner folders. **Patterns:** Slip joint folders (single and multiplied), lock-back folders, some fixed blades. Do own heat-treating; Rockwell test each blade. **Technical:** Carbon and stainless Damascus, some 1084, 1095, ATS-34. **Prices:** $200 to $1000 and up. **Remarks:** Sold first knife in 1997. Part-time maker. **Mark:** ADW enclosed in an oval or ADW.

WASHBURN JR., ROBERT LEE, 244 Lovett Scott Rd., Adrian, GA 31002, Phone: 475-275-7926, Fax: 475-272-6849
Specialties: Hand-forged period, Bowies, tactical, boot and hunters. **Patterns:** Bowies, tantos, loot hunters, tactical and folders. **Prices:** $100 to $2500. **Remarks:** All hand forged. 52100 being his favorite steel. **Mark:** Washburn Knives W of Dublin GA.

WATANABE, WAYNE, PO Box 3563, Montebello, CA 90640
Specialties: Straight knives in Japanese-styles. One-of-a-kind designs; welcomes customer designs. **Patterns:** Tantos to katanas, Bowies. **Technical:** Flat grinds A2, O1 and ATS-34. Offers hand-rubbed finishes and wrapped handles. **Prices:** Start at $200. **Remarks:** Part-time maker. **Mark:** Name in characters with flower.

WATERS, LU, 2516 Regency, Magnolia, AR 71753, Phone: 870-234-5409

WATERS, HERMAN HAROLD, 2516 Regency, Magnolia, AR 71753, Phone: 870-234-5409

WATERS, GLENN, 11 Shinakawa Machi, Hirosaki City 036-8183, JAPAN, Phone: 172-33-8881
Specialties: One-of-a-kind collector-grade highly embellished art knives. Folders, fixed blades, and automatics. **Patterns:** Locking liner folders, automatics and fixed art knives. **Technical:** Grinds blades from Damasteel, and selected Damascus makers, mostly stainless. Does own engraving, gold inlaying and stone setting, filework, and carving. Gold and Japanese precious metal fabrication. Prefers exotic material, high karat gold, silver, Shyaku Dou, Shibu Ichi Gin, precious gemstones. **Prices:** Upscale. **Remarks:** Designs and makes some-of-a-kind highly embellished art knives often with fully engraved handles and blades. A jeweler by trade for 20 years before starting to make knives. Full-time since 1999, first knife sold in 1994. **Mark:** Glenn Waters maker Japan, G. Waters or Glen in Japanese writing.

WATSON, PETER, 66 Kielblock St., La Hoff 2570, SOUTH AFRICA, Phone: 018-84942
Specialties: Traditional working and using straight knives and folders of his design. **Patterns:** Hunters, locking folders and utility/camp knives. **Technical:** Sandvik and 440C. **Prices:** $120 to $250; some to $1500. **Remarks:** Part-time maker; first knife sold in 1989. **Mark:** Buffalo head with name.

WATSON, TOM, 1103 Brenau Terrace, Panama City, FL 32405, Phone: 850-785-9209
Specialties: Liner-lock folders. **Patterns:** Tactical, utility and art investment pieces. **Technical:** Flat-grinds ATS-34, 440-V, Damascus. **Prices:** Tactical start at $250, investment pieces $500 and up. **Remarks:** In business since 1978. **Mark:** Name and city.

WATSON, BERT, PO Box 26, Westminster, CO 80036-0026, Phone: 303-426-7577
Specialties: Working/using straight knives of his design and to customer specs. **Patterns:** Hunters, utility/camp knives. **Technical:** Grinds O1, ATS-34, 440C, D2, A2 and others. **Prices:** $50 to $250. **Remarks:** Part-time maker; first knife sold in 1974. Doing business as Game Trail Knives. **Mark:** GTK stamped or etched, sometimes with first or last name.

WATSON, BILLY, 440 Forge Rd., Deatsville, AL 36022, Phone: 334-365-1482
Specialties: Working and using straight knives and folders of his design; period pieces. **Patterns:** Hunters, Bowies and utility/camp knives. **Technical:** Forges and grinds his own Damascus, 1095, 5160 and 52100. **Prices:** $40 to $1500. **Remarks:** Full-time maker; first knife sold in 1970. Doing business as Billy's Blacksmith Shop. **Mark:** Last name.

WATSON, DANIEL, 350 Jennifer Ln., Driftwood, TX 78619, Phone: 512-847-9679
Specialties: One-of-a-kind knives and swords. **Patterns:** Hunters, daggers, swords. **Technical:** Hand-purify and carbonize his own high-carbon steel, pattern-welded Damascus, cable and carbon-induced crystalline Damascus. European and Japanese tempering. **Prices:** $125 to $25,000. **Remarks:** Full-time maker; first knife sold in 1979. **Mark:** "Angel Sword" on forged pieces; "Bright Knight" for stock removal.

WATT III, FREDDIE, PO Box 1372, Big Spring, TX 79721, Phone: 915-263-6629
Specialties: Working straight knives, some fancy. **Patterns:** Hunters, fighters and Bowies. **Technical:** Grinds A2, D2, 440C and ATS-34; pre-

fers mirror finishes. **Prices:** $150 to $350; some to $750. **Remarks:** Full-time maker; first knife sold in 1979. **Mark:** Last name, city and state.

WATTELET, MICHAEL A., PO Box 649, 125 Front, Minocqua, WI 54548, Phone: 715-356-3069
Specialties: Working and using straight knives of his design and to customer specs; fantasy knives. **Patterns:** Daggers, fighters and swords. **Technical:** Grinds 440C and L6; forges and grinds O1. Silversmith. **Prices:** $75 to $1000; some to $5000. **Remarks:** Full-time maker; first knife sold in 1966. Doing business as M and N Arts Ltd. **Mark:** First initial, last name.

WATTS, WALLY, 9560 S. Hwy. 36, Gatesville, TX 76528, Phone: 254-487-2866
Specialties: Unique traditional folders of his design. **Patterns:** One- to five-blade folders and single-blade gents in various blade shapes. **Technical:** Grinds ATS-34; Damascus on request. **Prices:** $165 to $500; some to $500. **Remarks:** Full-time maker; first knife sold in 1986. **Mark:** Last name.

WATTS, JOHNATHAN, 9560 S State Hwy 36, Gatesville, TX 76528, Phone: 254-487-2866
Specialties: Traditional folders. **Patterns:** One and two blade folders in various blade shapes. **Technical:** Grinds ATS-34 and Damascus on request. **Prices:** $120 to $400. **Remarks:** Part-time maker; first knife sold in 1997. **Mark:** J Watts.

WEDDLE JR., DEL, 2703 Green Valley Rd., St. Joseph, MO 64505, Phone: 816-364-1981
Specialties: Working knives; some period pieces. **Patterns:** Hunters, fighters, locking folders, push knives. **Technical:** Grinds D2 and 440C; can provide precious metals and set gems. Offers his own forged wire-cable Damascus in his finished knives. **Prices:** $80 to $250; some to $2000. **Remarks:** Full-time maker; first knife sold in 1972. **Mark:** Signature with last name and date.

WEHNER, RUDY, 297 William Warren Rd, Collins, MS 39428, Phone: 601-765-4997
Specialties: Reproduction antique Bowies and contemporary Bowies in full and miniature. **Patterns:** Skinners, camp knives, fighters, axes and Bowies. **Technical:** Grinds 440C, ATS-34, 154CM and Damascus. **Prices:** $100 to $500; some to $850. **Remarks:** Full-time maker; first knife sold in 1975. **Mark:** Last name on Bowies and antiques; full name, city and state on skinners.

WEILAND JR., J REESE, PO Box 2337, Riverview, FL 33568, Phone: 813-671-0661
Specialties: Hawk bills; tactical to fancy folders. **Patterns:** Hunters, tantos, Bowies, fantasy knives, spears and some swords. **Technical:** Grinds ATS-34, 154CM, 440C, D2, O1, A2, Damascus. Titanium hardware on locking liners and button locks. **Prices:** $150 to $4000. **Other:** Full-time maker, first knife sold in 1978. Knifemakers Guild member since 1988.

WEILER, DONALD E., PO Box 1576, Yuma, AZ 85366-9576, Phone: 928-782-1159
Specialties: Working straight knives; period pieces. **Patterns:** Strong springbuck folders, blade and spring ATS-34. **Technical:** Forges O1, W2, 5160, ATS-34, D2, 52100, L6 and cable Damascus. Makes his own high-carbon steel Damascus. **Prices:** $150 to $1000. **Remarks:** Full-time maker; first knife sold in 1952. **Mark:** Last name, city.

WEINAND, GEROME M., 14440 Harpers Bridge Rd., Missoula, MT 59808, Phone: 406-543-0845
Specialties: Working straight knives. **Patterns:** Bowies, fishing and camp knives, large special hunters. **Technical:** Grinds O1, 440C, ATS-34, 1084, L6, also stainless Damascus, Aebl and 304; makes all-tool steel Damascus; Dendritic D2 from powdered steel. Heat-treats. **Prices:** $30 to $100; some to $500. **Remarks:** Full-time maker; first knife sold in 1982. **Mark:** Last name.

WEINSTOCK, ROBERT, PO Box 170028, San Francisco, CA 94117-0028, Phone: 415-731-5968
Specialties: Fancy and high-art straight knives of his design. **Patterns:** Daggers, folders, poignards and miniatures. **Technical:** Grinds A2, O1 and 440C. Chased and hand-carved blades and handles. Also using various Damascus steels from other makers. **Prices:** $3000 to 7,000+. **Remarks:** Full-time maker; first knife sold in 1994. **Mark:** Last name carved.

WEISS, CHARLES L., 18847 N. 13th Ave., Phoenix, AZ 85027, Phone: 623-582-6147
Specialties: High-art straight knives and folders; deluxe period pieces. **Patterns:** Daggers, fighters, boots, push knives and miniatures. **Technical:** Grinds 440C, 154CM and ATS-34. **Prices:** $300 to $1200; some to $2000. **Remarks:** Full-time maker; first knife sold in 1975. **Mark:** Name and city.

WERNER JR., WILLIAM A., 336 Lands Mill, Marietta, GA 30067, Phone: 404-988-0074

Specialties: Fantasy and working/using straight knives. **Patterns:** Bowies, daggers, fighters. **Technical:** Grinds 440C stainless, 10 series carbon and Damascus. **Prices:** $150 to $400; some to $750. **Remarks:** Part-time maker. Doing business as Werner Knives. **Mark:** Last name.

WERTH, GEORGE W., 5223 Woodstock Rd., Poplar Grove, IL 61065, Phone: 815-544-4408

Specialties: Period pieces, some fancy. **Patterns:** Straight fighters, daggers and Bowies. **Technical:** Forges and grinds O1, 1095 and his Damascus, including mosaic patterns. **Prices:** $200 to $650; some higher. **Remarks:** Full-time maker. Doing business as Fox Valley Forge. **Mark:** Name in logo or initials connected.

WESCOTT, CODY, 5330 White Wing Rd., Las Cruces, NM 88012, Phone: 505-382-5008

Specialties: Fancy and presentation-grade working knives. **Patterns:** Hunters, locking folders and Bowies. **Technical:** Hollow-grinds D2 and ATS-34; all knives file worked. Offers some engraving. Makes sheaths. **Prices:** $80 to $300; some to $950. **Remarks:** Full-time maker; first knife sold in 1982. **Mark:** First initial, last name.

WEST, CHARLES A., 1315 S. Pine St., Centralia, IL 62801, Phone: 618-532-2777

Specialties: Classic, fancy, high tech, period pieces, traditional and working/using straight knives and folders. **Patterns:** Bowies, fighters and locking folders. **Technical:** Grinds ATS-34, O1 and Damascus. Prefers hot blued finishes. **Prices:** $100 to $1000; some to $2000. **Remarks:** Full-time maker; first knife sold in 1963. Doing business as West Custom Knives. **Mark:** Name or name, city and state.

WEST, PAT, PO Box 9, Charlotte, TX 78011, Phone: 830-277-1290

Specialties: Classic working and using straight knives and folders. **Patterns:** Hunters, kitchen knives, slip-joint folders. **Technical:** Grinds ATS-34, D2 and Vascowear. Offers filework and decorates liners on folders. **Prices:** $300 to $600. **Remarks:** Spare-time maker; first knife sold in 1984. **Mark:** Name.

WESTBERG, LARRY, 305 S. Western Hills Dr., Algona, IA 50511, Phone: 515-295-9276

Specialties: Traditional and working straight knives of his design and in standard patterns. **Patterns:** Bowies, hunters, utility knives and miniatures. **Technical:** Grinds 440C, D2 and 1095. Heat-treats. Uses natural handle materials. **Prices:** $85 to $600; some to $1000. **Remarks:** Part-time maker; first knife sold in 1987. **Mark:** Last name-town and state.

WHEELER, ROBERT, 289 S Jefferson, Bradley, IL 60915, Phone: 815-932-5854

WHETSELL, ALEX, 1600 Palmetto Tyrone Rd., Sharpsburg, GA 30277, Phone: 770-463-4881

Specialties: Knifekits.com, a source for fold locking liner type and straight knife kits. Our kits are industry standard for folding knife kits. **Technical:** Many selections of colored G10 carbon fiber and wood handle material for our kits as well as bulk sizes for the custom knife maker, heat treated folding knife pivots, screws, bushings, etc.

WHIPPLE, WESLEY A., PO Box 3771, Kodiak, AK 99615, Phone: 907-486-6737

Specialties: Working straight knives, some fancy. **Patterns:** Hunters, Bowies, camp knives, fighters. **Technical:** Forges high-carbon steels, Damascus, offers relief carving and silver wire inlay. **Prices:** $200 to $800; some higher. **Remarks:** Part-time maker; first knife sold in 1989. **Mark:** Last name/JS. **Other:** A.K.A. Wilderness Knife and Forge.

WHITE, ROBERT J., RR 1, 641 Knox Rd. 900 N., Gilson, IL 61434, Phone: 309-289-4487

Specialties: Working knives, some deluxe. **Patterns:** Bird and trout knives, hunters, survival knives and locking folders. **Technical:** Grinds A2, D2 and 440C; commercial Damascus. Heat-treats. **Prices:** $125 to $250; some to $600. **Remarks:** Full-time maker; first knife sold in 1976. **Mark:** Last name in script.

WHITE, BRYCE, 1415 W Col. Glenn Rd., Little Rock, AR 72210, Phone: 501-821-2956

Specialties: Hunters, fighters, makes Damascus, file work, handmade only. **Technical:** L6, 1075, 1095, 01 steels used most. **Patterns:** Will do any pattern or use his own. **Prices:** $200 to $300. Sold first knife in 1995. **Mark:** White.

WHITE, LOU, 7385 Red Bud Rd. NE, Ranger, GA 30734, Phone: 706-334-2273

WHITE, RICHARD T., 359 Carver St, Grosse Pointe Farms, MI 48236, Phone: 313-881-4690

WHITE, GENE E., 6620 Briarleigh Way, Alexandria, VA 22315, Phone: 703-924-1268

Specialties: Small utility/gents knives. **Patterns:** Eight standard hunters; most other patterns on commission basis. Currently no swords, axes and fantasy knives. **Technical:** Stock removal 440C and D2; others on request. Mostly hollow grinds; some flat grinds. Prefers natural handle materials. Makes own sheaths. **Prices:** Start at $85. **Remarks:** Part-time maker; first knife sold in 1971. **Mark:** First and middle initials, last name.

WHITE, DALE, 525 CR 212, Sweetwater, TX 79556, Phone: 325-798-4178

Specialties: Working and using knives. **Patterns:** Hunters, skinners, utilities and Bowies. **Technical:** Grinds 440C, offers file pins and scrimshaw by Sherry Sellers. **Prices:** From $45 to $300. **Remarks:** Sold first knife in 1975. **Mark:** Full name, city and state.

WHITE JR., ROBERT J. BUTCH, RR 1, Gilson, IL 61436, Phone: 309-289-4487

Specialties: Folders of all sizes. **Patterns:** Hunters, fighters, boots and folders. **Technical:** Forges Damascus; grinds tool and stainless steels. **Prices:** $500 to $1800. **Remarks:** Spare-time maker; first knife sold in 1980. **Mark:** Last name in block letters.

WHITENECT, JODY, Elderbank, Halifax County, Nova Scotia, CANADA B0N 1K0, Phone: 902-384-2511

Specialties: Fancy and embellished working/using straight knives of his design and to customer specs. **Patterns:** Bowies, fighters and hunters. **Technical:** Forges 1095 and O1; forges and grinds ATS-34. Various filework on blades and bolsters. **Prices:** $200 to $400; some to $800. **Remarks:** Part-time maker; first knife sold in 1996. **Mark:** Longhorn stamp or engraved.

WHITLEY, L. WAYNE, 1675 Carrow Rd., Chocowinity, NC 27817-9495, Phone: 252-946-5648

WHITLEY, WELDON G., 1308 N Robin Ave., Odessa, TX 79764, Phone: 915-584-2274

Specialties: Working knives of his design or to customer specs. **Patterns:** Hunters, folders and various double-edged knives. **Technical:** Grinds 440C, 154CM and ATS-34. **Prices:** $150 to $1250. **Mark:** Name, address, road-runner logo.

WHITMAN, JIM, 21044 Salem St., Chugiak, AK 99567, Phone: 907-688-4575, Fax: 907-688-4278

Specialties: Working straight knives and folders; some art pieces. **Patterns:** Hunters, skinners, Bowies, camp knives, working fighters, swords and hatchets. **Technical:** Grinds AEB-L Swedish, 440C, 154CM, ATS-34, and Damascus in full convex. Prefers exotic hardwoods, natural and native handle materials—whale bone, antler, ivory and horn. **Prices:** Start at $150. **Remarks:** Full-time maker; first knife sold in 1983. **Mark:** Name, city, state.

WHITMIRE, EARL T., 725 Colonial Dr., Rock Hill, SC 29730, Phone: 803-324-8384

Specialties: Working straight knives, some to customer specs; some fantasy knives. **Patterns:** Hunters, fighters and fishing knives. **Technical:** Grinds D2, 440C and 154CM. **Prices:** $40 to $200; some to $250. **Remarks:** Full-time maker; first knife sold in 1967. **Mark:** Name, city, state in oval logo.

WHITTAKER, ROBERT E., PO Box 204, Mill Creek, PA 17060

Specialties: Using straight knives. Has a line of knives for buckskinners. **Patterns:** Hunters, skinners and Bowies. **Technical:** Grinds O1, A2 and D2. Offers filework. **Prices:** $35 to $100. **Remarks:** Part-time maker; first knife sold in 1980. **Mark:** Last initial or full initials.

WHITTAKER, WAYNE, 2900 Woodland Ct., Metamore, MI 48455, Phone: 810-797-5315

Specialties: Folders, hunters on request. **Patterns:** Bowies, daggers and hunters. **Technical:** ATS-34 S.S. and Damascus **Prices:** $300 to $500; some to $2000. **Remarks:** Full-time maker; first knife sold in 1985. **Mark:** Etched name on one side.

WHITWORTH, KEN J., 41667 Tetley Ave., Sterling Heights, MI 48078, Phone: 313-739-5720

Specialties: Working straight knives and folders. **Patterns:** Locking folders, slip-joints and boot knives. **Technical:** Grinds 440C, 154CM and D2. **Prices:** $100 to $225; some to $450. **Remarks:** Part-time maker; first knife sold in 1976. **Mark:** Last name.

WICKER, DONNIE R., 2544 E. 40th Ct., Panama City, FL 32405, Phone: 904-785-9158

Specialties: Traditional working and using straight knives of his design or to customer specs. **Patterns:** Hunters, fighters and slip-joint folders. **Technical:** Grinds 440C, ATS-34, D2 and 154CM. Heat-treats and does hardness testing. **Prices:** $90 to $200; some to $400. **Remarks:** Part-time maker; first knife sold in 1975. **Mark:** First and middle initials, last name.

WIGGINS, HORACE, 203 Herndon, Box 152, Mansfield, LA 71502, Phone: 318-872-4471
   Specialties: Fancy working knives. **Patterns:** Straight and folding hunters. **Technical:** Grinds O1, D2 and 440C. **Prices:** $90 to $275. **Remarks:** Part-time maker; first knife sold in 1970. **Mark:** Name, city and state in diamond logo.

WILCHER, WENDELL L., RR 6 Box 6573, Palestine, TX 75801, Phone: 903-549-2530
   Specialties: Fantasy, miniatures and working/using straight knives and folders of his design and to customer specs. **Patterns:** Fighters, hunters, locking folders. **Technical:** Hand works (hand file and hand sand knives), not grind. **Prices:** $75 to $250; some to $600. **Remarks:** Part-time maker; first knife sold in 1987. **Mark:** Initials, year, serial number.

WILE, PETER, RR 3, Bridgewater, Nova Scotia, CANADA B4V 2W2, Phone: 902-543-1373
   Specialties: Collector-grade one-of-a-kind file-worked folders. **Patterns:** Folders or fixed blades of his design or to customers specs. **Technical:** Grinds ATS-34, carbon and stainless Damascus. Does intricate filework on blades, spines and liners. Carves. Prefers natural handle materials. Does own heat treating. **Prices:** $350 to $2000; some to $4000. **Remarks:** Part-time maker; sold first knife in 1985; doing business as Wile Knives. **Mark:** Wile.

WILKINS, MITCHELL, 15523 Rabon Chapel Rd., Montgomery, TX 77316, Phone: 936-588-2696

WILLEY, W.G., R.D. 1, Box 235-B, Greenwood, DE 19950, Phone: 302-349-4070
   Specialties: Fancy working straight knives. **Patterns:** Small game knives, Bowies and throwing knives. **Technical:** Grinds 440C and 154CM. **Prices:** $225 to $600; some to $1500. **Remarks:** Part-time maker; first knife sold in 1975. Owns retail store. **Mark:** Last name inside map logo.

WILLIAMS, JASON L., PO Box 67, Wyoming, RI 02898, Phone: 401-539-8353, Fax: 401-539-0252
   Specialties: Fancy and high tech folders of his design, co-inventor of the Axis Lock. **Patterns:** Fighters, locking folders, automatics and fancy pocket knives. **Technical:** Forges Damascus and other steels by request. Uses exotic handle materials and precious metals. Offers inlaid spines and gemstone thumb knobs. **Prices:** $1000 and up. **Remarks:** Full-time maker; first knife sold in 1989. **Mark:** First and last initials on pivot.

WILLIAMS, MICHAEL L., Rt. 4, PO Box 64-1, Broken Bow, OK 74728, Phone: 405-494-6326
   Specialties: Plain to fancy working and dress knives. **Patterns:** Hunters, Bowies, camp knives and others. **Technical:** Forges 1084, L6, 52100 and pattern-welded steel. **Prices:** $295 and up. **Remarks:** Part-time maker; first knife sold in 1989. ABS Master Smith. **Mark:** Williams.

WILLIAMS JR., RICHARD, 1440 Nancy Circle, Morristown, TN 37814, Phone: 615-581-0059
   Specialties: Working and using straight knives of his design or to customer specs. **Patterns:** Hunters, dirks and utility/camp knives. **Technical:** Forges 5160 and uses file steel. Hand-finish is standard; offers filework. **Prices:** $80 to $180; some to $250. **Remarks:** Spare-time maker; first knife sold in 1985. **Mark:** Last initial or full initials.

WILLIAMSON, TONY, Rt. 3, Box 503, Siler City, NC 27344, Phone: 919-663-3551
   Specialties: Flint knapping—knives made of obsidian flakes and flint with wood, antler or bone for handles. **Patterns:** Skinners, daggers and flake knives. **Technical:** Blades have width/thickness ratio of at least 4 to 1. Hafts with methods available to prehistoric man. **Prices:** $58 to $160. **Remarks:** Student of Errett Callahan. **Mark:** Initials and number code to identify year and number of knives made.

WILLIS, BILL, RT 7 Box 7549, Ava, MO 65608, Phone: 417-683-4326
   Specialties: Forged blades, Damascus and carbon steel. **Patterns:** Cable, random or ladder lamented. **Technical:** Professionally heat treated blades. **Prices:** $75 to $600. **Remarks:** Lifetime guarantee on all blades against breakage. **Mark:** WF. **Other:** All work done by myself; including leather work.

WILLSON, WAYNE O., 11403 Sunflower Ln., Fairfax, VA 22030-6031, Phone: 703-278-8000

WILSON, JAMES G., PO Box 4024, Estes Park, CO 80517, Phone: 303-586-3944
   Specialties: Bronze Age knives; Medieval and Scottish-styles; tomahawks. **Patterns:** Bronze knives, daggers, swords, spears and battle axes; 12-inch steel Misericorde daggers, sgian dubhs, "his and her" skinners, bird and fish knives, capers, boots and daggers. **Technical:** Casts bronze; grinds D2, 440C and ATS-34. **Prices:** $49 to $400; some to

$1300. **Remarks:** Part-time maker; first knife sold in 1975. **Mark:** Wilson-Hawk.

WILSON, RON, 2639 Greenwood Ave., Morro Bay, CA 93442, Phone: 805-772-3381
   Specialties: Classic and fantasy straight knives of his design. **Patterns:** Daggers, fighters, swords and axes-mostly all miniatures. **Technical:** Forges and grinds Damascus and various tool steels; grinds meteorite. Uses gold, precious stones and exotic wood. **Prices:** Vary. **Remarks:** Part-time maker; first knives sold in 1995. **Mark:** Stamped first and last initials.

WILSON, JON J., 1826 Ruby St., Johnstown, PA 15902, Phone: 814-266-6410
   Specialties: Miniatures and full size. **Patterns:** Bowies, daggers and hunters. **Technical:** Grinds Damascus, 440C and O1. Scrimshaws and carves. **Prices:** $75 to $500; some higher. **Remarks:** Full-time maker; first knife sold in 1988. **Mark:** First and middle initials, last name.

WILSON, PHILIP C., SEAMOUNT KNIFEWORKS, PO Box 846, Mountain Ranch, CA 95246, Phone: 209-754-1990
   Specialties: Working knives; emphasis on salt water fillet knives and utility hunters of his design. **Patterns:** Fishing knives, hunters, kitchen knives. **Technical:** Grinds CPM S-30V, CPM10V, S-90V and 154CM. Heat-treats and Rockwell tests all blades. **Prices:** Start at $280. **Remarks:** First knife sold in 1985. Doing business as Sea-Mount Knife Works. **Mark:** Signature.

WILSON, R.W., PO Box 2012, Weirton, WV 26062, Phone: 304-723-2771
   Specialties: Working straight knives; period pieces. **Patterns:** Bowies, tomahawks and patch knives. **Prices:** $85 to $175; some to $1000. **Technical:** Grinds 440C; scrimshaws. **Remarks:** Part-time maker; first knife sold in 1966. Knife maker supplier. Offers free knife-making lessons. **Mark:** Name in tomahawk.

WILSON, MIKE, 1416 McDonald Rd., Hayesville, NC 28904, Phone: 828-389-8145
   Specialties: Fancy working and using straight knives of his design or to customer specs, folders. **Patterns:** Hunters, Bowies, utility knives, gut hooks, skinners, fighters and miniatures. **Technical:** Hollow-grinds 440C, L-6, 01 and D2. Mirror finishes are standard. Offers filework. **Prices:** $50 to $600. **Remarks:** Full-time maker; first knife sold in 1985. **Mark:** Last name.

WILSON (SEE SIMONELLA, GIANLUIGI)

WILSON, III, GEORGE H., 150-6 Dreiser Loop #6-B, Bronx, NY 10475

WIMPFF, CHRISTIAN, PO Box 700526, 70574 Stuttgart 70, GERMANY, Phone: 711 7260 749, Fax: 711 7260 749
   Specialties: High-tech folders of his design. **Patterns:** Boots, locking folders and liners locks. **Technical:** Offers meteorite, bolsters and blades. **Prices:** $1000 to $2800; some to $4000. **Remarks:** Full-time maker; first knife sold in 1984. **Mark:** First initial, last name.

WINBERG, DOUGLAS R., 19720 Hwy 78, Ramona, CA 92076, Phone: 760-788-8304

WINGO, PERRY, 22 55th St., Gulfport, MS 39507, Phone: 228-863-3193
   Specialties: Traditional working straight knives. **Patterns:** Hunters, skinners, Bowies and fishing knives. **Technical:** Grinds 440C. **Prices:** $75 to $1000. **Remarks:** Full-time maker; first knife sold in 1988. **Mark:** Last name.

WINGO, GARY, 240 Ogeechee, Ramona, OK 74061, Phone: 918-536-1067
   Specialties: Folder specialist. Steel 44OC, D2, others on request. Handle bone-stag, others on request. **Patterns:** Trapper three-blade stockman, four-blade congress, single- and two-blade barlows. **Prices:** 150 to $400. **Mark:** First knife sold 1994. Steer head with Wingo Knives or Straight Line Wingo Knives.

WINKLER, DANIEL, PO Box 2166, Blowing Rock, NC 28605, Phone: 828-295-9156
   Specialties: Forged cutlery styled in the tradition of an era past. **Patterns:** Fixed blades, friction folders, axes/tomahawks and war clubs. **Technical:** Forges and grinds carbon steels and his own Damascus. **Prices:** $200 to $4000. **Remarks:** Full-time maker since 1988. Exclusively offers leatherwork by Karen Shook. **Mark:** Initials connected. **Other:** ABS Master Smith; Knifemakers Guild voting member.

WINN, TRAVIS A., 558 E. 3065 S., Salt Lake City, UT 84106, Phone: 801-467-5957
   Specialties: Fancy working knives and knives to customer specs. **Patterns:** Hunters, fighters, boots, Bowies and fancy daggers, some miniatures, tantos and fantasy knives. **Technical:** Grinds D2 and 440C. Embellishes. **Prices:** $125 to $500; some higher. **Remarks:** Part-time maker; first knife sold in 1976. **Mark:** TRAV stylized.

WINSTON, DAVID, 1671 Red Holly St., Starkville, MS 39759, Phone: 601-323-1028
  Specialties: Fancy and traditional knives of his design and to customer specs. **Patterns:** Bowies, daggers, hunters, boot knives and folders. **Technical:** Grinds 440C, ATS-34 and D2. Offers filework; heat-treats. **Prices:** $40 to $750; some higher. **Remarks:** Part-time maker; first knife sold in 1984. Offers lifetime sharpening for original owner. **Mark:** Last name.

WINTER, GEORGE, 5940 Martin Hwy., Union City, TN 38261

WIRTZ, ACHIM, Mittelstrasse 58, WUERSELEN, D -52146, GERMANY, Phone: 0049-2405-2587
  Specialties: Period pieces, Scandinavian and middle east-style knives. **Technical:** Forges 5160, and own Damascus. Makes wootz and mokume gane. **Prices:** Start at $50. **Remarks:** Spare-time maker. First knife sold in 1997. **Mark:** Stylized initials.

WISE, DONALD, 304 Bexhill Rd., St. Leonardo-On-Sea, East Sussex, TN3 8AL, ENGLAND
  Specialties: Fancy and embellished working straight knives to customer specs. **Patterns:** Hunters, Bowies and daggers. **Technical:** Grinds Sandvik 12C27, D2 D3 and O1. Scrimshaws. **Prices:** $110 to $300; some to $500. **Remarks:** Full-time maker; first knife sold in 1983. **Mark:** KNIFE-CRAFT.

WITSAMAN, EARL, 3957 Redwing Circle, Stow, OH 44224, Phone: 330-688-4208
  Specialties: Straight and fantasy miniatures. **Patterns:** Wide variety—Randalls to D-guard Bowies. **Technical:** Grinds O1, 440C and 300 stainless; buys Damascus; highly detailed work. **Prices:** $85 to $300. **Remarks:** Part-time maker; first knife sold in1974. **Mark:** Initials.

WOLF, BILL, 4618 N. 79th Ave., Phoenix, AZ 85033, Phone: 623-846-3585, Fax: 623-846-3585
  Specialties: Investor-grade folders and straight knives. **Patterns:** Lockback, slip joint and side lock interframes. **Technical:** Grinds ATS-34 and 440C. **Prices:** $400 to $10,000. **Remarks:** Full-time maker; first knife sold in 1989. **Mark:** Name.

WOLF JR., WILLIAM LYNN, 4006 Frank Rd., Lagrange, TX 78945, Phone: 409-247-4626

WOOD, WILLIAM W., PO Box 606, Seymour, TX 76380, Phone: 817-888-5832
  Specialties: Exotic working knives with Middle-East flavor. **Patterns:** Fighters, boots and some utility knives. **Technical:** Grinds D2 and 440C; buys Damascus. Prefers hand-rubbed satin finishes; uses only natural handle materials. **Prices:** $300 to $600; some to $2000. **Remarks:** Full-time maker; first knife sold in 1977. **Mark:** Name, city and state.

WOOD, WEBSTER, 22041 Shelton Trail, Atlanta, MI 49709, Phone: 989-785-2996
  Specialties: Work mainly in stainless; art knives, Bowies, hunters and folders. **Remarks:** Full-time maker; first knife sold in 1980. Guild member since 1984. All engraving done by maker. **Mark:** Initials inside shield and name.

WOOD, OWEN DALE, 6492 Garrison St., Arvada, CO 80004-3157, Phone: 303-466-2748
  Specialties: Folding, knives and daggers. **Patterns:** Own Damascus, specialties in 456 composite blades. **Technical:** Materials: Damascus stainless steel, exotic metals, gold, rare handle materials. **Prices:** $1000 - $9000. **Remarks:** Folding knives in art deco and art noveau themes. **Other:** Full-time maker from 1981. **Mark:** OWEN WOOD.

WOOD, LARRY B., 6945 Fishburg Rd., Huber Heights, OH 45424, Phone: 513-233-6751
  Specialties: Fancy working knives of his design. **Patterns:** Hunters, buckskinners, Bowies, tomahawks, locking folders and Damascus miniatures. **Technical:** Forges 1095, file steel and his own Damascus. **Prices:** $125 to $500; some to $2000. **Remarks:** Full-time maker; first knife sold in 1974. Doing business as Wood's Metal Studios. **Mark:** Variations of last name, sometimes with blacksmith logo.

WOOD, ALAN, Greenfield Villa, Greenhead, Brampton CA8 7HH, ENGLAND, Phone: 016977-47303
  Specialties: High-tech working straight knives of his design. **Patterns:** Hunters, utility/camp and woodcraft knives. **Technical:** Grinds 12027, RWL-34, stainless Damascus and 01. Blades are cryogenic treated. **Prices:** $200 to $800; some to $750. **Remarks:** Full-time maker; first knife sold in 1979.Not currently taking orders **Mark:** Full name and state motif.

WOODARD, WILEY, 4527 Jim Mitchell W, Colleyville, TX 76034
  Specialties: Straight knives, Damascus carbon and stainless, all natural material.

WOODCOCK, DENNIS "WOODY", PO Box 416, Nehalem, OR 97131, Phone: 503-368-7511
  Specialties: Working knives. **Patterns:** Hunters, Bowies, skinners, hunters. **Technical:** Grinds ATS-34, D2, 440C, 440V. Offers filework; makes sheaths. **Prices:** $50 to $500. **Remarks:** Full-time maker; first knife sold in 1982. Doing business as Woody's Custom Knives. **Mark:** Nickname, last name, city, state.

WOODIWISS, DORREN, PO Box 396, Thompson Falls, MT 59873-0396, Phone: 406-827-0079

WOODWARD, WILEY, 4517 Jim Mitchell W, Colleyville, TX 76034, Phone: 817-267-3277

WOOTTON, RANDY, 83 Lafayett 254, Stamps, AR 71860, Phone: 870-533-2472

WORTHEN, BILL, 200 E 3rd, Little Rock, AR 72201-1608, Phone: 501-324-9351

WRIGHT, KEVIN, 671 Leland Valley Rd. W, Quilcene, WA 98376-9517, Phone: 360-765-3589
  Specialties: Fancy working or collector knives to customer specs. **Patterns:** Hunters, boots, buckskinners, miniatures. **Technical:** Forges and grinds L6, 1095, 440C and his own Damascus. **Prices:** $75 to $500; some to $2000. **Remarks:** Part-time maker; first knife sold in 1978. **Mark:** Last initial in anvil.

WRIGHT, TIMOTHY, PO Box 3746, Sedona, AZ 86340, Phone: 928-282-4180
  Specialties: High-tech folders and working knives. **Patterns:** Interframe locking folders, non-inlaid folders, straight hunters and kitchen knives. **Technical:** Grinds BG-42, AEB-L, K190 and Cowry X; works with new steels. All folders can disassemble and are furnished with tools. **Prices:** $150 to $1800; some to $3000. **Remarks:** Full-time maker; first knife sold in 1975. **Mark:** Last name and type of steel used.

WRIGHT, RICHARD S., PO Box 201, 111 Hilltop Dr., Carolina, RI 02812, Phone: 401-364-3579
  Specialties: Bolster release switchblades. **Patterns:** Folding fighters, gents pocket knives, one-of-a-kind high-grade automatics. **Technical:** Reforges and grinds various makers Damascus. Uses a variety of tool steels. Uses natural handle material such as ivory and pearl, extensive file-work on most knives. **Prices:** $2000 and up. **Remarks:** Part-time knife maker with background as a gunsmith. Made first folder in 1991. **Mark:** RSW on blade, all folders are serial numbered.

WRIGHT, L.T., 1523 Pershing Ave., Steubenville, OH 43952, Phone: 740-282-4947
  Specialties: Distressed finish on blades, filework, carved handles, hunting knives. **Patterns:** Drop point hunters, patch, lil skinner, Bowies. **Technical:** Grinds 440C. **Prices:** $15-$500. **Remarks:** Part-time maker. **Mark:** First, middle initials and last name w/house logo.

WUERTZ, TRAVIS, 2487 E. Hwy. 287, Casa Grande, AZ 85222, Phone: 520-723-4432

WYATT, WILLIAM R., Box 237, Rainelle, WV 25962, Phone: 304-438-5494
  Specialties: Classic and working knives of all designs. **Patterns:** Hunters and utility knives. **Technical:** Forges and grinds saw blades, files and rasps. Prefers stag handles. **Prices:** $45 to $95; some to $350. **Remarks:** Part-time maker; first knife sold in 1990. **Mark:** Last name in star with knife logo.

WYMAN, MARC L., 3325 Griffin Rd. Ste. 124, Ft Lauderdale, FL 33312, Phone: 754-234-5111, Fax: 954-964-4418
  Specialties: Custom pattern welded Damascus for stock removal. **Patterns:** Tactical fighters, combat and hunting knives. **Technical:** High-carbon steels. **Prices:** Upon request. **Remarks:** Part-time maker. **Mark:** MLW over skull and cross bones. **Other:** Florida fish and wildlife hunter safety education instructs.

y

YASHINSKI, JOHN L., 207 N Platt, PO Box 1284, Red Lodge, MT 59068, Phone: 406-446-3916
  Specialties: Native American Beaded sheathes. **Prices:** Vary.

YEATES, JOE A., 730 Saddlewood Circle, Spring, TX 77381, Phone: 281-367-2765
  Specialties: Bowies and period pieces. **Patterns:** Bowies, toothpicks and combat knives. **Technical:** Grinds 440C, D2 and ATS-34. **Prices:** $400 to $2000; some to $2500. **Remarks:** Full-time maker; first knife sold in 1975. **Mark:** Last initial within outline of Texas; or last initial.

YESKOO, RICHARD C., 76 Beekman Rd., Summit, NJ 07901

YORK, DAVID C., PO Box 3166, Chino Valley, AZ 86323, Phone: 928-636-1709
  Specialties: Working straight knives and folders. **Patterns:** Prefers small hunters and skinners; locking folders. **Technical:** Grinds D2 and 440C; buys Damascus. **Prices:** $75 to $300; some to $600. **Remarks:** Part-time maker; first knife sold in 1975. **Mark:** Last name.

YOSHIHARA, YOSHINDO, 8-17-11 TAKASAGO, KATSUSHI, Tokyo, JAPAN

YOSHIKAZU, KAMADA, , 540-3 Kaisaki Niuta-cho, Tokushima, JAPAN, Phone: 0886-44-2319

YOSHIO, MAEDA, , 3-12-11 Chuo-cho Tamashima Kurashiki-city, Okayama, JAPAN, Phone: 086-525-2375

YOUNG, GEORGE, 713 Pinoak Dr., Kokomo, IN 46901, Phone: 765-457-8893

Specialties: Fancy/embellished and traditional straight knives and folders of his design and to customer specs. **Patterns:** Hunters, fillet/camp knives and locking folders. **Technical:** Grinds 440C, CPM440V, and Stellite 6K. Fancy ivory, black pearl and stag for handles. Filework—all Stellite construction (6K and 25 alloys). Offers engraving. **Prices:** $350 to $750; some $1500 to $3000. **Remarks:** Full-time maker; first knife sold in 1954. Doing business as Young's Knives. **Mark:** Last name integral inside Bowie.

YOUNG, BUD, Box 336, Port Hardy, BC, CANADA V0N 2P0, Phone: 250-949-6478

Specialties: Fixed blade, working knives, some fancy. **Patterns:** Drop-points to skinners. **Technical:** Hollow or flat grind, 5160, 440-C, mostly ATS-34, satin finish. **Prices:** $150 to $500 CDN. **Remarks:** Spare-time maker; making knives since 1962; first knife sold in 1985. **Mark:** Name. **Other:** Not taking orders at this time, sell as produced.

YOUNG, CLIFF, Fuente De La Cibeles No. 5, Atascadero, San Miguel de Allende, GTO., MEXICO, Phone: 37700, Fax: 011-52-415-2-57-11

Specialties: Working knives. **Patterns:** Hunters, fighters and fishing knives. **Technical:** Grinds all; offers D2, 440C and 154CM. **Prices:** Start at $250. **Remarks:** Part-time maker; first knife sold in 1980. **Mark:** Name.

YOUNG, ERROL, 4826 Storey Land, Alton, IL 62002, Phone: 618-466-4707

Specialties: Traditional working straight knives and folders. **Patterns:** Wide range, including tantos, Bowies, miniatures and multi-blade folders. **Technical:** Grinds D2, 440C and ATS-34. **Prices:** $75 to $650; some to $800. **Remarks:** Part-time maker; first knife sold in 1987. **Mark:** Last name with arrow.

YOUNG, PAUL A., 168 Elk Ridge Rd., Boone, NC 28607, Phone: 704-264-7048

Specialties: Working straight knives and folders of his design or to customer specs; some art knives. **Patterns:** Small boot knives, skinners, 18th-century period pieces and folders. **Technical:** Forges O1 and file steels. Full-time embellisher—engraves and scrimshaws. Prefers floral designs; any design accepted. Does not engrave hardened metals. **Prices:** Determined by type and design. **Remarks:** Full-time maker; first knife sold in 1978. **Mark:** Initials in logo.

YOUNG, RAYMOND L., Cutler/Bladesmith, 2922 Hwy 188E, Mt. Ida, AR 71957, Phone: 870-867-3947

Specialties: Cutler-Bladesmith, Sharpening service. **Patterns:** Hunter, skinners, fighters, no guard, no ricasso, chef tools. **Technical:** Edge tempered 1095, 516C, Mosiac handles, water buffalo and exotic woods. **Prices:** $100 and up. **Remarks:** Federal contractor since 1995. Surgical steel sharpening. **Mark:** R.

YURCO, MIKE, PO Box 712, Canfield, OH 44406, Phone: 330-533-4928

Specialties: Working straight knives. **Patterns:** Hunters, utility knives, Bowies and fighters, push knives, claws and other hideouts. **Technical:** Grinds 440C, ATS-34 and 154CM; likes mirror and satin finishes. **Prices:** $20 to $500. **Remarks:** Part-time maker; first knife sold in 1983. **Mark:** Name, steel, serial number.

Z

ZACCAGNINO JR., DON, 2256 Bacom Point Rd., Pahokee, FL 33476-2622, Phone: 561-924-7032

Specialties: Working knives and some period pieces of their designs. **Patterns:** Heavy-duty hunters, axes and Bowies; a line of light-weight hunters, fillets and personal knives. **Technical:** Grinds 440C and 17-4 PH—highly finished in complex handle and blade treatments. **Prices:** $165 to $500; some to $2500. **Remarks:** Part-time maker; first knife sold in 1969 by Don Zaccagnino Sr. **Mark:** ZACK, city and state inside oval.

ZAHM, KURT, 488 Rio Casa, Indialantic, FL 32903, Phone: 407-777-4860

Specialties: Working straight knives of his design or to customer specs. **Patterns:** Daggers, fancy fighters, Bowies, hunters and utility knives. **Technical:** Grinds D2, 440C; likes filework. **Prices:** $75 to $1000. **Remarks:** Part-time maker; first knife sold in 1985. **Mark:** Last name.

ZAKABI, CARL S., PO Box 893161, Mililani Town, HI 96789-0161, Phone: 808-626-2181

Specialties: Working and using straight knives of his design. **Patterns:** Fighters, hunters and utility/camp knives. **Technical:** Grinds 440C and ATS-34. **Prices:** $90 to $400. **Remarks:** Spare-time maker; first knife sold in 1988. Doing business as Zakabi's Knifeworks LLC. **Mark:** Last name and state.

ZAKHAROV, CARLOS, R. Pernambuco175, Rio Comprido Jacarei, SP-12305-340, BRAZIL, Phone: 55 12 3958 4021, Fax: 55 12 3958 4103

Specialties: Using straight knives of his design. **Patterns:** Hunters, kitchen, utility/camp and barbecue knives. **Technical:** Grinds his own "secret steel." **Prices:** $30 to $200. **Remarks:** Full-time maker. **Mark:** Arkhip Special Knives.

ZBORIL, TERRY, 5320 CR 130, Caldwell, TX 77836, Phone: 979-535-4157

Specialties: ABS Journeyman Smith.

ZEMBKO III, JOHN, 140 Wilks Pond Rd., Berlin, CT 06037, Phone: 860-828-3503

Specialties: Working knives of his design or to customer specs. **Patterns:** Likes to use stabilized high-figured woods. **Technical:** Grinds ATS-34, A-2, D-2; forges O-1, 1095; grinds Damasteel. **Prices:** $50 to $400; some higher. **Remarks:** First knife sold in 1987. **Mark:** Name.

ZEMITIS, JOE, 14 Currawong Rd., Cardiff Hts., 2285 Newcastle, AUSTRALIA, Phone: 0249549907

Specialties: Traditional working straight knives. **Patterns:** Hunters, Bowies, tantos, fighters and camp knives. **Technical:** Grinds O1, D2, W2 and 440C; makes his own Damascus. Embellishes; offers engraving and scrimshaw. **Prices:** $150 to $3000. **Remarks:** Full-time maker; first knife sold in 1983. **Mark:** First initial, last name and country, or last name.

ZIMA, MICHAEL F., 732 State St., Ft. Morgan, CO 80701, Phone: 970-867-6078

Specialties: Working straight knives and folders. **Patterns:** Hunters; utility, locking and slip-joint folders. **Technical:** Grinds D-2, 440C, ATS-34, and Specialty Damascus. **Prices:** $150 to $300; some higher. **Remarks:** Full-time maker; first knife sold in 1982. **Mark:** Last name.

ZINKER, BRAD, BZ KNIVES, 1591 NW 17 St., Homestead, FL 33030, Phone: 305-216-0404

Specialties: Fillets, folders and hunters. **Technical:** Uses ATS-34 and stainless Damascus. **Prices:** $200-$600. **Remarks:** Voting member of Knifemakers Guild and Florida Knifemakers Association. **Mark:** Offset connected initials BZ.

ZIRBES, RICHARD, Neustrasse 15, D-54526 Niederkail, GERMANY, Phone: 0049 6575 1371

Specialties: Fancy embellished knives with engraving and self-made scrimshaw (scrimshaw made by maker). High-tech working knives and high-tech hunters, boots, fighters and folders. All knives made by hand. **Patterns:** Boots, fighters, folders, hunters. **Technical:** Uses only the best steels for blade material like CPM-T 440V, CPM-T 420V, ATS-34, D2, C440, stainless Damascus or steel according to customer's desire. **Prices:** Working knives and hunters: $200 to $600. Fancy embellished knives with engraving and/or scrimshaw: $800 to $3000. **Remarks:** Part-time maker; first knife sold in 1991. Member of the German Knife Maker Guild. **Mark:** Zirbes or R. Zirbes.

ZOWADA, TIM, 4509 E. Bear River Rd., Boyne Falls, MI 49713, Phone: 231-348-5446

Specialties: Working knives, some fancy. **Patterns:** Hunters, camp knives, boots, swords, fighters, tantos and locking folders. **Technical:** Forges O2, L6, W2 and his own Damascus. **Prices:** $150 to $1000; some to $5000. **Remarks:** Full-time maker; first knife sold in 1980.

ZSCHERNY, MICHAEL, 1840 Rock Island Dr., Ely, IA 52227, Phone: 319-848-3629

Specialties: Quality folding knives. **Patterns:** Liner-lock and lock-back folders in titanium, working straight knives. **Technical:** Grinds 440 and commercial Damascus, prefers natural materials such as pearls and ivory. **Prices:** Starting at $200. **Remarks:** Full-time maker, first knife sold in 1978. **Mark:** Last name, city and state; folders, last name with stars inside folding knife.

AK

Barlow, Jana Poirier	Anchorage
Brennan, Judson	Delta Junction
Breuer, Lonnie	Wasilla
Broome, Thomas A.	Kenai
Cannon, Raymond W.	Homer
Cawthorne, Christopher A.	Wrangell
Chamberlin, John A.	Anchorage
Dempsey, Gordon S.	N. Kenai
Dufour, Arthur J.	Anchorage
England, Virgil	Anchorage
Flint, Robert	Anchorage
Gouker, Gary B.	Sitka
Grebe, Gordon S.	Anchor Point
Hibben, Westley G.	Anchorage
Kommer, Russ	Anchorage
Lance, Bill	Eagle River
Little, Jimmy L.	Wasilla
Malaby, Raymond J.	Juneau
McFarlin, Eric E.	Kodiak
McIntosh, David L.	Haines
Mirabile, David	Juneau
Moore, Marve	Willow
Parrish III, Gordon A.	North Pole
Schmoker, Randy	Slana
Shore, John I.	Anchorage
Stegall, Keith	Anchorage
Trujillo, Adam	Anchorage
Trujillo, Miranda	Anchorage
Trujillo, Thomas A.	Anchorage
Van Cleve, Steve	Sutton
Whipple, Wesley A.	Kodiak
Whitman, Jim	Chugiak

AL

Andress, Ronnie	Satsuma
Batson, James	Madison
Baxter, Dale	Trinity
Bowles, Chris	Reform
Brend, Walter	Vinemont
Bullard, Bill	Andalusia
Coffman, Danny	Jacksonville
Conn Jr., C.T.	Attalla
Connell, Steve	Adamsville
Cutchin, Roy D.	Seale
Daniels, Alex	Town Creek
Di Marzo, Richard	Birmingham
Durham, Kenneth	Cherokee
Elrod, Roger R.	Enterprise
Fikes, Jimmy L.	Jasper
Fogg, Don	Jasper
Fowler, Ricky and Susan	Robertsdale
Fronefield, Daniel	Hampton Cove
Gilbreath, Randall	Dora
Green, Mark	Graysville
Hammond, Jim	Arab
Hodge, J.B.	Huntsville
Howard, Durvyn M.	Hokes Bluff
Howell, Len	Opelika
Howell, Ted	Wetumpka
Huckabee, Dale	Maylene
Hulsey, Hoyt	Attalla
Madison II, Billy D.	Remlap
McCullough, Jerry	Georgiana
Militano, Tom	Jacksonville
Monk, Nathan P.	Cullman
Morris, C.H.	Frisco City
Pardue, Melvin M.	Repton
Roe Jr., Fred D.	Huntsville
Russell, Tom	Jacksonville
Sandlin, Larry	Adamsville
Sinyard, Cleston S.	Elberta
Thomas, David E.	Lillian
Watson, Billy	Deatsville

AR

Alexander, Jered	Dierks
Anders, David	Center Ridge
Anders, Jerome	Center Ridge
Ardwin, Corey	North Little Rock
Barnes, Eric	Mountain View
Barnes Jr., Cecil C.	Center Ridge
Brown, Jim	Little Rock
Browning, Steven W.	Benton
Bullard, Tom	Flippin
Burnett, Max	Paris
Cabe, Jerry (Buddy)	Hattieville
Cook, James R.	Nashville
Copeland, Thom	Nashville
Crawford, Pat and Wes	West Memphis
Crowell, James L.	Mtn. View
Dozier, Bob	Springdale
Duvall, Fred	Benton
Echols, Roger	Nashville
Edge, Tommy	Cash
Ferguson, Lee	Hindsville
Fisk, Jerry	Nashville
Fitch, John S.	Clinton
Flournoy, Joe	El Dorado
Foster, Ronnie E.	Morrilton
Foster, Timothy L.	El Dorado
Frizzell, Ted	West Fork
Gadberry, Emmet	Hattieville
Greenaway, Don	Fayetteville
Herring, Morris	Dyer
Lane, Ben	North Little Rock
Lawrence, Alton	De Queen
Livesay, Newt	Siloam Springs
Martin, Bruce E.	Prescott
Martin, Hal W.	Morrilton
Massey, Roger	Texarkana
Newton, Ron	London
O'Dell, Clyde	Camden
Olive, Michael E.	Leslie
Passmore, Jimmy D.	Hoxie
Perry, Jim	Hope
Perry, John	Mayflower
Peterson, Lloyd (Pete) C.	Clinton
Polk, Clifton	Van Buren
Polk, Rusty	Van Buren
Quattlebaum, Craig	Searcy
Ramey, Marshall F.	West Helena
Red, Vernon	Conway
Sisemore, Charles Russel	Mena
Smoker, Ray	Searcy
Solomon, Marvin	Paron
Stanley, John	Crossett
Stout, Charles	Gillham
Sweaza, Dennis	Austin
Townsend, Allen Mark	Texarkana
Tycer, Art	Paron
Walker, Jim	Morrilton
Ward, Chuck	Benton
Waters, Herman Harold	Magnolia
Waters, Lu	Magnolia
White, Bryce	Little Rock
Wootton, Randy	Stamps
Worthen, Bill	Little Rock
Young, Raymond L.	Mt Ida

AZ

Ammons, David C.	Tucson
Amos, Chris	Tucson
Bennett, Glen C.	Tucson
Birdwell, Ira Lee	Bagdad
Boye, David	Dolan Springs
Bryan, Tom	Gilbert
Cheatham, Bill	Laveen
Choate, Milton	Somerton
Dodd, Robert F.	Camp Verde
Evans, Vincent K. and Grace	Show Low
Fuegen, Larry	Prescott
Goo, Tai	Tucson
Guignard, Gib	Quartzsite
Gundersen, D.F. "Doc"	Tempe
Hancock, Tim	Scottsdale
Hankins, R.	Tempe
Hoel, Steve	Pine
Holder, D'Alton	Peoria
Hull, Michael J.	Cottonwood
Karp, Bob	Phoenix
Kelley, Thomas P.	Cave Creek
Kopp, Todd M.	Apache Jct.
Lampson, Frank G.	Rimrock
Lee, Randy	St. Johns
Lively, Tim and Marian	Tucson
McFall, Ken	Lakeside
McFarlin, J.W.	Lake Havasu City
Murray, Bill	Green Valley
Newhall, Tom	Tucson
Norris, Don	Tucson
Purvis, Bob and Ellen	Tucson
Rybar Jr., Raymond B.	Phoenix
Snare, Michael	Phoenix
Tamboli, Michael	Glendale
Torgeson, Samuel L.	Sedona
Weiler, Donald E.	Yuma
Weiss, Charles L.	Phoenix
Wolf, Bill	Phoenix
Wright, Timothy	Sedona
Wuertz, Travis	Casa Grande
York, David C.	Chino Valley

CA

Abegg, Arnie	Huntington Beach
Abernathy, Paul J.	Eureka
Adkins, Richard L.	Mission Viejo
Aldrete, Bob	Lomita
Barnes, Gregory	Altadena
Barron, Brian	San Mateo
Benson, Don	Escalon
Berger, Max A.	Carmichael
Biggers, Gary	Ventura
Blum, Chuck	Brea
Bost, Roger E.	Palos Verdes
Boyd, Francis	Berkeley
Brack, Douglas D.	Camirillo
Breshears, Clint	Manhattan Beach
Brooks, Buzz	Los Angles
Browne, Rick	Upland
Brunetta, David	Laguna Beach
Butler, Bart	Ramona
Cabrera, Sergio B.	Harbor City
Cantrell, Kitty D.	Ramona
Caston, Darriel	Sacramento
Chelquist, Cliff	Arroyo Grande
Clark, R.W.	Corona
Cohen, Terry A.	Laytonville
Comus, Steve	Anaheim
Connolly, James	Oroville
Davis, Charlie	Santee
Davisson, Cole	Hemet
De Maria Jr., Angelo	Carmel Valley
Dion, Greg	Oxnard
Dixon Jr., Ira E.	Ventura
Doolittle, Mike	Novato
Driscoll, Mark	La Mesa
Dugan, Brad M.	San Marcos
Eaton, Al	Clayton
Ellis, Dave/ABS Master Smith	Vista
Ellis, William Dean	Fresno
Emerson, Ernest R.	Torrance
English, Jim	Jamul

Essegian, Richard	Fresno
Felix, Alexander	Torrance
Ferguson, Jim	Temecula
Fisher, Theo (Ted)	Montague
Flores, Henry	Santa Clara
Forrest, Brian	Descanso
Fox, Jack L.	Citrus Heights
Fraley, D.B.	Dixon
Francis, Vance	Alpine
Fred, Reed Wyle	Sacramento
Freer, Ralph	Seal Beach
Fulton, Mickey	Willows
Gamble, Frank	Fremont
Gofourth, Jim	Santa Paula
Golding, Robin	Lathrop
Green, Russ	Lakewood
Guarnera, Anthony R.	Quartzhill
Guidry, Bruce	Murrieta
Hall, Jeff	Los Alamitos
Hardy, Scott	Placerville
Harris, Jay	Redwood City
Harris, John	Riverside
Hartsfield, Phill	Newport Beach
Hayes, Dolores	Los Angeles
Helton, Roy	San Diego
Herndon, Wm. R. "Bill"	Acton
Hink III, Les	Stockton
Hockenbary, Warren E.	San Pedro
Holden, Larry	Ridgecrest
Hoy, Ken	North Fork
Humenick, Roy	Rescue
Jacks, Jim	Covina
Jackson, David	Lemoore
Jensen, John Lewis	Pasadena
Johnson, Randy	Turlock
Jones, Curtis J.	Palmdale
Jurgens, John	Torrence
Kazsuk, David	Perris
Keyes, Dan	Chino
Koster, Steven C.	Hunting Beach
Laner, Dean	Susanville
Lang, Bud	Orange
Larson, Richard	Turlock
Leland, Steve	Fairfax
Likarich, Steve	Colfax
Lockett, Sterling	Burbank
Loveless, R.W.	Riverside
Luchini, Bob	Palo Alto
Mackie, John	Whittier
Mallett, John	Ontario
Manabe, Michael K.	San Diego
Martin, Jim	Oxnard
Massey, Ron	Joshua Tree
Mata, Leonard	San Diego
Maxwell, Don	Fresno
McAbee, William	Colfax
McClure, Michael	Menlo Park
McGrath, Patrick T.	Westchester
Melin, Gordon C.	Whittier
Meloy, Sean	Lemon Grove
Montano, Gus A.	San Diego
Morgan, Jeff	Santee
Moses, Steven	Santa Ana
Mosier, Richard	Rollings Hills Est
Mountain Home Knives	Jamul
Naten, Greg	Bakersfield
Orton, Rich	Riverside
Osborne, Donald H.	Clovis
Packard, Bob	Elverta
Padilla, Gary	Auburn
Pendleton, Lloyd	Volcano
Perry, Chris	Fresno
Pfanenstiel, Dan	Modesto
Phillips, Randy	Ontario

Pitt, David F.	Anderson
Posner, Barry E.	N. Hollywood
Richard, Ron	Fremont
Richards Jr., Alvin C.	Fortuna
Rinaldi, T.H.	Winchester
Rodebaugh, James L.	Oak Hills
Rozas, Clark D.	Wilmington
St. Cyr, H. Red	Wilmington
Scarrow, Wil	San Gabriel
Schmitz, Raymond E.	Valley Center
Schroen, Karl	Sebastopol
Sibrian, Aaron	Ventura
Sjostrand, Kevin	Visalia
Slobodian, Scott	San Andreas
Sornberger, Jim	Volcano
Stapel, Chuck	Glendale
Steinberg, Al	Laguna Woods
Stimps, Jason M.	Orange
Stockwell, Walter	Redwood City
Stover, Howard	Pasadena
Strider, Mick	San Marcos
Taylor, Scott	Gardena
Terrill, Stephen	Lindsay
Tingle, Dennis P.	Jackson
Vagnino, Michael	Visalia
Van Riper, James N.	Citrus Heights
Ward, Ken	Weed
Warren, Al	Roseville
Watanabe, Wayne	Montebello
Weinstock, Robert	San Francisco
Wilson, Philip C.	Mountain Ranch
Wilson, Ron	Morro Bay
Winberg, Douglas R.	Ramona

CO

Anderson, Mel	Cedaredge
Appleton, Ray	Byers
Barrett, Cecil Terry	Colorado Springs
Booco, Gordon	Hayden
Brandon, Matthew	Denver
Brock, Kenneth L.	Allenspark
Burrows, Chuck	Durango
Campbell, Dick	Conifer
Davis, Don	Loveland
Dawson, Barry	Durango
Dawson, Lynn	Durango
Delong, Dick	Aurora
Dennehy, Dan	Del Norte
Dill, Robert	Loveland
Hatch, Ken	Dinosaur
High, Tom	Alamosa
Hockensmith, Dan	Crook
Hodgson, Richard J.	Boulder
Hughes, Ed	Grand Junction
Inman III, Paul R.	Glenwood Springs
Irie, Michael L.	Colorado Springs
Kitsmiller, Jerry	Montrose
Leck, Dal	Hayden
Lewis, Steve	Woodland Park
Miller, Hanford J.	Cowdrey
Miller, M.A.	Northglenn
Nolen, R.D. and Steve	Estes Park
Olson, Wayne C.	Bailey
Ott, Fred	Durango
Owens, John	Nathrop
Roberts, Chuck	Golden
Rollert, Steve	Keenesburg
Ronzio, N. Jack	Fruita
Sanders, Bill	Mancos
Thompson, Lloyd	Pagosa Springs
Tollefson, Barry A.	Gunnison
Topliss, M.W. "Ike"	Montrose
Vunk, Robert	Colorado Springs
Watson, Bert	Westminster

Wilson, James G.	Estes Park
Wood, Owen Dale	Arvada
Zima, Michael F.	Ft. Morgan

CT

Barnes, William	Wallingford
Buebendorf, Robert E.	Monroe
Chapo, William G.	Wilton
Framski, Walter P.	Prospect
Jean, Gerry	Manchester
Lepore, Michael J.	Bethany
Padgett Jr., Edwin L.	New London
Pankiewicz, Philip R.	Lebanon
Plunkett, Richard	West Cornwall
Putnam, Donald S.	Wethersfield
Rainville, Richard	Salem
Turecek, Jim	Ansonia
Vitale, Mace	Guilford
Zembko III, John	Berlin

DE

Antonio Jr., William J.	Newark
Daland, B. Macgregor	Harbeson
Schneider, Karl A.	Newark
Willey, W.G.	Greenwood

FL

Adams, Les	Hialeah
Angell, Jon	Hawthorne
Atkinson, Dick	Wausau
Bacon, David R.	Bradenton
Barry III, James J.	West Palm Beach
Bartrug, Hugh E.	St. Petersburg
Beckett, Norman L.	Satsuma
Beers, Ray	Lake Wales
Benjamin Jr., George	Kissimmee
Birnbaum, Edwin	Miami
Blackton, Andrew E.	Bayonet Point
Blackwood, Neil	Lakeland
Bosworth, Dean	Key Largo
Bradley, John	Pomona Park
Bray Jr., W. Lowell	New Port Richey
Brown, Harold E.	Arcadia
Burris, Patrick R.	Jacksonville
Butler, John	Havana
Chase, Alex	DeLand
Cole, Dave	Satellite Beach
Davenport, Jack	Dade City
Davis, Jim Jr.	Zephyrhills
Dietzel, Bill	Middleburg
Doggett, Bob	Brandon
Dotson, Tracy	Baker
Ellerbe, W.B.	Geneva
Enos III, Thomas M.	Orlando
Fagan, James A.	Lake Worth
Ferrara, Thomas	Naples
Ferris, Bill	Palm Beach Garden
Fowler, Charles R.	Ft. McCoy
Gamble, Roger	St. Petersburg
Gardner, Rob	Loxahatchee
Garner Jr., William O.	Pensacola
Gibson Sr, James Hoot	Bunnell
Goers, Bruce	Lakeland
Griffin Jr., Howard A.	Davie
Grospitch, Ernie	Orlando
Harris, Ralph Dewey	Brandon
Heitler, Henry	Tampa
Hodge III, John	Palatka
Holland, John H.	Titusville
Hughes, Dan	West Palm Beach
Humphreys, Joel	Bowling Green
Hunter, Richard D.	Alachua
Hytovick, Joe "Hy"	Dunnellon
Jernigan, Steve	Milton

Johanning Custom Knives, Tom Sarasota
Johnson, Durrell Carmon Sparr
Johnson, John R. Plant City
Kelly, Lance Edgewater
King, Bill Tampa
Krapp, Denny Apopka
Levengood, Bill Tampa
Leverett, Ken Lithia
Lewis, Mike DeBary
Long, Glenn A. Dunnellon
Lovestrand, Schuyler Vero Beach
Lozier, Don Ocklawaha
Lunn, Gail St. Petersburg
Lunn, Larry A. St. Petersburg
Lyle III, Ernest L. Chiefland
McDonald, Robert J. Loxahatchee
Miller, Ronald T. Largo
Mink, Dan Crystal Beach
Newton, Larry Jacksonville
Ochs, Charles F. Largo
Oller, Vince Miami
Owens, Donald Melbourne
Parker, Cliff Zephyrhills
Pendray, Alfred H. Williston
Piergallini, Daniel E. Plant City
Randall Made Knives, Orlando
Reed, John M. Oak Hill
Roberts, E. Ray Monticello
Robinson III, Rex R. Leesburg
Rodkey, Dan Hudson
Rogers, Rodney Wildwood
Ross, Gregg Lake Worth
Russ, Ron Williston
Schlomer, James E. Kissimmee
Schwarzer, Stephen Pomona Park
Simons, Bill Lakeland
Smart, Steaten Tavares
Smith, Michael J. Brandon
Stapleton, William E. Merritt Island
Steck, Van R. Orange City
Stephan, Daniel Valrico
Stipes, Dwight Palm City
Straight, Kenneth J. Largo
Sweder, Joram Ocala
Turnbull, Ralph A. Spring Hill
Vogt, Donald J. Tampa
Waldrop, Mark Summerfield
Wallace, Roger L. Tampa
Watson, Tom Panama City
Weiland Jr., J. Reese Riverview
Wicker, Donnie R. Panama City
Wyman, Marc L. Ft Lauderdale
Zaccagnino Jr., Don Pahokee
Zahm, Kurt Indialantic
Zinker, Brad Homestead

GA

Arrowood, Dale Sharpsburg
Ashworth, Boyd Powder Springs
Barker, Robert G. Bishop
Bentley, C.L. Albany
Bish, Hal Jonesboro
Black, Scott Covington
Bradley, Dennis Blairsville
Buckner, Jimmie H. Putney
Carey Jr., Charles W. Griffin
Cash, Terry Canton
Chamblin, Joel Concord
Cofer, Ron Loganville
Cole, Welborn I. Atlanta
Coughlin, Michael M. Winder
Crockford, Jack Chamblee
Davis, Steve Powder Springs
Dempsey, David Macon

Dunn, Charles K. Shiloh
Feigin, B. Marietta
Frost, Dewayne Barnesville
Gaines, Buddy Commerce
Glover, Warren D. Cleveland
Granger, Paul J. Kennesaw
Greene, David Covington
Halligan, Ed Sharpsburg
Hardy, Douglas E. Franklin
Harmon, Jay Woodstock
Hawkins, Rade Fayetteville
Haynie, Charles Toccoa
Hensley, Wayne Conyers
Hinson and Son, R. Columbus
Hoffman, Kevin L. Savannah
Hossom, Jerry Duluth
Hyde, Jimmy Ellenwood
Johnson, Harold "Harry" C. Trion
Jones, Franklin (Frank) W. Columbus
Kimsey, Kevin Cartersville
King, Fred Cartersville
Knott, Steve Rincon
Landers, John Newnan
Lonewolf, J. Aguirre Demorest
Mathews, Charlie and Harry Statesboro
McGill, John Blairsville
McLendon, Hubert W. Waco
Mitchell, James A. Columbus
Moncus, Michael Steven Smithville
Parks, John Jefferson
Poole, Marvin O. Commerce
Poole, Steve L. Stockbridge
Powell, Robert Clark Smarr
Poythress, John Swainsboro
Prater, Mike Flintstone
Price, Timmy Blairsville
Ragsdale, James D. Lithonia
Rogers Jr., Robert P. Acworth
Roghmans, Mark LaGrange
Rosenfeld, Bob Hoschton
Scofield, Everett Chickamauga
Sculley, Peter E. Rising Fawn
Smith Jr., James B. "Red" Morven
Snell, Jerry L. Fayetteville
Snow, Bill Columbus
Sowell, Bill Macon
Stafford, Richard Warner Robins
Thompson, Kenneth Duluth
Tomey, Kathleen Macon
Walters, A.F. TyTy
Washburn Jr., Robert Lee Adrian
Werner Jr., William A. Marietta
Whetsell, Alex Sharpsburg
White, Lou Ranger

HI

Bucholz, Mark A. Holualoa
Dolan, Robert L. Kula
Fujisaka, Stanley Kaneohe
Gibo, George Hilo
Lui, Ronald M. Honolulu
Mann, Tim Honokaa
Mayo Jr., Tom Waialua
Mitsuyuki, Ross Waipahu
Onion, Kenneth J. Kaneohe
Zakabi, Carl S. Mililani Town

IA

Brooker, Dennis Derby
Brower, Max Boone
Clark, Howard F. Runnells
Cockerham, Lloyd Denham Springs
Helscher, John W. Washington
Lainson, Tony Council Bluffs

Lewis, Bill Riverside
Miller, James P. Fairbank
Thie, Brian Sperry
Trindle, Barry Earlham
Westberg, Larry Algona
Zscherny, Michael Ely

ID

Alderman, Robert Sagle
Alverson, Tim (R.V.) Peck
Andrews, Don Coeur D'Alene
Burke, Bill Salmon
Eddy, Hugh E. Caldwell
Hawk, Grant and Gavin Idaho City
Hogan, Thomas R. Boise
Horton, Scot Buhl
Howe, Tori Athol
Kranning, Terry L. Pocatello
Mann, Michael L. Spirit Lake
Metz, Greg T. Cascade
Mullin, Steve Sandpoint
Nealey, Ivan F. (Frank) Mt. Home
Patton, Dick and Rob Nampa
Quarton, Barr McCall
Reeve, Chris Boise
Rohn, Fred Coeur d'Alene
Sawby, Scott Sandpoint
Schultz, Robert W. Cocolalla
Selent, Chuck Bonners Ferry
Sparks, Bernard Dingle
Spragg, Wayne E. Ashton
Steiger, Monte L. Genesee
Tippetts, Colten Ketchum
Towell, Dwight L. Midvale

IL

Abbott, William M. Chandlerville
Bloomer, Alan T. Maquon
Camerer, Craig Hettick
Cook, Louise Ozark
Cook, Mike Ozark
Detmer, Phillip Breese
Dicristofano, Anthony P. Northlake
Eaker, Allen L. Paris
Hawes, Chuck Weldon
Heath, William Bondville
Hill, Rick Maryville
Knuth, Joseph E. Rockford
Kovar, Eugene Evergreen Park
Lang, Kurt McHenry
Leone, Nick Pontoon Beach
Markley, Ken Sparta
Meier, Daryl Carbondale
Myers, Paul Wood River
Nevling, Mark Hume
Nowland, Rick Waltonville
Potocki, Roger Goreville
Pritchard, Ron Dixon
Rados, Jerry F. Grant Park
Rossdeutscher, Robert N. Arlington
Heights
Rzewnicki, Gerald Elizabeth
Schneider, Craig M. Claremont
Smale, Charles J. Waukegan
Smith, John M. Centralia
Steinbrecher, Mark W. Glenview
Thomas, Bob G. Thebes
Todd, Richard C. Chambersburg
Tompkins, Dan Peotone
Veit, Michael LaSalle
Voss, Ben Galesburg
Werth, George W. Poplar Grove
West, Charles A. Centralia
Wheeler, Robert Bradley

White, Robert J.	Gilson
White Jr., Robert J. Butch	Gilson
Young, Errol	Alton

IN

Ball, Ken	Mooresville
Barrett, Rick L. (Toshi Hisa)	Goshen
Bose, Reese	Shelburn
Bose, Tony	Shelburn
Chaffee, Jeff L.	Morris
Claiborne, Jeff	Franklin
Damlovac, Sava	Indianapolis
Darby, Jed	Greensburg
Fitzgerald, Dennis M.	Fort Wayne
Fraps, John R.	Indianpolis
Hunt, Maurice	Avon
Imel, Billy Mace	New Castle
Johnson, C.E. Gene	Portage
Kain, Charles	Indianapolis
Keeslar, Steven C.	Hamilton
Keeton, William L.	Laconia
Kinker, Mike	Greensburg
Largin, Kelgin Knives	Metamora
Mayville, Oscar L.	Marengo
Minnick, Jim	Middletown
Oliver, Todd D.	Spencer
Parsons, Michael R.	Indianapolis
Quakenbush, Thomas C.	Ft Wayne
Robertson, Leo D.	Indianpolis
Shostle, Ben	Muncie
Smock, Timothy E.	Marion
Snyder, Michael Tom	Zionsville
Stover, Terry "Lee"	Kokomo
Thayer, Danny O.	Romney
Young, George	Kokomo

KS

Bradburn, Gary	Wichita
Chard, Gordon R.	Iola
Courtney, Eldon	Wichita
Craig, Roger L.	Topeka
Culver, Steve	Meriden
Darpinian, Dave	Olathe
Dawkins, Dudley L.	Topeka
Dugger, Dave	Westwood
George, Les	Wichita
Greene, Steve	Rossville
Hegwald, J.L.	Humboldt
Herman, Tim	Overland Park
King, Jason M.	Eskridge
King Jr., Harvey G.	Eskridge
Kraft, Steve	Abilene
Lamb, Curtis J.	Ottawa
Magee, Jim	Salina
Petersen, Dan L.	Auburn

KY

Addison, Kyle A.	Murray
Barr, A.T.	Nicholasville
Baskett, Lee Gene	Eastview
Baumgardner, Ed	Glendale
Bodner, Gerald "Jerry"	Louisville
Bybee, Barry J.	Cadiz
Carson, Harold J. "Kit"	Vine Grove
Clay, J.D.	Greenup
Coil, Jimmie J.	Owensboro
Downing, Larry	Bremen
Dunn, Steve	Smiths Grove
Edwards, Mitch	Glasgow
Finch, Ricky D.	West Liberty
Fister, Jim	Simpsonville
France, Dan	Cawood
Frederick, Aaron	West Liberty
Gevedon, Hanners (Hank)	Crab Orchard

Greco, John	Greensburg
Hibben, Daryl	LaGrange
Hibben, Gil	LaGrange
Hibben, Joleen	LaGrange
Hoke, Thomas M.	LaGrange
Holbrook, H.L.	Sandy Hook
Howser, John C.	Frankfort
Keeslar, Joseph F.	Almo
Lott-Sinclair, Sherry	Campbellsville
Miller, Don	Lexington
Mize, Richard	Lawrenceburg
Obenauf, Mike	Vine Grove
Pease, W.D.	Ewing
Pierce, Harold L.	Louisville
Pulliam, Morris C.	Shelbyville
Rigney Jr., Willie	Bronston
Smith, Gregory H.	Louisville
Smith, John W.	West Liberty
Vowell, Donald J.	Mayfield
Walker III, John Wade	Paintlick
Wallingford Jr., Charles W.	Union

LA

Barker, Reggie	Springhill
Blaum, Roy	Covington
Caldwell, Bill	West Monroe
Calvert Jr., Robert W. (Bob)	Rayville
Capdepon, Randy	Carencro
Capdepon, Robert	Carencro
Chauvin, John	Scott
Culpepper, John	Monroe
Dake, C.M.	New Orleans
Dake, Mary H.	New Orleans
Diebel, Chuck	Broussard
Durio, Fred	Opelousas
Elkins, R. Van	Bonita
Faucheaux, Howard J.	Loreauville
Fontenot, Gerald J.	Mamou
Forstall, Al	Pearl River
Gorenflo, Gabe	Baton Rouge
Gorenflo, James T. (Jt)	Baton Rouge
Graffeo, Anthony I.	Chalmette
Holmes, Robert	Baton Rouge
Ki, Shiva	Baton Rouge
Laurent, Kermit	LaPlace
Leonard, Randy Joe	Sarepta
Mitchell, Max, Dean and Ben	Leesville
Phillips, Dennis	Independence
Potier, Timothy F.	Oberlin
Primos, Terry	Shreveport
Provenzano, Joseph D.	Chalmette
Randall Jr., James W.	Keithville
Randow, Ralph	Pineville
Reggio Jr., Sidney J.	Sun
Roath, Dean	Baton Rouge
Sanders, Michael M.	Ponchatoula
Tilton, John	Iowa
Trisler, Kenneth W.	Rayville
Wiggins, Horace	Mansfield

MA

Aoun, Charles	Wakefield
Dailey, G.E.	Seekonk
Entin, Robert	Boston
Frankl, John M.	Cambridge
Gaudette, Linden L.	Wilbraham
Gedraitis, Charles J.	Rutland
Grossman, Stewart	Clinton
Hinman, Ted	Watertown
Jarvis, Paul M.	Cambridge
Khalsa, Jot Singh	Millis
Kubasek, John A.	Easthampton
Lapen, Charles	W. Brookfield
Laramie, Mark	Fitchburg

Little, Larry	Spencer
Martin, Randall J.	Bridgewater
McLuin, Tom	Dracut
Moore, Michael Robert	Lowell
Olofson, Chris	Cambridge
Rebello, Indian George	New Bedford
Reed, Dave	Brimfield
Richter, Scott	S. Boston
Rizzi, Russell J.	Ashfield
Siska, Jim	Westfield
Smith, J.D.	Roxbury
Stoddard's, Inc., Copley Place	Boston
Szarek, Mark G.	Revere

MD

Bagley, R. Keith	White Plains
Barnes, Aubrey G.	Hagerstown
Barnes, Gary L.	New Windsor
Beers, Ray	Monkton
Bouse, D. Michael	Waldorf
Cohen, N.J. (Norm)	Baltimore
Dement, Larry	Prince Fredrick
Freiling, Albert J.	Finksburg
Fuller, Jack A.	New Market
Grossman, Scott	Forest Hill
Hart, Bill	Pasadena
Hendrickson, E. Jay	Frederick
Hendrickson, Shawn	Knoxville
Hudson, C. Robbin	Rock Hall
Hurt, William R.	Frederick
Kreh, Lefty	"Cockeysville"
Kretsinger Jr., Philip W.	Boonsboro
McCarley, John	Taneytown
McGowan, Frank E.	Sykesville
Merchant, Ted	White Hall
Mills, Michael	Lanham
Moran Jr., Wm. F.	Braddock Heights
Nicholson, R. Kent	Phoenix
Rhodes, James D.	
St. Clair, Thomas K.	Monrovia
Sentz, Mark C.	Taneytown
Smit, Glenn	Aberdeen
Sontheimer, G. Douglas	Potomac
Spickler, Gregory Noble	Sharpsburg
Walker, Bill	Stevensville

ME

Coombs Jr., Lamont	Bucksport
Corrigan, David P.	Bingham
Courtois, Bryan	Saco
Gray, Daniel	Brownville
Hillman, Charles	Friendship
Kravitt, Chris	Ellsworth
Leavitt Jr., Earl F.	E. Boothbay
Oyster, Lowell R.	Corinth
Sharrigan, Mudd	Wiscasset

MI

Ackerson, Robin E.	Buchanan
Andrews, Eric	Grand Ledge
Behnke, William	Kingsley
Bethke, Lora Sue	Grand Haven
Booth, Philip W.	Ithaca
Bruner, Rick	Jenison
Buckbee, Donald M.	Grayling
Canoy, Andrew B.	Hubbard Lake
Carlisle, Frank	Detroit
Carr, Tim	Muskegon
Carroll, Chad	Grant
Cashen, Kevin R.	Hubbardston
Cook, Mike A.	Portland
Costello, Dr. Timothy L.	Farmington Hills
Cousino, George	Onsted
Cowles, Don	Royal Oak

Dilluvio, Frank J.	Warren
Ealy, Delbert	Indian River
Erickson, Walter E.	Atlanta
Gordon, Larry B.	Farmington Hills
Gottage, Dante	Clinton Twp.
Gottage, Judy	Clinton Twp.
Harm, Paul W.	Attica
Hartman, Arlan (Lanny)	N. Muskegon
Hughes, Daryle	Nunica
Kalfayan, Edward N.	Ferndale
Krause, Roy W.	St. Clair Shores
Lankton, Scott	Ann Arbor
Leach, Mike J.	Swartz Creek
Lucie, James R.	Fruitport
Mankel, Kenneth	Cannonsburg
Mills, Louis G.	Ann Arbor
Nix, Robert T.	Wayne
Noren, Douglas E.	Springlake
Parker, Robert Nelson	Rapid City
Repke, Mike	Bay City
Sakmar, Mike	Rochester
Sandberg, Ronald B.	Browntown
Serven, Jim	Fostoria
Sigman, James P.	North Adams
Tally, Grant	Flat Rock
Van Eizenga, Jerry W.	Nunica
Vasquez, Johnny David	Wyandotte
Viste, James	Detroit
White, Richard T.	Grosse Pointe Farms
Whittaker, Wayne	Metamore
Whitworth, Ken J.	Sterling Heights
Wood, Webster	Atlanta
Zowada, Tim	Boyne Falls

MN

Davis, Joel	Albert Lea
Goltz, Warren L.	Ada
Griffin, Thomas J.	Windom
Hagen, Philip L.	Pelican Rapids
Hansen, Robert W.	Cambridge
Johnson, R.B.	Clearwater
Knipschield, Terry	Rochester
Maines, Jay	Wyoming
Mickley, Tracy	North Mankato
Rydbom, Jeff	Annandale
Shadley, Eugene W.	Bovey
Steffen, Chuck	St. Michael
Voorhies, Les	Faribault

MO

Ames, Mickey L.	Monett
Andrews II, E.R. (Russ)	Sugar Creek
Bolton, Charles B.	Jonesburg
Burrows, Stephen R.	Kansas City
Conner, Allen L.	Fulton
Cover, Raymond A.	Mineral Point
Cox, Colin J.	Raymore
Davis, W.C.	Raymore
Dippold, Al	Perryville
Driskill, Beryl	Braggadocio
Duvall, Larry E.	Gallatin
Ehrenberger, Daniel Robert	Shelbyville
Engle, William	Boonville
Hanson III, Don L.	Success
Harris, Jeffery A	St. Louis
Harrison, Jim (Seamus)	St. Louis
Jones, John A.	Holden
Kinnikin, Todd	House Springs
Knickmeyer, Hank	Cedar Hill
Knickmeyer, Kurt	Cedar Hill
Marks, Chris	Ava
Martin, Tony	Arcadia
Mason, Bill	Excelsior Springs
McCrackin, Kevin	House Spings

McCrackin and Son, V.J.	House Springs
McDermott, Michael	Defiance
McKiernan, Stan	Vandalia
Miller, Bob	Oakville
Muller, Jody and Pat	Pittsburg
Newcomb, Corbin	Moberly
Pryor, Stephen L.	Boss
Ramsey, Richard A.	Neosho
Rardon, A.D.	Polo
Rardon, Archie F.	Polo
Rice, Stephen E.	St. Louis
Riepe, Richard A.	Harrisonville
Scroggs, James A.	Warrensburg
Sonntag, Douglas W.	Nixa
Steketee, Craig A.	Billings
Stewart, Edward L.	Mexico
Stormer, Bob	St. Peters
Warden, Roy A.	Union
Weddle Jr., Del	St. Joseph
Willis, Bill	Ava

MS

Black, Scott	Picayune
Boleware, David	Carson
Davis, Jesse W.	Sarah
Evans, Bruce A.	Booneville
Lamey, Robert M.	Biloxi
Lebatard, Paul M.	Vancleave
Roberts, Michael	Clinton
Roberts, Mike	Clinton
Robinson, Chuck	Picayune
Shiffer, Steve	Leakesville
Skow, H. A. "Tex"	Senatobia
Taylor, Billy	Petal
Vandeventer, Terry L.	Terry
Wehner, Rudy	Collins
Wingo, Perry	Gulfport
Winston, David	Starkville

MT

Barnes, Jack	Whitefish
Barnes, Wendell	Missoula
Barth, J.D.	Alberton
Beam, John R.	Kalispell
Beaty, Robert B.	Missoula
Becker, Steve	Conrad
Bizzell, Robert	Butte
Boxer, Bo	Whitefish
Brooks, Steve R.	Walkerville
Caffrey, Edward J.	Great Falls
Carlisle, Jeff	Simms
Christensen, Jon P.	Shepherd
Colter, Wade	Colstrip
Conklin, George L.	Ft. Benton
Crowder, Robert	Thompson Falls
Dunkerley, Rick	Seeley Lake
Eaton, Rick	Shepherd
Ellefson, Joel	Manhattan
Fassio, Melvin G.	Lolo
Forthofer, Pete	Whitefish
Gallagher, Barry	Lewistown
Harkins, J.A.	Conner
Hill, Howard E.	Polson
Hintz, Gerald M.	Helena
Hollar, Bob	Great Falls
Hulett, Steve	West Yellowstone
Kajin, Al	Forsyth
Kauffman, Dave	Montana City
Kraft, Elmer	Big Arm
Luman, James R.	Anaconda
McGuane IV, Thomas F.	Bozeman
Mortenson, Ed	Darby
Moyer, Russ	Havre
Munroe, Deryk C.	Bozeman

Nedved, Dan	Kalispell
Patrick, Willard C.	Helena,
Peele, Bryan	Thompson Falls
Peterson, Eldon G.	Whitefish
Piorek, James S.	Rexford
Pursley, Aaron	Big Sandy
Robinson, Robert W.	Polson
Rodewald, Gary	Hamilton
Ruana Knife Works	Bonner
Sauer, Charles	Columbia Falls
Schmidt, Rick	Whitefish
Simonich, Rob	Clancy
Smallwood, Wayne	Kalispell
Smith, Josh	Frenchtown
Sweeney, Coltin D.	Missoula
Taylor, Shane	Miles City
Thill, Jim	Missoula
Weinand, Gerome M.	Missoula
Woodiwiss, Dorren	Thompson Falls
Yashinski, John L.	Red Lodge

NC

Baker, Herb	Eden
Bauchop, Peter	Cary
Britton, Tim	Winston-Salem
Busfield, John	Roanoke Rapids
Chastain, Wade	Horse Shoe
Coltrain, Larry D.	Buxton
Comar, Roger N.	Marion
Daniel, Travis E.	Chocowinity
Drew, Gerald	Asheville
Edwards, Fain E.	Topton
Fox, Paul	Claremont
Gaddy, Gary Lee	Washington
Goguen, Scott	Newport
Goode, Brian	Shelby
Greene, Chris	Shelby
Gross, W.W.	Archdale
Gurganus, Carol	Colerain
Gurganus, Melvin H.	Colerain
Guthrie, George B.	Bassemer City
Hazen, Mark	Charlotte
Kearney, Jarod	Brown Summit
Livingston, Robert C.	Murphy
Maynard, William N.	Fayetteville
McDonald, Robin J.	Fayetteville
McLurkin, Andrew	Raleigh
McNabb, Tommy	Winston-Salem
McRae, J. Michael	Mint Hill
Parrish, Robert	Weaverville
Patrick, Chuck	Brasstown
Patrick, Peggy	Brasstown
Scholl, Tim	Angier
Simmons, H.R.	Aurora
Snody, Mike	Liberty
Sprouse, Terry	Asheville
Sterling, Murray	Mount Airy
Summers, Arthur L.	Concord
Sutton, S. Russell	New Bern
Vail, Dave	Hampstead
Wagaman, John K.	Selma
Walker, Don	Burnsville
Warren, Daniel	Canton
Whitley, L. Wayne	Chocowinity
Williamson, Tony	Siler City
Wilson, Mike	Hayesville
Winkler, Daniel	Blowing Rock
Young, Paul A.	Boone

ND

Keidel, Gene W. and Scott J.	Dickinson
Pitman, David	Williston

NE

Jensen Jr., Carl A.	Blair
Jokerst, Charles	Omaha
Marlowe, Charles	Omaha
Mosier, Joshua J.	Edgar
Robbins, Howard P.	Elkhorn
Schepers, George B.	Shelton
Suedmeier, Harlan	Nebraska City
Syslo, Chuck	Omaha
Tiensvold, Alan L.	Rushville
Tiensvold, Jason	Rushville
Till, Calvin E. and Ruth	Chadron

NH

Carlson, Kelly	Antrim
Ellis, Willy B.	Litchfield
Gunn, Nelson L.	Epping
Hill, Steve E.	Goshen
Hitchmough, Howard	Peterborough
MacDonald, John	Raymond
Philippe, D. A.	Cornish
Saindon, R. Bill	Goshen

NJ

Eden, Thomas	Cranbury
Grussenmeyer, Paul G.	Cherry Hill
Licata, Steven	Garfield
Little, Guy A.	Oakhurst
McCallen Jr., Howard H.	So Seaside Park
Nelson, Bob	Sparta
Phillips, Jim	Williamstown
Polkowski, Al	Chester
Pressburger, Ramon	Howell
Quick, Mike	Kearny
Schilling, Ellen	Hamilton Square
Sheets, Steven William	Mendham
Slee, Fred	Morganville
Viele, H.J.	Westwood
Yeskoo, Richard C.	Summit

NM

Black, Tom	Albuquerque
Cherry, Frank J.	Albuquerque
Coleman, Keith E.	Albuquerque
Cordova, Joseph G.	Peralta
Cumming, R.J.	Cedar Crest
Digangi, Joseph M.	Santa Cruz
Duran, Jerry T.	Albuquerque
Dyess, Eddie	Roswell
Fisher, Jay	Clouis
Goode, Bear	Navajo Dam
Gunter, Brad	Tijeras
Hethcoat, Don	Clovis
Hume, Don	Albuquerque
Jones, Bob	Albuquerque
Kimberley, Richard L.	Santa Fe
Lewis, Tom R.	Carlsbad
MacDonald, David	Los Lunas
Rogers, Richard	Magdalena
Schaller, Anthony Brett	Albuquerque
Stalcup, Eddie	Gallup
Terzuola, Robert	Santa Fe
Trujillo, Albert M.B.	Bosque Farms
Walker, Michael L.	Rancho de Taos
Ware, Tommy	Datil
Wescott, Cody	Las Cruces

NV

Barnett, Van	Reno
Beasley, Geneo	Wadsworth
Blanchard, G.R. (Gary)	Las Vegas
Cameron, Ron G.	Logandale
Defeo, Robert A.	Henderson
Dellana	Reno
Duff, Bill	Reno
George, Tom	Henderson
Hrisoulas, Jim	Las Vegas
Kreibich, Donald L.	Reno
Mount, Don	Las Vegas
Nishiuchi, Melvin S.	Las Vegas
Norton, Don	Las Vegas
Thomas, Devin	Panaca
Tracy, Bud	Reno
Washburn, Arthur D.	Pioche

NY

Baker, Wild Bill	Boiceville
Champagne, Paul	Mechanicville
Cute, Thomas	Cortland
Davis, Barry L.	Castleton
Farr, Dan	Rochester
Faust, Dick	Rochester
Hobart, Gene	Windsor
Isgro, Jeffery	West Babylon
Johnston, Dr. Robt.	Rochester
Levin, Jack	Brooklyn
Loos, Henry C.	New Hyde Park
Ludwig, Richard O.	Maspeth
Lupole, Jamie G.	Kirkwood
Maragni, Dan	Georgetown
McCornock, Craig	Willow
Meerdink, Kurt	Barryville
Meshejian, Mardi	E. Northport
Page, Reginald	Groveland
Palazzo, Tom	Bayside
Pattay, Rudy	Long Beach
Peterson, Karen	Brooklyn
Phillips, Scott C.	Gouverneur
Rachlin, Leslie S.	Elmira
Rappazzo, Richard	Cohoes
Rotella, Richard A.	Niagara Falls
Scheid, Maggie	Rochester
Schippnick, Jim	Sanborn
Schlueter, David	Syracuse
Serafen, Steven E.	New Berlin
Skiff, Steven	Broadalbin
Smith, Lenard C.	Valley Cottage
Smith, Raymond L.	Erin
Summers, Dan	Whitney Pt.
Szilaski, Joseph	Wappingers Falls
Turner, Kevin	Montrose
Wilson III, George H.	Bronx

OH

Babcock, Raymond G.	Vincent
Bailey, Ryan	Galena
Bendik, John	Olmsted Falls
Busse, Jerry	Wauseon
Click, Joe	Swanton
Collins, Harold	West Union
Collins, Lynn M.	Elyria
Coppins, Daniel	Cambridge
Cottrill, James I.	Columbus
Downing, Tom	Cuyahoga Falls
Downs, James F.	Londonderry
Etzler, John	Grafton
Foster, R.L. (Bob)	Mansfield
Francis, John D.	Ft. Loramie
Franklin, Mike	Aberdeen
Geisler, Gary R.	Clarksville
Gittinger, Raymond	Tiffin
Glover, Ron	Mason
Greiner, Richard	Green Springs
Guess, Raymond L.	Mechanicstown
Hinderer, Rick	Wooster
Hudson, Anthony B.	Amanda
Imboden II, Howard L.	Dayton
Jones, Roger Mudbone	Waverly

Kiefer, Tony	Pataskala
Kubaiko, Hank	Beach City
Longworth, Dave	Hamersville
Loro, Gene	Crooksville
Maienknecht, Stanley	Sardis
McDonald, Rich	Columbiana
McGroder, Patrick J.	Madison
Mercer, Mike	Lebanon
Messer, David T.	Dayton
Morgan, Tom	Beloit
Panak, Paul S.	Kinsman
Potter, Billy	Nashport
Ralph, Darrel	Galena
Rose, Derek W.	Gallipolis
Rowe, Fred	Amesville
Salley, John D.	Tipp City
Shinosky, Andy	Canfield
Shoemaker, Carroll	Northup
Shoemaker, Scott	Miamisburg
Spinale, Richard	Lorain
Stevens, Barry B.	Cridersville
Stoddart, W.B. Bill	Forest Park
Strong, Scott	Beavercreek
Summers, Dennis K.	Springfield
Thomas, Kim	Seville
Thourot, Michael W.	Napoleon
Tindera, George	Brunswick
Votaw, David P.	Pioneer
Ward, J.J.	Waverly
Ward, Ron	Loveland
Warther, Dale	Dover
Witsaman, Earl	Stow
Wood, Larry B.	Huber Heights
Wright, L.T.	Steubenville
Yurco, Mike	Canfield

OK

Baker, Ray	Sapulpa
Barngrover, Jerry	Afton
Brown, Troy L.	Park Hill
Burke, Dan	Edmond
Crenshaw, Al	Eufaula
Darby, David T.	Cookson
Dill, Dave	Bethany
Englebretson, George	Oklahoma City
Gepner, Don	Norman
Griffith, Lynn	Tulsa
Johns, Rob	Enid
Kennedy Jr., Bill	Yukon
Kirk, Ray	Tahlequah
Lairson Sr, Jerry	Ringold
Martin, John Alexander	Okmulgee
Miller, Michael E.	El Reno
Sanders, A.A.	Norman
Spivey, Jefferson	Yukon
Tomberlin, Brion R.	Norman
Williams, Michael L.	Broken Bow
Wingo, Gary	Ramona

OR

Bell, Michael	Coquille
Bochman, Bruce	Grants Pass
Brandt, Martin W.	Springfield
Buchman, Bill	Bend
Buchner, Bill	Idleyld Park
Cameron House	Salem
Clark, Nate	Yoncalla
Coon, Raymond C.	Gresham
Davis, Terry	Sumpter
Dowell, T.M.	Bend
Ferdinand, Don	Shady Cove
Fox, Wendell	Springfield
Frank, Heinrich H.	Seal Rock
Goddard, Wayne	Eugene

Harsey, William H.	Creswell
Hilker, Thomas N.	Williams
Horn, Jess	Eugene
Kelley, Gary	Aloha
Lake, Ron	Eugene
Lindsay, Chris A.	Bend
Little, Gary M.	Broadbent
Lockett, Lowell C.	North Bend
Lum, Robert W.	Eugene
Martin, Gene	Williams
Martin, Walter E.	Williams
Miller, Michael K.	Sweet Home
Olson, Darrold E.	Springfield
Osterman, Daniel E.	Junction City
Rider, David M.	Eugene
Schoeningh, Mike	North Powder
Schrader, Robert	Bend
Sevey Custom Knife	Gold Beach
Sheehy, Thomas J.	Portland
Shoger, Mark O.	Beaverton
Smith, Rick	Rogue River
Thompson, Leon	Gaston
Thompson, Tommy	Portland
Vallotton, Butch and Arey	Oakland
Vallotton, Rainy D.	Umpqua
Vallotton, Shawn	Oakland
Vallotton, Thomas	Oakland
Veatch, Richard	Springfield
Wahlster, Mark David	Silverton
Woodcock, Dennis "Woody"	Nehalem

PA

Amor Jr., Miguel	Lancaster
Anderson, Gary D.	Spring Grove
Anderson, Tom	Manchester
Appleby, Robert	Shickshinny
Besedick, Frank E.	Ruffsdale
Candrella, Joe	Warminster
Chavar, Edward V.	Bethlehem
Clark, D.E. (Lucky)	Mineral Point
Corkum, Steve	Littlestown
D'Andrea, John	East Stroudsberg
Darby, Rick	Levittown
Evans, Ronald B.	Middleton
Frey Jr., W. Frederick	Milton
Goldberg, David	Blue Bell
Goodling, Rodney W.	York Springs
Gottschalk, Gregory J.	Carnegie
Heinz, John	Upper Black Eddy
Hudson, Rob	Northumberland
Janiga, Matthew A.	Hummelstown
Malloy, Joe	Freeland
Marlowe, Donald	Dover
Mensch, Larry C.	Milton
Milford, Brian A.	Knox
Miller, Rick	Rockwood
Moore, Ted	Elizabethtown
Morett, Donald	Lancaster
Navagato, Angelo	Camp Hill
Nealy, Bud	Stroudsburg
Neilson, J.	Wyalusing
Nott, Ron P.	Summerdale
Ogden, Bill	Avis
Ortega, Ben M.	Wyoming
Parker, J.E.	Clarion
Rupert, Bob	Clinton
Sass, Gary N.	Hermitage
Scimio, Bill	Spruce Creek
Sinclair, J.E.	Pittsburgh
Steigerwalt, Ken	Orangeville
Stroyan, Eric	Dalton
Valois, A. Daniel	Lehighton
Vaughan, Ian	Manheim
Whittaker, Robert E.	Mill Creek

Wilson, Jon J.	Johnstown

RI

Bardsley, Norman P.	Pawtucket
Burak, Chet	E Providence
Dickison, Scott S.	Portsmouth
McHenry, William James	Wyoming
Olszewski, Stephen	Coventry
Potter, Frank	Middletown
Williams, Jason L.	Wyoming
Wright, Richard S.	Carolina

SC

Barefoot, Joe W.	Liberty
Beatty, Gordon H.	Seneca
Branton, Robert	Awendaw
Campbell, Courtnay M.	Columbia
Cannady, Daniel L.	Allendale
Cox, Sam	Gaffney
Defreest, William G.	Barnwell
Denning, Geno	Gaston
Easler Jr., Russell O.	Woodruff
Fecas, Stephen J.	Anderson
Gainey, Hal	Greenwood
Gaston, Ron	Woodruff
George, Harry	Aiken
Gregory, Michael	Belton
Hendrix, Jerry	Clinton
Hendrix, Wayne	Allendale
Herron, George	Springfield
Kaufman, Scott	Anderson
Kay, J. Wallace	Liberty
Kessler, Ralph A.	Fountain Inn
Knight, Jason	Harleyville
Langley, Gene H.	Florence
Lewis, K.J.	Lugoff
Lutz, Greg	Greenwood
Majer, Mike	Hilton Head
Manley, David W.	Central
McManus, Danny	Taylors
Montjoy, Claude	Clinton
Odom, Vic	North
Page, Larry	Aiken
Parler, Thomas O.	Charleston
Peagler, Russ	Moncks Corner
Perry, Johnny	Spartanburg
Sears, Mick	Sumter
Thomas, Rocky	Moncks Corner
Tyser, Ross	Spartanburg
Whitmire, Earl T.	Rock Hill

SD

Boysen, Raymond A.	Rapid Ciy
Ferrier, Gregory K.	Rapid City
Sarvis, Randall J.	Fort Pierre
Thomsen, Loyd W.	Oelrichs

TN

Bailey, Joseph D.	Nashville
Baker, Vance	Riceville
Breed, Kim	Clarksville
Byrd, Wesley L.	Evensville
Canter, Ronald E.	Jackson
Casteel, Dianna	Monteagle
Casteel, Douglas	Monteagle
Centofante, Frank	Madisonville
Claiborne, Ron	Knox
Clay, Wayne	Pelham
Conley, Bob	Jonesboro
Coogan, Robert	Smithville
Copeland, George Steve	Alpine
Corby, Harold	Johnson City
Dickerson, Gordon S.	Hohenwald
Elder Jr., Perry B.	Clarksville

Ewing, John H.	Clinton
Harley, Larry W.	Bristol
Harley, Richard	Bristol
Heflin, Christopher M.	Nashville
Hurst, Jeff	Rutledge
Hutcheson, John	Chattanooga
Johnson, David A.	Pleasant Shade
Johnson, Ryan M.	Hixson
King, Herman	Millington
Levine, Bob	Tullahoma
Marshall, Stephen R.	Mt. Juliet
McCarty, Harry	Blaine
McDonald, W.J. "Jerry"	Germantown
McNeil, Jimmy	Memphis
Moulton, Dusty	Loudon
Raley, R. Wayne	Collierville
Ramey, Larry	Chapmansboro
Rollick, Walter D.	Maryville
Ryder, Ben M.	Copperhill
Sampson, Lynn	Jonesborough
Smith, Newman L.	Gatlinburg
Taylor, C. Gray	Fall Branch
Vanderford, Carl G.	Columbia
Walker, John W.	Bon Aqua
Ward, W.C.	Clinton
Williams Jr., Richard	Morristown
Winter, George	Union City

TX

Adams, William D.	Burton
Alexander, Eugene	Ganado
Allen, Mike "Whiskers"	Malakoff
Ashby, Douglas	Dallas
Bailey, Kirby C.	Lytle
Barnes, Marlen R.	Atlanta
Barr, Judson C.	Irving
Batts, Keith	Hooks
Blasingame, Robert	Kilgore
Blum, Kenneth	Brenham
Boatright, Basel	New Braunfels
Bradshaw, Bailey	Diana
Bratcher, Brett	Plantersville
Brightwell, Mark	Leander
Broadwell, David	Wichita Falls
Brooks, Michael	Lubbock
Bullard, Randall	Canyon
Burden, James	Burkburnett
Cairnes Jr., Carroll B.	Palacios
Callahan, F. Terry	Boerne
Cannon, Dan	Dallas
Carpenter, Ronald W.	Jasper
Carter, Fred	Wichita Falls
Champion, Robert	Amarillo
Chase, John E.	Aledo
Churchman, T.W.	San Antonio
Cole, James M.	Bartonville
Connor, John W.	Odessa
Connor, Michael	Winters
Cosgrove, Charles G.	Arlington
Costa, Scott	Spicewood
Crain, Jack W.	Granbury
Darcey, Chester L.	College Station
Davidson, Larry	Cedar Hill
Davis, Vernon M.	Waco
Dean, Harvey J.	Rockdale
Dietz, Howard	New Braunfels
Dominy, Chuck	Colleyville
Dyer, David	Granbury
Edwards, Lynn	W. Columbia
Eldridge, Allan	Ft. Worth
Elishewitz, Allen	Canyon Lake
Epting, Richard	College Station
Eriksen, James Thorlief	Garland
Evans, Carlton	Aledo

Fant Jr., George	Atlanta	Roberts, Jack	Houston
Ferguson, Jim	San Angelo	Robinson, Charles (Dickie)	Vega
Fortune Products, Inc.,	Marble Falls	Rogers, Charles W.	Douglas
Foster, Al	Magnolia	Ruple, William H.	Charlotte
Foster, Norvell C.	San Antonio	Ruth, Michael G	Texarkana
Fowler, Jerry	Hutto	Scott, Al	Harper
Fritz, Jesse	Slaton	Self, Ernie	Dripping Springs
Fuller, Bruce A.	Baytown	Shipley, Steven A.	Richardson
Garner, Larry W.	Tyler	Sims, Bob	Meridian
Gault, Clay	Lexington	Sloan, Shane	Newcastle
Goytia, Enrique	El Paso	Smart, Steve	McKinney
Graham, Gordon	New Boston	Stokes, Ed	Hockley
Green, Bill	Garland	Stone, Jerry	Lytle
Griffin, Rendon and Mark	Houston	Stout, Johnny	New Braunfels
Hamlet Jr., Johnny	Clute	Theis, Terry	Harper
Hand, Bill	Spearman	Thuesen, Ed	Damon
Hawkins, Buddy	Texarkana	Treiber, Leon	Ingram
Hayes, Scotty	Tesarkana	Turcotte, Larry	Pampa
Haynes, Jerry	San Antonio	Watson, Daniel	Driftwood
Hays, Mark	Austin	Watt III, Freddie	Big Spring
Hearn, Terry L.	Lufkin	Watts, Johnathan	Gatesville
Hemperley, Glen	Willis	Watts, Wally	Gatesville
Hesser, David	Dripping Springs	West, Pat	Charlotte
House, Lawrence	Canyon Lake	White, Dale	Sweetwater
Howell, Jason G.	Lake Jackson	Whitley, Weldon G.	Odessa
Howell, Robert L.	Kilgore	Wilcher, Wendell L.	Palestine
Hudson, Robert	Humble	Wilkins, Mitchell	Montgomery
Hughes, Bill	Texarkana	Wolf Jr., William Lynn	Lagrange
Hughes, Lawrence	Plainview	Wood, William W.	Seymour
Jackson, Charlton R.	San Antonio	Woodard, Wiley	Colleyville
Jaksik Jr., Michael	Fredericksburg	Woodward, Wiley	Colleyville
Johnson, Gorden W.	Houston	Yeates, Joe A.	Spring
Johnson, Ruffin	Houston	Zboril, Terry	Caldwell
Kerby, Marlin W.	Brashear		
Kern, R. W.	San Antonio	**UT**	
Kious, Joe	Kerrville	Allred, Bruce F.	Layton
Knipstein, R.C. (Joe)	Arlington	Baum, Rick	Lehi
Ladd, Jim S.	Deer Park	Black, Earl	Salt Lake City
Ladd, Jimmie Lee	Deer Park	Ence, Jim	Richfield
Lambert, Jarrell D.	Granado	Ennis, Ray	Ogden
Laplante, Brett	McKinney	Erickson, L.M.	Liberty
Lay, L.J.	Burkburnett	Hunter, Hyrum	Aurora
Leblanc, John	Winnsboro	Johnson, Steven R.	Manti
Lemcke, Jim L.	Houston	Maxfield, Lynn	Layton
Lister Jr., Weldon E.	Boerne	Nielson, Jeff V.	Monroe
Locke, Keith	Watauga	Nunn, Gregory	Castle Valley
Love, Ed	San Antonio	Palmer, Taylor	Blanding
Luchak, Bob	Channelview	Peterson, Chris	Salina
Luckett, Bill	Weatherford	Rapp, Steven J.	Midvale
Marshall, Glenn	Mason	Strickland, Dale	Monroe
Martin, Michael W.	Beckville	Velarde, Ricardo	Park City
McConnell Jr., Loyd A.	Odessa	Warenski, Buster	Richfield
Mellard, J. R.	Houston	Winn, Travis A.	Salt Lake City
Merz III, Robert L.	Katy		
Miller, R.D.	Dallas	**VA**	
Mitchell, Wm. Dean	Warren	Apelt, Stacy E.	Norfolk
Moore, James B.	Ft. Stockton	Arbuckle, James M.	Yorktown
Neely, Greg	Bellaire	Ballew, Dale	Bowling Green
Nelson, Dr. Carl	Texarkana	Batley, Mark S.	Wake
Obrien, George	Katy	Batson, Richard G.	Rixeyville
Odgen, Randy W.	Houston	Beverly II, Larry H.	Spotsylvania
Ogletree Jr., Ben R.	Livingston	Callahan, Errett	Lynchburg
Osborne, Warren	Waxahachie	Catoe, David R.	Norfolk
Overeynder, T.R.	Arlington	Chamberlain, Charles R.	Barren Springs
Ownby, John C.	Plano	Compton, William E.	Sterling
Pardue, Joe	Spurger	Conkey, Tom	Nokesville
Patterson, Pat	Barksdale	Davidson, Edmund	Goshen
Pierce, Randall	Arlington	Douglas, John J.	Lynch Station
Pollock, Wallace J.	Cedar Park	Foster, Burt	Bristol
Polzien, Don	Lubbock	Frazier, Ron	Powhatan
Powell, James	Texarkana	Harris, Cass	Bluemont
Pugh, Jim	Azle	Hawk, Jack L.	Ceres
Ray, Alan W.	Lovelady	Hawk, Joey K.	Ceres
Richardson Jr., Percy	Hemphill	Hedrick, Don	Newport News

Hendricks, Samuel J.	Maurertown		
Holloway, Paul	Norfolk		
Jones, Barry M. and Phillip G.	Danville		
Jones, Enoch	Warrenton		
Kellogg, Brian R.	New Market		
McCoun, Mark	DeWitt		
Metheny, H.A. "Whitey"	Spotsylvania		
Murski, Ray	Reston		
Norfleet, Ross W.	Richmond		
Parks, Blane C.	Woodbridge		
Pawlowski, John R.	Newport News		
Richter, John C.	Chesapeake		
Ryan, C.O.	Yorktown		
Tomes, P.J.	Shipman		
Vanhoy, Ed and Tanya	Abingdon		
White, Gene E.	Alexandria		
Willson, Wayne O.	Fairfax		

VT

Haggerty, George S.	Jacksonville
Kelso, Jim	Worcester

WA

Amoureux, A.W.	Northport
Baldwin, Phillip	Snohomish
Begg, Todd M.	Spanaway
Ber, Dave	San Juan Island
Berglin, Bruce D.	Mount Vernon
Bloomquist, R. Gordon	Olympia
Boguszewski, Phil	Lakewood
Boyer, Mark	Bothell
Bromley, Peter	Spokane
Brothers, Robert L.	Colville
Brown, Dennis G.	Shoreline
Brunckhorst, Lyle	Bothell
Bump, Bruce D.	Walla Walla
Butler, John R.	Shoreline
Chamberlain, John B.	Wenatchee
Chamberlain, Jon A.	E. Wenatchee
Conti, Jeffrey D.	Port Orchard
Crain, Frank	Spokane
Crossman, Daniel C.	Blakely Island
Crowthers, Mark F.	Rolling Bay
D'Angelo, Laurence	Vancouver
Davis, John	Selah
Diskin, Matt	Freeland
Dole, Roger	Buckley
Ferry, Tom	Auburn
Frey, Steve	Snohomish
Gallagher, Sean	Monroe
Goertz, Paul S.	Renton
Gray, Bob	Spokane
Greenfield, G.O.	Everett
Hansen, Lonnie	Spanaway
Higgins, J.P. Dr.	Coupeville
House, Gary	Ephrata
Hurst, Cole	E. Wenatchee
Mosser, Gary E.	Kirkland
O'Malley, Daniel	Seattle
Sanderson, Ray	Yakima
Schempp, Ed	Ephrata
Schempp, Martin	Ephrata
Schirmer, Mike	Rosalia
Smith, D. Noel	Poulsbo
Stegner, Wilbur G.	Rochester
Swyhart, Art	Klickitat
Wright, Kevin	Quilcene

WI

Bostwick, Chris T.	Burlington
Brandsey, Edward P.	Milton
Bruner Jr., Fred, Bruner Blades	Fall Creek
Delarosa, Jim	Mukwonago
Fiorini, Bill	DeSoto

Garrity, Timothy P.	Waukesha
Genske, Jay	Fond du Lac
Haines, Jeff,	Wauzeka
Haines Custom Knives	
Hembrook, Ron	Neosho
Johnson, Richard	Germantown
Kanter, Michael	New Berlin
Kohls, Jerry	Princeton
Kolitz, Robert	Beaver Dam
Lary, Ed	Mosinee
Lerch, Matthew	Sussex
Maestri, Peter A.	Spring Green
Martin, Peter	Waterford
Millard, Fred G.	Richland Center
Nelson, Ken	Pittsville
Niemuth, Troy	Sheboygan
Ponzio, Doug	Pleasant Prairie
R. Boyes Knives,	Menomonee Falls
Revishvili, Zaza	Madison
Ricke, Dave	West Bend
Rochford, Michael R.	Dresser
Schrap, Robert G.	Wauwatosa
Wattelet, Michael A.	Minocqua

WV

Bowen, Tilton	Baker
Carnahan, Charles A.	Green Spring
Dent, Douglas M.	S. Charleston
Derr, Herbert	St. Albans
Drost, Jason D.	French Creek
Drost, Michael B.	French Creek
Elliott, Jerry	Charleston
Jeffries, Robert W.	Red House
Liegey, Kenneth R.	Millwood
Maynard, Larry Joe	Crab Orchard
McConnell, Charles R.	Wellsburg
Morris, Eric	Beckley
Pickens, Selbert	Liberty
Reynolds, Dave	Harrisville
Shaver II, James R.	Parkersburg
Sigman, Corbet R.	Liberty
Small, Ed	Keyser
Straight, Don	Points
Tokar, Daniel	Shepherdstown
Wilson, R.W.	Weirton
Wyatt, William R.	Rainelle

WY

Alexander, Darrel	Ten Sleep
Ankrom, W.E.	Cody
Archer, Ray and Terri	Medicine Bow
Banks, David L.	Riverton
Bartlow, John	Sheridan
Bennett, Brett C.	Cheyenne
Draper, Audra	Riverton
Draper, Mike	Riverton
Fowler, Ed A.	Riverton
Friedly, Dennis E.	Cody
Justice, Shane	Sheridan
Kilby, Keith	Cody
Kinkade, Jacob	Carpenter
Rexroat, Kirk	Wright
Reynolds, John C.	Gillette
Ross, Stephen	Evanston
Walker, George A.	Alpine

ARGENTINA

Ayarragaray, Cristian L.	(3100)
	Parana-Entre Rios
Bertolami, Juan Carlos	Neuquen
Gibert, Pedro	San Rafael Mendoza
Kehiayan, Alfredo	CP B1623GXU
	Buenos Aires
Rho, Nestor Lorenzo	Buenos Aires

AUSTRALIA

Bennett, Peter	Engadine N.S.W. 2233
Crawley, Bruce R.	Croydon 3136 Victoria
Cross, Robert	Tamworth 2340
Del Raso, Peter	Mt. Waverly,
	Victoria, 3149
Gerus, Gerry	Qld. 4870
Giljevic, Branko	N.S.W.
Green, William (Bill)	View Bank Vic.
Harvey, Max	Perth 6155
Husiak, Myron	Victoria
Jones, John	Manly West, QLD 4179
K B S, Knives	Vic 3450
Maisey, Alan	Vincentia 2540
Rowe, Stewart G.	Brisbane 4306
Tasman, Kerley	Western Australia
Zemitis, Joe	2285 Newcastle

BELGIUM

Dox, Jan	B 2900 Schoten
Monteiro, Victor	1360 Maleves Ste Marie

BRAZIL

Bodolay, Antal	Belo Horizonte
	MG-31730-700
Bossaerts, Carl	14051-110,
	Ribeirao Preto
Campos, Ivan	Tatui, SP
Dorneles, Luciano	Nova Petropolis, RS
	Oliverira
Gaeta, Angelo	SP-17201-310
Gaeta, Roberto	05351 Sao Paulo
Garcia, Mario Eiras	Sao Paulo
	SP-05516-070
Ikoma, Flavio Yuji,	108 SP-19031-220
R. Manoel, R. Teixeira	
Lala, Paulo Ricardo P.	SP-19031-260
and Lala, Roberto P.	
Neto Jr., Nelson and	SP-12900-000
De Carvalho, Henrique M.	
Paulo, Fernandes R.	Sao Paulo
Petean, Francisco	SP-16200-000
and Mauricio	
Ricardo Romano, Bernardes	Itajuba MG
Rosa, Pedro Gullherme	SP-19065-410
Teles	
Sfreddo, Rodrito	Nova Petropolis,
Menezes	RS
Villa, Luiz	Sao Paulo, SP-04537-081
Villar, Ricardo	S.P. 07600-000
Vilar, Ricardo Augusto	Mairipora
Ferreira	Sao Paulo
Zakharov, Carlos	SP-12305-340

CANADA

Arnold, Joe	London, Ont.
Beauchamp, Gaetan	Stoneham, PQ
Beets, Marty	Williams Lake, BC
Bell, Donald	Bedford, Nova Scotia
Berg, Lothar	Kitchener, Ont.
Beshara, Brent	Stayner, Ont.
Bold, Stu	Sarnia, Ont.
Boos, Ralph	Edmonton, Alberta
Bourbeau, Jean Yves	Ile Perrot, Quebec
Bradford, Garrick	Kitchener, Ont.
Dallyn, Kelly	Calgary, AB
Debraga, Jose C.	Aux Lievres, Quebec
Deringer, Christoph	Cookshire, Quebec
Diotte, Jeff	LaSalle, Ontario
Doiron, Donald	Messines, PQ
Doussot, Laurent	Montreal, Quebec
Downie, James T.	Port Franks, Ont.
Dublin, Dennis	Enderby, BC
Freeman, John	Cambridge, Ont.

Frigault, Rick	Niagara Falls, Ont.
Garvock, Mark W.	Balderson, Ontario
Gilbert, Chantal	Quebec City, Quebec
Harildstad, Matt	Edmonton, AB
Haslinger, Thomas	Calgary, AB
Hayes, Wally	Orleans, Ont.
Hofer, Louis	Rose Prairie, BC
Hoffmann, Uwe H.	Vancouver, BC
Jobin, Jacques	Levis Quebec
Kaczor, Tom	Upper London, Ont.
Lay, R.J.(Bob)	Falkland, BC
Leber, Heinz	Hudson's Hope, BC
Lightfoot, Greg	Kitscoty, AB
Linklater, Steve	Aurora, Ont.
Loerchner, Wolfgang	Bayfield, Ont.
Lyttle, Brian	High River, AB
Maneker, Kenneth	Galiano Island, BC
Martin, Robb	Elmira, Ontario
Marzitelli, Peter	Langley, BC
Massey, Al	Mount Uniacke, Nova Scotia
McKenzie, David Brian	Campbell River
Miville-Deschenes, Alain	Parent, QC
O'Hare, Sean	Fort Simpson, NT
Olson, Rod	High River, AB
Patrick, Bob	S. Surrey, BC
Pepiot, Stephan	Winnipeg, Man.
Piesner, Dean	St. Clements, Ont.
Pugh, Vernon	Saskatoon, SK
Roberts, George A.	Whitehorse, YT
Ross, Tim	Thunder Bay, Ont.
Schoenfeld, Matthew A.	Galiano Island,
	BC
St. Amour, Murray	Pembroke, Ont.
Stancer, Chuck	Calgary, AB
Storch, Ed	Alberta
Stuart, Steve	Gores Landing, Ont.
Tichbourne, George	Mississauga, Ont.
Tighe, Brian	Ridgeville, Ont.
Toner, Roger	Pickering, Ont.
Treml, Glenn	Thunder Bay, Ont.
Trudel, Paul	Ottawa, Ont.
Whitenect, Jody	Nova Scotia
Wile, Peter	Bridgewater, Nova Scotia
Young, Bud	Port Hardy, BC

DENMARK

Andersen, Henrik Lefolii	3480,
	Fredensborg
Anso, Jens	116, 8472 Sporup
Carlsson, Marc Bjorn	4000 Roskilde
Dyrnoe, Per	DK 3400 Hilleroed
Henriksen, Hans J.	DK 3200 Helsinge
Strande, Poul	Dastrup 4130 Viby Sj.
Vensild, Henrik	DK-8963 Auning

FRANCE

Bennica, Charles	34190 Moules
	et Baucels
Bertholus, Bernard	Antibes
Chauzy, Alain	21140 Seur-en-Auxios
Doursin, Gerard	Pernes les Fontaines
Ganster, Jean-Pierre	F-67000 Strasbourg
Graveline, Pascal	29350
and Isabelle	Moelan-sur-Mer
Headrick, Gary	Juane Les Pins
Madrulli, Mme Joelle	Salon De Provence
Reverdy, Pierre	Romans
Thevenot, Jean-Paul	Dijon
Viallon, Henri	Thiers

GERMANY

Balbach, Markus	35789
	Weilmunster-Laubuseschbach/TS.
Becker, Franz	84533, Marktl/Inn

Boehlke, Guenter   56412 Grossholbach
Borger, Wolf   76676 Graben-Neudorf
Dell, Wolfgang   D-73277 Owen-Teck
Faust, Joachim   95497 Goldkronach
Fruhmann, Ludwig   84489 Burghausen
Greiss, Jockl   D 77773 Schenkenzell
Hehn, Richard Karl   55444 Dorrebach
Hennicke, Metallgestaltung   55578
    Wallertheim
Herbst, Peter   91207 Lauf a.d. Pegn.
Joehnk, Bernd   24148 Kiel
Kaluza, Werner   90441 Nurnberg
Kressler, D.F.   Odetzhausen
Neuhaeusler, Erwin   86179 Augsburg
Rankl, Christian   81476 Munchen
Rinkes, Siegfried   Markterlbach
Selzam, Frank   Bad Koenigshofen
Steinau, Jurgen   Berlin 0-1162
Tritz, Jean Jose   20255 Hamburg
Wimpff, Christian   70574 Stuttgart 70
Wirtz, Achim   D-52146
Zirbes, Richard   D-54526 Niederkail

GREECE

Filippou, Ioannis-Minas   Athens 17122

ISRAEL

Shadmot, Boaz   Arava

ITALY

Albericci, Emilio   24100, Bergamo
Ameri, Mauro   16010 Genova
Ballestra, Santino   18039 Ventimiglia (IM)
Bertuzzi, Ettore   24068 Seriate (Bergamo)
Bonassi, Franco   Pordenone 33170
Fogarizzu, Boiteddu   07016 Pattada
Giagu, Salvatore and   07016
    Deroma Maria Rosaria   Pattada (SS)
Pachi, Francesco   17046 Sassello (SV)
Puddu, Salvatore   Quartu s Elena (CA)
Scordia, Paolo   Roma
Simonella, Gianluigi   33085 Maniago
Toich, Nevio   Vincenza
Tschager, Reinhard   I-39100 Bolzano

JAPAN

Aida, Yoshihito   Itabashi-ku, Tokyo
    175-0094
Carter, Murray M.   Kumamoto
Ebisu, Hidesaku   Hiroshima City
Fujikawa, Shun   Osaka 597 0062
Fukuta, Tak   Seki-City, Gifu-Pref
Hara, Kouji   Gifu-Pref. 501-32
Hirayama, Harumi   Saitama
    Pref. 335-0001
Hiroto, Fujihara   Hiroshima
Isao, Ohbuchi   Fukuoka
Ishihara, Hank   Chiba Pref.
Kagawa, Koichi   Kanagawa
Kanda, Michio   Yamaguchi 7460033
Kanki, Iwao   Hydugo
Kansei, Matsuno   Gitu-city
Kato, Kiyoshi   Tokyo 152
Kato, Shinichi   Moriyama-ku,
    Nagoya, Aichi
Katsumaro, Shishido   Hiroshima
Kawasaki, Akihisa   Kobe
Keisuke, Gotoh   Ohita
Koyama, Captain   Nagoya City
    Bunshichi   453-0817
Mae, Takao   Toyonaka, Osaka
Makoto, Kunitomo   Hiroshima
Matsusaki, Takeshi   Nagasaki

Michinaka, Toshiaki   Tottori 680-0947
Micho, Kanda   Yamaguchi
Ryuichi, Kuki   Saitama
Sakakibara, Masaki   Tokyo 156-0054
Shikayama, Toshiaki   Saitama 342-0057
Sugihara, Keidoh   Osaka, F596-0042
Sugiyama, Eddy K.   Ohita
Takahashi, Kaoru   Kamoto Kumamoto
Takahashi, Masao   Gunma 371 0047
Terauchi, Toshiyuki   Fujita-Cho Gobo-Shi
Toshifumi, Kuramoto   Fukuoka
Uchida, Chimata   Kumamoto
Uekama, Nobuyuki   Tokyo
Wada, Yasutaka   Nara prefect 631-0044
Waters, Glenn   Hirosaki City 036-8183
Yoshihara, Yoshindo   Tokyo
Yoshikazu, Kamada   Tokushima
Yoshio, Maeda   Okayama

MEXICO

Scheurer, Alfredo E. Faes   C.P. 16010
Sunderland, Richard   Puerto Escondido,
    Oaxaca
Young, Cliff   San Miguel,
    De Allende, GTO

NETHERLANDS

Gatherwood   1851VE Heiloo
Van De Manakker, Thijs   5759 px
    Helenaveen
Van Den Elsen, Gert   5012 AJ Tilburg
Van Eldik, Frans   3632BT Loenen
Van Rijswijk, Aad   3132 AA Vlaardingen

NEW ZEALAND

Gerner, Thomas   Oxford
Pennington, C.A.   Kainga Christchurch
    8009
Reddiex, Bill   Palmerston North
Ross, D.L.   Dunedin
Sands, Scott   Christchurch 9

NORWAY

Bache-Wiig, Tom   Eivindvik
Jorgensen, Gerd   N-3262 Larvik
Momcilovic, Gunnar   Waipahu
Sellevold, Harald   N5834 Bergen
Vistnes, Tor

RUSSIA

Kharlamov, Yuri   300007

SAUDI ARABIA

Kadasah, Ahmed Bin   Jeddah 21441

SINGAPORE

Tay, Larry C-G.   Singapore 9145

SLOVAKIA

Bojtos, Arpa D.   98403 Lucenec
Pulis, Vladimir   96 701 Kremnica

SOUTH AFRICA

Baartman, George   Limpopo
Bauchop, Robert   Kwazulu-Natal 4278
Beukes, Tinus   Vereeniging 1939
Bezuidenhout, Buzz   Malvern,
    Queensburgh, Natal 4093
Boardman, Guy   New Germany 3619
Brown, Rob E.   Port Elizabeth
Burger, Fred   Kwa-Zulu Natal
De Villiers, Andre   Cascades 3202
    and Kirsten

Dickerson, Gavin   Petit 1512
Fellows, Mike   Velddrie 7365
Grey, Piet   Naboomspruit 0560
Harvey, Heather   Belfast 1100
Harvey, Kevin   Belfast 1100
Horn, Des   7700 Cape Town
Kojetin, W.   Germiston 1401
Lagrange, Fanie   Table View 7441
Lancaster, C.G.   Free State
Liebenberg, Andre   Bordeauxrandburg
    2196
Mackrill, Stephen   Johannesburg
Mahomedy, A. R.   Marble Ray KZN,
    4035
Nelson, Tom   Gauteng
Pienaar, Conrad   Bloemfontein 9300
Rietveld, Bertie   Magaliesburg 1791
Russell, Mick   Port Elizabeth 6070
Schoeman, Corrie   Danhof 9310
Shoebotham, Heather   Belfast 1100
Theuns Prinsloo Knives   Bethlehem,
    9700
Watson, Peter   La Hoff 2570

SWEDEN

Bergh, Roger   12051 Arsta
Billgren, Per
Eklund, Maihkel   S-820 41 Farila
Embretsen, Kaj   S-82821 Edsbyn
Hogstrom, Anders T.
Johansson, Anders   S-772 40
    Grangesberg
Lundstrom, Jan-Ake   66010 Dals-Langed
Nilsson, Johnny Walker
Nordell, Ingemar   82041 Färila
Persson, Conny   820 50 Loos
Ryberg, Gote   S-562 00 Norrahammar
Vogt, Patrik   S-30270 Halmstad

SWITZERLAND

Gagstaetter, Peter   9306 Freidorf TG
Roulin, Charles   1233 Geneva
Soppera, Arthur   CH-9631 Ulisbach

UNITED KINGDOM

Boden, Harry   Derbyshire DE4 2AJ
Elliott, Marcus   Llandudno Gwynedd
Farid R., Mehr   Kent
Hague, Geoff   Wilton Marlborough,
    Wiltshire
Harrington, Roger   East Sussex
Heasman, H.G.   Llandudno
Horne, Grace   Sheffield Britian
Jackson, Jim   Chapel Row
    Bucklebury RG7 6PU
Jones, Charles Anthony   No. Devon
    E31 4AL
Lamprey, Mike   Devon EX38 7BX
Maxen, Mick   "Hatfield, Herts"
Morris, Darrell Price   Devon
Penfold, Mick   Tremar,
    Cornwall PL14 5SJ
Wardell, Mick   N Devon EX39 3BU
Wise, Donald   East Sussex TN3 8AL
Wood, Alan   Brampton CA8 7HH

URUGUAY

Gonzalez, Leonardo Williams   CP 20000
Symonds, Alberto E.   Montevideo 11300

ZIMBABWE

Burger, Pon   Bulawayo

Not all knifemakers are organization-types, but those listed here are in good standing with these organizations.

the knifemakers' guild

2004 voting membership

a Les Adams, Yoshihito Aida, Mike "Whiskers" Allen, Michael Anderson, W.E. Ankrom, Joe Arnold, Boyd Ashworth, Dick Atkinson

b Joseph D. Bailey, Santino Ballestra, Norman Bardsley, Van Barnett, A.T. Barr, James J. Barry III, John Bartlow, Gene Baskett, James Batson, Gaetan Beauchamp, Norman Beckett, Raymond Beers, Charlie Bennica, Tom Black, Andrew Blackton, Gary Blanchard, Alan T. Bloomer, Arpad Bojtos, Phillip Booth, Wolf Borger, Tony Bose, Dennis Bradley, Edward Brandsey, W. Lowell Bray Jr., Clint Breshears, Tim Britton, David Broadwell, David Brown, Harold Brown, Rick Browne, Jimmie Buckner, R.D. "Dan" Burke, John Busfield

c Bill Caldwell, Errett Callahan, Ron Cameron, Daniel Cannady, Ronald Canter, Robert Capdepon, Harold J. "Kit" Carson, Fred Carter, Dianna Casteel, Douglas Casteel, Frank Centofante, Jeffrey Chaffee, Joel Chamblin, William Chapo, Alex Chase, Edward Chavar, William Cheatham, Howard F. Clark, Wayne Clay, Lowell Cobb, Keith Coleman, Vernon Coleman, Blackie Collins, Bob Conley, Gerald Corbit, Harold Corby, Joe Cordova, Jim Corrado, George Cousino, Raymond Cover, Colin Cox, Pat & Wes Crawford, Dan Cruze, Roy Cutchin

d George E. Dailey, Charles M. Dake, Alex Daniels, Jack Davenport, Edmund Davidson, Barry Davis, Terry A. Davis, Vernon M. Davis, W.C. Davis, Harvey Dean, Robert DeFeo, Dellana, Dan Dennehy, Herbert Derr, Howard Dietz, William Dietzel, Robert Dill, Frank Dilluvio, Allen Dippold, David Dodds, T.M. Dowell, Larry Downing, Tom Downing, Bob Dozier, Bill Duff, Melvin Dunn, Steve Dunn, Jerry Duran, Fred Durio, Dwayne Dushane

e Russell & Paula K. Easler, Rick Eaton, Allen Elishewitz, Jim Elliott, David Ellis, Kaj Embretsen, Ernest Emerson, Jim Ence, Virgil England, William Engle, James T. Eriksen

f Howard Faucheaux, Stephen Fecas, Lee Ferguson, Bill Fiorini, Jay Fisher, Jerry Fisk, Joe Flournoy, Pete Forthofer, Paul Fox, Derek Fraley, Henry Frank, Michael H. Franklin, Ron Frazier, Aaron Frederick, Ralph Freer, Dennis Friedly, Daniel Fronefield, Larry Fuegen, Shun Fujikawa, Stanley Fujisaka, Tak Fukuta, Bruce Fuller, Shiro Furukawa

g Frank Gamble, Roger Gamble, William O. Garner Jr., Ron Gaston, Clay Gault, James "Hoot" Gibson Sr., Warren Glover, Stefan Gobec, Bruce Goers, David Goldberg, Warren Goltz, Greg Gottschalk, Roger M. Green, Jockl Greiss, Carol Gurganus, Melvin Gurganus, Kenneth Guth

h Philip L. "Doc" Hagen, Geoffrey Hague, Ed Halligan & Son, Tomonori Hamada, Jim Hammond, James E. Hand, M.D., Shaun Hansen, Kouji Hara, J.A. Harkins, Larry Harley, Ralph D. Harris, Rade Hawkins, Richard Hehn, Henry Heitler, Earl Jay Hendrickson, Wayne Hendrix, Wayne G. Hensley, Peter Herbst, Tim Herman, George Herron, Don Hethcoat, Gil Hibben, Howard Hill, Steve E. Hill, R. Hinson & Son, Harumi Hirayama, Howard Hitchmough, Steve Hoel, Kevin Hoffman, D'Alton Holder, Jess Horn, Jerry Hossum, Durvyn Howard, Jeff Howlett, Daryle Hughes, Roy Humenick, Joel Humphreys, Gerald Hurst, Joseph Hytovick

i Billy Mace Imel, Michael Irie

j Jason Jacks, Jim Jacks, Paul Jarvis, John Jensen, Steve Jernigan, Tom Johanning, Brad Johnson, Ronald Johnson, Ruffin Johnson, Steven R. Johnson, W.C. Johnson, Enoch D. Jones, Robert Jones

k Edward N. Kalfayan, William Keeton, Bill Keller, Bill Kennedy Jr., Jot Singh Khalsa, Bill King, Russell Klingbeil, Terry Knipschield, R.C. Knipstein, Mick Koval, Roy W. Krause, D.F. Kressler, John Kubasek

l Ron Lake, Ken Largin, Kermit Laurent, Mike Leach, William Letcher, Matthew J. Lerch, Bill Levengood, Yakov Levin, Bob Levine, Tom Lewis, Greg Lightfoot, Steve Linklater, Wolfgang Loerchner, Juan A. Lonewolf, R.W. Loveless, Schuyler Lovestrand, Don Lozier, Robert Lum, Larry Lunn, Ernest Lyle

m Joe Malloy, Dan Maragni, Peter Martin, Randall J. Martin, Roger Massey, Charles McConnell, Loyd McConnell, Richard McDonald, Robert J. McDonald, W. J. McDonald, Ken McFall, Frank McGowan, Thomas McGuane, W.J. McHenry, Tommy McNabb, Kurt Meerdink, Mike Mercer, Ted Merchant, Robert L. Merz III, Toshiaki Michinaka, James P. Miller, Steve Miller, Louis Mills, Dan Mink, Jim Minnick, Gunnar Momcilovic, Sidney "Pete" Moon, James B. Moore, Jeff Morgan, C.H. Morris, Dusty Moulton

n Bud Nealy, Corbin Newcomb, Larry Newton, Ron Newton, R.D. & Steve Nolen, Ingemar Nordell, Ross Norfleet, Rick Nowland

o Charles Ochs, Ben R. Ogletree Jr., Raymond Frank Oldham, Warren Osborne, T.R. Overeynder, John Owens

p Francesco Pachi, Larry Page, Robert Papp, Joseph Pardue, Melvin Pardue, Robert Patton, W.D. Pease, Alfred Pendray, John L. Perry, Eldon Peterson, Kenneth Pfeiffer, Daniel Piergallini, David Pitt, Leon & Tracy Pittman, Al Polkowski, Joe Prince, Jim Pugh, Morris Pulliam

r Jerry Rados, James D. Ragsdale, Steven Rapp, Chris Reeve, John Reynolds, Ron Richard, David Ricke, Bertie Rietveld, Willie Rigney, Dean Roath, Howard Robbins, Rex Robinson III, Fred Roe, Richard Rogers, Charles Roulin, Ron Russ, A.G. Russell

s Masaki Sakakibara, Mike Sakmar, Hiroyuki Sakurai, John Salley, Scott Sawby, Michael Schirmer, Maurice & Alan Schrock, Mark C. Sentz, Yoshinori Seto, Eugene W. Shadley, John I. Shore, Bill Simons, R.J. Sims, Cleston Sinyard, Jim Siska, Fred Slee, Scott Slobodian, J.D. Smith, John W. Smith, Michael J. Smith, Ralph Smith, Jerry Snell, Marvin Solomon, Arthur Soppera, Jim Sornberger, Ken Steigerwalt, Jurgen Steinau, Daniel Stephan, Murray Sterling, Barry B. Stevens, Johnny

Stout, Keidoh Sugihara, Arthur L. Summers, Russ Sutton, Charles Syslo, Joseph Szilaski

t Grant Tally, Robert Terzuola, Leon Thompson, Brian Tighe, P.J. Tomes, Dan Tompkins, John E. Toner, Bobby L. Toole, Dwight Towell, Leon Treiber, Barry Trindle, Reinhard Tschager, Jim Turecek, Ralph Turnbull

v Michael Vagnino, Frans Van Eldik, Edward T. Van Hoy, Aad Van Rijswijk, Michael Veit, Ricardo Velarde, Howard Viele, Donald Vogt

w James Walker, John W. Walker, George Walker, Michael Walker, Charles S. Ward, Tommy Ware, Buster

Warenski, Daniel Warren, Dale Warther, Thomas J. Watson, Charles Weeber, John S. Weever, Reese Weiland, Robert Weinstock, Charles L. Weiss, Weldon Whitley, Wayne Whittaker, Donnie R. Wicker, R.W. Wilson, Daniel Winkler, Earl Witsaman, Frank Wojtinowski, William Wolf, Owen Wood, Webster Wood, Tim Wright

y Joe Yeates, Yoshindo Yoshihara, George Young, Mike Yurco

z Brad Zinker

american bladesmith society

a Robin E. Ackerson, Lonnie Adams, Kyle A. Addison, Charles L. Adkins, Anthony "Tony" Aiken, Yoichiro Akahori, Douglas A. Alcorn, David Alexander, Mike Alexander, Eugene Alexander, Daniel Allison, Chris Amos, David Anders, Jerome Anders, Gary D. Anderson, Ronnie A. Andress Sr, E. R. (Russ) Andrews II, James M Arbuckle, Doug Asay, Boyd Ashworth, Ron Austin

b David R. Bacon, Robert Keith Bagley, Marion Bagwell, Brent Bailey, Larry Bailey, Bruce Baker, David Baker, Stephen A. Baker, Randall Baltimore, Dwayne Bandy, Mark D. Banfield, David L. Banks, Robert G. Barker, Reggie Barker, Aubrey G. Barnes Sr., Cecil C. Barnes Jr., Gary Barnes, Marlen R. Barnes, Van Barnett Barnett International, Judson C. Barr, Nyla Barrett, Rick L. Barrett, Michael Barton, Hugh E. Bartrug, Paul C. Basch, Nat Bassett, James L. Batson, R. Keith Batts, Michael R. Bauer, Rick Baum, Dale Baxter, Geneo Beasley, Jim Beaty, Robert B. Beaty, Steve Becker, Bill Behnke, Don Bell, John Bendik, Robert O. Benfield Jr., George Benjamin Jr., Brett Bennett, Rae Bennett, Bruce D. Berglin, Brent Beshara, Chris Bethke, Lora Sue Bethke, Gary Biggers, Ira Lee Birdwell, Hal Bish, William M. Bisher, Jason Bivens, Robert Bizzell, Scott Black, Randy Blair, Dennis Blankenheim, Robert Blasingame, R. Gordon Bloomquist, Josh Blount, Otto Bluntzer, David Bolton, David Boone, Roger E. Bost, Raymond A. Boysen, Bailey Bradshaw, Sanford (Sandy) Bragman, Martin W. Brandt, Robert Branton, Brett Bratcher, W. Lowell Bray Jr., Steven Brazeale, Charles D. Breme, Arthur Britton, Peter Bromley, Charles E. Brooks, Christopher Brown, Dennis G. Brown, Mark D. Brown, Rusty Brown, Troy L. Brown, Steven W. Browning, C. Lyle Brunckhorst, Aldo Bruno, Jimmie H. Buckner, Nick Bugliarello-Wondrich, Bruce D. Bump, Larry Bundrick, Bill Burke, Paul A. Burke, Stephen R. Burrows, John Butler, John R. Butler, Wesley L. Byrd

c Jerry (Buddy) Cabe, Sergio B. Cabrera, Ed Caffrey, Larry Cain, F. Terry Callahan, Robt W. Calvert Jr., Craig Camerer, Ron Cameron, Courtnay M. Campbell, Dan Cannon, Andrew B. Canoy, Jeff Carlisle, Chris Carlson, Eric R. Carlson, William Carnahan, Ronald W. Carpenter, James V. Carriger, Chad Carroll, George Carter, Murray M. Carter, Shayne Carter, Terry Cash, Kevin R. Cashen, P. Richard Chastain, Milton Choate, Jon Christensen, Howard F. Clark, Jim Clary, Joe Click, Russell Coats, Charles Cole, Frank Coleman, Wade Colter, Larry D. Coltrain, Roger N. Comar, Roger Combs, Wm. E. (Bill) Compton, Larry Connelley, John W. Connor, Michael Connor, Charles W. Cook, III, James R.

Cook, Robert Cook, James Roscoe Cooper, Jr., Ted Cooper, Joseph G. Cordova, David P. Corrigan, Dr. Timothy L. Costello, William Courtney, Collin Cousino, Gregory G. Covington, Monty L. Crain, Dawnavan M. Crawford, George Crews, Jim Crowell, Peter J. Crowl, Steve Culver, George Cummings, Kelly C. Cupples, John A. Czekala

d George E. Dailey, Mary H. Dake, B. MacGregor Daland, Kelly Dallyn, Sava Damlovac, Alex Daniels, David T. Darby, Chester L. Darcey, David Darpinian, Jim Davidson, Richard T. Davies, Barry Davis, John Davis, Patricia D. Davis, Dudley L. Dawkins, Michael de Gruchy, Angelo De Maria Jr., Harvey J. Dean, Anthony Del Giorno, Josse Delage, Clark B. DeLong, William Derby, Christoph Deringer, Dennis E. Des Jardins, Chuck Diebel, Bill Dietzel, Eric Dincauze, Jason Dingledine, Al Dippold, Matt Diskin, Michael Distin, Luciano Dorneles, Patrick J. Downey, Audra L. Draper, Mike Draper, Joseph D. Drouin, Paul Dubro, Ron Duncan, Calvin Duniphan, Rick Dunkerley, Steve Dunn, Eric Durbin, Kenneth Durham, Fred Durio, David Dyer

e Rick Eaton, Roger Echols, Mike Edelman, Thomas Eden, Gregory K. Edmonson, Randel Edmonson, Mitch Edwards, Lynn Edwards, Joe E. Eggleston, Daniel Robert Ehrenberger, Fred Eisen, Perry B. Elder Jr., Allen Elishewitz, R. Van Elkins, Rickie Ellington, Gordon Elliott, Carroll Ellis, Darren Ellis, Dave Ellis, Roger R. Elrod, Kaj Embretsen, Edward Engarto, Al Engelsman, Richard Epting, David Etchieson, Bruce E. Evans, Greg Evans, Ronald B. Evans, Vincent K. Evans, Wyman Ewing

f John E. Faltay, George Fant Jr., Daniel Farr, Alexander Felix, Gregory K. Ferrier, Robert Thomas Ferry III, Michael J. Filarski, Steve Filicietti, Ioannis-Minas Filippou, Jack Fincher, John Fincher, Ray Fincher, Perry Fink, Sean W. Finlayson, William Fiorini, Jerry Fisk, James O. Fister, John S. Fitch, Dawn Fitch, Mike Fletcher, Joe Flournoy, Charles Fogarty, Don Fogg, Stanley Fortenberry, Burt Foster, Edward K. Foster, Norvell C. Foster, Ronnie E. Foster, Timothy L. Foster, C. Ronnie Fowler, Ed Fowler, Jerry Fowler, Kevin Fox, Walter P. Framski, John M. Frankl, John R. Fraps, Aaron Frederick, Steve Freund, Steve Frey, Rolf Friberg, Rob Fritchen, Daniel Fronefield, Dewayne Frost, Larry D. Fuegen, Bruce A. Fuller, Jack A. Fuller, Richard Furrer

g Barry Gallagher, Jacques Gallant, Jesse Gambee, Tommy Gann, Tommy Gann, Rodney Gappelberg, Jim L. Gardner, Robert J. Gardner, Larry W. Garner, Mike Garner, Timothy P. Garrity, Mark W. Garvock, Bert

Gaston, Brett Gatlin, Darrell Geisler, Thomas Gerner, James Gibson, Fabio Giordani, Joel Gist, Kevin Gitlin, Gary Gloden, Wayne Goddard, Jim Gofourth, Scott K. Goguen, David Goldberg, Rodney W. Goodling, Tim Gordon, Thomas L. Gore, Gabe Gorenflo, James T. Gorenflo, Greg Gottschalk, Rayne Gough, Edward Graham, Paul J. Granger, Daniel Gray, Don Greenaway, Jerry Louis Grice, Michael S. Griffin, Larry Groth, Anthony R. Guarnera, Bruce Guidry, Christian Guier, Tom & Gwen Guinn, Garry Gunderson, Johan Gustafsson

h Cyrus Haghjoo, Ed Halligan, N. Pete Hamilton, Timothy J. Hancock, Bill Hand, Don L. Hanson III, Douglas E. Hardy, Larry Harley, Sewell C. Harlin, Paul W. Harm, Brent Harper-Murray, Cass Harris, Jeffrey A. Harris, Tedd Harris, Bill Hart, Sammy Harthman, Heather Harvey, Kevin Harvey, Robert Hatcher, Buddy Hawkins, Rade Hawkins, Rodney Hawkins, Wally Hayes, Charlie E. Haynes, Gary Headrick, Kelly Healy, Chad Heddin, Dion Hedges, Win Heger, Daniel Heiner, John Heinz, E. Jay Hendrickson, Bill Herndon, Harold Herron, Don Hethcoat, Jim B. Hill, John M. Hill, Amy Hinchman, Vance W. Hinds, Donald R. Hinton, Dan Hockensmith, Dr. Georg Hoellwarth, William G. Hoffman, Thomas R. Hogan, Troy Holland, Michael Honey, Un Pyo Hong, John F. Hood, John Horrigan, Robert M. Horrigan, Lawrence House, Gary House, Michael Houston, Jason G Howell, F. Charles Hubbard, Dale Huckabee, Gov. Mike Huckabee, C. Robbin Hudson, Anthony B. Hudson, Bill Hughes, Daryle Hughes, Tony Hughes, Brad Humelsine, Maurice Hunt, Raymon E. Hunt, Richard D. Hunter, K. Scott Hurst, William R. Hurt, David H. Hwang, Joe Hytovick

i Gary Iames, Hisayuki Ishida

j David Jackson, Jim L. Jackson, Chuck Jahnke, Jr., Karl H. Jakubik, Melvin Jennings Jr., John Lewis Jensen, Mel "Buz" Johns, David A. Johnson, John R. Johnson, Ray Johnson, Thomas Johnson, Clayton W. Johnston, Dr. Robt. Johnston, William Johnston, Chris E. Jones, Enoch Jones, Franklin W. Jones, John Jones, Roger W. Jones, William Burton Jones, Terry J. Jordan, Shane Justice

k Charles Kain, Al J. Kajin, Gus Kalanzis, Barry Kane, David Kazsuk, Jarod Kearney, Robert Keeler, Joseph F. Keeslar, Steven C. Keeslar, Jerry Keesling, Dale Kempf, Larry Kempf, R. W. Kern, Joe Kertzman, Lawrence Keyes, Charles M. Kilbourn, Jr., Keith Kilby, Nicholas Kimball, Richard L. Kimberley, Herman King, David R. King, Fred J. King, Harvey G. King Jr., Kenneth King, Frederick D. Kingery, Donald E. Kinkade, Ray Kirk, Todd Kirk, John Kish, Brad Kliensmid, Russell K. Klingbeil, Hank Knickmeyer, Kurt Knickmeyer, Jason Knight, Steven C. Koster, Bob Kramer, Lefty Kreh, Phil Kretsinger

l Simon Labonti, Jerry Lairson Sr., Curtis J. Lamb, J. D. Lambert, Robert M. Lamey, Leonard D. Landrum, Warren H. Lange, Paul Lansingh, Rodney Lappe, Kermit J. Laurent, Alton Lawrence, Randell Ledbetter, Denis H. LeFranc, Jim L. Lemcke, Jack H. Leverett Jr., Wayne Levin, Bernard Levine, Steve Lewis, Tom Lewis, John J. Lima, Lindy Lippert, Guy A. Little, Tim Lively, Keith Locke, Lowell C. Lockett, Anthony P. Lombardo, Phillip Long, Jonathan A. Loose, Eugene Loro, Jim Lott, Sherry Lott, Jim Lovelace, Ryan Lovell, Steven Lubecki, Bob Luchini, James R. Lucie, James R. Luman, William R. Lyons

m John Mackie, Madame Joelle Madrulli, Takao Mae, Mike Majer, Raymond J. Malaby, John Mallett, Bob Mancuso, Kenneth Mankel, Matt Manley, James Maples, Dan

Maragni, Ken Markley, J. Chris Marks, Stephen R. Marshall, Tony Martin, John Alexander Martin, Hal W. Martin, Alan R. Massey, Roger D. Massey, Mick Maxen, Lynn McBee, Daniel McBrearty, Howard H. McCallen Jr., Michael McClure, Sandy McClure, Frederick L. McCoy, Kevin McCrackin, Victor J. McCrackin, Richard McDonald, Robert J. McDonald, Robin J. McDonald, Frank McGowan, Donald McGrath, Patrick T. McGrath, Eric McHugh, Don McIntosh, Neil H. McKee, Tim McKeen, David Brian McKenzie, Hubert W. McLendon, Tommy McNabb, J. Michael McRae, David L. Meacham, Maxie Mehaffey, J. R. Mellard, Walter Merrin, Mardi Meshejian, Ged Messinger, D. Gregg Metheny, Dan Michaelis, Tracy Mickley, Gary Middleton, Bob Miller, Hanford J. Miller, Michael Mills, David Mirabile, Wm. Dean Mitchell, Jim Molinare, Michael Steven Moncus, Charlie Monroe, Keith Montgomery, Lynn Paul Moore, Marve Moore, Michael Robert Moore, Shawn Robert Moore, William F Moran Jr., Jim Moyer, Russell A. Moyer, James W. Mueller, Jody Muller, Deryk C. Munroe, Jim Mutchler, Ron Myers

n Ryuji Nagoaka, Evan Nappen, Maj. Kendall Nash, Angelo Navagato, Bob Neal, Darby Neaves, Gregory T. Neely, Thomas Conor Neely, James Neilson, Bill Nelson, Lars Nelson, Mark Nevling, Corbin Newcomb, Ron Newton, Tania Nezrick, John Nicoll, Marshall Noble, Douglas E. Noren, H.B. Norris, Paul T. Norris, William North, Vic Nowlan

o Charles F. Ochs III, Julia O'Day, Clyde O'Dell, Vic Odom, Michael O'Herron, Hiroaki Ohta, Michael E. Olive, Todd D. Oliver, Joe Olson, Kent Olson, Richard O'Neill, Robert J. O'Neill, Rich Orton, Philip D. Osattin, Donald H. Osborne, Warren Osborne, Fred Ott, Mac Overton, Donald Owens

p Anthony P. Palermo, Rik Palm, Paul Papich, Ralph Pardington, Cliff Parker, Earl Parker, John Parks, Jimmy D. Passmore, Rob Patton, Jerome Paul, Gary Payton, Michael Peck, Alfred Pendray, Christopher A. Pennington, Johnny Perry, John L. Perry, Conny Persson, Dan L. Petersen, Lloyd Pete C. Peterson, Dan Pfanenstiel, Jim Phillips, Benjamin P. Piccola, Ray Pieper III, Diane Pierce, Dean Piesner, Dietrich Podmajersky, Dietmar Pohl, Clifton Polk, Rusty Polk, Jon R. "Pop" Poplawski, Timothy Potier, Dwight Povistak, James Powell, Robert Clark Powell, Jake Powning, Houston Price, Terry Primos, Jeff Prough, Gerald Puckett, Martin Pullen

q Thomas C. Quakenbush

r Michael Rader, John R. Radford Jr., R. Wayne Raley, Darrel Ralph, Richard A. Ramsey, Gary Randall, James W. Randall Jr., David L. Randolph, Ralph Randow, Mike Reagan, George R. Rebello, Lee Reeves, Roland R. "Rollie" Remmel, Zaza Revishvili, Kirk Rexroat, Scott Reyburn, John Reynolds, Linden W. Rhea, Jim Rice, Stephen E. Rice, Alvin C. Richards Jr., James Richardson, David M. Rider, Richard A. Riepe, Dennis Riley, E. Ray Roberts, Jim Roberts, Don Robertson, Leo D. Robertson, Charles R. Robinson, Michael Rochford, James L. Rodebaugh, James R. Rodebaugh, Gary Rodewald, Charles W. Rogers, Richard Rogers, Willis "Joe" Romero, Frederick Rommel, Troy Ronning, N. Jack Ronzio, Steven Roos, Doun T. Rose, Robert Rosenfeld, Robert N. Rossdeutscher, George R. Roth, Charles Roulin, Kenny Rowe, Clark D. Rozas, Ronald S. Russ, Michael G. Ruth, Michael G. Ruth Jr., Brad Rutherford,

Tim Ryan, Wm. Mike Ryan, Raymond B. Rybar Jr., Gerald Rzewnicki

s David Sacks, William Sahli, Ken Sands, Paul Sarganis, Charles R. Sauer, James P. Saviano, Ed Schempp, Ellen Schilling, Tim Scholl, Robert Schrader, Stephen C. Schwarzer, James A. Scroggs, Bert Seale, Turner C. Seale, Jr., David D. Seaton, Steve Seib, Mark C. Sentz, Jimmy Seymour, Rodrigo Menezes Sfreddo, Steve Shackleford, Gary Shaw, James F. Shull, Robert Shyan-Norwalt, Ken Simmons, Brad Singley, Cleston S. Sinyard, Charles Russel Sisemore, Charles J. Smale, Charles Moran Smale, Carel Smith, Clifford Lee Smith, Corey Smith, J.D. Smith, Joshua J. Smith, Lenard C. Smith, Raymond L. Smith, Timothy E. Smock, Michael Tom Snyder, Max Soaper, John E. Soares, Arthur Soppera, Bill Sowell, Randy Spanjer Sr., David R. Sparling, H. Red St. Cyr, Chuck Stancer, Craig Steketee, Daniel Stephan, Tim Stevens, Edward L. Stewart, Rhett & Janie Stidham, Jason M. Stimps, Walter Stockwell, J.B. Stoner, Bob Stormer, Mike Stott, Charles Stout, John K. Stout Jr., Johnny L. Stout, Howard Stover, John Strohecker, Robert E. Stumphy Jr., Harlan Suedmeier, Wayne Suhrbier, Alan L. Sullivan, Fred Suran, Tony Swatton, John Switzer, John D. Switzer, Arthur Swyhart, Mark G. Szarek, Joseph Szilaski

t Scott Taylor, Shane Taylor, Danny O. Thayer, Jean-Paul Thevenot, Brian Thie, David E. Thomas, Devin Thomas, Guy Thomas, Scott Thomas, Hubert Thomason, Robert Thomason, Kinzea L. Thompson, Alan L. Tiensvold,

Jason Tiensvold, John Tilton, George Tindera, Dennis Tingle, Dennis P. Tingle, Brion Tomberlin, P. J. Tomes, Kathleen C. Tomey, Mark Torvinen, Lincoln Tracy, Joe E. Travieso III, James J. Treacy, Craig Triplett, Kenneth W Trisler, James Turpin, Ross Tyser

v Michael V. Vagnino, Jr,, Butch Vallotton, Steve Van Cleve, Jerry W. Van Eizenga, Terry L. Vandeventer, Robert Vardaman, Chris Vidito, Michael Viehman, Gustavo Colodetti Vilal, Ricardo Vilar, Mace Vitale, Patrik Vogt, Bruce Voyles

w Steve "Doc" Wacholz, Lawrence M. Wadler, Adam Waldon, Bill Walker, Don Walker, James L. Walker, Carl D. Ward, Jr., Ken Warner, Robert Lee Washburn Jr., Herman Harold Waters, Lu Waters, Robert Weber, Charles G. Weeber, Fred Weisenborn, Ronald Welling, Eddie Wells, Gary Wendell, Elsie Westlake, Jim Weyer, Nick Wheeler, Wesley Whipple, John Paul White, Lou White, Richard T. White, L. Wayne Whitley, Randy Whittaker, Timothy L. Wiggins, William Burton Wiggins, Jr., Scott Wiley, Dave Wilkes, Craig Wilkins, A. L. Williams, Charles E. Williams, Linda Williams, Michael L. Williams, Edward Wilson, George H. Wilson III, Jeff Wilson, Daniel Winkler, Randy Winsor, George Winter, Ronald E. Woodruff, Steve Woods, Bill Worthen, Terry Wright, Derrick Wulf

z Mark D. Zalesky, Kenneth Zarifes, Matthew Zboray, Terry Zboril, Karl Zimmerman

miniature knifemaker's society

Paul Abernathy, Joel Axenroth, Blade Magazine, Dennis Blaine, Gerald Bodner, Gary Bradburn, Brock Custom Knives, Ivan Campos, Mitzi Cater, Don Cowles, Creations Yvon Vachon, Dennis Cutburth, David Davis, Robert Davis, Gary Denms, Dennis Des Jardins, Eisenberg Jay Publishers, Allen Eldridge, Peter Flores, David Fusco, Eric Gillard, Wayne Goddard, Larah Gray, Gary Greyraven, Tom & Gwen Guinn, Karl Hallberg, Ralph Harris, Richard Heise, Laura Hessler, Wayne Hensley, Tom Hetmanski, Howard Hosick, Albert Izuka, Garry Kelley, Knife World Publishers, R F Koebbeman, Terry Kranning, Gary Lack, John LeBlanc, Mike Lee, Les Levinson, Jack Lewis, Mike Ley, Ken Liegey, Henry Loos, Jim Martin, Howard Maxwell, McMullen & Yee

Publishing, Ken McFall, Mal Mele, Paul Meyers, Toshiaki Michinaka, Allen G Miller, Wayne & June Morrison, Mullinnix & Co, National Knife Collectors Assoc., Allen Olsen, Charles Ostendorf, Mike Pazos, Jim Pear, Gordon Pivonka, Jim Pivonka, Prof. Knifemakers Assoc, Jim Pugh, Roy Quincy, John Rakusan, A D Rardon, Dawin Richards, Stephen Ricketts, Mark Rogers, Alex Rose, Hank Rummell, Helen Rummell, Sheffield Knifemakers Supply, Sporting Blades, Harry Stalter, Udo Stegemann, Mike Tamboli, Hank Rummell, Paul Wardian, Ken Warner, Michael Wattelet, Ken Wichard Jr. Charles Weiss, Jim Whitehead, Steve Witham, Shirley Whitt, G T Williams, Ron Wilson, Dennis Windmiller, Carol Winold, Earl Witsaman, James Woods

professional knifemaker's association

Mike "Whiskers" Allen, John Anthon, Ray Archer, Eddie Baca, Cecil Barret, John Bartlow, Paul Basch, Brett Bennett, Nico Bernard, Phillip Booth, Kenneth Brock, Craig Camerer, Tim Cameron, Rod Carter, Jeff Chaffee, Roger Craig, Bob Cumming, Dave Darpinian, Michael Donato, Mike Draper, Audra Draper, Ray Ennis, Jim Eriksen, Jack Feder, John Fraps, Bob Glassman, Sal Glesser, John Greco, Jim Griksen, John Harbuck, Marge Hartman, Mike Henry, Gary Hicks, Guy Hielscher, Howard Hitchmough, Terrill Hoffman, Robert Hunter, Mike Irie, Donald Jones, Jot Singh Khalsa, Harvey King, Jason King, Steve Kraft, Jim Largent, Jim Lemcke (Texas Knifemakers Supply), WSSI (Mike Ludeman), Jim

Magee, Daniel May, Jerry McClure, Mac McLaughlin, Larry McLaughlin, Clayton Miller, Mark Molnar, Ty Montell, Mike Mooney, NC Tool Company, Bill Noehren, Steve Nolen, Rick Nowland, Fred Ott, Dick Patton, Rob Patton, PKA, Pop Knives, Dennis Riley, Rocky Mountain Blade Collectors, Steve Rollert, Clint Sampson, Charles Sauer, Jerry Schroeder, Craig Steketee, Joe Stetter, Big Mike Taylor, Bob Terzuola, Loyd Thomsen, James Thrash, Ed Thuesen, Chuck Trice, Louis Vallet, Louis Vinquist, Bill Waldrup, Tommy Ware, David Wattenberg, Joe Wheeler, Dan Wittman, Owen Wood, Mike Zima, Daniel Zvonek

state/regional associations

alaska knifemakers association

A.W. Amoureux, John Arnold, Bud Aufdermauer, Robert Ball, J.D. Biggs, Lonnie Breuer, Tom Broome, Mark Bucholz, Irvin Campbell, Virgil Campbell, Raymond Cannon, Christopher Cawthorne, John Chamberlin, Bill Chatwood, George Cubic, Bob Cunningham, Gordon S. Dempsey, J.L. Devoll, James Dick, Art Dufour, Alan Eaker, Norm Grant, Gordon Grebe, Dave Highers, Alex Hunt, Dwight Jenkins, Hank Kubaiko, Bill Lance, Bob Levine, Michael Miller, John Palowski, Gordon Parrish, Mark W. Phillips, Frank Pratt, Guy Recknagle, Ron Robertson, Steve Robertson, Red Rowell, Dave Smith, Roger E. Smith, Gary R. Stafford, Keith Stegall, Wilbur Stegner, Norm Story, Robert D. Shaw, Thomas Trujillo, Ulys Whalen, Jim Whitman, Bob Willis

arizona knifemakers association

D. "Butch" Beaver, Bill Cheatham, Dan Dagget, Tom Edwards, Anthony Goddard, Steve Hoel, Ken McFall, Milford Oliver, Jerry Poletis, Merle Poteet, Mike Quinn, Elmer Sams, Jim Sornberger, Glen Stockton, Bruce Thompson, Sandy Tudor, Charles Weiss

arkansas knifemakers association

David Anders, Auston Baggs, Don Bailey, Reggie Barker, Marlen R. Barnes, Paul Charles Basch, Lora Sue Bethke, James Black, R.P. Black, Joel Bradford, Gary Braswell, Paul Brown, Shawn Brown, Troy L. Brown, Jim Butler, Buddy Cabe, Allen Conner, James Cook, Thom Copeland, Gary L. Crowder, Jim Crowell, David T Darby, Fred Duvall, Rodger Echols, David Etchieson, Lee Ferguson, Jerry Fisk, John Fitch, Joe & Gwen Flournoy, Dewayne Forrester, John Fortenbury, Ronnie Foster, Tim Foster, Emmet Gadberry, Larry Garner, Ed Gentis, Paul Giller, James T. Gilmore, Terry Glassco, D.R. (Rick) Gregg, Lynn Griffith, Arthur J. Gunn, Jr., David Gunnell, Morris Herring, Don "Possum" Hicks, Jim Howington, B. R. Hughes, Ray Kirk, Douglas Knight, Lile Handmade Knives, Jerry Lairson Sr., Claude Lambert, Alton Lawrence, Jim Lemcke, Michael H. Lewis, Willard Long, Dr. Jim Lucie, Hal W Martin, Tony Martin, Roger D. Massey, Douglas Mays, Howard McCallen Jr., Jerry McClure, John McKeehan, Joe McVay, Bart Messina, Thomas V. Militano, Jim Moore, Jody Muller, Greg Neely, Ron Newton, Douglas Noren, Keith Page, Jimmy Passmore, John Perry, Lloyd "Pete" Peterson, Cliff Polk, Terry Primos, Paul E Pyle Jr, Ted Quandt, Vernon Red, Tim Richardson, Dennis Riley, Terry Roberts, Charles R. Robinson, Kenny Rowe, Ken Sharp, Terry Shurtleff, Roy Slaughter, Joe D. Smith, Marvin Solomon, Hoy Spear, Charles Stout, Arthur Tycer, Ross Tyser, James Walker, Chuck Ward, Herman Waters, Bryce White, Tillmon T Whitley III, Mike Williams, Rick Wilson, Terry Wright, Ray Young

australian knifemakers guild inc.

Peter Bald, Wayne Barrett, Peter Bennett, Wayne Bennett, Wally Bidgood, David Brodziak, Neil Charity, Terry Cox, Bruce Crawley, Mark Crowley, Steve Dawson, Malcolm Day, Peter Del Raso, John Dennis, Michael Fechner, Steve Filicietti, Barry Gardner, Thomas Gerner, Branko Giljevic, Eric Gillard, Peter Gordon, Stephen Gregory-Jones, Ben Hall, Mal Hannan, Lloyd Harding, Rod Harris, Glen Henke, Michael Hunt, Robert Hunt, Myron Husiak, John Jones, Simeon Jurkijevic, Wolf Kahrau, Peter Kandavnieks, Peter Kenny, Tasman Kerley, John Kilby, Murrary Lanthois, Anthony Leroy, Greg Lyell, Paul Maffi, Maurice McCarthy, Shawn McIntyre, Ray Mende, Dave Myhill, Adam Parker, John

Pattison, Mike Petersen, Murray Shanaughan, Kurt Simmonds, Jim Steele, Rod Stines, David Strickland, Kelvin Thomas, Doug Timbs, Hardy Wangemann, Brendon Ware, Glen Waters, Bob Wilhelm, Joe Zemitis

california knifemakers association

Arnie Abegg, George J. Antinarelli, Elmer Art, Gregory Barnes, Mary Michael Barnes, Hunter Baskins, Gary Biggers, Roger Bost, Clint Breshears, Buzz Brooks, Steven E. Bunyea, Peter Carey, Joe Caswell, Frank Clay, Richard Clow, T.C. Collins, Richard Corbaley, Stephanie Engnath, Alex Felix, Jim Ferguson, Dave Flowers, Logwood Gion, Peter Gion, Joseph Girtner, Tony Gonzales, Russ Green, Tony Guarnera, Bruce Guidry, Dolores Hayes, Bill Herndon, Neal A. Hodges, Richard Hull, Jim Jacks, Lawrence Johnson, David Kazsuk, James P. Kelley, Richard D. Keyes, Michael P. Klein, Steven Koster, John Kray, Bud Lang, Tomas N. Lewis, R.W. Loveless, John Mackie, Thomas Markey, James K. Mattis, Toni S. Mattis, Patrick T. McGrath, Larry McLean, Jim Merritt, Greg Miller, Walt Modest, Russ Moody, Emil Morgan, Gerald Morgan, Mike Murphy, Thomas Orth, Tom Paar, Daniel Pearlman, Mel Peters, Barry Evan Posner, John Radovich, James L. Rodebaugh, Clark D. Rozas, Ron Ruppe, Brian Saffran, Red St. Cyr, James Stankovich, Bill Stroman, Tony Swatton, Gary Tamms, James P. Tarozon, Scott Taylor, Tru-Grit Inc., Tommy Voss, Jessie C. Ward, Wayne Watanabe, Charles Weiss, Steven A. Williams, Harlan M. Willson, Steve Wolf, Barry B. Wood

canadian knifemakers guild

Gaetan Beauchamp, Shawn Belanger, Don Bell, Brent Beshara, Dave Bolton, Conrad Bondu, Darren Chard, Garry Churchill, Guillaume J. Cote, Christoph Deringer, Jeff Diotte, Randy Doucette, Jim Downie, John Dorrell, Eric Elson, Lloyd Fairbairn, Paul-Aime Fortier, Rick Frigault, John Freeman, Mark Garvock, Brian Gilbert, Murray Haday, Tom Hart, Thomas Haslinger, Ian Hubel, Paul Johnston (London, Ont.), Paul Johnston (Smith Falls, Ont.), Jason Kilcup, Kirby Lambert, Greg Lightfoot, Jodi Link, Wolfgang Loerchner, Mel Long, Brian Lyttle, David Macdonald, Michael Mason, Alan Massey, Leigh Maulson, James McGowan, Edward McRae, Mike Mossington, Sean O'Hare, Rod Olson, Neil Ostroff, Ron Post, George Roberts, Brian Russell, Murray St. Armour, Michael Sheppard, Corey Smith, David Smith, Jerry Smith, Walt Stockdale, Matt Stocker, Ed Storch, Steve Stuart, George Tichbourne, Brian Tighe, Robert Tremblay, Glenn Treml, Steve Vanderkloff, James Wade, Bud Weston, Peter Wile

florida knifemaker's association

Dick Atkinson, Albert F. "Barney" Barnett, James J. Barry III, Howard Bishop, Andy Blackton, Stephen A. Bloom, Dean Bosworth, John Boyce, W. Lowell Bray Jr., Harold Brown, Douglas Buck, Dave Burns, Patrick Burris, Norman J. Caesar, Peter Channell, Mark Clark, Lowell Cobb, David Cole, Mark Condron, William (Bill) Corker, Ralph L. D'Elia, Jack Davenport, Kevin Davey, J.D. Davis, Kenny Davis, Bill Dietzel, Bob Doggett, William B. Douglas, John B. Durham, Jim Elliot, Tom M. Enos, Bob Ferring, Todd Fischer, Mike Fisher, Ricky Fowler, Mark Frank, Roger Gamble, Tony Garcia, John Gawrowski, James "Hoot" Gibson, Pedro Gonzalez, Ernie Grospitch, Pete Hamilton, Dewey Harris, Henry Heitler, David Helton, Phillip Holstein, John Hodge, Kevin Hoffman, Edward O. Holloway, Joel Humphreys, Joe Hytovick,

Tom Johanning, Raymond C. Johnson II, Paul S. Kent, Bill King, F.D. Kingery, Russ Klingbeil, John E. Klingensmith, William S. Letcher, Bill Levengood, Tim Logan, Glenn A. Long, Gail Lunn, Larry Lunn, Ernie Lyle, Bob Mancuso, Randy Mason, R.J. McDonald, Faustina Mead, Maxie Mehaffey, Dennis G. Meredith, Steve Miller, Dan Mink, Steven Morefield, Martin L. "Les" Murphy, Toby Nipper, Cliff Parker, L.D. (Larry) Patterson, James Perry, Dan Piergallini, Martin Prudente, Carlo Raineri, Ron Russ, Rusty Sauls, Dennis J. Savage, David Semones, Ann Sheffield, Brad Shepherd, Bill Simons, Stephen J. Smith, Kent Swicegood, Louis M. Vallet, Donald Vogt, Roger L. Wallace, Tom Watson, Andrew M. Wilson, Stan Wilson, Hugh E. Wright III, Brad Zinker

knifemakers' guild of southern africa

Jeff Angelo, George Baartman, Francois Basson, Rob Bauchop, George Beechey, Arno Bernard, Buzz Bezuidenhout, Chris Booysen, Ian Bottomley, Peet Bronkhorst, Rob Brown, Fred Burger, Sharon Burger, William Burger, Larry Connelly, Z. Andre de Beer, Andre de Villiers, Melodie de Witt, Gavin Dickerson, Roy H. Dunseith, Leigh Fogarty, Andrew Frankland, Ettore Gianferrari, Stan Gordon, Nick Grabe, John Grey, Piet Grey, Heather Harvey, Kevin Harvey, Dries Hattingh, Gawie Herbst, Thinus Herbst, Greg Hesslewood, Des Horn, Billy Kojetin, Mark Kretschmer, Fanie La Grange, Steven Lewis, Garry Lombard, Steve Lombard, Ken Madden, Edward Mitchell, Gunther Muller, Tom Nelson, Jan Olivier, Christo Ooosthuizen, Cedric Pannell, Willie Paulsen, Nico Pelzer, Conrad Pienaar, David Pienaar, Jan Potgieter, Lourens Prinsloo, Theuns Prinsloo, Hilton Purvis, Derek Rausch, Chris Reeve, Bertie Rietveld, Dean Riley, John Robertson, Corrie Schoeman, Eddie Scott, Mike Skellern, Toi Skellern, Carel Smith, Ken Smythe, Graham Sparks, Andre E. Thorburn, Fanie Van Der Linde, Johan van der Merwe, Van van der Merwe, Marius Van der Vyver, Louis Van der Walt, Cor Van Ellinkhuijzen, Danie Van Wyk, Ben Venter, Willie Venter, Gert Vermaak, Rene Vermeulen, Erich Vosloo, Desmond Waldeck, John Wilmot, Wollie Wolfaardt, Owen Wood

midwest knifemakers association

E.R. Andrews III, Frank Berlin, Charles Bolton, Tony Cates, Mike Chesterman, Ron Duncan, Larry Duvall, Bobby Eades, Jackie Emanuel, James Haynes, John Jones, Mickey Koval, Ron Lichlyter, George Martoncik, Gene Millard, William Miller, Corbin Newcomb, Chris Owen, A.D. Rardon, Archie Rardon, Max Smith, Ed Stewart, Charles Syslo, Melvin Williams

montana knifemaker's association

Bill Amoureux, Wendell Barnes, James Barth, Bob Beaty, Brett C. Bennett, Arno & Zine Bernard, Robert Bizzell, Peter Bromley, Bruce Bump, Ed Caffrey, C Camper, John Christensen, Roger Clark, Jack Cory, Bob Crowder, Roger Dole, Rick Dunkerley, Mel Fassio, Tom Ferry, Gary Flohr, Vern Ford, Barry Gallagher, Doc Hagen, Ted Harris, Thomas Haslinger, Sam & Joy Henson, Gerald Hintz, Tori Howe, Al Inman, Dan Kendrick, Doug Klaudt, Mel Long, James Luman, Mike Mann, Jody Martin, Neil McKee, Larry McLaughlin, Mac & Nancy McLaughlin, Gerald Morgan, Ed Mortenson, Deryk Munroe, Dan Nedved, Joe Olson, Daniel O'Malley, Patton Knives, Eldon Peterson, Jim Raymond, Lori Ristinen, James Rodebaugh, Gary Rodewald, Gordon St. Clair, Andy Sarcinella, Charles Sauer, Dean Schroeder, Art Swyhart, Shane Taylor, Jim Thill, Frank Towsley, Bill Waldrup, Michael Wattelet, Darlene & Gerome Weinand, Daniel Westlind, Nick Wheeler, Michael Young, Fred Zaloudek

new england bladesmiths guild

Phillip Baldwin, Gary Barnes, Paul Champagne, Jimmy Fikes, Don Fogg, Larry Fuegen, Rob Hudson, Midk Langley, Louis Mills, Dan Maragni, Jim Schmidt, Wayne Valachovic and Tim Zowada

north carolina custom knifemakers' guild

Mark Amon, Marion Bagwell, Herbert M. Baker, Robert E. Barber, Dr. James Batson, Wayne Bernauer, William M. Bisher, Dave Breme, Tim Britton, John (Jack) H. Busfield, E. Gene Calloway, Terry Cash, R. C. Chopra, Thomas Clegg, Joe Corbin, Harry Cosgrove, Robert (Bob) J. Cumming, Travis Daniel, Rob Davis, Geno Denning, Dexter Ewing, Brent Fisher, Charles F. Fogarty, Don Fogg, Alan Folts, Norman A. Gervais, Nelson Gimbert, Scott Goguen, Mark Gottesman, Ed Halligan, Koji Hara, Mark Hazen, George Herron, Daniel C. Hilgenberg, Terrill Hoffman, Stacey Holt, B.R. Hughes, Jack Hyer, Steve James, Dan Johnson, Tommy Johnson, Barry & Phillip Jones, Tony Kelly, Robert Knight, Ben Lumpkin, Lavra Marshall, Tom Matthews, Andrew McLurkin, Tommy McNabb, J. Michael McRae, Charlie & Maureen Monroe, Bill Moran, Ron Newton, Victor L. Odom Jr., Charles Ostendorf, Bill Pate, James Poplin, Harry S. Powell, John W. Poythress, M. Perry Price, Darrel Ralph, Bruce M. Ryan, Robert J. Schmidt, Tim & Kathy Scholl, Danks Seel, Daryl Shelby, Rodney N. Shelton, J. Wayne Short, Harland & Karen Simmons, Ken & Nancy Simmons, Johnnie Sorrell, Chuck Staples, Murray Sterling, Carl Strickland, Russ Sutton, Kathleen Tomey, Bruce Turner, Kaiji & Miki Uchida, Dave Vail, Edward & Tanya VanHoy, Wayne Whitley, James A. Williams, Daniel Winkler, Rob Wotzak

ohio knifemakers association

Raymond Babcock, Van Barnett, Harold A. Collins, Larry Detty, Tom Downing, Jim Downs, Patty Ferrier, Jeff Flannery, James Fray, Bob Foster, Raymond Guess, Scott Hamrie, Rick Hinderer, Curtis Hurley, Ed Kalfayan, Michael Koval, Judy Koval, Larry Lunn, Stanley Maienknecht, Dave Marlott, Mike Mercer, David Morton, Patrick McGroder, Charles Pratt, Darrel Ralph, Roy Roddy, Carroll Shoemaker, John Smith, Clifton Smith, Art Summers, Jan Summers, Donald Tess, Dale Warther, John Wallingford, Earl Witsaman, Joanne Yurco, Mike Yurco

south carolina association of knifemakers

Bobby Branton, Gordo Brooks, Daniel L. Cannady, Thomas H. Clegg, John Conn, Geno Denning, Charlie Douan, Jerry G. Hendrix, Wayne Hendrix, George H. Herron, T.J. Hucks, Johnny Johnson, Lonnie Jones, Jason Knight, Col. Thomas D. Kreger, Gene Langley, Eddie Lee, David Manley, William (Bill) Massey, David McFalls, Claude Montjoy, Larry Page, Ricky Rankin, John (Mickey) Reed, Gene Scaffe, Mick Sears, Ralph Smith, S. David Stroud, Robert Stuckey, Rocky Thomas, Woodrow W. Walker, Charlie Webb, Thomas H. Westwood

tennessee knifemakers association

John Bartlow, Doug Casteel, Harold Crisp, Larry Harley, John W. Walker, Harold Woodward, Harold Wright

etchers/carvers

Bell, Donald, 139, 143, 144
Chamblin, Joel, 140
Cook, James, 144
Dippold, Al, 139
Frank, H.H., 142
Fuegen, Larry, 142, 145
Fuller, Jack, 143
Grussenmeyer, Paul, 142
Hirayama, Harumi, 141
Hoffman, Kevin, 143
Horn, Des, 61
Ishihara, Hank, 141
Knickmeyer, Hank, 142

Knight, Jason, 144
Larstein, Francine, 144
Lunn, Larry, Front Cover
McRae, Mike, 145
Norris, Don, 141, 144
O'Connor, Carol Ann, 30, 33, 35
Olszewski, Stephen, 140, 145
Palm, Rik, 143
Poythress, John, 139
Robinson, Rex, 140
Sandar, 141, 144
Sellevold, Harald, 142
Shaw, Bruce, 97

Smith, D. Noel, 140
Smith, Everett, 97
Steigerwalt, Ken, 140, 144
Sunderland, Richard, 144
Szilaski, Joe, 141
Taylor, Shane, 145
Tighe, Brian, 145
Turecek, Jim, 141
Vinnecombe, P., 106
Wada, Yasutaka, 143, 144
Weinstock, Robert, 140

engravers

Aasland, Bertil, 149
Bates, Billy, 151, 155
Bell, Donald, 153
Branham, Mike, 159
Brend, Walter, 152
Cai, C.J., 153
Davidson, Jere, 149, 150, 153
Dellana, 149
El Hadi, Rashid, 30, 32
Fassio, Mel, 153
Foster, N.C., 149
Frank, H.H., 151
George, Tim, 154
Gibo, George, 151

Hansen, Sharla, 150
Hansen, Shaun, 150
Herman, Tim, 151
Holder, Pat, 152
Keeslar, Joe, 152
Kommer, Russ, 151
Levin, Jack, 152
Liege, Lovenberg, 155
Limings, Harry, 153, 158
Lytton, Simon, 153
Minnick, Joyce, 150
Moulton, Dusty, 153
Muller, Jody, 152
Muller, Pat, 152

Nilsson, Jonny Walker, 154
Nott, Ron, 124, 150
Overeynder, T.R., 151
Pulis, Vladimir, 154
Rudolph, Gil, 154
Smith, John W., 154
Smith, Warren, 150
Stedanyan, Amayak, 155
Towell, Dwight, 155
Van Rijswijk, Aad, 149, 155
Vinnecombe, P., 121
Warenski, Julie, 155
Waters, Glenn, 155
Whitehead, Jim, 150

knifemakers

Allred, Bruce, 73
Anders, Jerome, 123, 131, 136
Anderson, Mel, 119
Ankrom, W.E., 154
Anso, Jens, 65, 117
Ashworth, Boyd, 105, 161
Baar, A.T., 53
Baartman, George, 85, 136, 162
Banks, David, 75
Bardsley, Norman, 62, 78
Barnes, Jim, 149
Barnett, Van, 25
Barker, Reggie, 76
Barry III, James, 62
Barth, J.D., 67, 156
Baskett, Gene, 131, 147, 153, 158
Batson, Jim, 98, 100
Baumgardner, Ed, 74, 132, 159
Beaty, Robert, 72
Begg, Todd, 84, 112, 136
Behnke, Bill, Back Cover, 81
Bell, Don, 162

Bell, Michael, 95
Bertholus, Bernard, 64, 97
Beshara, Brent, 90, 92
Bishop, Ron, 127
Bizzell, Bob, 61, 67, 121
Black, Tom, 121
Blasingame, Robert, 54, 55
Boguszewski, Phil, 68
Bojtos, Arpad, Front Cover
Booysen, Chris, 133
Bose, Tony, 184
Boye, David, 85, 147
Brandsey, Edward, 90, 124
Bray, Lowell, 116
Brodziak, David, 30, 31, 32, 33, 34, 35
Brunckhorst, C. Lyle, 162
Buchanan, Thad, 73
Bump, Bruce, 88, 133
Burke, Dan, 109, 110
Caffrey, Ed, 106, 162, 163
Calvin, Ruth, 97
Calvin, Till, 97

Camerer, Craig, 123
Cameron, Ron, 133
Cannon, Chad, 26
Cannon, Dale, 26
Carlson, Kelly, 159
Carrillo, Dwaine, 117
Carroll, Chad, 72, 163
Carson, Kit, 69
Cashen, Kevin, 79, 134
Caston, Darriel, 71
Cawthrone, Christopher, 124
Centofante, Frank, 149
Chamblin, Joel, 102, 130
Chard, Gordon, 71
Chisan, C., 89, 134
Choate, Milton, 122
Christensen, Jon, 163
Claiborne, Jeff, 110, 148
Colter, Wade, 61, 64, 137
Connolly, James, 123
Cook, James, 134
Coombs Jr., Lamont, 107

Parker, Robert Nelson, 76
Parquet, Ponzio, 103
Patrick, Bob, 87, 119, 122
Pease, William D., 103
Pendray, Al, 165
Perry, John, Front Cover
Persson, Conny, 154
Peterson, E.G., 151
Polk, Cliff, 97, 166
Polk, Rusty, 77
Polzien, Don, 79, 159, 160
Poythress, John, 90, 105, 113
Pozien, Don, 96
Prinsloo, Theuns, 59
Puddu, Salvatore, 103, 131
Rados, Jerry, 37, 71, 112, 140
Ralph, Darrel, 53, 69, 91
Randall, J.W., 67, 166
Red, Vernon, 97
Rexroat, Kirk, 131, 138
Richards, A.C., 77, 86, 107
Rigney, Willie, 158
Roberts, Jack, 157, 159
Robinson, Charles "Dickie", 77
Rogers, Ray, 71
Rogers, Richard, 110
Rossdeutscher, Robert, 83, 88
Rowe, Fred, 73, 82
Ruple, Bill, 66, 111
Ryan, Steve, 180
Rybar, Ray, 166
Sakmar, Mike, 124
Sanders, Michael M., 125, 148
Sauer, Charles, 136
Sawby, Scott, 154
Schempp, Ed, 139, 144
Schoeman, Corrie, 167
Schwarzer, Steve, 37

Scordia, Paolo, 86
Scroggs, James, 123
Sellevold, Harald, 96
Selzam, Frank, 78
Shadley, Eugene, 153
Sharrigan, Mudd, 62, 91, 123
Sigman, Corbet, 80
Simonich, Rob, 178
Sinyard, Cleston, 98
Skow, Tex, 93, 101
Slobodian, Scott, 79, 94, 95
Smit, Glen, 62, 82
Smith, Carel, 92
Smith, John W., 60
Smith, Josh, 58, 104
Smith, Raymond L., 83, 101
Smith, Rick, 63, 99, 121
Smollen, Nick, 89
Snow, Bill, 118
Solomon, Marvin, 78, 125
Sprokholt, Denise, 80
Sprokholt, Rob, 80
Stalcup, Eddie, 83
Steck, Van, 59, 95
Steigerwalt, Ken, 130
Steinau, Jurgen, 129
Sterling, Murray, 109, 167
Suedmeier, Harlan, 135
Sunderland, Richard, 91
Sutton, Russ, 67, 73, 104, 167
Sword, Angel, 79
Takeshi, Matsusaki, 105, 110, 111
Tamboli, Mike, 85, 97, 119, 122
Taylor, Shane, 60, 66, 148, 167
Thomas, Devin, Front Cover, 66, 78, 94, 113, 125, 130, 132, 133, 146, 156, 164, 167
Thomsen, Loyd, 12, 13, 14, 59, 82, 119
Thourot, Mike, 182

Tichbourne, George, 73, 93, 117
Tiensvold, Jason, 58, 135, 166
Tighe, Brian, 69
Tippette, Colten, 81
Tomberlin, Brian, 81
Treiber, Leon, 64, 66, 160
Trudel, Paul, 90
Tschager, Reinhard, 131, 132
Turnbull, Ralph, 69, 82, 167
Tycer, Art, 72, 101, 137, 155
Vagnino, Michael, 100, 105
Van Den Elsen, Gert, 76, 93, 96, 122
Van Der Merwe, Johan, 83, 103, 165
Van Eldik, Frans, 108, 155
Van Rijswijk, Aad, 66, 132
Vitale, Mace, 116
Wada, Yasutaka, 93, 119
Walker, Jim, 124
Walker, John, 90
Walker, Michael, 61, 69
Ward, Chuck, 86
Wardell, Mick, 120
Waters, Glenn, 127
Watson, Billy, 76, 124
Watson, Daniel, 79, 94
Wattelet, Michael, 128
Watts, Johnathan, 27, 110
Watts, Wally, 27, 73
Weinand, Gerome, 136
Welling, Ron, 98, 99
Werth, George, 38
Winkler, Daniel, 64, 169
Wood, Gary, 32, 35
Wood, Owen, 155
Wood, Webster, 127
Wright, Richard S., 71, 112, 147
Zima, Mike, 85
Zscherny, Mike, 161, 166

leatherworkers/sheathmakers

Begg, Todd, 169
Bruner, Rick, 168
Burrows, Chuck, 169
Calvin, Ruth, 170
Calvin, Till, 170
Carroll, Chad, 169
Choate, Judy, 168, 169
Cole, David, 170

Guignard, Gib, 169
Harrison, Carol, 26
Haslinger, Thomas, 168
Jones, Roger, 170
Jones, Teresa, 170
Kelly, Joann, 170
Kravitt, Chris, 171
Maines, Jay, 170

Neilson, Tess, 169, 171
Nix, Robert, 168, 169
O'Connor, Carol Ann, 34
Polk, Rusty, 168
Rowe, Kenny, 171
Schrap, Bob, 168, 171
Shook, Karen, 169
Thomsen, Loyd, 171

scrimshanders

Beauchamp, Gaetan, 157, 158
Conover, Carina, 156
Eklund, Maihkel, 157, 158
Hergert, Bob, 156, 158, 160
Holland, Dennis, 159, 160

Hutchings, Hutch, 159
Lay, Bob, 160
Ristinen, Lori, 160
Roberts, Barbara, 157, 159
Stone, Linda Karst, 159, 160

Stothart, Matt, 159
Tonkin, Gary, 30, 32
White, Dale, 156
Williams, Gary, 158

sporting cutlers

The firms listed here are special in the sense that they make or market special kinds of knives made in facilities they own or control either in the U.S. or overseas. Or they are special because they make knives of unique design or function. The second phone number listed is the fax number.

A.G. RUSSELL KNIVES INC
1920 North 26th St.
Lowell, AR 72745-8489
479-631-0130 800-255-9034; 749-631-8493
ag@agrussell.com; www.agrussell.com
The oldest knife mail-order company, highest quality. Free catalog available. In these catalogs you will find the newest and the best. If you like knives, this catalog is a must.

AL MAR KNIVES
PO Box 2295
Tualatin, OR 97062-2295
503-670-9080; 503-639-4789
www.almarknives.com
Featuring our ultralight™ series of knives. Sere 2000™ Shirke, Sere™, Operator™, Nomad™ and Ultralight series ™.

ALCAS COMPANY
1116 E. State St.
Olean, NY 14760
716-372-3111; 716-373-6155
www.cutco.com
Household cutlery / sport knives

ANZA KNIVES
C. Davis
Dept. BL 12, PO Box 710806
Santee, CA 92072
619-561-9445; 619-390-6283
sales@anzaknives.com; www.anzaknives.com

B&D TRADING CO.
3935 Fair Hill Rd.
Fair Oaks, CA 95628

BARTEAUX MACHETES, INC.
1916 SE 50th St.
Portland, OR 97215
503-233-5880
barteaux@machete.com; www.machete.com
Manufacture of machetes, saws, garden tools

BEAR MGC CUTLERY
1111 Bear Blvd. SW
Jacksonville, AL 36265
256-435-2227; 256-435-9348
Lockback, commemorative, multi tools, high tech & hunting knives

BECK'S CUTLERY & SPECIALTIES
McGregor Village Center
107 Edinburgh South Dr.
Cary, NC 27511
919-460-0203; 919-460-7772
beckscutlery@mindspring.com;
www.beckscutlery.com

BENCHMADE KNIFE CO. INC.
300 Beaver Creek Rd.
Oregon City, OR 97045
503-655-6004; 503-655-6223
info@benchmade.com; www.benchmade.com
Sports, utility, law enforcement, military, gift and semi custom

BERETTA U.S.A. CORP.
17601 Beretta Dr.
Accokeek, MD 20607
800-528-7453
www.berettausa.com
Full range of hunting & specialty knives

BLACKJACK KNIVES
PO Box 3
Greenville, WV 24945
304-832-6878
www.knifeware.com

BLUE GRASS CUTLERY CORP
20 E. Seventh St., PO Box 156
Manchester, OH 45144
937-549-2602; 937-549-2709 or 2603
sales@bluegrasscutlery.com;
www.bluegrasscutlery.com
Manufacturer of Winchester Knives, John Primble Knives and many contract lines

BOKER USA INC.
1550 Balsam St.
Lakewood, Co 80214-5917
303-462-0662; 303-462-0668
sales@bokerusa.com; www.bokerusa.com
Wide range of fixed blade and folding knives for hunting, military, tactical and general use

BROWNING
One Browning Pl.
Morgan, UT 84050
801-876-2711; 801-876-3331
www.browning.com
Outdoor hunting & shooting products

BUCK KNIVES INC.
1900 Weld Blvd.
El Cajon, CA 92020
800-735-2825; 619-562-2285
www.buckknives.com
Sports cutlery

BULLDOG BRAND KNIVES
PO Box 23852
Chattanooga, TN 37422
423-894-5102; 423-892-9165
Fixed blade and folding knives for hunting and general use

BUSSE COMBAT KNIFE CO.
11651 Co. Rd. 12
Wauseon, OH 43567
419-923-6471; 419-923-2337
www.bussecombat.com
Simple & very strong straight knife designs for tactical & expedition use

CAMILLUS CUTLERY CO.
54 Main St.
Camillus, NY 13031
315-672-8111; 315-672-8832
customerservice@camillusknives.com;
www.camillusknives.com

CAS IBERIA INC
650 Industrial Blvd.
Sale Creek, TN 37373
423-332-4700; 423-332-7248
www.casiberia.com
Extensive variety of fixed-blade and folding knives for hunting, diving, camping, military and general use

CASE CUTLERY
W R & Sons
Owens Way
Bradford, PA 16701
800-523-6350; 814-368-1736
consumer-relations@wrcase.com;
www.wrcase.com
Folding pocket knives

CHICAGO CUTLERY CO.
9234 W. Belmont Ave.
Franklin Park, IL 60131
847-678-8600
www.chicagocutlery.com
Sport & utility knives

CHRIS REEVE KNIVES
11624 W. President Dr. No.B
Boise, ID 83713
208-375-0367; 208-375-0368
crknifo@chrisreeve.com; www.chrisreeve.com

Makers of the award winning Yarborough/ Green Beret Knife; the One Piece Range; and the Sebenza and Mnandi folding knives

COAST CUTLERY CO.
2045 SE Ankeny St.
Portland, OR 97214
800-426-5858 or 503-234-4545; 503-234-4422
www.coastcutlery.com
Variety of fixed-blade and folding knives and multi-tools for hunting, camping and general use

COLD STEEL INC.
3036 Seaborg Ave. Suite A
Ventura, CA 93003
800-255-4716 or 805-650-8481; 805-642-9727
art@coldsteel.com; www.coldsteel.com
Wide variety of folding lockbacks and fixed-blade hunting, fishing and neck knives, as well as bowies, kukris, tantos, throwing knives and kitchen knives

COLONIAL KNIFE COMPANY
Division of Colonial Cutlery International
K.M. Paolantonio
PO Box 960
North Scituate, RI 02857
866-421-6500; 401-421-6500
colonialcutlery@aol.com
www.colonialcutlery@aol.com;
www.colonialknifecompany.com
Collectors edition specialty knives. Special promotions

COLUMBIA RIVER KNIFE & TOOL
9720 SW Hillman Ct.
Wilsonville, OR 97070
800-891-3100; 503-682-9680
info@crkt.com; www.crkt.com
Complete line of sport, work and tactical knives

CRAWFORD KNIVES
205 N. Center
West Memphis, AR 72301
870-732-2452
Folding knives for tactical and general use

DAVID BOYE KNIVES
PO Box 1238
Dolan Springs, AZ 86441
800-853-1617, 928-767-4273; 928-767-3030
boye@ctaz.com; www.boyeknives.com
Boye Dendritic Cobalt boat knives

DUNN KNIVES
Steve Greene
PO Box 204
Rosville, KS 66533
785-584-6856; 785-584-6856
sigreene@earthlink.net; www.dunnknives.com
Custom knives

EMERSON KNIVES, INC.
PO Box 4180
Torrance, CA 90510-4180
310-212-7455; 310-212-7289
www.emersonknives.com
Hard use tactical knives; folding & fixed blades

WXTREME RATIO S.A.S.
Mauro Chiostri/Maurizio Castrati
Viale Montegrappa 298
59100 Prato ITALY
0039 0574 58 4639; 0039 0574 58 1312
Tactical/military knives and sheaths, blades and sheaths to customer's specs

FALLKNIVEN AB
Havrevagen 10
S-96142 Boden
SWEDEN
46-92154422; 46-92154433
info@fallkniven.se; www.fallkniven.com
High quality stainless knives

FROG TOOL CO.
PO Box 600
Getzville, NY 14068-0600
716-877-2200; 716-877-2591
gatco@buffnet.net; www.frogtool.net
Precision multi tools

FROST CUTLERY CO.
PO Box 22636
Chattanooga, TN 37422
800-251-7768 or 423-894-6079; 423-894-9576
www.frostcutleryco.com
Wide range of fixed-blade and folding knives with a multitude of handle materials

GATCO SHARPENERS
PO Box 600
Getzville, NY 14068
716-877-2200; 716-877-2591
gatcosharpeners.com
Precision sharpening systems, diamond sharpening systems, ceramic sharpening systems, carbide sharpening systems, natural Arkansas stones

GENUINE ISSUE INC.
949 Middle Country Rd.
Selden, NY 11784
631-696-3802; 631-696-3803
gicutlery@aol.com
Antique knives, swords

GERBER LEGENDARY BLADES
14200 SW 72nd Ave.
Portland, OR 97223
503-639-6161
www.gerberblades.com
Knives, multi-tools, axes, saws, outdoor products

GIGAND USA
701 Penhoun Ave.
Secaucus, NJ 07094
201-583-5968
Imports designed by Fred C.

GROHMANN KNIVES LTD.
PO Box 40
Pictou Nova Scotia B0K 1H0
CANADA
888-756-4837 or 902-485-4224; 902-485-5872
Fixed-blade belt knives for hunting and fishing, folding pocket knives for hunting and general use

GT KNIVES
7734 Arjons Dr.
San Diego, CA 92126
858-530-8766; 858-530-8798
gtknives@gtknives.com; www.gtknives.com
Law enforcement & military automatic knives

H&B FORGE CO.
235 Geisinger Rd.
Shiloh, OH 44878
419-895-1856
Tomahawks & throwing knives

HISTORIC EDGED WEAPONRY
1021 Saddlebrook Dr.
Hendersonville, NC 28739
828-692-0323; 828-692-0600
histwpn@bellsouth.net
Antique knives from around the world; importer of puukko and other knives from Norway, Sweden, Finland and Lapland

HONEYCUTT MARKETING, INC., DAN
3165 C-4 S Campbell
Springfield, MO 65807
417-887-2635
danhoneycutt@sbcglobal.net
All kinds of cutlery, military, Randalls

IMPERIAL SCHRADE CORP.
7 Schrade Ct.
Ellenville, NY 12428
800-2-Schrade
www.schradeknives.com

JOY ENTERPRISES-FURY CUTLERY
1862 M.L. King Blvd.
Riviera Beach, FL 33404
800-500-3879 or 561-863-3205; 561-863-3277
mail@joyenterprises.com;;
www.joyenterprises.com; www.furycutlery.com
Fury ™, Mustang™, extensive variety of fixed-blade and folding knives for hunting, fishing, diving, camping, military and general use; novelty key ring knives. Muela Sporting Knives

KA-BAR KNIVES INC.
200 Homer St.
Olean, NY 14760
800-282-0130
www.ka-bar.com

KATZ KNIVES, INC.
PO Box 730
Chandler, AZ 85224-0730
480-786-9334; 480-786-9338
katzkn@aol.com; www.katzknives.com

KELLAM KNIVES CO.
902 S. Dixie Hwy.
Lantana, FL 33462
800-390-6918; 561-588-3185; 561-588-3186
info@kellamknives.com; www.kellamknives.com
Largest selection of Finnish knives; handmade & production

KERSHAW/KAI CUTLERY CO.
25300 SW Parkway
Wilsonville, OR 97070

MESSEV KLOTZLI
Hohengasse E CH 3400
Burgdorf
SWITZERLAND
(34) 422-2378; (34) 422-7693
info@klotzli.com; www.klotzli.com
High-tech folding knives for tactical and general use

KNIFEWARE INC
PO Box 3
Greenville, WV 24945
304-832-6878
www.knifeware.com
Black Jack brand knives

KNIGHTS EDGE LTD.
5696 N Northwest Hwy.
Chicago, IL 60646-6136
773-775-3888; 773-775-3339
sales@knightsedge.com;
www.knightsedge.com
Medieval weaponry, swords, suits of armor, katanas, daggers

KNIVES OF ALASKA, INC.
Charles or Jody Allen
3100 Airport Dr.
Denison, TX 75020 8623
903-786-7366, 800-752-0980; 903-786-7371
info@knivesofalaska.com;
www.knivesofalaska.com
High quality hunting & outdoorsmen's knives

KUTMASTER KNIVES
Div. of Utica Cutlery Co.
820 Noyes St.
Utica, NY 13502
315-733-4663; 315-733-6602
www.kutmaster.com
Manufacturer and importer of pocket, lockback, tool knives and multi-purpose tools

LAKOTA
620 E. Monroe
Riverton, WY 24945
307-856-6559; 307-856-1840
AUS 8-A high-carbon stainless steel blades

LEATHERMAN TOOL GROUP, INC.
PO Box 20595
Portland, OR 97294
503-253-7826; 503-253-7830
mktg@leatherman.com; www.leatherman.com
Multi-tools

LONE WOLF KNIVES
Doug Hutchens
17400 SW Upper Boones Ferry Rd., Suite 240
Portland, OR 97224
503-431-6777

MARBLE'S OUTDOORS
420 Industrial Park
Gladstone, MI 49837
906-428-3710; 906-428-3711
marble@up.net
www.marblesoutdoors.com

MASTERS OF DEFENSE KNIFE CO.
4850 Brookside Ctt
Norfolk, VA 23502
800-694-5263; 888-830-2013
cs@blackhawk.com; www.modknives.com
Fixed-blade and folding knives for tactical and general use

MEYERCO MANUFACTURING
4481 Exchange Service Dr.
Dallas, TX 75236
214-467-8949; 214-467-9241
www.meyercousa.com
Folding tactical,rescue and speed-assisted pocket knives; fixed-blade hunting and fishing designs; multi-function camping tools and machetes

MCCANN INDUSTRIES
132 S 162nd, PO Box 641
Spanaway, WA 98387
253-537-6919; 253-537-6993
McCann.machine@worldnet.att.net;
www.mccannindustries.com

MICRO TECHNOLOGY
932 36th Ct. SW
Vero Beach, FL 32968
772-569-3058; 772-569-7632
sales@microtechknives.com;
www.microtechknives.com
Manufacturers of the highest quality production knives

MORTY THE KNIFE MAN, INC.
4 Manorhaven Blvd.
Pt Washington, NY 11050
516-767-2357; 516-767-7058

MUSEUM REPLICAS LTD.
PO Box 840, Dept. PQ
Conyers, GA 30012
800-883-8838
www.museumreplicas.com
Historically accurate & battle-ready swords & daggers

MYERCHIN MARINE CLASSICS
14185 Regina Dr., Ste G
Rancho Cucamonga, CA 91739
909-463-6741; 909-463-6751
myerchin@myerchin.com; www.myerchin.com
Rigging / Police knives

NATIONAL KNIFE DISTRIBUTORS
PO Box 188
Forest City, NC 28043
800-447-4342, 828-245-4321; 828-245-5121
Benchmark pocket knives from Solingen, Germany

NORMARK CORP.
10395 Yellow Circle Dr.
Minnetonka, MN 55343
800-874-4451; 612-933-0046
Hunting knives, game shears and skinning ax

ONTARIO KNIFE CO.
26 Empire St.
Franklinville, NY 14737
800-222-5233; 800-299-2618
salesokc@aol.com; www.ontarioknife.com
Fixed blades, tactical folders, military & hunting knives, machetes

OUTDOOR EDGE CUTLERY CORP.
4699 Nautilus Ct. S #503
Boulder, Co 80301
800-447-EDGE; 303-530-7020
info@outdooredge.com; www.outdooredge.com

PARAGON CUTLERY CO.
2015 Asheville Hwy.
Hendersonville, Nc 28791
828-697-8833; 828-697-5005
www.paragonweb.com
Knife making furnaces

PILTDOWN PRODUCTIONS
Errett Callahan
2 Fredonia Ave.
Lynchburg, VA 24503

QUEEN CUTLERY COMPANY
PO Box 500
Franklinville, NY 14737
800-222-5233; 800-299-2618
salesokc@aol.com; www.queencutlery.com
Pocket knives, collectibles, Schatt & Morgan, Robeson, club knives

QUIKUT
PO Box 29
Airport Industial Park
Walnut Ridge, AR 72476
870-886-6774; 870-886-9162

RANDALL MADE KNIVES
PO Box 1988
Orlando, Fl 32802-1988
407-855-8075; 407-855-9054
grandall@randallknives.com;
www.randallknives.com
Handmade fixed-blade knives for hunting, fishing, diving, military and general use

REMINGTON ARMS CO., INC.
870 Remington Drive
PO Box 700
Madison, NC 27025-0700
800-243-9700
www.remigton.com

SANTA FE STONEWORKS
3790 Cerrillos Rd.
Santa Fe, NM 87507
800-257-7625; 505-471-0036
knives@rt66.com; www.santafestoneworks.com
Gem stone handles

SARCO CUTLERY LLC
449 Lane Dr.
Florence AL 35630
256-766-8099; 256-766-7246
sarcoknives@earthlink.net;
www.sarcoknives.com
Fixed-blade camping knife

SOG SPECIALTY KNIVES & TOOLS, INC.
6521 212th St. SW
Lynwood, Wa 98036
425-771-6230; 425-771-7689
info@sogknives.com; www.sogknives.com

SOG assisted technology, Arc-Lock, folding knives, specialized fixed blades, multi-tools

SPYDERCO, INC.
820 Spyderco Way
Golden, Co 80403
800-525-7770; 303-278-2229
sales@spyderco.com; www.spyderco.com
Knives and sharpeners

SWISS ARMY BRANDS INC.
PO Box 874
One Research Dr.
Shelton, CT 06484-0874
800-243-4045; 800-243-4006
www.swissarmy.com
Folding multi-blade designs and multi-tools for hunting, fishing, camping, hiking, golfing and general use. One of the original brands (Victorinox) of Swiss Army Knives

TAYLOR CUTLERY
1736 N Eastman Rd.
PO Box 1638
Kingsport, TN 37662-1638
800-251-0254, 423-247-2406; 423-247-5371
taylor@preferred.com; www.taylorcutlery.com
Fixed-blade and folding knives for tactical, rescue, hunting and general use

TIGERSHARP TECHNOLOGIES
1002 N Central Expwy., Suite 499
Richardson, TX 75080
469-916-2861; 972-907-0716
claudettehead@hotmail.com

TIMBERLINE KNIVES
PO Box 600
Getzville, NY 14068-0600
716-877-2200; 716-877-2591
gatco@buffnet.net; timberlineknives.com
High Technology production knives for professionals, sporting, tradesmen & kitchen use

TINIVES
1725 Smith Rd.
Fortson, GA 31808
888-537-9991; 706-322-9892
info@tinives.com; www.tinives.com
High-tech folding knives for tactical, law enforcement and general use

TRU-BALANCE KNIFE CO.
PO Box 140555
Grand Rapids, MI 49514

TURNER, P.J., KNIFE MFG., INC.
PO Box 1549
Afton, Wy 83110
307-885-0611
pjtkm@silverstar.com; www.eknife.net

UTICA CUTLERY CO.
820 Noyes St.
Utica, NY 13503-1537
800-888-4223; 315-733-6602
sales@kutmaster.com
Wide range of folding and fixed-blade designs, multi-tools and steak knives

WARNER K.
PO Box 3
Greenville, WV 24945
304-832-6878

WENGER NORTH AMERICA
15 Corporate Dr.
Orangeburg, NY 10962
800-431-2996 or 845-365-3500; 845-365-3558
www.wengerna.com
One of the official makers of folding multi-blade Swiss Army knives

WILD BOAR BLADES
1701 Broadway PMB 282
Vancouver, WA 98666
888-735-8483 or 360-735-0570; 360-735-0390
Wild Boar Blades is pleased to carry a full line of Kopromed knives and kitchenware imported from Poland

WILLIAM HENRY FINE KNIVES
3200 NE Rivergate
McMinnville, OR 97128
888-563-4500 or 503-434-9700; 503-434-9704
www.williamhenryknives.com
Semi-custom folding knives for hunting and general use; some limited editions

WORLD SURVIVAL INSTITUTE
C. Janowsky
Dept. BL 12, Box 394
Tok, AK 99780
907-883-4243

WUU JAU CO INC
2600 S Kelly Ave.
Edmond, OK 73013
800-722-5760 or 405-359-5031
877-256-4337 or 405-340-5965
mail@wuujau.com; www.wuujau.com
Wide variety of imported fixed-blade and folding knives for hunting, fishing, camping, and general use. Wholesale to knife dealers only

WYOMING KNIFE CORP.
101 Commerce Dr.
Ft. Collins, CO 80524

XIKAR INC.
PO Box 025757
Kansas City MO 64102
888-266-1193
info@xikar.com; www.xikar.com

importers

A. G. RUSSELL KNIVES INC.
1920 North 26th St.
Lowell, AR 72745-8489
479-631-0130, 479-631-8493; 800-255-9034
ag@agrussell.com; www.agrussell.com
The oldest knife mail-order company, highest quality. Free catalog available. In these catalogs you will find the newest and the best. If you like knives, this catalog is a must. Celebrating 40 years in the industry

ADAMS INTERNATIONAL KNIFEWORKS
8710 Rosewood Hills
Edwardsville, IL 62025
Importers & foreign cutlers

AITOR-BERRIZARGO S.L.
P.I. Eitua PO Box 26
48240 Berriz Vizcaya
SPAIN
946826599
94602250226
info@aitor.com
www.aitor.com
Sporting knives

ATLANTA CUTLERY CORP.
2143 Gees Mill Rd.
Box 839FD
Conyers, GA 30207
770-922-3700; 770-388-0246
www.atlantacutlery.com

BAILEY'S
PO Box 550
Laytonville, CA 95454

BELTRAME, FRANCESCO
Via Molini 27
33085Maniago PN
ITALY
39 0427 701859
www.italianstiletto.com

BOKER USA, INC.
1550 Balsam St.
Lakewood, CO 80214-5917
303-462-0662; 303-462-0668
sales@bokerusa.com; www.bokerusa.com
Ceramic blades

CAMPOS, IVAN DE ALMEIDA
R. Stelio M. Loureiro, 205
Centro, Tatui
BRAZIL
00-55-15-33056867
www.ivancampos.com

C.A.S. IBERIA, INC.
650 Industrial Blvd.
Sale Creek, TN 37373
423-332-4700; 423-332-7248
cas@casiberia.com; www.casiberia.com
Paul Chen/Hanwei Swords, Muela, Ajtor, Replica weaponry

CATOCTIN CUTLERY
PO Box 188
Smithsburg, MD 21783

CLASSIC INDUSTRIES
1325 Howard Ave., Suite 408
Burlingame, CA 94010

COAST CUTLERY CO.
2045 SE Ankeny St.
Portland, OR 97214

COLUMBIA PRODUCTS CO.
PO Box 1333
Sialkot 51310
PAKISTAN

COLUMBIA PRODUCTS INT'L
PO Box 8243
New York, NY 10116-8243
201-854-3054, 201-854-8504; 201-854-7058
nycolumbia@aol.com; http://
columbiaproducts.homestead.com/cat.html
Pocket, hunting knives and swords of all kinds

COMPASS INDUSTRIES, INC.
104 E. 25th St.
New York, NY 10010

CONAZ COLTELLERIE
Dei F.LLI Consigli-Scarperia
Via G. Giordani, 20
50038 Scarperia (Firenze)
ITALY
conaz@dada.it; www.conaz.com

CONSOLIDATED CUTLERY CO., INC.
696 NW Sharpe St.
Port St. Lucie, FL 34983

CRAZY CROW TRADING POST
PO Box 847 Dept. 96
Pottsboro, TX 75020
903-786-2287; 903-786-9059
info@crazycrow.com; www.crazycrow.com
*Solingen blades, knife making parts &
supplies*

**DER FLEISSIGEN BEAVER
(THE BUSY BEAVER)**
Harvey Silk
PO Box 1166
64343 Griesheim
GERMANY
49 6155 2231; 49 6155 2433
Der.Biber@t-online.de

EMPIRE CUTLERY CORP.
12 Kruger Ct.
Clifton, NJ 07013

EXTREME RATIO SAS
Mauro Chiostri
Maurizio Castrat, Viale
Montegrappa 298
59100 Prato
ITALY
0039 0574 58 4639; 0039 0574 58 1312
chios@iol.it; www.extremaratio.com
Tactical & military knives manufacturing

FALLKNIVEN AB
Havrevagen 10
S-96142 Boden
SWEDEN
46 92154422; 46 92154433
info@fallkniven.se; www.fallkniven.com
High quality knives

FREDIANI COLTELLI FINLANDESI
Via Lago Maggiore 41
I-21038 Leggiuno
ITALY

GIESSER MESSERFABRIK GMBH, JOHANNES
Raiffeisenstr 15
D-71349 Winnenden
GERMANY
49-7195-18080; 49-7195-64466
info@giesser.de; www.giesser.de
Professional butchers and chef's knives

HIMALAYAN IMPORTS
3495 Lake Side Dr.
Reno, NV 89509
775-825-2279
himimp@aol.com
http://members.aol.com/himinp/index.html

IVAN DE ALMEIDA CAMPOS-KNIFE DEALER
R. Xi De Agosto
107, Centro, Tatui, SP 18270
BRAZIL
55-15-251-8092; 55-15-251-4896
campos@bitweb.com.br
Custom knives from all Brazilian knifemakers

JOY ENTERPRISES
1862 M.L. King Blvd.
Riviera Beach, FL 33404
561-863-3205, 800-500-3879; 561-863-3277
mail@joyenterprises.com;
www.joyenterprises.com
Fury™, Mustang™, Hawg Knives, Muela

KELLAM KNIVES CO.
902 S. Dixie Hwy.
Lantana, FL 33462
561-588-3185, 561-588-3186; 800-390-6918
info@kellamknives.com; www.kellamknives.com
Knives from Finland; own line of knives

KNIFE IMPORTERS, INC.
PO Box 1000
Manchaca, TX 78652
800-561-5301;800-266-2373
Wholesale only

KNIGHTS EDGE
5696 N. Northwest Hwy
Chicago, IL 60646
773-775-3888;773-775-3339
*Exclusive designers of our Rittersteel,
Stagesteel and Valiant Arms lines of
weaponry*

LEISURE PRODUCTS CORP.
PO Box 1171
Sialkot-51310
PAKISTAN

L. C. RISTINEN
Suomi Shop
17533 Co Hwy 38
Frazee MN 56544
218-538-6633; 218-538-6633
icrist@wcia.net
*Scandinavian cutlery custom antique and
books*

LINDER, CARL NACHF.
Erholungstr. 10
42699 Solingen
GERMANY
212 330856; 212 337104
info@linder.de; www.linder.de

MARTTIINI KNIVES
PO Box 44 (Marttiinintie 3)
96101 Rovaniemi
FINLAND

MATTHEWS CUTLERY
4401 Sentry Dr., Suite K
Tucker, GA 30084

MESSER KLÖTZLI
PO Box 104
Hohengasse 3, Ch-3402 Burgdorf
SWITZERLAND
034 422 2378; 034 422 7693
info@klotzli.com; www.klotzli.com

MURAKAMI, ICHIRO
Knife Collectors Assn. Japan
Tokuda Nishi 4 Chome, 76 Banchi, Ginancho
Hashimagun, Gifu
JAPAN
81 58 274 1960; 81 58 273 7369
www.gix.orjp/~n-resin/

MUSEUM REPLICAS LIMITED
2147 Gees Mill Rd., Box 840 PQ
Conyers, GA 30012
800-883-8838
www.museumreplicas.com

NICHOLS CO.
PO Box 473, #5 The Green
Woodstock, VT 05091
802-457-3970; 802-457-2051
janjesse@sover.net
*Import & distribute knives from EKA
(Sweden), Helle (Norway), Brusletto
(Norway), Roselli (Finland). Also market Zippo
products and Snow & Neally axes*

NORMARK CORP.
Craig Weber
10395 Yellow Circle Dr.
Minnetonka, MN 55343

PRO CUT
9718 Washburn Rd.
Downey, CA 90241
562-803-8778; 562-803-4261
sales@procutdist.com
*Wholesale only. Full service distributor of
domestic & imported brand name cutlery.
Exlusive U.S. importer for both Marto Swords
and Battle Ready Valiant Armory edged
weapons*

PRODUCTORS AITOR, S.A.
Izelaieta 17
48260 Ermua
SPAIN
943-170850; 943-170001
info@aitor.com
Sporting knives

RUSSELL, A. G. KNIVES INC
1920 North 26th St.
Lowell, AR 72745-8489
479-631-0130, 479-631-8493; 800-255-9034
ag@agrussell.com; www.agrussell.com

SCANDIA INTERNATIONAL INC.
5475 W. Inscription Canyon Dr.
Prescott, AZ 86305
928-442-0140; 928-442-0342
frosts@cableone.net; www.frosts-scandia.com
Frosts Knives of Sweden

STAR SALES CO., INC.
1803 N. Central St., PO Box 1503
Knoxville, TN 37901

SVORD KNIVES
Smith Rd., Rd. 2
Waiuku, South Auckland
NEW ZEALAND

SWISS ARMY BRANDS LTD.
The Forschner Group, Inc.
One Research Drive
Shelton, CT 06484
203-929-6391; 203-929-3786
www.swissarmy.com

TAYLOR CUTLERY
PO Box 1638
1736 N. Eastman Rd.
Kingsport, TN 37662
*Colman Knives along with Smith & Wesson,
Cuttin Horse, John Deere, Zoland knives*

UNITED CUTLERY CORP.
1425 United Blvd.
Sevierville, TN 37876
865-428-2532; 865-428-2267
order@unitedcutlery.com;
www.unitedcutlery.com
*Harley-Davidson™, Colt™, Stanley™ hunting,
camping, fishing, collectible & fantasy knives*

UNIVERSAL AGENCIES INC.
4690 S. Old Peachtree Rd., Ste C
Norcross, GA 30071-1517
678-969-9147, 678-969-9148; 678-969-9169
info@uai.org; www.knifesupplies.com;
www.thunderforged.com; www.uai.org
*Serving the cutlery industry with the finest
selection of India Stag, Buffalo Horn,
Thunderforged ™ Damascus. Mother of pearl,
knife kits and more*

VALOR CORP.
1001 Sawgrass Corp. Pkwy.
Sunrise, FL 33323-2811
954-377-4925; 954-377-4941
www.valorcorp.com
Wide variety of imported & domestic knives

WENGER N. A.
15 Corporate Dr.
Orangeburg, NY 10962
800-431-2996
www.wengerna.com
Swiss Army Knives

WILD BOAR BLADES
1701 Broadway, Suite 282
Vancouver, WA 98663
888-735-8483; 360-735-0570, 360-735-0390
usakopro@aol.com; www.wildboarblades.com
*Wild Boar Blades is plesed to carry a full line
of Kopromed knives and kitchenware
imported from Poland*

ZWILLING, J.A.
Henckels Inc.
171 Saw Mill River Rd.
Hawthorne, NY 10532
914-742-1850
info@jahenckels.com
*Kitchen cutlery, scissors, gadgets, and
flatware*

knife making supplies

AFRICAN IMPORT CO.
Alan Zanotti
22 GoodWin Rd.
Plymouth, MA 02360
508-746-8552; 508-746-0404
africanimport@aol.com
Ivory

AMERICAN SIEPMANN CORP.
65 Pixley Industrial Parkway
Rochester, NY 14624
585-247-1640; 585-247-1883
www.siepmann.com
*CNC blade grinding equipment, grinding
wheels, production blade grinding services*

ANCHORAGE CUTLER
Greg Gritten
801 Airport Hts. #351
Anchorage, AK 99508
907-277-5843
cutlery@artic.net; www.anchoragecutlery.com
*Custom knife making supplies; ivory,
gemstones, antler, horn, bone*

ART JEWEL ENTERPRISES, LTD.
460 Randy Rd.
Carol Stream, IL 60188

ATLANTA CUTLERY CORP.
2147 Gees Mill Rd., Box 839XE
Conyers, GA 30012
800-883-0300

BATAVIA ENGINEERING
PO Box 53
Magaliesburg, 1791
SOUTH AFRICA
27-14-5771294
bertie@batavia.co.za; www.batavia.co.za
*Contact wheels for belt grinders and surface
grinders; damascus and mokume*

BILL'S CUSTOM CASES
PO Box 65
Etna, CA 96027
530-467-3783; 530-467-3903
billscases@sisqtel.net
Knife cases

BOONE TRADING CO., INC.
PO Box 669
Brinnon, WA 98320
800-423-1945
www.boonetrading.com
Ivory of all types, bone, horns

BORGER, WOLF
Benzstrasse 8
76676 Graben-Neudorf
GERMANY
wolf@messerschmied.de;
www.messerschmied.de

BOYE KNIVES
PO Box 1238
Dolan Springs, AZ 86441
800-853-1617; 928-767-3030
boye@ctaz.com; www.boyeknives.com
Dendritic steel and Dendritic cobalt

BRONK'S KNIFEWORKS
C. Lyle Brunckhorst
23706 7th Ave. SE
Country Village, Suite B
Bothell, WA 98021
425-402-3484
bronks@net-tech.com;
www.bronksknifeworks.com
Damascus steel

CHRISTOPHER MFG., E.
PO Box 685
Union City, TN 38281

CRAZY CROW TRADING POST
PO Box 847 Dept. 96
Pottsboro TX 75076
903-786-2287; 903-786-9059
info@crazycrow.com; www.crazycrow.com
*Solingen blades, knife making parts &
supplies*

CUSTOM FURNACES
PO Box 353
Randvaal, 1873
SOUTH AFRICA
27 16 365-5723; 27 16 365-5738
johnlee@custom.co.za
Furnaces for hardening & tempering of knives

CUSTOM KRAFT
PO Box 2337
Riverview, FL 33568
813-671-0661; 727-595-0378
RWPHIL413@earthlink.net;
www.rwcustomknives.com
*Specialize in precision screws and hardware
for folders. Also carrying gemstones and
cabochons for inlay work. Catalog available*

CUTLERY SPECIALTIES
Dennis Blaine
4296 SE Cove Lake Circle Ste #104
Great Neck, NY 11024-1707
800-229-5530; 772-219-6436, 772-219-7674
dennis13@aol.com;
www.restorationproduct.com
*US agent/distributor for Renaissance-wax/
polish and other restoration products. Dealer
in medium to high end custom-made knives,
Antique knives and hard-to-find knives and
related items, and extraordinary cutlery*

DAMASCUS-USA CHARLTON LTD.
149 Deans Farm Rd.
Tyner, NC 27980-9718
252-221-2010
damascussusa.com

DAN'S WHETSTONE CO., INC.
130 Timbs Place
Hot Springs, AR 71913
501-767-1616; 501-767-9598
questions@danswhetstone.com;
www.danswhetstone.com
Produce natural abrasive stone products

DIAMOND MACHINING TECHNOLOGY, INC. DMT
85 Hayes Memorial Dr.
Marlborough, MA 01752
800-481-5944; 508-485-3924
dmtsharp@dmtsharp.com; www.dmtsharp.com
*Knife and tool sharpeners - diamond and
ceramic*

DIXIE GUN WORKS, INC.
PO Box 130
Union City, TN 38281
731-885-0700; 731-885-0440 or 800-238-6785
info@dixiegun.com; www.dixiegun.com
Knife and knife making supplies

E. CHRISTOPHER MFG
PO Box 685
Union City, TN 38281
731-885-0374; 731-885-0440
*Solingen blades from Germany (ground and
polished)*

EZE-LAP DIAMOND PRODUCTS
3572 Arrowhead Dr.
Carson City, NV 89706
775-888-9500; 775-888-9555
sales@eze-lap.com; www.eze-lap.com
Diamond coated sharpening tools

FIELDS, DONALD
790 Tamerlane St.
Deltona, FL 32725
386-532-9070
donaldfields@aol.com

FLITZ INTERNATIONAL, LTD.
821 Mohr Ave.
Waterford, WI 53185
800-558-8611; 262-534-2991
info@flitz.com; www.flitz.com
Metal polish, buffing pads, wax

FORTUNE PRODUCTS, INC.
205 Hickory Creek Rd.
Marble Falls, TX 78654
830-693-6111; 830-693-6394
www.accusharp.com
AccuSharp knife sharpeners

GILMER WOOD CO.
2211 NW ST. Helens Rd.
Portland, OR 97210
503-274-1271
www.gilmerwood.com

GOLDEN AGE ARMS CO.
115 E. High St.
PO Box 366
Ashley, OH 43003

GRS CORP.
D.J. Glaser
PO Box 1153
900 Overlander St.
Emporia, KS 66801
620-343-1084, 620-343-9640; 800-835-3519
glendo@glendo.com; www.glendo.com
*Engraving, equipment, tool sharpener, books/
videos*

HALPERN TITANIUM INC
Les and Marianne Halpern
PO Box 214
Three Rivers, MA 01080
413-283-8627; 413-289-2372
info@halperntitanium.com
*Titanium, carbon fiber, G-10, fasteners; CNC
milling*

HARMON, JOE T.
8014 Fisher Drive
Jonesboro, GA 30236

HAWKINS CUSTOM KNIVES & SUPPLIES
110 Buckeye Rd.
Fayetteville, GA 30214
770-964-1177; 770-306-2877
radeh@bellsouth.net
www.radehawkinscustomknives.com
All styles

HILTARY DIAMOND INDUSTRIES
7303 E. Earll Dr.
Scottsdale, AZ 85251
480-945-0700, 480-994-5752; 480-945-3333
usgrc@qwest.net; www.bigbrainsdont.com

HOUSE OF TOOLS LTD.
#136, 8228 Macleod Tr. S.E.
Calgary, AB CANADA
T2H 2B8

HOV KNIVES & SUPPLIES
Box 8005
S-700 08 Orebro
SWEDEN

INDIAN JEWELERS SUPPLY CO.
601 E Coal Ave
Gallup, NM 87301
505-722-4451; 888-722-4172
www.ijsinc.com
Gems, metals, tools

INTERAMCO INC.
5210 Exchange Dr.
Flint, MI 48507
810-732-8181; 810-732-6116
solutions@interamco.com
Knife grinding and polishing

JANTZ SUPPLY
PO Box 584-K4
Davis, OK 73030-0584
800-351-8900; 580-369-3082
jantz@brightok.net; www.knifemaking.com
*Pre-shaped blades, kit knives, complete
knifemaking supply line*

JOHNSON, R.B.
I.B.S. Int'l. Folder Supplies
Box 11
Clearwater, MN 55320
320-558-6128; 320-558-6128
hclark@radiks.net; www.customknives.com/
r.b.johnson
Threaded pivot pins, screws, taps, etc.

JOHNSON WOOD PRODUCTS
34968 Crystal Rd.
Strawberry Point, IA 52076

K&G FINISHING SUPPLIES
PO Box 458
Lakeside, AZ 85929
928-537-8877; 928-537-8066
www.knifeandgun.com
Full service supplies

KOVAL KNIVES, INC.
5819 Zarley St.
New Albany, OH 43054
614-855-0777; 614-855-0945
koval@kovalknives.com; www.kovalknives.com
Knife making supplies & equipment

KOWAK IVORY
Roland and Kathy Quimby
PO Box 350
Ester, AK 99725
520-723-5827
rlqiv@yahoo.com
Fossil ivories

LITTLE GIANT POWER HAMMER
420 4th Corso
Nebraska City, NE 68410

LIVESAY NEWT
3306 S Dogwood St.
Siloam Springs, AR 72761
479-549-3356; 479-549-3357
newt@newtlivesay.com; www.newtlivesay.com
*Combat utility knives, titanium knives,
sportsmen knives, custom-made orders taken
on knives and after-market Kydex© sheaths
for commercial or custom cutlery*

LOHMAN CO., FRED
3405 N.E. Broadway
Portland, OR 97232

MARKING METHODS, INC.
Sales
301 S. Raymond Ave.
Alhambra, CA 91803-1531
626-282-8823; 626-576-7564
sales@markingmethods.com;
www.markingmethods.com
Knife etching equipment & service

MASECRAFT SUPPLY CO.
254 Amity St.
Meriden, CT 06450
203-238-3049; 203-238-2373
masecraft.supply@snet.net;
www.masecraft@masecraftsupply.necoxmail.com
*Natural & specialty synthetic handle materials
& more*

MEIER STEEL
Daryl Meier
75 Forge Rd.
Carbondale, IL 62901

MOTHER OF PEARL CO.
Joe Culpepper
PO Box 445, 293 Belden Cir.
Franklin, NC 28734
828-524-6842; 828-369-7809
www.knifehandles.com;
www.stingrayproducts.com
Mother of pearl, bone, abalone, stingray

NICHOLAS EQUIPMENT CO.
730 E. Washington St.
Sandusky, OH 44870

NICO BERNARD
PO Box 5151
Nelspruit 1200
SOUTH AFRICA
011-2713-7440099
bernardn@iafrica.com

NORRIS, MIKE
35925 City Lake Dr
Albermarle, NC 28001
704-982-8445
*Forges stainless steel Damascus for sale to
knife makers and production compaines.
William Henry and Schrade, etc.*

OREGON ABRASIVE & MFG. CO.
12345 NE Sliderberg Rd
Brush Prairie, WA 98606
360-892-1142; 360-892-3025
Triple grit 3 stone sharpening system

OSO FAMOSO
Box 654
Ben Lomond,CA 95005
831-336-2343
oso@osofamoso.com; www.osofamoso.com
Mammoth ivory bark

OZARK KNIFE & GUN
3165 C-4 S. Campbell
Springfield, MO 65807
417-886-CUTT; 417-887-2635
danhoneycutt@sbcglobal.net
Randall and custom folders

PAPAI, ABE
5013 N. 800 E.
New Carlisle, IN 46552

PARAGON INDUSTRIES, INC. L. P.
2011 South Town East Blvd.
Mesquite, TX 75149-1122
972-288-7557; 800-876-4328
paragonind@att.net; www.paragonweb.com
Heat treating furnaces for knife makers

POPLIN, JAMES/POP KNIVES & SUPPLIES
103 Oak St.
Washington, GA 30673

PUGH, JIM
PO Box 711
Azle, TX 76098
817-444-2679; 817-444-5455
*Rosewood ebony Micarta blocks-handle rivets
for Kydex sheath, 0-80 screws for folders*

RADOS, JERRY
PO Box 531
7523E 5000 N Rd.
Grant Park, IL 60940
815-405-5061
jerryr@favoravi.com
Damascus steel

REACTIVE METALS STUDIO, INC.
PO Box 890
Clarkdale, AZ 86324
928-634-3434; 928-634-6734
reactive@commspeed.net;
www.reactivemetals.com

REPRODUCTION BLADES
17485 SW Pheasant Ln.
Beaverton, OR 97006
503-649-7867
*Period knife blades for hobbyists &
re-enactors*

RICK FRIGAULT CUSTOM KNIVES
3584 Rapidsview Dr.
Niagara Falls, Ontario L2G 6C4
CANADA
905-295-6695
rfrigaultknives.com; www.rftigaultknive.som
*Selling padded zippered knife pouches with
an option to personalize the outside with the
marker, purveyor, stores - address, phone
number, email web-site or any other
information needed. Available in black
cordura, mossy oak camo in sizes 4"X2" to
20"X4.5"*

RIVERSIDE MACHINE
201M W Stillwell
Dequeen, AR 71832
870-642-7643; 870-642-4023
uncleal@ipa.net; www.riversidemachine.net

ROCKY MOUNTAIN KNIVES
George L. Conklin
PO Box 902, 615 Franklin
Ft. Benton, MT 59442
406-622-3410
bbgrus@ttc-cmc.net
Working knives

RUMMELL, HANK
10 Paradise Lane
Warwick, NY 10990

SAKMAR, MIKE
1451 Clovelly Ave.
Rochester, MI 48307
248-852-6775; 248-852-8544
Mokume bar stock. Retail & wholesale

SANDPAPER, INC. OF ILLINOIS
270 Eisenhower Ln. N, Unit 5B
Lombard, IL 60148
630-629-3320; 630-629-3324
www.sandpaperinc.com
Abrasive belts, rolls, sheets & discs

SCHEP'S FORGE
PO Box 395
Shelton, NE 68876-0395

SENTRY SOLUTIONS LTD
33 S Commercial St #401
Manchester, NH 03101-2626
603-626-8888, 603-626-8889; 800-546-8049
knives2002@sentrysolutions.com;
www.sentrysolutions.com
Knife care products

SHEFFIELD KNIFEMAKERS SUPPLY, INC.
PO Box 741107
Orange City, FL 32774-1107
386-775-6453; 386-774-5754
www.sheffieldsupply.com

SHINING WAVE METALS
PO Box 563
Snohomish, WA 98290-0563
425-334-5569
phb@u.washington.edu
*A full line of Mokume-Gane in precious and
non-precious metals for knife makers,
jewelers and other artists*

SMITH ABRASIVES, INC.
1700 Sleepy Valley Rd.
Hot Springs, AR 71901

SMITH WHETSTONE, INC.
1700 Sleepy Valley Rd.
Hot Springs, AR 71901

SMOLEN FORGE, INC.
Nick Smolen
S1735 Vang Rd.
Westby, WA 54667
608-634-3569; 608-634-3869
www.smolenforge.com
Damascus billets & blanks, Mokume gane billets

SOSTER SVENSTRUP BYVEJ 16
Dastrup 4130 VIBY SJ
Denmark
45 46 19 4305; 45 46 19 5319
www.poulstrande.com

STAMASCUS KNIFEWORKS INC
Mike Norris
35925 City Lake Dr
Albermarle, NC 28001
704-982-8445
Blade steels

STOVER, JEFF
PO Box 43
Torrance, CA 90507
310-532-2166
edgedealer@aol.com
Fine custom knives — top makers

TEXAS KNIFEMAKERS SUPPLY
Thuesen, Kevin
10649 Haddington, Suite 180
Houston TX 77043
713-461-8632
Working straight knives. Hunters including upswept skinners and custom walking sticks

TRU-GRIT, INC.
760 E. Francis St. #N
Ontario, CA 91761
909-923-4116, 909-923-9932; 800-532-3336
trugrit@aol.com; www.trugrit.com
The latest in Norton and 3/M ceramic grinding belts. Also Super Flex, Trizact, Norax and Micron belts to 3000 grit. All of the popular belt grinders. Buffers and variable speed motors. ATS-34, 440C, BG-42, CPM S-30V, 416 and Damascus steel

UNIVERSAL AGENCIES, INC
4690 S. Old Peachtree Rd. Ste C
Norcross, GA 30071-1517
678-969-9147,678-969-9169; 678-969-9148
info@uai.org; www.knifesupplies.com
www.thunderforged.com; www.uai.org
Serving the cutlery industry with the finest selection of India Stag, Buffalo Horn, Thunderforged ™ Damascus. Mother of Pearl, knife kits and more

WASHITA MOUNTAIN WHETSTONE CO.
PO Box 20378
Hot Springs, AR 71903
501-525-3914; 501-525-0816
wmw@hsnp

WEILAND, J REESE
PO Box 2337
Riverview, FL 33568
813-671-0661; 727-595-0378
rwphil413@earthlink.net;
www.rwcustomknives.com
Folders, straight knives, etc.

WILD WOODS
Jim Fray
PO Box 104
Monclova, OH 43542
419-866-0435

WILSON, R.W.
113 Kent Way
Weirton, WV 26062

WOOD CARVERS SUPPLY, INC.
PO Box 7500-K
Englewood, FL 34295-7500
800-284-6229; 941-698-0329
www.woocarverssupply.com
Over 2,000 unique wood carving tools

WOOD STABILIZING SPECIALISTS INT'L.
Mike & Cara Ludemann
2940 Fayette Ave.
Ionia, IA 50645
641-435-4746; 641-435-4759
Mike@stabilizedwood.com;
www.stabilizedwood.com
Processor of acrylic impregnated materials

WYVERN INDUSTRIES
PO Box 1564
Shady Cove, OR 97539-1564

ZOWADA CUSTOM KNIVES
Tim Zowada
4509 E Bear River Rd.
Boyne Falls, MI 49713
231-348-5416
knifeguy@nmo.net; www.tzknives.com
Damascus, pocket knives, swords, lower case gothic tz logo

mail order sales

A. G. RUSSELL KNIVES INC
1920 North 26th St.
Lowell, AR 72745-8489
479-631-0130; 479-631-8493
ag@agrussell.com; www.agrussell.com
The oldest knife mail-order company, highest quality. Free catalog available. In these catalogs you will find the newest and the best. If you like knives, this catalog is a must

ARIZONA CUSTOM KNIVES
Jay and Karen Sadow
8617 E. Clydesdale
Scottsdale, AZ 85258
480-951-0699
sharptalk@aol.com;
www.arizonacustomknives.com
Color catalog $5 U.S. / $7 Foreign

ATLANTA CUTLERY CORP.
2147 Gees Mill Rd., Box 839DY
Conyers, GA 30012
800-883-0300
www.atlantacutlery.com
Special knives & cutting tools

ATLANTIC BLADESMITHS/PETER STEBBINS
50 Mill Rd.
Littleton, MA 01460
978-952-6448
j.galt1100@verizon.ent;
www.atlanticbladesmiths.com
Sell, trade, buy; carefully selected handcrafted, benchmade and factory knives

BALLARD CUTLERY
1495 Brummel Ave.
Elk Grove Village, IL 60007

BECK'S CUTLERY SPECIALTIES
MacGregor Village #109
107 Edinburgh S.
Cary, NC 27511
919-460-0203
www.beckscutlery.com
Knives

BLADEGALLERY.COM
107 Central Way
Kirkland, WA 98033
877-56-blade
www.bladegallery.com
Bladegallery.com specializes in hand-made one-of-a-kind knives from around the world. We have an emphasis on forged knives and high-end gentlemen's folders

BLUE RIDGE KNIVES
166 Adwolfe Rd.
Marion, VA 24354-6664
276-783-6143; 276-783-9298
www.blueridgeknives.com
Wholesale distributor of knives

BOB NEAL CUSTOM KNIVES
PO Box 20923
Atlanta, GA 30320
770-914-7794; 770-914-7796
bob@bobnealcustomknives.com;
www.bobnealcustomknives.com
Exclusive limited edition custom knives—sets & single

BOONE TRADING CO., INC.
PO Box 669
Brinnon, WA 98320
800-423-1945
www.boonetrading.com
Ivory scrimshaw horns

CARMEL CUTLERY
Dolores & 6th; PO Box 1346
Carmel, CA 93921
831-624-6699; 831-624-6780
ccutlery@ix.netcom.com;
www.carmelcutlery.com
Quality custom and a variety of production pocket knives, swords; kitchen cutlery; personal grooming items

CLASSIC CUTLERY
5 Logan Rd.
Nashua, NH 03063
603-881-3776
yesdragonfly@earthlink.net
Custom knives, gemstones, high quality factory knives

CORRADO CUTLERY
39 Old Orchard Center, C39
Skokie, IL 60077
847-329-9770
www.corradocutlery.com
Knives, nippers, scissors, gifts, optical goods

CREATIVE SALES & MFG.
Box 111
Whitefish, MT 59937
406-849-5174; 406-849-5130
www.creativesales.com

CUTLERY SHOPPE
357 Steelhead Way
Boise, ID 83704
800-231-1272; 208-672-8588
www.cutleryshoppe.com
Discount pricing on top quality brands

CUTTING EDGE, THE
1920 North 26th St.
Lowell, AR 72745-8489
479-631-0055; 479-631-8734
editor@cuttingedge.com; www.cuttingedge.com
After-market knives since 1968. They offer about 1,000 individual knives for sale each month. Subscription by first class mail, in U.S. $20 per year, Canada or Mexico by air mail, $25 per year. All overseas by air mail, $40 per year. The oldest and the most experienced in the business of buying and selling knives. They buy collections of any size, take knives on consignment. Every month there are 4-8 pages in color featuring the work of top makers

DENTON, J.W.
102 N Main St., Box 429
Hiawassee, GA 30546
706-896-2292; 706-896-1212
jwdenton@alltel.net
Loveless knives

DUNN KNIVES INC.
PO Box 204
Rossville, KS 66533
785-584-6856

directory

EPICUREAN EDGE, THE
107 Central Way
Kirkland, WA 98033
425-889-5980
www.epicureanedge.com
*The Epicurean Edge specializes in high-end
chef's knives from around the world. They
have an empasis on handmade and hard-to-
find knives*

FAZALARE, ROY
PO Box 1335
Agoura Hills, CA 91376
818-879-6161 after 7:00 pm
ourfaz@aol.com
*Handmade multiblades; older case; Fight'n
Rooster; Bulldog brand & Cripple Creek*

FROST CUTLERY CO.
PO Box 22636
Chattanooga, TN 37422

GENUINE ISSUE, INC.
949 Middle Country Rd.
Selden, NY 11784
516-696-3802; 516-696-3803
g.i._cutlery.com
All knives

GODWIN, INC., G. GEDNEY
2139 Welsh Valley Rd.
Valley Forge, PA 19481
610-783-0670; 610-783-6083
www.gggodwin.com
18th century reproductions

GUILD KNIVES
320 Paani Place, 1A
Paia, HI 96779
808-877-3109; 808-877-3524
donguild1@aol.com; www.guildknives.com
Purveyor of Custom Art Knives

HAWTHORN GALLERIES, INC.
PO Box 6071
Branson, MO 65616
417-335-2170; 417-335-2011
hg_inc@hotmail.com

HERITAGE ANTIQUE KNIVES
Bruce Voyles
PO Box 22171
Chattanooga, TN 37422
423-238-6753; 423-238-6711
bruce@jbrucevoyles.com;
www.jbrucevoyles.com
Knives, knife auctions

HOUSE OF TOOLS LTD.
#136, 8228 MacLeod Tr. SE
Calgary, Alberta, CANADA
T2H 2B8

HUNTER SERVICES
Fred Hunter
PO Box 14241
Parkville, MD 64152

JENCO SALES, INC.
PO Box 1000
Manchaca, TX 78652
800-531-5301; 800-266-2373
jencosales@sbcglobal.net
Wholesale only

KELLAM KNIVES CO.
902 S Dixie Hwy.
Lantana, FL 33462
561-588-3185, 561-588-3186; 800-390-6918
info@kellamknives.com; www.kellamknives.com
*Largest selection of Finnish knives; own line
of folders and fixed blades*

KNIFEART.COM
13301 Pompano Dr.
Little Rock, AR 72211
501-221-1010; 501-221-2695
www.knifeart.com
*Large internet seller of custom knives &
upscale production knives*

KNIFE IMPORTERS, INC.
PO Box 1000
Manchaca, TX 78652

KNIFEMASTERS CUSTOM KNIVES/J&S FEDER
PO Box 208
Westport, CT 06881
203-226-5211; 203-226-5312
Investment grade custom knives

KNIVES PLUS
2467 I 40 West
Amarillo, TX 79109
800-687-6202
*Retail cutlery and cutlery accessories since
1987*

KRIS CUTLERY
PO Box 133 KN
Pinole, CA 94564
510-223-8968
kriscutlery@attbl.com; www.kriscutlery.com
Japanese, medieval, Chinese & Philippine

LDC CUSTOM KNIVES
PO Box 20923
Atlanta, GA 30320
770-914-7794; 770-914-7796
bob@bobnealcustomknives.com
*Exclusive limited edition custom knives —
sets & single*

LES COUTEAUX CHOISSIS DE ROBERTS
Ron Roberts
PO Box 273
Mifflin, PA 17058

LONE STAR WHOLESALE
PO Box 587
Amarillo, TX 79105
806-356-9540; 806-359-1603
*Wholesale only; major brands and
accessories*

MATTHEWS CUTLERY
4401 Sentry Dr., Suite K
Tucker, GA 30084

MORTY THE KNIFE MAN, INC.
4 Manorhaven Blvd.
Port Washington, NY 11050

MUSEUM REPLICAS, LTD.
2143 Gees Mill Rd., Box 840PQ
Conyers, GA 30207
800-883-8838
www.museumreplicas.com
*Historically accurate and battle -eady swords
& daggers*

NORDIC KNIVES
1634CZ Copenhagen Dr.
Solvang, CA 93463
805-688-3612
info@nordicknives.com; www.nordicknives.com
Custom and Randall knives

OAKES WINSTON
431 Deauville Dr.
Dayton, OH 45429
937-434-3112
*Dealer in Bose, Jess Horn, Michael Walker &
other quality knives. Some tactical folders.
$100-$7000*

PARKER'S KNIFE COLLECTOR SERVICE
6715 Heritage Business Ct.
Chattanooga, TN 37422
423-892-0448
bbknife@bellsouth.net

PEN AND THE SWORD LTD., THE
PO Box 290741
Brooklyn, NY 11229-0741
718-382-4847; 718-376-5745
info@pensword.com
*Custom folding knives, engraving, scrimshaw,
Case knives, English fruit knives, antique
pocket knives*

PLAZA CUTLERY, INC.
3333 S. Bristol St., Suite 2060
South Coast Plaza
Costa Mesa, CA 92626
714-549-3932
plazacutlery@earthlink.net;
www.plazacutlery.com
*Largest selection of knives on the west coast.
Custom makers from beginners to the best.
All customs, William Henry, Strider, Reeves,
Randalls & others available online by phone*

ROBERTSON'S CUSTOM CUTLERY
PO Box 1367
Evans, GA 30809-1367
706-650-0252; 706-860-1623
customknives@comcast.net;
www.robertsoncustomcutlery.com
*World class custom knives, Vanguard knives
— Limited exclusive design*

ROBINSON, ROBERT W.
1569 N Finley Pt.
Polson, MT 59860

RUSSELL, A.G. KNIVES INC
1920 North 26th St.
Lowell, AR 72745-8489
479-631-0130; 479-631-8993
ag@agrussell.com; www.agrussell.com

SHAW, GARY
24 Central Ave.
Ridgefield Park, NJ 07660
201-641-8801; 201-641-0872
gshaw@carroll.com
Investment grade custom knives

SMOKY MOUNTAIN KNIFE WORKS
2320 Winfield Dunn Pkwy
Sevierville, TN 37876
865-453-5871; 800-251-9306
info@smkw.com; www.eknifeworks.com
*The world's largest knife showplace, catalog
and website*

**STIDHAM'S KNIVES/DBA MEADOWS' EDGE
KNIFE SHOP**
PO Box 160
Meadows of Dan, VA 24120
276-952-2500; 276-952-6245
rstidham@gate.net;
www.randallknifesociety.com
*Randall, Loveless, Scagel, moran, antique
pocket knives*

STODDARD'S, INC.
Copley Place 25
100 Huntington Ave.
Boston, MA 02116
617-536-8688; 617-536-8689
*Cutlery (kitchen, pocket knives, Randall-made
knives, custom knives, scissors & manicure
tools) binoculars, lwo vision aids, personal
care items (hair brushes, manicure sets
mirrors)*

appraisers

Levine, Bernard, PO Box 2404, Eugene, OR, 97402, 541-484-0294, brlevine@ix.netcom.com

Russell, A.G., Knives inc, 1920 North 26th St, Lowell, AR, 72745-8489, 800-255-9034 479-631-0130, fax: 479-631-8493, ag@agrussell.com, www.agrussell.com

Vallini, Massimo, Via G. Bruno 7, 20154 Milano, ITALY, 02-33614751, massimo_vallini@yahoo.it, Knife expert

custom grinders

Beauchamp, Gaetan, 125 de la Riviere, Stoneham, PQ, CANADA, G0A 4P0, 418-848-1914, (418) 848-6859, knives@gbeauchamp.ca, ww.beauchamp.cjb.net

High, Tom, Rocky Mountain Scrimshaw & Arts, 5474 S. 112.8 Rd., Alamosa, CO, 81101, www.rockymountainscrimshaw.com

McGowan Manufacturing Company, 25 Michigan St., Hutchinson, MN, 55350, 800-342-4810, fax: 320 587-7966, info@mcgowanmfg.com, www.mcgowanmfg.com, Knife sharpeners, hunting axes

McLuin, Tom, 36 Fourth St., Dracut, MA, 01826, 978-957-4899, tmcluin@attbi.com, www.people.ne.mediaone.net/tmcluin

Peele, Bryan, The Elk Rack, 215 Ferry St. PO Box 1363, Thompson Falls, MT, 59873

Schlott, Harald, Zingster Str. 26, 13051 Berlin, GERMANY, 049 030 9293346, harald.schlott@T-online.de, Custom grinder, custom handle artisan, display case/box maker, etcher, scrimshander

Wilson, R.W., PO Box 2012, Weirton, WV, 26062

custom handles

Burrows, Chuck, dba Wild Rose Trading Co., PO Box 5174, Durango, CO, 81301, 970-259-8396, chuck@wrtcleather.com, www.wrtcleather.com

Cooper, Jim, 1221 Cook St, Ramona, CA, 92065-3214, 760-789-1097, fax: 760 788-7992, jamcooper@aol.com

Eccentric Endeavors, Michel Santos and Peggy Quinn, PO Box 97, Douglas Flat, CA, 95229

Grussenmeyer, Paul G., 310 Kresson Rd, Cherry Hill, NJ, 08034, 856-428-1088, fax: 856-428-8997, pgrussentne@comcast.net, www.pgcarvings.com

High, Tom, Rocky Mountain Scrimshaw & Arts, 5474 S. 112.8 Rd., Alamosa, CO, 81101, www.rockymountainscrimshaw.com

Holden, Larry, PO Box 2017, Ridgecrest, CA, 93556-2017, lardog44@yahoo.com, Custom knifemaker

Holland, Dennis K., 4908-17th Pl., Lubbock, TX, 79416

Imboden II, Howard L., Hi II Originals, 620 Deauville Dr., Dayton, OH, 45429

Kelso, Jim, 577 Collar Hill Rd, Worcester, VT, 05682, 802-229-4254, fax: 802 223-0595

Knack, Gary, 309 Wightman, Ashland, OR, 97520

Marlatt, David, 67622 Oldham Rd., Cambridge, OH, 43725, 740-432-7549

Mead, Dennis, 2250 E. Mercury St., Inverness, FL, 34453-0514

Miller, Robert, 216 Seminole Ave., Ormond Beach, FL, 32176

Myers, Ron, 6202 Marglenn Ave., Baltimore, MD, 21206, 410-866-6914

Saggio, Joe, 1450 Broadview Ave. #12, Columbus, OH, 43212, jvsag@webtv.net, www.j.v.saggio@worldnet.att.net

Schlott, Harald, Zingster Str. 26, 13051 Berlin, GERMANY, 049 030 9293346, harald.schlott@T-online.de, Custom grinder, custom handle artisan, display case/box maker, etcher, scrimshander

Snell, Barry A., 4801 96th St. N., St. Petersburg, FL, 33708-3740

Vallotton, A., 621 Fawn Ridge Dr., Oakland, OR, 97462

Watson, Silvia, 350 Jennifer Lane, Driftwood, TX, 78619

Wilderness Forge, 315 North 100 East, Kanab, UT, 84741, 435-644-3674, bhatting@xpressweb.com,

Williams, Gary, (GARBO), PO Box 210, Glendale, KY, 42740-2010

display cases

Bill's Custom Cases, PO Box 603, Montague, CA, 96064, 530-459-5968, billscustomcases@snowcrest.net

Brooker, Dennis, Rt. 1, Box 12A, Derby, IA, 50068

Chas Clements' Custom Leathercraft, Chas, 1741 Dallas St., Aurora, CO, 80010-2018, 303-364-0403, GRYPHONS@HOME.NET, Display case/box maker, Leatherworker, Knife appraiser

Gimbert, Nelson, PO Box 787, Clemmons, NC, 27012

Haydu, Thomas G., Tomway Products, 750 E Sahara Ave, Las Vegas, NV, 89104, 8884 Tomway, fax: 702 366-0626, tom@tomway.com, tomway.com

McLean, Lawrence, 18361 Larkstone Circle, Huntington Beach, CA, 92646, 714-848-5779, lmclean@socal.rr.com

Miller, Michael K., M&M Kustom Krafts, 28510 Santiam Highway, Sweet Home, OR, 97386

Miller, Robert, PO Box 2722, Ormond Beach, FL, 32176

Retichek, Joseph L., W9377 Co. TK. D, Beaver Dam, WI, 53916

Robbins, Wayne, 11520 Inverway, Belvidere, IL, 61008

S&D Enterprises, 20 East Seventh St, Manchester, OH, 45144, 937-549-2602, 937-549-2602, sales@s-denterprises.com, www.s-denterprises.com. Display case/box maker. Manufacturer of aluminum display, chipboard type displays, wood displays. We do silk screening or acid etching for logos on product.

Schlott, Harald, Zingster Str. 26, 13051 Berlin, GERMANY, 049 030 9293346, harald.schlott@T-online.de, Custom grinder, custom handle artisan, display case/box maker, etcher, scrimshander

engravers

Adlam, Tim, 1705 Witzel Ave., Oshkosh, WI, 54902, 920-235-4589, www.adlamngraving.com

Alfano, Sam, 36180 Henry Gaines Rd., Pearl River, LA, 70452

Allard, Gary, 2395 Battlefield Rd., Fishers Hill, VA, 22626

Alpen, Ralph, 7 Bentley Rd., West Grove, PA, 19390, fax: 610-869-7141

Baron, David, Baron Technology Inc., 62 Spring Hill Rd., Trumbull, CT, 06611, 203-452-0515, bti@baronengraving.com, www.baronengraving.com, Polishing, plating, inlays, artwork

Bates, Billy, 2302 Winthrop Dr. SW, Decatur, AL, 35603

Bettenhausen, Merle L., 17358 Ottawa, Tinley Park, IL, 60477

Blair, Jim, PO Box 64, 59 Mesa Verde, Glenrock, WY, 82637, 307-436-8115, jblairengrav@msn.com

Bonshire, Benita, 1121 Burlington, Muncie, IN, 47302

Boster, A.D., 3000 Clarks Bridge Rd Lot 42, Gainesville, GA, 30501, 770-532-0958

Brooker, Dennis B., Rt. 1 Box 12A, Derby, IA, 50068

Churchill, Winston G., RFD Box 29B, Proctorsville, VT, 05153

Collins, Michael, Rt. 3075, Batesville Rd., Woodstock, GA, 30188

Cupp, Alana, PO Box 207, Annabella, UT, 84711

Dashwood, Jim, 255 Barkham Rd., Wokingham, Berkshire ENGLAND RG11 4BY

Dean, Bruce, 13 Tressider Ave., Haberfield, N.S.W. 2045, AUSTRALIA

DeLorge, Ed, 6734 W Main St, Houma, LA, 70360, 504-223-0206

Dickson, John W., PO Box 49914, Sarasota, FL, 34230

Dolbare, Elizabeth, PO Box 502, Dubois, WY, 82513-0502

Downing, Jim, PO Box 4224, Springfield, MO, 65808, 417-865-5953, www.thegunengraver.com, Scrimshander

Drain, Mark, SE 3211 Kamilche Pt. Rd., Shelton, WA, 98584

Duarte, Carlos, 108 Church St., Rossville, CA, 95678

Dubben, Michael, 414 S. Fares Ave., Evansville, IN, 47714

Dubber, Michael W., 8205 Heather Pl, Evansville, IN, 47710-4919

Eklund, Maihkel, Föne 1111, S-82041 Färila, SWEDEN, www.art-knives.com

Eldridge, Allan, 1424 Kansas Lane, Gallatin, TN, 37066

Engel, Terry (Flowers), PO Box 96, Midland, OR, 97634

Jeff, Flannery Engraving Co., 11034 Riddles Run Rd., Union, KY, 41091, engraving@fuse.net, http://home.fuse.net/engraving/

Foster, Norvell, Foster Enterprises, PO Box 200343, San Antonio, TX, 78220

Fountain Products, 492 Prospect Ave., West Springfield, MA, 01089

Gipe, Sandi, Rt. 2, Box 1090A, Kendrick, ID, 83537

Glimm, Jerome C., 19 S. Maryland, Conrad, MT, 59425

Gournet, Geoffroy, 820 Paxinosa Ave., Easton, PA, 18042, 610-559-0710, www.geoffroygournet.com

Hands, Barry Lee, 26192 E. Shore Rte., Bigfork, MT, 59911

Harrington, Fred A., Winter: 3725 Citrus, Summer: 2107 W Frances Rd Mt Morris, MI 48458-8215, St. James City, FL, 33956, Winter: 239-283-0721 Summer: 810-686-3008

Henderson, Fred D., 569 Santa Barbara Dr., Forest Park, GA, 30297, 770-968-4866

Hendricks, Frank, 396 Bluff Trail, Dripping Springs, TX, 78620, 512-858-7828

Holder, Pat, 7148 W. Country Gables Dr., Peoria, AZ, 85381

Hudson, Tommy, 1181 E 22nd St. Suite #18, Marysville, CA, 95901, 530-681-6531, twhunson@attbi.com, www.picturetrail.com/tommyhudson

Ingle, Ralph W., 151 Callan Dr., Rossville, GA, 30741, 706-858-0641, riengraver@aol.com, Photographer

Johns, Bill, 610 Yellowstone Ave, Cody, WY, 82414, 307-587-5090

Kelly, Lance, 1723 Willow Oak Dr., Edgewater, FL, 32132

Kelso, Jim, RD 1, Box 5300, Worcester, VT, 05682

Koevenig, Eugene and Eve, Koevenig's Engraving Service, Rabbit Gulch, Box 55, Hill City, SD, 57745-0055

Kostelnik, Joe and Patty, RD #4, Box 323, Greensburg, PA, 15601

Kudlas, John M., 55280 Silverwolf Dr, Barnes, WI, 54873, 715-795-2031, jkudlas@cheqnet.net, scrimshander

Limings Jr., Harry, 959 County Rd. 170, Marengo, OH, 43334-9625

Lindsay, Steve, 3714 West Cedar Hills Drive, Kearney, NE, 68847

Lyttle, Brian, Box 5697, High River AB CANADA, T1V 1M7

Lytton, Simon M., 19 Pinewood Gardens, Hemel Hempstead, Herts. HP1 1TN, ENGLAND

McCombs, Leo, 1862 White Cemetery Rd., Patriot, OH, 45658

McDonald, Dennis, 8359 Brady St., Peosta, IA, 52068

McKenzie, Lynton, 6940 N Alvernon Way, Tucson, AZ, 85718

McLean, Lawrence, 18361 Larkstone Circle, Huntington Beach, CA, 92646, 714-848-5779, lmclean@socal.rr.com

Meyer, Chris, 39 Bergen Ave., Wantage, NJ, 07461, 973-875-6299

Minnick, Joyce, 144 N. 7th St., Middletown, IN, 47356

Morgan, Tandie, PO Box 693, 30700 Hwy. 97, Nucla, CO, 81424

Morton, David A., 1110 W. 21st St., Lorain, OH, 44052

Moulton, Dusty, 135 Hillview Ln, Loudon, TN, 37774, 865-408-9779

Muller, Jody & Pat, PO Box 35, Pittsburg, MO, 65724, 417-852-4306/417-752-3260, mullerforge@hotmail.com,

Nelida, Toniutti, via G. Pasconi 29/c, Maniago 33085 (PN), ITALY

Nott, Ron, Box 281, Summerdale, PA, 17093

Parsons, Michael R., McKee Knives, 7042 McFarland Rd, Indianapolis, IN, 46227, 317-784-7943

Patterson, W.H., PO Drawer DK, College Station, TX, 77841

Peri, Valerio, Via Meucci 12, Gardone V.T. ITALY 25063

Pilkington Jr., Scott, PO Box 97, Monteagle, TN, 37356, 931-924-3400, scott@pilkguns.com, www.pilkguns.com

Poag, James, RR1, Box 212A, Grayville, IL, 62844

Potts, Wayne, 912 Poplar St., Denver, CO, 80220

Rabeno, Martin, Spook Hollow Trading Co., 92 Spook Hole Rd., Ellenville, NY, 12428

Raftis, Andrew, 2743 N. Sheffield, Chicago, IL, 60614

Roberts, J.J., 7808 Lake Dr., Manassas, VA, 20111, 703-330-0448, jjrengraver@aol.com, www.angelfire.com/va2/engraver

Robidoux, Roland J., DMR Fine Engraving, 25 N. Federal Hwy. Studio 5, Dania, FL, 33004

Rosser, Bob, Hand Engraving, 1824 29th Ave. South, Suite 214, Birmingham, AL, 35209, www.hand-engravers.com

Rudolph, Gil, 20922 Oak Pass Ave, Tehachapi, CA, 93561, 661-822-4949, www.gtraks@csurfers.net

Rundell, Joe, 6198 W. Frances Rd., Clio, MI, 48420

Schickl, L., Ottingweg 497, A-5580 Tamsweg, AUSTRIA, 0043 6474 8583, Scrimshander

Schlott, Harald, Zingster Str. 26, 13051 Berlin, GERMANY, 049 030 9293346, harald.schlott@T-online.de, Custom grinder, custom handle artisan, display case/box maker, etcher, scrimshander

Schönert, Elke, 18 Lansdowne Pl., Central, Port Elizabeth, SOUTH AFRICA

Shaw, Bruce, PO Box 545, Pacific Grove, CA, 93950, 831-646-1937, fax: 831-644-0941

Shostle, Ben, 1121 Burlington, Muncie, IN, 47302

Sinclair, W.P., The Orchard, Church Lane, Fovant, Wiltshire SP3 5LA, ENGLAND, 44 1722 714692, wsinclair@clara.net

Smith, Ron, 5869 Straley, Ft. Worth, TX, 76114

Smitty's Engraving, 800 N. Anderson Rd., Choctaw, OK, 73020, 405-769-3031, www.smittys-engraving.us

Spode, Peter, Tresaith Newland, Malvern, Worcestershire, ENGLAND WR13 5AY

Swartley, Robert D., 2800 Pine St., Napa, CA, 94558

Takeuchi, Shigetoshi, 21-14-1-Chome kamimuneoka Shiki shi, 353 Saitama, JAPAN

Theis, Terry, 21452 FM 2093, Harper, TX, 78631, 830-864-4438

Valade, Robert B., 931 3rd Ave., Seaside, OR, 97138, 503-738-7672, fax: 503 738-7672

Waldrop, Mark, 14562 SE 1st Ave. Rd., Summerfield, FL, 34491

Wallace, Terry, 385 San Marino, Vallejo, CA, 94589

Warenski, Julie, 590 East 500 N., Richfield, UT, 84701, 435-896-5319, julie@warenskiknives.com, www.warenskiknives.com

Warren, Kenneth W., PO Box 2842, Wenatchee, WA, 98807-2842, 509-663-6123, fax: 509 663-6123

Whitehead, James D., 204 Cappucino Way, Sacramento, CA, 95838

Whitmore, Jerry, 1740 Churchill Dr., Oakland, OR, 97462

Williams, Gary, 221 Autumn Way, Elizabeth, KY, 42701

Winn, Travis A., 558 E. 3065 S., Salt Lake City, UT, 84106

Wood, Mel, PO Box 1255, Sierra Vista, AZ, 85636

Zietz, Dennis, 5906 40th Ave., Kenosha, WI, 53144

etchers

Baron Technology Inc., David Baron, 62 Spring Hill Rd., Trumbull, CT, 06611

Fountain Products, 492 Prospect Ave., West Springfield, MA, 01089

Hayes, Dolores, PO Box 41405, Los Angeles, CA, 90041

Holland, Dennis, 4908 17th Pl., Lubbock, TX, 79416

Kelso, Jim, RD1, Box 5300, Worcester, VT, 05682

Larstein, Francine, FRANCINE ETCHINGS & ETCHED KNIVES, 368 White Rd, Watsonville, CA, 95076, 800-557-1525/831-426-6046, 831-684-1949, francine@francinetchings.com, www.francineetchings.com

Lefaucheux, Jean-Victor, Saint-Denis-Le-Ferment, 27140 Gisors, FRANCE

Leibowitz, Leonard, 1025 Murrayhill Ave., Pittsburgh, PA, 15217

(Acid), Mead, Faustina L., 2550 E. Mercury St., Inverness, FL, 34453-0514, 352-344-4751, scrimsha@infionline.net, www.scrimshaw-by-faustina.com

Myers, Ron, 6202 Marglenn Ave., Baltimore, MD, 21206, Display Cases & Boxes, Schlott, Harald, Zingster Str. 26, 13051 Berlin, GERMANY, 049 030 9293346, harald.schlott@T-online.de, Custom grinder, custom handle artisan, display case/box maker, etcher, scrimshander

Vallotton, A., Northwest Knife Supply, 621 Fawn Ridge Dr., Oakland, OR, 97462

Watson, Silvia, 350 Jennifer Lane, Driftwood, TX, 78619

heat treaters

Bay State Metal Treating Co., 6 Jefferson Ave., Woburn, MA, 01801

Bos Heat Treating, Paul, Shop: 1900 Weld Blvd., El Cajon, CA, 92020, 619-562-2370 / 619-445-4740 Home, PaulBos@BuckKnives.com

Kazou, Okaysu, 12-2 1 Chome Higashi, Ueno, Taito-Ku, Tokyo, JAPAN, 81-33834-2323, fax: 81-33831-3012

Progressive Heat Treating Co, 2802 Charles City Rd, Richmond, VA, 23231, 804-545-0010, fax: 804-545-0012

Holt, B.R., 1238 Birchwood Drive, Sunnyvale, CA, 94089

Metal Treating Bodycote Inc, 710 Burns St., Cincinnati, OH, 45204

O&W Heat Treat Inc., One Bidwell Rd., South Windsor, CT, 06074, 860-528-9239, fax: 860 291-9939, owht1@aol.com,

Texas Heat Treating Inc., 303 Texas Ave., Round Rock, TX, 78664

Texas Knifemakers Supply, 10649 Haddington, Suite 180, Houston, TX, 77043

The Tinker Shop, 1120 Helen, Deer Park, TX, 77536

Valley Metal Treating Inc., 355 S. East End Ave., Pomona, CA, 91766

Wilderness Forge, 315 North 100 East, Kanab, UT, 84741, 435-644-3674, bhatting@xpressweb.com,

Wilson, R.W., PO Box 2012, Weirton, WV, 26062

leather workers

Abramson, David, 116 Baker Ave, Wharton, NJ, 07885, lifter4him1@aol.com,

Burrows, Chuck, dba Wild Rose Trading Co, PO Box 5174, Durango, CO, 81301, 970-259-8396, chuck@wrtcleather.com,

Clements' Custom Leathercraft, Chas, 1741 Dallas St., Aurora, CO, 80010-2018

Congdon, David, 1063 Whitchurch Ct., Wheaton, IL, 60187

Cooper, Harold, 136 Winding Way, Frankfort, KY, 40601

Cooper, Jim, 1221 Cook St, Ramona, CA, 92065-3214, 760-789-1097, fax: 760-788-7992, jamcooper@aol.com,

Cow Catcher Leatherworks, 3006 Industrial Dr, Raleigh, NC, 27609

Cubic, George, GC Custom Leather Co., 10561 E. Deerfield Pl., Tucson, AZ, 85749, 520-760-0695, gcubic@aol.com

Dawkins, Dudley, 221 N. Broadmoor, Topeka, KS, 66606-1254, 785-235-0468, dawkind1@junocom, ABS member/ knifemaker forges straight knives

Evans, Scott V, Edge Works Mfg, 1171 Halltown Rd, Jacksonville, NC, 28546, 910-455-9834, fax: 910 346-5660, edgeworks@coastalnet.com, www.tacticalholsters.com

Genske, Jay, 283 Doty St, Fond du Lac, WI, 54935, 920-921-8019/Cell Phone 920-579-0144, jaygenske@hotmail.com, Custom Grinder, Custom Handle Artisan

Hawk, Ken, Rt. 1, Box 770, Ceres, VA, 24318-9630

Homyk, David N., 8047 Carriage Ln., Wichita Falls, TX, 76306

John's Custom Leather, John R. Stumpf, 523 S. Liberty St, Blairsville, PA, 15717, 724-459-6802, fax: 724-459-5996

knife services

Kravitt, Chris, HC 31 Box 6484, Rt 200, Ellsworth, ME, 04605-9805, 207-584-3000, fax: 207-584-3000, sheathmkr@aol.com, www.treestumpleather.com, , Reference: Tree Stump Leather

Larson, Richard, 549 E. Hawkeye, Turlock, CA, 95380

Layton, Jim, 2710 Gilbert Avenue, Portsmouth, OH, 45662

Lee, Randy, PO Box 1873, St. Johns, AZ, 85936, 928-337-2594, fax: 928-337-5002, info@randylee.knives.com, www.randyleeknives.com, , Custom knifemaker

Mason, Arne, 258 Wimer St., Ashland, OR, 97520, 541-482-2260, fax: 541 482-7785, www.arnemason.com

McGowan, Liz, 12629 Howard Lodge Dr., Sykesville, MD, 21784, 410-489-4323

Metheny, H.A. "Whitey", 7750 Waterford Dr., Spotsylvania, VA, 22553

Miller, Michael K., 28510 Santiam Highway, Sweet Home, OR, 97386

Mobley, Martha, 240 Alapaha River Road, Chula, GA, 31733

Morrissey, Martin, 4578 Stephens Rd., Blairsville, GA, 30512

Niedenthal, John Andre, Beadwork & Buckskin, Studio 3955 NW 103 Dr., Coral Springs, FL, 33065-1551, 954-345-0447, a_niedenthal@hotmail.com,

Neilson, Tess, RR2 Box 16, Wyalusing, PA, 18853, 570-746-4944, www.mountainhollow.net, doing business as Neilson's Mountain Hollow

Parsons, Michael R., McKee Knives, 7042 McFarland Rd, Indianapolis, IN, 46227, 317-784-7943

Poag, James H., RR #1 Box 212A, Grayville, IL, 62844

Red's Custom Leather, Ed Todd, 9 Woodlawn Rd., Putnam Valley, NY, 10579, 845-528-3783

Rowe, Kenny, 3219 Hwy 29 South, Hope, AR, 71801, 870-777-8216, fax: 870-777-0935, rowesleather@yahoo.com, www.knifeart.com or www.theedgeequipment.com

Ruiz Industries Inc., 1513 Gardena Ave., Glendale, CA, 91204

Schrap, Robert G., 7024 W. Wells St., Wauwatosa, WI, 53213-3717, 414-771-6472, fax: 414 479-9765, knifesheaths@aol.com, www.customsheaths.com, *Custom Knife Sheathes,

Strahin, Robert, 401 Center St., Elkins, WV, 26241

Stuart, V. Pat, Rt. 1, Box 447-S, Greenville, VA, 24440

Tierney, Mike, 447 Rivercrest Dr., Woodstock ON CANADA N4S 5W5

Turner, Kevin, 17 Hunt Ave., Montrose, NY, 10548

Velasquez, Gil, 7120 Madera Dr., Goleta, CA, 93117

Walker, John, 17 Laber Circle, Little Rock, AR, 72209

Watson, Bill, #1 Presidio, Wimberly, TX, 78676

Whinnery, Walt, 1947 Meadow Creek Dr., Louisville, KY, 40218

Williams, Sherman A., 1709 Wallace St., Simi Valley, CA, 93065

miscellaneous

Kydex Sheath Maker, Hendryx Design, Scott, 5997 Smokey Way, Boise, ID, 83714, 208-377-8044, www.shdsheaths@msn.com,

Robertson, Kathy, Impress by Design, PO Box 1367, Evans, GA, 30809-1367, 706-650-0982, fax: 706 860-1623, impressbydesign@comcast.net, Advertising/graphic designer

Custom Knife Sheaths, Strahin, Robert, 401 Center St., Elkins, WV, 26241

photographers

Alfano, Sam, 36180 Henery Gaines Rd., Pearl River, LA, 70452

Allen, John, Studio One, 3823 Pleasant Valley Blvd., Rockford, IL, 61114

Bilal, Mustafa, Turk's Head Productions, 908 NW 50th St., Seattle, WA, 98107-3634, 206-782-4164, fax: 206 783-5677, mustafa@turkshead.com, www.turkshead.com, Graphic design, marketing & advertising

Bogaerts, Jan, Regenweg 14, 5757 Pl., Liessel, HOLLAND

Box Photography, Doug, 1804 W Main St, Brenham, TX, 77833-3420

Brown, Tom, 6048 Grants Ferry Rd., Brandon, MS, 39042-8136

Butman, Steve, PO Box 5106, Abilene, TX, 79608

Calidonna, Greg, 205 Helmwood Dr., Elizabethtown, KY, 42701

Campbell, Jim, 7935 Ranch Rd., Port Richey, FL, 34668

Cooper, Jim, Sharpbycoop.com photography, 9 Mathew Court, Norwalk, CT, 06851, jcooper@sharpbycoop.com, www.sharpbycoop.com

Courtice, Bill, PO Box 1776, Duarte, CA, 91010-4776

Crosby, Doug, RFD 1, Box 1111, Stockton Springs, ME, 04981

Danko, Michael, 3030 Jane Street, Pittsburgh, PA, 15203

Davis, Marshall B., PO Box 3048, Austin, TX, 78764

Dikeman, Lawrence, 17571 Parkplace Cir, Spring Lake, MI, 49456-9148

Earley, Don, 1241 Ft. Bragg Rd., Fayetteville, NC, 28305

Ehrlich, Linn M., 2643 N. Clybourn Ave., Chicago, IL, 60614

Ellison, Troy, PO Box 94393, Lubbock, TX, 79493, tellison@hiplains.net

Etzler, John, 11200 N. Island Rd., Grafton, OH, 44044

Fahrner, Dave, 1623 Arnold St., Pittsburgh, PA, 15205

Faul, Jan W., 903 Girard St. NE, Rr. Washington, DC, 20017

Fedorak, Allan, 28 W. Nicola St., Amloops BC CANADA V2C 1J6

Forster, Jenny, 534 Nantucket Way, Island Lake, IL, 60042, www.thesilkca.msn.com

Fox, Daniel, Lumina Studios, 6773 Industrial Parkway, Cleveland, OH, 44070, 440-734-2118, fax: 440 734-3542, lumina@en.com

Freiberg, Charley, PO Box 42, Elkins, NH, 03233, 603-526-2767, charleyfreiberg@tos.net,

Gardner, Chuck, 116 Quincy Ave., Oak Ridge, TN, 37830

Gawryla, Don, 1105 Greenlawn Dr., Pittsburgh, PA, 15220

Goffe Photographic Associates, 3108 Monte Vista Blvd., NE, Albuquerque, NM, 87106

Graham, James, 7434 E Northwest Hwy, Dallas, TX, 75231, 214-341-5138, jamie@jamiepoto.com, www.jamiephoto.com, , Product photographer

Graley, Gary W., RR2 Box 556, Gillett, PA, 16925

Griggs, Dennis, 118 Pleasant Pt Rd, Topsham, ME, 04086, 207-725-5689

Hanusin, John, Reames-Hanusin Studio, PO Box 931, Northbrook, IL, 60065 0931

Hardy, Scott, 639 Myrtle Ave., Placerville, CA, 95667

Hodge, Tom, 7175 S US Hwy 1 Lot 36, Titusville, FL, 32780-8172

Holter, Wayne V., 125 Lakin Ave., Boonsboro, MD, 21713

Hopkins, David W, Hopkins Photography inc, 201 S Jefferson, Iola, KS, 66749, 620-365-7443, nhoppy@netks.net,
Kelley, Gary, 17485 SW Pheasant Lane, Aloha, OR, 97006
Kerns, Bob, 18723 Birdseye Dr., Germantown, MD, 20874
LaFleur, Gordon, 111 Hirst, Box 1209, Parksville BC CANADA V0R 270
Lear, Dale, 11342 State Route 588, Rio Grande, OH, 45674, 740-245-5007, dalelear@yahoo.com, Web page designer
LeBlanc, Paul, No. 3 Meadowbrook Cir., Melissa, TX, 75454
Lester, Dean, 2801 Junipero Ave Suite 212, Long Beach, CA, 90806-2140
Leviton, David A., A Studio on the Move, PO Box 2871, Silverdale, WA, 98383, 360-697-3452
Long, Gary W., 3556 Miller's Crossroad Rd., Hillsboro, TN, 37342
Long, Jerry, 402 E. Gladden Dr., Farmington, NM, 87401
Lum, Billy, 16307 Evening Star Ct., Crosby, TX, 77532
McCollum, Tom, PO Box 933, Lilburn, GA, 30226
Moake, Jim, 18 Council Ave., Aurora, IL, 60504
Moya Inc., 4212 S. Dixie Hwy., West Palm Beach, FL, 33405
Norman's Studio, 322 S. 2nd St., Vivian, LA, 71082
Owens, William T., Box 99, Williamsburg, WV, 24991
Palmer Studio, 2008 Airport Blvd., Mobile, AL, 36606
Parsons, 15 South Mission, Suite 3, Wenatchee, WA, 98801
Payne, Robert G., PO Box 141471, Austin, TX, 78714
Peterson Photography, Kent, 230 Polk St., Eugene, OR, 97402, kdp@pond.net, www.pond.net/kdp
Pigott, John, 231 Heidelberg Drive, Loveland, OH, 45140, 513-683-4875
Point Seven, 810 Seneca St., Toledo, OH, 43608
Rasmussen, Eric L., 1121 Eliason, Brigham City, UT, 84302
Rhoades, Cynthia J., Box 195, Clearmont, WY, 82835
Rice, Tim, PO Box 663, Whitefish, MT, 59937
Richardson, Kerry, 2520 Mimosa St., Santa Rosa, CA, 95405, 707-575-1875, kerry@sonic.net, www.sonic.net/~kerry
Ross, Bill, 28364 S. Western Ave. Suite 464, Rancho Palos Verdes, CA, 90275
Rubicam, Stephen, 14 Atlantic Ave., Boothbay Harbor, ME, 04538-1202
Rush, John D., 2313 Maysel, Bloomington, IL, 61701
Schreiber, Roger, 429 Boren Ave. N., Seattle, WA, 98109
Semmer, Charles, 7885 Cyd Dr., Denver, CO, 80221
Silver Images Photography, 2412 N Keystone, Flagstaff, AZ, 86004
Slobodian, Scott, 4101 River Ridge Dr., PO Box 1498, San Andreas, CA, 95249, 209-286-1980, fax: 209 286-1982, www.slobodianswords.com
Smith, Earl W., 5121 Southminster Rd., Columbus, OH, 43221
Smith, Randall, 1720 Oneco Ave., Winter Park, FL, 32789
Storm Photo, 334 Wall St., Kingston, NY, 12401
Surles, Mark, PO Box 147, Falcon, NC, 28342
Third Eye Photos, 140 E. Sixth Ave., Helena, MT, 59601
Thurber, David, PO Box 1006, Visalia, CA, 93279
Tighe, Brian, RR 1, Ridgeville ON CANADA L0S 1M0, 905-892-2734, www.tigheknives.com
Towell, Steven L., 3720 N.W. 32nd Ave., Camas, WA, 98607
Troutman, Harry, 107 Oxford Dr., Lititz, PA, 17543
Valley Photo, 2100 Arizona Ave., Yuma, AZ, 85364
Vara, Lauren, 4412 Waples Rd., Granbury, TX, 76049
Verno Studio, Jay, 3030 Jane Street, Pittsburgh, PA, 15203
Wells, Carlene L., 1060 S. Main Sp. 52, Colville, WA, 99114

Weyer International, 2740 Nebraska Ave., Toledo, OH, 43607, 800-448-8424, fax: 419 534-2697, law-weyerinternational@msn.com, Books
Wise, Harriet, 242 Dill Ave., Frederick, MD, 21701
Worley, Holly, 6360 W David Dr, Littleton, CO, 80128-5708

scrimshanders

Adlam, Tim, 1705 Witzel Ave., Oshkosh, WI, 54902, 920-235-4589, www.adlamngraving.com
Alpen, Ralph, 7 Bentley Rd., West Grove, PA, 19390, fax: 610-869-7141
Anderson, Terry Jack, 10076 Birnamwoods Way, Riverton, UT, 84065-9073
Bailey, Mary W., 3213 Jonesboro Dr., Nashville, TN, 37214, mbscrim@aol.com, www.members.aol.com/mbscrim/scrim.html
Baker, Duane, 2145 Alum Creek Dr., Cambridge Park Apt. #10, Columbus, OH, 43207
Barrows, Miles, 524 Parsons Ave., Chillicothe, OH, 45601
Brady, Sandra, PO Box 104, Monclova, OH, 43542, 419-866-0435, fax: 419 867-0656, sandyscrim@hotmail.com, www.knifeshows.com
Beauchamp, Gaetan, 125 de la Riviere, Stoneham, PQ, CANADA, G0A 4P0, 418-848-1914, fax: 418 848-6859, knives@gbeauchamp.ca, www.beauchamp.cjb.net
Bellet, Connie, PO Box 151, Palermo, ME, 04354 0151, 207-993-2327, phwhitehawk@gwl.net,
Benade, Lynn, 2610 Buckhurst Dr, Beachwood, OH, 44122, 216-464-0777, llbnc17@aol.com,
Bonshire, Benita, 1121 Burlington Dr., Muncie, IN, 47302
Boone Trading Co. Inc., PO Box 669, Brinnon, WA, 98320, 800-423-1945, www.boonetrading.com
Bryan, Bob, 1120 Oak Hill Rd., Carthage, MO, 64836
Byrne, Mary Gregg, 1018 15th St., Bellingham, WA, 98225-6604
Cable, Jerry, 332 Main St., Mt. Pleasant, PA, 15666
Caudill, Lyle, 7626 Lyons Rd., Georgetown, OH, 45121
Cole, Gary, PO Box 668, Naalehu, HI, 96772, 808-929-9775, fax: 808-929-7371, www.community.webshots.com/album/11836830uqyeejirsz
Collins, Michael, Rt. 3075, Batesville Rd., Woodstock, GA, 30188
Conover, Juanita Rae, PO Box 70442, Eugene, OR, 97401, 541-747-1726 or 543-4851, juanitaraeconover@yahoo.com,
Courtnage, Elaine, Box 473, Big Sandy, MT, 59520
Cover Jr., Raymond A., Rt. 1, Box 194, Mineral Point, MO, 63660
Cox, J. Andy, 116 Robin Hood Lane, Gaffney, SC, 29340
Dietrich, Roni, Wild Horse Studio, 1257 Cottage Dr, Harrisburg, PA, 17112, 717-469-0587, ronimd@aol
DiMarzo, Richard, 2357 Center Place, Birmingham, AL, 35205
Dolbare, Elizabeth, PO Box 502, Dubois, WY, 82513-0502
Eklund, Maihkel, Föne 1111, S-82041 Färila, SWEDEN, +46 6512 4192, maihkel.eklund@swipnet.se, www.art-knives.com
Eldridge, Allan, 1424 Kansas Lane, Gallatin, TN, 37066
Fields, Donald, 790 Tamerlane St, Deltona, FL, 32725, 386-532-9070, donaldfields@aol.com, Scrimshander; selling ancient ivories; mammoth & fossil walrus,
Fisk, Dale, Box 252, Council, ID, 83612, dafisk@ctcweb.net,

Foster Enterprises, Norvell Foster, PO Box 200343, San Antonio, TX, 78220

Fountain Products, 492 Prospect Ave., West Springfield, MA, 01089

Gill, Scott, 925 N. Armstrong St., Kokomo, IN, 46901

Halligan, Ed, 14 Meadow Way, Sharpsburg, GA, 30277, ehkiss@bellsouth.net

Hands, Barry Lee, 26192 East Shore Route, Bigfork, MT, 59911

Hargraves Sr., Charles, RR 3 Bancroft, Ontario CANADA K0L 1C0

Harless, Star, c/o Arrow Forge, PO Box 845, Stoneville, NC, 27048-0845

Harrington, Fred A., Summer: 2107 W Frances Rd, Mt Morris MI 48458 8215 Winter: 3725 Citrus, St. James City, FL, 33956, Winter: 239-283-0721, Summer: 810-686-3008

Hergert, Bob, 12 Geer Circle, Port Orford, OR, 97465, 541-332-3010, hergert@harborside.com, www.scrimshander.com

Hielscher, Vickie, 6550 Otoe Rd, PO Box 992, Alliance, NE, 69301, 308-762-4318, hielscher@premaonline.com

High, Tom, 5474 S. 112.8 Rd., Alamosa, CO, 81101, 719-589-2108, scrimshaw@vanion.com, www.rockymountainscrimshaw.com

Himmelheber, David R., 11289 40th St. N., Royal Palm Beach, FL, 33411

Holland, Dennis K., 4908-17th Place, Lubbock, TX, 79416

Imboden II, Howard L., 620 Deauville Dr., Dayton, OH, 45429, 937-439-1536, Guards by the "Last Wax Technic"

Johnson, Corinne, W3565 Lockington, Mindora, WI, 54644

Johnston, Kathy, W. 1134 Providence, Spokane, WA, 99205

Karst-Stone, Linda, 402 Hwy. 27 E., Ingram, TX, 78025-3317, 830-896-4678, fax: 830-257-6117, karstone@ktc.com,

Kelso, Jim, RD 1, Box 5300, Worcester, VT, 05682

Kirk, Susan B., 1340 Freeland Rd., Merrill, MI, 48637

Koevenig, Eugene and Eve, Koevenig's Engraving Service, Rabbit Gulch, Box 55, Hill City, SD, 57745-0055

Kostelnik, Joe and Patty, RD #4, Box 323, Greensburg, PA, 15601

Lemen, Pam, 3434 N. Iroquois Ave., Tucson, AZ, 85705

Martin, Diane, 28220 N. Lake Dr., Waterford, WI, 53185

McDonald, René Cosimini-, 14730 61 Court N., Loxahatchee, FL, 33470

McFadden, Berni, 2547 E Dalton Ave, Dalton Gardens, ID, 83815-9631

McGowan, Frank, 12629 Howard Lodge Dr., Sykesville, MD, 21784

McGrath, Gayle, PMB 232 15201 N Cleveland Ave, N Ft Myers, FL, 33903

McLaran, Lou, 603 Powers St., Waco, TX, 76705

McWilliams, Carole, PO Box 693, Bayfield, CO, 81122

Mead, Faustina L., 2550 E. Mercury St., Inverness, FL, 34453-0514, 352-344-4751, scrimsha@infionline.net, www.scrimshaw-by-faustina.com

Mitchell, James, 1026 7th Ave., Columbus, GA, 31901

Moore, James B., 1707 N. Gillis, Stockton, TX, 79735

Ochonicky, Michelle "Mike", Stone Hollow Studio, 31 High Trail, Eureka, MO, 63025, 636-938-9570, www.bestofmissourihands.com

Ochs, Belle, 124 Emerald Lane, Largo, FL, 33771, 727-530-3826, chuckandbelle@juno.com, www.oxforge.com

Pachi, Mirella, Via Pometta 1, 17046 Sassello (SV), ITALY, 019 720086, www.pachi-knives.com

Parish, Vaughn, 103 Cross St., Monaca, PA, 15061

Peterson, Lou, 514 S. Jackson St., Gardner, IL, 60424

Poag, James H., RR #1 Box 212A, Grayville, IL, 62844

Polk, Trena, 4625 Webber Creek Rd., Van Buren, AR, 72956

Purvis, Hilton, PO Box 371, Noordhoek, 7979 SOUTH AFRICA, 27 21 789 1114, hiltonp@telkomsa.net, www.kgsa.co.za/member/hiltonpurvis

Ramsey, Richard, 8525 Trout Farm Rd, Neosho, MO, 64850

Ristinen, Lori, 14256 County Hwy 45, Menahga, MN, 56464, 218-538-6608, lori@loriristinen.com, www.loriristinen.com

Roberts, J.J., 7808 Lake Dr., Manassas, VA, 22111, 703-330-0448, jjrengraver@aol.com, www.angelfire.com/va2/engraver

Rudolph, Gil, 20922 Oak Pass Ave, Tehachapi, CA, 93561, 661-822-4949, www.gtraks@csurfers.net

Rundell, Joe, 6198 W. Frances Rd., Clio, MI, 48420

Saggio, Joe, 1450 Broadview Ave. #12, Columbus, OH, 43212, jvsag@webtv.net, www.j.v.saggio@worldnet.att.net

Sahlin, Viveca, Konstvaktarevagem 9, S-772 40 Grangesberg SWEDEN, 46 240 23204, www.scrimart.use

Satre, Robert, 518 3rd Ave. NW, Weyburn SK CANADA S4H 1R1

Schlott, Harald, Zingster Str. 26, 13051 Berlin, 929 33 46, GERMANY

Schulenburg, E.W., 25 North Hill St., Carrollton, GA, 30117

Schwallie, Patricia, 4614 Old Spartanburg Rd. Apt. 47, Taylors, SC, 29687

Selent, Chuck, PO Box 1207, Bonners Ferry, ID, 83805

Semich, Alice, 10037 Roanoke Dr., Murfreesboro, TN, 37129

Shostle, Ben, 1121 Burlington, Muncie, IN, 47302

Sinclair, W.P., 3, The Pippins, Warminster, Wiltshire BA12 8TH, ENGLAND

Smith, Peggy, 676 Glades Rd., #3, Gatlinburg, TN, 37738

Smith, Ron, 5869 Straley, Ft. Worth, TX, 76114

Stahl, John, Images In Ivory, 2049 Windsor Rd., Baldwin, NY, 11510, 516-223-5007, imivory@msn.com, www.imagesinivory.org

Steigerwalt, Jim, RD#3, Sunbury, PA, 17801

Stuart, Stephen, 15815 Acorn Circle, Tavares, FL, 32778, 352-343-8423, fax: 352 343-8916, inkscratch@aol.com

Talley, Mary Austin, 2499 Countrywood Parkway, Memphis, TN, 38016, matalley@midsouth.rr.com,

Thompson, Larry D., 23040 Ave. 197, Strathmore, CA, 93267

Toniutti, Nelida, Via G. Pascoli, 33085 Maniago-PN, ITALY

Tucker, Steve, 3518 W. Linwood, Turlock, CA, 95380

Tyser, Ross, 1015 Hardee Court, Spartanburg, SC, 29303

Velasquez, Gil, Art of Scrimshaw, 7120 Madera Dr., Goleta, CA, 93117

Warren, Al, 1423 Santa Fe Circle, Roseville, CA, 95678, 916-257-5904, al@warrenknives.com, www.warrenknives.com

Wilderness Forge, 315 North 100 East, Kanab, UT, 84741, 435-644-3674, bhatting@xpressweb.com

Williams, Gary, (Garbo), PO Box 210, Glendale, KY, 42740-0210

Winn, Travis A., 558 E. 3065 S., Salt Lake City, UT, 84106

Young, Mary, 4826 Storeyland Dr., Alton, IL, 62002

Zima, Russell, 7291 Ruth Way, Denver, CO, 80221

organizations & publications

organizations

AMERICAN BLADESMITH SOCIETY
c/o Jim Batson, PO Box 977, Peralta, NM 87042

AMERICAN KNIFE & TOOL INSTITUTE***
Dave Kowalski, Comm. Coordinator, AKTI, DEPT BL2, PO Box 432, Iola WI 54945-0432; 715-445-3781;715-445-5228; communications@akti.org; www.akti.org

AMERICAN KNIFE THROWERS ALLIANCE
c/o Bobby Branton,4976 Seewee Rd.,Awendaw, SC 29429

ART KNIFE COLLECTOR'S ASSOCIATION
c/o Mitch Weiss, Pres.,2211 Lee Road, Suite 104,Winter Park, FL 32789

CALIFORNIA KNIFEMAKERS ASSOCIATION
c/o Clint Breshears, Membership Chairman, 1261 Keats St., Manhattan Beach CA 90266

CANADIAN KNIFEMAKERS GUILD
c/o Peter Wile, RR # 3, Bridgewater N.S., B4V 2W2; 902-543-1373; www.ckg.org

CUTTING EDGE, The
1920 N 26th St., Lowell AR 72745; 479-631-0055; 479-631-8734; buyer@cuttingedge.com
After-market knives since 1968. We offer about 1,000 individual knives each month. Subscription by first class mail, in U.S. $20 per year, Canada or Mexico by air mail, $25 per year. All overseas by air mail, $40 per year. The oldest and the most experienced in the business of buying and selling knives. We buy collections of any size, take knives on consignment or we will trade. Every month there are eight pages in color featuring the work of top makers.

JAPANESE SWORD SOCIETY OF THE U.S.
PO Box 712, Breckenridge, TX 76424

KNIFE COLLECTORS CLUB INC, THE
1920 N 26th St., Lowell AR 72745; 479-631-0055; 479-631-8734; ag@agrussell.com Web:www.club@k-c.com
The oldest and largest association of knife collectors. Issues limited edition knives, both handmade and highest quality production, in very limited numbers. The very earliest was the CM-1, Kentucky Rifle.

KNIFEMAKERS GUILD
c/o Al Pendray, President, 13950 N.E. 20th St., Williston FL 32696; 352-528-6124; 352-528-6124; bpendray@aol.com

KNIFEMAKERS GUILD OF SOUTHERN AFRICA, THE
c/o Carel Smith, PO Box 1744, Delmars 2210, SOUTH AFRICA; carelsmith@therugby.co.za Web:www.kgsa.co.za

MONTANA KNIFEMAKERS' ASSOCIATION, THE
14440 Harpers Bridge Rd., Missoula, MT 59808; (406) 543-0845
Annual book of custom knife makers' works and directory of knife making supplies; $19.99

NATIONAL KNIFE COLLECTORS ASSOC.
PO Box 21070, Chattanooga, TN 37424; 423-892-5007; 423-899-9456
nkca@aol.com Web: nationalknive.org

NEO-TRIBAL METALSMITHS
PO Box 44095, Tucson, AZ 85773-4095

NEW ENGLAND CUSTOM KNIFE ASSOCIATION
George R. Rebello, President, 686 Main Rd., Brownville, ME 04414; Web:www.kinvesby.com/necka.html

NORTH CAROLINA CUSTOM KNIFEMAKERS GUILD
c/o Tommy McNabb, Pres., 4015 Brownsboro Rd., Winston-Salem, NC 27106; tommy@tmcnabb.com; Web:www.nckniveguild.org

PROFESSIONAL KNIFEMAKERS ASSOCIATION
2905 N. Montana Ave., Ste. 30027, Helena, MT 59601

TRIBAL NOW!
Neo-Tribal Metalsmiths, PO Box 44095, Tucson, AZ 85733-4095

UNITED KINGDOM BLADE ASSOCIATION (UKBA)
PO Box 1, Brampton, CA67GD, ENGLAND

publications

BLADE
700 E. State St., Iola, WI 54990-0001; 715-445-22214; www.blademag.com
The world's No. 1 knife magazine.

KNIFE WORLD
PO Box 3395, Knoxville, TN 37927

KNIVES ILLUSTRATED
265 S. Anita Dr., Ste. 120, Orange, CA 92868; 714-939-9991; knivesillustrated@yahoo.com Web:www.knivesillustrated.com
All encompassing publication focusing on factory knives, new handmades, shows and industry news.

RESOURCE GUIDE AND NEWSLETTER / AUTOMATIC KNIVES
2269 Chestnut St., Suite 212, San Francisco, CA 94123; 415-731-0210; Web:www.thenewsletter.com

TACTICAL KNIVES
Harris Publications, 1115 Broadway, New York, NY 10010

WEYER INTERNATIONAL BOOK DIVISION
2740 Nebraska Ave., Toledo, OH 43607-3245

Add to Your Knifemaking Know-How

How to Make Knives
by Richard W. Barney & Robert W. Loveless
Learn how with "the bible of knife-making." Gives complete instructions on making high quality handmade knives. Forging and stock removal, mirror polishing, sheath making, safety techniques, required tools and supplies and more.
Softcover • 8½ x 11 • 182 pages
448 b&w photos
Item# KHM01 • $13.95

Wayne Goddard's $50 Knife Shop
by Wayne Goddard
Outfitting a knifemaking shop doesn't have to cost a fortune and Wayne Goddard shows you how to do it on a budget. This book expands on information from his popular column in Blade magazine to help you create helpful gadgets and obtain useful supplies. You will learn how to acquire the tools you need to make a knife shop for less than the cost of some knives.
Softcover • 8½ x 11 • 160 pages
75 b&w photos • 8-page color section
Item# WGBW • $19.95

Antique American Switchblades
by Mark B. Erickson
Master how to realistically grade and price switchblades and learn inside information on the hobby, including slang and jargon specific to this field, as well as a reliable history on how they were developed and profiling the companies that manufactured them. This comprehensive reference offers detailed listings-manufacturer/model section, color photographs, detailed descriptions, and accurate prices-with an honest appraisal of more than 250 individual models.
Softcover • 8-¼ x 10-7/8 • 160 pages
300 color photos
Item# AAMS • $24.99

How to Make Folding Knives
A Step-By-Step How-To
by Ron Lake, Frank Centofante and Wayne Clay
Follow easy instructions by on how to make your own folding knife. Includes safety tips, suppliers lists and answers many questions from three top custom makers.
Softcover • 8½ x 11 • 193 pages
350 b&w photos
Item# KMF01 • $15.95

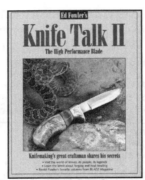

Knife Talk II: The High Performance Blade
by Ed Fowler
Blade magazine's Ed Fowler presents 65 of his Knife Talk columns in a second new volume. He takes you on a journey visiting industry legends and presents his knife-making philosophies. He also discusses the major steps of knife making, including function, design, types of blade materials, heat treating, how to grind blades, and knife maintenance. This second volume chronicles the latest four years of Knife Talk columns.
Softcover • 8½ x 11 • 200 pages
250 b&w photos • 8-page color section
Item# KNTA2 • $19.99

The Wonder of Knifemaking
by Wayne Goddard
Do you want to know how to make a knife? Wayne Goddard has the answers to your questions. As a columnist for *Blade* magazine, Goddard has been answering real questions from real knifemakers for the past eight years. With its question-and-answer format, this book gives you the answers to real-world problems like heat-treating, choosing the best steel and finding the right tools for your knifemaking shop.
Softcover • 8½ x 11 • 160 pages
150 b&w photos • 16-page color section
Item# WOKN • $19.95

Custom Knifemaking
10 Projects From a Master Craftsman
by Tim McCreight
Ten increasingly difficult projects that together constitute a survey of knifemaking skills. Within the project format, readers learn how to cut, shape, heat, treat and finish a knife.
Softcover • 7 x 9 • 224 pages
75 b&w photos • 100 line drawings
Item# CK01 • $17.95

2005 Sporting Knives
4th Edition
Edited by Joe Kertzman
Hundreds of factory-made sporting knives are arranged alphabetically according to manufacturer with each listing containing retail prices, knife specifications, features, styles, appropriate sheaths, handle components, and collaborating custom knifemakers. All-new feature articles and field reports from well-known experts cover the best and latest the commercial knife industry has to offer.
Softcover • 8-½ x 11 • 256 pages
500 b&w photos
Item# DGK04 • $22.99

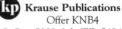